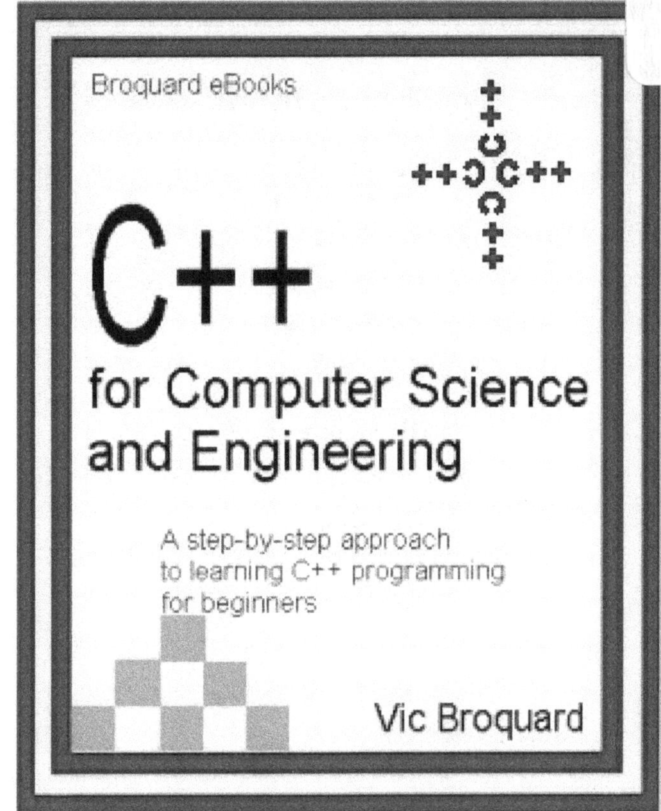

C++ for Computer Science and Engineering

(5th Edition)

Vic Broquard

C++ for Computer Science and Engineering
Vic Broquard

Fifth Edition
ISBN: 978-1-941415-53-5
Broquard eBooks
103 Timberlane
East Peoria, IL 61611
author@Broquard-eBooks.com
www.Broquard-eBooks.com

To all of my dedicated, persevering students,
and to L. Ron Hubbard, who taught me to "Simplify"

Preface

This book assumes you have no previous programming background. It uses a step-by-step building block approach to gradiently learn how to solve computer science and engineering problems in the C++ language. Each chapter has three sections. Section A presents the basic theory and principles of the current topic. Section B illustrates these basic principles by using applications that are often found in computer science. Section C illustrates these basic principles by using applications that may be found in the various engineering disciplines. You should study the basic theory Section A and then study the appropriate application section. Of course, anyone can benefit by also reviewing the other application area, since they are frequently interrelated.

The book comes with a self-extracting zip file containing all of the sample programs in the book along with all of the test data required for the programming assignments. Download them at:
http://www.Broquard-eBooks.com/pb/cpp-cs-engr and use the link there.

At the end of each chapter are **Design Exercises**, **Stop Exercises** and **Programming Problems**. Before you tackle any programming assignments, you should do both the Design and Stop exercises. The Design Exercises are paper and pencil activities that assist in solidifying the basic design principles covered in the chapter. The Stop Exercises cover the new syntax of the language, illustrating many of the more common errors beginners make in coding the language. If you dutifully do these two sets of exercises **before** you start in on your programming assignments, you will have a much better chance of success with drastically lower frustration level.

If you find any errors or have any suggestions or comments, please email me at author@Broquard-eBooks.com

Contents

Chapter 1—Introduction to Programming

Section A: Basic Theory

Introduction

Few areas of study have more specialized terms and abbreviations to know than in the computer field. As you study the text, key words and abbreviations are given good action definitions as they occur. If a section of a chapter is blank in your mind, stop and look back earlier and see if you can find a word or abbreviation that is not fully understood. Once the word is fully understood, reread that blank section and it should now make sense.

At the end of each chapter are two practice sections designed to solidify the theory just studied. The "Design Exercises" enhance your problem solving skills. The "Stop! Do These Exercises Before Programming" exercises illustrate many of the common errors that a programmer can make. Thus, if you work these exercises before you begin the actual programming problems, you should make far fewer goofs, should have a much more enjoyable time doing the programming, should greatly reduce the amount of time it takes to do your assignments, and should definitely lower the frustration level.

What is a Computer?

A definition of a **computer** is an electronic device that can input data, process data and output data, accurately and at great speed. **Data** are any kind of information that can be codified in some manner and input into the computer. Normally, we think of data as facts and numbers such as a person's name and address or the quantity or cost of an item purchased. However, data can also be graphical images, sound files, movies and more.

A computer is capable of inputting information such as the quantity ordered and the cost of that item. Processing data means to do something with it. Often we think of processing as performing some kind of calculations. If the quantity and cost have been input, then the obvious calculation would be to multiply cost times quantity to produce the total cost. However, processing data can mean more than just calculations. Perhaps you have entered the series of friends and their phone numbers. Processing the data can also mean sorting the friends' information into alphabetical order by last names. Finally, to be useful, the computer needs to be able to output information, the results, to the user in an accurate and timely manner. The user is anyone that is making use of the results that the computer is producing.

However, an abacus can input, process and output data. There must be more in this definition. It is the qualifier, accurately and at great speed, that makes computers so powerful. Let's look at each of these in turn.

A computer is accurate and reliable; they do not make mistakes. However, it did not used to be this way. Back in the first generation of computers in the early 1950's, computers were built from some 18,000 vacuum tubes. In addition, tubes frequently burned out forcing their replacement. Statistically, when one has 18,000 of these tubes in one machine, one expects one tube failure every fifteen seconds! This is where the idea that computers are not reliable has its genus. There was no reliability in those days. However, with modern computers now built from silicon and germanium integrated circuits or chips (a device consisting of a number of connected electronic circuit elements such as transistors fabricated on a single chip of silicon crystal), the failure rate is about one chip failure ever thirty-three million hours of operation. Of course, if you drop a computer or run it during an electrical storm, you can significantly shorten its lifetime. Thus, modern computers are reliable. However, the software that runs on them is not necessarily error proof.

The other qualifier is at great speed. Just how fast is a computer? Let's compare the time that it takes various computers to add two integer whole numbers. The unit of time measurement is the nanosecond, which is 10^{-9} of a second, or 1/1,000,000,000 of a second. Electricity travels approximately 11.4 inches down a copper wire in a nanosecond. The following chart approximates how long it takes some computers to add two numbers. (MHz is short for **megahertz** or a million cycles per second, GHz is **gigahertz** (1024 MHz), and ns is nanoseconds.)

```
IBM-PC      4.77 MHz   600 ns
386           33 MHz    60 ns
486          100 MHz    10 ns
Pentium      200 MHz     5 ns
P-3          500 MHz     2 ns
P-4            2 GHz    .5 ns
```

In other words, if you have one of the newer Pentium-3 500 MHz machines, in one second the computer could perform many billions of additions. (Note that the addition instruction is one of the fastest instructions the computer has. Many other instructions take substantially longer to perform.)

Thus, it is the ability of the modern computer to perform reliably and to perform at great speed that has made it so powerful.

Computers have a fixed set of **instructions** that they can perform for us. The specific instruction set depends upon the make and model of a computer. However, these instructions can be broadly grouped into four basic categories:

Math instructions
Comparison instructions
Movement of data instructions
Input and output instructions

When one thinks of math instructions, the add, subtract, multiply and divide operations immediately come to mind. However, for a mathematician, there are more complex math operations as well, such as finding the trigonometric sine of an angle or the square root of a number. Comparison instructions permit the computer to tell if one number is greater than, less than or equal to another number. The computer can move data from one location in its memory to another area. And of course, the computer can input and output data.

That is all that a computer knows how to do. I sometimes joke that a computer is basically a "moronic idiot." That is, it is an "idiot" because of its limited instruction set, in other words, what it knows how to do. The "moronic" adjective comes from the fact that the computer always attempts to do precisely what you tell it to do. Say, for example, you tell the computer to divide ten by zero, it tries to do so and fails at once. If you tell the computer to calculate a person's wages by multiplying their hours worked by their hours worked, say, forty hours this week, the computer accurately and at great speed does the multiply instruction, and outputs their pay as $1600!

Thus, we have this rule: If you tell the computer to do something stupid, the computer accurately and at great speed does that stupid action! Your idea of a computer either malfunctioning or making a mistake is likely coming from this aspect.

What is a **program**? A computer program is a series of instructions that tell the computer every step to take in the proper sequence in order to solve a problem for a user. A **programmer** is one who writes the computer program. When the computer produces a wrong or silly result, it can be traced to an improper sequence of instructions or incorrect data being input to the program. That is, the responsibility or blame lies on either the original programmer who wrote out the instructions for the computer to follow or the user who has entered incorrect data.

For example, the latest Mars explorer satellite, after flawlessly traveling all the way to Mars, disintegrated on attempting to go into orbit around the planet. The reason NASA discovered is that the computer program controlling the satellite expected measurements to be in English units and someone supplied those measurements in the metric system.

Thus, I have a new term for programs that have one or more errors in them—"mostly working software." When a program has an error in it, that error is often called a "**bug**." And the process of getting all of the errors out of a program is called **debugging**. The term originates in the first generation of computers when someone removed a fly that had gotten into the computer circuitry and shorted it out - they were "debugging" the computer. In fact, mostly working software is a pet peeve of mine. Mostly working software—a program with one or more errors in it—is indicative of a programmer who has not done their job thoroughly for whatever reason. What would you think about having an operation done by a mostly working surgeon?

Designing Solutions—the Cycle of Data Processing

Perhaps the single most important aspect of solving a problem on the computer is the initial design phase in which one lays out with paper and pencil the precise steps the computer must take. Nearly every significant program follows the same fundamental design and it is called the **Cycle of Data Processing**, Figure 1.1.

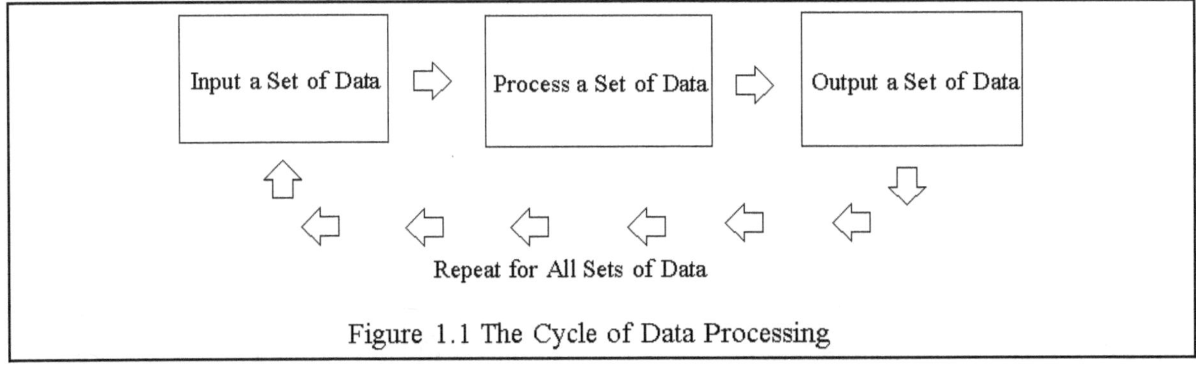

Figure 1.1 The Cycle of Data Processing

The Cycle of Data Processing is Input, Process, Output. First, the computer must input a set of data on which to work. Once the data has been input into the computer, it can then process that data, often performing some calculations on that information. When the calculations are finished, the computer outputs that set of data and the results.

For example, suppose that we wanted to write a program that would calculate someone's wages. First, the computer must be instructed to input the person's hours worked and their pay rate. Next, the computer uses the values it has just input to calculate the wages. Now that the wages are known, the computer can output the answer.

The Cycle of Data Processing is called IPO for short. IPO is the most basic design of a program. Thus, when you are confronting a computer problem to solve, IPO is the starting point! Input a set of information first. Then do the requisite processing steps using that information. Last, output the results.

Also, notice that in general, once that set of data and results have been output, the program would repeat the entire process on the next set of data until there are no more sets of data to be processed. It will be several chapters before we can implement all these steps.

Any deviation from the IPO sequence generally yields silly results. Suppose that someone tried to write a program to calculate a person's wages by doing OPI instead? That is, have the program output the answer before it knew what the hours that were worked or who was the person for whom the wages were to be found! Nonsense. Have the program calculate the pay before it has input the hours worked? How can it? You see, worked in reverse, it just makes no sense at all.

Occasionally, by accident someone writes an IP program. That is, it inputs the data and does the calculations, but fails to output the result. For example, you want a soda, so you input your quarters into the pop machine, Input. You press the button and the internal machinery makes lots of noise as it processes your request. But no can of soda ever appears, no Output! Or take a PO program. You walk by the soda machine and all of a sudden you hear it making noises and a can of soda appears! Or you walk by a piano and it starts playing—spooky when there is no input! Occasionally, someone writes an O program by accident. Suppose the program needed to print some headings at the top of a page and suppose the programmer made a booboo and continually printed headings over and over and over. You would have an O program. Or take a P program, the program just calculates, calculates, calculates, endlessly. This is sometimes called an infinite processing loop.

Whenever you are trying to design a program, remember that it usually must follow the IPO cycle. Now there are some exceptions, but they are rare. A possible exception might be producing a mathematical table of trigonometric function values. For example, suppose that you wanted to produce a table of the values of the sine and cosine of all angles from zero to ninety degrees. In such a case, there would be no input, just a process-output series as the program calculated each set of results and displayed them.

Building a Program

The computer internally operates on the **binary number system**. In the binary number system, the only valid digits are 0 and 1. For example, if you add in binary 1 plus 1, you get 10, just as if you added 9 + 1 => 10 in the decimal or base 10 system.

Why does the computer use binary? Electronic circuits can either have some electricity in them or not. If a circuit element, such as a transistor, has electricity, it can be said to contain a 1; if none, then a 0. This is the basis for computer operations. The actual instructions that make up a program are all in binary, long strings of binary digits. But no one wants to try to write out these long tedious series of 1's and 0's to try to direct the computer to solve a problem. Rather a high-level language is used. In this case, we use the C++ language.

In a high-level language, we use various symbols and mathematical notations to create the program, which is called the source program. A **source program** is the precise series of high-level language statements in the proper order for the computer to follow to solve the problem. For us, that source file has the file extension of .cpp.

Another piece of software called the **compiler** inputs our source program and converts it into the machine language, binary equivalent. If you make some typos, these show up as **syntax errors** when the compiler tries to convert the source program. A syntax error just means that you have coded the C++ instruction incorrectly. When you first compile a program and suddenly see a large number of compile errors, don't panic. Often it is just one small syntax error that cascades into many errors. Fix the original error and the others are automatically fixed. The output from a successful compile run is called an **object file** with the .obj file extension. The obj file contains the binary machine language instructions to control the computer in solving your problem. However, it is not the final program; object files are missing something.

Although we know nothing about the C++ programming language at this point, we can still understand what is missing in the object files. Suppose that as part of your program you needed to input some value, then compute the square root of that value and lastly print out that original number and its square root. Ignoring for the moment the input and output situation, how can you calculate the square root of any given number? If you have a strong math background, you probably are beginning to think of a method for doing just this. However, the C++ language has already provided that coding necessary to calculate the square root of any number for us. Why reinvent the wheel? We should use the solution provided by the compiler manufacturer. These short solutions to common needs such as finding the square root of a number are called functions.

A **function** is a subprogram, a collection of instructions that does a very precise action. Our program invokes or calls the function. When we do so, the computer temporarily halts execution of our instructions, goes to the instructions of the function, and carries out the function's instructions. When the function has completed its task, it issues a return instruction. The **return** instruction instructs the computer to go back to from where the function was called and resume execution there. So in short, our program calls the square root function, which then does its thing and returns back to us with the answer for our program to use as we wish. Functions are a vital part of any programming language.

So in the above example of inputting a number, finding its square root and then printing it, the object file as created by the compiler does not have in it the provided functions that are built into the language for our use. Specifically in this case, it is lacking the input, output, and the square root functions. These are located in the compiler's Lib folder. In order to make the final executable program, the .exe file, another piece of software called the Linker, must be run. The **Linker** program inputs our object files and finds all the needed system functions, such as the square root function, and builds the actual .exe file for us.

Finally, in order to make the entire process easy for us, from the initial editing or typing of the cpp file, through compilation and linking phases, most compiler manufacturers provide an **i**ntegrated **d**evelopment platform or **e**nvironment known as an IDE. An **IDE** is simply a software application that provides a convenient common environment to create, compile, link, and test execute our programs.

However, the price that the IDEs command for all this convenience is a project file. A **project file** (also called a **solution** in .NET) is a compiler manufacturer specific file(s) that tell the IDE everything it needs to know in order for it to build the final exe file. For example, it needs to know the name and location of our source file(s), where to place the exe final program, where the system libraries are located that contain all the system functions such as the square root function, and so on.

The Steps Needed to Create a Program—or — How to Solve a Problem on the Computer

The following steps represent an optimum procedure to follow to solve any problem on the computer. Every time you begin to tackle another programming assignment, this IS the procedure you should follow **slavishly**. In fact, I am letting you in on an inside programmer's secret. This series of steps, if followed precisely and honestly, results in the finished program in perfect working order with the least amount of your time spent on it and with the least frustration on your part. The reverse is true as well. If you want to spend vast amounts of time trying to get a programming assignment completed with maximal frustrations on your part, simply completely ignore these steps.

Here is the tale of one of my former students. She actually believed me about these steps and followed them slavishly. In her programming class, whenever a new assignment was handed out, she was known as the **last** person to ever get the problem coded into the computer, to get the cpp source file created. She was teased about this, but only briefly. She was always the very first person to have the assignment completed and ready to turn in! Soon, everyone in the class was turning to her for "help." She was looked upon as a programming goddess.

Now that I have your attention, what are the steps to developing a program?

Step 1. Fully understand the problem to be solved. Begin by looking over the output, what the program is supposed to be producing, what are the results? Then look over the input that the program will be receiving. Finally, determine what general processing steps are going to be needed to turn that input into the required output. If something about the problem is not clear, usually your instructor can assist you in understanding what is to be done. It is pointless to try to go on to the subsequent steps, if you are not 100% certain what must be done.

Part of this step of understanding the problem involves determining the algorithm to be used. An **algorithm** is a finite series of steps for solving a logical or mathematical problem. In computer programming, there are a large number of algorithms or methods that have been designed to assist us. Many of the Computer Science examples are illustrating common algorithms often needed in such programming. Likewise, many of the Engineering applications are concerned with numerical analysis algorithms. Some are used to find statistical averages, others to find roots of equations (where the graph crosses the x-axis), some for numerical integration, and so on. Part of learning how to program problems on the computer is learning about algorithms or methods to use.

Step 2. Design a solution using paper and pencil. This process involves two distinct activities.

The first action is to design what function(s) would best aid in the solution. Note these are functions that you must write, not those like the square root that are provided by the compiler manufacturer. This process is greatly aided by a design technology called Top-down Design, which is covered in Chapter 6 where you first learn how to write your own functions. Until then, no additional functions of our own design are needed and this action can be skipped until then.

The second action is crucial. Write out on paper the precise steps needed to solve the problem in the precise sequence. This is often called **pseudocode**. It is done by using English and perhaps some C++ like statements. You are trying at this point to say in English the correct sequence of steps that must be followed to produce the result.

Even though we know nothing about C++ at this point, given only the Cycle of Data Processing, we can still solve problems by writing out the pseudocode for them. Let's do so now. Suppose that the problem is to ask the user to input a number and then display the square root of that number. Here is some beginning pseudocode to solve this simple problem.

Display on the screen: "Enter a number: "
Input the user's number and store it in **Number**
Let **Answer** equal the square root of **Number**
Display on the screen **Answer**

Notice one crucial aspect of the solution above—in bold print. I have indicated where in the computer's memory to place the user's inputted number; it is going to be placed into a memory area known as **Number**. I have also shown that the result is going to be placed in a memory area known as **Answer**. Both **Number** and **Answer** are known as program variables. A **variable** is a memory location in which to store something. It is vital that the variable names are 100% consistent from line to line in your solution.

One common problem all programmers face is slightly different names. For example, suppose I had sloppily coded this solution as follows.

Display on the screen: "Enter a number: "
Input the user's number and store it in **Number**
Let **Answer** equal the square root of **Num**
Display on the screen **Ansr**

Remember that the computer is an idiot. It is going to try to do precisely what you tell it to do. In the above coding, the user's data in input and stored in a variable called **Number**. However, the variable used in the next line is not **Number** but **Num**. To us, it is obviously referring to **Number**, but to the compiler and the computer, **Number** and **Num** are two completely different things! Ditto on the result variable. **Answer** contains the square root return value, but I try to display the contents of the variable **Ansr**—a completely different name! Both yield instant compiler errors or produce erroneous garbage results. This then brings us to the most important step in this entire process!

Step 3. Thoroughly desk check the solution. Desk check means to play computer and follow slavishly and precisely the steps written down in the solution. You are looking for errors at this point. When you desk check, you must learn to play the role of a moronic idiot. That is, you do precisely what is written down, not what should be there, not what was intended, not what ought to be there—just what **is** there, as it is. To desk check, one really needs to draw a picture of the memory of the computer and place the variables as boxes in it so you can write in them. Let's see how the above incorrect solution could be desk checked. First we construct a picture of memory with all the variable names found in the solution and place a ??? in each box as shown in Figure 1.2.

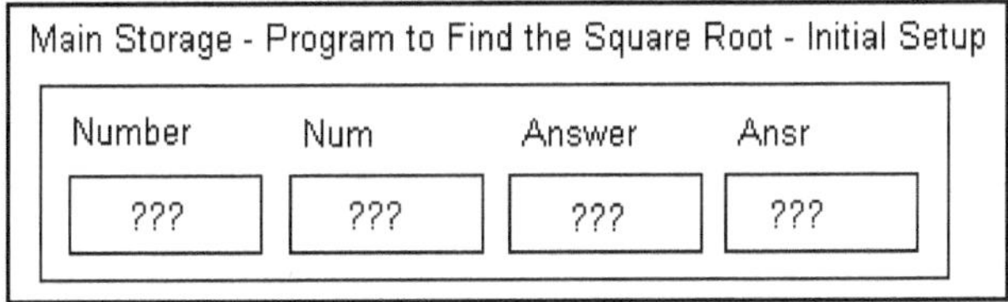

Figure 1.2 Main Storage — Initial Setup

Then, as you step through each line of the solution, make needed changes in the boxes. Assume the user enters 100. The square root is 10. But what does my erroneous coding do? Following the precise steps, we get the following results as shown in Figure 1.3.

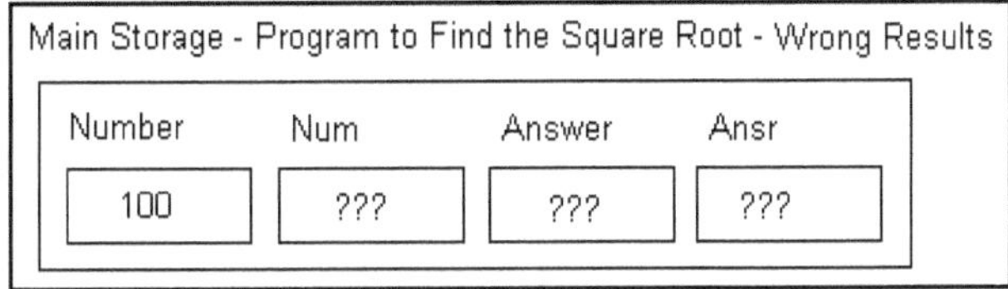

Figure 1.3 Main Storage — Wrong Results

Obviously, the solution is wrong. Here is how the correct version would be desk checked. Again the starting point is to draw boxes to represent all the variables in the solution and give them their initial values of ??? or unknown as shown in Figure 1.4.

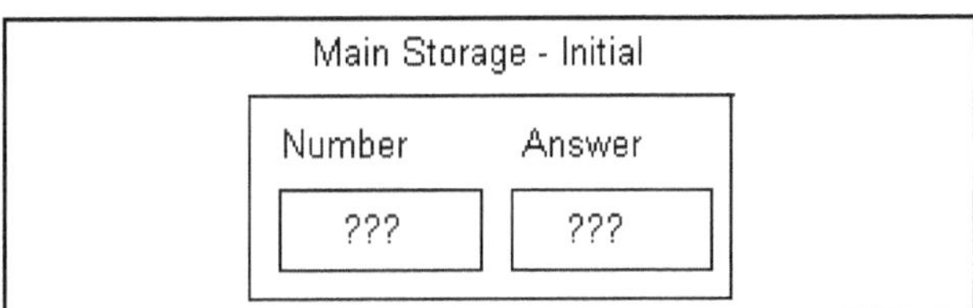

Figure 1.4 Main Storage — Correct Initial Setup

And when one has gone through the series of pseudocode steps, the following results as shown in Figure 1.5.

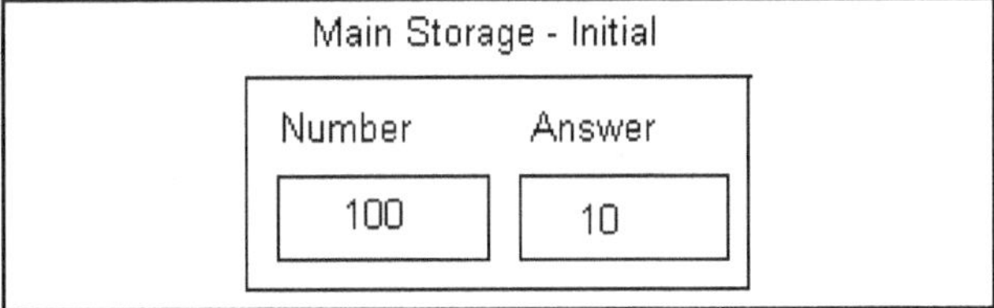

Figure 1.5 Main Storage — Correct - Final Results

The benefits of desk checking cannot be undervalued! The whole purpose of desk checking is to find all errors in the solution. Do not go on to Step 4 until you have thoroughly tested the solution. The key word is **thoroughly**. This is the point that so many veterans fail to do. Thoroughly means 100% completely under all conditions, all possibilities and so on. If you mostly desk check your program, then you have a mostly working program!

Step 4. Code the solution into the programming language, C++ in our case. With the pseudo coding and memory drawings at hand, it becomes a simple matter to convert the solution into a C++ source program. Your biggest challenge at this point is to get the syntax correct.

Step 5. Compile the program. If there are any errors found by the compiler, these are called **syntax errors**. Again, a syntax error is just incorrect coding. Just fix up the mistyping and recompile. Once you have a clean compile and built the program (and have an executable file), go on to the next step.

Step 6. Test the program with one set of data. Try inputting one set of test data only. Examine the output and verify it is correct. If you have done a good job with Step 3, Desk Checking, there are no surprises; the results are correct. If they are not correct, this is a more serious problem. An error here is called a runtime **logic error**. If the results are not correct, then you have missed something. It is back to Step 1 or 2 to figure out what was missed. After you discover what was missed, you then need to fix up the solution and re-desk check, then re-code, then recompile and try the single set of test data again. Obviously, you cannot go on to the next step until you have the program producing the right results for one set of test data.

Step 7. Thoroughly test the program. At this point, one tests the program thoroughly and completely. Often the problems in this text have some supplied test data sets you must use. These are designed to thoroughly test your program. If in testing, you discover another error, it is again a logic error. And it is once more back to Step 1 and 2. Then you have to redo all the steps in order to get back here to this step. Now, if you have done a thorough job of desk checking your pseudo coding, there are no more surprises—the program works perfectly no matter what tests you do. Once more, you cannot go on to the next step until the program is working perfectly.

Step 8. Put the program into production. In the real world, this means that the program is given to the users who now run it to solve their problems. In the case of student programs, they are handed in to be graded by the instructor who plays the role of the user. I guarantee you that users will indeed thoroughly test that program; users are known for doing all sorts of unexpected things with programs! What happens if the user finds an error? It is once again all the way back to Steps 1 and 2 once more. But if you have done a thorough job of desk checking and testing the program itself, the users will find nothing wrong.

In the industry, dollar costs have been calculated in this bug finding process. If it costs the company $1 to locate and find an error during Step 3 Desk Checking, then if that bug is found in Step 6, it costs $10. If that same error is found during Step 7, the thorough testing phase, it costs the company $100. However, if the program goes into production and the users find the error, then it costs the company $1,000! Hence, there is a major incentive to find all the program's errors early in the development cycle.

The Early Retirement Program

Let's apply the how to solve a problem logic to a simple problem. The Acme company wants to have a listing of all their employees that might consider a new early retirement plan. The input comes from their employee file, which consists of one line per employee, which contains the following information: the employee's id, their age, and the years they have been employed at Acme. To be considered a candidate, the employee must have worked for Acme for ten years and be at least 55 years old. The report should display the id number, age and years employed. The last line should contain the total number of possible candidates.

Looking over the input lines, three variables or fields are needed to store the incoming data, **id**, **age,** and **years_employed**. The output consists of these three fields. However, the last line is a count, which we can call **total_number**. Each time we discover that an employee is qualified for early retirement, we need to display their information and add one to the **total_number**. Our Main Storage diagram contains the three input fields and the **total_number** and is shown in Figure 1.6.

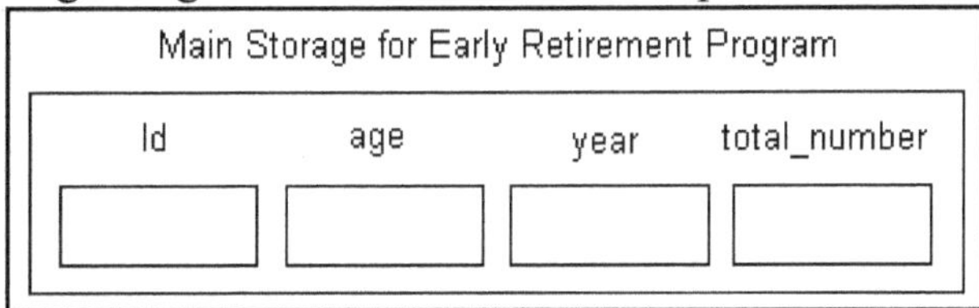

Figure 1.6 Main Storage — Early Retirement

Here is the English solution.
set **total_number** to 0
input an **id**, **age** and **years**
as long as there is a set of data, do the following
    if the **age** is greater than or equal to 55 and
      the **years** is greater than or equal to 10, then do the following
        display the **id**, **age** and **years**
        add one to **total_number**
    end of the then clause
    try to input another **id**, **age** and **years**
end of the do the following loop
display "The total number of possible early retirement candidates is "
display **total_number**

We can test the program with the following information.

```
123 60 21
234 44 10
266 55 10
275 55 9
284 56 9
345 25 5
```

```
344 34 12
```

And the output of the program is

```
123 60 21
266 55 10
The total number of possible early retirement candidates is 2
```

The Mechanical Robot Problem

To illustrate these design principles and to help you to get the feel for what is needed to be able to write programs, consider the Mechanical Robot Problem. Your company has been given a multimillion dollar robot in the shape of a person. For a demo test, you are to write out the solution of the following problem. The robot is initially seated an unknown distance from the wall. It has sensors in its fingers so that if its arms are raised, it fingers can tell if it is touching any obstruction, such as a wall. You are to instruct the robot to stand up and walk forward until it finds the wall, turn around and retrace its steps until it reaches the chair, at which point it should turn around and sit down.

Sounds simple when said in normal English. But the problem is that the robot does not understand English. Rather, as a computer, it understands a basic set of instructions. Here are the **only** commands the robot understands.

Stand up
Sit down
Raise arms
Lower arms
Turn around
Are your fingers touching anything? It replies yes or no.
Take one step (all steps are a uniform distance)
Set an internal counter to 0
Add one to the internal counter
Subtract one from the internal counter
Is the internal counter 0? It replies yes or no.

And these are the only commands it knows how to do. If you give it a command other than these precise ones, it stands there and does nothing.

Your job is to use only these commands and write out a solution that will work with all possible distances the robot might be from the wall. For simplicity, assume that the robot is always an integral number of steps from the wall. That is, the robot distance from the wall could be 0, 1, 2, 3, 4 or more steps. All steps are uniform in size. Thoroughly desk check your solution. Be sure it works if the robot is 0 steps from the wall as well as 5 steps. Note that if the robot is 0 steps from the wall, it still has room to raise its arms, at which point its raised arms would be touching the wall, if asked.

Be prepared to share your solution with others.

The Mechanical Mouse Problem

A mechanical mouse must run through a maze. The maze has only four "cells." Two outside walls of the maze are fixed as shown in Figure 1.7

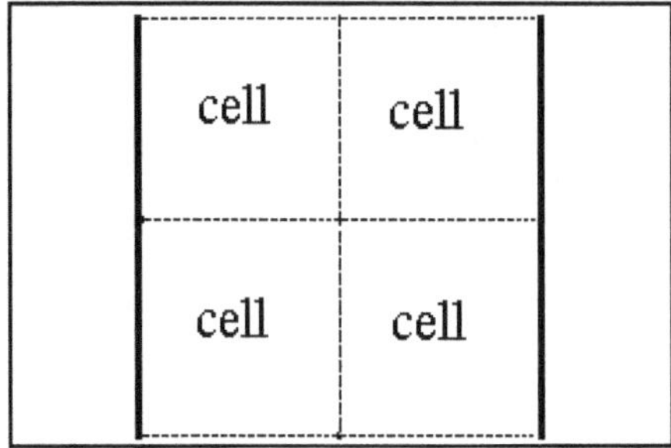

Figure 1.7 Mouse in a Maze Cell

Baffle walls may be erected on any of the dotted lines, but a maze is valid only if it meets these conditions:

1. One (only one) entry point on the entry side of the maze.
2. One (only one) exit point on the exit side of the maze.
3. An open passage from the entry point to the exit point.
4. Two of the four sides are open; two are closed on each cell that must be traversed.

Figure 1.8 shows three valid mazes.

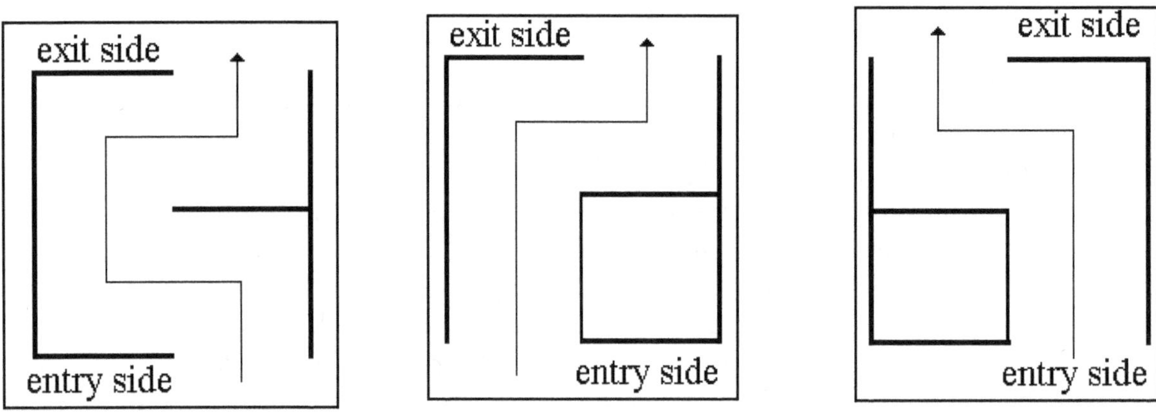

Figure 1.8 Three Valid Mouse Mazes

At the beginning, an operator will place the mouse on the entry side of the maze, in front of the entry point, facing the maze. The instruction, "Move to the Next Cell," causes the mouse to move into the middle of the entrance cell.

After that, the job is to move from cell to cell until the mouse emerges on the exit side. If the mouse is instructed to "Move to the Next Cell" when there is a wall in front of it, it hits the wall. In this case, there will be a sharp explosion, and both the mouse and maze will disappear in a cloud of blue smoke (and the game is lost). Obviously, the mouse must be instructed to test if it is "Facing a Wall?" before any "Move."

Your assignment: Write out a sequence of these permissible instructions, which navigates the mouse through any valid maze. The only permissible instructions are the following.

The Mechanical Mouse's Instruction Set

A. Physical Movement

Move to the Next Cell (the mouse will move in the direction it is facing).
2. Turn Right
3. Turn Left (all turns are made in place, without moving to another cell).
4. Turn Around

B. Logic

1. Facing a Wall? (through this test the mouse determines whether there is a wall immediately in front of it; that is, on the border of the cell it is occupying, and in the direction it is facing).
2. Outside the Maze?

If the mouse is outside the maze, it can also make the following decisions:

3. On the Entry Side? (If so, it gets frustrated and detonates in an explosion as well.)
4. On the Exit Side?

When your solution works on the above three mazes, test it on this last maze, Figure 1.9.

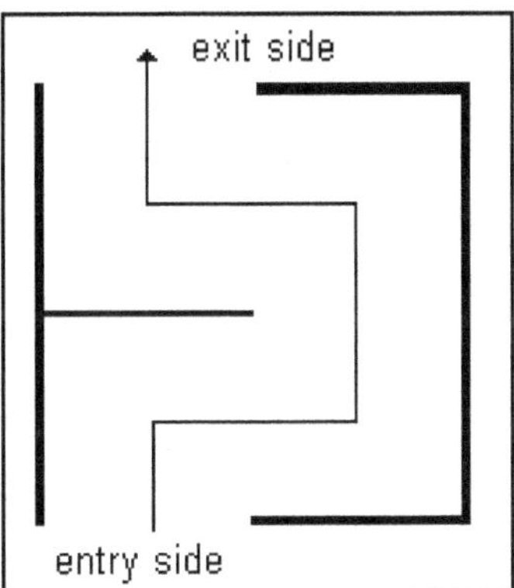

Figure 1.9 Test Maze

Basic Computer Architecture

In order effectively to write programs on the computer, some basic knowledge of computer architecture is required. The computer can be viewed as having two major components, the Central Processing Unit or CPU and main storage or memory. The **CPU** handles all of the mathematical operations, comparisons and input and/or output actions. **I/O** is often used to mean input and/or output operations. That portion of the CPU that carries out the mathematical operations and the comparisons is called the **ALU**, arithmetic and logic unit.

Main storage or memory is a vast collection of storage units called a byte. A **byte** is capable of storing one character of information. A byte is composed of eight connected bits. A **bit** is the tiniest storage element and consists of a circuit element that can be either on or off, representing a one or zero. A bit could be a tiny transistor located on a computer chip, for example. A single bit cannot be accessed directly; rather memory is accessed in terms of one or more bytes at a time. The term 1K or kilobyte represents 1024 bytes. It is 2^{10} bytes, which is why it is not an even 1,000 bytes. The term 1M or megabyte represents 1024K. Personal computers now typically have between 64M and 256M of main memory.

The computer can read and write the contents of a byte. But in order to do so, it must specify which byte is to be referenced. Bytes are located by their **memory addresses**. The first byte in memory is given the address 0. The next sequential byte is at address 1, and so on, rather like post office box numbers. However, no two bytes can ever have the same address. Each is at a distinct location. See Figure 1-9a below.

When data is to be input into the computer, it must be placed into some location in its memory. When data is to be displayed on the screen, for example, that data normally comes from some memory location. From the point of view of the high-level languages, such as C++, these memory locations are known as **variables**. Some variables might occupy only a single byte, for instance the letter grade you receive for the course. Other variables occupy many consecutive bytes, such as a person's name or address. Some kinds of variables always occupy the same number of bytes; the numerical types of data are a prime example.

When the power to the computer is turned off, the contents of the computer memory bytes are lost permanently. When power is subsequently turned back on, all of the main memory bytes are reset to zero. This kind of computer memory is known as **RAM**, random access memory; RAM is normal memory which can be both read and written—that is we can store something in memory and then later retrieve it back. Some computers have a small amount of **ROM**, read-only memory. This specialized type of memory has some permanent information stored or burned into it so that when power is reapplied, the contents reappear. ROM is used to store parts of the computer's operating system code in some PCs. The key point is that data stored in memory is gone once the program finishes its execution.

Attached to the computer are many I/O devices. The keyboard is an input device while the display screen, the CRT (cathode ray tube), is normally an output device. Floppy disks and hard disk drives are called auxiliary storage devices because they can store vast amounts of data on a semipermanent basis. Typically, programs read files of data stored on disk and can write files of results back to disk.

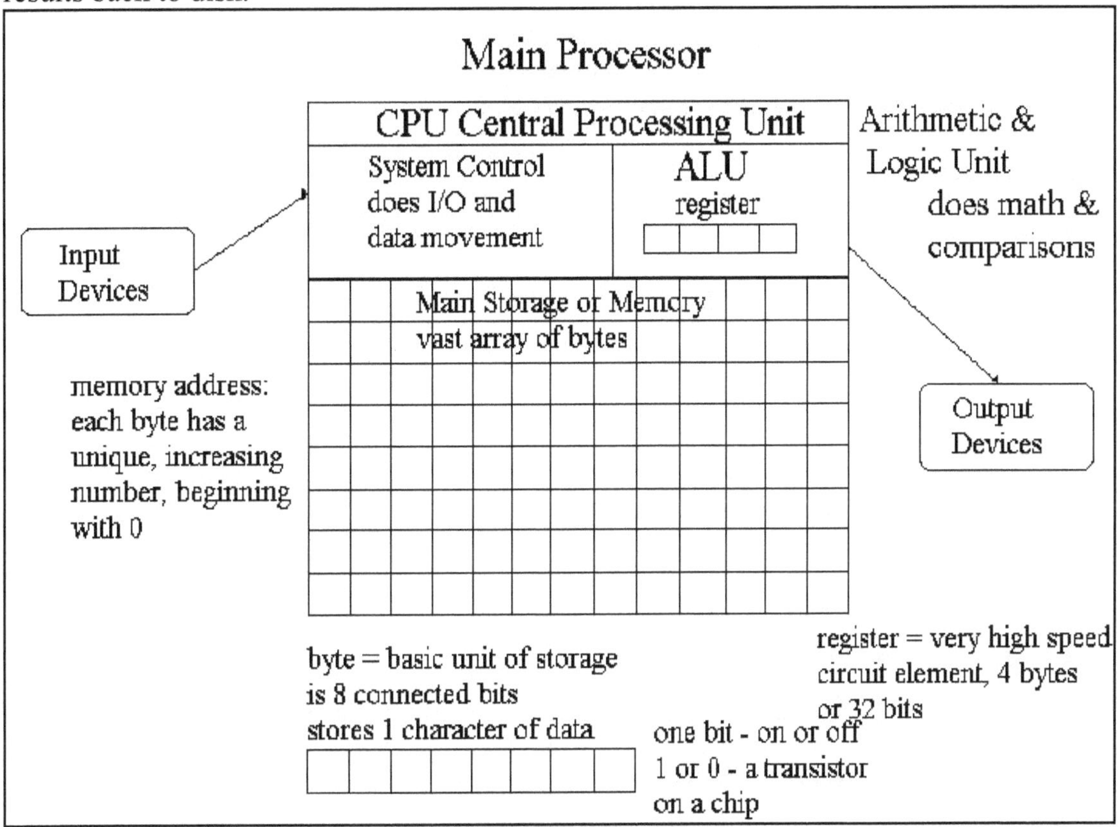

Figure 1-9a Parts of a Computer

The C++ Language and the Hello World Program

The C programming language was developed at Bell Labs in 1972 by Dennis Ritchie. C as a language makes extensive use of functions. The concepts of structured programming were pioneered during this era. **Structured programming** defines specific ways that computer instructions ought to be organized. Instead of coding instructions in any manner that suited the programmer, structured programming dictates that all the instructions are organized into one of three main groups: the sequence structure, the decision structure and the iterative structure.

The **sequence structure** represents one or more instructions that are to be executed one after the other in the sequence they are written. The short program to calculate the square root of a number was one sequence structure with four instructions in it.

The **decision structure** allows one to ask a question that can be answered yes/no or true/false. If some question is true, then the program can execute a series of instructions that are only done when the question is true. If it is false, the computer can optionally execute a different series of instructions.

The **iterative structure** performs a series of instructions over and over, a loop in other words, while some condition is true. These are shown in Figure 1.10.

It has been mathematically proven that any problem that can be solved on the computer can be solved using only these three organizations of instructions.

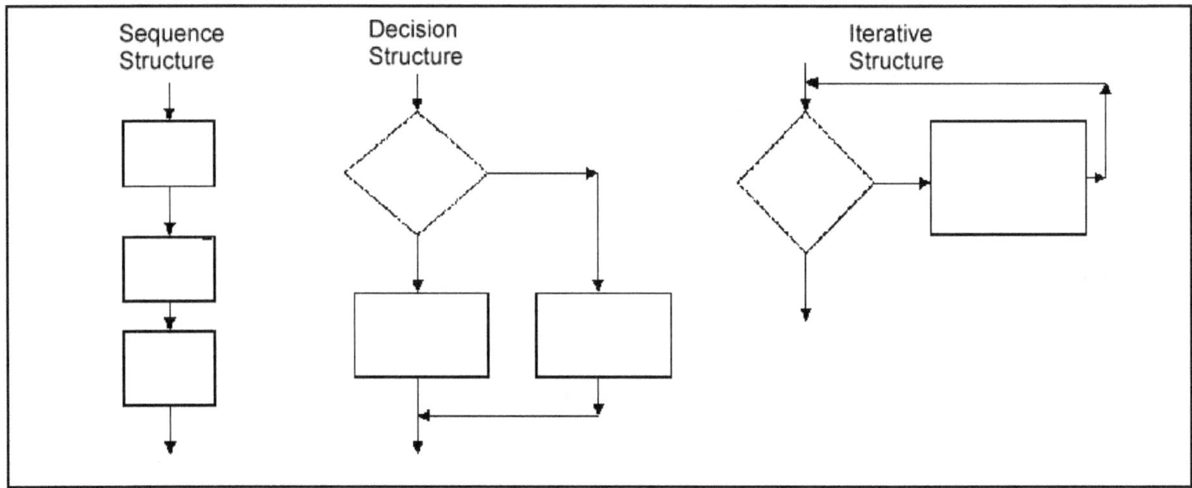

Figure 1.10 The Three Structured Programming Sequences

Over the years, it was realized that, while exceedingly powerful, C had some aspects that made it hard to learn and error prone. Further, while complex problems were successfully broken down into smaller functional units in C, the idea of treating the data and the functions that operate on that data as an object or entity led to the development of C++.

Bjarne Stroustrup, also at Bell Labs, in 1985 developed the C++ language as an extension of the C language. C++ encompasses most of the C language and adds new features to bypass the more error prone coding sequences of C and added support for working with objects, or Object Oriented Programming, OOP for short.

The adage you must learn to crawl before you can walk and run holds true. Before you can dive into the OOP portion of the language, you must master the basics, that is, the C portion.

In 1998, the C++ language was formally standardized by ISO (International Standards Organization). This means that now your C++ program can be written and compiled on any computer platform (PCs, minicomputers, mainframe computers) that has a standard C++ compiler.

In this chapter, we are going to examine the basic format of C++ so that we can write a simple program to display the message **"Hello World"** on the screen.

Rule 1. C++ is a case-sensitive language. Each of these "cost" identifiers is considered totally different from each other. Always be alert for the case of the various identifiers that are used.

```
cost   COST   Cost   cosT   cOSt
```

Rule 2. All C++ programs must have a main() function. When DOS launches your program, some compiler supplied coding known as the **C++ startup code** is what actually begins executing first. The startup code prepares the C++ environment for your program. Once it has everything set up, it then calls a function known as **main()**. Remember a function is like a subprogram, it does its required processing steps and then returns back to the calling point. Take the square root function, for example. When it is invoked, it finds the desired root and returns that answer back to the calling program, which can then use that answer as it chooses.

Notice that it is a lowercase **main()**. Notice also that there are () after it. Between the () one would pass to that function any values that function needed to do its work. In the case of the square root function, we would have to pass it the number of which we wanted to find the root. While the **main()** function is indeed passed some parameters from the C++ startup coding, we must wait until a later chapter to be able to understand and utilize those parameters. When an empty set of () are used, it means either that we are ignoring all the parameters or that the function really does not have anything passed to it. With the **main()** function, we are ignoring them for now.

Rule 3. A block of coding is surrounded by { } braces. The { brace indicates the start of a block of instructions. The } brace indicates where it ends. All of the instructions that we wish to have in our **main()** function must be surrounded by the pair { }.

Rule 4. The main() function does indeed return a value back to the C startup program. That return value is a completion code, which is in turn given back to DOS, and it indicates whether the program ran successfully. A value of zero is interpreted by DOS to mean that the program ran successfully. Any non-zero value indicates the program did not complete successfully. Normally, DOS ignores that return code. These return codes are integers or whole numbers—a number with no decimal point. And the kind of data the function is to return is coded preceding the name of the function. Thus, we have the basic shell as

```
int main () {
 ... our instructions go here
}
```

Here the **int** is short for integer. The first line says that this is the **main()** function, that it is accepting no parameters and that it returns an integer back to the caller which is the C++ startup program. This first line is also called the **function header**, for it marks the beginning of the function.

```
int main () { <- the function header
 ... our instructions <- the function body
}
```

All three lines above are called the **main() function**. The first line is the **function header**. All lines between the { and } braces are known as the **function body**.

Definition: **White space**, abbreviated **ws**, is a consecutive series of blanks, tabs, carriage returns, line feeds, printer page ejects and vertical tabs (found only on mainframe computer terminals, not on PCs).

Rule 5. White space is the delimiter in C++. That is, white space is used to separate things. Notice the function header for main just above. White space separates the return type of data (**int**) from the name of the function (**main**). When you press the enter key while editing a program, it generates a carriage return and a line feed. (A carriage return, as in a typewriter, goes back to column one, while the linefeed advances to the next line.) Since white space is used to separate things in C++ coding, you can use as much white space as you desire.

Rule 6. When coding a block of instructions, you need to use a consistent style of indentation. In C++, we have an inside joke: C++ is a write once, never read language. That is, a C++ program can be rather hard to read to see what it is doing. Thus, anything you can do to make your program more readable, the better it is. There are two major coding styles in common use. Here are the two.

Style A:

```
int main () {
  ... our instructions go here
  ... our instructions go here
}
```

Style B:

```
int main ()
   {
   ... our instructions go here
   ... our instructions go here
   }
```

Notice in each of these, our instructions are uniformly indented some constant amount. That way, one can tell at a glance the "block structure" of your program or what instructions are in what block of coding. Yes, soon our programs will have many begin—end braces as the logic becomes more complex.

How much do you indent? It is a matter of style. I prefer Style A with a uniform indentation of one space or blank. Through much experience, I have found that if one accidentally has one too few or one too many } braces, with Style A, it is much easier to find and fix than it is in Style B. I also indent one space because I prefer to see as much of the line of coding without horizontal scrolling as possible. Since I often put in lots of comments on lines of code to make them more understandable, my lines tend to be long.

One caution. Many editors, such as the Microsoft Visual C++ editor, insert tab codes to assist in maintaining the consistent indentation. Sometimes by accident, one enters some blanks or spaces by pressing the space bar to force things to line up. However, blanks and tab codes are two different things. Tabs are often expanded by different amounts between a screen and a printer. If you get tab codes and spaces (blanks) intermingled, while your source program may look perfect displayed on the screen, when you print it, jagged edges in the indentation may appear. The first action I always take when installing a new C++ compiler is to find the setting that replaces all tabs with a fixed amount of actual blanks (1 blank in my case). Realize that none of this affects the actual operation of the program. It only affects its visual appearance in a program editor.

Rule 7. Since the **main()** function is supposed to return back to the C++ startup code an integer indicating a successful execution, we must code a **return** instruction and give it the integer to return, a zero, to indicate that all is ok.

```
return 0;
```

Rule 8. All C/C++ statements end in a ; (semicolon). If it does not end in a semicolon, it is not a C statement. The function header for **main()—int main () {**—is not a C statement. Rather, it is a function header. Shortly we will see another example that is not a C statement.

Where do you place the **return 0;** instruction? It should be the last line of the **main()** function because when it is executed, the computer passes control back to the C++ startup program to terminate the program. Putting this together, we have thus far:

```
int main () {
 ... our instructions go here
 return 0;
}
```

Rule 9. C++ supports literal constants. In the above return instruction, the 0 is an integer constant or literal value. Some other literal numerical values are: 42, –10, 3.1415926 for example. If you want to have a single character literal value, enclose that letter within a single set of quote marks. 'A' might be a literal that represents the desired grade in this course. An 'F' might denote the sex of a customer. A literal string of characters must be enclosed within a set of double quote marks ("series of characters").

If we want to write a program to display **Hello World** on the screen, then this is precisely what we need, a literal character string. We can code the message we want to display on the screen as

```
"Hello World"
```

Literal constants are covered more completely in the next chapter. All we now need is the output instruction that displays the message on the screen.

C++ views the consecutive series of characters being displayed on the screen as a program executes an **output stream**, rather similar to the water stream coming from a garden hose. Instead of water, characters appear on the screen, one after the other, in sequence. Treating the output to the screen as an object to be manipulated is actually an OOP (object oriented program) construct. An **object** in C++ consists of all the data and functions to operate on that data - all taken together as an entity. The blueprint for the compiler to follow to make an actual instance of an object is called a

class in C++. In simple terms, a class is just the model that defines how a real object is to be constructed when one is needed.

For example, if one were to create a Car class in C++, one would want various informational items or data to be a part of the object, including such things as the make, model, color, VIN number, size of the gas tank, current amount of gas and miles per gallon. Also, the class or model defines functions to operate on those items, such as **FillGasTank()**. Given the class definition, then one can actually make a car object, say a Ford Bronco, and fill it with gas and so on. The Bronco is then an instance of the Car class.

In a similar manner, C++ defines the class **ostream** to represent output to the screen. The class has various informational items and most importantly a way to output data to the screen. The specific instance of that **ostream** class that we use to display information on the screen is called **cout**. The function we use to output data is called the **insertion operator** or <<. The line of code to output our literal string message is then

```
cout << "Hello World";
```

The insertion operator displays exactly the characters as we have them in the string. Visualize the insertion operator as a directional arrow that is sending or flowing the data to its right to the destination on its left, **cout**, which is the screen.

However, remember that the computer does precisely what you tell it to do. If we ask it to display the above message, this is what appears on the screen. When the instruction is done, notice where the cursor is located.

```
Hello World_
```

The cursor is positioned after the 'd'. Normally, like a typewriter, when we have finished displaying all the characters on a line, we want the cursor to be in column one of the next line. In C++, we have to tell the **ostream** to go to a new line. This can be done in one of two ways.

The first way to generate a carriage return and line feed is to display the new line code in our string. The **new line code** is **\n**. Thus, a better version of our message would be

```
cout << "Hello World\n";
```

Wherever the new line code is found, there is a new line at that point.

What would be the output from the following instruction?

```
cout << "Hello\n\n World\n";
```

Remember that it displays exactly what you tell it to display. The output is

```
Hello

 World
_
```

Two **\n** codes in a row cause double spacing. The 'W' character does not line up with the 'H' character because there is a blank or space before the 'W' character after the second new line code.

The second way to generate the new line is to insert **endl**, the end line, value into the output stream. This method is not as convenient in this example, but is coded this way.

```
cout << "Hello World" << endl;
```

The **endl** is called an output **manipulator** because it is manipulating the output stream in some way, here adding a new line code at the point that it appears. If we wanted to have each word on a separate line, code

```
cout << "Hello" << endl << "World" << endl;
```

The above line of coding is an example of **chaining** several separate pieces together into a single output instruction. It could also be done with separate lines as follows

```
cout << "Hello";
cout << endl;
cout << "World";
cout << endl;
```

There is no limit to how many lines of output are displayed in a single **cout** instruction. To chain, just code another insertion operator followed by the next piece of information to be displayed.

Here is how our first program appears thus far, though we are not yet finished.

```
int main () {
 cout << "Hello World\n";
 return 0;
}
```

How does the compiler know what **cout** is or that **endl** is an output manipulator? It doesn't unless we provide the compiler with the blueprints to follow. As it stands, if we were to compile this program, we would get a bunch of error messages saying that the compiler does not know what these two things are.

It is our job to include in our programs the needed blueprints for the compiler to use. These blueprints are the class definitions and function prototypes. A **function prototype** is a blueprint or model for the compiler to follow when it wants to call a function. A function prototype looks very similar to the function header line. It gives the name of the function, its parameters (if any) and what kind of information the function will be returning (if any). Until Chapter 6, we use functions provided by the compiler manufacturer, the standard functions of the C++ language. However, in Chapter 6, we will learn to write our own functions; function prototypes are explored there in depth.

In our beginning program, we need to tell the compiler to include the definitions of the **ostream** class and the manipulators. This is done by issuing an order to the compiler to copy the contents of some files into our program—the **#include directive**. Its syntax is

```
#include <filename>
```

The **#include** tells the compiler to copy a file into our program at this place in the program. The <> tells the compiler to look for the file in its own \INCLUDE folders. Each compiler has one or more include folders in which the various class definitions and standard C++ function prototypes are located. Included files usually have the **.h** file extension, h for header file. However, many of the newer C++ headers have no file extension. In our first program, we must code the following

```
#include <iostream>
```

```
#include <iomanip>
using namespace std;
```

The header file **iostream** contains the definition of the output stream class; the **iomanip** file contains the definitions of the manipulators (for **endl** in this case). Notice that these are compiler directives and not C++ statements and therefore do not end in a semicolon.

With all the possible identifiers in C++, a way to manage their use was added to the C++ language recently. A **namespace** is a collection of identifiers, class definitions and functions grouped together for a program's use. The C++ language provides the **namespace std** that refers to all the normal C++ classes and function prototypes. When a program uses the standard **namespace**, the header file includes take on an abbreviated form. The using statement notifies the compiler that a particular **namespace** is to be used in this program. It is coded as follows.

```
using namespace std;
```

Where are header file includes placed in programs? The answer is simple.

Rule 10. Header file includes must be physically before the first usage of what they define or contain. Thus, nearly always, the includes are the very first thing in the source program. Here is our complete first program that displays **Hello World** on the screen.

```
#include <iostream>
#include <iomanip>
using namespace std;

int main () {

 cout << "Hello World\n";

 return 0;
}
```

Notice one small detail. I have added **blank lines** to separate key lines of coding to make it more readable. Please use blank lines in your coding to assist the readers of your program. A blank line in a source program acts the same way a blank line does in a book, marking the end of paragraphs. In a book, the reader knows that they may take a breather when they reach the end of a paragraph. It is the same way when reading a program. One can safely pause when a blank line is encountered. In programming, we use blank lines to group related instructions to make the reading of the program easier.

Rule 11. Comments in C++ take two forms. The short form is //. When the // is not part of a literal character string, everything after the // to the end of that line is considered a comment by the compiler. The long form or C style comment is everything between a /* and a */ is considered a comment, when not inside a string literal constant. For example

```
cout << endl; // display a blank line here
/* this is a comment */
/* this is a
   longer
```

```
comment */
```

The following are not comments because they are imbedded in a character string literal value.

```
cout << "This is a // strange message\n";
cout << "This is also strange /* not a comment */ \n";
```

To help document a program, I use block comments that look like this.

```
/***************************************************************/
/*                                                             */
/* First Program in C++: display Hello World on the screen     */
/*                                                             */
/***************************************************************/
```

Why? Imagine someone hands you a C++ program that has no comments in it. How can you figure out what that program does—what its purpose is? You would have to read through the program coding to attempt to find out.

Now suppose someone handed you the following program. Notice you can tell at a glance what it does without having to read a line of C++ coding.

```
/***************************************************************/
/*                                                             */
/* First Program in C++: display Hello World on the screen     */
/*                                                             */
/***************************************************************/
#include <iostream>
#include <iomanip>
using namespace std;

int main () {

   cout << "Hello World\n";

   return 0;
}
```

Rule 12. Always document your program. Include some form of comment at the very beginning outlining in twenty-five words or less what the purpose of the program is. Also include additional comments where they are needed to help someone follow the logic and operation of your program. Throughout the text, you will see numerous examples of what I think a well-documented program ought to look like. Some of you may not care for the impressive visual impact that my block comments make; in that case use a more gentle style. Style is not at issue, but the comments are.

It has been said many times in this industry that a complex program with no internal comments at all is practically worthless because it is nearly impossible for someone other than the author to maintain. Please develop good habits by documenting your programs as you write them.

What should you do next? Get your compiler installed and see if you can get this Hello World program entered and to execute successfully.

CPP for Computer Science and Engineering

Note that this chapter does not have the Computer Science or Engineering Examples sections.

Design Exercises

1. How would you solve this problem? What is the answer? A bug wishes to climb to the top of a 12-foot tall telephone pole. During the day, it climbs 3 feet. However, while it sleeps at night, the bug slides back down 2 feet. How many days does it take the bug to reach its objective, the top of the pole?

2. Sketch a solution in pseudocode or English to solve this problem. A math teacher wishes to have a program that displays the multiplication tables for her fourth graders. She wants the program to accept any whole number (integer) from 1 to 9. The program then displays the multiplication tables from 1 to that number. A sample run might be as follows. Note she enters the underlined number 4.

```
Enter a number from 1 to 9: 4
1 x 1 = 1 x 1 = 1
1 x 2 = 2 x 1 = 2
1 x 3 = 3 x 1 = 3
1 x 4 = 4 x 1 = 4
2 x 2 = 2 x 2 = 4
2 x 3 = 3 x 2 = 6
2 x 4 = 4 x 2 = 8
3 x 3 = 3 x 3 = 9
3 x 4 = 4 x 3 = 12
4 x 4 = 4 x 4 = 16
```

3. Sketch a solution in pseudocode or English to solve this problem. A manager of some carpet store wishes a program that calculates the square footage of carpet a customer requires and determines his cost for installation based on the square footage. The program first asks him to enter the length and width of the room. It then displays the square footage. His installation cost is found by multiplying the square footage by 7.5%. A test run might be:

```
Enter the length and width of the carpet: 10 20
The square footage is 200 and the service charge is $15.00
```

Stop! Do These Exercises Before Programming

Correct the errors in the following programs. If you are having trouble determining what is wrong, you can always make a test program, enter this coding and see what the compiler indicates is wrong.

1. Why does this program not compile? Show what must be done to fix it?

```
int main () {
  cout << "Hi there!\n";
  return 0;
}
#include <iostream>
#include <iomanip>
```

2. Why does this program not compile? Show what must be done to fix it?

```
#include <iostream>
#include <iomanip>
Int Main () {
  Cout << "Great day outside!!\n";
  return 0;
}
```

3. Why does this program not compile? Show what must be done to fix it?

```
#include <iostream>
#include <iomanip>
using namespace std;
int main () {
  cout << Hi there! << endl;
  return 0;
}
```

4. Why does this program not produce any output? Show what must be done to fix it.

```
#include <iostream>
#include <iomanip>
Using Namespace Std;
int main () {
  return 0;
  cout << "John Jones successfully made this" << endl;
}
```

5. Why does this program not compile? Show what must be done to fix it?

```
#include <iostream>
#include <iomanip>
using namespace std
int main ()
  cout << "Something is very wrong here" << endl;
  return 0;
}
```

6. Why does this program not compile? Show what must be done to fix it?

```
#include <iostream>
#include <iomanip>
using namespace std;
int main (){
  c out >> "Something is still wrong here" << endl;
  Return zero;
}
```

7. Why does this program not compile? Show what must be done to fix it?

```
#include <iostream>
#include <manip>
using namespace std;
int main (){
  cout << 'I cannot get this program to work!' << << endl;
  return 0;
}
```

8. This program compiles, but what is stylistically wrong? Show what must be done to fix it?

```
#include <iostream>
#include <iomanip>
using namespace std;
int main () {
cout << "Something is not quite right here" << endl;
return 0;}
```

9. A programmer has written the following solution to calculate wages for their company's weekly payroll. The programmer is convinced it will work just fine and has submitted it to you for verification and approval. This means you must thoroughly desk check their solution. How many errors can you find in it? Show how they could be repaired so that it would work.

Each line of input contains the employee's number, the hours they have worked, and their pay rate. Any hours more than 40 are to be paid at time and a half.

Set **total_payroll** to 0
input **employee_id** and **hours** and **payrate**
as long as we got a set of data, do the following
    multiply **hours** by **payrate** and store it in **pay**
    if the **hours** is greater than 40 then do this
        Pay = (**hours** - 40) times **rate** times 1.5
    end the if
    add the **pay** to the **TotalPayroll**
    display the **id number** and the **pay**
    try to input another **employee_id** and **hours** and **payrate**

end the do series here
display the **total_payroll**

Test the program with the following input lines of data
123455 40 5.00
245346 20 7.50
535323 60 6.00

Hint: draw a picture of what main storage or memory should be. Pay attention to the names of the variables used in the solution.

What is the precise output from these output instructions? Fill in the boxes to indicate the results. Each box represents one column on the screen and each row represents one line on the screen.

10.

```
cout << "One";
cout << "Two";
cout << "Three";
```

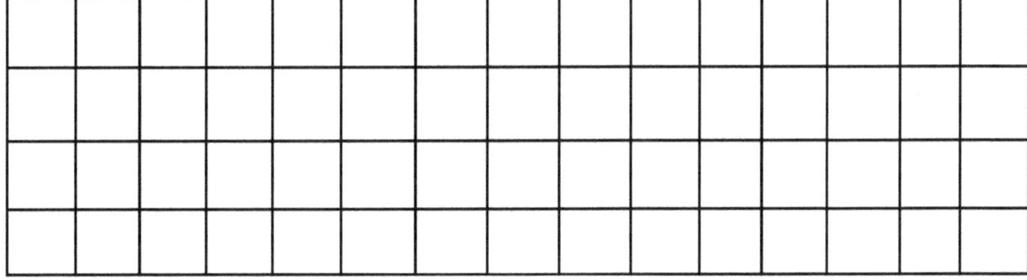

11.

```
cout << "One ";
cout << "Two ";
cout << "Three";
```

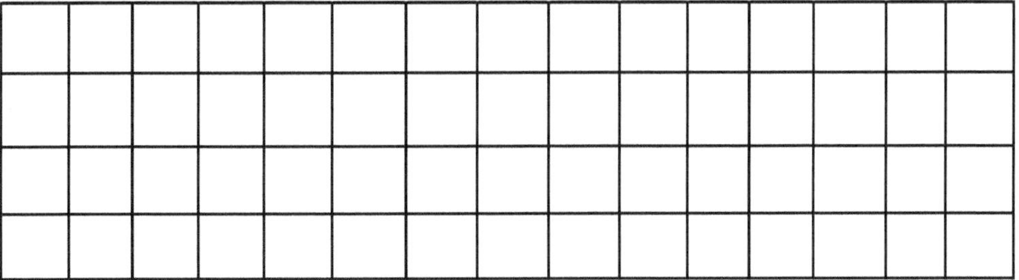

12.

```
cout << "One" << endl;
cout << "Two"<< endl;
cout << "Three" << endl;
```

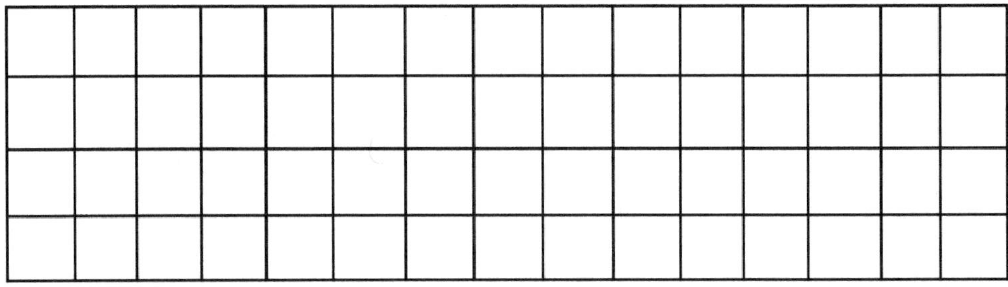

13.

```
cout << "One\n";
cout << "\nTwo\n";
cout << "Three";
```

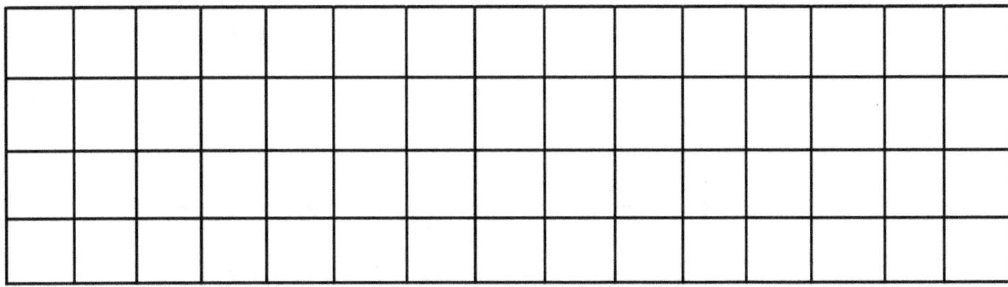

14.

```
cout << "One\nTwo\nThree\n";
```

Programming Problems

Although we do not know enough about C++ to actually write programs yet, we have all the skills needed to write out English step by step solutions and to desk check them. Developing the skill to write out the sequential steps needed to solve a problem on the computer is always the first step to solving a programming problem.

Problem Cs01-1—Make a Sandwich

Write the steps that someone can follow to make a peanut butter–jelly sandwich. The bread, peanut butter and jelly are located in the refrigerator. Utensils are located in a cabinet drawer. Be as specific as you can. Imagine a 6-year-old trying to follow your instructions. That is, the person is going to follow your instructions to the letter. Assume that the person has no prior knowledge about how it should be done. As a guide, you probably do not need to use more than fifty different words in the solution. (Note this is not supposed to be written as a computer program.)

Problem Cs01-2—Directions

A friend from out of town is staying with you and needs directions to the nearest bus station. Write out the series of steps necessary to direct them from your house to the station. While they are not likely to walk all the way, assume that they are navigating themselves, either on foot or by car (a bit unrealistic). The object is to give directions to enable someone to get from your house to the station. If you do not have a bus station, use the nearest train station or airport. (Note this is not supposed to be written as a computer program.)

Problem Cs01-3—Cost of Goods Sold

Using English statements, write out a solution to the Cost of Goods Sold problem. Acme company has a file of sales data. Each line in the file contains the quantity sold and the cost of that item. The report should look like the following

```
Qty     Cost     Total Cost
  42    10.00      420.00
  10     4.99       49.90

Grand Total Cost of Goods is 469.90
```

Use the Cycle of Data Processing as your guide. The basic steps are Input, Process, Output, and then back to Input until there is no more data to be processed. (Note this is not supposed to be written as a computer program.)

Problem Cs01-4—Your First Actual Real Computer Program

Write a program that outputs your personal information in a card-like format. Your card information should be a series of lines containing the title line, your name, address, city, state, zip, and phone number. Format it similar to mine:

```
Program Cs01-4 by Vic Broquard

Name:     Vic Broquard

Address:  10305 Ridge Line Road
          East Some City, IL
          61611

Phone:    (309) 699-9999
```

Note that this program has no "variables" and consists of one or more **cout** lines. You can output the information using six **cout** instructions or jam it all into a single **cout**.

Create the cpp source program, compile, and execute the program.

Problem Engr01-1—Converting Degrees to Radians

Write out the steps to solve the following problem. Use English or mathematical equations as needed. Follow the Cycle of Data Processing, Input, Process, Output, and repeat until the user is done. Do not actually write the C++ program.

The user enters an angle in degrees; the program converts it into radians and displays the results. The program should convert as many angles as desired until the user enters a -999 for the angle at which point the program stops. Here is a sample run of how the program should work.

Enter an angle in degrees: 0
0 degrees is 0 radians
Enter an angle in degrees: 180
180 degrees is 3.14158 radians
Enter an angle in degrees: -999
Thanks for using the Converter Program

Pay particular attention to what is constant literal character string information and what is variable information on the input and output processes. (Note this is not supposed to be written as a computer program.)

Chapter 2—Numerical Processing

Section A: Basic Theory

Introduction

When one begins to write a program, the first action should be to define the variables that the program needs; variables are places in memory in which to store data items. Next, one writes the instructions to input values from the user (say, via the keyboard) and store those values in the variables. Now that the variables have values, one can write the needed calculation instructions and finally the instructions to display the results. This chapter concentrates on numeric type of variables and constants along with their basic input and output instructions.

Variables and Constants

In C++, a **data object** is a region in memory in which to store data. A **data value** is the contents of that object. A place to hold the quantity purchased, say 42, could be called **qty** but the actual contents of **qty**, its data value, would be 42 in this case. A variable in C++ is a **modifiable data object**, that is, it is a place to store data, and the value stored there can change, as we desire.

The opposite of a variable is a constant data object. With a **constant data object**, once the initial value is defined, it can never be changed in any way. If we created a variable to hold the number of months in a year, it should be a constant data object because its value, 12, ought not ever be changed. Similarly, if we defined a variable to hold the value of PI, it should be a constant as well, 3.14159.

Integer versus Floating Point (Real) Numbers

Thinking about the number of months in a year and the value of PI illustrates that there are inherently two types of numerical data, integer (whole numbers) and real (floating point) numbers. Integer numbers are discrete values on the number system; they never contain any fractional part. Some examples of integer numbers are 10, 42, 84, 99, and –88. Real numbers or floating point numbers contain a possible fractional amount. Any number with a decimal point is a floating point number. Some examples include 3.14159, 123.55, 10. and –.00123. Notice that the addition of the decimal point on the 10. **has** changed it into a real number from an integer.

When entering some real or floating point constant numbers, often they are very large or very small, with many leading or trailing 0's. In such cases, use the scientific notational form. For example, 123.45 could be rewritten as $.12345 \times 10^3$ and entered as a constant as .12345E3, where the E stands for "exponent" and the 3 digit is the power of ten. Here are some other examples.

123000000.0 could also be coded as .123e9 or 1.23e8 or 12.3e7 or 123.e6

.000123 could also be coded as .123e–3 or 1.23e–4

Scientific notation closely resembles how the computer will store floating point numbers. Specifically, if we had 1.23e+002 representing 123.00, then the 1.23 is called the mantissa; the e stands for exponent power of 10; and the +002 is the exponent, meaning 10^2. When the computer stores a floating point number, it stores both the exponent and the mantissa.

In summary, 123.00 represents the fixed point notation while 1.23e+002 represents that same number in scientific notation. They are the same number. Which way the computer displays them to us is controlled by the program. See the Insertion of Floating Point Numbers into an Output Stream section below.

Which Type of Data Do You Use for Which Variable?

Now which data type you use when defining a variable is significant. The computer's integer math instructions are some of the fastest executing instructions. On the other hand, floating point math instructions are some of the slowest. Furthermore, some variables represent discrete integral values. How could one have 5.5249 months in a year? Similarly, a count of the number of employees in a company would be an integer (how could you have 10.3487 employees)? The quantity of cans of soup purchased would be an integer. However, the cost of one can of soup would need to be stored in a floating point variable ($0.49).

One cannot just make all the numerical data fields in a program arbitrarily a floating point number any more than you can make them arbitrarily all integers. The deciding factor is "will this field or variable ever possibly have a fractional part?" If so, it must be defined as a floating point number. If not, it should be an integer type.

Definition of Variables

The syntax to define a variable is actually quite simple.

```
datatype variable_name;
```

Let's begin with the two most commonly used data types, the **int** and the **double**. The **int** is a short form of the word **integer**. (Yes, you could spell it out, but most programmers simply use **int**.) An **int** variable can only contain an integer or whole number. A **double** specifies a floating point number, a number with a decimal point and possible fractional portion. Thus, in the definition of a variable, the data type can be either an **int** or a **double**. In the ensuing chapters, we explore other possibilities.

After the data type comes the name you wish to call this variable. What are the rules for names in C++?

1. Names can be from one character long to as many characters as desired; however, only the first thirty-one characters are used by the compiler.

2. The name must begin with a letter of the alphabet or the _ character. (However, names beginning with an _ generally have a special purpose meaning and should be avoided.)

3. Each name must be unique.

4. Remember also that C++ is case sensitive.

5. The _ character can be used to separate compound names.

6. A blank cannot be used in a variable name because a blank is a form of white space and white space is the delimiter between language elements.

7. Numerical digits can be a part of the name after the first character of the name.

The following are valid names in C++: **cost**, **Cost**, **COST**, **qty**, **quantityOnHand**, **PI**, **department5**, **invoiceNumber**, **firstName**, **R2D2**, **resistance**, **ohms** and **grade**.

These are invalid names in C++: **invoice number** and **3-d**. Why? A blank cannot be part of the name in the first one, and a name can neither begin with a digit nor contain a minus sign (which is interpreted by the compiler to mean a subtraction operation).

8. There are some reserved words in C++ and these words are the language "verbs" and components. A variable cannot be a reserved word.

For example, a variable name could not be **int** or **double** because these are the reserved words for the two data types. While I could compile a list of all known reserved words, such is not needed for two important reasons. Both are discussed under the next rule.

9. All variable names in a program must be meaningful names.

This rule is true in every programming language. The names you choose to call the variables of your program absolutely must be representative of their meaning. Someone, you included, must be able to read the program's instructions and make sense of them. If your program needed to have a variable to represent the quantity ordered and the item's cost, then there is nothing to prevent you from calling them Fred and Wilma, respectively, or x and y, or v1 and v2. However, doing so makes the program nearly impossible for another to decipher! In this example, what would be good meaningful names? It is a matter of taste and clarity. If I were naming them in my program, I would likely call them **qty** and **cost** because I tend to favor shorter names. However, if you are having trouble following coding sequences, longer more descriptive names can aid you; try calling them **quantityOnHand** and **costOfGoods**, for example.

When solving Engineering problems, often a mathematical equation is involved. Suppose we need to calculate the force on an object given its mass and acceleration. The equation is f = m a. In such cases, it is acceptable to name the variables f, m and a. However, it is also acceptable to call them force, mass and acceleration. It would not be meaningful to call them x, y and z. In programming, when a programmer sees variables x, y and z, they often visualize a three-dimensional coordinate system!

The key point is that no language element that is a reserved word would be a meaningful variable name in most programming applications.

The second reason that it is not important to have a large list of reserved words is that most compilers today provide an editor in which to type in a program. The editors have chroma-color syntax highlighting systems. This system operates as you type in characters. Suppose that you type in the following two letters: in. They appear in a normal font. However, the second that you type the letter t as the next character, the editor turns the three letters into some form of color-highlighting: ***int***. It is trying to show you that this is a key C++ identifier. If you then type a fourth letter, say you intend to spell out interest, as soon as you enter the letter e next, the color-highlighting reverts back to plain text as it is now not that key identifier: inte. Once you have typed in a couple programs, you will instinctively make use of that color-highlighting system. Since the editor displays reserved words in a fancy manner, there is no need to have a lengthy list of names to avoid.

The Issue of the Case of a Variable Name

What about case and compound variable names such as a variable to represent a person's first name? One could use any of the following: **firstname, FirstName first_name, firstName**. Of course, there are many more possibilities than these four. However, these four are sufficient to define the issue at hand. Take the first version, **firstname**. When a variable name is actually a compound name formed from two words, using all lowercase letters all run together makes the name harder to read. Programmers usually avoid that if possible.

A better solution is to use the _ character: **first_name**. However, using a form of capitalization is often seen as an even better way to make compound variable names more readable: **FirstName** and **firstName**. However, it is my personal suggestion that you avoid capitalizing the first word of a compound variable name or the first letter of any variable name. That is, don't use **FirstName** or **Quantity**, rather capitalize the second and subsequent words in the compound name: **firstName** and **quantity**. Why?

I am assuming that you are all going to master the beginning C++ programming and move on into the advanced C++ courses and perhaps even into Windows programming as well. In almost all of Windows programming and in much of advanced C++ work, the key identifiers and function names often must be capitalized. Thus, if you capitalize your variable names, eventually you will not easily be able to tell at a glance whether a given identifier is your variable or a C++ or Windows identifier. It is called "name space pollution" in the industry. The word name space here means the universe of identifier names of the program. Throughout this text, when I use a variable name that is formed from two or more words, the second and subsequent words are capitalized. No normal variable name of mine ever begins with a capital letter unless there is no better alternative.

Similarly, for two reasons, do not code all of your variable names in all uppercase letters, such as **QUANTITY**. First, when you use all uppercase letters in a variable name, others tend to perceive it as "shouting." THIS SENTENCE IS VIEWED BY MOST READERS AS SHOUTING. Second, an identifier in all uppercase letters tends to stick out readily when viewed in a sea of lowercase letters. However, in our programs, we are soon going to have some special identifiers used to represent very special items. By convention amongst all programmers, these special identifiers are always fully upper-cased so that they do stick out as special items.

Defining More Than One Variable in the Same Statement

One can also define multiple variables of the same data type with a single statement. This alternate syntax is:

```
data type name1, name2, name3, ... name_n;
```

If the problem required three integers, one for quantity, product id, and year, one could code:

```
int quantity, productId, year;
```

or

```
int quantity,
    productId,
    year;
```

or

```
int quantity;
int productId;
int year;
```

Suppose that one needed some **double** variables to hold the charge, voltage, and resistance of a circuit element. One could code either of these to define the variables.

```
double charge, voltage, resistance;
```

or

```
double charge,
       voltage,
       resistance;
```

or

```
double charge;
double voltage;
double resistance;
```

Which style is preferred? Again, questions of style are best answered by each individual programmer. Here are common arguments for and against each. Statistically, a programmer has fewer errors in coding when they can see all of the coding on the screen at one time. Defining multiple variables on one line reduces the total lines of a program thereby making more of the program visible before you have to scroll. The disadvantage is twofold.

When multiple variables are defined on one line, it is very hard to find any specific variable in the list. Consider for a minute the following set of lines that define a series of variables.

```
int qty, hours, idNumber, minutes, prodId, seconds, count;
double cost, hoursWorked, payRate, yearToDatePay, pay;
```

How fast can one spot the variable for product id number or the person's rate of pay? You have to read through each line searching for them.

The other disadvantage is that one cannot insert comments to better document the meaning of that variable. Frequently in the coding examples in this text, you will see comments beside the variable definitions providing further information about its meaning. For example,

```
int quantity;   // quantity purchased under warranty
int productId;  // manufacturer's id number of these
int year;       // purchase year for start of warranty
```

Adding comments to variable definitions can provide a means to identify the units of the values the variable holds. Consider these variable definitions.

```
double distanceTraveled; // in miles
double frequency;        // in kilohertz
int    time;             // in seconds
```

Can you see the extra clarity the comments can provide? Also notice a subtle formatting action I used. I aligned all the variable names in the same column because it greatly aids readability. For aesthetics and readability, I aligned the comments as well. Finally, what happens if you need to change the data type of a variable, which has been defined along with four others on one line?

Where Are Variable Definitions Placed in a Program?

Where are the variable definitions placed within a program? The answer is that a variable must be defined before its first use in an instruction. Normally, the variables to be used for input, those for calculation results and those for output are defined at the beginning of the **main()** function.

For example, suppose that our program needed to define variables for a cost, a quantity and a total. The program up to this point is as follows.

```
#include <iostream>
#include <iomanip>
using namespace std;

int main () {
  int    qty;   // quantity ordered
  double cost;  // cost of one item
```

```
  double total; // total cost of the order
 ...
```

Initializing Variables and the Assignment Operator

When a variable is defined, it has no starting or initial value. We refer to it as containing "core garbage" or just random data. For some variables, this is perfectly fine. Suppose that the first use of a variable is to store the data entered by the user in response to an input instruction. Storing new data into the variable wipes out whatever was previously contained in that memory location.

It serves no purpose to initialize variables that are going to be used for input. Any such initial value is going to be replaced by the incoming data. In fact, many compilers issue a warning message notifying you that no use is being made of that initial value. Likewise, any variable that is going to hold the result of a calculation need not be initialized.

However, any variable that is used as a counter or a total value must be initialized to zero. That is, if your first use of a counter is to add one to it, then that counter must have a value initially.

A variable whose value is not to be inputted from the keyboard can be given an initial value in one of two ways. Both methods use the **assignment operator**, which is an = sign.

The assignment operator copies the data value on the right side of the operator to the variable on the left side of it.

One method to assign values is to code an assignment instruction. For example, to place a 42 into **quantity** and 10.99 into **cost**, we code

```
quantity = 42;
cost     = 10.99;
```

then the first line removes any previous value in **quantity** and places the integer value of 42 in it. Likewise, the **double** value of 10.99 is placed into the variable **cost**.

Please note that the assignment operator should not be confused with the mathematical equals sign that is also an equal sign. Assignment means to copy a data value on the right into the variable on the left.

The second method that a variable can be initialized to a starting value is at the time the variable is being defined. The syntax is:

```
datatype name = value;
```

Thus, we could have coded:

```
int    quantity = 42;    // quantity ordered
double cost     = 10.99; // cost of one item
```

Several variables can be initialized as they are defined. Consider this line.

```
double cost = 10.99, total = 0, tax, grandTotal = 0;
```

Here when the compiler sets up memory for **cost**, it gives it the starting value of 10.99. Then it sets up memory for **total** and gives it a value of zero. Next, it sets up memory for **tax** and gives it no starting value (presumably, it is going to have to be calculated somehow). Finally, it sets up memory for **grandTotal**, giving it a value of zero. Figure 2.1 shows what computer memory looks like after the above variable definitions are completed.

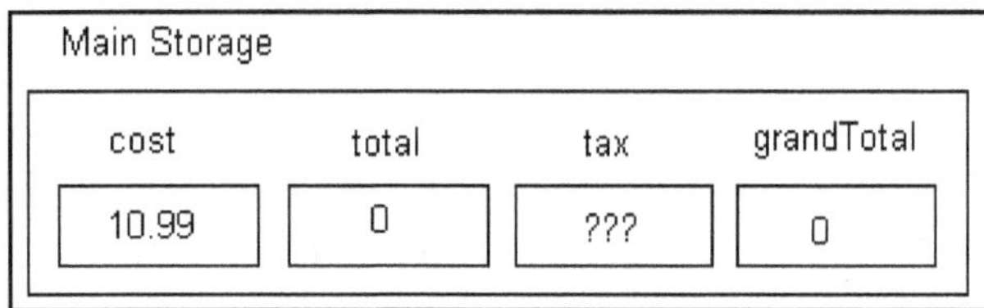

Figure 2.1 Main Storage after Data Definitions

In programming, you will see variables being initialized or given a value both ways. By initializing variables that must have a starting value when you define them, you eliminate one extra line (the assignment instruction). This means that you can see more lines of the program on the screen at one time, which lessens the potential for errors.

Rule: When assigning data with the assignment operator, the data value on the right must be compatible with the data type of the variable on its left side.

Consider this incorrect assignment.

```
double cost = "Hello World";
```

Coding the above like causes a compile time error. How can the character string "Hello World" be converted into a numerical value? It cannot and such attempts generate error messages. One can code

```
double cost = 0;
```

Here **cost** is a **double** but the number being assigned to **cost** is an integer—no decimal point. However, the compiler can easily convert an integer into a **double** for us. This is known as **data conversion**, a process in which data of one type is converted into another data type. Data conversion and its rules are discussed in the next chapter.

In the above example, if we now assign tax a value, by coding

```
tax = 8.84;
```

then memory appears as shown in Figure 2.2.

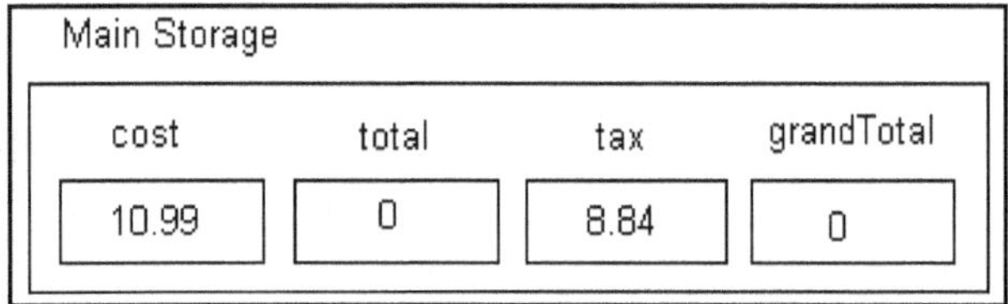

Figure 2.2 Main Storage after Assignments

Multiple Assignments—Chaining the Assignment Operator

Just as we can chain insertion operators into a single output operation, so can the assignment operator be chained.

Suppose that we have three total fields defined to hold the purchase price of tickets. Children and senior citizens get a price reduction. Their ticket costs are defined as follows.

```
double costAdultTickets;
double costChildTickets;
double costSeniorTickets;
```

Suppose further that the program needed to set these for cost fields to 0. One could do so with four assignment statements, such as this one.

```
costAdultTickets = 0;
```

Or one could initialize these to zero as they are defined as shown here.

```
double costAdultTickets = 0;
```

However, one can also chain and make a **multiple assignment** of 0 to each of these as follows.

```
costAdultTickets = costChildTickets = costSeniorTickets = 0;
```

This moves a 0 into **costSeniorTickets** first and then copies that 0 into **costChildTickets** and finally copies that 0 into **costAdultTickets**. While not commonly used, multiple assignments occur mostly when setting variables to 0.

Input of Data Values into Variables

C++ defines an input stream that retrieves data from the keyboard as a consecutive series of characters. The class or blueprint is called an **istream** and the specific instance that we use to obtain keyboard input is called **cin**. This definition of **cin**, as an instance of the **istream**, is parallel to our use of cost as an instance of the intrinsic **double** data type. It is the same with **cout** being an instance of the **ostream** class of data. The **istream** class and the definition of **cin** are contained in the header file **iostream.h**. The operator that causes transfer of data from the keyboard into our variable is called the **extraction operator**, which is >>. The extraction operator can be thought of as extracting the next data item from the input stream of characters as they are entered on the keyboard.

The extraction operator's syntax is similar to the insertion operator that is used to send data to the screen.

```
cin >> variable;
```

Assume that we have defined both **qty** and **cost** as an **integer** and a **double** as above. If we code

```
cin >> qty;
```

then the input stream waits until the user has entered their data and pressed the enter key. Once the enter key is pressed, the extraction operator attempts to extract the data requested, which is given by the data type of the variable. If it is successful, then that data is placed into the variable, erasing what was previously contained in the variable. Thus, if the user enters 10 and presses the enter key, the extraction operator above places 10 into our **qty** field in memory. If we next code

```
cin >> cost;
```

and the user types in 42.99 and presses the enter key, then the extraction operator attempts to input a **double** value, since **cost** is a **double**. If successful, **cost** now contains 42.99. What happens when incorrect data is entered is discussed in a later chapter. Until then, assume that no user ever makes a mistake typing in any data. (I know, this is highly unlikely, but we need more C++ language elements to sort it all out.)

Chaining Extraction Operators

Just as the insertion operator can be chained with other insertion operators to output more than one item at a time, so can the extraction operator. For example, one can code

```
cin >> qty >> cost;
```

There is no limit on the number of data items that can be input on a single **cin** input operation, just as there is none on **cout**.

However, just how must the user enter the two values? The answer is simple; white space must be used to separate the two numerical values. Recall that white space is any consecutive series of blanks, tabs, carriage returns, and line feeds for example. Pressing the enter key generates both a carriage return and a line feed. For most purposes, the two numerical values would be separated by a blank. Thus, the user could enter both values as

```
10 42.99<CR>
```

where <CR> means press the enter key. In the following, b means a blank or space and t means a tab key was pressed. The user could also enter these two values in any of the following ways.

```
10<CR>
bbttbbtbtbtbtbt<CR>
bttt42.99bttbbt<CR>
```

or

```
10<CR>
42<CR>
```

Only when that last <CR> is pressed does the extraction operator finally get to input the two values. Realistically, no one is going to be that silly when typing in numerical data. Just a single blank is commonly typed.

Always Prompt the User Before Inputting the Data

This is an important concept. Typically, our programs must have the user's desired input before calculations and the output of results can occur. But you cannot just start the program with

```
cin >> qty >> cost;
```

Why? Imagine what the user sees. They launch the program, which immediately displays a blinking cursor and sits there waiting for them to enter the input data. What are they supposed to enter?

When inputting data from the keyboard, a program must always prompt the user notifying them what data is to be entered at this point. A prompt is nothing more than a simple **cout** line. For example, one could code

```
cout << "Enter the quantity: ";
cin >> qty;
cout << "Enter the cost:      ";
cin >> cost;
```

On the screen, the user sees the messages and responds by entering the keystrokes shown in boldface below.

```
Enter the quantity: 10<CR>
Enter the cost:     42.99<CR>
```

Notice one nice touch. I put sufficient blanks in the "enter cost" prompt message so that the first character of the user's entry (the 4) aligned with the first character of the quantity (the 1). This makes a more aesthetic appearance.

What would the prompt look like if the user was supposed to enter both values at the same time? That depends on the "computer savvy" of your program's users. The following might be sufficient.

```
cout << "Enter quantity and cost, separated by a blank\n";
cin >> qty >> cost;
```

Here I am implicitly assuming that the users know that, after they have entered the two desired values, they need to press the enter key. If they might not know that, then you should add even more directions in your prompt message. In this example, the user sees and responds as follows.

```
Enter quantity and cost, separated by a blank
10 42.99<CR>
```

In both of these input operations, the final result is our variables **qty** and **cost** now contain the 10 and the 42.99.

Now let's examine some common errors a programmer can make. Can you spot the errors?

```
Cin >> qty;
cin qty;
cin >> >> qty;
cin > qty;
cin >> 10 >> 42.99;
```

In the first line, **cin** was capitalized, which makes it an unknown item. In the second line, there is no extraction operator coded. In the third line, there are two extraction operators in a row. In the fourth line, there is no extraction operator; the single > is the greater than sign that is used in comparison operations. In the fifth line, there are no variables to store the inputted values; the programmer is confusing the variables **qty** and **cost** with the user entered data values.

Now we are ready to continue with our program. Before we tackle the calculations, let's examine the output operation in more depth. That way, when we do get to the calculations, we can display the answers.

Output of a Variable

Let's assume that these three variables are defined and initialized as follows.

```
int    qty   = 10;
double cost  = 1.99;
double total = 19.99;
```

To display output on the screen, **cout** is used similar to the Hello World Program of Chapter 1. The insertion operator (<<) is used to send one or more variables to the output stream onto the screen. To display the contents of the **cost** variable, code

```
cout << cost;
```

Further, chaining can be used just as it was in the Hello World Program. To display the person's order represented by the **qty**, **cost** and **total** variables, one could code

```
cout << qty << cost << total << endl;
```

However, there are some other aspects that must be considered because the above line does not produce usable results.

Specifically, unless instructed otherwise, the insertion of a number into the stream includes all significant digits of the value. Given the above values of these three variables, the output from the above **cout** line is

```
101.9919.99
```

Oops. Notice that it does display all the significant digits in the values. However, there is no spacing between each value! One advantage of the output stream is that it gives us total control over the formatting aspects.

The first thing we need to do is to put some spaces between the numbers. There are two ways to do this. The first method is quick and dirty; output a string with some blanks in it between the numbers; here I used two blanks.

```
cout << qty << "  " << cost << "  " << total << endl;
```

This now yields the following.

```
10  1.99  19.99
```

For simple results, this can be perfectly fine.

However, soon the program may need to display a several sets of these values. Suppose these represent a person's order. What if the program processed several sets of orders displaying the results for each using the above **cout** instruction? Here is an example of four orders being displayed with this method.

```
10  1.99  19.99
1 .25 .25
100 .49 49.00
20 2.00 40.00
```

Can you read the columns of numbers?

Obviously, the data should be aligned. With numbers, columns of data are aligned on the right. If decimals are involved, usually the decimal points are aligned on successive rows. The desired results for this sample are

```
  10  1.99  19.99
   1   .25    .25
 100   .49  49.00
  20  2.00  40.00
xxxxyyyyyyzzzzzzz
```

Now the results are readable. Notice that in this example, the maximum width of the quantity column shown by the series of x's is four. The width of the cost column shown by the y's is six; the total column shown by the z's is seven.

The setw() Function

The **setw()** or set width function can be used to set the total width for the **next** item being displayed. It applies solely and only to the next item to be displayed. The function takes one parameter, the total width of the next item. For numeric types, the values are right justified within the total specified width.

A more optimum way to display the line is as follows.

```
cout << setw (4) << qty
     << setw (6) << cost
     << setw (7) << total << endl;
```

This is in fact exactly what was used in the above proper columnar alignment example.

If you misjudge a needed width and make it too small, then the output stream ignores your width and displays all of the significant digits. Suppose that I used a width of four columns for the **total** variable,

```
cout << setw (4) << qty
     << setw (6) << cost
     << setw (4) << total << endl;
```

then, the output would have been

```
  10  1.9919.99
   1   .25 .25
 100   .4949.00
  20  2.0040.00
```

Also note that the **setw()** only applies to the very next item to be output! This would also fail.

```
cout << setw (7) << qty << cost << total << endl;
```

Here the width of seven columns applies only to the **qty** variable; the others display only the actual digits in them with no blanks between them.

In general, always use the **setw()** function to control the maximum width of numbers.

Insertion of Floating Point Numbers into an Output Stream - setprecision and fixed

We have seen that the **setw()** function is used to define the total width of a field on output. Included in the width is any negative sign and all significant digits. However, on output, floating point numbers pose an additional problem. The output problem is twofold. First, since a double has 15 possible decimal digits in it, how many of those do we desire to display? Do we show 4.0 or 4.0000000000000 or something in between? Second, when the value is large or the value is a tiny decimal fraction, the **ostream** default is to show the result in scientific notation. Thus, we are likely to see $4e+006 instead of $4000000. Or we see 4e–6 instead of .000004.

The first problem of the number of decimal digits to show is easily solved using the **setprecision()** function. When not displaying numbers in scientific format, this function sets the number of decimal digits to the right of the decimal point that we desire to see in the result. Unlike **setw()**, the precision once set, applies to all floating point numbers that are output until a new **setprecision()** function call occurs if any. Thus, if we desire that all the numbers in our output contain two decimal digits, such as found in financial calculations, we need only to make one call to **setprecision()** at the start of the program as shown below.

```
cout << setprecision (2);
```

An added benefit of using the **setprecision()** function is that it rounds the number as it is displayed to that precision. Suppose that variable result contained 12.456789. Here are several runs with different precisions; notice the effect of rounding. Notice with a precision of zero digits, the fractional .4 is not .5 or greater so that the unit's digit remains at 2.

```
double a = 12.456789;
cout << setprecision (5) << a << endl;
```
outputs: 12.45679
```
cout << setprecision (4) << a << endl;
```
outputs: 12.4568
```
cout << setprecision (3) << a << endl;
```
outputs: 12.457
```
cout << setprecision (2) << a << endl;
```
outputs: 12.46
```
cout << setprecision (1) << a << endl;
```
outputs: 12.5
```
cout << setprecision (0) << a << endl;
```
outputs: 12.

If the precision is not set, the output stream has a default of six digits. The **setprecision()** function is a manipulator and requires the inclusion of the **iomanip** header file.

The second problem requires more work. We must tell the output stream that we do not want to see floating point numbers in the scientific notational format, but rather in the fixed point format that we are more used to seeing. The output stream contains a number of flags or switches that indicate, which format it is to use. The **setf()** or set flags function can be used to directly alter those flags. The coding we need is

```
cout.setf (ios::fixed, ios::floatfield);
cout.setf (ios::showpoint);
```

These two work on any manufacturer's compiler. However, Microsoft and others provide an even more convenient way using the **fixed** manipulator function.

```
cout << fixed;
cout.setf (ios::showpoint);
```

The first function call to **setf()** or to **fixed** tells the **cout** stream to display all float fields in the fixed point format, not in the scientific format. The second call tells the **cout** stream to show the decimal point in all floating point numbers being displayed whenever the precision is set to 0 digits. Notice that the compiler must show a decimal point as long as the precision is greater than 0. However, when it is 0, do you or don't you want to see the decimal point. **showpoint** forces the decimal point to be displayed when the precision is 0. The identifiers prefixed with **ios::** are key identifiers found in the input/output stream class.

These two lines need to be coded before the first output of a floating point number to the **cout** stream. Commonly, they are coded just after the variables are defined.

If one needed to return to the scientific notation for floating point numbers, one can code

```
cout.setf (ios::scientific, ios::floatfield);
```

There is yet another way to control the selection of fixed and scientific formatting of floating point numbers. C++ standard namespace has a pair of manipulators to do this.

```
cout << fixed;
```

and

```
cout << scientific;
```

Once used, all floating point numbers are output in the fixed point format in the first case or the scientific format in the second case. However, there is one small difference. If the variable **a** from the above example that contained 12.456789 was subsequently output this way

```
cout << fixed << setprecision (0) << a << endl;
```

then the output is just 12 with no decimal point.

A final note. If the **setprecision()** function is used without using either the **ios::fixed** or **ios::scientific** flags set by either of the two methods, then the precision passed to **setprecision()** specifies the total number of digits to be displayed including those to the left of the decimal point. If the **setprecision()** function call comes after specifically setting either fixed or scientific formats, then the precision passed refers only to the number of digits to the right of the decimal point.

Labeling Output

Commonly, output is labeled to make the meaning of the results clear to the reader. Let's display a single customer order given by the following variable definitions:

```
int    qty   = 10
double cost  = 1.99
double total = 19.99;
```

When a program is to display a single set of results, it can be done as follows.

```
cout << "The quantity is:              " << qty << endl
     << "The cost of each is:        $ " << cost << endl
     << "The total of the order is: $" << total << endl;
```

And the result that this produces is this.

```
The quantity is:            10
The cost of each is:      $ 1.99
The total of the order is: $19.99
```

Notice that I used sufficient blanks in the character string messages to make the numbers align in a column and look good.

When displaying variables, it is important also to display the units of the resultant numbers, if any. Suppose that the result of the calculations yielded the resistance of a circuit. The output might be done as follows.

```
cout << "The resistance needed is "
     << resistance << " ohms.\n";
```

If the value currently in the variable **resistance** is 125, then the screen displays

```
The resistance needed is 125 ohms.
```

Similarly if a distance measurement resulted from calculations, one must output also the units of that distance, otherwise it is a meaningless number.

```
cout << "The distance is " << distance << " km\n";
```

If the variable **distance** contains 125, this yields

```
The distance is 125 km
```

When displaying floating point numbers, there are some other additional details involved. See the section below called Insertion of Floating Point Numbers into an Output Stream.

Math Operators—Calculations

The math operators in C++ consist of the following.

```
operator     name            Example    Yields
   +       addition          10 + 3       13
   -       subtraction       10 - 3        7
   *       multiplication    10 * 3       30
   /       division          10 / 3        3
   %       remainder or      10 % 3        1
           mod operator - applies only for integer types
```

Most of these operators are self-evident, except the integer divide and remainder operators.

When doing an integer division, the divide operator gives only the integer quotient. Thus, 10/3 gives 3 not 3.33333 because 3.33333 is a floating point or real number. If one did a floating point division, as 10./3., then the result would be 3.33333.

The remainder operator gives the remainder of the integer division. When one codes `10 % 3`, then quotient of 3 is discarded and the remainder of 1 is returned. From a mathematical point of view, the remainder operator is sometimes called the mod operator. The remainder operator cannot be applied to real or floating point numbers because there is no remainder because the decimal fractional part is part of the result already.

Thus, if one wanted to calculate the **totalCost**, one could code

```
totalCost = cost * quantity;
```

This assumes that the variables **cost** and **quantity** have previously been given a value.

Assuming that the needed variables have been both defined and either given their initial values or inputted from the user, many formulae can be computed. Here are some common ones.

```
force = mass * acceleration;
areaTriangle = .5 * base * height;
perimeterTriangle = side1 + side2 + side3;
salesCommission = sales * commissionRate;
average = sum / count;
```

Notice that in each of these lines, I surround every operator with one blank. It greatly aids readability of the formula. Also note that all of the variables found on the right side of these equations must have been previously given a value. The variables on the left side of the assignment operator are given their values by the calculation results from the right side.

Precedence or Priority of Operators

Normally, the compiler performs the calculations from left to right as it works out the final value of an equation. In the preceding example of calculating the perimeter of a triangle, the contents of **side1** are first added to the contents of **side2** and then that result is added to the contents of **side3** and the final result placed into **perimeterTriangle**.

However, multiply, divide and the remainder operators have a higher precedence or priority than do the add and subtract operators. What is the order that the compiler follows in this calculation?

```
e = a + b * c - d;
```

Here, the multiplication of **b** and **c** are done first. Next, the content of **a** is added to that result and then the content of **d** is subtracted. Finally, the result is stored in **e**.

Use () to override the precedence of operators when it is needed. In the previous example, if the result of **a + b** was supposed to be multiplied by the results of **c - d**, then parentheses are required.

```
e = (a + b) * (c - d);
```

Here are some other examples that require parentheses.

```
sum = n * (n - 1) / 2;
x = a * ( b + c);
result = x * y / (z + 1);
```

Do not get parentheses happy and use parentheses where they are not needed. Why? A common syntax error is one too many begin parentheses or one too few end parentheses. Consider the following messy calculation.

```
result = (((a + b) + c) / (d - (e - (f * g)));
```

Can you spot the missing parentheses? The equation should have been written as follows.

```
result = (a + b + c ) / (d - e + f * g);
```

Now the intention of the programmer is quite clear.

Constant Data Objects

Frequently a program needs the use of a variable whose value is inherently a constant value, such as the number of months in a year. In geometry problems, the value of **PI** is frequently needed; it is a constant. In financial calculations, there are 100 pennies per dollar. Certainly one can simply use a literal value, such as 12, for the number of months wherever that value is needed in a program. Likewise, one can simply code 100 as needed in money problems. However, from a program maintenance point of view, it is superior to have an actual constant identifier associated with that value. It avoids confusion, aids program readability, and facilitates changes when they are required. Let's see how.

Suppose a program that calculates monetary results also calculated some percentages. For example, one might have the following.

```
percentLoss = Loss * 100 / Gross;
dollars = pennies / 100;
```

Now suppose that inflation strikes and the treasury decided that a dollar now requires 200 pennies. When changing the program, one might opt to change globally all 100 values into 200. Yet, if that is done, suddenly all the percentage calculations are quite incorrect!

To alleviate the problem, one could define a variable **penniesPerDollar** as

```
int penniesPerDollar = 100;
```

and then the monetary calculations could make use of that variable like this.

```
percentLoss = Loss * 100 / Gross;
dollars = pennies /penniesPerDollar;
```

However, since **penniesPerDollar** is a variable, there is nothing to prevent the programmer from accidentally coding

```
penniesPerDollar = 42;
```

Now the program produces correct results up to this point where the accidental assignment occurred. What is needed is a way to denote that some variable is holding a constant value that cannot be changed. This is known as a **constant data object**.

The syntax is quite simple—place the keyword **const** before the data type when defining the variable. However, when making a variable a constant data object, one must at that time give that variable the constant value that it is to contain. We could define the constant data object, **PenniesPerDollar** and use it as follows.

```
const int PenniesPerDollar = 100;

percentLoss = Loss * 100 / Gross;
dollars = pennies /PenniesPerDollar;
```

There are two small points to be understood about using constant data objects. The first is the case of the item's name. By convention, programmers desire these constant objects to have a clearly distinguishable name. Sometimes, all uppercase letters are used. However, in the case above, the compound name would be unreadable, **PENNIESPERDOLLAR**. However, capitalizing all of the words in a compound name works well.

The second point concerns the placement of the definition itself. Obviously, the definition must occur before the first usage of that constant data object. Since these constant objects are special, place them at the beginning of the **main()** function before all other variable definitions. This location of a constant object will be changed later on in Chapter 6, when we learn to write our own functions. Since the constants might well be used within these additional functions, they have to be moved to the global namespace area above the function header for the **main()** function.

Both of the following are correct.

```
#include <iostream>
#include <iomanip>
using namespace std;

const int PenniesPerDollar = 100;

int main () {
 double pennies;
 double dollars;

 cout << "Enter the number of pennies: ";
 cin >> pennies;

 dollars = pennies / PenniesPerDollar;

 cout << pennies << " equals $" << dollars << endl;
 return 0;
}
```

and

```
#include <iostream>
#include <iomanip>
using namespace std;

int main () {
```

```
  const int PenniesPerDollar = 100;

  double pennies;
  double dollars;

  cout << "Enter the number of pennies: ";
  cin >> pennies;

  dollars = pennies / PenniesPerDollar;

  cout << pennies << " equals $" << dollars << endl;
  return 0;
}
```

However, the following is incorrect since the variables of **main()** are now defined outside of **main()**.

```
#include <iostream>
#include <iomanip>
using namespace std;

const int PenniesPerDollar = 100;
double pennies;    // error defining outside of main
double dollars;    // error defining outside of main

int main () {
 cout << "Enter the number of pennies: ";
 cin >> pennies;

 dollars = pennies / PenniesPerDollar;

 cout << pennies << "equals $" << dollars << endl;
 return 0;
}
```

The above actually produces the correct results but is very bad program design. This is covered in Chapter 7 at length. For now, making the variables of a program defined before the **main()** function makes those variables known to the entire program everywhere. These two variables are intended to be used only within **main()**'s calculations and nowhere else.

Math Library Functions

C++ has a large number of mathematical functions available for our use. To use any of the math functions, be sure to use the **#include <cmath>** for the math header file.

For example, suppose that we needed to find the square root of a number. The built-in square root function is called **sqrt()**.

```
root = sqrt (number);
```

The prototype that is contained in the **cmath** header file defines the **sqrt()** function as taking one **double** type parameter returning the square root of that parameter as a **double** type.

Have you noticed that there is no exponentiation operator in the C++ language? Suppose that you needed to calculate x^y or x raised to the yth power. The **pow()** (power) function is used to handle exponentiation. The syntax of the **pow()** function is

```
double result = pow (base number, exponent number);
```

To calculate x^y, we code

```
double answer = pow (x, y);
```

The **pow()** function has many uses, especially with scientific and Engineering formulae. Suppose that we needed to find the 4th root of a number. We can code the following

```
double root = pow (number, .25);
```

Many trigonometric functions are provided; among these are **sin()**, **cos()**, **tan()**, **asin()**, **acos()** and **atan()**. The **sin()**, **cos()** and **tan()** functions take an angle (of **double** type) in radians and return a **double** result. To convert an angle in the more familiar degree units into radians, remember that there are two PI radians in 360 degrees.

Suppose that one needed a program that would input an angle in degrees and display the cosine of that angle. One could code the following; notice the comments help readability.

```
#include <iostream>
#include <iomanip>
#include <cmath>
using namespace std;

int main () {
 const double PI = 3.14159;

 double angle;      // in degrees
 double radians;    // angle converted to radians
 double result;

 cout << "Enter the angle in degrees: ";
 cin >> angle;

 radians = angle * PI / 180.; // 2PI radians in 360 degrees
 result = cos (radians);

 cout << result << endl;
 return 0;
}
```

Often it is clearer to solve the problem one step at a time. However, one could have coded this problem with far fewer lines.

```
#include <iostream>
#include <iomanip>
#include <cmath>
using namespace std;
int main () {
 const double PI = 3.14159;
 double angle; // in degrees
 cout << "Enter the angle in degrees: ";
 cin >> angle;
 cout << cos (angle * PI / 180.) << endl;
 return 0;
}
```

Here the return value from the cosine function is immediately sent to the screen. No blank lines are used to separate the distinct groups of thoughts either, running it all together. It is shorter but much harder to read and write.

The Most Nearly Accurate Value of PI

Sometimes, one needs the most nearly accurate value of PI in a **double**, that is, the value of PI is needed to 15 digits. Since there are 2 PI radians in 360 degrees, or PI radians in 180 degrees and since the cosine of 180 degrees is –1., we can get PI to 15 digits by coding

```
PI = acos (-1.);
```

Thus, one of the best ways to define the most nearly accurate PI is

```
const double PI = acos (-1.);
```

Other Math Functions

Some other math functions include the following

```
Name   Meaning                          Usage

abs    absolute value of an integer     int j = -3;
                                        int x = abs(j);// x = 3

fabs   floating point absolute value

exp    expotential function e^x         double x = 1;
                                        double y = exp (x);

log    natural log                      double x = 9000.;
                                        y = log (x); // 9.105

log10  log base 10                      Y = log10(x);// 3.954
```

Some Additional Insertion Operator Details

The insertion operator << can be used to output either a constant, the contents of a variable or an expression. Some examples are as follows.

```
// constants
cout << 42;                // displays the integer 42
cout << "Hello World\n";   // displays a string "Hello World"

// variables
const double PI = 3.14159;
cout << PI;                // displays 3.14159
int x = -123;
cout << x;                 // displays -123

// expressions
double angle = 60.;
cout << cos (angle * PI / 180); // displays .5
```

It is much easier to debug a program that does not output expressions but rather calculates the result and outputs the result variable. Jamming everything into one line, like the above cosine expression, is an "all or nothing" proposition. Either it comes out right or it doesn't. If it doesn't, finding the error can be harder if there are no intermediate results to check manually.

Breaking a Complex Calculation Down into Smaller Portions

To illustrate the idea of breaking a complex equation down into more manageable portions or sub-expressions, let's consider an example from astronomy. Find the period of a satellite in an orbit 100 kilometers above the earth. Here is the formula for determining the time for one revolution or period.

$$\text{period} = 2\pi\sqrt{\frac{\text{Re}}{g}}(1+\frac{h}{\text{Re}})^{\frac{3}{2}}$$

In the equation Re is the earth's radius of 6.378E6 meters, g is the force of gravity of 9.8 m/sec/sec and h is the height of the satellite in meters. In this case if a satellite is in orbit 100 km above the earth, its period is about 1.4 hours, which means that it passes by a ground-based observer about 16 times a day. Note, it is not important how to derive this formula—that is the arena of astronomy and orbital physics. Often, programmers are given a formula for some problem and asked to write a computer program to solve it.

The best way to solve this complex equation is to first calculate various expressions and then put the pieces together. First, define the constants in the problem, those that cannot vary. This one has three

```
const double PI = acos (-1.);
```

```
const double Re = 6.378e6; // radius of earth
const double g = 9.8;      // gravitational acceleration
```

Now define the variables and answer areas. The height of the satellite should be considered a variable since we could easily change it.

```
double h = 100 * 1000;     // convert using 1000 m per km
double period;             // objective: find the period
```

Next, break the lengthy calculation into smaller pieces, defining a variable to hold each piece.

```
double a = 2 * PI;
double b = sqrt (Re / g);
double c = 1. + h / Re;
double d = pow (c, 1.5);
```

Finally, put the smaller pieces together to form the result

```
period = a * b * d;
cout << period;
```

If anything goes wrong, you can add in debugging steps so that you can manually determine, which ones are incorrect.

```
cout << "a = " << a << endl
     << "b = " << b << endl
     << "c = " << c << endl
     << "d = " << d << endl;
```

However, one could also code a much shorter version as follows.

```
cout << 2 * PI * sqrt (Re / g) * pow(1.+h/Re, 1.5) << endl;
```

Here, one hopes that nothing goes wrong! Thus, unless there are some other overriding concerns, always break complex calculations down into smaller more manageable units.

Here is the complete period of an orbiting satellite program. Notice the placement of the various instructions.

Basic02a - Calculate the Period of a Satellite

```
/***************************************************************/
/*                                                             */
/* Basic02a Calculate the period of a satellite in orbit       */
/*                                                             */
/***************************************************************/

#include <iostream>
#include <iomanip>
#include <cmath>
using namespace std;

int main () {
 const double PI = acos (-1.);
```

```
const double Re = 6.378e6; // radius of earth
const double g = 9.8;      // gravitational acceleration
double h;                  // convert using 1000 m per km
double period;             // objective: find the period

// setup floating point format for output
cout << fixed << setprecision (2);

cout << "Enter the height of the satellite in Km: ";
cin >> h;

h = h * 1000; // convert to meters

// compute subterms of the equation
double a = 2 * PI;
double b = sqrt (Re / g);
double c = 1. + h / Re;
double d = pow (c, 1.5);

// compute final answer in terms of the subtrerms
period = a * b * d;        // period in seconds

// output the results in km and in hours
cout << "\nA satellite orbiting at a height of "
     << h / 1000 << " kilometers\nhas a period of "
     << period / 3600. << " hours\n";

return 0;

```

And here is the output from a test execution.

```
Basic02a - Calculate the Period of a Satellite

Enter the height of the satellite in Km: 100

A satellite orbiting at a height of 100.00 kilometers
has a period of 1.44 hour
```

Section B: Computer Science Example

Cs02a—Ticket Prices for a Concert

Acme Box Office requires a program to calculate the total cost of a customer's tickets. Ticket prices vary. Children less than 12 are charged 1/4 of the normal rate. Senior citizens pay 1/2 the normal rate. Anyone person buying tickets could purchase a variable number of tickets from the three categories. The program should display the number of tickets for each category along with the cost for those tickets. A final line should contain the total cost for all of the tickets. Test the program with a normal rate of $10.00 with two children, two adult and two senior citizen tickets purchased.

Always design the solution first before attempting to program it. The starting point is to determine what variables are going to be needed and draw the main storage or memory box. The problem specifies that there is a basic ticket price; let's call it **basicPrice**. However, since there are two discount rates involved, let's make those constant data objects, **RateChild** and **RateSenior**. What other variables are needed? Three variables must hold the number of tickets purchased in the categories. While the two rates and the basic price must be **doubles**, no one can purchase .5967 of a ticket. The three number of purchased tickets should be integers. Let's call them **numAdultTickets, numChildTickets** and **numSeniorTickets**. Next, the problem indicates we must display the total price of tickets purchased in each of these three categories. We will need a **double** variable for each of these, say **costAdult, costChild** and **costSenior**. Finally, the grand total cost of all tickets purchased can be called **grandTotal**. Figure 2.3 shows what main storage for the program should be.

Now that we have drawn the picture and solidified the variable names, the program must follow the Cycle of Data Processing. Thus, the next step is to input the data required. The following accomplish this.

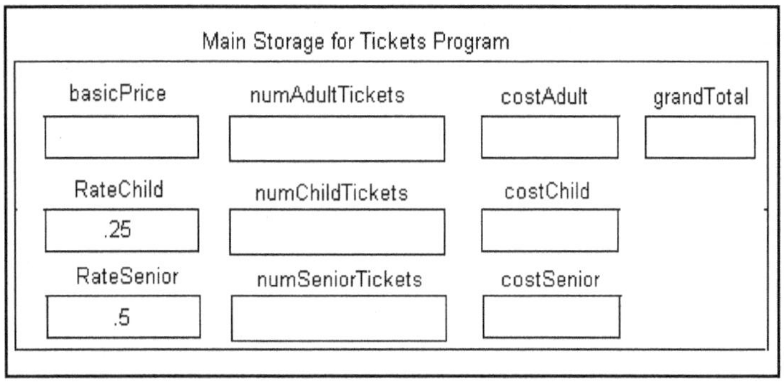

Main Storage for Tickets Program

basicPrice	numAdultTickets	costAdult	grandTotal
RateChild: .25	numChildTickets	costChild	
RateSenior: .5	numSeniorTickets	costSenior	

Figure 2.3 Main Storage for Tickets Sold Program

prompt "enter basic price of a ticket"
input **basicPrice** of a ticket
prompt "enter the number of adult tickets purchased"
input the **numAdultTickets**

prompt "enter the number of children's tickets purchased"
input the **numChildTickets**
prompt "enter the number of senior citizen tickets purchased"
input the **numSeniorTickets**

With the input instructions finished, now work out the calculations that are required. In this case, there are four simple ones. One can use English statements or pseudo-C++ lines. I'll use the latter to get the following:

costAdult = numAdultTickets * basicPrice;
costChild = numChildTickets * basicPrice * RateChild;
costSenior = numSeniorTickets * basicPrice * RateSenior;
grandTotal = costAdult + costChild + costSenior;

With the calculations complete, write a series of output instructions to display the title and the results. Something like this should suffice.

print a nice heading
print identifier for adult tickets, **numAdultTickets** and **costAdult**
print identifier for child tickets, **numChildTickets** and **costChild**
print identifier for senior tickets, **numSeniorTickets** and **costSenior**
print identifier for grand total and **grandTotal**

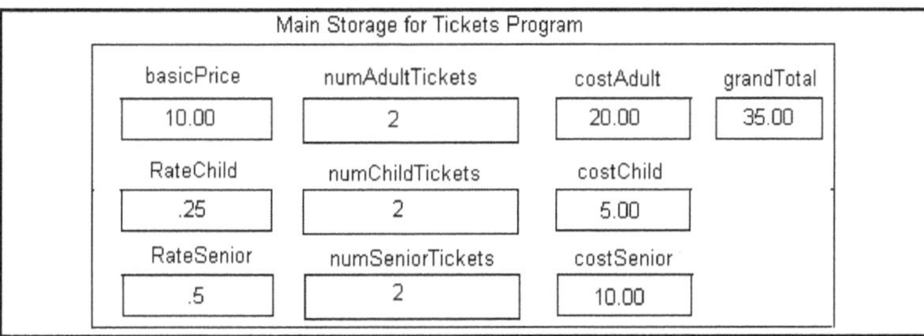

Figure 2.4 Main Storage after the Program Is Desk Checked

When the design is complete, we must desk check the program for accuracy. Use the main storage drawing as a sketchpad during desk checking. First, place the constant data value of .25 in the **RateChild** box; .5 in the **RateSenior** box. Pretend you are running the program and follow the series of prompt and input steps to input $10 in the **basicPrice** box and a 2 in each of the three number of tickets variables. As you execute each line in the above calculations, carry out that operation using the contents of the various boxes referred to in the calculation, placing the result in the indicated box. For example, into the **costAdult** box place 2 * 10.00 or 20.00. Into the **costChild** box goes 2 * 10.00 * .25 or 5.00. Into the **costSenior** box goes 2 * 10.00 * .5 or 10.00. In the **grandTotal** box, place the results of adding up the three cost boxes, 35.00. Finally, carry out the print instructions. Look over the results displayed. Are they correct? If so, thoroughly desk check the solution. Experiment with other initial starting values. Only when the solution is 100% correct, do we then convert it into a C++ program. Figure 2.4 shows what the main storage diagram should contain when this initial set of test data has been processed by the program.

Here are the completed program and the output from the test run.

Cs02a—Calculate Ticket Prices

```
/***************************************************************/
/*                                                             */
/* Cs02a: calculate concert ticket prices                      */
/*                                                             */
/***************************************************************/

#include <iostream>
#include <iomanip>
using namespace std;
int main () {
 const double RateChild = .25;  // children's rate
 const double RateSenior = .5;  // senior citizen's rate

 double basicPrice;          // basic price of a ticket
 int    numAdultTickets;     // number of adult tickets purchased
 int    numChildTickets;     // number of child tickets purchased
 int    numSeniorTickets;    // number of senior citizen tickets

 double costAdult;     // the cost of all adult tickets purchased
 double costChild;     // the cost of all child tickets purchased
 double costSenior;    // the cost of all senior tickets purchased
 double grandTotal;    // the grand total cost of all tickets

 // setup floating point format for output of dollars
 cout << fixed << setprecision (2);

 // output a title
 cout << "Acme Box Office Ticket Sales\n\n";

 // prompt and input the user's data
 cout << "Enter the basic price of a ticket: ";
 cin >> basicPrice;
 cout << "Enter the number of adult tickets purchased:  ";
 cin >> numAdultTickets;
 cout << "Enter the number of child tickets purchased:  ";
 cin >> numChildTickets;
 cout << "Enter the number of senior tickets purchased: ";
 cin >> numSeniorTickets;

 // compute ticket costs
 costAdult = numAdultTickets * basicPrice;
 costChild = numChildTickets * basicPrice * RateChild;
 costSenior = numSeniorTickets * basicPrice * RateSenior;

 // compute grand total cost
 grandTotal = costAdult + costChild + costSenior;

 // output the results
```

```
51   cout << endl;
52   cout << "Number of adult tickets:                "
53        << setw(4) << numAdultTickets << " = $"
54        << setw (6) << costAdult << endl;
55   cout << "Number of child tickets:                "
56        << setw(4) << numChildTickets << " = $"
57        << setw (6) << costChild << endl;
58   cout << "Number of senior citizen tickets: "
59        << setw(4) << numSeniorTickets << " = $"
60        << setw (6) << costSenior << endl;
61   cout << "Total purchase price:                         $"
62        << setw (6) << grandTotal << endl;
63
64   return 0;
65
```

```
Output from a Sample Run of Cs02a—Calculate Ticket Prices
```

```
Acme Box Office Ticket Sales

Enter the basic price of a ticket: 10.00
Enter the number of adult tickets purchased:  2
Enter the number of child tickets purchased:  2
Enter the number of senior tickets purchased: 2

Number of adult tickets:            2 = $ 20.00
Number of child tickets:            2 = $  5.00
Number of senior citizen tickets:   2 = $ 10.00
Total purchase price:                   $ 35.00
```

There are a number of things about the completed program to notice. First, the extensive use of comments greatly aids readability along with the use of descriptive names. Second, line breaks separate each logical group of actions, such as variable definitions from calculations from output operations. Third, lines 25-27 set up the **cout** output stream for proper floating point output of dollars. Finally, lines 52-62 carefully control spacing so that all of the output results form consistent columns making the report easy to read.

Section C: Engineering Example

Engr02a—Pressure Drop in a Fluid Flowing Through a Pipe (Civil Engineering)

Consider the problem of an incompressible fluid being pumped through a pipe at a steady rate. The drop in pressure from point one to point two in the pipe is given by

pressureDrop = P1 - P2 = d (g h + Eloss)

where d is the fluid density, g the gravitational constant, h the difference in height between points one and two, and Eloss is the energy loss per kilogram from internal friction with the walls of the pipe. The energy loss expression is

$$Eloss = \frac{4 f v^2 L}{D}$$

where f is the friction factor, v is the velocity of flow, L is the length of the pipe and D is the pipe's diameter. The velocity of fluid flow is given by

$$v = \frac{4Q}{\pi D^2}$$

where is the volume flow rate. Finally, for smooth pipes, the friction factor f depends only on the Reynold's number R given by

$$R = \frac{dvD}{u}$$

and u is the viscosity of the fluid. If R is less than or equal to 2,000, then the friction factor is f=8/R for laminar flow (non-turbulent).

Calculate the pressure drop of ethyl alcohol whose density is 789.4 kg/m^3, whose viscosity u is 0.0012 kg/m-sec through a pipe that is .01 meters in diameter and 100 meters long with a height difference of 10 meters at a volume flow rate Q of 0.00002 m^3/sec.

The starting point is to design a solution on paper. In this problem, there are a large number of constant initial values. They can be either constants or actual input values. Since the problem did not specifically state that they must be input, we can store them as constant data objects. Let's identify those and their values first. The constant **Density** is 789.4; the constant **Viscosity** is 1.2E–3; the constant **Height** is 10.; the constant **Diameter** is .01; the constant **Length** is 100.; the constant **Q** is 2.0E–5; the gravitational constant **g** is 9.8; and finally **PI**. Draw a series of memory boxes for each of these and place these constant values in them. Next, identify the variables needed for the calculations. Here I have called them **velocity**, **reynolds**, **friction**, **eloss** and **pressureDrop**. Make up another five boxes and label them with the chosen names. Figure 2.5 shows the completed Main Storage box.

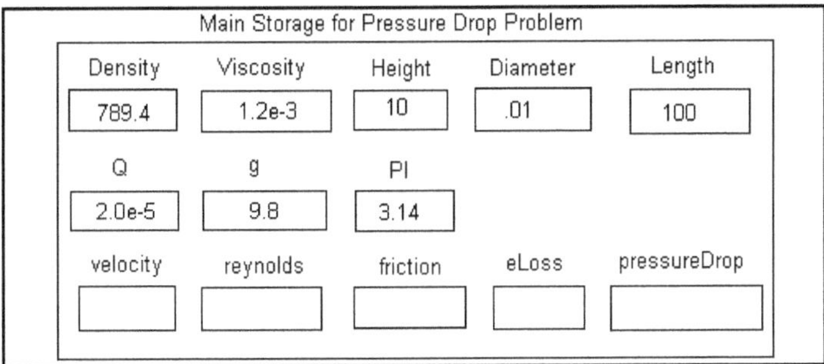

Figure 2.5 Main Storage for Pressure Drop Problem

Next, write out in English or pseudo C++ the calculations that are required in the order to find the resultant pressure drop.

velocity = 4. * **Q** / (**PI** * **Diameter** * **Diameter**)
reynolds = **Density** * **velocity** * **Diameter** / **Viscosity**
friction = 8. / **reynolds**
eloss = 4. * **friction** * **velocity** * **velocity** * **Length** / **Diameter**
pressureDrop = **Density** * (**g** * **Height** + **eloss**)

Finally, design how the results are to be displayed and code those instructions. It is an excellent idea to echo these starting values or constants before displaying the final answer, the pressure drop. Also, for debugging purposes, let's also display the results of the four intermediate calculations. So we should sketch the following:

print a title, the **Density**, **Viscosity**, **Diameter**, **Length**, **Height** and
    the flow rate **Q** all appropriately labeled
print the **velocity**, **reynolds**, **friction** and **eloss** results, also labeled
print the final answer **pressureDrop** nicely labeled

Now desk check the solution. Using the numbers placed in the constant object boxes, step through the program line by line, doing each calculation, and placing the results in the corresponding box, beginning with velocity. Use your handy-dandy pocket calculators as needed. When you have verified the solution works, then convert it into a program. In our case, the only difficulties are in the formatting of the printed results.

Here are the final program and the output from the test run.

Engr02a - Calculate the Pressure Drop of Ethyl Alcohol in a Pipe

```
/***************************************************************/
/*                                                             */
/* Engr02a: Calc pressure drop of Ethyl Alcohol in a pipe      */
/*                                                             */
/***************************************************************/

#include <iostream>
#include <iomanip>
```

```
#include <cmath>
using namespace std;
int main () {
 const double Density = 789.4;     // fluid density in kg/m/m/m
 const double Viscosity = 1.2E-3;// fluid viscosity in kg/m-sec
 const double Height = 10.;        // height between P1 and P2 in m
 const double Diameter = .01;      // pipe diameter in m
 const double Length = 100.;       // pipe length in m
 const double Q = 2.0E-5;          // volume flow rate- cubic m/sec
 const double g = 9.8;             // gravity acceleration constant
 const double PI = acos (-1.);

 double velocity;       // velocity in the pipe
 double reynolds;       // Reynold's number
 double friction;       // friction factor
 double eloss;          // energy loss
 double pressureDrop;   // the pressure drop between P1 and P2

 // setup floating point format for output - set for 4 dec digits
 cout <<fixed << setprecision (4);

 // perform the calculations
 velocity = 4. * Q / (PI * Diameter * Diameter);
 reynolds = Density * velocity * Diameter / Viscosity;
 friction = 8. / reynolds;
 eloss = 4. * friction * velocity * velocity * Length / Diameter;
 pressureDrop = Density * (g * Height + eloss);

 // display the initial specifications
 cout << "Ethyl Alcohol Pressure Drop in a Pipe\n";
 cout << "  of density  = " << setw (9) << Density
      << " kg/cubic meter\n";
 cout << "  viscosity   = " << setw(9)<<Viscosity<<" kg/m-sec\n";
 cout << "  pipe specs\n";
 cout << "    diameter  = " << setw (9) << Diameter << " m\n";
 cout << "    length    = " << setw (9) << Length << " m\n";
 cout << "  from height = " << setw (9) << Height << " m\n";
 cout << setprecision (5);
 cout << "  flow rate   = " <<setw(9)<<Q<<" cubic meter/sec\n\n";

 // display the intermediate results
 cout << "Velocity:      " << setw (12) << velocity << endl;
 cout << "Reynolds:      " << setw (12) << reynolds << endl;
 cout << "Friction:      " << setw (12) << friction << endl;
 cout << "Energy Loss:   " << setw (12) << eloss << endl;

 // display the desired final pressure drop
 cout << "Pressure Drop: " << setw (12) << pressureDrop << endl;

 return 0;
```

```
Output from Engr02a - Calculate the Pressure Drop
```

```
Ethyl Alcohol Pressure Drop in a Pipe
  of density   =  789.4000 kg/cubic meter
  viscosity    =    0.0012 kg/m-sec
  pipe specs
    diameter   =    0.0100 m
    length     =  100.0000 m
  from height  =   10.0000 m
  flow rate    =   0.00002 cubic meter/sec

Velocity:              0.25465
Reynolds:           1675.15883
Friction:              0.00478
Energy Loss:          12.38723
Pressure Drop:     87139.67970
```

All the constant data objects begin with a capital letter except **g** for gravity. One could have uppercased all of these. However, **g** is the universal symbol for gravity; it is far better to use universal symbolic names when they are available as legal C++ variable names.

Notice that the comments greatly aid the readability of the program and that the line breaks tend to group the different logical actions such as defining constants, variables, calculations, and outputting results.

Observe how the uniform spacing of the output fields and text was achieved. By placing each output line on a separate line, one can align the literal text strings. Also, use a uniform field width whenever possible. Finally, notice lines 30 and 48. Initially, the precision was set to four decimal digits. This was sufficient for all the constant initial values except the flow rate, **Q**, which needed five digits. By having five digits in the result values, the friction result is well displayed, but the Reynolds number and the final pressure drop certainly do not need so many digits to the right of the decimal point. It was done this way so that the column of result numbers aligned on their decimal points.

Design Exercises

1. Mysterious “crop circles” sometimes appear in a farmer’s cornfield. A crop circle is an area in the middle of his cornfield in which all of the corn stalks have been trampled flat, yielding some design visible only from the air. Farmer Jones discovered just such a circle in his field. Since the plants were smashed, Farmer Jones suffers a crop yield loss. His crop insurance covers some of his lost income by paying him a rate of $2.25 per bushel of corn lost. His yield on the remainder of that field is 125 bushels per acre. He measured the crop circle and found it was 50 feet in diameter. How much money does he get from the crop insurance? Hint, the area of a circle is given by PI times the square of the radius and an acre is 4840 square yards.

2. It's party time. You are planning a party and have $40 with which to buy as many refreshments as possible. But not every guest prefers the same refreshments. Six guests prefer pizza while eight prefer to eat a hot dog. Four guests like Pepsi, eight prefer Coca-Cola, and two want Dr. Pepper. A pizza comes with eight large slices and costs $9.00. Hot dogs cost $1.25 each. A six-pack of any kind of soda pop costs $3.50. The rules you must follow are:

All guests must have something they like to eat and drink.
Soda pop can only be purchased in six-packs.
Pizza can only be bought as a whole pizza with eight slices.

What is the minimum that you must buy to satisfy these criteria? Do you have enough money to pay for it? (Ignore sales taxes.)

Stop! Do These Exercises Before Programming

1. The programmer was having a bad day writing this program. Correct the errors so that there are no compile time errors. Make whatever assumptions you can about data types that need fixing up.

```
#includ <iostrea>
Const int TOTAL 100;
int main () {
 Double costOfItem;
 quantity = 42;
 double total cost;
 cupon_discount int;
 const double AmountPaid;
 cost of item = 4.99
 AmountPaid = 9.99;
 ...
```

2. Circle the variable names that are **invalid** C++ variable names. Do not circle ones that are legal, even though they might not represent the best naming convention.

```
CostOfGoodsSold
total Price
C3P0
3D-Movie
distance Traveled
sin
fAbs
Log
qty_sold
qty sold
qtySold
```

3. Convert each of these formulas into a proper C++ statement.

a. F = m a (Force = mass times acceleration)

b. A = PI R^2 (area of a circle)

c. $total = \frac{n(n+1)}{2}$

d. x = sin (2 PI y);

e. $z = \sqrt{x^2 + y^2}$

f. $x = \frac{-B + \sqrt{B^2 - 4AC}}{2A}$

g. $x = \sqrt[4]{z}$

h. $y = ae^x + b$

4. Correct the errors in these C++ calculations.

```
a. cost = qty unitPrice;        // cost is qty times unitPrice
b. sum = sum + + count;         // add count to sum
c. count + 1 = count            // add one to count
d. root = sqrt x * x + y * y;
    // x is the square root of x squared + y squared
e. xy = Pow (x, y);   // calculate x raised to the yth power
f. count + 1;         // increment count
```

5. The equation to be solved is this

$$percent1 = \frac{salesTotal1}{salesTotal1 + salesTotal2} 100$$

Assuming all variables are **doubles**, which of the following correctly calculates the percentage? Next, assuming all variables are **integers**, which of the following correctly calculates the percentage? Indicate which work for doubles and which work for integers by placing an I or a D before each letter.

a. percent1 = salesTotal1 / salesTotal1 + salesTotal2 * 100;

b. percent1 = salesTotal1 / (salesTotal1 + salesTotal2 * 100);

c. percent1 = salesTotal1 / (salesTotal1 + salesTotal2) * 100;

d. percent1 = ((salesTotal1) / (salesTotal1 + salesTotal2)) * 100;

e. percent1 = salesTotal1 * 100 / salesTotal1 + salesTotal2;

f. percent1 = salesTotal1 * 100 / (salesTotal1 + salesTotal2);

6. Show the precise output from the following series of **cout** instructions. Assume these are the initial values of the variables. Assume the **ios::fixed** has been set along with **ios::showpoint**. The precision has not been set to any value initially.

```
int x = 123;
double z = 42.35353;
```

a. `cout << setw (5) << x << x;`

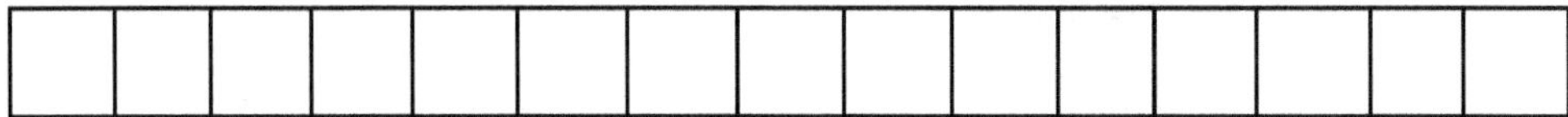

b. `cout << x << setw (5) << x;`

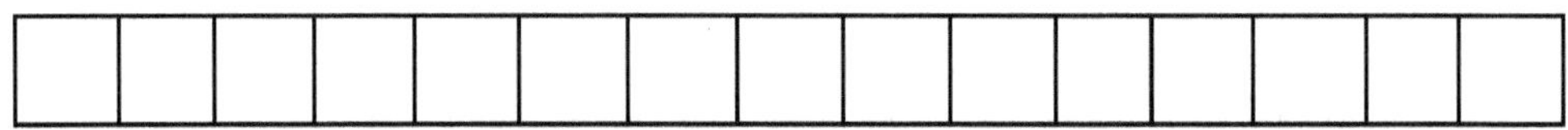

c.
```
cout << setprecision (2) << z
     << setw (7) << setprecision (3) << z;
```

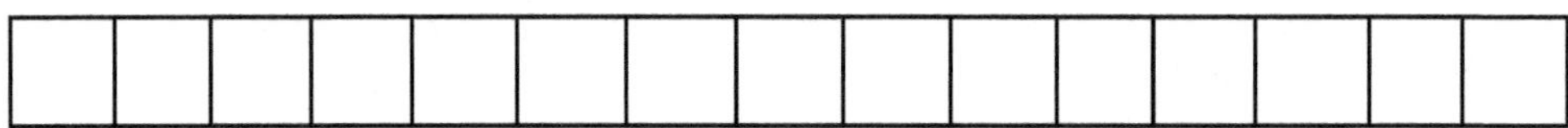

d. `cout << setprecision (4) << setw (8) << z;`

7. For each of these short calculations, show the result that is displayed. Assume that **ios::fixed** and **ios::showpoint** have been set on **cout** and that the precision is set to two decimal digits unless overridden.

a.

```
int x = 10;
int y = 4;
cout << x / y;
```

b.

```
int pennies = 123;
const int QUARTERS = 25;
int quarters;
quarters = pennies / QUARTERS;
pennies = pennies % QUARTERS;
cout << quarters << " " << pennies;
```

c.

```
double number = 100;
cout << sqrt (number);
```

d.

```
double num = 10;
double bignum;
bignum = pow (num, 2);
cout << setprecision (0) << bignum;
```

Programming Problems

Problem Cs02-1—Conversion of a Fahrenheit Temperature to Celsius

When dealing with temperatures, one common problem is the conversion of a temperature in Fahrenheit degrees into Celsius degrees. The formula is

$$C = \frac{5}{9}(F - 32)$$

Write a program that converts a constant Fahrenheit temperature into the corresponding Celsius temperature. Prompt the user to enter a Fahrenheit temperature. Then, calculate the Celsius equivalent and display the results using the format shown below. You should produce precisely these results; observe the formatting. Make three test runs of the program entering the indicated Fahrenheit temperatures.

```
     100.0 F =  37.8 C
      32.0 F =   0.0 C
     212.0 F = 100.0 C
```

Problem Cs02-2—Format Control

Write a program that inputs two integers and outputs their difference and their product using this precise format.

```
    123          123
-   -10     X    -10
-------....-------
    133        -1230
```

Assume that both integers, their difference, and their product do not exceed five digits. Either or both may be negative. Test the program by entering the two integer values shown above. Then test the program with these two additional sets.

–12345 and 2

1234 and –6

Problem Cs02-3—Monthly Mortgage Payment Calculator

How much will my monthly payments be? This is a common question new home buyers frequently need answered. The following formula calculates the monthly payment

$$P = \frac{Ar}{1-(1+r)^{-n}}$$

where P is the monthly payment, A is the loan amount, r is the monthly interest rate and n is the number of monthly payments to be made.

Unfortunately, the loan statistics are not often in these units. Prompt the user to enter the values for the loan amount, the **annual** interest rate **percentage** and the loan length in **years**. Then compute the monthly payment and output the results as shown below. Note that you must convert the initial data as entered by the user into the proper quantities needed in the formula. The monthly interest rate is 1/12th of the annual rate and is not in percentage format. All variables should be doubles.

Make four test runs of the program entering the indicated values shown below. The output should look like this

```
----------Input--------------           Results
     Loan    Annual      Length         Monthly
   Amount      Rate    in Years         Payment
$   50000    11.50%        25.0        $ 508.23
```

2nd run

```
----------Input--------------           Results
     Loan    Annual      Length         Monthly
   Amount      Rate    in Years         Payment
$   24800     7.80%        25.0        $ 188.14
```

3rd run

```
----------Input--------------           Results
     Loan    Annual      Length         Monthly
   Amount      Rate    in Years         Payment
$1000000      5.00%        30.0        $5368.22
```

4th run

```
----------Input--------------           Results
     Loan    Annual      Length         Monthly
   Amount      Rate    in Years         Payment
$    9500    14.75%         5.0        $ 224.76
```

Problem Engr02-1 Falling Objects

The equation that describes the height of a falling object as a function of time is

$$y = y_0 + v_0 t - \frac{g}{2} t^2$$

where

y_0 is the initial height of the object
v_0 is the initial velocity of the falling object
y is the final height of the object
t is the time
g is the gravitational acceleration: 9.8 m/s/s

Write a program that, prompts the user to input a set of values for the initial height, initial velocity, and the final height. Then calculate and display the number of seconds until the object reaches the final height. All data are in the metric system. Assume that the final height is less than the initial height. All program variables should be doubles. Use the quadratic equation to solve for t. However, you must determine whether to use the + or – root.

For the first run, use these values for the initial height, initial velocity and final height: 100., 0., 0. Then when that is producing the correct results, rerun the program and enter these three: 1000., 100., 100.

With the program now verified as operational, use it to solve this problem. An astronomer has detected an asteroid that is on a collision course toward the earth. When it is detected, the asteroid is located 80,000,000 m away or about 50,000 miles moving directly toward the earth at a speed of 20 m/s or 45 mph. How much time do we have to take preventive measures, such as launching a nuclear strike to break the asteroid into small fragments? (Assume the final height is zero for a collision; ignore orbital considerations as well as air friction effects.)

Turn in the output of the two initial test runs as well as the asteroid run.

Chapter 3—Additional Processing Details

Section A: Basic Theory

Introduction

This chapter introduces more of the numerical data types. How these data are stored in memory is discussed. This leads to a discussion of the effects of data types upon calculations or, more precisely, data conversion. Finally, some additional C++ math operators are presented.

The Complete Integer Data Types

There are actually eight different integer data types. Integers fall into two categories, **signed** and **unsigned**. A signed integer may have a sign—either + or –; if no sign is present, it is assumed to be positive. Unsigned integers cannot ever be negative; they are assumed to be positive.

Some examples of a signed integer are: +10, –32, +42, and 11 where this last one is assumed to be +11. Some examples of an unsigned integer are: 11, 42, 88, 1.

Each type of integer comes in four sizes. The following Table 3.1 shows these data types, the number of bytes they occupy and the range of values that each can hold. This list will be expanded when the new 64-bit computers arrive.

Note that the **int** and **unsigned int** are both platform dependent. Under old DOS, they are 2 bytes, but under Win32 console applications and similar 32-bit platforms like mainframe computers and Unix, they are 4 bytes in size.

Table 3.1 The Integer Data Types

```
Data Type          Number         Range of values
                   of Bytes

signed:
char                 1            +127 to -128
short                2            +32,767 to -32,768
int*               2 or 4         as a short or a long
long                 4            +2,147,483,647 to -2,147,483,648

unsigned:
unsigned char        1            0 to 255
unsigned short       2            0 to 65,535
unsigned int*      2 or 4         as an unsigned short or unsigned long
unsigned long        4            0 to 4,294,967,295

* int and unsigned int: platform dependent
```

Why does C++ have all these different sizes? Would not one size, the **long**, serve all of them? The major reason for the different sizes, besides backwards compatibility with existing applications and databases, is to reduce total memory requirements of a program and of files on disk. While our programs are extremely simple at this point, it does not take much imagination to envision a program storing vast quantities of similar data to be processed.

Suppose that no one could order more than 127 of any given item. Then, defining the quantity as a **char** would make sense. If there were 1,000,000 customer orders in the data base, the amount of memory saved by making the quantity be a **char** instead of a **long** would be
(4 – 1) * 1,000,000 or three million bytes!

Some variables are inherently small in range. Take for example the x and y screen coordinates of a colored pixel dot on the CRT. In high resolution mode, there are 1024 dots horizontally and 768 vertically. If your program were plotting points, it would make sense to store those (x,y) coordinates as **shorts** not **longs**.

Here is another example; companies often give their departments a number to identify them. Typically, the department numbers are stored as a **char** because few companies have more than 127 departments.

Which Type of Data Do I Use in My Program?

Well, that all depends on the maximum value that each integer variable is to hold. Sometimes the size is given in the problem specifications. If it is not, then it is the programmer's task to determine the best choice to use. There is no escaping the fact that the programmer must know what the range of values for any given variable is expected to contain.

However, if you do not know which to use, try using an **int**. In fact, the **int** is the most commonly used integer data type, even though it is platform dependent. Why is the **int** so commonly used? The reason is that C++ language specifications allow the compiler makers to create the fastest possible executing integer math instructions for the **int** type of data. Thus, program developers who use an **int** data type are guaranteed the best performance on any platform. For example, under old DOS, performing math operations on **long** variables is significantly slower than if **int** variables are used. However, if the program is compiled and run on a Win32 console platform, then the **long**s and **int**s are entirely equivalent in terms of speed.

The decisions are destined to become even more complex. The newer computers just now coming out have these high speed, work register, circuit elements 64-bits or 8 bytes in size. Look for full support of 8-byte integers in the next release of the compilers. Following that in the not so distant future are the 128-bit or 16-byte computers.

How Integer Data Is Stored in Memory

While a detailed knowledge of exactly how an integer is stored in memory circuits is not needed for most programming applications, it greatly aids one's understanding of the details of integer math. Recall that the computer is really a binary machine, that is, everything is either on or off, electricity or no electricity, 1 or 0. Suppose that one defined a **char** variable called **x** and stored a 1 in it.

```
char x = 1;
```

Since a **char** occupies one byte of memory and since a byte consists of eight connected bits or circuit elements capable of storing a 0 or a 1, the decimal number 1 is stored in **x** as follows

0000 0001

where each binary digit represents a power of two. The 1 is in the 2^0 position and means 1 times 2^0—anything to the 0th power is 1. So we have 1 as the decimal number.

The number 2 would be stored as

0000 0010

where the 1 means 1 times 2^1 or 2 in decimal.

The number 5 is stored as

0000 0101

which is 1x 2^2 plus 0x 2^1 plus 1x 2^0, which is 4 + 0 + 1 or 5.

The sign is always the first bit of the entire field, here the left-most bit. A 0 means the number is positive and a 1 means it is negative. What is the largest number that can be stored in a

char? The left-most bit must remain a 0 so that the number is positive, but the rest of the bits are 1's.

0111 1111

which is $1x2^6 + 1x2^5 + 1x2^4 + 1x2^3 + 1x2^2 + 1x2^1 + 1x2^0 = 64 + 32 + 16 + 8 + 4 + 2 + 1$, which is +127.

Curiously, what happens if you add one to a **char** number that currently has +127 in it? Let's perform that binary addition problem and see.

```
 0111 1111
+0000 0001
----------
 1000 0000
```

In binary, 1 + 1 is 10, or a 0 and carry your 1. A carry and 1 is 10, or 0 and another carry. It works just like elementary addition in the decimal system. But look what happened to the sign bit! It is now a 1 bit, which means the whole number is negative! In fact, this is actually how a –128 is stored! What has happened is that the result has **overflowed** the contents of a **char** sized variable.

On the other hand, if we define y to be an **unsigned char**, now the leftmost bit is part of the number. A 1 bit here means $1x2^7$ or 128 added into the total. So the maximum value that can be stored in an **unsigned char** is 255

1111 1111

which is $1x2^7 + 1x2^6 + 1x2^5 + 1x2^4 + 1x2^3 + 1x2^2 + 1x2^1 + 1x2^0$
or 128 + 64 + 32 + 16 + 8 + 4 + 2 + 1 or 255.

Ok. What happens if we add one to an **unsigned char** that holds 255 currently? We have the following

```
 1111 1111
+0000 0001
----------
 0000 0000
```

The leftmost carry is going into a nonexistent 9th bit and is simply pitched by the circuitry. Again, this is called an **overflow**.

Integer Variable Overflow

When integer math is done, the programmer must be alert for the possibility of overflow. Failure to do so can result in silly results. Let's see how this comes about. Suppose that the programmer has defined the following variables and does the indicated calculation

```
short quantity = 10;
short cost = 10000;
short total;
total = cost * quantity; // potential error is here
```

Clearly, a **short** is an excellent choice for the quantity ordered and the cost of the item (say a used car for example) is fine as is. Both numbers, 10 and $10,000, fit nicely in a **short**. But what happens when the multiply instruction is executed? The numerical result is 100,000. However, a **short** can only hold a maximum of 32,767. What occurs during this multiply operation is overflow—namely all bits beyond the 16 bits that a 2-byte **short** can hold are discarded. It is even worse, because in this case, the result has a 1 in the left-most bit position of the **short** result, indicating the result is some negative number when it was supposed to mean $1x2^{15}$ added into the result. In fact, if you displayed the result, it is –31072.

How can it be fixed? The crudest way to fix the overflow problem is to make all variables a **long**. But in the real world this is not often possible. In a later chapter our programs input master files from disk where the data is stored in a **short** and must be input that way (See the Binary File section in Chapter 13.). Thus, we must find a way to make this work short of making all variables a **long**. After examining the floating point data types, we will examine this conversion problem fully.

The Complete Floating Point Data Types

Just as there is more than one size of integer data types, so also there are additional floating point data types. There are actually three types of floating point numbers as shown in Table 3.2.

Table 3.2 The Floating Point Data Types

Data Type	Number of Bytes	Range of values	Decimal Digits	Powers of Ten
float	4	$\pm 3.4x10^{-38}$ $\pm 3.4x10^{+38}$	6 3/4	10^{+38} - 10^{-38}
double	8	$\pm 1.7x10^{-308}$ $\pm 1.7x10^{+308}$	15	10^{+308} - 10^{-308}
long double	10	$\pm 3.4x10^{-4932}$ $\pm 1.7x10^{+4932}$	19	10^{+4932} - 10^{-4932}

These values are for the Microsoft Visual C++ compiler, but most implementations are similar. Note: in VC6, to get the long double as 10 bytes, you need to link to LIB/FP10.obj and include it before LIBC.LIB, LIBCMT.LIB, MSVCRT.LIB on the linker command line.

As you look over these data types, pay careful attention to the number of decimal digits a variable of that type can hold. The basic **float** data type is seldom used because it only offers six decimal digits of accuracy. Suppose that you made the grand total monthly sales variable be a **float** type. Only six digits can be accurately stored, $9,999.99 would be the largest total accurately represented. In financial calculations, this would be considered a disaster!

Thus, the most frequently used floating point data type is the **double**. A **double** gives 15 digits of accuracy, which is usually totally sufficient. Notice that the exponent or power of ten is seldom a problem with any of these. 10^{38} is a very large number; a one with 38 zeros after it. Also, math operations with the **long double** are the slowest math instructions on any computer and are exceedingly rarely used.

Principles of Data Conversion

When math is performed on two variables or constants, the C++ rules specify that both must be of the same data type. Thus, C++ can add two **ints**, two **shorts**, two **chars**, two **unsigned longs**, for example. But it cannot do math on unlike items. Consider what happens when the compiler encounters this calculation.

```
short quantity;
long  cost;
long  total;
total = cost * quantity;
```

The compiler is forced to do some data conversion, because it cannot do the **long * short** multiplication. (Note: the C++ data conversion rules are a bit different from the older C conversion rules.)

Data Conversion Rule 1. All types of **char** and **short** (signed and unsigned) are automatically promoted to an **int** in calculations. (On an old DOS platform where an **int** is only 2 bytes, then an **unsigned short** is converted to an **unsigned int** instead because an **unsigned short** can contain a larger value than can be held in a 2-byte **int**.)

This makes calculations involving a mixture of the smaller sized integer types very convenient. For example, assume the following definitions and calculation.

```
char  a;
short b;
int   c;
c = a + b;
```

Here the compiler automatically promotes both **a** and **b** to an **int** by temporarily creating a pair of **int** variables and converting **a** and **b** into these temporary variables. Then, it does the calculation, which results in an **int** answer and stores that answer into **c**, which is also an **int**. Finally, it deletes the memory that was used by these temporary variables. Table 3.3 Data Type Ranking shows the ranking of the different data types from the worst at the top to the least at the bottom.

long double
double
float
unsigned long
long
unsigned int
int

Table 3.3 Data Type Ranking

Data Conversion Rule 2. When an operator joins two values that have different data types, it converts the one of the lesser rank into a temporary instance of the data type of the higher rank. Now math can be performed on data of the same data type. Another way of saying this is that the compiler always converts to the worst data type. Unsigned numbers are worse than signed numbers; **long**s are worse than **int**s; **float**s are worse than **long**s and so on.

This conversion is precisely what happens when the compiler encounters the first example in this section.

```
total = cost * quantity;
```

Since **quantity** is a **short** and **cost** is a **long**, the **short** is promoted to the higher rank, a **long**. The compiler allocates a temporary **long** variable and converts **quantity** into that temporary **long** variable. The calculation is then **long * long** yielding a **long** result, which is assigned to **total**, which is also a **long**.

Consider this messy conversion problem.

```
char a;
short b;
int c;
long d;
long result = a * b + c * d;
```

Since there are no parentheses, the normal precedence of operators applies. First, the compiler does **a** times **b**, but it cannot multiply **char** times **short**. Data Conversion Rule 1 applies to both operands. The compiler converts both the **char a** and the **short b** into a temporary **int** variables. It then does **int * int** giving an **int** result. Next, it cannot multiply **int** times **long**. Here, Data Conversion Rule 2 applies. The worse type is **long**. It converts the **int c** variable into a temporary **long** and does **long** times **long** yielding a **long** result. Now it goes back to add the two partial results and discovers it cannot add an **int** result of the first multiplication and a **long** result of the second one, so the **int** intermediate result of **a * b** is converted into a **long**. The compiler can then add **long** plus **long** yielding a **long** final result. At last, it copies the **long** answer into the **result** variable, which is also a **long** and the compiler deletes all of the temporary variables it used.

Assigning Smaller Sized Integers to Larger Sized Integers

One can always assign a smaller sized integer value to a larger sized integer variable. For example, a **long** can easily hold the maximum value that any **int**, **short** or **char** can hold. Similarly, a **short** can hold any possible value that a **char** might contain.

The following assignments are always safe.

```
char a;
unsigned char b;
short c;
unsigned short d;
int e;
long f;
c = a;
c = b;
e = c;
e = d;
f = e;
```

Assigning Larger Sized Integers to Smaller Sized Integer Variables (The Typecast)

Data conversion is often automatically done by the compiler as needed during calculations and during assignments. However, the programmer must also force conversions at other times. Consider the following calculation to find the average number of students per section of a course that has a lot of sections in it.

```
char  numberOfSections;
short totalStudentsEnrolled;
char  studentsPerSection;
studentsPerSection = totalStudentsEnrolled/numberOfSections;
```

While the total number of students taking a course could be large, the number of course sections is not likely to exceed +127 so a **char** is appropriate. The average number of students in a course section is also not large; a **char** should hold the result nicely. However, when we compile this program, the calculation line generates a compile-time warning message—possible truncation of data.

Data Conversion Rule 3. The compiler always converts the final value of an expression to the data type of the result variable. However, if there is a chance that data conversion may result in a loss of accuracy, the compiler also issues a warning message so stating.

In the above example, data conversion rules show that the **char numberOfSections** is going to be converted into a temporary **int** as well as the **short** variable. Then, the compiler can do the divide of **int** by **int**, yielding an **int** result. However, the assignment is to a **char** sized variable. What happens?

The compiler copies only those bytes that can fit in the answer variable, beginning with the bytes on the right of the sending field. The following illustrates this; each x represents one bit of data. An **int** is four bytes or 16 bits long while a **char** is one byte or 8 bits.

```
studentsPerSection    =    Result
   xxxx xxxx        <---   0000 0000 0000 0000 0000 0000 xxxx xxxx
```

In other words, the high order three bytes of the **int** result are simply pitched. If part of the answer were stored there, where the zeros are located above, then the answer variable, **studentsPerSection**, would have a bogus value in it. Hence, the compiler issues a warning message, possible loss of precision. Nevertheless, the compiler is going to go ahead and make the assignment.

In this particular case, we know by the nature of the calculation that the answer is going to be small and will always fit within the smaller **char** variable. But the compiler does not.

A program should compile error and warning message free when it is done. Never leave warning messages in a program. If you leave these warnings in a program, then every time anyone compiles the program, they have to go back and re-evaluate whether or not those warnings are significant or not. This is very bad programming style indeed.

So how can we get rid of the warning in this case? True, there is a compiler option to disable such warning messages. But that is playing Russian Roulette; if you do that, then you will not be notified of assignments that will cause trouble! The answer is to insert some coding that tells the compiler that this is ok that we are assuming full responsibility for this particular assignment statement. This is called a **typecast**.

A **typecast** consists of the desired data type surrounded by parentheses. The typecast applies to what comes **immediately** after it.

To remove the warning message in the above example, code

```
studentsPerSection = (char) (totalStudentsEnrolled /
                              numberOfSections);
```

The typecast tells the compiler to convert the **int** final result into a **char** and that we say it is ok to do so. Notice that the parenthesis is around the complete result, not just in front of the total students variable. Coding only this

```
studentsPerSection = (char) totalStudentsEnrolled /
                            numberOfSections;
```

causes the compiler to convert the **short** into a **char**, likely truncating the number, causing even more problems.

There are also times when this warning indicates a fundamental design flaw. Consider the problem of calculating the total cost of an order.

```
int  quantity = 10;
long cost = 10000;
int  total;
total = quantity * cost;
```

Here the compiler again does data conversion when performing the multiply operation. It promotes the **int quantity** to a **long** temporary value and multiplies **long** times **long** yielding a **long** result. Next, the assignment is a **long** to an **int**. Since an **int** type could be two bytes not four, the compiler issues the warning message and then moves what it can of the resulting product into **total**. When compiled and run on a 32-bit platform such as Win32 console applications, the **int** is really four bytes and all is well. When that same code is compiled as an older DOS application, the results are garbage in **total**.

Thus, whenever assigning a large sized result into a smaller sized variable, you must analyze the situation and determine whether the best course is to make the answer variable larger or put in the typecast because the answer really is not that large.

Assigning smaller sized floating point values to larger sized floating point variables is always acceptable and totally safe. Obviously, if a **float** value contains 6 digits, it can be assigned to a **double**, which has 15 digits. The exponents are safe as well, since the **double** can handle a much larger exponent.

Assigning a large sized floating point value to a smaller sized floating point variable raises the same compiler warning about truncation as with integers. Consider this assignment

```
float a;
double b = 1.23456789012345;
a = b;
```

Variable **a** cannot store more than 6 digits accurately. Thus, there is going to be a loss of precision. If, however, this is acceptable, then supply the typecast

```
a = (float) b;
```

and the warning message is handled.

However, there is an additional consideration, the exponent or power of ten. Consider this version.

```
float a;
double b = 1.23456789012345E100;
a = (float) b;
```

By using the typecast, the warning goes away but when the program actually executes this assignment line, trouble occurs. A **float** can only store an exponent of 10^{38} and the computer cannot store 10^{100} in **float** variable **a** and promptly issues a floating point overflow error message and terminates the program.

Thus, always consider both the needed number of digits as well as the possible magnitude of the number.

Calculations Involving Multiple Floating Point Data Types

Just as with the integer family, the compiler must perform data conversion when an instruction involves floating point numbers of different data types. Consider the following.

```
float a;
double b;
float c;
c = b * a;
```

The compiler must convert the contents of **float a** variable into a temporary **double** so that it can perform the multiply operation. It also issues the warning message about possible truncation when it gets to the assignment portion since the answer variable is a **float** and the result of the calculation is a **double**. If the **double**'s exponent exceeds that of a smaller **float**, a math exception is raised and the program is terminated. Even if the exponent of the result is small enough to fit in a **float**, one is trying to place 15 digits of accuracy into a number that can only hold a little more than 6 digits!

If you knew by the nature of the problem that the exponent was in range and the loss of precision was not a factor, then the following removes the compiler warning.

```
c = (float) (b * a);
```

What happens if integer data types and floating point types are used in the same calculation? A situation such as this is called mixed mode math.

Mixed Mode Math

Mixed mode math occurs any time both integer data types and floating point types occur in the same calculation. Any floating point type is worse than any of the integer types. Consider the following mixed mode calculation.

```
char a;
float b;
int c;
double d;
double answer;
answer = a / b + c * d;
```

The computer cannot divide **char** by **float**, so the **char** variable **a** is converted into a temporary **float** and the division is done, yielding a **float** result. Next, the multiplication is done, but the **int c** variable's contents are converted into a temporary **double** variable and then the multiplication is done, yielding a **double**. Then, the addition of the two intermediate results is performed, but the **float** result of the division must first be converted into a **double**. The final result is a **double**. At last, the assignment can be made, which goes without a hitch because the right side result value is a **double** and the left side answer variable is a **double**.

When making an assignment from a floating point type to any of the integer types, a new problem arises. Let's examine the problem and then see how it can be rectified. Suppose that the grading scale for the course is 90-up is an A. Suppose that in calculating your final grade the following was done.

```
int totalPoints = 899;
int numParts = 10;
int grade;
grade = totalPoints / numParts;
```

If this was your final grade, would you be happy and content getting an 89 or a B? But you say you actually had an 89.9. Ah, the above was integer division. We can fix that easily using a typecast.

```
grade = (double) totalPoints / numParts;
```

Just typecast to a **double** either of the two variables and the division now must be done using floating point numbers. The result is 89.9 and then the assignment is done.

When the computer assigns a floating point number to any of the integer types, it issues first a warning message about possible loss of data. It is possible for a float value to overflow a long, not by digits, but by the power of ten involved. Consider a float value of 1×10^{38}—it would totally overflow a **long**. But in this case, student grades should range between 0 and 100 and would even fit in a **char** type. So now, our typecast fix looks like this.

```
grade = (int) ( (double) totalPoints / numParts);
```

Now the warning message is gone. But one major problem remains.

Data Conversion Rule 4. When assigning any floating point type to any of the integer types, the computer assigns only the digits to the left of the decimal point. It drops all decimal fractions.

Thus in the above assignment, even though the result is now clearly 89.9, the compiler places the whole number portion only into **grade**, the 89. What we want it to do is to round up!

Corollary: when assigning any float data type to any of the integer data types, add +.5 before the assignment to round up.

The correct calculation is

```
grade = (int) ( (double) totalPoints / numParts + .5);
```

This line says to convert **totalPoints** to a **double** and do the division using **doubles**; then, add .5; then, convert the **double** result into an **int** and copy it into **grade**. In the case of 89.9, adding .5 yields 90.4 but the conversion to an **int** copies only the 90 portion, yielding the desired result.

Constants and Data Types

When numerical constants are coded, such as 10 and 123.45, the compiler assumes that they are of data types **int** and **double** respectively. That is, the compiler assumes you desire the fastest math possible on integers and the 6 digits of accuracy is not enough with floating point numbers. In general, these are wise decisions.

Occasionally, you might wish to override those assumed data types to specify that the constant is a **long** or is an **unsigned int** or **unsigned long**. These are the only overrides available. Suppose that you are dealing with a graphics problem in which only positive x and y values are allowed. Further, suppose that you wanted to move the point one pixel to the right along the x-axis. Here, the compiler assumes a data type of **int** for the constant value of 1. It would be better if we could force it to be an **unsigned int** of value 1.

```
unsigned int x;
unsigned int y;
x = x + 1;
```

The integer constant data type can be specified by adding a one or two letter suffix to the number. The possible suffixes are U or u for unsigned and L or l for long or UL or ul for unsigned long.

We can rewrite the above addition as follows

```
x = x + 1U;
```

and now the constant 1 is of type **unsigned int**.

When making a constant a **long** value, please do not use the lowercase l for it is easily confused with a digit of 1. Look at these two attempts to make a 1000 into a **long** constant.

```
1000l
1000L
```

Notice that the first one looks more like ten thousand and one.

Suppose that we needed to add 100,000 to a **long total** variable. Coding

```
long total;
total = total + 100000;
```

often gives the compiler warning message the constant is a **long**. To remove the compiler warning, simply append the suffix L to the constant.

```
total = total + 100000L;
```

Notice that one major use of constant suffixes is within calculations. Suppose that our calculation is the number of ounces in a variable number of tons. There are 16 ounces in a pound and 2000 pounds in a ton. Here is the problem.

```
int numTons;
long totalOunces;
totalOunces = numTons * 2000 * 16;
```

Assume that the user has entered something easy to calculate, say 10 tons. What results? Can you spot the error? The calculation involves all **int**s and thus can result in an overflow for any number of tons above one. 2000 times 16 is 32000. If **numTons** is above one, it may overflow an **int** result if the program is compiled to run under old DOS where an **int** is only 2 bytes in size. The calculation can be fixed by using a typecast as we have learned earlier.

```
totalOunces = (long) numTons * 2000 * 16;
```

But using a long suffix is much easier.

```
totalOunces = numTons * 2000L * 16;
```

Notice that I applied the L suffix to the 2000 constant.

What would likely happen if I had coded it this way?

```
totalOunces = numTons * 2000 * 16L;
```

If **numTons** had been the initial 10, all would have been fine, since an **int** result can hold 20,000. But what if the user entered 20 tons? Overflow. Here is a case where position of the override is important.

The data type of floating point constants can similarly be altered by two suffixes: f or F for **float** and L or l for **long double**. Coding

123.5f

creates a **float** constant instead of a **double**.

The f suffix is quite useful if all of your variables are of type **float**. Assume that we are dealing with weather temperatures. Storing such a temperature in a **double** is overkill, since we would not need more than say four digits, as in 101.5 degrees. Suppose that we needed to add one degree to a temperature measurement.

```
float temp;
temp = temp + 1.;
```

This again yields a possible loss of precision warning message because the 1.0 is a **double** constant, forcing the addition to be done using **doubles**. By forcing the 1.0 to be of type **float**, the calculation is done using **float** types.

```
temp = temp + 1.f;
```

Here's another common goof. What is wrong with this one?

```
int   x = 10;
int   y = 10055;
float ansr;
ansr = (float) x + y / x;
```

Have you spotted the error? Which operation is done first? The divide operator has precedence over the add operator. Thus, the compiler performs **int** divided by **int** and discards the remainder. Next, it converts **x** into a **float** and then converts the division result into a **float** so that they can be added. The fractional portion is not therefore present in the answer variable. Here is a corrected version.

```
ansr = x + (float) x / y;
```

By now you are probably thinking why not make everything in the program a **double** variable and forget about it? Master files of data on disk very often use these smaller sized integer values to conserve disk space. Turning every integer variable into a **double** is also wasteful of computer memory within your program. Perhaps even more importantly, math operations on floating point data are much slower than math on integer data.

Additional Operators

The Increment and Decrement Operators

An extremely common operation in programs is adding one to a counter. Perhaps less common is the need to subtract one from a counter. The **increment operator** ++ and the **decrement operator** – – do exactly these common actions.

```
int count = 0;
int tally = 42;
count = count + 1;
tally = tally - 1;
```

These can be replaced with just

```
count++;
tally--;
```

After these are executed, **count** contains 1 and **tally** contains 41.

The operators can be placed after or before the variable on which it applies. These are called the **prefix inc** or **postfix inc**. The meanings are different. The prefix inc or dec means to increment/decrement the variable before that variable is used in the statement. The postfix inc or dec means to go ahead and use the current contents of the variable in the statement and when the statement is done, go ahead and increment/decrement the variable.

In the case above, both

```
count++;
tally--;
```

and

```
++count;
--tally;
```

produce the same results because no use of the current contents of either **count** or **tally** is made (other than the increment/decrement operation).

However, that is not always the case. Consider these two

```
int count1 = 42;
int count2 = 42;
int sum1 = 0;
int sum2 = 0;
sum1 = count1++;
sum2 = ++count2;
```

In both cases, **count1** and **count2** contain 43 when the instructions are finished. Variable **sum1** contains 42 while **sum2** contains 43.

These two calculation lines are equivalent to writing

```
sum1 = count1;
count1 = count1 + 1;
```

```
count2 = count2 + 1;
sum2 = count2;
```

The Compound Assignment Operators

Another common coding action is to add a value to a total. Consider the problem of accumulating the total cost of an order.

```
int quantity;
double cost;
double totalCost = 0;
totalCost = totalCost + quantity * cost;
```

The lengthy calculation line can be shortened by use of the += operator.

The += operator adds the result to the right of the operator to the variable to the left of the operator. The total cost calculation can be shortened to just

```
totalCost += quantity * cost;
```

Here is another example. Suppose we need to accumulate the student scores on a test.

```
double score;
double sum = 0;
sum += score;
```

The calculation says to add the contents of **score** to the current contents of **sum** and then place the revised value back into **sum**. It is equivalent to writing

```
sum = sum + score;
```

Please note that in both the above examples, variables **sum** and **totalCost** must be initialized to zero because the first use of those variables is to add something to them.

The use of the += operator is widespread. However, there are also –=, *=, /= and %= operators available for use. The %= operator only applies to integer types values, of course, since floating point values already have a decimal point.

Suppose that we wished to calculate 3!—that is, 3 * 2 * 1. One way to do this is

```
int fact = 3;
fact *= (fact - 1);
```

This says to multiply **fact** by the quantity **fact–1** and place the result back in **fact**. It is a short cut for

```
fact = fact * (fact - 1);
```

Ok. I admit that I could have determined 3! in my head; however, soon you will get to find N! in which the user enters a value for N.

Suppose that we wished to divide a number by 10. We could code

```
int num = 123;
num /= 10;
```

This results in 12 in **num** when the operation is complete.

Just be alert for possible uses of these short cut type of operators.

Section B: Computer Science Examples

CS03a—Vote Tally Program

Input the vote count received by each of the three candidates running for election. Output the percentage of the votes received by each candidate. Call the candidates Mr. Jones, Ms. Baker, and Ms. Smith. Test the program using 19345, 23673, and 34128 votes respectively.

Design the solution first. We need three variables to hold the input vote counts. These should be **long**s since vote counts can be rather large numbers. Let's call them **votesJones**, **votesBaker**, and **votesSmith**. To find the percentage each candidate has, the total vote count must be found; it also must be a **long** variable. Let's call it **totalVotes**. Given the total votes cast, the percentage each candidate received can then be calculated. So we need three result variables, say called **percentJones**, **percentBaker** and **percentSmith**. These must be **double**s if they are to hold a result such as 10.5%. Draw up a picture of main storage with small boxes for each of these variables. Figure 3.1 shows the main storage diagram.

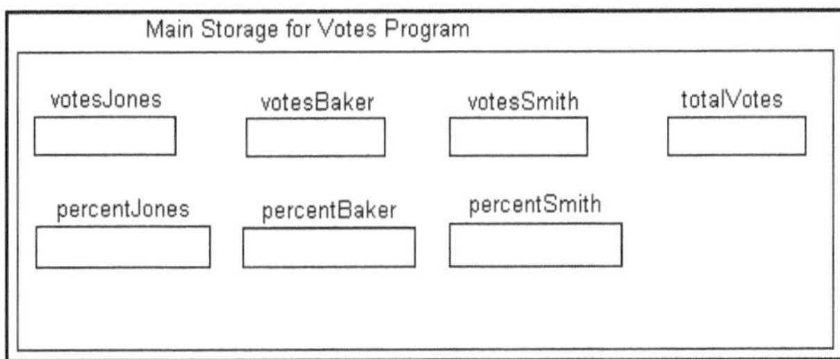

Figure 3.1 Main Storage for Votes Program

Now using these names for the variables, write out the sequence of processing steps needed, following the Cycle of Data Processing, IPO.

prompt and input the vote count for Jones placing it in **votesJones**
prompt and input the vote count for Baker placing it in **votesBaker**
prompt and input the vote count for Smith placing it in **votesSmith**
set **totalVotes** to 0
add **votesJones** to **totalVotes**
add **votesBaker** to **totalVotes**
add **votesSmith** to **totalVotes**
set **percentJones** = **votesJones** * 100. / **totalVotes**
set **percentBaker** = **votesBaker** * 100. / **totalVotes**
set **percentSmith** = **votesSmith** * 100. / **totalVotes**

Notice that I force the calculation to use **doubles** by first multiplying by 100. and not 100!

Finally, output the results nicely formatted
displaying **percentJones**, **percentBaker** and **percentSmith**.

Now desk check it using the input test vote counts. When you have convinced yourself that there are no errors, go ahead and code it into a C++ program. Here is the completed program.

Cs03a - Vote Count Program

```
/***************************************************************/
/*                                                             */
/* Cs03a: vote tally program                                   */
/*                                                             */
/***************************************************************/

#include <iostream>
#include <iomanip>
using namespace std;
int main () {
 long votesJones; // total votes for Jones
 long votesBaker; // total votes for Baker
 long votesSmith; // total votes for Smith

 long totalVotes = 0; // total votes cast in the election

 double percentJones; // results for Jones
 double percentBaker; // results for Baker
 double percentSmith; // results for Smith

 // prompt and input the three vote counts
 cout << "Enter the vote count for Mr. Jones: ";
 cin >> votesJones;
 cout << "Enter the vote count for Ms. Baker: ";
 cin >> votesBaker;
 cout << "Enter the vote count for Ms. Smith: ";
 cin >> votesSmith;

 // find the total votes cast
 totalVotes += votesJones;
 totalVotes += votesBaker;
 totalVotes += votesSmith;

 // calculate the percentages
 percentJones = votesJones * 100. / totalVotes;
 percentBaker = votesBaker * 100. / totalVotes;
 percentSmith = votesSmith * 100. / totalVotes;

 // setup floating point format for output of percentages
 cout << fixed << setprecision (1);

```

```
// output a title
cout << "\nVoting Results\n\n";
cout << "Mr. Jones: " << setw(5) << percentJones << "%\n";
cout << "Ms. Baker: " << setw(5) << percentBaker << "%\n";
cout << "Ms. Smith: " << setw(5) << percentSmith << "%\n";

return 0;

```

```
Output from Cs03a - Vote Count Program
```

```
Enter the vote count for Mr. Jones: 19345
Enter the vote count for Ms. Baker: 23673
Enter the vote count for Ms. Smith: 34128

Voting Results

Mr. Jones:  25.1%
Ms. Baker:  30.7%
Ms. Smith:  44.2%
```

Section C: An Engineering Example

Engr03a—Calculating the Power Supplied to a Load (Electrical Engineering)

An AC power supply of V volts is applied to a circuit load with impedance of Z (Ø) with current I. Display the real power P, the reactive power R, the apparent power A and the power factor PF of the load. Test the program with a voltage of 120 volts and an impedance of 8 ohms at 30 degrees.

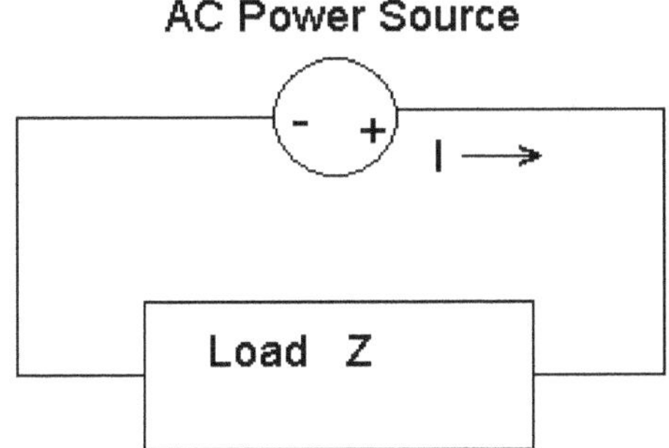

Here are the formulae that define these power values

$I = V/Z$

$P = V\,I \cos Ø$

$R = V\,I \sin Ø$

A = VI
PF = cos Ø

where V is the root mean square (RMS) voltage of the AC power source in volts, Z is the impedance in ohms, Ø is the angle of impedance in degrees, I is the current in amperes, P is the real power in watts, R is the reactive power in volt–amperes–reactive (VAR), A is the apparent power in volt–amperes and PF is the power factor of the load.

The starting point is to design the solution on paper. We begin by identifying the input variables. Here we must input the volts, impedance, and its angle. Let's call these variables **V**, **Z** and **angle**. Draw main three storage boxes and label them with these names. Next look at the output and create main storage boxes for what is needed. Let's call them **P**, **R**, **A** and **PF**. Finally, we must have some intermediate result variables. The angle must be converted to radians and the current is needed. Let's call those boxes, **radAngle** and **I**. To convert to radians, we need the constant **PI**. This is shown in Figure 3.2 below.

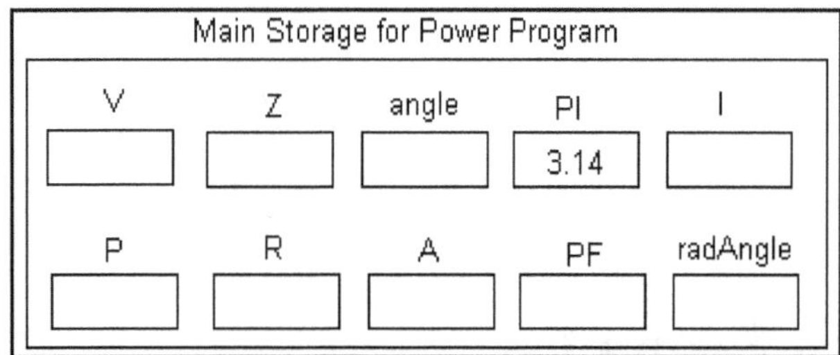

Figure 3.2 Main Storage for Power Program

Now follow the Cycle of Data Processing, IPO, and write out the sequences we need to solve this problem making sure we use the same variable names as we have in the main storage boxes. First, we need to input the three variables.

prompt and input the voltage and store it in **V**
prompt and input the impedance and store it in **Z**
prompt and input the angle and store it in **angle**

Next, calculate the intermediate values we are going to need in the main power calculations.

radAngle = **angle** * **PI** / 180
I = **V** / **Z**

Now calculate the various power values.

P = **V** * **I** * cos **radAngle**
R = **V** * **I** * sin **radAngle**
A = **V** * **I**
PF = cos **radAngle**

And lastly, display the results

print nicely labeled the input situation: **V**, **Z** and **angle**
print nicely labeled the four results: **P**, **R**, **A**, and **PF**

Here are the completed program and the sample run.

Engr03a - Calculate the Power Supplied to a Load

```
/***************************************************************/
/*                                                             */
/* Engr03a: Calculate the power delivered to a load            */
/*                                                             */
/***************************************************************/

#include <iostream>
#include <iomanip>
#include <cmath>
using namespace std;
const double PI = acos (-1.);

int main () {

 double V;     // initial volts of AC power supply
 double Z;     // initial impedance of load
 double angle; // initial angle of impedance of load

 double I;        // current flow in amperes
 double radAngle; // angle in radians

 double P;  // real power in watts
 double R;  // reactive power in VAR
 double A;  // apparant power in VA
 double PF; // power factor

 // prompt and input the initial values of V, Z and angle
 cout << "Enter the AC power supply voltage:       ";
 cin >> V;
 cout << "Enter the impedance of the load in ohms: ";
 cin >> Z;
 cout << "Enter the angle in degrees:              ";
 cin >> angle;

 // calculate intermediate needed values
 radAngle = angle * PI / 180;
 I = V / Z;

 // calculate the four resulting power factors
 P = V * I * cos (radAngle);
 R = V * I * sin (radAngle);
 A = V * I;
 PF = cos (radAngle);

 // setup floating point format for output
 cout << fixed << setprecision (3);

 // echo print the input
 cout << "\n Power Supplied to a Load Results\n";
 cout << "AC voltage supplied:     " << setw(8) << V<<" volts\n";
```

```
 cout << "Load impedance of:          " << setw(8) << Z <<" ohms\n";
 cout << "      at an angle of:       " << setw(8) << angle
      << " degrees\n";
 cout << "Yields these power factors\n";
 cout << "Real power supplied:        " << setw(8) << P<<" watts\n";
 cout << "Reactive power supplied: " << setw(8) << R
      << " volt-amperes-reactive\n";
 cout << "Apparant power supplied: " << setw(8) << A
      << " volt-amperes\n";
 cout << "Power factor is:            " << setw(8)
      << PF << endl;

 return 0;
}
```

```
Output from Engr03a - Calculate the Power Supplied to a Load
```

```
Enter the AC power supply voltage:       120
Enter the impedance of the load in ohms: 8
Enter the angle in degrees:              30

 Power Supplied to a Load Results
AC voltage supplied:       120.000 volts
Load impedance of:           8.000 ohms
     at an angle of:        30.000 degrees
Yields these power factors
Real power supplied:      1558.846 watts
Reactive power supplied:   900.000 volt-amperes-reactive
Apparant power supplied: 1800.000 volt-amperes
Power factor is:             0.866
```

Design Exercises

1. Sketch the pseudocode to solve this problem. The user enters some even integer greater than two, called say number. The program determines the next higher even integer from number and the next lower even integer from number. Display the sum of the three numbers, the product of the three numbers, and the average of the three numbers.

2. Sketch the pseudocode to solve this problem. The user wishes to enter six temperature observations taken at four-hour intervals throughout the day. Compute and print the average temperature for the day.

Stop! Do These Exercises Before Programming

1. What is in the variable **result** when the calculation is finished?
```
double result = 123 / 10 + .5;
```

2. What is in the variable **result** when the calculation is finished?
```
double result = 123 / 10. + .5;
```

3. What is in the variable **result** when the calculation is finished?
```
char a = 2;
short b = 3;
long c = 100000L;
double result = b / a + c;
```

4. What is in the variable **result** when the calculation is finished?
```
char a = 2;
short b = 3;
long c = 100000L;
double result = (double) b / a + c;
```

5. What is in the variable **result** when the calculation is finished?
```
char a = 2;
short b = 3;
long c = 100000L;
double result = b / a + (double) c;
```

On the next two problems, fix the errors by changing the calculation line; do not change the data types of the variables.

6. Fix the compiler truncation warning message.
```
int itemsOrdered;
double totalCost;
double unitCost;
itemsOrdered = totalCost / unitCost;
```

7. Repair the equation so that **totalBytes** contains the correct amount even on old DOS systems.
```
short k = 1024; // 1k bytes = 1024, 1m bytes = 1024k
short numMegs;
long totalBytes;
totalBytes = numMegs * k * k;
```

8. What is in **sum** and **count** after these instructions complete.

```
int count = 99;
int sum = 10;
sum += (++count)++;
```

9. What is in **sum** and **count** after these instructions complete.

```
int count = 99;
int sum = 10;
sum *= count++;
```

10. What is in **sum** and **count** after these instructions complete.

```
int count = 10;
int sum = 99;
sum /= count++;
```

Programming Problems

Problem Cs03-1—Height of a Rainbow

How high is a rainbow? Interestingly enough, when light is refracted by the water droplets just after a storm, the angle between the level of your eye and the top of a rainbow is always the same, 42.3333333 degrees. From trigonometry, if we know the distance to the rainbow, then using the **tan()** function, we can calculate the unknown height.

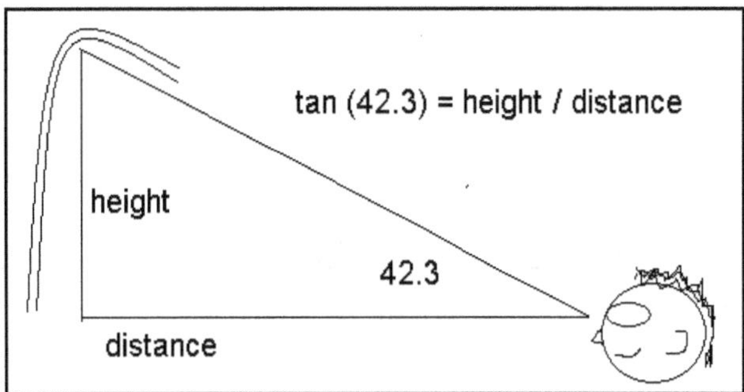

Thus, given the distance and the angle, the height is distance * tan (angle). Note that the trig functions of the C++ library all take the angle in radians. Use radians = angle * PI / 180 to convert.

Sometimes you can see a second rainbow just above the first one. The magic angle for this secondary rainbow is 52.25 degrees. (I have actually once seen seven rainbows at one time.)

Write a program that inputs the distance in miles from the rainbow and displays the height of the primary and secondary rainbows. Display the distance and heights with two decimal digits and appropriately labeled. Test your program with a distance of 2 miles, 1 mile and .5 miles.

Cs03-2—Area of a Triangle

The perimeter of a triangle is the sum of the lengths of all three sides. The semi-perimeter is ½ of the perimeter. Given a triangle, the area of the triangle is as follows, where s is the semi-perimeter.

$$area = \sqrt{s(s - side1)(s - side2)(s - side3)}$$

Write a program that inputs the three sides of a triangle and displays the area of that triangle. Display the area to three decimal digits. Test the program with these three test runs.

10 15 20
10 7.5 12.5
25.25 18.5 21.77

Cs03-3—Dollar Conversion Program

Input a dollar amount as a double, such as 1.23 for $1.23. Convert it into the number of pennies in that amount and store it in a long. Next, print out the minimum number of dollars, quarters, dimes, nickels and pennies in that amount. Prompt the user like this:

Enter the amount of money (such as 1.23 for $1.23): 1.23

Your output should show the following lines.

```
$1.23 contains
  1 dollar
  0 quarter(s)
  2 dime(s)
  0 nickel(s)
  3 penny/pennies
```

Test the program with these values as well as 1.23: 4.18, 8.88, 0.22.

Problem Engr03-1—Carbon–14 Dating

Radioactive isotopes of elements are not a stable form and they spontaneously decay into another element over time. This radioactive decay is an exponential function over time and is given by

$$Q(t) = Q_0 e^{-lambda*t}$$

where Q_0 is the initial quantity of a radioactive substance at time t = 0 and lambda is the radioactive decay constant.

Now the reverse process is valuable. That is, since the decay is at a known rate, if we observe a given quantity of radioactive substance in a sample and we know the initial quantity that was there to begin with, then the time for that initial quantity to have decayed into the current amount can be calculated, yielding the date of the sample.

$$t = -\frac{1}{lambda} \ln \frac{Q}{Q_0}$$

Archaeologists use Carbon–14 isotopes to determine the age of samples. Plants and animals continuously absorb Carbon–14 while they are living. Once they die, nothing new is absorbed and the slow decay process begins. Thus, assumptions can be made about the initial quantity of Carbon–14 in a sample and the current amount of Carbon–14 in a sample can be measured in the lab. Samples are commonly trees used as building materials and campfire remains, for example. The decay constant lambda of Carbon–14 is well known to be 0.00012097 per year. Typical lab measurements report the percentage of Carbon–14 remaining in a sample.

Write a program that inputs the percentage of Carbon–14 in a sample and displays the age of that sample in years. Note that the formula uses a ratio not a percentage. Test the program with these percentages: 50%, 25%, and 12.5%. Display the year results to one decimal. Echo print the original inputted percentage. Label all values appropriately.

Finally, suppose that the percentage ratios are only sufficiently accurate to measure 1.0% because with concentrations that low, field contamination plays a more significant role. What would the oldest date that the Carbon–14 process be able to yield?

Engr03-2—Railroad Track Design (Transportation Engineering)

When a train travels over a straight section of track, it exerts a downward force on the rails. But when it rounds a level curve, it also exerts a horizontal force outward on the rails. Both of these forces must be considered when designing the track. The downward force is equivalent to the weight of the train. The horizontal force, known as centrifugal force, is a function of the weight of the train, the speed of the train as it rounds the curve, and the radius of the curve. The equation to compute the horizontal force, in pounds, is:

$$force = \left(\frac{weight * 2000}{32}\right)\left(\frac{(1.4667 * mph)^2}{radius}\right)$$

where weight is the weight of the train in tons, mph is the speed of the train in miles per hour and radius is the radius of the curve in feet.

Write a program to input the weight, mph and radius. Compute and print the corresponding horizontal force generated along with the initial three values, appropriately labeled. Test the program using these situations:

a). use weight = 405.7 tons at a speed of 30.5 mph on a curve of radius 2005.33 feet
b). run again increasing the speed
c). run again increasing the radius

d). run again decreasing the radius

Write two sentences describing what happens to the force when the speed and curve vary. For example, what happens when either the speed or radius is doubled or is cut in half?

Engr03-3—Period of an Oscillating Pendulum

The period of an oscillating pendulum on the surface of the earth is given by

$$T = 2PI\sqrt{\frac{L}{g}}$$

where the period T is in seconds, L is the length of the pendulum in meters and g is the gravitational acceleration of the earth on the surface, 9.8 m/s/s.

Write a program that first prompts the user to input the length of the pendulum and then calculates its period. Display both the length and the period appropriately labeled and with their units.

Analysis: Suppose that the length of a pendulum was carefully constructed to be 0.24824m long so that the period was one second. Suppose that the space shuttle took that pendulum into orbit around the earth. What would happen to the period of that pendulum?

Chapter 4—Decisions

Section A: Basic Theory

Introduction

A decision asks a question that can be answered true or false, yes or no. Decisions are widely used in most programs. If a question is true, then often one or more actions are to be performed. However, if the question is false or not true, then one might have some alternative processing steps to be performed instead.

A decision can be thought of as having three parts: a test condition to be examined, one or more instructions to follow when the test condition is true, and one or more instructions to follow when the test condition is false. When considered from this point of view, the test condition itself can be used in far more C++ constructs than just a simple decision structure.

In C++, the decision structure is called an If-Then-Else.

The Components of an If-Then-Else Decision Structure

The decision structure is shown below in Figure 4.1. Notice that flow of control comes in at the top and after branching and doing one of two alternative sets of statements, control leaves out the bottom. The statements to do when the test is true are called the then-clause. The statements to do when the test is false are called the else-clause.

The If-Then-Else Syntax

The If-Then-Else basic syntax to implement the decision structure is as follows.

```
if (test condition) {
  0, 1 or more statements to do if the test condition is true
}
else {
  0, 1, or more stmts to do if the test condition is false
}
```

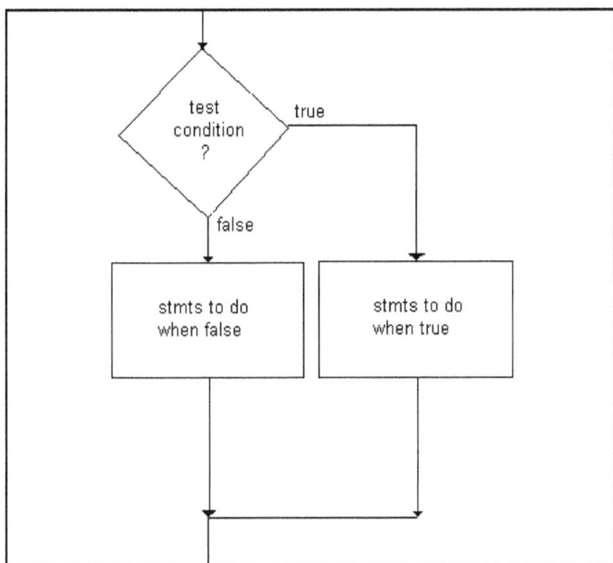

Figure 4.1 The Decision Structure

The keyword **if** begins the decision. It is followed by a test condition surrounded by parentheses. Note that there is no "then" keyword but that there is an **else** keyword.

The else-clause is strictly optional; if nothing needs to be done when the test condition is false, the else-clause does not need to be coded.

Notice that the statements to be done are surrounded by a begin-end block { }. I prefer to place the begin block { on the line that is launching that block. All statements within that block are uniformly indented. The end block } must align with the start of the line that is launching the block.

The other commonly used style looks like this.

```
if (test condition)
  {
  0, 1 or more statements to do if the test condition is true
  }
else
  {
  0, 1, or more stmts to do when the test condition is false
  }
```

In this style, the begin block { and all statements within that block and the end block } are all uniformly indented the uniform amount. Choose one style or the other and remain consistent in its use throughout the program.

The else-clause is optional. If there is nothing to do when the test condition is false, it can be omitted as shown below.

```
if (test condition) {
  0, 1 or more stmts to do when the test condition is true
```

```
}
```

Further, if there is only a single statement to do, the begin-end pair {} can be omitted.

```
if (test condition)
  a single statement when true;
else
  a single statement when false;
```

Or if there is nothing to do when the statement is false, it can be simply

```
if (test condition)
  a single statement when true;
```

Note that a single statement can be a null statement consisting of just a semicolon.

```
if (test condition)
  a single statement when true;
else
 ;
```

The Test Condition

Test conditions can be very complex and the rules, likewise. However, let's start with simple ones and add onto the complexity as we gain understanding of what they are and how they are used. A test condition asks some kind of question that can be answered true or false. In its most basic form, it parallels how we ask a question in English. For example

is the quantity less than or equal to five?
is x greater than y?
is count not equal to zero?
is sum equal to zero?

Notice in these examples that the comparison operators are less than or equal to, greater than, not equal to, and equal to. Observe that there is some quantity to the left and also to the right of each comparison operator. In English, the following would make no sense

if quantity greater than

"Greater then what" is the immediate reply. This gives us the basic format of a simple test condition:

```
operand1 comparison-operator operand2
```

In C++, there are six comparison operators. They are

```
>    greater than
>=   greater than or equal to
<    less than
<=   less than or equal to
!=   not equal to
==   equal to
```

Pay particular attention to the comparison equals operator! Notice it is a double equals sign (==); it is not a single equals sign (=). A single equal sign (=) is **always** an assignment operator in C++.

Using these operators, we can translate the above four English comparisons into C++ as follows.

```
if (quantity <= 5) {
   // do these things if true
}

if (x > y) {
   // do these things if true
}

if (count != 0) {
   // do these things if true
}

if (sum == 0) {
   // do these things if true
}

if (hoursWorked > 40) {
   // calculate overtime pay
}
```

Let's apply just this much to some programming situations. Suppose that we wanted to print a message if an employee was eligible for early retirement. That is, if their **age** was greater than or equal to 55. One could code the following to do this.

```
int age;
long employeeID;
cout << "Enter the employee id number and age\n";
cin >> employeeID >> age;
if (age >= 55) {
   cout << employeeID
        << " is eligible for early retirement\n";
}
```

Suppose that we wanted to determine whether a person was eligible to vote. We can input their **citizenship** status, which contains a one if they are a citizen and a zero if they are not a citizen.

```
int citizenship;
cout << "Enter citizenship status: ";
cin >> citizenship;
if (citizenship == 1) {
   cout << "You are eligible to vote\n";
}
else {
   cout << "Non-citizens are not eligible to vote\n";
}
```

Ok. So far it looks fairly simple, but complexity can arise swiftly. Decisions can be nested inside each other.

Nested Decisions

There is no limit to the complexity of statements that can be contained in the then-clause or the else-clause of a decision. Hence, another decision structure could be found inside of the then-clause, for example. However, such nested decisions must be entirely contained within the then-clause. This gives us the ability to choose from among several choices, not just between two.

In the above voting example, a citizen must also be 18 or older to be eligible to vote. So realistically inside the then-clause, which is executed if the person is a citizen, we need to further test to see if the person is old enough to vote. And here programmers can get into trouble.

Consider this version in which I have manually added line numbers for reference.

```
1.    if (citizenship == 1)
2.         if (age < 18)
3.            cout << "You must be 18 to be eligible to vote\n";
4.    else
5.       cout << "Non-citizens are not eligible to vote\n";
```

Notice the nice block structure. It "looks" reasonable. However, it is not correct. Suppose that the **citizenship** is a one and the **age** is 50. What actually prints out is "Non-citizens are not eligible to vote." Why? White space is the delimiter in C++. Thus, the nice alignment of line 4's else with line 1's if statement makes no difference to the compiler. Line 4's else-clause actually is the else-clause of line 2's if statement!

There are several ways to code the nested if statements correctly. One way is to provide the missing else-clause for line 2's **if** statement.

```
if (citizenship == 1)
     if (age < 18)
        cout << "You must be 18 to be eligible to vote\n";
     else
        ;
else
   cout << "Non-citizens are not eligible to vote\n";
```

Here the else-clause has been provided and consists of a null statement, that is, a simple semicolon.

However, the real genus of the coding error came from not using begin-end braces {} around the two clauses. If you always use the braces, you will be far less likely to code these inadvertent errors. Here is perhaps the best way to repair the coding.

```
if (citizenship == 1) {
     if (age < 18) {
        cout << "You must be 18 to be eligible to vote\n";
     }
}
else {
   cout << "Non-citizens are not eligible to vote\n";
}
```

By using the begin-end braces on the then-clause of the citizenship test, the compiler knows for certain that there can be no else-clause on the age test because the age decision must be contained within the then-clause of the citizenship test.

Let's look at an even more complex decision structure. Suppose that our company is asked to check up on its hiring practices. After inputting the information on an employee, we are to display a message if that person is over age 50 or is physically challenged or if their race is not Caucasian. The input fields consist of age, disability (1 if so), and race (1 if white). We can code the decisions as follows.

```
if (age > 50) {
   cout << "Over 50 ";
}
else if (disability == 1) {
   cout << "Disabled ";
}
else if (race != 1) {
   cout << "Non-white ";
}
```

Notice how the else-clauses use a single statement, which is itself another If-Then-Else statement. It could also be coded this way.

```
if (age > 50) {
  cout << "Over 50 ";
}
else {
   if (disability == 1) {
     cout << "Disabled ";
   }
   else {
      if (race != 1) {
          cout << "Non-white ";
      }
   }
}
```

It could also be coded this way

```
if (age > 50)
   cout << "Over 50 ";
else
   if (disability == 1)
     cout << "Disabled ";
   else
      if (race != 1)
         cout << "Non-white ";
```

Probably the first way is the easiest to read. Okay. What does the program display for output if one enters a 55-year-old African-American who has a limp? The age test is checked first and out comes the fact that this employee is over 50. There is no mention of the other aspects. Suppose that we restate the problem to display all of the possible aspects an employee might have. How would the coding change? Notice that the reason the second test was never performed with the current employee is that all the other tests began with an else, meaning only check further if the age was not more than 50. If we just remove the else's, we are left with three independent decisions that are not nested in any way.

```
if (age > 50) {
   cout << "Over 50 ";
}
if (disability == 1) {
   cout << "Disabled ";
}
if (race != 1) {
   cout << "Non-white ";
}
```

Now the output would be "Over 50 Disabled Non-white."

When programming decisions, one must be very careful to duplicate precisely the problem's specifications.

Suppose that we are running a dating service. A client wishes to see if a specific person would be a possible match for them. The client wishes to see if this candidate is a single male between the ages of 20 and 25. Assume that we have input the **age**, **maritalStatus** (0 for single), and **sex** (1 for male). In this example, to be a possible match, the candidate must satisfy all four tests, single, male, age greater than or equal to 20 and age less than or equal to 25. Notice that you cannot write

```
if (20 <= age => 25){
```

It requires two separate test conditions. Notice also that all four of these test conditions must be true for us to display the message. Here is how this might be coded.

```
if (age >= 20)
   if (age <= 25)
      if (maritalStatus == 0)
         if (sex == 1)
            cout << "Is a potential match\n";
```

It could also be written this way.

```
if (age >= 20) {
   if (age <= 25) {
      if (maritalStatus == 0) {
         if (sex == 1) {
            cout << "Is a potential match\n";
         }
      }
   }
}
```

It could also be written this way.

```
if (age >= 20)
   {
   if (age <= 25)
      {
      if (maritalStatus == 0)
```

```
            {
            if (sex == 1)
               {
               cout << "Is a potential match\n";
               }
            }
         }
      }
```

Here is another example. Suppose that the month has been input. Display the message "Summer Vacation" if the month is June, July or August. For any other months, print "School in session." Please note that you cannot code

```
     if (month == 6, 7, 8) // does not compile
```

Each value must be a complete test condition. If the month is 6 or if the month is 7 or if the month is 8, then print the message.

```
     if (month == 6)
        cout << "Summer Vacation\n";
     else if (month == 7)
        cout << "Summer Vacation\n";
     else if (month == 8)
        cout << "Summer Vacation\n";
     else
        cout << "School in session\n";
```

Notice that an else verb connects each decision after the first one.

Now suppose that we did not have to output the last message if school was in session. One might be tempted to code the following.

```
     if (month == 6)
        cout << "Summer Vacation\n";
     if (month == 7)
        cout << "Summer Vacation\n";
     if (month == 8)
        cout << "Summer Vacation\n";
```

Yes, it still produces the correct answer. But this raises a serious efficiency concern. If the **month** contains a six, then after printing the message, control passes to the next decision. But since it contained a six, it cannot under any circumstances also contain a seven or an eight! Yet, the program wastes time retesting the **month** for a seven and then for an eight. This kind of programming is wasteful of computer resources and is generally frowned upon in the industry. It shows a distinct lack of thought on the part of the programmer. Don't do it.

Compound Test Conditions

The previous test conditions have become rather lengthy and a bit unwieldy. There is a much better alternative to so much coding. A test condition can be a compound one. That is, two or more tests can be joined together to form a larger test using either the **AND** or **OR** relational operators. First, let's define AND and OR logic.

AND logic says that both tests must be true to get a true result. This is often expressed using boolean (two-valued) logic.

```
        true         true         false        false
    AND true     AND false    AND true     AND false
        -----        -----        -----        -----
        true         false        false        false
```

OR logic says that if either one or both of the tests are true, the result is true. Expressed in boolean logic, OR logic appears as follows.

```
        true         true         false        false
     OR true      OR false     OR true      OR false
        -----        -----        -----        -----
        true         true         true         false
```

In C++ these two operators are **&&** for AND and **||** for OR. To either side of these operators must be a test condition. I often refer to these two operators as the "joiner ops" since they are used to join two tests together. Figuratively, if we code

```
if (test1 && test2)
```

then this is saying that if test1 **and** test2 are both true, then execute the then-clause. Again, figuratively if we code

```
if (test1 || test2)
```

then this is saying that if either test1 **or** test2 is true, then execute the then-clause.

We can greatly simplify the previous examples using these compound joiner operators. In the dating service example, all the tests had to be true before the program printed the potential match message. This means AND logic is used and the joiner would be **&&**. Rewriting those four decisions into one greatly simplifies that decision.

```
if (age >= 20 && age <= 25 && maritalStatus == 0 && sex == 1)
 cout << "Is a potential match\n";
```

The summer vacation decision is an example of OR logic, since if either of the three month tests is true, it is a summer month. It can be simplified as follows using the || operator.

```
if (month == 6 || month == 7 || month == 8)
   cout << "Summer Vacation\n";
else
   cout << "School in session\n";
```

These two operators are actually even more efficient. Take the AND operator **&&** for example. Suppose that the age of the person in the above dating service problem was 19. When the very first test condition is executed, the age is not greater than or equal to 20. Thus, a false results. Since the **&&** operator is joining all of these other test conditions, C++ immediately knows the final outcome of the compound test, false. Remember, AND logic says that they all have to be true to get a true result. And that is exactly how C++ behaves. As soon as one of the joined tests yields a false result, the compiler stops doing the remaining tests and immediately goes to the else-clause if there is one. The remaining tests are not even executed! C++ is being as efficient as it can with compound test conditions. Programmers often take advantage of just this behavior, terminating remaining tests joined with the **&&** operator when a false result is encountered. We will do just that in Chapter 9.

The same efficiency applies to test conditions that are joined with OR **| |** operators. Consider the summer vacation tests. If the month is indeed six, then the result of the first test is true. Since the remaining tests are joined with **| |** operators, the compiler immediately knows the final result, true, and does not bother to perform the remaining tests, jumping immediately into the then-clause.

Thus, when we join our related decisions using **AND** and **OR** operators to form longer tests, we gain a measure of efficiency from the language itself.

The **AND** operator has a higher precedence than does the **OR** operator and both are lower than the six relational operators. In the dating service example, we could have used parentheses as shown below, but because the **&&** is at a lower precedence, they are not needed.

```
if ( (age >= 20) && (age <= 25) &&
     (maritalStatus == 0) && (sex == 1))
  cout << "Is a potential match\n";
```

Both **&&** and **| |** operators can be used in the same decision. If so, the **&&** is done before the **| |** operation.

```
if (a > 5 && b > 5 || c > 5)
```

This is the same as if we had coded

```
if ( (a > 5 && b > 5) || c > 5)
```

Sometimes, parentheses can aid readability of a program. There is no harm in using them in this manner.

Also note that the six relational operators have a lower precedence than all of the math operators. Thus, if we coded the following

```
if (a + b > c + d)
```

then this would group as if we had used parentheses:

```
if ((a + b) > (c + d))
```

However, I tend to use the parentheses anyway because it aids program readability. Without them, the reader must know that the relational operator > is of lower precedence.

The Logical Not Operator—!

The last of the logical operators is the not (**!**) operator. This operator reverses the condition to its right. Suppose that one coded the following.

```
if ( ! (x > y) )
```

The **!** reverses the result. If **x** contains 10 and **y** contains 5, then the test **x > y** is true, but the **!**

reverses it; the true becomes false and the else branch is taken. However, if **x** equals **y** or is actually less than **y**, then the test **x > y** is false; the **!** reverses that to true and the then-clause is executed.

Confusing? Likely so. I have more than 35 years' experience in the programming world. One thing that I have found to be uniformly true among all programmers is confusion over not-logic. While no one has any trouble with test conditions like **x != y**, there is uniform non-comprehension about not-logical conditions, such as the one above. In fact, the chances of mis-coding a complex not-logical expression are exponential! My advice has always been "Reverse it; say the test in the positive and adjust the clauses appropriately."

Here is another example to illustrate what I mean. In the dating service match test condition, the age is to be between 20 through and including 25. That is, an age that is less than 20 or an age that is more than 25 are not candidates for a match. Thus, one could test for those using

```
    age < 20 || age > 25
```

But if these were true, then this person is not a match and we are looking for a match, so not logic would reverse it.

```
  if ( !((age < 20) || (age > 25)) &&
       (maritalStatus == 0) && (sex == 1))
   cout << "Is a potential match\n";
```

This is much more difficult to read for the average programmer. Unless your mathematical background is well attuned to these kinds of logical expressions, it is much better to reverse the not logic and say it in the positive as in the following.

```
  if ( (age >= 20) && (age <= 25) &&
       (maritalStatus == 0) && (sex == 1))
   cout << "Is a potential match\n";
```

There are a few times where not logic improves the coding by making it tighter, shorter and more compact, mostly in the area of controlling the iterative or looping process (next chapter). I use not logic sparingly throughout this text, preferring always to try to say it in the positive manner.

Data Type and Value of Relational Expressions—The bool Data Type

In C++, the result of any test condition or relational expression is always an **int** data type whose value is either 0 for false or 1 for true.

When the test condition evaluation is completed by the compiler, the result is an **int** whose value is either 0 or 1. Assume that integer variable **x** contains 10 and integer variable **y** contains 5. In the following **if** statement

```
    if (x > y)
```

the test condition **x > y** evaluates to true or an integer 1. The compiler then sees just

```
    if (1)
```

and so does the then-clause. If however, we reverse the contents of variables **x** and **y**, then the test results in a false and the compiler sees just

```
if (0)
```

and takes the else-clause if present.

This means that one could define an integer variable to hold the result of a relational expression. Consider the following code.

```
int result = x > y;
```

At first, it may look a bit bizarre. To the right of the assignment operator is a test condition. After the test is complete, the result is either 0 or 1 and that **int** value is what is being assigned to the variable **result**. Another way of looking at the variable **result** is that it is holding a true/false value.

The bool Data Type

However, there is a far better data type to use if only a true/false value is desired. This is the new data type called **bool**, which represents boolean data or two-valued logic. A variable of type **bool** can have only two possible values, **true** and **false**. Some examples of variables that can effectively utilize this data type include the following.

```
bool isWindowVisible; // true if this window is visible
bool isMoving;        // true if this object is in motion
bool isAvailable;     // true if available for work
bool isFoodItem;      // true if this item is classified as
                      //      food for tax purposes
```

Consider the readability of this section of coding that deals with moving objects.

```
bool isMoving;
...
if (speed > 0)
  isMoving = true;
else
  isMoving = false;
...
if (isMoving) {
 ...
}
```

If the variable **speed** contains say 45 miles an hour, then the test is true and a true value is assigned to **isMoving**. Notice that the test condition could also have been written

```
if (isMoving == true) {
 ...
}
```

But since a **bool** already contains the needed 1 or 0 value (**true** or **false**), it is not needed.

Using **bools** can add a measure of readability to a program. Consider using a **bool** whenever the variable can be expressed in a true/false manner.

The compiler can always convert an integer relational expression result into a **bool** data type. The above coding can be rewritten even simpler as follows.

```
isMoving = speed > 0;
...
if (isMoving) {
  ...
}
```

This leads us to the two vitally important shortcut test conditions that are widespread in C++ coding. To summarize, if we code

```
if (x < y)
```

then this results in an integer value 1 or 0, which is then evaluated to see if the then-clause or else-clause is taken

```
if (1)
```

or

```
if (0)
```

Notice that the then-clause is executed if the test result is not 0. The else-clause is taken if the result is equal to 0. This is commonly extended by coding these two shortcuts

```
if (x)
```

or

```
if (!x)
```

where **x** is a variable or expression.

When the compiler encounters

```
if (x)
```

it checks the contents of variable **x**. If **x**'s contents are non-zero, the then-clause is executed. Similarly, when the compiler encounters

```
if (!x)
```

it checks the contents of variable **x**. If **x**'s contents are zero, then the then-clause is taken. Thus,

```
if (x)
```

is a shortcut way of saying

```
if (x != 0)
```

and

```
if (!x)
```

is a shortcut way of saying

```
if (x == 0)
```

I commonly keep track of these two shortcuts by using this scheme. If something does not exist, it is zero. So **if (!apples)** means not apples means no apples or that apples is zero. And **if (apples)** means if apples exist and apples exist if apples is not zero. However, you choose to remember these two shortcuts, make sure you understand them for their use is widespread in advanced C++ programming.

The Most Common Test Condition Blunder Explained

Finally, we can finally understand the most common error made by programmers when coding test conditions. And that error is shown here.

```
if (quantity = 0)
```

or

```
if (x = y)
```

The error is coding an assignment operator instead of the conditional equality operator ==. This is not a syntax error and does compile and execute, but the results are disastrous. Why? It is first and foremost an assignment operator. When either of the above two if instructions are executed, the first action is to replace the value in **quantity** with a 0 and to replace the contents of variable **x** with the contents of variable **y**. This is therefore destructive of the contents of **quantity** and **x**! Secondly, once the value has been copied, the compiler is left with just evaluating

```
if (quantity)
```

and

```
if (x)
```

But we now know what that actually becomes. If the newly updated **quantity** is not zero, take the then-clause. If the newly updated **x** is not zero, take the then-clause.

This coding action is exceedingly rarely used. Thus, many compilers actually issue a warning message along the lines of "assignment in a test condition!"

Always be extra careful to make sure you use the equality relational operator == and not the assignment operator = when making your test conditions.

The Conditional Expression

The conditional expression operators **? :** provide a shortcut to the normal If-Then-Else coding. Let's calculate the car insurance premium for a customer. The rates are based on the age of the insured. The following calculates the insured's premium using If-Then-Else logic.

```
double premium;
if (age > 55)
  premium = 100.00;
else
  premium = 250.00;
```

Notice in both clauses, something is being assigned to the same variable, **premium**, in this case. That is the key that the conditional expression can be used. It would be coded like this

```
double premium = age > 55 ? 100.00 : 250.00;
```

The syntax of the conditional expression is

```
test condition ? true expression : false expression
```

The test condition is the same test condition we have been discussing this whole chapter. It can be simple or compound. It is followed by a ? After the ? comes the then or true expression. The expression can be as simple as a constant as in this case or it can be a variable or an expression that results in a value to be used. After the true expression comes a : to separate the true and false expressions and the false expression follows.

Here is a more complex version. Suppose that younger drivers pay a higher rate. We now have the following.

```
double premium;
if (age > 55)
  premium = 100.00;
else if (age < 21)
  premium = 1000;
else
  premium = 250.00;
```

This can be rewritten as follows

```
double premium = age > 55 ? 100 : (age < 20 ? 1000 : 250);
```

Here the false portion of the first conditional expression is another entire conditional expression! But more importantly, we have reduced seven lines of coding into one line.

The conditional expression is not limited to assignments, though it is commonly used in such circumstances. Suppose that we need to make a very fancy formatted line indicating the higher temperature for the day. The line is to be shown on the 10 o'clock weather. Assume that we have already calculated the morning and evening temperatures and need now to display the larger of the two temperatures as the higher temperature. We could do the following.

```
if (am_temp > pm_temp)
  cout << ...fancy formatting omitted << am_temp << endl;
else
  cout << ...fancy formatting omitted << pm_temp << endl;
```

While this works well, as you have undoubtedly discovered at this point, making output look good requires a lot of trial and error, fiddle, fiddle, to get it to look good. Here in this example, we have precisely the same fancy formatting to do twice! As you tweak the first output, you must remember to do the same exact things to the second output instruction. I have enough trouble getting it right once. The conditional expression comes to our rescue. This can be rewritten as

```
cout << ...fancy formatting omitted
     << (am_temp > pm_temp ? am_temp : pm_temp)
     << endl;
```

This then displays the larger of the two temperatures. Note the () are required with the insertion operator.

The Precedence of Operators

Table 4.1 shows the precedence of operators from highest at the top to the lowest at the bottom. Each row is at a different level. A function call must always be done first so that the value the function returns is available for the rest of the expression's evaluation. Assignments are always last. Of course, parentheses can be used to override the normal precedence.

Notice that the postfix operator (after inc or dec) and prefix operator (before inc and dec) have high precedence so that their use can be detected early and properly applied after the current value is used.

The unary - is used in instructions such as

```
x = - y;
```

The address operator & returns the memory location of the item that follows it. So if we coded

```
&x
```

this returns where in memory variable **x** is located. We deal with addresses in a later chapter.

Table 4.1 The Precedence of Operators

Operator	Name	Associates
functionName (...)	function call	left to right
++ and --	postfix increment and decrement operators	left to right
++ and --	prefix increment and decrement operators	right to left
-, +, !, &	unary -, unary +, logical not, and address of operators	right to left
(datatype)	typecast	right to left
*, / and %	multiply, divide and remainder operators	left to right
+ and -	add and subtract operators	left to right
>, >=, <, <=	greater than, greater than or equal, less than, less than or equal to operators	left to right
== and !=	equal to and not equal to operators	left to right
&&	logical and	left to right
||	logical or	left to right
? :	conditional expression	right to left
=, +=, -=, *=, /=, %=	assignment operators	right to left

Testing of Real Numbers

There remains one additional test condition situation that must be understood. This applies only to floating point or real numbers. Recall that a floating point number is only an approximation of a specific real number, as close as the computer can get in the finite number of binary decimal bits. Further, when calculations are done on these floating point numbers, small roundoff errors and precision effects begin appearing.

For example, let's take a variable **x** of **float** data type. Suppose that it is initialized to 4.0. The computer stores this number as close as it can get to 4.0. It might be 3.99999 or it might be 4.00001. Now assume that we do the following to **x**

```
x = x - y
```

where **y** contains 3.99998. At this point, variable **x** contains 0.00001 or 0.00003, depending upon the above values. What happens if we do the following test condition?

```
if (x == 0)
```

Clearly, the else-clause is taken because **x** is not zero. But it sure is close to zero! The question is "is **x** sufficiently close to zero to be actually considered zero?" Or wilder still, suppose **x** was a **double** that contained 0.000000000000000123456789012345. A **double** has fifteen digits of accuracy and that is what is stored here—.123456789012345E-15. Is this version of **x** zero? Nope.

When testing floating point numbers, to avoid this kind of error, always test in such a manner to see if it is sufficiently close to the desired value. Use the floating point absolute value function.

```
if (fabs (x) <= .000001)
```

This takes the absolute value of **x** and compares it to the desired degree of closeness. If you have no idea how close is close enough, try one part in a million or .000001.

Similarly when comparing two floating point values for equality, always compare the absolute value of their difference to the desired degree of closeness. Instead of coding

```
if (x == y)
```

code

```
if (fabs (x - y) <= .000001)
```

How close is "close enough" depends on the problem at hand. Suppose that **x** represents the cubic yards of concrete to place into a concrete truck to deliver to a construction site. Probably .1 is highly accurate enough!

Section B: Computer Science Example

Cs04a—Compute the Total Bill By Finding the Sales Tax Rate

Acme Company sells products in two states. Typically, state codes of 13 for Illinois and 14 for Iowa are used to determine the tax rates. Assume that the Illinois tax rate is 7.5% and the Iowa rate is 8%. Additionally, if 10 or more than of the same item are purchased, a discount of 4% is given on the total cost of those items. If the total sale is $100.00 or more, shipping costs are free. Otherwise, the customer pays shipping, which is $4.00 or .5% of the total order before taxes, whichever is larger. Write a program that inputs one order consisting of the customer number (up to six digits long), the state code number, the item number of the product ordered, the quantity ordered, and the unit cost. Print out a nice billing form showing the order details and final total cost to the customer.

The design begins as usual by identifying the input fields. Here we need **custNumber**, **stateCode**, **itemNumber**, **quantity**, and **cost**. Draw a set of main storage boxes for these and label them with their chosen names. Figure 4.2 shows the complete main storage diagram.

Now using these names, write out the steps to solve this problem.

Prompt and input **custNumber**, **stateCode**, **itemNumber**, **quantity**, and **cost**

The first calculation is to find the total cost of the quantity purchased. Then we can apply discounts. Let's call this one **subTotal**; add another box in the main storage diagram for it and write

subTotal = **quantity** * **cost**;

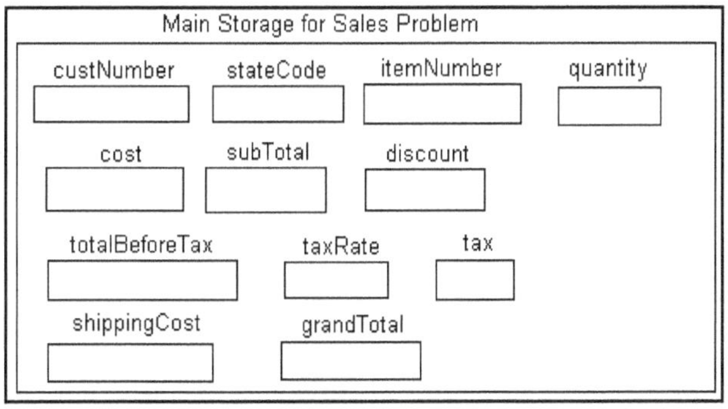

Figure 4.2 Main Storage for Sales Tax Problem

Next, check the **quantity** ordered and see if there is a discount to be applied.

if the **quantity** is greater than or equal to 10, then do the following

discount = **subTotal** * .04;

otherwise

discount is 0;

Next, figure the total before tax, calling it **totalBeforeTax**

totalBeforeTax is **subTotal** minus **discount**

To figure the tax, we need to get the rate. Let's call it **taxRate**; make a box for it and **tax**. Then calculate them by

if **stateCode** is equal to 13 then
    taxRate = .075
else check if **stateCode** is equal to 14 if so then
    taxRate = .08
tax = **totalBeforeTax** * **taxRate**

To get the shipping costs, we need a field to hold it, say **shippingCost** and it is calculated as follows

if **totalBeforeTax** is greater than or equal to 100 then
    shippingCost is 0
otherwise
    shippingCost = **totalBeforeTax** * .005
    but if **shippingCost** < 4.00 then
        shippingCost = 4;

Finally, the grand total due, say called **grandTotal**, is given by the sum of the following partial totals.

grandTotal = **totalBeforetax** + **shippingCost** + **tax**
now display all these results nicely formatted

One should thoroughly desk check the design. Make up various input sets of data so that all possible situations can occur and be verified.

```
customer  state  item     qty    cost
number    code   number
 12345      13    1111      5    10.00 // no discounts
 12345      13    1111     10    10.00 // only 4%
 12345      13    1111     15    10.00 // 4% & free shipping
123456      14    1111      5    10.00 // other state rate
```

Here are the completed program and the output from the above four test executions.

Cs04a: Customer Order Program

```
/***************************************************************/
/*                                                             */
/* Cs04a: Customer Order                                       */
/*                                                             */
/***************************************************************/

#include <iostream>
#include <iomanip>
using namespace std;
int main () {

 // input variables
```

```
long   custNumber;  // customer name
int    stateCode;   // state code 13 or 14
long   itemNumber;  // item number ordered
int    quantity;    // quantity ordered
double cost;        // cost of one item

// prompt and input a set of data
cout << "Enter Customer Id number: ";
cin >> custNumber;
cout << "Enter state code:         ";
cin >> stateCode;
cout << "Enter Item number:        ";
cin >> itemNumber;
cout << "Enter quantity ordered:   ";
cin >> quantity;
cout << "Enter cost of one item:   ";
cin >> cost;

// the calculation fields needed
double subTotal;       // basic cost of these items
double discount = 0;   // 4% discount if quantity >= 10
double totalBeforeTax; // total ordered with discount applied
double taxRate;        // tax rate based on state code
double tax;            // total tax on totalBeforeTax
double shippingCost = 0; // shipping free if totalBeforetax>=100
double grandTotal;     // total due from customer

// the calculations section
subTotal = quantity * cost; // figure basic cost

if (quantity >= 10)         // apply 4% if quantity large enough
 discount = subTotal * .04; // if not, leave original 0 in it
totalBeforeTax = subTotal - discount; // total before taxes

if (stateCode == 13)        // find the right tax rate to use
 taxRate = .075;            // state Illinois rate
else if (stateCode == 14)
 taxRate = .08;             // state Iowa rate
else {                      // oops, not a valid state code
 cout << "Invalid state code. It was " << stateCode << endl;
 return 1;
}

tax = totalBeforeTax * taxRate; // calc the tax owed

if (totalBeforeTax < 100) {    // need to figure shipping costs
 shippingCost = totalBeforeTax * .005;
 if (shippingCost < 4.00)      // if it is less than minimum amt
  shippingCost = 4.00;         // reset shipping to minimum amt
} // no else is needed since shippingCost was initialized to 0

grandTotal = totalBeforeTax + shippingCost + tax;

```

```
// setup floating point format for output of dollars
cout << fixed << setprecision (2);

// display the results section
cout << endl << endl << "Acme Customer Order Form\n";
cout << "Customer Number: " << custNumber << " in State: "
     << stateCode << endl;
cout << "Item Number   Quantity   Cost       Total\n";
cout << setw (8) << itemNumber << setw (11) << quantity
     << setw(11) << cost << setw (11) << subTotal <<endl <<endl;
cout << "Total after discount:"<<setw(20)<<totalBeforeTax<<endl;
cout << "Tax:                  "<<setw(20)<<tax << endl;
cout << "Shipping costs:       "<<setw(20)<<shippingCost << endl;
cout << "Grand Total Due:      "<<setw(20)<<grandTotal << endl;

return 0;

```

Output from 4 test runs of Cs04a: Customer Order Program

```
Test Run # 1 Results

Enter Customer Id number: 12345
Enter state code:         13
Enter Item number:        1111
Enter quantity ordered:   5
Enter cost of one item:   10


Acme Customer Order Form
Customer Number: 12345 in State: 13
Item Number   Quantity   Cost       Total
    1111          5      10.00      50.00

Total after discount:               50.00
Tax:                                 3.75
Shipping costs:                      4.00
Grand Total Due:                    57.75

========================================
Test Run # 2 Results

Enter Customer Id number: 12345
Enter state code:         13
Enter Item number:        1111
Enter quantity ordered:   10
Enter cost of one item:   10


Acme Customer Order Form
Customer Number: 12345 in State: 13
Item Number   Quantity   Cost       Total
```

```
    1111          10      10.00     100.00

Total after discount:                96.00
Tax:                                  7.20
Shipping costs:                       4.00
Grand Total Due:                    107.20

=========================================
Test Run # 3 Results

Enter Customer Id number: 12345
Enter state code:         13
Enter Item number:        1111
Enter quantity ordered:   15
Enter cost of one item:   10


Acme Customer Order Form
Customer Number: 12345 in State: 13
Item Number   Quantity   Cost       Total
    1111          15      10.00     150.00

Total after discount:               144.00
Tax:                                 10.80
Shipping costs:                       0.00
Grand Total Due:                    154.80

=========================================
Test Run # 4 Results

Enter Customer Id number: 123456
Enter state code:         14
Enter Item number:        1111
Enter quantity ordered:   5
Enter cost of one item:   10


Acme Customer Order Form
Customer Number: 123456 in State: 14
Item Number   Quantity   Cost       Total
    1111           5      10.00      50.00

Total after discount:                50.00
Tax:                                  4.00
Shipping costs:                       4.00
Grand Total Due:                     58.00
```

Section C: An Engineering Example

Engr04a—Quadratic Root Solver

A major usage of decisions is to avoid doing calculations when one or more variables are out of range for that calculation. For example, an attempt to divide by zero causes a program crash. Passing values out of range to the arcsine function cause the **asin()** function to crash the program. Commonly, decisions protect programs from such attempts. This example explores these uses.

Write a program that displays the roots of the quadratic equation, $\mathbf{ax^2 + bx + c}$, given any user inputted values for **a**, **b** and **c**.

Analyzing the problem, the equation we need to solve is

$$\frac{-b \pm \sqrt{b^2 - 4ac}}{2a}$$

But the complicating factor is that the user might enter values such that imaginary roots occur or even division by zero if **a** is zero. To make a totally general program, we must handle all the possibilities. The first consideration is "Is the value the user entered for the **a** term 0?" If so, there is no solution. Next if the discriminant, $\mathbf{b^2{-}4ac}$, is negative, then there are two imaginary roots given by

$$-\frac{b}{2a} \pm \frac{\sqrt{b^2 - 4ac}}{2a} i \ldots where \ldots i = \sqrt{-1}$$

Further, if $\mathbf{b^{2-}4ac}$ is 0, then there are two identical real roots.

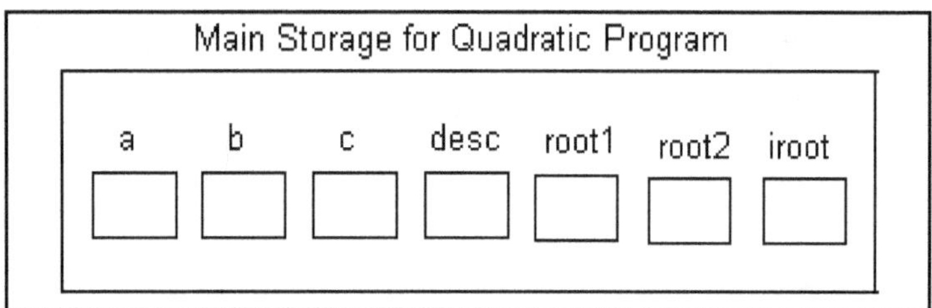

Figure 4.3 Main Storage for Quadratic Root Program

Designing our solution first, we must make main storage variables for the input values. Let's call them **a**, **b** and **c**. Since the discriminant, $\mathbf{b^2{-}4ac}$, must be evaluated, let's also make a variable to hold it, say **desc**. Finally, the result variables might be **root1** and **root2**. But in the case of the imaginary roots, there are going to be an imaginary part, so let's also define **iroot** to hold the imaginary portion. Figure 4.3 shows the main storage diagram.

Now write out the sequence of operations needed to solve this problem using our variable names. We have

prompt and input **a**, **b** and **c**
if **a** is 0 then display no solution
otherwise to the following
    calculate **desc** = $\mathbf{b^2–4ac}$
    if **desc** is 0 then do the following
        find **root1** = **–b/(2a)**
        display two roots at **root1**
    otherwise if **desc** is negative then do the following
        root1 = **–b/(2a)**
        iroot = **sqrt** (|**desc**|) / (2**a**)
        display one imaginary root as **root1** + **iroot** * i
        display the other imag root as **root1** – **iroot** * i
    otherwise
        root1 = (–b+sqrt (desc))/(2a)
        root2 =(–b-sqrt (desc))/(2a)
        display **root1** and **root2**
    end otherwise
end otherwise

Next, make up some test values to thoroughly check out the program. For example, we might use these sets

0, 1, 2 - for no solution
3, 4, 5 - for imaginary roots
2, 8, 6 - for two real roots
4, 4, 1 - for multiple roots

Here are the program and the test runs.

Engr04a - Quadratic Roots Solver

```
/***************************************************************/
/*                                                             */
/* Engr04a: Quadratic Equation Roots                           */
/*                                                             */
/***************************************************************/

#include <iostream>
#include <iomanip>
#include <cmath>
using namespace std;
int main () {

 // input variables
 double a;
 double b;
 double c;

```

```
// result variables
double desc;
double root1;
double root2;
double iroot;

// prompt and input the user's coefficients for a, b and c
cout << "Quadratic Equation Root Solver Program\n\n";
cout<<"Enter the quadratic equation's coefficients a, b and c\n"
    << "separated by a blank\n";
cin >> a >> b >> c;

// setup floating point format for output of roots
cout << fixed << setprecision (4) << endl;

// check for division by 0 or not a quadratic case
if (fabs (a) < .000001) {
 cout <<"Since a is zero, there is no solution-not quadratic\n";
}
// here it is a quadratic equation, sort out roots
else {
 desc = b * b - 4 * a * c;
 // is desc basically 0 indicating multiple roots at one value?
 if (fabs (desc) <= .000001) {
  root1 = - b / (2 * a);
  cout << "Multiple roots at " << setw (12) << root1 << endl;
 }
 // is the desc positive indicating two real roots
 else if (desc > 0) {
  root1 = (-b + sqrt (desc)) / (2 * a);
  root2 = (-b - sqrt (desc)) / (2 * a);
  cout << "Two real roots at: " << setw (12) << root1 << endl;
  cout << "                   " << setw (12) << root2 << endl;
 }
 // desc is negative indicating two imaginary roots
 else {
  desc = fabs (desc);
  root1 = -b / (2 * a);
  iroot = sqrt (desc) / (2 * a);
  cout << "Two imaginary roots at :" << setw (12) << root1
       << " + i * " << setw (12) << iroot << endl;
  cout << "                        " << setw (12) << root1
       << " - i * " << setw (12) << iroot << endl;
 }
}

return 0;
```

Output from Four Test Runs of Engr04a - Quadratic Roots Solver

```
Results of test tun #1
```

```

Quadratic Equation Root Solver Program

Enter the quadratic equation's coefficients a, b and c
separated by a blank
0 1 2

Since a is zero, there is no solution - not a quadratic

Quadratic Equation Root Solver Program

=========================================================
Results of test tun #2

Enter the quadratic equation's coefficients a, b and c
separated by a blank
3 4 5

Two imaginary roots at :      -0.6667 + i *       1.1055
                              -0.6667 - i *       1.1055

=========================================================
Results of test tun #3

Quadratic Equation Root Solver Program

Enter the quadratic equation's coefficients a, b and c
separated by a blank
2 8 6

Two real roots at:       -1.0000
                         -3.0000

=========================================================
Results of test tun #4

Quadratic Equation Root Solver Program

Enter the quadratic equation's coefficients a, b and c
separated by a blank
4 4 1

Multiple roots at      -0.5000
```

Design Exercises

1. Avoiding a Mostly Working Program.

Programs usually accept some kind of user input. Here we are dealing with numerical input data. When a specific program uses numerical data, the programmer must be alert for particular numerical values which, if entered, cause problems for the algorithm or method that is being used. The programmer must check for possible incorrect values and take appropriate actions. Sometimes the program specifications tell the programmer what to do if those "bad values" are entered; other times, it is left to the good sense of the programmer to decide what to do.

For each of the following, assume that the input instruction has been executed. You are to sketch in pseudocode the rest of the needed instructions.

a. The program accepts a day of the week from one to seven. It displays Sunday when the day is one; Monday, when two; Saturday, when seven.

```
Input a dayNumber
```

b. Housing Cost Program. When buying a house, the seller specifies the length and width of the outside of the home, the number of stories it has and the asking price. This program calculates the actual cost per square foot of real living area within that home. Usually, 25% of the home area is non-liveable, being occupied by doors, closets, garages and so on. Using this program, a buyer can evaluate, which home offers the best living area value. Using pseudocode, indicate what should be done to make this program work appropriately for all possible numerical inputs.

```
input the length, width, numberStories and cost
let grossArea = length * width * numberStories
let nonLivingArea = grossArea * .25
let liveableArea = grossArea – nonLivingArea
let realCostPerLiveableFoot = cost / liveableArea
output the realCostPerLiveableFoot
```

2. Comparison of Cereal Prices. Grocery store shoppers are often looking for the best value for their money. For example, a given type of cereal may come in several different sized boxes, each with a different price. A shopper wants to purchase the most cereal they can for the least money; that is, they want the best value for their money. A further complexity arises with coupons. Specific size boxes may have a coupon available to lower the total cost of that box. This program inputs the data for two different boxes and displays, which one has the better value (most cereal for the least money). Write the rest of the pseudocode to determine for each box, the actual cost per ounce. Then, display the actual cost per ounce of each box and which is the better value, box1 or box2.

```
Input box1Weight, box1Cost, box1CouponAmount
Input box2Weight, box2Cost, box2CouponAmount
```

Stop! Do These Exercises Before Programming

1. Given the following variable definitions, what is the result of each of the following test conditions? Mark each result with either a t (for true or 1) or f (for false or 0).

```
      int x = 10, y = 5, z = 42;
_____ a. if (x > 0)
_____ b. if (x > y)
_____ c. if (x == 0)
_____ d. if (x == z)
_____ e. if (x + y > z)
_____ f. if (x / y == z)
_____ g. if (x > z / y)
_____ h. if (x > 0 && z < 10)
_____ i. if (x > 0 && z >= 10)
_____ j. if (x > 0 || z < 10)
_____ k. if (x > 0 || z >= 10)
_____ l. if (x)
_____ m. if (!x)
```

2. Using the definitions in 1. above, what is the output of the following code?

```
if (z <= 42)
 cout << "Hello\n";
else
 cout << "Bye\n";
```

3. Using the definitions in 1. above, what is the output of the following code?

```
int t = y > x ? z : z + 5;
cout << t;
```

4. Correct all the errors in the following coding. The object is to display the fuel efficiency of a car based on the miles per gallon it gets, its **mpg**.

```
if (mpg > 25.0) {
  cout << Gas Guzzler\n";
else
  cout << "Fuel Efficient\n";
```

In the next three problems, repair the If-Then-Else statements. However, maintain the spirit of each type of If-Then-Else style. Do not just find one way to fix it and copy that same “fix” to all three problems. Rather fix each one maintaining that problem’s coding style.

5. Correct all the errors in the following coding. The object is to display "equilateral triangle" if all three sides of a triangle are equal.

```
if (s1 == s2 == s3);
   {
   cout << "equilateral triangle\n";
   }
else;
   cout >> "not an equilateral triangle\n";
```

6. Correct all the errors in the following coding. The object is to display "equilateral triangle" if all three sides of a triangle are equal.

```
if (s1 == s2)
   if (s2 == s3)
      cout << "equilateral triangle\n";
cout >> "not an equilateral triangle\n";
```

7. Correct all the errors in the following coding. The object is to display "equilateral triangle" if all three sides of a triangle are equal.

```
if (s1 == s2) {
   if (s2 == s3) {
      cout << "equilateral triangle\n";
   }
   else {
      cout >> "not an equilateral triangle\n";
   }
}
```

8. Correct this grossly inefficient set of decisions so that no unnecessary decisions are made.

```
if (day == 1)
   cout << "Sunday\n";
if (day == 2)
   cout << "Monday\n";
if (day == 3)
   cout << "Tuesday\n";
if (day == 4)
   cout << "Wednesday\n";
if (day == 5)
   cout << "Thursday\n";
if (day == 6)
   cout << "Friday\n";
if (day == 7)
   cout << "Saturday\n";
```

9. Correct this non-optimum solution. Consider all of the numerical possibilities that the user could enter for variable **x**. Rewrite this coding so that the program does not crash as a result of the numerical value entered by the user. You may display appropriate error messages to the user. Ignore the possibility of the user entering in nonnumerical information by accident.

```
double x;
double root;
double reciprocal;
cin >> x;
root = sqrt (x);
reciprocal = 1 / x;
cout << x << " square root is " << root
     << " reciprocal is " << reciprocal << endl;
```

10. Correct this inherently unsound calculation.

```
double x;
double y;
cin >> x;
y = x * x + 42.42 * x + 84.0 / (x * x * x + 1.);
if (!y || y == x) {
 cout << "x's value results in an invalid state.\n"
 return 1;
}
```

Programming Problems

Problem Cs04-1—Easter Sunday

Given the year inputted by the user, calculate the month and day of Easter Sunday. When the program executes, it should produce output similar to this.

Easter Sunday Calculator
Enter the year: 1985
Easter Sunday is April 7, 1985

The formula is a complex one and produces the correct day for any year from 1900 through 2099. I have broken it down into intermediate steps as follows. Frequently, Easter Sunday is in March, but occasionally it is in April. The following formula calculates the day of the month in March of Easter Sunday.

let a = year % 19
let b = year % 4
let c = year % 7
now start to put these pieces together
let d = (19 * a + 24) % 30
let e = (2 * b + 4 * c + 6 * d + 5) % 7
finally, the day of the month of Easter Sunday is

let day = 22 + d + e

However, if the day is greater than 31, then subtract 31 days and the resulting value in day is in April instead. But the equation is off by exactly 7 days if these years are used: 1954, 1981, 2049 and 2076. Thus, when the calculation is finished, if the year is one of these four, you must subtract 7 days from the day variable. The subtraction does not cause a change in the month.

Test your program on the following years—I have shown the day you should obtain in parentheses:

1985 (April 7)
1999 (April 4)
1964 (March 29)
2099 (April 12)
1900 (April 15)
1954 (April 18)
1981 (April 19)
2049 (April 18)
2076 (April 19)
1967 (March 26)

Problem Cs04-2—Calculating Wages

Calculate a person's wages earned this week. Prompt and input the person's social security number (nine digits with no dashes), their hourly pay rate, the hours worked this week, and the shift worked. The shift worked is 0 for days, 1 for second shift and 2 for the "graveyard shift". The company pays time and a half for all hours worked above 40.00. The additional shift bonus is a 5% for second shift and 15% for the graveyard shift. Format the output as follows:

```
Employee Number:       999999999
Hours Worked:              99.99
Base Pay:              $ 9999.99
Overtime Pay:          $ 9999.99
Shift Bonus:           $ 9999.99
Total Pay This Week:   $99999.99
```

Make the following test runs of the program.

```
Employee   rate  hours shift
123456789  5.00  40.00   0
123456788  5.00  40.00   1
123456787  5.00  40.00   2
123456786  5.00  60.00   0
123456785  5.00  60.00   1
123456784  5.00  60.00   2
123456783  5.00   0.00   2
```

Problem Cs04-3—Scholastic GPA Results

The program inputs a student id number that can be nine digits long and their grade point average, GPA. The program is to display that student's status, which is based only on their GPA. If the GPA is less than 1.0, the status is Suspended. If the GPA is less than 2.0 but greater than or equal to 1.0, then the status is Probation. If the GPA is greater than or equal to 2.0 and less than 3.0, the status is Satisfactory. If the GPA is greater than or equal to 3.0 and less than 4.0, then the status is Dean's List. If the GPA is 4.0, then the status is President's List. Display the results as follows.

```
    Id         GPA      Status
123456789     3.25     Dean's List
```

Make sure that no unneeded tests are made. That is, if you find that the GPA is that for Suspended, then do not additionally test for the other conditions. Once you have found a match, when finished displaying the results, do not subject that set of input data to additional test conditions.

Test your program with several test runs. The following series of values should thoroughly test the program.

```
123456789 0.5
123456788 1.0
123456787 1.1
123456786 2.0
123456785 2.1
123456784 3.0
123456783 3.1
123456782 3.9
123456781 4.0
```

Problem Engr04-1—Snell's Law—Optical Engineering

Snell's Law gives the angle that light is bent when it passes through a region with an index of refraction n_1 into another region with a different index of refraction n_2. An example is a light ray that passes through water in a crystal bowl. As the ray passes from the water through the clear crystal glass sides of the container, it is bent according to Snell's Law.

n_1 sin angle$_1$ = n_2 sin angle$_2$

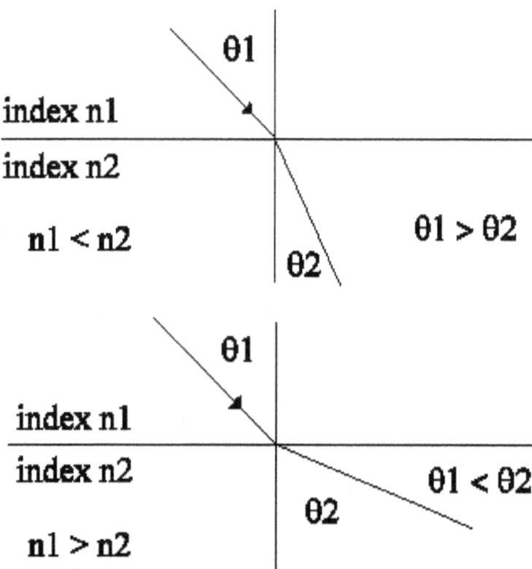

When a ray passes from a region with a low index of refraction n_1 into a region with a higher index n_2, the exit angle is smaller than the entrance angle or the light bends toward the vertical. When passing from a region with a higher index of refraction into a region of lower index of refraction, the angle of exit is greater than the entrance angle or the angle bends away from the vertical. This is shown in the above drawing.

Write a program that calculates the exit angle of incidence angle$_2$, given the entrance angle of incidence angle$_1$ and the two indices of refractions, n_1 and n_2. Prompt the user to enter these three values; the angle input should be in degrees. Display the original input data along with the exit angle nicely formatted. The equation to be solved is

$$\theta_2 = \sin^{-1}\left(\frac{n_1}{n_2}\sin\theta_1\right)$$

Caution: if $n_1 > n_2$, then for some angles, the absolute value passed to the arcsine is greater than 1.0. This means that all light is reflected back in the direction it came from and none goes into the region two.

Test your program using a crystal bowl of water. The bowl is made of Crown Glass whose index of refraction is 1.52326. The water has an index of 1.33011.

Test 1 θ_1 is 30 degrees coming from the glass and going into the water
Test 2 θ_1 is 90 degrees coming from the glass and going into the water
Test 3 θ_1 is 90 degrees coming from the water and going into the glass
Test 4 θ_1 is 30 degrees coming from the water and going into the glass

Problem Engr04-2—Power Levels

Decibels (dB) are often used to measure the ratio of two power levels. The equation for the power level in decibels is

$$dB = 10\log_{10}\frac{P_2}{P_1}$$

where P_2 is the power level being monitored and P_1 is some reference power. Prompt the user for the two power levels; then calculate and display the resulting decibels. You must guard against all ranges of numerical entries for the two power levels. Test your program with these inputs for P_1 and P_2.

```
1.0     5.0
1.0     50.0
496.64 1932.4
0.0     42.
```

Problem Engr04-3—Formula Evaluation

Write a program to evaluate the following function for all possible numerical values of x that the user can input.

$$y(x) = \ln\frac{1}{1-x}$$

Show sufficient test runs to demonstrate that all possible situations are handled by your program.

Chapter 5 —Files and Loops

Section A: Basic Theory

Introduction

Up to this point, our programs have been severely limited to inputting only one set of data. This chapter introduces the various iterative instructions that allow a program to perform a series of instructions repetitively until the ending condition is reached. Iterative instructions are figuratively called looping instructions. Now programs can input as many sets of data as required. Programs can perform a series of instructions many times until the desired result is achieved.

Often the input consists of many sets of input data. In all of the previous programs in the first four chapters, there was only one set of input data. In those programs, it was a simple matter to key in the input data from the keyboard. However, suppose that there were fifty such sets of data? Of course, you only needed one test run of your programs, right? They all worked perfectly on the very first test run, so that you only had to enter the test data one time, right? Okay. Okay. I am teasing. But this could have happened if one designed on paper and thoroughly desk checked before coding it in C++. But more than likely, you needed to run the program several times, if only to get the output looking good. If there are going to be 50 sets of test data, would you like to enter all that data numerous times?

Of course not! Hence, this chapter begins by showing you how you can use existing files of data for input as well as writing the program's output to a **result.txt** file that can then be printed from Notepad in its entirety.

How are the input files created in the first place? For those that come with this text, I used Notepad. You can make your own using Notepad as well. I would suggest that you use the **.txt** file extension so that you can just double click on the data file and have Notepad open it up automatically. Within Notepad, just type the lines as if you were going to enter them into the program from the keyboard.

Input Files

To input data from a file instead of from the keyboard is extremely easy. It requires minimal changes on your part. Input files, in C++, make use of the already existing **istream** class. Recall that a class in C++ is just a blueprint or model to follow when the compiler needs to make an object of that kind. The class contains all the data it needs to do its job plus all of the functions we need to use it effectively. The input file class, called **ifstream**, is built upon the simple **istream** class, extending it to operate on a file of data. Thus, everything you currently know about an **istream** instance, **cin**, applies totally to an instance you make of the **ifstream**.

To use a file for input, you must include another header **<fstream>**. This header file includes the definitions of both input and output files.

Next, you need to define an instance of the **ifstream** class. Unlike the **istream** class in which we the used built-in instance called **cin**, here we can name the file variable anything desired. I often call mine **infile**. One codes just

```
ifstream infile;
```

or

```
ifstream myfile;
```

Any descriptive name is fine.

Next, you need to have the program actually open the input file by calling the **open()** function. The open process is where you provide the actual filename to use. The system then finds that file, attempts to open it for read operations and get everything ready for your first actual input operation. Hence, you must know the actual filename of the data file on disk that you want to use for input—its precise name and file extension, if any. You must also know the drive and path to the file as well. If you have any doubts, use the Explorer, navigate, and find the actual file you want to use for input operations. The single biggest problem that students have when using input files instead of directly inputting data from the keyboard is getting the location and filename correct.

Let's say that the filename is **test1.txt** and it is located on disk drive D: in the folder **\ComputerScience\TestData**. The full path to the file stored in a literal character string is then "**d:\\ComputerScience\\TestData\\test1.tx**t". Did you notice the double \\? In C++, a single backslash \ indicates an **escape sequence** character is coming next. We have used the **\n** escape sequence to create a new line. There are a number of other escape sequences. Since a single \ means here comes an escape sequence code, we cannot code as a filename string "**d:\ComputerScience\TestData\test1.txt**"! It assumes each of the \C, \T and \t are escape sequences, which they are not! (A **\t** is the escape sequence for a tab code.) Thus, if you forget the double backslashes, the system will never find your file, ever. In my opinion, this is the single most klutzy feature of the language. I won't tell you how many times I have accidentally forgot the double backslashes in my filenames.

Now there is a point to all this effort to get the filename string coded properly. If the filename is not found during the open process, then the stream winds up in the fail state and nothing can be input. Usually, this is simply a case of coding the wrong path, misspelling the filename, omitting the file extension, omitting the double backslashes and so on.

The **open()** function is coded as follows.

```
infile.open ("d:\\ComputerScience\\TestData\\test1.txt");
```

The parameter is the name of the file and is usually a character string literal until we get to the chapter on character string variables.

Here is the complete opening sequence.

```
ifstream infile;
infile.open ("d:\\ComputerScience\\TestData\\test1.txt");
```

As usual, there is a shortcut to coding both these two lines. The commonly used shortcut is to define the variable and initialize it at the same time.

```
ifstream infile("d:\\ComputerScience\\TestData\\test1.txt");
```

I highly recommend that the test data files be copied into the project's folder residing alongside of the cpp files. Then the coding is simpler.

```
ifstream infile ("test1.txt");
```

This is saying to open the file **test1.txt** located in the current default disk drive in the current default subfolder. When running Microsoft Visual C++, for example, that current drive and folder is the folder of the project containing the cpp file. Seldom are one's data files in that folder. But there is nothing to keep you from using Explorer to copy the test data files into the project folder to simplify the filenames for the opening process.

There is, of course, one small detail that I mentioned and did not elaborate upon when I said it above. If the file cannot be opened for whatever reason, the file system goes into the bad state. This means that no input operations can be done on using it. All attempts to input data fail. Hence, after creating and opening an input file, one must check to see if the file was successfully opened and ready for input operations.

I/O Stream States

Any I/O stream has several state flags that indicate the current state of affairs within that stream. There are simple access functions to retrieve these status flags. The functions take no parameters. The more frequently used ones include

```
good (); // returns true if all is well
bad ();  // returns true if a serious I/O error occurred
eof ();  // returns true if it is at the end of the file
fail (); // returns true if bad data has been encountered
```

To use any of these, place the stream variable and a dot to the left of the function; the following are all valid test conditions.

```
if (cin.good ())
if (cin.bad ())
if (cin.eof ())
```

```
if (cin.fail ())
if (infile.good ())
if (infile.bad ())
if (infile.eof ())
if (infile.fail ())
```

Notice we can test **cin** as well as our files. Each of these must be examined in detail.

Testing for Goodness

After opening the file, if the process has failed because the filename is misspelled, we should display a message and terminate the program. This can be done as follows.

```
ifstream infile ("test1.txt");
if (!infile.good ()) {
  cout << "Error: cannot open the input file\n";
  return 1;
}
```

Since the **good()** function returns **true** if all is ok, we must check for the opposite, hence the ! in the test condition. Notice that to abort the program, I return back to DOS but this time I returned a non-zero value. DOS does not care what you return. However, by convention, a value of zero being returned means all is ok and any non-zero value means the program failed in some way. Alternatively, one can test the fail bit.

```
ifstream infile ("test1.txt");
if (infile.fail ()) {
  cout << "Error: cannot open the input file\n";
  return 1;
}
```

There is a shortcut way to do the above same coding and this is what most programmers use.

```
ifstream infile ("test1.txt");
if (!infile) {
  cout << "Error: cannot open the input file\n";
  return 1;
}
```

It is just the expression **!infile**. Recall that the test condition **!x** can be interpreted to mean if **x** does not exist. Here **!infile** is **true** if the input stream is not in the good state for whatever reason. The reverse test can also be used and shortly becomes a workhorse for us.

```
if (infile)
```

This is a shortcut for asking if the input file stream is still in the good state.

Any given stream at any given time might not be in the good state for several reasons. It has encountered bad data, it has reached the end of the file, or a serious I/O error occurred, such as running out of disk space on an output file.

Testing for Bad Data Entry

Suppose that we attempt to input the integer **quantity** by coding

```
cin >> quantity;
```

and assume the user enters

```
A0<cr>
```

That is, the A key is pressed instead of the 1 key. The input stream locks up at this point and goes into the fail state since it was asked to input an integer and it failed to do so. The stream remains in the fail state and no further input operations are attempted. (In advanced programming situations, there are ways to reset the state flags, remove the offending data, and resume, but these techniques as far beyond the beginning level.)

So at this point, we must examine in detail how the extraction operator works on the stream of data coming into the computer. The key to extraction operations is an internal **current position within the stream pointer**, which keeps track of where we are within the input stream of characters. Let's say that we have coded the following input instruction.

```
int quantity;
double cost;
cin >> quantity >> cost;
```

Let's also imagine all the ways one could correctly and incorrectly enter the data. Recall that white space (consecutive series of blanks, tabs, carriage returns, and line feeds, for example) is the delimiter between the values. Here is the first way.

```
10 42.50<cr>
```

Initially the current position in the stream is pointing to the 1 digit. The extraction operator first skips over any white space. In this case, there is none. Next, it must extract an integer. So it inputs successive characters that meet the requirements of an integer (that is, the digits 0 through 9 and the + and – signs). It stops whenever it encounters any character that cannot be a part of a valid integer number. In this case, the blank between the 0 and 4 digits terminates the extraction of **quantity**. Note that the current position in the input stream is now pointing to that blank.

The next input operation, the extracting of the **double cost**, resumes at the current position in the input stream. It again skips over white space to the first non-white space character, here the 4 digit. Next, it extracts successive characters that can be part of a **double** until it encounters any character that cannot be part of the **double**. In this case, the CR and LF codes (the enter key) end the extraction. Again, the current position in the input stream is updated to point to the CRLF pair. The next input operation resumes here at this location, usually skipping over white space if an extraction operator is used.

Now consider this erroneous input.

```
10 A2.45<cr>
```

After inputting the **quantity**, the current position in the input stream is pointing to the blank between the 0 and A characters. When the extraction of the **double** begins, it skips over white space to the A character. It then inputs all characters that can be a part of a **double**. Here the A character ends it;

there are none. The input stream now goes into the fail state and all further input operations are not done. Clearly, we must check on this state after all of our input operations are done and point out the error in user input.

But what about this circumstance?

```
10 4A.45<cr>
```

When the extraction operator is to begin the process for the **double cost**, the current position is at the blank between the 0 and 4 digits. It skips over white space and begins extracting characters that can be in a **double**. It successfully inputs the 4 digit. It stops on the A character and the current position in the input stream is on the A, but it then believes it has successfully input a **double** whose value is 4.0. If we perform another input operation that is not asking for a letter, the stream then goes into the fail state.

The End of File

DOS marks the physical end of a file with a special byte whose value is a decimal 26 or a CTRL-Z code, ^Z as it is displayed on the screen. (Hold down the control key and press Z.) Most editors do not display this end of file marker byte, but display all bytes up to that point. On a keyboard data entry, one could press Ctrl-Z to simulate the end of file. When reading in information from a file, we must be able to detect when we have reached the end of that file.

Consider the following input operation of **quantity** and **cost**.

```
infile >> quantity >> cost;
```

and the file contains

```
10 42.50^Z
```

The extraction operator retrieves 10 for **quantity** and 42.50 for **cost**. The ^Z code is where the current position in the input stream is pointing. If we do an additional input operation, then the end of file condition occurs.

Suppose that a premature end of file exists because someone forgot to enter the **cost**.

```
10^Z
```

The instruction was asked to input two values. Clearly the **quantity** is successfully inputted, but when the extraction operator attempts to skip over white space and find the first non-white space character to begin inputting the **double cost**, the end of file is reached and the stream goes into the EOF state and the operation fails.

After we discuss the iterative looping instructions, we will see how to actually test for these circumstances in our programs.

Closing a File

When a program is finished working with a file, it should call the **close()** function. The **close()** function makes the file available for other programs to use. If the file is an output file, any remaining data not yet physically written to the disk are actually written and the end of file marker is written.

C++ and DOS automatically close all files should the programmer forget to close them. It is bad programming style to fail to close the files that you open. On some operating systems, error messages are generated if you fail to close your files. The **close()** function is very simple.

```
infile.close ();
```

Here is a complete sample program that inputs a single set of data from a file and displays the total cost of an order. Notice the placement of the new instruction.

```
#include <iostream>
#include <iomanip>
#include <fstream>
using namespace std;

int main () {
 // input variables and total
 int    quantity;
 double cost;
 double total;

 // define the file and open it
 ifstream infile ("Test1.txt");
 if (!infile) { // unable to open file, display msg and quit
  cout << "Error: cannot open test1.txt file\n";
  return 1;
 }

 // try to input a set of data
 infile >> quantity >> cost;
 if (!infile) { // check if input was successful
  cout << "Error: unable to input quantity and cost\n";
  infile.close (); // close the opened file
  return 2;
 }

 // calculate total cost of order
 total = cost * quantity;

 // display the results
 cout << "The quantity is:              " << quantity << endl
      << "The cost of each is:        $ " << cost << endl
      << "The total of the order is: $" << total << endl;
 infile.close ();
 return 0;
}
```

The Iterative Instructions

There are three iterative instructions available in C++. They are used to create programming loops so that a series of instructions can be executed more than once. The typical program follows the Cycle of Data Processing, Input a set of data, Process that set of data in some manner, Output that set of data and then repeat the entire process until there are no more sets of data, in other words, the end of the file has been reached.

The first of the three is the Do While structure, which is implemented with the **while** instruction. The Do While structure shown in Figure 5.1 illustrates how the looping process works. First, a test condition is checked. While that test condition is true, a series of things to do are performed. Then the test is checked again. The loop continues until the test condition becomes false. Of vital importance is that something in the series of things to do must somehow eventually alter the test condition so that the loop can end. If not, an infinite loop results.

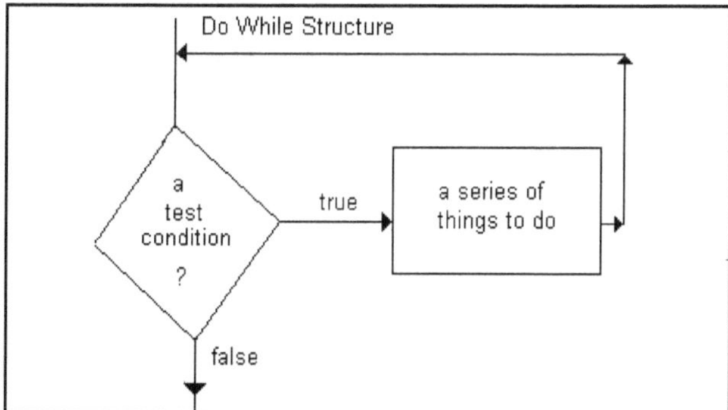

Figure 5.1 The Do While Structure

The syntax of the **while** statement that implements the Do While Structure is

```
while (test condition) {
  0, 1, or more things to do while the condition is true
}
```

If there is only one instruction or even a null instruction to do, it can be shortened to

```
while (test condition)
  1 statement;
```

The alternative indentation would be

```
while (test condition)
  {
  0, 1, or more things to do while the condition is true
  }
```

The test condition is exactly the same test condition that was used with If-then-else instructions. There is no change to it whatsoever. A **while** instruction actually is rather simple, yet powerful instruction. Using it, many different kinds of processing loops can be built.

Loops That Are to Be Executed a Known Number of Times

Let's apply the **while** statement to one of the simplest forms of looping. Sometimes one must perform a loop a known number of times. For example, let's sum all the odd integers from one to twenty-five. Here is a way it can be done.

```
int number = 1;
int sum = 0;
while (number <= 25) {
  sum += number;
  number += 2;
}
cout << "The sum of all odd integers from 1 to 25 is "
     << sum << endl;
```

This short program contains a number of very key elements of the looping process in general. First, notice how **sum** is defined. The **sum** variable must be initialized to 0 before the loop begins. Inside the loop, the next number is added into **sum**; then the next odd integer is calculated. When the loop is finished, **sum** contains the answer and is then displayed. This gives some general guidelines for creating the sum or total of some quantity.

To develop a **total** or **sum** of some quantity, follow these steps.
a. Before the loop begins, initialize the sum or total to 0
b. Inside the loop, add the next value to the total or sum
c. When the loop is done, display the contents of that total or sum

The next key point with this loop is that the variable **number** is used as the **loop control variable**, which is a variable that is used to control the number of times the loop is executed. Here are the steps involved.
a. A loop control variable must be initialized before the loop begins.
b. A loop control variable is tested for the ending value in the while clause
c. A loop control variable is incremented or decremented at the very end of the loop.

Consider what would happen if we used this incorrect sequence.

```
int number = 1;
int sum = 0;
while (number <= 25) {
  number += 2;     // wrong order
  sum += number;
}
```

It is obvious that we fail to add the initial value of **number**, a 1 in this case, to **sum**. But worse still, when **number** is incremented the last time to 27, that value is then erroneously added into **sum** before the test condition gets a chance to shut the loop down.

When designing a loop, ask yourself "What is going to control the number of times the loop is to execute?" Here, it was "keep going while number is less than or equal to 25," the last odd number to be used. Next, before the **while** statement, initialize the control variable to its first or initial value. Finally, at the very end of the loop, do what is necessary to get the loop control variable ready for its next iteration.

Here is another example. Suppose that we needed the sum of the reciprocals of all integers from one to twenty. That is, compute the sum of 1 + 1/2 + 1/3 + 1/4 + ... + 1/20. Here is a way it can be done following the design guidelines. The current integer **num** controls the number of times the loop is to be done. So we have this far

```
int num;
...
while (num < 21) {
```

What should the initial value for **num** be? 1, in this case. And at the very end of the loop, the next value is given by incrementing **num**. So now, we have

```
int num = 1;
...
while (num < 21) {
  ...
  num++;
}
```

Finally, write the body of the loop. Here we need to sum the reciprocal of **num**. We cannot just write **sum += 1/num**. Can you spot why? Integer division yields zero for all terms but the first. The **sum** must be a **double**. Here is the final version.

```
int num = 1;
double sum = 0.;
while (num < 21) {
  sum += 1./num;
  num++;
}
cout << "Result is " << sum << endl;
```

Loops to Input All Data in a File

By far the most common **while** loop in any program is one setup to process all of the sets of data in a file or entered by hand from the keyboard. The input loops can be constructed in several different ways, depending upon the circumstances.

Sentinel Controlled Input Loops

A sentinel value is a unique, special value that has been placed in the data to signal that there are no more sets of data. Suppose that the file contains lines that have the **quantity** ordered and the unit **cost** of them. There are an unknown number of lines. One way to let the program know that the end has been reached is to enter some unique value for the **cost** and **quantity**. Two common sentinel values are 999 and –999, though they have to be chosen with the problem in mind. If you do not expect that anyone would return 999 of the items (which would be the meaning of entering a **quantity** of –999), then this would work to define the end of the data. In other words, if you opened the data file with Notepad, you would see

```
10 42.50
 3 10.99
-999 -999
```

The program should then input sets of **quantity** and **cost** until the **quantity** becomes –999.

How do we structure the program to do this? Following the loop design guidelines, the **while** clause is

```
while (quantity != -999) {
```

So before the **while** statement, **quantity** must have its initial value; this means we must read in the first set of data so that **quantity** has a value. Then, at the very end of the loop, we must attempt to input another set of data. Here is the complete program; notice the locations of the different statements.

```
#include <iostream>
#include <iomanip>
#include <fstream>
using namespace std;

int main () {
 int quantity; // quantity ordered
 double cost;  // price of one item
 double total; // total cost of this order

 // define, open the input file--display error if fails
 ifstream infile ("test.txt");
 if (!infile) {
   cout << "Error: cannot open test.txt\n";
   return 1;
 }

 // setup floating point format for output of dollars
 cout << fixed << setprecision (2);

 infile >> quantity >> cost; // input first set of data

 // a quantity of -999 marks last set of data
 while (quantity != -999) {
   // calculate this sale and display results
   total = quantity * cost;
   cout << setw (4) << quantity << setw (10) << cost
        << setw (12) << total << endl;
   // attempt to get the next set of data
   infile >> quantity >> cost;
 }
```

```
 infile.close ();
 return 0;
}
```

As coded, this is a prime example of mostly working software! Consider what this program does if the last line of the file contains -99 -99 by accident instead of the expected -999? Or what happens if we reach the end of the file unexpectedly because the user forgot to insert the sentinel values line? Or what happens if the file contains bad data, such as A2 instead of a quantity of 42? Look at the while statement. Under what circumstances is the loop actually ended? Only when the quantity is -999. And in the above situations, it never will contain that ending value! So our loop continues to run endlessly, an infinite loop, displaying the same garbage over and over.

So how could we change the while statement to guard against erroneous situations? In this example, the file should always be in the good state. If it is ever in the fail state for whatever reason, in this problem, it is an error. So we could remedy this mostly working program this way.

```
while (quantity != -999 && infile) {
  // calculate this sale and display results
  total = quantity * cost;
  cout << setw (4) << quantity << setw (10) << cost
       << setw (12) << total << endl;
  // attempt to get the next set of data
  infile >> quantity >> cost;
}
if (!infile)
  cout << "An error occurred processing test.txt\n";
```

Sentinel controlled loops are often programmed by novice programmers who have not learned how to check for and handle the end of file condition. The input streams are perfectly capable of detecting and reporting that there are no more sets of data. Where sentinel controlled loops shine are in keyboard data entry and in menu processing.

Keyboard Data Entry Sentinel Controlled Loops

Consider this sequence displayed on the screen.

```
Enter another student grade or -1 to quit: -1<cr>
```

The loop's test condition must be

```
while (grade != -1) {
```

This also means that before the **while** statement, we must input a student **grade** to have one for which to test in the **while** statement. This also means that there must be another input a student **grade** instruction at the very end of the loop. Here is what the loop looks like.

```
double grade;
cout << "Enter a student grade or -1 to quit: ";
cin >> grade;
while (grade != -1. && cin) {
  ...do something with this grade - process & output
```

```
  cout << "Enter a student grade or -1 to quit: ";
  cin >> grade;
}
if (!cin)
  cout << "An error was encountered in the input\n";
```

One aside. Even though **grade** is a **double** floating point type, I did not use the **fabs()** function to check for equality. Why? Well, if –1 is entered, however it may be stored in **grade**, when comparing it to –1., which is also a **double**, they are both going to be stored identically. However, had grade been the result of a calculation, then **fabs()** would have been prudent.

Menus as Sentinel Controlled Loops

Menus are commonly found in applications. Consider the following screen display and single digit user entry from the keyboard.

```
Acme File Services

     1. Produce the Daily Sales Report
     2. Produce the Weekly Sales Summary Report
     3. Produce the Salesperson Ranking Report
     4. Quit the program

Enter the number of your choice: 4<cr>
```

The **while** test condition is to keep doing the loop as long as **choice != 4** where 4 is the sentinel value. Here is how the menu can be done. In a later chapter, we will see how this large amount of duplicate coding can be reduced.

```
cout << "Acme File Services\n\n"
     << "   1. Produce the Daily Sales Report\n"
     << "   2. Produce the Weekly Sales Summary Report\n"
     << "   3. Produce the Salesperson Ranking Report\n"
     << "   4. Quit the program\n\n"
     << "Enter the number of your choice: ";
cin >> choice;
while (choice != 4) {
  if (choice == 1) {
     ...do the daily sales report
  }
  else if (choice == 2) {
     ...do the weekly summary report
  }
  else if (choice == 3) {
     ...do the salesperson ranking report
  }
  else {
     cout << "Choice is out of range, reenter 1 through 4";
```

```
  }
  cout << "Acme File Services\n\n"
       << "    1. Produce the Daily Sales Report\n"
       << "    2. Produce the Weekly Sales Summary Report\n"
       << "    3. Produce the Salesperson Ranking Report\n"
       << "    4. Quit the program\n\n"
       << "Enter the number of your choice: ";
  cin >> choice;
}
```

Okay. But what happens in the above loop if the user enters the letter A for a choice or presses Ctrl-Z signaling the end of file? Under what conditions does the while loop terminate? Only when **choice** contains a 4 does it end. And if bad data or eof occurs, the loop continues on endlessly in an infinite loop and the menus fly by on the screen at a rapid rate. It is a nice "light show," but not productive. How can we alter the while loop so that this cannot occur?

```
while (choice != 4 && cin) {
```

By simply adding an additional check that the **cin** stream is still in the good state will prevent silly things occurring.

Primed Input Loops that Detect End of File

This example is the easiest method for beginning programmers to implement. It is called a **primed loop** approach because we must input the first set of data before the **while** statement. Why? We know that the input streams have a way to check for EOF. Available to us are

```
while (!infile.eof()) {
```

and

```
while (infile) {
```

In the first **while** statement, we check directly for the end of file condition; and, if it has not yet occurred, continue the loop. However, the second **while** statement is a better choice. It is checking to see if the input stream is still in the good state. If the end of file has been reached or if bad data has caused the stream to lock up or freeze on the bad character, the loop ends. Since bad data can and does occur, it is wiser to use the second test condition for our loops.

Following the loop design guidelines, if **while (infile)** is the test, then before the **while** statement, **infile** must be initialized. This means we need to attempt to input the first set of data. Then, we would input the next set of data at the very end of the loop. Here is the main loop portion of the preceding program.

```
infile >> quantity >> cost; // input first set of data
while (infile) { // stop at eof or bad data
  // calculate this sale and display results
  total = quantity * cost;
  cout << setw (4) << quantity << setw (10) << cost
       << setw (12) << total << endl;
  // attempt to get the next set of data
  infile >> quantity >> cost;
}
```

This is called a **primed loop** because there is an initial "Get the First Set of Data" that is done before the loop begins. The loop only continues as long as the input stream is in the good state. At the very end of the loop, an identical input instruction is coded. This identical second input instruction is known as the "Get Next Set of Data" instruction.

Here is a common way to mess up the loop coding. Can you spot what is going to happen at the end of file or if bad data is encountered?

```
while (infile) { // stop at eof or bad data
  infile >> quantity >> cost;
  total = quantity * cost;
  cout << setw (4) << quantity << setw (10) << cost
       << setw (12) << total << endl;
}
```

When the end of file is reached, the input stream goes into the not good state and nothing is inputted for **quantity** or **cost**. However, the next two lines ignore this and go right ahead calculating a total and displaying the data as if it actually had another set of data. This often results in the last record in the file being processed and output twice! It is even worse if bad data were encountered as the contents of **quantity** and **cost** are unpredictable.

And this brings up the testing that we must perform when the loop actually ends. The while statement terminates when the file is no longer in the good state. That is, it is the end of file (**eof**), it has run into a bad spot on the disk and is unable to read the data (**bad**), or has detected bad data in the input lines (the **fail** bit is on but not **eof** and not **bad**). Of the three ways the while loop terminates, only the eof situation is normal and to be expected. The other two represent an error situation. We must alert the user to any errors that we encounter.

Error checking can be done in many ways. Here is one simple version that does not discriminate between a physically bad disk drive and bad data entered.

```
 infile >> quantity >> cost; // input first set of data
 while (infile) { // stop at eof or bad data
   ...
   infile >> quantity >> cost;
 }
if (infile.eof())
  cout << "All data processed successfully\n";
else
  cout << "Bad data was encountered, output is incorrect\n";
```

Or one can check this way.

```
if (!infile.eof())
  cout << "Bad data was encountered, output is incorrect\n";
```

Or one can check this way.

```
if (!infile.eof()) {
  if (infile.bad()) {
    cout << " The disk cannot be read. Use a backup copy\n";
  else
    cout << "Bad data was encountered\n";
```

```
}
```

I highly recommend using the Primed Loop approach when processing a file of data. It is an easy one to design, code, and test. However, there is a shorter way that most experienced C++ programmers are going to use.

A More Compact Loop That Detects End of File

Seasoned programmers balk at coding the same instructions twice. Here, we take advantage of the extraction operator's return value. We know that we can chain extraction operators.

```
cin >> quantity >> cost;
```

This means that the extraction operator must be returning the input stream so that it is available for the next extraction operator to its right. In other words, the first portion

```
cin >> quantity
```

when completed must return back **cin** so that the next extraction would be

```
cin >> cost;
```

Since the **while** clause desires to test the goodness of the stream, the shortcut version merges the input operation into the **while** clause test condition!

```
while (cin >> quantity >> cost) {
```

This first does the indicated input operations. When that is finished, the last extraction operator returns **cin** and the test condition becomes the expected **while (cin)**. Clever, but complex. Here is the entire looping process, this time using a file of data.

```
while (infile >> quantity >> cost) {
  total = quantity * cost;
  cout << setw (4) << quantity << setw (10) << cost
       << setw (12) << total << endl;
}
```

Notice that the loop is now more compact, not necessarily more readable.

This is one of the most common forms of input loops you will see. It does have one drawback, besides complexity. And that is, the entire input process must be able to be stated in one long chain of extraction operators. This is not always possible, as we will see later on.

Now that we can write loops, what can we do with them? The next section covers some of the many uses for loops.

Applications of Loops

The Summation of a Series

Summations are a very common action in numerical analysis. The preceding summation of the reciprocal (1/num) from one to twenty lacks one very important feature. Just running the loop through the first twenty terms is not sufficient to guarantee any kind of accuracy. Let's formalize the problem as seen in numerical analysis: the summation of a series. Further, let's sum $1/x^2$ instead.

$$result = \sum_{x=1}^{N} \frac{1.}{x^2}$$

where N can be infinity.

What is needed is a result that is sufficiently accurate, not just the first twenty terms. Let's say that we need the result accurate to .001. That is, keep on adding in the next **term** until the value of that next **term** is less than or equal to .001. Within the loop body, the next **term** to add into the **sum** is **1./x²** using the current value of the loop control variable **x**. We could change the **while** test condition to just

```
while (term > .001) {
```

However, one safety factor should always be considered. Certainly **1./x²** is going to become small rapidly as the value of **x** increases. If **x** is 10, the **term** is .01; if **x** is 100, the **term** is .0001, which is more accuracy than was requested. The **while** clause certainly would stop long before **x** is up to 100.

However, what if we summed this one

$$result = \sum_{x=1}^{N} x^2$$

Oops! This one would never converge on an answer. Each term gets significantly larger than the previous one! If our only ending condition was to continue while the term is greater than .001, we would have an infinite loop that would run forever, until we found a way to abort the program. Thus, in all summation programs, some kind of alternate loop termination is **always** installed, just in case something goes terribly wrong with the process.

In this example, if **x** ever reached 1000, for example, something must be very wrong. If **x** becomes that large, terminate the loop and give it further study. So now, our test condition becomes

```
while (x < 1000 && term > .001) {
```

Following the loop construction guidelines, both **x** and **term** must be given their starting values before the **while** clause. Both must be assigned their next value at the end of the loop.

Here is the complete loop.

```
int x = 1;
double term = 1; // 1/x/x = 1 for the first term
```

```
double sum = 0;
while (x < 1000 && term > .001) {
 sum += term;
 x++;
 term = 1. / (x * x);
}
cout << "Sum yields " << sum << endl;
```

The summation is a powerful technique that is found both in Computer Science and Engineering applications.

Counters and Totals—Grand Totals

In many applications, the count of the number of sets of data is needed. If, for example, each line represents a single sales, then the count of the number of lines input would be the number of sales. If each line of input represented the data for a single policyholder, then the count of the number of lines input would be the number of policyholders. In a bowling score-keeping program, if each line contained the data for one game, then a count of the lines would be the number of bowling games played.

Commonly, when the end of file is reached, the application is required to display grand totals. Using the sales example of **quantity** and **cost**, for each set of data, we calculate and display the total of that sales. However, at the end of the file, the grand total sales ought to be shown along with the number of sales and even perhaps an average sale.

Here is how the user would like the report to appear.

```
   Acme Daily Sales Report

Quantity    Cost          Total
  Sold    Per Item        Sales

  9999    $9999.99     $99999.99
  9999    $9999.99     $99999.99
  9999    $9999.99     $99999.99
                       ---------
                       $99999.99
  Number sales:             9999
  Average Sales:       $99999.99
```

First, identify what is new from the previous version of the program above. Headings have been added along with some specific columnar alignments and dollar signs. What is significant is the ----- line and what comes after it. When are all these final lines displayed? Clearly, they are displayed after the main loop terminates at the end of the file. A grand total sales variable is needed, and this is officially called a **total**. A variable must be added to add up the number of sales, which is really a count of the number of lines inputted, this is known as a **counter**.

The rules for **counters** and **totals** are simple. Repeating the previous guidelines

a. Before the loop begins, counters and totals must be initialized to their starting values, usually zero.

b. Within the loop, counters must be incremented and totals added to.

c. When the loop ends, counters and totals are often displayed.

Here are the completed program and the output from a sample run. Notice carefully the placement of the new instructions.

Basic05a - Acme Sales Report with Grand Totals

```
/***************************************************************/
/*                                                             */
/* Basic05a Acme Sales Report with grand totals                */
/*                                                             */
/***************************************************************/

#include <iostream>
#include <iomanip>
#include <fstream>
using namespace std;

int main () {
 int    quantity; // quantity ordered
 double cost;     // price of one item
 double total;    // total cost of this order

 int    numSales = 0;    // total number of sales
 double grandTotal = 0; // grand total sales
 double avgSales;       // the average sales amount

 // define, open the input file - display error if fails
 ifstream infile ("sales.txt");
 if (!infile) {
   cout << "Error: cannot open sales.txt\n";
   return 1;
 }

 // setup floating point format for output of dollars
 cout << fixed << setprecision (2);

 // display headings and column heading lines
 cout << "   Acme Daily Sales Report\n\n"
      << "Quantity    Cost          Total\n"
      << "  Sold    Per Item        Sales\n\n";

 // main loop - process all input lines in the file
 while (infile >> quantity >> cost) {
   // calculate this sale
```

```
      total = quantity * cost;

      // increment counters and totals
      numSales++;
      grandTotal += total;

      // display this report line
      cout << "   " << setw (4) << quantity
           << "    $" << setw (7) << cost
           << "    $" << setw (8) << total << endl;
    }

    // display grand total lines
    cout << "                         --------\n";
    cout << "                        $" << setw (8)
         << grandTotal << endl;
    cout << "  Number Sales:               " << setw (4)
         << numSales << endl;

    // find and display the average sales
    avgSales = grandTotal / numSales;
    cout << "  Average Sales:      $" << setw (8)
         << avgSales << endl;

    infile.close ();
    return 0;
   }
```

```
Output from Basic05a - Sales Report with Grand Totals
```

```
    Acme Daily Sales Report

 Quantity    Cost          Total
   Sold     Per Item       Sales

     10     $  42.00     $  420.00
      1     $  10.00     $   10.00
     20     $  15.00     $  300.00
      2     $  14.50     $   29.00
      7     $  30.00     $  210.00
      5     $  10.00     $   50.00
                          --------
                         $ 1019.00
   Number Sales:                 6
   Average Sales:        $  169.80
```

Finding the Maximum and Minimum Values

Often when processing a set of data, the maximum and minimum values are desired. In the previous sales report, two additional lines could be added at the end of the report.

```
     Highest Sales:      $99999.99
     Lowest Sales:       $99999.99
```

To produce these, we need another pair of **doubles** to hold these, say **hiSales** and **lowSales**.

How are they found? Within the loop, each time a new **total** is found by multiplying **cost** times **quantity**, we must compare that new **total** to what is currently in **hiSales** and **lowSales**. If the new **total** is larger than the current **hiSales**, replace **hiSales** with this new value. Likewise, if the new **total** is lower than the current value in **lowSales**, replace **lowSales** with this lower value. When the loop ends, these two fields, **hiSales** and **lowSales**, contain the largest and smallest sales.

But to what do we initialize these two variables? In this problem, the finding of the maximum and minimum values is overly simplified. Due to the nature of the problem, there can be no negative values (unless we can expect refunds to be in this file). One might suspect that all we need do is to initialize both **hiSales** and **lowSales** to 0. Wrong. Let's see what happens after we input the very first sales line. The total is 420.00. That is certainly larger than the 0 in **hiSales**, so **hiSales** is now updated to contain 420.00. But look what happens to the **lowSales**; its initial value of 0 is certainly smaller than 420.00 and thus **lowSales** is **not** updated. In fact, none of the totals are below 0 and thus, **lowSales** is never updated and ends up being 0!

Rule: when finding the maximum or minimum values, initialize the two variables that are to contain the maximum and minimum to the actual data contained in the first set of data.

Since we must have the first set of data to use to get the initial values for the high and low sales, we should use the primed loop approach. Since much of the program is the same, only excerpts are shown here. Pay careful attention to the location of the various steps. In the main processing loop, after the total sales is calculated, the new **total** is compared to the **maxSales** and then to the **minSales** variables.

Basic05b - Acme Sales Report with Grand Totals and High/Low Sales

```
/***************************************************************/
/*                                                             */
/* Basic05b Acme Sales with grand totals and max/min sales */
/*                                                             */
/***************************************************************/

#include <iostream>
#include <iomanip>
#include <fstream>
using namespace std;

int main () {
```

```
int    quantity; // quantity ordered
double cost;     // price of one item
double total;    // total cost of this order

int    numSales = 0;    // total number of sales
double grandTotal = 0; // grand total sales
double avgSales;        // the average sales amount
double maxSales = 0;    // the largest sales - if file is empty
double minSales = 0;    // the smallest sales - if file is empty

// define, open the input file - display error if fails
ifstream infile ("sales.txt");
if (!infile) {
  cout << "Error: cannot open sales.txt\n";
  return 1;
}

// setup floating point format for output of dollars
cout << fixed << setprecision (2);

// display headings and column heading lines
cout << "   Acme Daily Sales Report\n\n"
     << "Quantity    Cost          Total\n"
     << "  Sold    Per Item       Sales\n\n";

// get first set of data to initialize max/min values
infile >> quantity >> cost;
if (infile) // only assign if there was a set of data
 maxSales = minSales = quantity * cost;

// main loop - process all input lines in the file
while (infile) {
 // calculate this sale
 total = quantity * cost;

 // check on min and max values
 if (total > maxSales) {
  maxSales = total;
 }
 else if (total < minSales) {
  minSales = total;
 }

 // increment counters and totals
 numSales++;
 grandTotal += total;

 // display this report line
 cout << "  " << setw (4) << quantity
      << "    $" << setw (7) << cost
      << "    $" << setw (8) << total << endl;

 // get next set of data
```

```
67     infile >> quantity >> cost;
68    }
69
70    // display grand total lines
71    cout << "                       --------\n";
72    cout << "                      $" << setw (8)
73         << grandTotal << endl;
74    cout << "  Number Sales:           " << setw (4)
75         << numSales << endl;
76
77    // find and display the average sales - guard against no data
78    if (numSales)
79     avgSales = grandTotal / numSales;
80    else
81     avgSales = 0;
82    cout << "  Average Sales:      $" << setw (8)
83         << avgSales << endl;
84
85    // display max/min sales values
86    cout << "  Highest Sales:      $" << setw (8)
87         << maxSales << endl;
88    cout << "  Lowest Sales:       $" << setw (8)
89         << minSales << endl;
90
91    infile.close ();
92    return 0;
93  }
```

Bulletproofing Programs

Once you have the basics of looping down, the next thing to consider is what about all the things that can go wrong while inputting data.

The first thing you must always consider is that sometimes a file can have no data in it yet. Suppose that Acme Company has a Daily Sales File that contains all of the sales data for its salespeople for one day. What happens to our program if someone runs it before anyone has made a sale for the day? The file is empty. What does your program do at that point? Certainly, it should not do calculations on nonexistent data!

What does **Basic05b** program do if there are no data in the file? Look at lines 20, 21 and 40 through 42. I initialized the maximum and minimum sales variables to 0 so that they have a starting value. On line 40, the input operation encounters the end of file. Was it checked for? Yes, on line 41, only if the input stream is in the good state do the assignments to the maximum and minimum sales variables take place. And when line 45 is executed, the **while** test condition fails because the stream is not in the good state, rather it is at the end of file. The main loop is never executed.

Ok. Now look over the display of all the totals and results. First, look at lines 77 through 81. Here, I slid in a bit more protection. The program must calculate the average sales, but the divisor, **numSales** could be 0, and is, if there the file is empty. If I did not guard against this possibility, then, should such occur, the program would crash with a divide exception at this point! Notice that the maximum and minimum sales correctly display their 0 initial values.

So **Basic05b** is in good shape if there are no data in the file. Always double check your programs to be certain that all works if there are no data inputted. A situation of no input data can and does happen in the real world.

Ok. Next, what happens if bad data is encountered? Ah ha, **Basic05b** is not ready for bad data events! If there is bad data on the very first line, the program simply prints all zeros for the fields and quits without any notice to the user that there was anything wrong! Worse still, suppose the bad data was on line one hundred of the sales file! Now we get a report that actually looks like it is a valid one, at least for the first ninety nine sets of data that are shown and used in the calculations! This can completely mislead the user who is not aware that bad data was encountered. The report gives no indication whatsoever that the results are not valid. This is totally **unacceptable** for a program to do. We must at the least let the user know that bad data was encountered and the results shown are not valid.

Where can we take care of this detail? The main loop is testing the goodness of the stream and terminates whenever it is not good, either end of file or bad data. Thus, the proper place to check is immediately after the main loop terminates and before we begin displaying the totals. Insert after line 68, the end brace of the main processing loop, the following bulletproofing code.

```
if (!infile.eof()) {
  cout << "Error: bad data encountered on line: "
       << numSales + 1 << endl;
  infile.close();
  return 1;
}
```

Sometimes programmers even go so far as to add one more line after these four.

```
cout << "All data successfully processed\n";
```

Thus, whenever you write a program that has an input processing loop, you should **always** bulletproof your coding, allowing for files with no data in them and for encountering bad data.

Creating Output Files

When programs process all of the sets of data in a file, very often the number of output lines exceeds the amount that can be shown on the screen without having the screen scroll. This makes it much more difficult to verify the output is correct. Instead, programs that produce a lot of output lines often write the lines to an output file and later that file can be viewed with Notepad or printed.

Switching from **cout** to an actual output file is very easy. The output file class is **ofstream**. Similar to input files, an instance must be created, and the file opened for output. The only information that is really needed is the filename you wish it to create. My suggestion is to use a file extension of txt so that simply double clicking the file in Explorer launches Notepad to open it for viewing or printing.

Similar to an input file, the output file can be defined and opened with a single statement or explicitly opened with a second instruction. Here are both methods.

```
ofstream outfile ("results.txt");
```

or

```
ofstream outfile;
outfile.open ("results.txt");
```

If the file does not exist, a new one is built, and initially it contains 0 bytes. If the file exists, it is emptied of its prior contents and now contains 0 bytes. As the program outputs to the **outfile** stream, the system stores the data in the file. When the program is done, it should call the **close()** function. The close operation on an output file writes any remaining data and places the end of file marker in it.

One should also check for failure to open the file successfully. If the disk is full, the open fails. If you should use an invalid path or folder name, the open fails. If you should use an invalid filename, the open fails. So it is always wise to check. Thus, we follow the opening of the output file with

```
if (!outfile) {
  cout << "Error: unable to open output file: result.txt\n";
  // possibly close any open input files here
  return 2;
}
```

How do you write data to the file? It's done exactly the same way you write data to the **cout** stream.

```
outfile << "Hello World\n";
```

This writes the text **Hello World** and a new line code to the file just as it does when sent to the screen with **cout**.

There is, however, one detail to remember. Just as we must setup the floating point flags with the **cout** stream, we must do the same with the output file stream.

```
// setup floating point format for output of dollars
outfile.setf (ios::fixed, ios::floatfield);
outfile << setprecision (2);
```

An output file is closed in exactly the same manner as an input file.

```
outfile.close ();
```

Basic05c is a rewrite of program **Basic05b** using an output file instead of using **cout**. I have also taken the liberty to insert bulletproofing for bad data this time. To save pages, some of the coding that is exactly the same as the previous example has been removed.

Basic05c - Acme Sales - Output Goes to a File

```
/***************************************************************/
/*                                                             */
/* Basic05c Acme Sales Report using an output file             */
/*                                                             */
/***************************************************************/

#include <iostream>
#include <iomanip>
#include <fstream>
using namespace std;

int main () {
 int    quantity; // quantity ordered
 double cost;     // price of one item
 double total;    // total cost of this order

 int    numSales = 0;    // total number of sales
 double grandTotal = 0; // grand total sales
 double avgSales;        // the average sales amount
 double maxSales = 0;    // the largest sales - if file is empty
 double minSales = 0;    // the smallest sales - if file is empty

 // define, open the input file - display an error msg if fails
 ifstream infile ("sales.txt");
 if (!infile) {
   cout << "Error: cannot open sales.txt\n";
   return 1;
 }

 // define and open the output file
 ofstream outfile ("results.txt");
 if (!outfile) {
   cout << "Error: cannot open results.txt for output\n";
   infile.close ();
   return 2;
 }

 // setup floating point format for output of dollars
 outfile << fixed << setprecision (2);

 // display headings and column heading lines
 outfile << "   Acme Daily Sales Report\n\n"
         << "Quantity    Cost         Total\n"
         << "  Sold    Per Item       Sales\n\n";

 // get first set of data to initialize max/min values
```

```
infile >> quantity >> cost;
if (infile) // only assign if there was a set of data
 maxSales = minSales = quantity * cost;

// main loop - process all input lines in the file
while (infile) {
 // calculate this sale
 total = quantity * cost;

 // check on min and max values
 if (total > maxSales) {
  maxSales = total;
 }
 else if (total < minSales) {
  minSales = total;
 }

 // increment counters and totals
 numSales++;
 grandTotal += total;

 // display this report line
 outfile << "  " << setw (4) << quantity
         << "    $" << setw (7) << cost
         << "    $" << setw (8) << total << endl;

 // get next set of data
 infile >> quantity >> cost;
}

// check for bad data in the input file - if found, display an
// error message to screen and in the output file - abort pgm
if (!infile.eof()) {
 cout << "Error: bad data encountered in the input file\n"
      << "The line containing the error is " << numSales + 1
      << endl;
 outfile << "Error: bad data encountered in the input file\n"
         << "The line containing the error is " << numSales + 1
         << endl;
 infile.close ();
 outfile.close ();
 return 3;
}

// display grand total lines
outfile << "                       --------\n";
outfile << "                      $" << setw (8) << grandTotal
        << endl;
outfile << "  Number Sales:               " << setw (4)
        << numSales << endl;

// find and show average sales - guard against empty input file
if (numSales)
```

```
  avgSales = grandTotal / numSales;
 else
  avgSales = 0;
 outfile << "  Average Sales:       $" << setw (8)
         << avgSales << endl;

 // display max/min sales values
 outfile << "  Highest Sales:       $" << setw (8)
         << maxSales << endl;
 outfile << "  Lowest Sales:        $" << setw (8)
         << minSales << endl;

 infile.close ();
 outfile.close ();
 return 0;
}
```

The Do Until Instruction—An Alternative to the Do While

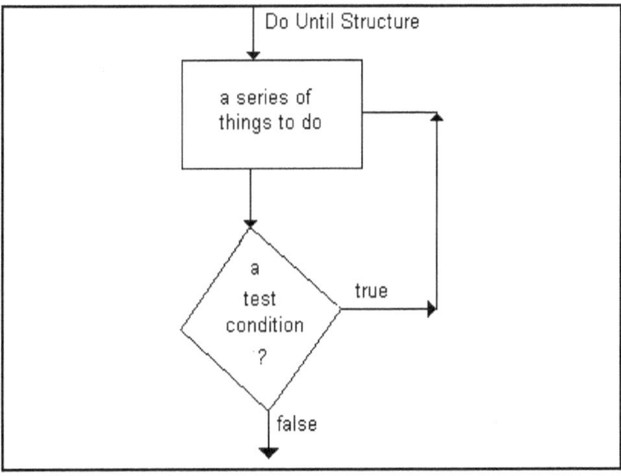

Figure 5.2 The Do Until Structure

The Do Until iterative structure is different from the Do While in that the body of the loop is always done once and then the test condition is checked. The Do Until is shown above.

What is the difference between a Do While and a Do Until structure? By way of an analogy, imagine you are driving down Main Street on a Friday night. You decide to turn left. The Do Until says to turn left. Now apply the test condition—was it ok to turn left—no oncoming cars—not a one way street—not a red light—no pedestrians? In contrast, the Do While says to check to see if it is ok to turn left and if so, then turn left. Ok. This is a bit of an extreme viewpoint on the two structures, but it serves to drive home the main point of difference, the Do Until always executes the series of things to do one time. Why is this important? Consider reading a file of data using a Do Until. If there are no data in the file, the test for that condition does not occur until after all the processing of the nonexistent set of data is done and the results of the calculations on the nonexistent set of data are output! Thus, a Do Until is a specialized form of looping to be used in those circumstances in which one can guarantee in all circumstances the body of the loop must be done one time.

The syntax of the Do Until is

```
do {
  0, 1 or more statements
} while (test condition);
```

or

```
do
  {
  0, 1 or more statements
  } while (test condition);
```

While one can always use a Do While to solve a programming problem, there are a few times that a Do Until is more convenient. Here is one such time. Suppose that we need to display the following on the screen and get the user response.

```
Enter a numerical choice of 1 through 4: _
```

Once the user has entered a number, it might not be in the correct range. The program should then insist on a proper entry be made.

```
Enter a numerical choice of 1 through 4: 5
Enter a numerical choice of 1 through 4: 6
Enter a numerical choice of 1 through 4: -42
Enter a numerical choice of 1 through 4: 4
```

The program must provide a loop that repeatedly prompts and gets the user's choice until it is within the valid range. While this could be done with a Do While, a Do Until is more convenient.

```
int choice;
do {
  cout << "Enter a numerical choice of 1 through 4: ";
  cin >> choice;
} while (choice < 1 || choice > 4);
```

The corresponding Do While takes a bit more coding.

```
int choice;
cout << "Enter a numerical choice of 1 through 4: ";
cin >> choice;
while (choice < 1 || choice > 4) {
  cout << "Enter a numerical choice of 1 through 4: ";
  cin >> choice;
}
```

The Do Loop or for Statement

Frequently, a program needs to perform a series of instructions a known, finite number of times. We have seen that a **while** loop can easily be used to sum the reciprocals of the numbers from one to ten, for example. Here is the **while** version.

```
int num;
double sum;
num = 1;
sum = 0;
while (num < 21) {
 sum += 1./num;
 num++;
}
cout << "Result is " << sum << endl;
```

The **for** loop is a shortcut way to do the same thing. Here is how that same reciprocal sum program could have been written using a **for** statement.

```
int num;
double sum = 0.;
for (num=1; num<21; num++)
 sum += 1./num;
cout << "Result is " << sum << endl;
```

The **for** syntax is

```
for (0, 1 or more initial expressions separated by a comma;
     test condition;
     0, 1 or more bump expressions) {
 body of the loop
}
```

The initial expressions represent all statements that occur before the **while** statement. If there are more than one, separate them with commas. The initial expression is ended with a semicolon. The test condition is the same test condition we have been using and is ended with another semicolon. The bump expressions represent the incrementing of the loop control variables, but are not so limited. We could have written this same for loop more compactly.

```
double sum;
for (int num=1, sum=0; num<21; num++)
 sum += 1./num;
cout << "Result is " << sum << endl;
```

Here the initialization of **sum** has been moved into the **for** statement as one of the initial expressions. Also note that I am now defining the loop control variable **num** within the initial expression. This variable then is technically only available within the loop itself and should not be used later on after the loop ends.

But we could condense this for loop even further.

```
double sum;
for (int num=1, sum=0; num<21; sum += 1./num, num++) ;
```

```
cout << "Result is " << sum << endl;
```

Now I have moved the **sum** calculation into the first bump expression location. Notice that **num** is incremented after the sum is calculated using the original value in **num** before the increment takes place.

But it could be consolidated even further.

```
double sum;
for (int num=1, sum=0; num<21; sum += 1./num++) ;
cout << "Result is " << sum << endl;
```

Here **sum** is calculated using the current contents of **num** and the ++ after increment then takes place. And now, we have a very compact line of code!

Here is another example. Suppose that we had the following coding.

```
double x, y, sum;
x = 1;
y = 10;
sum = 0;
while (x < y) {
  sum += x * y;
  x++;
  y--;
}
```

This could be rewritten using a **for** loop as follows.

```
double x, y, sum;
for (x=1, y=10, sum = 0; x < y; x++, y--) {
  sum += x * y;
}
```

Notice that all statements above the **while** clause can be considered initialization statements. Here there are three. There are two bump expressions since both **x** and **y** can be considered loop control variables in this case. This leaves then only one statement in the loop's body.

However, this can be condensed even more by moving the remaining statement into the bump expressions.

```
double x, y, sum;
for (x=1, y=10, sum = 0; x < y; sum += x * y, x++, y--) ;
```

Notice that the **sum** instruction must be done before the incrementing and decrementing of **x** and **y**.

This can be condensed even further.

```
double x, y, sum;
for (x=1, y=10, sum = 0; x < y; sum += x++ * y--) ;
```

Again notice that this uses the postfix ++ and – – operators so that the current values of **x** and **y** are used in the calculation before they are altered.

Rule. All **while** loops can be rewritten as a more compact **for** loop. All **for** loops can be rewritten as a more understandable and readable **while** loop.

By now you are probably wondering why anyone would want to write such a compact, dense line of code as the **for** loop with **x** and **y** instead of the more readable **while** version. Job security, no—just kidding. The reason lies with compiler guidelines and speed of execution. In all circumstances, the compiler is allowed to create the fastest, best possible machine instruction sequence for one C++ statement. Take the summation of the **x*y** example. The **while** version has seven separate executable instructions. The condensed **for** version has one statement. Thus, in all circumstances the **for** version is guaranteed to have the best possible, fastest executing set of machine instructions generated by the compiler. How much faster? In this case the **for** statement version is perhaps 5% faster in execution.

However, most compilers have a "global optimize for speed" compiler option. Microsoft Visual C++ has a Debug build and a Release build option, with Debug as the default. A Debug version of a program contains lots of debugging information to assist in finding programming errors. When a Release build is chosen, the compiler by default optimizes for speed. No debugging information is included in the resulting exe file, which is therefore drastically smaller in size. The Release version of a program executes substantially faster than the Debug version, which tends to check for all sorts of internal errors as well as those committed by the program directly. When global optimize for speed is in effect, the compiler can then do anything it wishes to any statement in the entire program. Typically, the compiler rearranges program statements into somewhat different order to gain speed of execution. Of course, when you let the compiler begin to move lines of coding around, it is entirely possible the compiler will move a line that it should not have moved, and a new bug that was not there in the Debug version now appears. In large programs, this can happen, and sometimes global optimization is disabled for a section of the program.

By writing these compact for loops, you are guaranteeing that in all circumstances the compiler creates the fastest possible execution speed for the loop. However, is this really significant? It all depends. If the entirety of the program was the summation of **x*y** above, the amount of time actually saved in measured in nanoseconds—it's insignificant. However, if this calculation was being done 10,000,000 times, then that speed increase is observably significant.

Since speed of execution is the primary concern with programs today, programmers usually code for speed.

By the way, you read a condensed **for** statement by decomposing it back into the **while** loop of which it is equivalent. However, condensed **for** loops are very hard to read. So many companies prefer the more verbose **while** versions because they are more readable and therefore more maintainable.

Also, **for** loops have other purposes than consolidating **while** loops. In subsequent chapters, we will see that a major use of a **for** loop is to do a large series of instructions a known number of times. Typical coding that we will see in later chapters is like this.

```
for (int i=0; i<limit; i++) {
  a significant body of things to do
}
```

In these cases, the **for** loops are easy to follow.

Here is a more practical use of a **for** loop. Suppose we need to calculate a table of 101 values of the sine function from an angle of 0 to PI in uniform steps. Here is a good use of a **for** loop.

```
const double PI = acos (-1.);
const double delta = PI / 100;
double angle = 0;
double sinAngle;
cout << setprecision (4);
for (int i=0; i<101; i++) {
 sinAngle = sin (angle);
 cout << setw (5) << angle << " "
      << setw (6) << sinAngle << endl;
 angle += delta;
}
```

The uniform increment in the **angle** is calculated and the loop done 101 times. Each iteration through the loop, the sine is calculated and the **angle** and sine are displayed. The **angle** is incremented as the last instruction to get it ready for the next loop iteration. While I could also have moved the **angle** increment into the bump expressions, keeping it in the loop's body kept the **for** statement more readable.

Efficient Loops

Often loop bodies are executed a large number of times. In such cases, it is important to keep things that do not need to be in the body out of it. For example, consider this assignment to variable **z**.

```
int x, z;
double y = 0;
for (x=0; x<100; x++) {
  y += x * x / 42.;
  z = 100;
}
```

In this case, the assignment of 100 to **z** is done 100 times. How many times does **z** need to be assigned its value of 100? Once. Since variable **z** is not used within the loop body, it could be moved either before the loop or after the end } of the loop. In fact, this is precisely one thing that the compiler does during global optimizations for speed in Release builds of a program. It moves these **loop invariants**, as they are called, out of the loop, either before the loop if it is needed within the loop or after it is done if it is not needed within the loop.

Loop control variables should be of the integer data type whenever possible. The integer math instruction set on any computer is the fastest executing math types. The floating point math instruction set is one of the slowest. If the loop has to be done a large number of times, the difference in speed is noticeable when the loop control variable is an integer type versus a floating point type.

For example, I could have rewritten the display of 101 sines program above using the variable **angle** to control the loop. However, having the loop control variable be a **double** slows down the overall speed of execution.

```
const double PI = acos (-1.);
const double delta = PI / 100;
double angle = 0;
double sinAngle;
cout << setprecision (4);
for (; fabs(angle - PI)> .0001; angle += delta;) {
 sinAngle = sin (angle);
 cout << setw (5) << angle << "  "
      << setw (6) << sinAngle << endl;
}
```

Notice that if there are no initial conditions, the semicolon must still be coded. The same is true if there are no bump expressions. What does this loop do?

```
for (; true; ) {
 ...
}
```

It is equivalent to writing

```
while (true) {
 ...
}
```

Nesting of Loops

Loops can be nested. The rules are simple. The inner loop must be entirely contained within the outer loop. If there are If-Then-Else statements within a loop, the entire If-Then-Else must be within the loop. Here is a correct nested loop.

```
int j = 0, k;
while (j < 100) {
  // some outer loop statements can be here
  for (k=0; k<100; k++) {
    // inner loop statements
  }
  // some more outer loop statements
  j++;
}
```

If you try to nest a loop incorrectly with an If-Then-Else, the compiler catches this and gives an error messages. Here is an example.

```
int j, k;
for (j=0; j<10; j++) {
   // some loop statements
   if (k < 10) {
     // then-clause
```

```
    }
} <---- this ends the for loop and there is no else-clause
else { <---- compiler error cannot find the corresponding if
  // else clause of k<10
}
```

An Example of Nested Loops

Very often programs use nested loops. In this next example, a student's average grade is calculated. The sentinel controlled inner loop inputs test scores, and accumulates the total points. When the user enters a **score** of –99, the inner loop terminates, calculates, and displays the average grade. Wrapped around this process is an outer loop asks the user if there is another student to grade. If there is, the inner loop is repeated for that student. Assume that floating point fixed format has been setup on **cout** and the precision set to 1.

```
long id;
cout << "Enter Student ID number or -1 to quit: ";
while (cin >> id && id != -1)
  {
  double sum = 0;
  int count = 0;
  double score;
  cout << "Enter test score or -99 when finished: ";
  while (cin >> score && score != -99)
    {
    sum += score;
    count++;
    cout << "Enter test score or -99 when finished: ";
    }
  if (count > 0)
    {
    cout << "Student " << id << " grade: "
         << setw (4) << sum/count <<endl;
    }
  cout << "Enter Student ID number or -1 to quit: ";
  }
```

This example illustrates a vital detail when using nested loops. Inside the outer loop and before the inner loop begins, notice that **sum** and **count** must be reinitialized to 0 to get ready for the next student's set of test scores. A common error is to code this as follows.

```
long id;
double sum = 0;
int count = 0;
double score;
cout << "Enter Student ID number or -1 to quit: ";
while (cin >> id && id != -1)
  {
```

```
   cout << "Enter test score or -99 when finished: ";
   while (cin >> score && score != -99)
     {
     sum += score;
     count++;
     cout << "Enter test score or -99 when finished: ";
     }
...
```

This correctly calculates the first student's average. But what happens when the second student's scores are entered? Since **sum** and **count** are not reset to 0, the second student's scores are added to the first and so on.

Section B: Computer Science Examples

Cs05a—Acme Ticket Sales Summary Program

Back in Chapter 2, we wrote a program to calculate the price of tickets that a customer purchased in which a discount is given for children and senior citizens. In such sales applications, it is vital that some form of a transaction log is also written at the time of purchase documenting that purchase. Assume that just such a log has been produced, called **trans-log.txt**. The log file contains three integers that represent the number of regular tickets purchased, the number of children's tickets purchased, and the number of senior citizens' tickets purchased by a single customer. After those three integers comes a **double** that contains the total purchase price of all those tickets.

Management now wishes to have a summary report of the sales. This program inputs the transaction log file and builds a daily ticket sales summary report, which is actually written to a file called **results.txt**. The Ticket Sales Summary Report contained in that file looks like this.

```
       Acme Ticket Sales Summary Report

       Number of Tickets Sold     Total Cost
       Adult   Child   Senior     Of Tickets

          99      99       99     $ 999.99
          99      99       99     $ 999.99
          99      99       99     $ 999.99
         ---     ---      ---     --------
Totals:  999     999      999     $9999.99
Percents: 99%     99%      99%

Average cost of ticket:           $ 999.99
```

When the end of the sales input occurs, after displaying a line of dashes, the totals of each of the four columns are shown. Then, the percentage sold in each of the three categories is displayed. Finally, the average price of a ticket is calculated and presented.

As usual, begin by defining the input fields and the needed calculation and output fields. Let's call the three number of tickets variables **numAdult**, **numChild** and **numSenior**. The input total cost of the tickets is just **cost**. Make four main storage boxes so labeled with these names. Next, what are we going to need to calculate the first total line after the line of dashes? Four total variables are needed, one for each column. Let's call them **totNumAdult**, **totNumChild**, **totNumSenior** and **totalCost**. How do we calculate the percent results? We can add up the three total tickets' results to find the **grandTotalTicketsSold** integer. Knowing that, the seniors' ticket percentage is just **totNumSenior** * 100. / **grandTotalTicketsSold**. Let's call these **percentAdult**, **percentChild**, **percentSenior**. Finally, the average ticket cost, **avgCost**, is just the **totalCost** / **grandTotalTicketsSold**. After making labeled main storage boxes for all of these, we can then write the sequence of instruction we need. The final main storage diagram is shown in Figure 5.3.

Since there is both an input file and an output file, we need two file variables; these could also be added to the main storage diagram if desired. Following the usual design procedure, now sketch out the solution in pseudocode or pseudo English using these variable names.

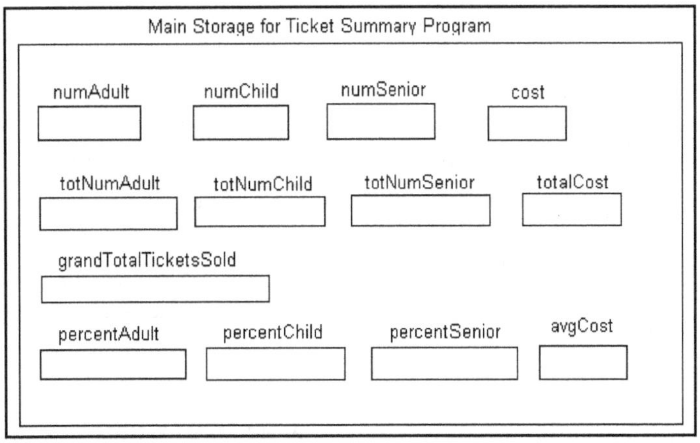

Main Storage for Ticket Summary Program

numAdult numChild numSenior cost

totNumAdult totNumChild totNumSenior totalCost

grandTotalTicketsSold

percentAdult percentChild percentSenior avgCost

Figure 5.3 Main Storage for Ticket Summary Program

The initial steps and the main loop are as follows.

open the input file, **infile**
if it fails to open, display an error message and quit
open the output file, **outfile**
if it fails to open, display an error message, close the input file and quit
setup floating point format with two decimal digits for dollars on **outfile**
display the heading line on **outfile**
display the two column heading lines on **outfile**
set **totNumAdult**, **totNumChild**, **totNumSenior** and **totalCost** to 0
input **numAdult**, **numChild** and **numSenior** and **cost** from **infile**
if there are no data, display a message, close the files and quit
while (input operation is successful) {
  add **numAdult** to **totNumAdult**
  add **numChild** to **totNumChild**
  add **numSenior** to **totNumSenior**

add cost to **totalCost**
display the **numAdult**, **numChild** and **numSenior** and **cost** variables on **outfile**
input **numAdult**, **numChild** and **numSenior** and **cost** from **infile**
}

When we get to this point, all the data have been input, if any. We should guard against bad input data. Thus, we can add the following to handle such eventualities. Then we move onto the final calculations and display.

if **infile** is in the bad state, display an error message, close the files and quit
display on outfile the dashes line
display on outfile **totNumAdult**, **totNumChild**, **totNumSenior** and **totalCost**
let **grandTotalTicketsSold** = **totNumAdult** + **totNumChild** + **totNumSenior**
let **percentAdult** = **totNumAdult** * 100 / **grandTotalTicketsSold**
let **percentChild** = **totNumChild** * 100 / **grandTotalTicketsSold**
let **percentSenior** = **totNumSenior** * 100 / **grandTotalTicketsSold**
display on **outfile** the **percentAdult**, **percentChild**, **percentSenior**
let **avgCost** = **totalCost** / **grandTotalTicketsSold**
display on **outfile** the **avgCost**
close **infile** and **outfile**

With the simple sequence written, make up some test data and thoroughly desk check the solution to verify it works perfectly on paper. Then, code it into a C++ program. Notice how easily this one converts into C++. A good design makes programming much easier to do.

Here are the complete program and a test run.

Cs05a - Acme Ticket Sales Summary Program

```
/***************************************************************/
/*                                                             */
/* Cs05a Acme Ticket Sales Summary Program                     */
/*                                                             */
/***************************************************************/

#include <iostream>
#include <iomanip>
#include <fstream>
using namespace std;

int main () {

 // input fields
 int    numAdult;  // number adult tickets sold to this customer
 int    numChild;  // number child tickets sold to this customer
 int    numSenior; // number senior tickets sold to this customer
 double cost;      // total cost of this customer's tickets

 // calculation fields
```

```
int    totNumAdult = 0;  // total adult tickets sold
int    totNumChild = 0;  // total child tickets sold
int    totNumSenior = 0; // total senior tickets sold
double totalCost = 0;    // total cost of all tickets sold

// final totals and results
int    grandTotalTicketsSold;// total number of all tickets sold
double percentAdult;         // percent adult of total tickets
double percentChild;         // percent child of total tickets
double percentSenior;        // percent senior of total tickets
double avgCost;              // average cost of one ticket

// attempt to open the input file
ifstream infile ("trans-log.txt");
if (!infile) { // failed, so display an error message and quit
 cout << "Error: cannot open file trans-log.txt\n";
 return 1;
}

// attempt to open the output file
ofstream outfile ("results.txt");
if (!outfile) { // failed, so display error, close and quit
 cout << "Error: cannot open the output file results.txt\n";
 infile.close ();
 return 2;
}

// setup floating point format for output of dollars
outfile << fixed << setprecision (2);

// display heading line and two column heading lines
outfile << "      Acme Ticket Sales Summary Report\n\n"
        << "       Number of Tickets Sold    Total Cost\n"
        << "       Adult   Child   Senior    Of Tickets\n\n";

// try to get the first set of data
infile >> numAdult >> numChild >> numSenior >> cost;
if (!infile) { // fails, no data or bad data in the file
 cout << "Error: file is empty or has bad data in first line\n";
 infile.close ();
 outfile.close ();
 return 3;
}

// process all the input sets of data
while (infile) {
 // accumulate totals
 totNumAdult += numAdult;
 totNumChild += numChild;
 totNumSenior += numSenior;
 totalCost += cost;
 // display this set of data
 outfile << setw (12) << numAdult <<  setw (8) << numChild
```

```
          << setw (9)  << numSenior << "    $" << setw (7)
          << cost << endl;
  // input next set of data
  infile >> numAdult >> numChild >> numSenior >> cost;
 }
 if (!infile.eof()) { // oops, bad data encountered
  cout << "Error: bad data in the input file\n";
  infile.close ();
  outfile.close ();
  return 4;
 }

 // display first totals line
 outfile << "          ---     ---      ---    --------\n";
 outfile << "Totals:" << setw (5) << totNumAdult << setw (8)
         << totNumChild << setw (9) << totNumSenior
         << "    $" << setw (7) << totalCost << endl;

 // calculate and display the percentages line
 grandTotalTicketsSold = totNumAdult + totNumChild +totNumSenior;
 percentAdult = totNumAdult * 100. / grandTotalTicketsSold;
 percentChild = totNumChild * 100. / grandTotalTicketsSold;
 percentSenior = totNumSenior * 100. / grandTotalTicketsSold;
 outfile << setprecision (0);
 outfile << "Percents:" << setw (3) << percentAdult << "%"
         << setw (7) << percentChild << "%" << setw (8)
         << percentSenior << "%" << endl << endl;
 outfile << setprecision (2);

 // calculate and display the average cost of a ticket
 avgCost = totalCost / grandTotalTicketsSold;
 outfile << "Average cost of ticket:         $" << setw (7)
         << avgCost << endl;

 // close files
 infile.close ();
 outfile.close ();
 return 0;
}
```

results.txt from Cs05a - Acme Ticket Sales Summary Program

```
       Acme Ticket Sales Summary Report

        Number of Tickets Sold    Total Cost
        Adult   Child   Senior    Of Tickets

            2       2        2    $  42.00
            2       0        0    $  20.00
            1       8        0    $  30.00
            0       2        2    $  15.00
            2       0        0    $  20.00
```

```
                1          0          0      $  10.00
                1          2          0      $  15.00
                6          8          0      $  80.00
                2          0          0      $  20.00
               ---        ---        ---     --------
 Totals:       17         22          4      $ 252.00
 Percents:    40%        51%         9%

 Average cost of ticket:                     $   5.86
```

Since I stored the percentage results in a **double** and since the specifications called for no decimal points on the display of the percentages, I did not set the **ios::showpoint** flag this time. Thus, on line 98 when the precision is set to 0 digits, no decimal point results and the numbers are rounded to the nearest whole number. On line 102, the precision is set back to two digits for the next dollar amount.

Cs05b—Calculating N! (N factorial)

N! is commonly needed in equations, particularly in statistical type applications and probability calculations. If the user needs 5!, then we must calculate 5*4*3*2*1. In this problem, the user wishes to enter an integer and we are to display the factorial of that integer. For example, the user enters 5 and we must calculate 5! Here is the way the screen display is to appear.

```
Acme Factorial Program
Enter a number or -1 to quit: 5
5! = 120

Enter a number or -1 to quit: 4
4! = 24
```

Analyzing the problem a bit, two loops are going to be needed. The outer loop prompts and inputs the user's number. The inner loop does the actual factorial calculation. When designing a solution that involves nested looping as this one does, it is sometimes useful to design the outer loop first and make sure it works and then come back and design the inner loop.

The outer loop is responsible for the user input. Let's call the input value **number** and the result, **factor**. What kind of data ought **factor** be? If we make it only an **int**, then on some platforms the largest value is 32,767, which is not a very large n! value. So let's make it a **long**. If we knew that very large factorials needed to be calculated, then we could use a **double** and limit them to only 15 digits of accuracy. So make two main storage boxes for these two variables. (Since there are so few variables, I have omitted the figure of main storage this time.) Now let's design the program through the outer loop, leaving the actual details of how to calculate the factorial to last.

No files are required. One time only the title of the program is displayed. Then, a prompt and input loop is needed.

output the title
prompt "Enter a number or –1 to quit: "
input **number**
while (**number** is not equal to –1) do the following
  calculate factor
  output **number** and **factor** and double space
  prompt "Enter a number or –1 to quit: "
  input **number**
end the while loop

Okay. The main loop is simple enough. Now how do we calculate the factorial? Care must be taken here. 0! is defined to be 1. 1! = 1. We need to be able to handle all circumstances. What would the basic working line of this inner loop be? We can try something like

factor = **factor** * **term**

where **term** is the next number by which to multiply. Add a main storage box for **term**. Suppose we initialize **factor** to 1. Then, a loop can be used to calculate all terms above one until we have done number of them.

let **factor** = 1
let **term** = 2
while **term** is less than or equal to **number** do the following
  factor = **factor** * **term**
  term = **term** + 1
end the while loop

Will this work for all numbers whose results do not exceed what can fit in a **long** integer? Suppose the user enters a 0. Then, **factor** is set to 1 and **term** is 2, but the **while** test is **false** because **term** is not less than or equal to **number**. The answer in **factor** is 1, which is correct.

Now test it further. What is the result if the user enters a 1 or 2 or 3 or 4? Does it work correctly? It does. When we convert this inner loop into C++, a **for** loop can be used. We might have this short loop.

```
for (term=2; term <= number; term++)
  factor = factor * term;
```

This could be shortened to just

```
for (factor=1, term=2; term <= number; factor = factor * term++);
```

Here is the completed program. Notice the coding of the **for** loop.

```
Cs05b - Calculating N!
```

```
/***************************************************************/
/*                                                             */
/* Cs05b Calculation of N!                                     */
/*                                                             */
/***************************************************************/

#include <iostream>
#include <iomanip>
```

```
#include <fstream>
using namespace std;
int main () {

 long number; // the number to use to calculate its factorial
 long factor; // the factorial of the number

 long term;    // next term to use in the calculation

 // prompt and get the first number
 cout << "Enter a number or -1 to quit: ";
 cin >> number;

 while (number >= 0 && cin) {
  // calculate number factorial
  factor = 1;
  for (term=2; term <= number; term++) {
   factor *= term;
  }
  // the following is the short-cut version
  //for (term=2, factor=1; term <= number; factor *= term++);

  // output number and its factorial
  cout << number << "! = " << factor <<endl << endl;

  // get another number to do
  cout << "Enter a number or -1 to quit: ";
  cin >> number;
 }

 return 0;
}
```

Sample Run of Cs05b - Calculating N!

```
Enter a number or -1 to quit: 0
0! = 1

Enter a number or -1 to quit: 1
1! = 1

Enter a number or -1 to quit: 2
2! = 2

Enter a number or -1 to quit: 3
3! = 6

Enter a number or -1 to quit: 4
4! = 24

Enter a number or -1 to quit: 5
5! = 120
```

```

Enter a number or -1 to quit: -1
```

Section C: Engineering Examples

Engr05a—Summation of Infinite Polynomials

One major use of loops is to evaluate the summation of infinite series. Examine first the **Cs05b** N Factorial program just above. Sometimes summations are to be done over a finite range. For example, one might be asked what is the sum of the square roots of all the numbers from one to fifty.

$$\sum_{x=1}^{50} \sqrt{x} = \sqrt{1} + \sqrt{2} + \sqrt{3} + \ldots \sqrt{50}$$

However, often the summation is an infinite one, or rather it is an infinite series of terms or polynomials. From mathematical textbooks, the series expansion for the exponential function is

$$e^x = 1 + x + \frac{x^2}{2!} + \frac{x^3}{3!} + \ldots + \frac{x^n}{n!} + \ldots = \sum_{n=0}^{\infty} \frac{x^n}{n!}$$

Suppose that we needed to write a program to calculate e^x by adding up the sum of the terms. How would it be done? We need to formulate this into something that can be done inside a loop. What we need is to be able to say **sum = sum + term** within the loop. Thus, we need to find how to calculate the next term in the series. But wait; if we have just calculated say the $x^3/3!$ term and are going on to the $x^4/4!$ term, we are redoing nearly all the calculations! While this would work, it is horribly inefficient and wasteful of computer time. Instead, is there a way that we can calculate the next term based on the previous term?

Yes, there is. Examine the ratio of the n+1 term to the n term. It is

$$ratio = \frac{\dfrac{x^{n+1}}{(n+1)!}}{\dfrac{x^n}{n!}} = \frac{x^{n+1}}{(n+1)!} \cdot \frac{n!}{x^n} = x \frac{n!}{(n+1)n!} = \frac{x}{(n+1)}$$

And since (n+1)! = (n+1)n!, the ratio becomes just x/(n+1). In other words, the next term is equal to the previous term times x/(n+1). Okay. Let's see how this would work in a loop to calculate e^x. Assuming that **x** is a **double**, we can sketch

input **x**
let **sum** = 0

let **term** = 1
let **n** = 0
while (not sure what ending condition is yet) do the following
  sum = **sum** + **term**
  ratio = **x** / (**n**+1)
  term = **term** * **ratio**
  n = **n** + 1
end the **while**

Since this looks good so far, make up main storage boxes for **x**, **sum**, **term** and **n**. All we have to do is determine how to end the loop. Main Storage is shown in Figure 5.4.

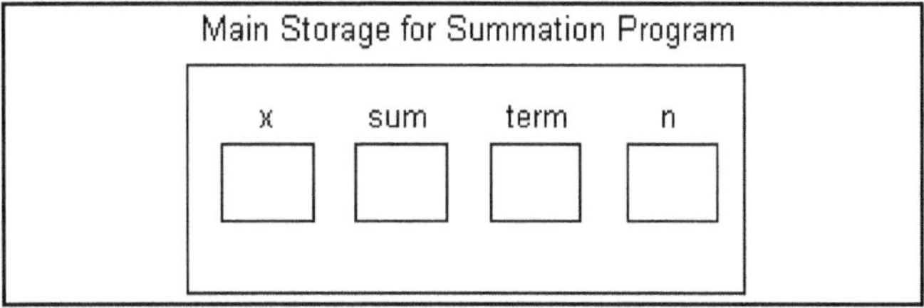

Figure 5.4 Main Storage for Summation Program

Now mathematically speaking, this process must be carried out to infinity to produce the precise identity of e^x. However, nothing on the computer can go to infinity—that would be an infinite loop. Here is where numerical analysis on a computer diverges from pure mathematics. If **n** is sufficiently large, the divisor (**n!**) becomes so large that from that **term** onwards no appreciable amount is added into the **sum**. This is called a **converging series**. The opposite is called a **diverging series**, such as the sum from one to infinity of x; in this case, x just keeps on getting bigger and bigger.

Since the series is converging, there will come a point at which the next term is so small that it can be neglected and we are done. The question is "what is the desired degree of accuracy that we need for e^x?" The answer is that it depends on the problem we are solving. If the desired degree of accuracy, often called the **error precision** or **eps**, is not specified, .000001 is commonly assumed.

Realize that numerical methods are nearly always going to give an approximate answer or rather it gives an answer sufficiently accurate for our needs. The ending condition in this case is given by the following.

```
while (term > .000001)
```

However, one should always bulletproof coding to guard against unexpected events, such as a slight mis-coding of the series in this example. If we make an error in calculating the ratio or the next term, then it is possible that by accident we now have a diverging series. That means, our ending test condition would never be met and our program would execute forever until we manually abort it.

Rule. In numerical analysis, always provide a backdoor way for a loop to end if it does not find an answer.

In this problem, **n** begins at 0 and works its way steadily up by 1 through each iteration of the loop. The significance of **n** is that we are evaluating **n!** and for large values of **n**, the term must become smaller and smaller as **n** increases. A backdoor shut down might also be to stop the loop if **n** becomes sufficiently large. If **n** was say 100, then 100! is quite large.

100! =
93326215443944152681699238856266700490715968264381621468592963895217599993229
9156089414639761565182862536979208272237582511852109168640000000000000000000000
00

If we divide by that number (100!), that term has to be infinitesimal in this case. So the loop now should have two ways to terminate

```
while (n < 100 && term > .000001)
```

Here are the completed program and a sample run.

Engr05a - Finding e to x by Summation

```
/***************************************************************/
/*                                                             */
/* Engr05a Calculate e to the x power using summation technique*/
/*                                                             */
/***************************************************************/

#include <iostream>
#include <iomanip>
#include <cmath>
using namespace std;

int main () {

 double x;       // the number to use
 double sum;     // holds the result of e to x
 double term;    // next term in the series
 double ratio;   // multiplicative factor to get next term
 int    n;       // the current term to do

 // setup floating point output for 6 digits of accuracy
 cout << fixed << setprecision (6);

 // prompt and input the user's value
 cout << "Enter the number to use or Ctrl-Z to quit: ";
 cin >> x;

 // loop through all the user's values
 while (cin) {
  // reset to initial starting point
  sum = 0;
  term = 1;
  n = 0;
```

```

   // permit 100 tries to get it accurate to .000001
   while (n < 100 && term > .000001) {
    sum += term;          // add in this term
    ratio = x / (n + 1); // find next term to use
    term = term * ratio;
    n++;
   }

   // display results
   if (n >= 100) { // check for diverging result
    cout << "Error: after " << n
         << " tries, the result is not sufficiently accurate\n"
        << "The series might be diverging. The result so far is\n"
         << sum << endl << "The built-in function yields\n"
         << exp (x) << endl << endl;
   }
   else { // converged result
    cout << "e to x = " << sum << " and was found after "
         << n << " iterations\nThe built-in function yields "
         << exp (x) << endl << endl;
   }

   // get the next user's value to calculate
   cout << "Enter the number to use or Ctrl-Z to quit: ";
   cin >> x;
  }

  return 0;
}
```

```
Sample Run of Engr05a - Finding e to x by Summation
```

```
Enter the number to use or Ctrl-Z to quit: 2
e to x = 7.389056 and was found after 14 iterations
The built-in function yields 7.389056

Enter the number to use or Ctrl-Z to quit: 20
e to x = 485165195.409790 and was found after 65 iterations
The built-in function yields 485165195.409790

Enter the number to use or Ctrl-Z to quit: 42
Error: after 100 tries, the result is not sufficiently accurate
The series might be diverging. The result so far is
1739274941520462800.000000
The built-in function yields
1739274941520501000.000000

Enter the number to use or Ctrl-Z to quit: ^Z
```

Notice that I also displayed the value given by the built-in function **exp()**. In the sample run, I purposely entered an **x** value of 42 to generate a giant result. In that case, we have 13 digits correct after 100 iterations, clearly more are needed when the value of **x** is large.

Engr05b—Artillery Shell Trajectory

An artillery shell is fired from a howitzer at a velocity of V at some angle. If we ignore air friction and the curvature of the earth, the path of the projectile is a parabola. At any point in its flight, the shell's coordinates with respect to the firing point are

$$y(t) = V_y t + .5 g t^2$$

$$x(t) = V_x t$$

where

$$V_x = V \cos \theta$$

$$V_y = V \sin \theta$$

Here, g is the gravitational acceleration or –32 feet/sec/sec in this coordinate system. The problem is to plot the trajectory until the shell hits. That is, display successive values of x, y and t until the projectile hits. Since the number of lines can be lengthy, write the results to a file called **results.txt**.

In this problem, could easily be solved mathematically. However, let's do it iteratively to illustrate some additional looping techniques. The variables are **x**, **y**, **V**, **angle**, **Vx**, **Vy** and **g** (gravitational acceleration). To convert the angle into radians, we need **PI** and a variable **rangle** to hold it along with **t** for time and **outfile** for the file. Main Storage is shown in Figure 5.5.

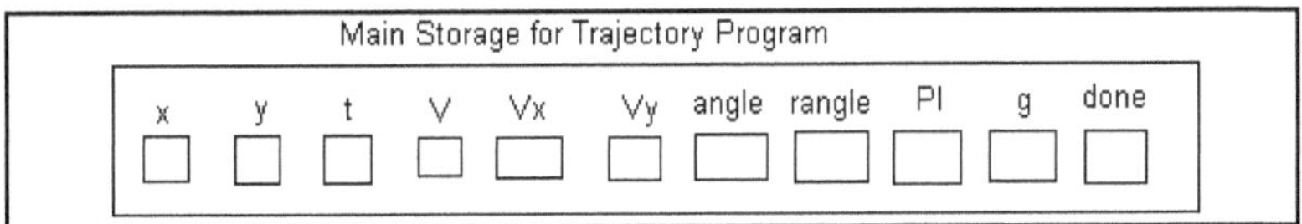

Figure 5.5 Main Storage for Shell Trajectory Program

Calculating the current coordinates as a function of time is the iterative approach that I use in this problem. Time begins at 0; with each iteration, time is incremented by one second. A new position is calculated using this new time and written to the output file. The beginning design is

open **outfile** using the filename "results.txt" and display an error msg if it fails
prompt and input **V** and **angle**
while there is a set of values to use
    display to **outfile** **V** and **angle**
    let **t** = 1
    rangle = **angle** * **PI** / 180
    calculate the **Vx** as **V** cos (**rangle**) and **Vy** as **V** sin (**rangle**) components

while (some ending condition as yet unknown) do the following
calculate **x** and **y**
display to **outfile** **x**, **y**, and **t**
increment **t** by one second
end the inner **while**
prompt and input the **V** and **angle**
end the outer **while**
close **outfile**

This is a simple design. But how do we know when to end the loop? It must be when the projectile has landed. When a shell has landed, the **y** value becomes zero or negative. This suggests that we could use **while (y>0)**. However, at the starting point in the above solution, **y** has not yet been calculated. We could set **y** to some positive value initially just to force the test condition to permit the loop to be entered the first time.

Since some problems that we may want to solve have very complex ending criteria, which are hard to express in a single test condition, I use a different approach here. Suppose that we also define a variable called **done** and set it to 0. Let the test condition be **while (!done)**. It does read well. Inside the loop after **y** is found, we can then check the ending criteria. If **y** is zero or less, set **done** to 1. On the next iteration, the loop ends. This is a useful technique if the ending criteria are complex. Note that **done** could also be a **bool** variable.

Here are the completed program and a sample test run.

Engr05b - Plotting the Trajectory of a Projectile

```
/***************************************************************/
/*                                                             */
/* Engr05b Plotting the trajectory of an artillery shell       */
/*                                                             */
/***************************************************************/

#include <iostream>
#include <iomanip>
#include <cmath>
#include <fstream>
using namespace std;
int main () {

 double V;     // velocity of the shell as it leaves the howitzer
 double angle; // the initial angle of the firing

 double x;     // position of the shell as a function of time
 double y;
 long   t;     // time in seconds since the firing

 double Vx;    // velocity along the x axis
 double Vy;    // velocity along the y axis
```

```
double rangle;  // angle in radians
const double PI = acos (-1.);
const double g = -32.2;
ofstream outfile ("results.txt");
if (!outfile) {
 cout << "Error: cannot open output file\n";
 return 1;
}
// setup floating point output for 2 digits of accuracy
outfile << fixed << setprecision (2);
// prompt and input the initial velocity and angle
cout << "Enter the initial velocity (feet/sec)\n"
     << "and the angle in degrees (0-90)\n"
     << "or Ctrl-Z to quit\n";
cin >> V >> angle;
// loop through all the user's test firings
while (cin) {
 // display initial settings
 outfile << endl << "Trajectory of a shell fired at "
         << setw (5) << angle << " degrees\n"
         << "With initial velocity of "
         << setw (10) << V << " feet/sec\n\n"
         << "     Time         X           Y\n\n";
 // calculate initial Vx and Vy
 rangle = angle * PI / 180;
 Vx = V * cos (rangle);
 Vy = V * sin (rangle);
 t = 1;           // initialize time
 int done = 0;    // done will be non-zero when shell lands
 while (!done) {  // repeat until shell lands
  // calculate new position
  x = Vx * t;
  y = Vy * t + .5 * g * t * t;
  // display new position on report
  outfile <<setw(8)<< t << setw(12) << x << setw(12) << y<<endl;
  // check for ending criteria
  if (y <= 0)
   done = 1;   // will terminate loop
  else
   t++;        // add one second for next position
 }
 // prompt for next attempt
 cout << "Enter the initial velocity (feet/sec)\n"
      << "and the angle in degrees (0-90)\n"
      << "or Ctrl-Z to quit\n";
 cin >> V >> angle;
}
```

```
 outfile.close ();
 return 0;
}
```

```
Sample output from Engr05b - Plotting the Trajectory of a Projectile
```

```

Trajectory of a shell fired at 10.00 degrees
With initial velocity of     1000.00 feet/sec

     Time          X            Y

        1       984.81       157.55
        2      1969.62       282.90
        3      2954.42       376.04
        4      3939.23       436.99
        5      4924.04       465.74
        6      5908.85       462.29
        7      6893.65       426.64
        8      7878.46       358.79
        9      8863.27       258.73
       10      9848.08       126.48
       11     10832.89       -37.97
```

Design Exercises

1. Write a short loop that inputs integers from the user and sums them until the user enters any negative number. When the loop ends, display the sum of the numbers and the average value of the numbers that were entered.

2. The migration flight of a flock of birds has been observed by scientists. From data returned by electronic tracking devices attached to the birds' legs, they have created a file consisting of the number of miles traveled each day by the birds. The first line in **migrate.txt** is the number of days of observations. Each subsequent line consists of the miles traveled that day. For example, if the first number in the file is 30, then there are 30 lines after that first line representing the number of miles traveled each day. Write the pseudocode to input the file and compute the average daily distance the birds have traveled.

Stop! Do These Exercises Before Programming

Correct all errors in these programs. The first six illustrate different basic methods of creating the input looping process. However, they contain one or more errors. When you correct them, do NOT just convert them all to a single method—retain the intended input method. In other words, on the first three problems, the **while** loop was intended to not only input the values but also to control the looping process. Problems 4, 5 and 6 use a different method; they should not be rewritten as duplicates of Problem 1.

1. This program is to input pairs of integers from a file called **integers.txt**.

```
#include <iostream>
#include <fstream>
using namespace std;
int main(){
 ifstream infile;
 if (infile) {
  cout << "Error cannot open file integers.txt\n"
  return 1;
 }
 int i, j;
 while (infile << i << j) {
  process them and output results
  ...
 }
 infile.close ();
 return 0;
}
```

2. This program is to input pairs of integers from a file called **d:\testdata\data.txt**.

```
#include <iostream>
#include <fstream>
using namespace std;
int main(){
 ifstream infile ("d:\testdata\data.txt");
 if (!infile) {
  cout << "Error cannot open file data.txt\n"
  return 1;
 }
 int i, j;
 while (infile >> i >> j) {
  process them and output results
  ...
 }
 infile.close ();
 return 0;
}
```

3. This program is to input pairs of integers from a file called **inputdata.txt**.

```
#include <iostream>
#include <fstream>
using namespace std;
int main(){
 ifstream infile ("inputdata.txt");
 if (!infile) {
  cout << "Error cannot open file inputdata.txt\n"
  return 1;
 }
```

```
 int i, j;
 while (cin >> i >> j) {
  process them and output results
  ...
 }
 infile.close ();
 return 0;
}
```

4. This program is to input pairs of integers from a file called **filedata.txt**.

```
#include <iostream>
#include <fstream>
using namespace std;
int main(){
 ifstream infile ("filedata.txt"
 if (!infile) {
  cout << "Error cannot open filedata.txt\n"
  return 1;
 }
 int i, j;
 infile >> i >> j;
 while (infile) {
  infile  >> i >> j
  process them and output results
  ...
 }
 infile.close ();
 return 0;
}
```

5. This program is to input pairs of integers from a file called **filedata.txt**.

```
#include <iostream>
#include <fstream>
using namespace std;
int main(){
 ifstream infile ("filedata.txt");
 if (!infile) {
  cout << "Error cannot open filedata.txt\n"
  return 1;
 }
 int i, j;
 while (cin) {
  process them and output results
  ...
  infile  >> i >> j
 }
```

```
 infile.close ();
 return 0;
}
```

6. This program is to input pairs of integers from a file called **filedata.txt**.

```
#include <iostream>
#include <fstream>
using namespace std;
int main(){
 ifstream infile ("filedata.txt");
 if (!infile) {
  cout << "Error cannot open filedata.txt\n"
  return 1;
 }
 int i, j;
 while (infile.good());{
  infile  >> i >> j
  process them and output results
  ...
 }
 infile.close ();
 return 0;
}
```

The next four questions refer to this short program. Note the user enters CTL-Z to signal the end of file or input.

```
#include <iostream>
using namespace std;
int main(){
 int i, j;
 while (cin >> i >> j)
  cout << i << " " << j << " ";
 return 0;
}
```

7. What is the output if this is the input: 5 6 7 8 CTRL-Z

8. What is the output if this is the input: 5 6 A 7 8 CTRL-Z

9. What is the output if this is the input: 1 2 3.4 5 6 CTRL-Z

10. What is the output if this is the input: 1 2 3 A 5 6 CTRL-Z

11. A programmer wrote this program to input five numbers from the user. What is wrong with this program? How can it be fixed?

```
#include <iostream>
using namespace std;
int main(){
 double number;  // number from user
 int    count;   // stop after 5 numbers inputted
 while (count <= 5) {
  cout << "Enter a number: ";
  cin >> number;
  count++;
 }
```

12. Since the previous version did not work, he rewrote it believing this version would input five numbers from the user. What is wrong with this program? How can it be fixed?

```
#include <iostream>
using namespace std;
int main(){
 double number;  // number from user
 int    count;   // stop after 5 numbers inputted
 for (count=1; count<6; count++) {
  cout << "Enter a number: ";
  cin >> number;
  count++;
 }
```

13. Since the first two versions did not work, he then tried to write this program to input five numbers from the user. What is wrong with this program? How can it be fixed?

```
#include <iostream>
using namespace std;
int main(){
 double number;  // number from user
 int    count;   // stop after 5 numbers inputted
 do {
  cout << "Enter a number: ";
  cin >> number;
 } while (count < 6);
```

14. This program is supposed to write the sum of the odd integers from one to fifty to the file **sum.txt**. What is wrong with it? How can it be fixed?

```
#include <fstream>
using namespace std;
int main(){
 ofstream outfile ("sum.txt"
```

```
 if (!outfile) {
  cout << "Error cannot open sum.txt\n"
  return 1;
 }
 int j = 1, sum;
 while (j < 50) {
  sum += j;
  j++;
 }
 cout << sum << endl
 return 0;
}
```

15. What is printed by this program?

```
#include <iostream>
#include <iomanip>
using namespace std;
int main(){
 int a = 5;
 while (a) {
  cout << a << endl;
  --a;
 }
 cout << a << endl;
 return 0;
}
```

16. What is printed by this program where the decrement has been moved into the test condition as a postfix decrement?

```
#include <iostream>
#include <iomanip>
using namespace std;
int main(){
 int a = 5;
 while (a--) {
  cout << a << endl;
 }
 cout << a << endl;
 return 0;
}
```

17. What is printed by this program where the decrement has been moved into the test condition as a prefix decrement?

```
#include <iostream>
#include <iomanip>
```

```
using namespace std;
int main(){
 int a = 5;
 while (--a) {
  cout << a << endl;
 }
 cout << a << endl;
 return 0;
}
```

Programming Problems

Problem Cs05-1—Roots Table

The user wishes to make a table of square roots and cube roots for whole numbers from one to some upper value that the user chooses. Write a program that prompts and inputs the user's choice of an upper limit. Then, from one to that number, display the current number, square root, and cube root of that current number. Display the results in columns as shown:

```
Number   Square Root   Cube Root
   1        1.0000       1.0000
   2        1.4142       .....
```

and so on through the number entered by the user. Repeat the process until the user enters a negative number or a zero.

Problem Cs05-2—Series Summation—Fibonacci Sequence

Write a program to sum the series given by

1, 1, 2, 3, 5, 8, 13, 21, 34, 55, ...

This is called the Fibonacci sequence. The first two numbers are one. Each one after that is the sum of the two preceding numbers. Thus, the fourth number is 2 + 1; the fifth number is 2 + 3; the eighth number is 8 + 13.

Prompt the user to enter an integer to which to find the Fibonacci number. Then display the result. Continue until the user enters a zero or negative number to quit. Test your program with this test run.

```
Enter a number (0 or negative to quit): 10<cr>
Fibonacci (10) = 55
Enter a number (0 or negative to quit): 3<cr>
Fibonacci (3) = 2
Enter a number (0 or negative to quit): 9<cr>
Fibonacci (9) = 34
Enter a number (0 or negative to quit): 1<cr>
```

```
Fibonacci (1) = 1
Enter a number (0 or negative to quit): 20<cr>
Fibonacci (20) = 6765
Enter a number (0 or negative to quit): 0<cr>
```

Problem Cs05-3—Programming Your CD Changer

You are holding a dance party next Friday night and you need to get 60 minutes of music lined up to play. The CD player can be programmed with a sequence of songs to play one after another. The objective is to write a program to generate a play list to be used to program the CD player. The input file consists of one line per song you have chosen. Each song line contains the song number and the song's total play time as two integers, minutes and seconds.

As each song is input, display its information on the output report along with the total accumulated play time after that song is finished. However, should that song force a total play time to exceed 60 minutes, print an error message and terminate the program.

The output should appear something like this.

```
          Proposed CD Play List
Song    Song Time           Total Play Time
Number  Minutes   Seconds   Minutes Seconds
------  -------   -------   ------- -------
  1        2        44         2      44
  2        3        16         6      00
```

Test the program with the two test data files provided, **SongTest1.txt** and **SongTest2.txt**.

Problem Cs05-4—Acme Sales Report

Write a program to input and display a sales file. Each input line contains an integer ID number and a sales amount. When the end of the file occurs, print the high sales amount and the number of times that amount occurred. Print also the second highest sales amount and the number of times that one occurred. Print the results like this:

```
Acme Sales Report
 ID       Sales

9999    $9999.00
9999    $9999.00
9999    $9999.00
9999    $9999.00
High sales amount: $9999.99 occurs: 99 times.
Second highest sales amount: $9999.99 occurs: 99 times.
```

Test your program with the provided data files: **sales1.txt**, **sales2.txt** and **sales3.txt**. Be sure to verify the accuracy of your program output. The program should make only one pass through the file to determine the results. Do not close and reopen or otherwise read in the file a second time in order to find the second high sales and count. One pass through the file should result in both sets of results. Hint: pseudocode out the logic needed to determine the highest and second highest vales. Then thoroughly desk check it before coding the solution.

Problem Engr05-1—The Great Motorcycle Jump

A well-known daredevil stunt man is planning a spectacular canyon jump on his motorcycle. After staring at the canyon and its walls, he has asked you for help in determining how to set up the jump. Assume that the air drag is proportional to his velocity, where k is the proportional constant. The following equations determine his position (x = horizontal distance, y = height) as a function of time, t.

$$x = \frac{V_0 \cos(a)}{k}(1 - e^{-kt})$$

$$y = \frac{-g}{k}t + \frac{1}{k}\left(V_0 \sin(a) + \frac{g}{k}\right)\left(1 - e^{-kt}\right)$$

where g is acceleration due to gravity of 32.2 ft/sec/sec, V_0 is the initial takeoff speed, a is the angle of takeoff from the ramp and k is the air drag constant of 0.15.

The canyon is 1000 feet across and 100 feet deep. The ramp is 20 feet high at the takeoff point. Note the trig functions require the angle to be in radians.

Write a program that prompts and inputs the initial values for the takeoff speed and angle (in degrees) at time zero as he leaves the top of the 20-ft. high jump ramp. Print heading lines identifying the input values for this case and then a column heading for distance, height, and seconds. Then, print out three values, x, y, and t in formatted columns of data, as t varies from zero by .5 second intervals. Stop the loop when either he makes it successfully to the other side displaying "Successful Jump" or he crashes displaying "Crash."

Then, allow the user to restart by entering another set of takeoff parameters and repeat the process. When the user enters a takeoff speed of –1, terminate the program. Test the program with these three test cases.

v = 330 ft/sec at a = 45 degrees
v = 200 ft/sec at a = 45 degrees
v = 260 ft/sec at a = 40 degrees

Hint: Draw a figure illustrating the problem; note carefully the origin of the coordinate system that the equations are using. Then, determine the ending conditions; there are more than one.

Extra Credit: determine whether the stuntman lands at the bottom of the canyon or hits the side of the canyon. (I'm not sure which would be preferable!)

Problem Engr05-2—A Summation of an Infinite Series

The value of e can be found from the series

$$e = 1 + \frac{1}{1} + \frac{1}{2!} + \frac{1}{3!} + \ldots \frac{1}{n!} \ldots$$

Determine the ratio of the $(n+1)^{th}$ term to the nth term. Then write a program that uses this equation to calculate the value of e. Prompt and input the desired degree of accuracy desired. The user might enter the desired accuracy or error precision as 1.0E-10. After finding the value of e to that desired degree of accuracy, repeat the process until the user enters a 0 or a negative number. Also quit that specific summation, if there have been 3000 iterations with no solution yet. Display the value of e and the number of iterations it took like this.

```
Enter the Accuracy of e or 0 to quit: 1.0e-5<cr>
e = 2.71828 (with 9999 iterations required)

Enter the Accuracy of e or 0 to quit: 1.0e-9<cr>
e = 2.718281828 (with 9999 iterations required)

Enter the Accuracy of e or 0 to quit: 0<cr>
```

Problem Engr05-3—Diode Current Flow (Electrical Engineering)

The current flow through a semiconductor diode is given by

$$i_d = I_0\left(e^{\frac{qv_d}{kT}} - 1\right)$$

where i_d is the current flow through the diode in amps, v_d is the voltage across the diode in volts, I_0 is the leakage current of the diode in amps, q is the charge on an electron of $1.602\text{x}10^{-19}$, k is Boltzmann's constant of $1.38\text{x}10^{-23}$ J/K and T is the temperature of the diode in kelvin. Assume that the leakage current is 2.0 microamps (10^{-6} amps). The temperature in kelvin is given by

$$T_k = \frac{5}{9}(T_F - 32) + 273.15$$

Write a program that prompts and inputs the temperature in Fahrenheit of the diode. Using a columnar form of output showing voltage and current, calculate and display the current flowing through the diode for voltages ranging from –1.0 through +0.8 volts in .02 volt steps. Repeat the entire process until the user enters a –1 for the temperature. Test your program with these temperatures: 75, 100 and 125 degrees Fahrenheit. Note the results are very small values.

Chapter 6 —Writing Your Own Functions

Section A: Basic Theory

Introduction

As programs become longer and do more sophisticated actions, **main()** functions tend to exceed even a printed page. One must scroll many screens just to view the entirety of the program. The more one has to scroll to view the function, the greater the chance for errors and the more difficult it is for someone to read the code. It is my own observation based on over thirty years in this business that the chance for errors is non-linear as the number of lines in a function increase. With new programmers, my guess is that it is nearly exponential.

The industry has adopted the guideline that no function, or module as they are sometimes called, should ever exceed fifty lines of code. Of course, programmers immediately ask: does that include variable definitions or even comment lines? My answer is "try to keep the whole function, counting every line, to one screen—no scrolling, in other words." I have found that when a programmer can see the entirety of a function on the screen, the chance for errors drops significantly.

We have been using many of C++'s built-in functions, such as **sqrt()**, **sin()**, **acos()**, **pow()**, and so on. C++ encourages you to develop your own functions to break the more complex activities down into more manageable units. In fact, this idea of breaking the total workload down into smaller pieces is a fundamental design principle of modern programming. The general term to describe this process of breaking a complex problem down into more manageable units is **functional decomposition**. One of the simplest design tools to assist functionally decomposing a problem is **Top-down Design**.

This chapter begins with a discussion of the principles of Top-Down design. Once a problem can be broken down into functional modules or just functions, and then the principles of how to write C++ functions are thoroughly presented. Since the topic is extremely broad, two chapters are devoted to writing our own functions.

Principles of Top-Down Design

The Cycle of Data Processing has been our workhorse for designing programs up to this point. Nearly every program you write inputs a set of data, processes that set of data in some way, outputs that set of data and/or results and then repeats the process until there are no more sets of data. However, as problems become more complex, the volume of instructions involved increases rapidly. Sometimes the process a set of data operation can involve a huge number of instructions. Top-Down Design provides a logical method for breaking complex problems down into more manageable units, called modules or functions.

The basic principle of Top-Down Design, or functional decomposition as it is sometimes called, begins with a statement of the problem to be solved. Let's take a simple non-data processing problem to illustrate the principles. The problem to solve is to "Bake a Loaf of Bread." Draw a top box around this statement. Notice that each statement must contain one and only one verb and one and only one object of that verb. The problem to solve is not "Bake a Loaf of Bread and Vacuuming the House and Tuning Up the Car." That is one common mistake—each statement must contain one action to do on one thing. Confusion results with a program that tries to do the daily sales report, update the master file, and print monthly bills. These represent three separate programs.

You can have all the adjectives, adverbs, and prepositional phrases desired. For example, "Bake a loaf of pumpernickel bread quickly." Use only one verb and object of that verb. You are after one specific function, one action to do per box.

Next, ask yourself "What broad, large scale actions must I do to accomplish the task in the top box?" In this case, I would have Gather Materials, Mix Ingredients and Bake Bread as the major steps needed to Bake a loaf of bread. Draw a box for each of these and connect them to the top box. Our solution so far appears as shown in Figure 6.1.

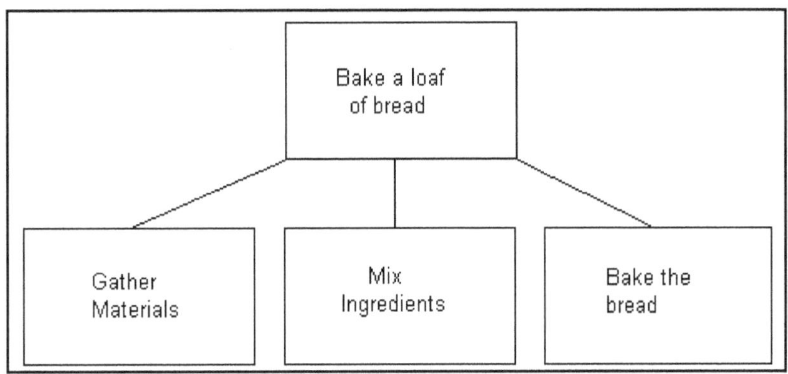

Figure 6.1 Initial Top-Down Design to Bake a Loaf of Bread

One level of the break down is complete when you ask "If I Gather Materials, Mix Ingredients, and Bake Bread, have I accomplished 'Bake a Loaf of Bread'?" and the answer is yes. Then, focus on one of the subordinate boxes, Gather Materials. Now ask, "What do I need to do in order to accomplish that?" My solution requires a breakdown into two functions: Get Ingredients and

Get Utensils. Mix Ingredients requires three functions: Make milk mixture, Mix dry ingredients, Do a final mix. The solution now is shown in Figure 6.2.

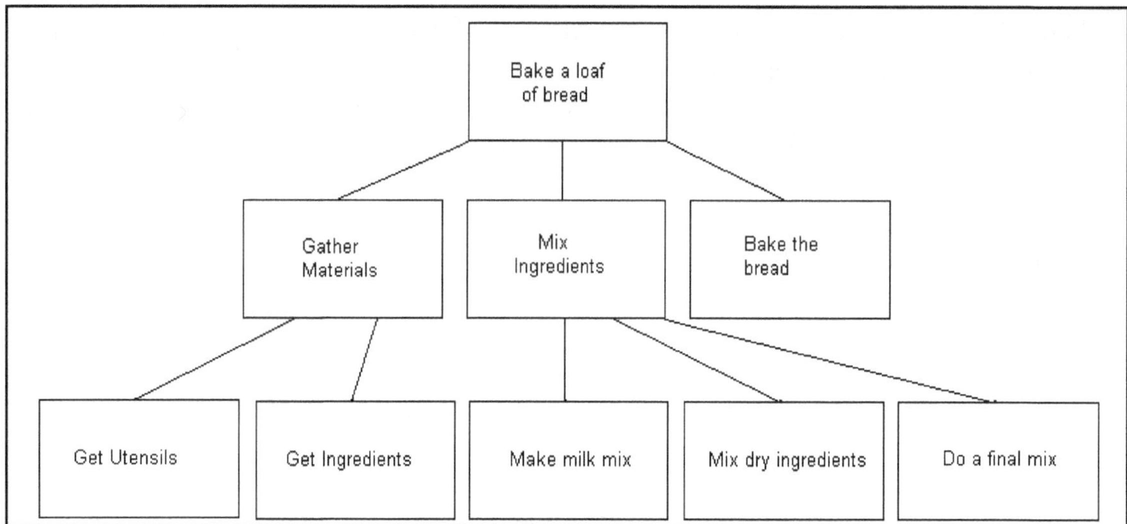

Figure 6.2 Complete Top-Down Design for Make a Loaf of Bread

At this point, we have decomposed Gather Materials and Mix Ingredients into the subfunctions that are needed to accomplish those tasks. When do you stop decomposing, breaking a box or function down into smaller steps? The answer is simple. The time to stop breaking a function down further occurs when you can envision in your head the simple sequence of steps that a box or function requires.

The Bake Bread function is not broken down because it represents the simple sequence of actually doing the baking, such as: turn on the oven, set to 350°, when preheated, insert pans, set timer for 45 minutes and so on. Likewise, as we look at each of the remaining lower level boxes, each one represents a simple sequence. Well, perhaps your solution might need another function below Get Ingredients, such as Go to the Store.

A Top-Down Design solution represents an optimum solution to the problem at hand. Each of the boxes represents a function or module in the program. Each box should be a simple sequence of instructions or steps to accomplish that smaller task. Certainly each box or function should be significantly less than the industry guideline of 50 lines of code per module.

There are two common errors one can make when functionally decomposing a problem. The first is omitting a function. Actually, this is rather common. Sometimes when the design is being converted into the actual program coding, changes need to be made to the design because of aspects that were not thought about initially. This is really not an error, just add onto the design as needed. Often the design can be evolutionary.

The second error is the single most commonly made error even by experienced programmers. The design error is shown in Figure 6.3.

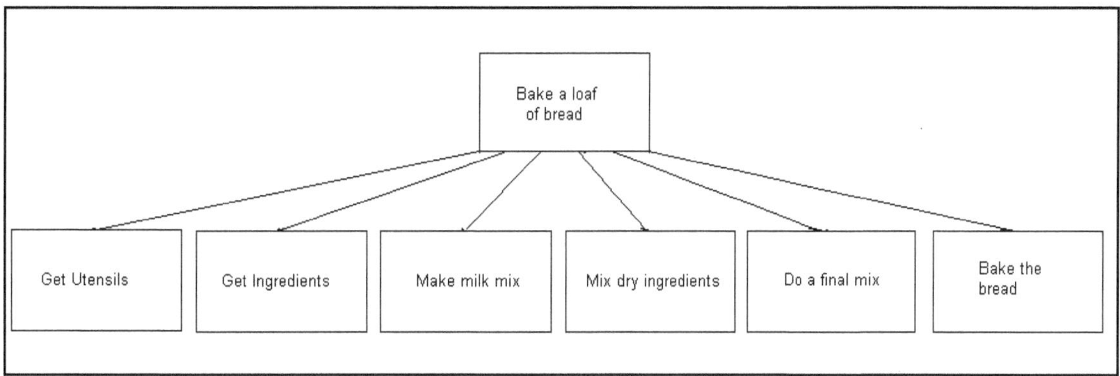

Figure 6.3 A Common Top-Down Design Error

The error is jumping from a clean statement of the problem immediately into ALL of the details needed to solve the problem, omitting all the higher-level functions or abstractions. You can spot this person a mile away. You give them a problem to solve, and at once, they are totally enmeshed in all of the details. Ah, to solve this one, you need to do this and this and that and that and this and on and on. They see all the trees in the forest at once, and the problem sure looks huge and unconfrontable to them. What is missed is taking a more general look first. What are the major steps needed? It is rather like peeling an onion; you design layer by layer.

Let's do another non-data processing example. Suppose on your way to class you have a flat tire. So the problem to solve is Change a Flat Tire. There are numerous solutions to this problem including ignoring it and continuing to drive on to class. However, let's design an optimum solution. Begin with a top box, which contains a clean statement of the problem, Change a Flat Tire. Now peel the onion. Ask what major functions need to be done? Get the Materials (such as a spare tire and tools), Change the Tire, Put Tools Away, Clean Self Up and Take Tire To Be Fixed might represent the first layer of the design shown in Figure 6.4.

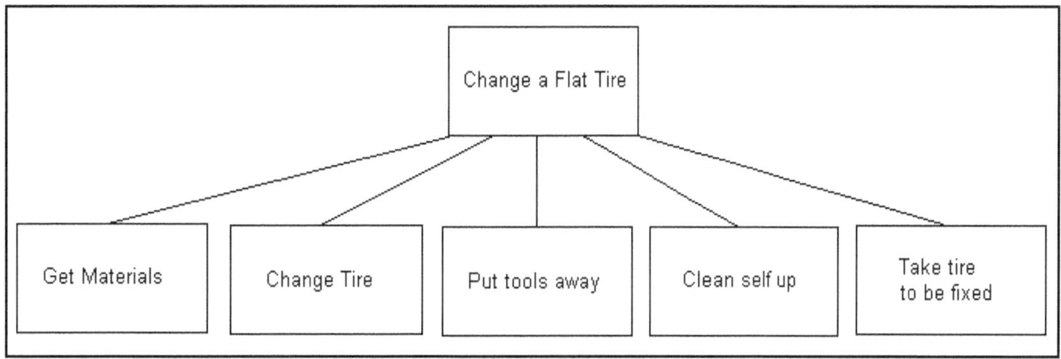

Figure 6.4 Initial Top-Down Design to Change a Flat Tire

Next, concentrate on just one of the subfunctions and break that one down. For example, Get Materials involve Get Tools and Get Spare Tire. Similarly, Change Tire can be broken down into these functions: Jack Up the Car, Remove Flat, Install New Tire and Lower Car. The other functions would not need to be further broken down, assuming that you have a spare tire in the car. The final design is shown in Figure 6.5.

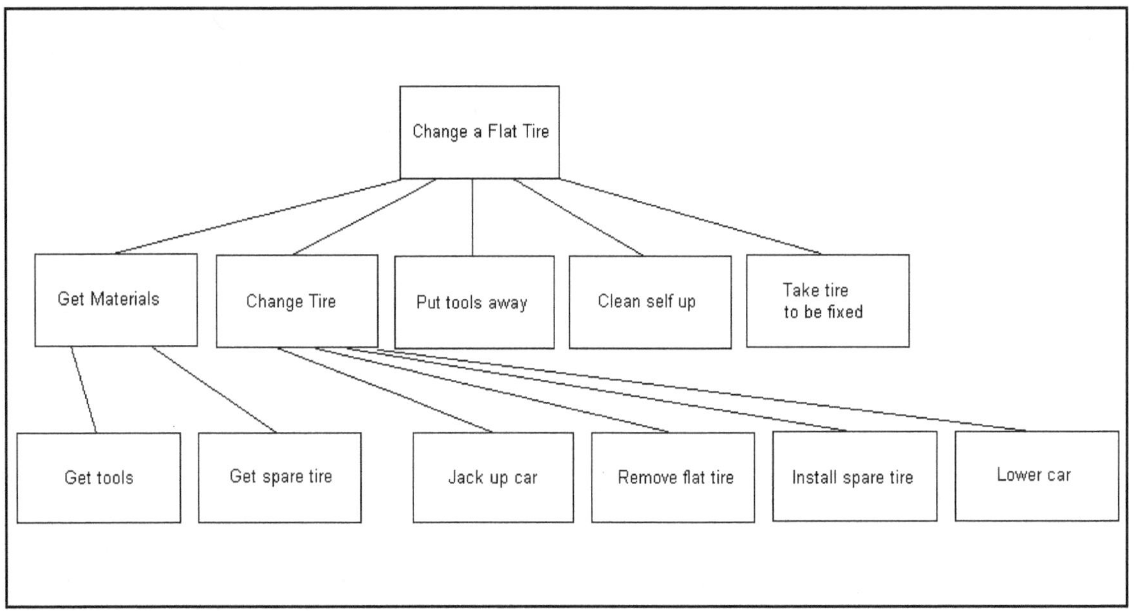

Figure 6.5 Complete Top-Down Design to Fix a Flat Tire

Try your hand at creating a Top-Down Design for these problems.
1. Cook dinner for four, two of which are your parents.
2. Tune-up the engine of a car.
3. Photograph a model for a magazine cover.
4. Prepare an income tax return.
5. Do laundry for a family of five.

Writing your own functions

Each box in the Top-Down Design represents one function in the program. The top box is the **main()** function. For the first example of writing our own functions, let's take an overly simple one in which the coding should be obvious. Suppose that the **main()** function had defined two **double**s, **x** and **y**. Further, **main()** wishes to store the larger of the two numbers in a **double** called **bigger**. It should be obvious that this could be done with a simple If-Then-Else statement. But to illustrate how to write functions, let's say that we need a function called **higher()** whose purpose is to return the larger of two numbers. The Top-Down Design for this program is shown in Figure 6.6.

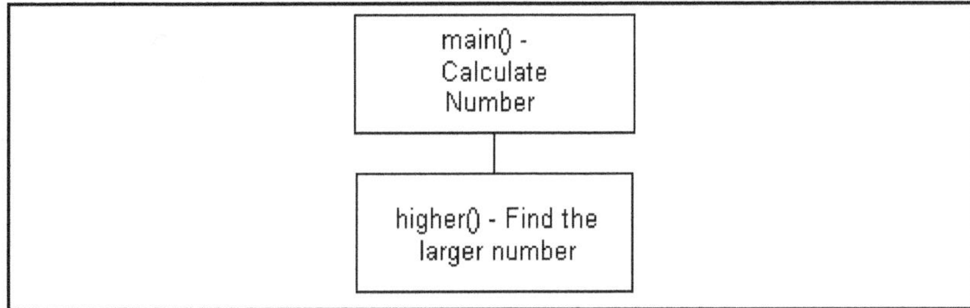

Figure 6.6 Top-Down Design for Higher Program

Here is the main program up to the point where the new function **higher()** is needed.

```
#include <iostream>
#include <iomanip>
using namespace std;

int main () {
 double x;         // a number entered by user
 double y;         // a second number entered by user
 double bigger;    // a place to store the larger of x and y

 cout << "Enter two numbers: ";
 cin >> x >> y;

 bigger = ....
```

Writing your own functions is a simple task if you follow the procedure step by step.

Step A. Define the Function's Prototype

Every function in C++ must have a prototype, model, or blueprint for the compiler to use when it needs to call or invoke that function. Knowing a function's prototype enables the compiler to handle any necessary data conversions. For example, in this problem, both the two numbers are **doubles**. Our function should expect to receive a pair of **doubles** as its parameters. If we passed a pair of integers instead, the compiler can automatically convert the integers into temporary **doubles** and pass the correct data.

If one did not use a prototype, then the compiler would have no choice but to pass the pair of integer values, which would become a disaster. When the function accesses what it believes to be a pair of **doubles**, the memory is actually integers. Since a **double** occupies 8 bytes and an integer takes up 4 bytes (on a 32-bit platform), clearly the function is going to access data beyond the boundaries of each integer value. Wildly unpredictable results occur. Hence, C++ requires every function to have a prototype so that such goofs can be avoided.

To create a function prototype, first invent a good name for the function and place parentheses after it along with a semicolon. In this case, a good name for the function is **higher()**.

```
...higher (...);
```

Next, determine what items must be passed to the function so that it can do its job. List the items, their data types and the order in which you want to pass them to the function. In this example, there are two items that **higher()** must have in order to do its job: the doubles **x** and **y**. Place the items in the parameter list in the order you want them to be passed, code their data type first, then the name of the parameter and separate them with commas. So now, we have

```
...higher (double x, double y);
```

The final step is to determine what the function is to return—what kind of data. In this case, it must return the larger number, which must be a **double** as well. Place the return data type before the name of the function. Here is the complete prototype for our **higher()** function.

```
double higher (double x, double y);
```

All that remains is where to place the prototype in our program. Obviously, if the prototype is to be used by the compiler as a model to follow when invoking the function, it must be physically before the actual call to the **higher()** function. However, the vast majority of the time, function prototypes are placed after the **#includes** and before the start of the **main()** function. This way, you never have to worry about if you have the prototype ahead of the function call that uses it. Here is the revised beginning of the program.

```
#include <iostream>
#include <iomanip>
using namespace std;

double higher (double x, double y);

int main () {
 double x;          // a number entered by user
 double y;          // a second number entered by user
 double bigger;     // a place to store the larger of x and y

 cout << "Enter two numbers: ";
 cin >> x >> y;

 bigger = ....
 return 0;
}
```

In a function prototype, the names of the parameters are optional. Names are provided for good documentation and convenience.

In other words, the compiler could also use this as the prototype.

```
double higher (double, double);
```

If names are provided for good documentation, they are ignored by the compiler. However, always provide good names for the parameters. Why?

Consider the prototype for a **calctax()** function whose purpose is to calculate the sales tax depending upon the state code. A reasonable prototype might be

```
double calctax (double cost, int quantity, int statecode);
```

However, the compiler is content with just

```
double calctax (double, int, int);
```

This shortened form with no parameter names can cause trouble. When you are going to call the function, do you pass **cost, quantity** and **statecode** or do you pass **cost, statecode** and **quantity**? From the short form prototype above, you cannot tell. Imagine the tax returned if the purchaser bought one new car for $20,000 in state 13 (which is often Illinois) and the **main()** function passed the **cost, statecode** and the **quantity**. The tax calculated would be for 13 cars in state 1 (often Alabama)!

With no parameter names coded on the prototypes, you have no choice but to find where the actual function is coded and see what is the real order; this is no fun if the source file is a large one.

Step B. Define the Function Header

The actual coding of the function begins with a **function header**. The function header follows the exact same format as the prototype except that the ending semicolon is replaced with a beginning { and ending } indicating here come the actual statements that the function represents.

The function header for the **higher()** function is

```
double higher (double x, double y) {
  ...
}
```

Notice that the only difference is the ending semicolon is replaced with a begin-end block set of braces.

Thus, it is highly recommended that you simply copy the prototype and paste it where the function is to be coded. That way, fewer errors can occur.

Where in the program do the function headers get placed? Since the function header is the start of the actual instructions of that function, the real question is where does the code for the functions go?

Rule: The function coding must be outside of any other block of coding.

In other words, each function in a program including **main()** must be outside of any other function. While there are no limits on where you can call or invoke functions, their actual definitions cannot be nested within other functions like an inner **while** loop contained within an outer loop. Each function definition must be by itself. There are several possibilities. Here is the order that I prefer, **main()** comes first and then the functions that **main()** directly calls and then the functions that those functions call and so on.

```
#includes
const ints go here
prototypes go here
```

```
double higher (double x, double y);

int main () {
 ...
}

double higher (double x, double y) {
 ...
}
```

This is a Top-down point of view. The reader sees the overall **main()** function first so that the big picture of the program is the starting point.

Here is an alternative. The functions are coded first and **main()** last.

```
#includes
const ints go here
prototypes go here

double higher (double x, double y) {
 ...
}

int main () {
 ...
}
```

This is called the Bottom-up Style. The programming language, Pascal, must be coded in this style in which the **main()** function is last. Notice one small detail. Since the entire body of the function occurs before **main()** and before any other call to **higher()**, the function header can serve as the prototype because the compiler has now seen the entirety of the function and knows how to call or invoke it later on when it encounters references to **higher()** in **main()**.

The following is illegal because the function definition itself is within the body of the **main()** function. If compiled, it often generates an error message that **local functions** are not supported.

```
#includes
const ints
prototypes
int main () {
 ...
double higher (double x, double y) { // illegal
 ...
}
 ...
}
```

A third possibility is that one or more functions are contained in their own separate cpp files. This is examined in the next chapter.

Step C. Code the Function's Body

With the prototype coded at the top and the function header coded after the **main()** function, the next step is to code the actual instructions that the function is to perform.

In the case of the **higher()** function, here is where the coding to determine which number is the larger is written. There are a number of ways that this function can be implemented. Let's examine the simplest and then see some variations. Define another **double**, **big**, to hold the larger number. Then, a simple If-Then-Else can place the larger of **x** and **y** into it.

```
double higher (double x, double y) {
 double big;
 if (x > y)
   big = x;
 else
   big = y;
 ...
}
```

The last step is to return what is now in **higher()**'s **big** variable back to the calling program. This is done with the **return** instruction. The **return** instruction syntax is

```
return;
return constant;
return variable;
return expression;
```

We have already been using the return of a constant in all of our **main()** functions.

```
return 0;
```

or if the file could not be opened

```
return 1;
```

Here we need to code

```
return big;
```

This instruction copies the current contents of variable **big** and returns that value back to the calling or invoking function.

Here is the complete **higher()** function.

```
double higher (double x, double y) {
 double big;
 if (x > y)
   big = x;
 else
   big = y;
 return big;
}
```

We can use the ?: shortcut to reduce the amount of coding we need. Notice in both clauses of the **if** statement a value is assigned to variable **big**. Thus, we can also implement **higher()** this way.

```
double higher (double x, double y) {
 double big;
 big = x > y ? x : y;
 return big;
}
```

However, we can get it even shorter by returning an expression. Here is the ultimate version of the **higher()** function.

```
double higher (double x, double y) {
 return x > y ? x : y;
}
```

We have gotten the function body reduced to a one-liner!

Are there any benefits to using the one-line version of **higher()** versus the original one that stored the larger in **big**, which was then returned? Yes and no. Yes, in that the compiler can create the fastest possible machine instructions for one line of code in all circumstances. The longer version also wastes memory for the variable **big**, 8 bytes in this case. The fewer the lines, the more of the program that can be seen on the screen at one time and the lower the chance for errors.

No, in that the one line version is harder to read. Debugging a one line function body is difficult at best. The one line is either right or wrong. The debugger can trace through your program one line at a time; after each line has been executed, it can show you the contents of each variable. In other words, the longer versions allow you to inspect intermediate results along the way toward the final value the function is to return. When it is all jammed into one line of code, the debugger cannot assist much.

C++ programs in the real world tend to have numerous functions reduced to one line of coding. So be prepared to read them when they occur. However, for beginning programmers, I highly recommend coding the function one step at a time and not trying to produce one-liners. By the way, the technique used to create the one line function is the same that I used here. Begin with a straightforward implementation; get it working producing the correct answer. Then come back and see if any of the shortcuts you have learned can be applied to your coding, just as was done here with **higher()**.

Step D. Invoke or Call the Function

With the prototype and function coded, now go back to the calling function, **main()** in this case, and write the line of code that is to call or invoke the function, line 20 in the Basic06a figure below. In **main()** variable **bigger** is to hold the larger value, which is the returned value from **higher()**.

```
bigger = higher (x, y);
```

Here is the complete program, **Basic06a**.

```
Basic06a - Finding the larger of two numbers - function higher
```

```
/***************************************************************/
/*                                                             */
/* Basic06a Finding the larger of two numbers - function higher*/
/*                                                             */
/***************************************************************/

#include <iostream>
#include <iomanip>
using namespace std;
double higher (double x, double y);

int main () {
 double x;        // a number entered by user
 double y;        // a second number entered by user
 double bigger;   // a place to store the larger of x and y

 cout << "Enter two numbers: ";
 cin >> x >> y;

 bigger = higher (x, y);//call higher &store return val in bigger

 cout << bigger << endl;
 return 0;
}

/***************************************************************/
/*                                                             */
/* higher: a function to return the larger of two numbers      */
/*                                                             */
/***************************************************************/

double higher (double x, double y) {
 double big;
 big = x > y ? x : y;
 return big;
}
```

Notice that **main()** could also make use of **higher()** this way:

```
cout << higher (x, y);
```

just as we could write

```
cout << sqrt (number);
```

In other words, when the function call is done, the coding **higher (x, y)** is replaced by the value it returns. That value can then be used in any manner desired, such as assigning it to **bigger** or sending it to the output stream on the screen.

You could also use that returned value in a calculation such as

```
double z = 42 * higher (x, y) / sqrt ( higher (x, y));
```

In this weird line, the larger value of **x** and **y** is multiplied by 42 and then divided by the square root of that larger value.

When you call a function, the function call in the invoking statement is replaced by the value that the function returns; then the remaining actions of that original line are done.

Here is a common mistake beginners can make. Can you spot the error here in **main()**?

```
higher (x, y);
```

This is a function call. The compiler passes the contents of **x** and **y** to the **higher()** function, which calculates the larger value and returns or gives it back to the calling program. What does the calling program then do with that answer? Nothing. It is simply pitched or ignored. It is the same thing as doing the following

```
sqrt (x);
acos (-1.);
```

The first function call computes the square root of variable **x** and then no use is made of that answer. The second computes **PI** and then no use is made of it. Both answers are pitched by the compiler. You need to make some use of the value being returned from the functions, such as

```
cout << sqrt (x) / 42.;
const double PI = acos (-1.);
bigger = higher (x, y);
```

A Second Example, calcTax()

Let's review the steps needed to create our own functions by working another problem. Suppose that our company is currently selling items in two states but that we shortly plan to go nationwide. Tax on the sales is dependent upon each state's rate. Thus, in the **main()** function if we calculated the tax on the sales, **main()** would be cluttered up with many lines of code making it harder to read and follow. So a function, **calcTax()**, is to be written migrating all of the detailed work of actually calculating the tax into a separate function, thereby streamlining the **main()** function. The **main()** function coding goes as follows.

```
#includes go here
const ints go here
prototypes go here

int main () {
 double cost;        // cost of one item
 int quantity;       // number of items purchased
 int statecode;      // state of purchase
 double subtotal;    // total of items purchased
 double tax;         // total tax on this purchase
 double total;       // total of order

 ...input a set of data

 subtotal = cost * quantity;
 tax = calcTax (...
 total = subtotal + tax;
 output the results
```

```
 return 0;
}
```

At the boldfaced location above, we need to call our new function. Applying *Step A*, invent a good name, surround it with parenthesis, and end it with a semicolon.

```
... calcTax (...);
```

Next, determine the number of parameters that must be passed to **calcTax()** so that it may fulfill its purpose. Note their data types and decide upon the order you wish to pass them. Here the **subtotal** and the **statecode** must be passed, a **double** and an integer in that order. So our prototype is now

```
... calcTax (double total, int statecode);
```

What, if anything, should **calcTax()** return to the caller? It must return the tax, which is a **double**. Here is the complete prototype.

```
double calcTax (double total, int statecode);
```

Place it above the start of **main()**.

```
#includes go here
const ints go here

double calcTax (double total, int statecode);

int main () {
```

Step B. Now, copy it and paste it below the end of the **main()** function and change the semicolon to a set of begin-end braces. Now we have the function header coded.

```
#includes go here
const ints go here

double calcTax (double total, int statecode);

int main () {

}

double calcTax (double total, int statecode) {
}
```

Step C. Here we must code the body of the function. I've allowed for just two initial state codes. Presumably, later on all fifty states will be represented in this function.

```
double calcTax (double total, int statecode) {
 double rate;
 if (statecode == 13)
  rate = .075;
 else if (statecode == 1)
  rate = .065;
 return total * rate;
}
```

Step D. Back in the **main()** function, code the call for **calcTax()**. Here is the complete shell.

```
#includes go here
const ints go here

double calcTax (double total, int statecode);

int main () {
 double cost;        // cost of one item
 int quantity;       // number of items purchased
 int statecode;      // state of purchase
 double subtotal;    // total of items purchased
 double tax;         // total tax on this purchase
 double total;       // total of order

 ...input a set of data

 subtotal = cost * quantity;
 tax = calcTax (subtotal, statecode);
 total = subtotal + tax;
 output the results
 return 0;
}

double calcTax (double total, int statecode) {
 double rate;
 if (statecode == 13)
  rate = .075;
 else if (statecode == 1)
  rate = .065;
 return total * rate;
}
```

Again, we have **mostly working** software. Consider what the function returns when the client program passes it a state code that is not 1 or 13. As it stands, rate is uninitialized. So wildly unpredictable things occur. If that garbage is not decipherable as a floating point number, a runtime error and program crash results. If it is interpretable as a number, a wildly wrong tax is returned. How can it be repaired? Here is one way.

```
double calcTax (double total, int statecode) {
 double rate = 0;
 if (statecode == 13)
  rate = .075;
 else if (statecode == 1)
  rate = .065;
 else
  cout << "Error: bad state code: " << statecode << endl;
 return total * rate;
}
```

How Parameters Are Passed to Functions

Just how do the values get passed to the invoked function? Look again at line 20 in the Basic06a program above. In C++, all parameters are **passed by value**, never by **address**. **Passing by value** means that a copy of the contents of the caller's variable is made and the copy passed to the function's parameter variable. Some languages **pass parameters by address**, which means the memory location or address of the caller's variable is what is passed to the function's parameter variable. What is the difference? Figure 6.7, Passing by Value Versus Passing by Address, shows the major differences.

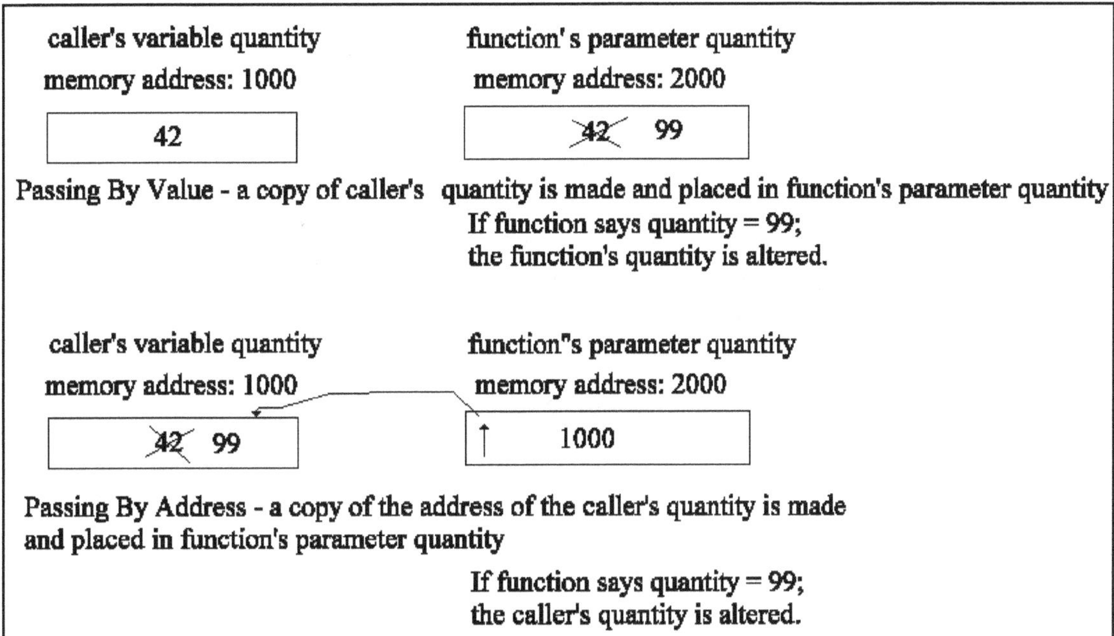

Figure 6.7 Passing by Value Versus Passing by Address

When a variable is passed by value, a copy of its contents is made and given to the function. If the function should try to alter it, only the function's copy is changed. However, when passing by address, if the function should attempt to change it, the calling program's variable is actually changed.

Let's step through the sequence of events that occur in Basic06a's line 20 call to **higher()**. Suppose that the user has input 10 for **x** and 42 for **y**. Figure 6.8 shows the circumstances in memory as C++ executes line 20,

```
bigger = higher (x, y);
```

A copy of **main()**'s **x** and **y** values are placed into **higher()**'s parameters **x** and **y**. Next, **higher()** places the larger value, 42, into its **big** variable and returns **big**'s contents back to the **main()** function. The returned value 42 is then copied into **main()**'s **bigger** variable as shown in the next figure. Notice that the function call to **higher()** is replaced with the return value of 42 and then the assignment is done to **bigger**.

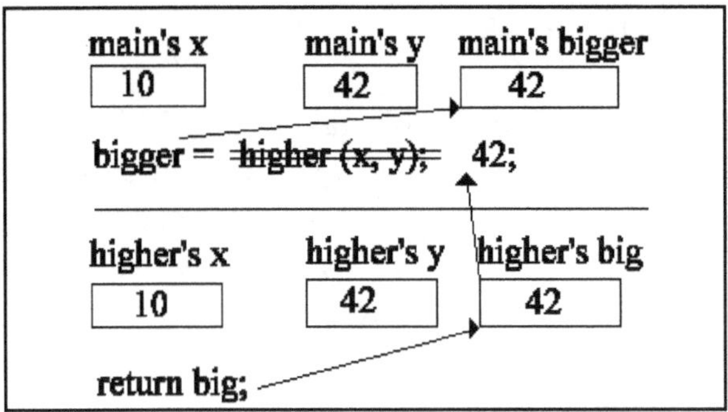

Figure 6.8 Invocation of Function higher

The Types, Scope, and Storage Classes of Variables

C++ has three main **types** of variables: **local**, **parameter,** and **global**. A **local** variable is any variable that is defined within a function. A **parameter** variable is any variable in the parameter list of a function header. A **global** variable is any variable defined outside of any other block of coding; global variables are examined in the next chapter.

The type of variable determines the **scope** of that variable. The scope of a variable is that portion of the program in which it is available for use by using its name. In other words, the scope of a variable is the area within a program in which that variable can be referenced just by coding its name.

Scope Rule 1. For local type variables, the scope is from the point of their definition to the end of the defining block of code.

The scope of **x** and **y** in the **main()** function is from the point of their definitions to the end of the defining block or the end brace } of **main()**. The scope of **big** in the **higher()** function is from the point of its definition in **higher()** to the end brace of **higher()**.

Scope Rule 2. For parameter type variables, the scope is from the point of their definition within the function header to the end brace of the function.

Thus, the scope of **higher()**'s parameters **x** and **y** is from their definition points in the function header to the end of the defining block, or }, of **higher()**.

A variable's name can only be used when it is in scope. This means that once the end brace } of **main()** is reached, all of **main()**'s variables go out of scope and cannot be accessed by using their names. Thus, within **higher()** we could not write

```
bigger = big;
```

because **main()**'s **bigger** is now out of scope.

Another way of looking at this is that a local or parameter type of variable belongs exclusively to the function in which it is defined. Its name is not known outside of that function or earlier in the same function before it is defined. The following Figure 6.9 illustrates the scope of both local and parameter types of variables.

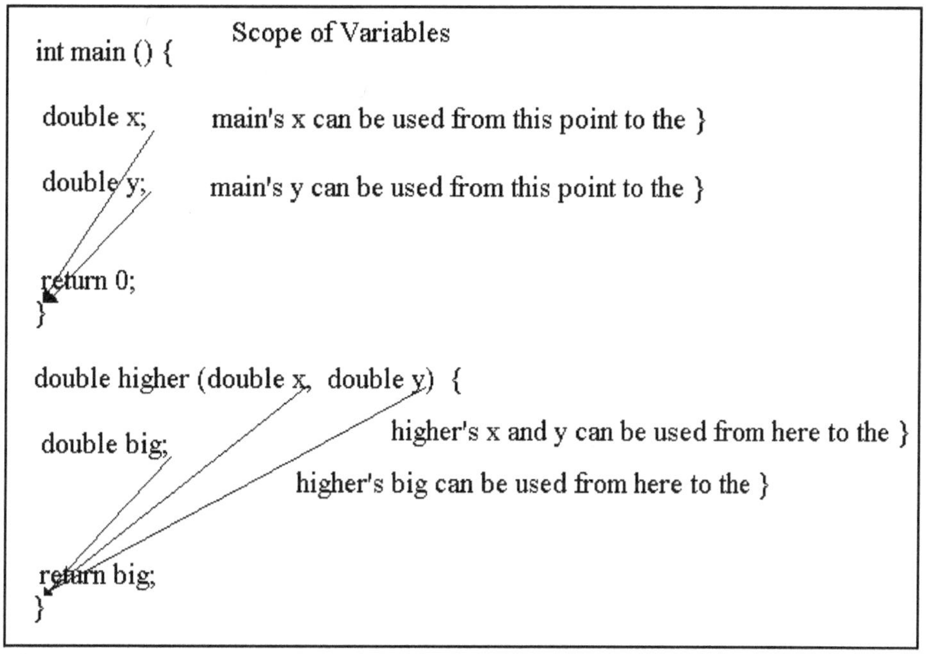

```
                Scope of Variables
int main () {

 double x;      main's x can be used from this point to the }

 double y;      main's y can be used from this point to the }

 return 0;
}

double higher (double x, double y) {

 double big;           higher's x and y can be used from here to the }
                  higher's big can be used from here to the }

 return big;
}
```

Figure 6.9 The Scope of Local and Parameter Variables

Sometimes variables are defined within smaller blocks. Consider this example.

```
int main () {
 ...
 if (x == y) {
    int z = 0;
    ...
 }
```

Whenever the then-clause is executed, variable **z** comes into scope and can be used. It is the then-clause's variable **z**. It goes out of scope when the end brace } of the then-clause is reached.

Here is another example.

```
for (j=0; j<count; j++ ) {
  int sum = 0;
 ...
}
```

The scope of the **for** loop's **sum** is from its point of definition to the end brace } of the **for** loop.

Scope rules can also cause variables to become hidden within blocks of coding. In this example, **main()** defines a local variable named **x** and initializes it to 0. Within a **while** clause, another local variable, local to the body of the **while** loop, defines a variable **x**. Note that the assignment of 42 goes to the **while** loop's **x** and not **main()**'s **x** because **main()**'s **x** is hidden by the local block's variable **x**.

```
int main () {
 int x = 0;
 int j = 0;
 while (j < 10) {
  int x;  // hides main's x from this point on to the }
  x = 42; // assignment is to while loop's x
  j++;
}
```

This hiding effect can create problems. Consider this block of coding.

```
int main () {
 int i = 0;
 while (i<10) {
  int i = 0;
  i++;
 }
```

When this code is executed, an infinite loop is created. **main()**'s local variable **i** is initialized to zero and the **while** loop test condition is testing **main()**'s **i**. However, within the **while** loop, a local variable to the **while** block is created also called **i**, hiding **main()**'s **i** from this point through the end of the **while** block. Thus, the wrong variable is incremented and **main()**'s **i** is never incremented and the loop repeats endlessly.

The C++ **storage classes** define further properties of variables in terms of memory usage methods. The storage class of a variable determines the **lifetime** of a variable and its initialization method, if any. The **lifetime** of a variable represents the duration of its existence, from the point that its memory is created to the point of its destruction.

The two storage classes that have been used in the book thus far are **automatic** and **parameter** storage. The storage class automatic is the default; all variables that we have defined thus far in our programs are automatic storage variables, with the exception of the parameter variables within function headers. Variables of **automatic** storage have their memory allocated for them by the compiler upon entry to the defining block of code. When the program execution leaves that block (reaches the end brace }), the storage for that variable is destroyed.

All parameter variables in a function header are of the **parameter** storage class. Parameter class variables have their memory allocated for them by the compiler when the function is invoked and before actual entry into to the function's body. When the program execution leaves that function (i.e., reaches the end brace }), the storage for parameter variables is destroyed.

Notice that automatic and parameter storage lifetimes are nearly identical, with parameter storage coming into existence just before the automatic storage variables defined within a function.

The storage class affects a variable's **initialization** as well. Parameter storage variables are initialized by the compiler when the function is invoked. It first creates memory for the parameter variables and then copies the values to be passed from the calling function into the newly created variables. Thus, we say that parameter storage variables are automatically initialized by the compiler with a copy of the variables to be passed as the function is invoked.

Similarly, automatic storage variables are initialized by the compiler at run time every time the block is entered. In the following loop, the local variable **sum** is held in automatic storage and is initialized 100 times, each time the body of the loop is executed.

```
j = 0;
while (j<100) {
  int sum = 0; // created and initialized 100 times
  ...
  j++;
}              // sum is destroyed here 100 times
```

Registers and the Stack—a Bit of Computer Architecture

Most beginners find that the storage classes are a bit of an abstract concept—just something to memorize and file away for future use. However, if you understand a bit of computer architecture that underlies these storage classes, their rules become totally obvious.

A **register** is a high-speed circuit element, usually capable of holding 32 bits or 4 bytes of information. When you hear that a computer is a "a 32-bit" computer, they are describing the size of these high-speed registers. The original PCs were 16-bit computers, meaning that the registers were only 2 bytes in size (16 bits). Computer instructions operating upon data held within one of these registers is done in a few nanoseconds (10^{-9} sec). Unfortunately, there are only a few of these registers available, so registers are a scarce resource not to be squandered. When the compiler is creating the machine instructions for your programs, it tries to have your program's instructions make effective use of the registers so that your program runs fast.

How a Function Returns a Value

One way the program can run more quickly is to place the values being returned by functions into a known register; then, when back at the invoking point in the calling function, that return value is sitting in a high-speed register ready for the usage that is to be made of it. Typically on a PC, one register known as **EAX**, extended accumulator register, is used to hold return values from functions in C++ and in many other languages as well. Register EAX is 4 bytes in size. Within this 4-byte register, the lower 2-byte portion or the rightmost two bytes is called register **AX.** Original PCS only had register AX available, which is 16 bits in size. The rightmost byte of register AX or EAX is also accessible or subdividable as register **AL**, accumulator lower byte register. From these three portions of register EAX, C++ handles the high-speed return of values as follows.

```
size of the value    return value
to be returned       is in register
     4                  EAX
     2                  AX
     1                  AL
 any other size         special on the stack
```

A **stack** is a last-in-first-out save area, abbreviated LIFO. That is, the last item placed onto the stack is the first item that can be taken off the stack. An analogy is a stack of plates on a stainless steel serving cart at a local buffet. When a new diner enters, he or she can take only the top plate off the stack—that plate was the last one placed on top of the stack. Often a spring then pushes the remaining plates upwards. When the next diner enters, he or she then takes the next plate from the stack, which is on top. Only the top plate can be removed. When a clean plate is placed back onto the stack, it is placed on the top of the stack; the others are "pushed down"; this new plate now becomes the new top of the stack.

Every C++ program has a stack save area. In fact, most all programs that run on the computer have a stack save area.

Rule 3. All automatic and parameter storage class variables are stored on the stack save area.

To see how this works, let's return to the higher program, Basic06a, and follow how the computer actually handles the function call to **higher()** from **main()**. When the **main()** function is called at the start of the program, the automatic storage variables of **main()** are allocated on the stack. Figure 6.10 represents the stack as it appears at the time of the call to function **higher()**.

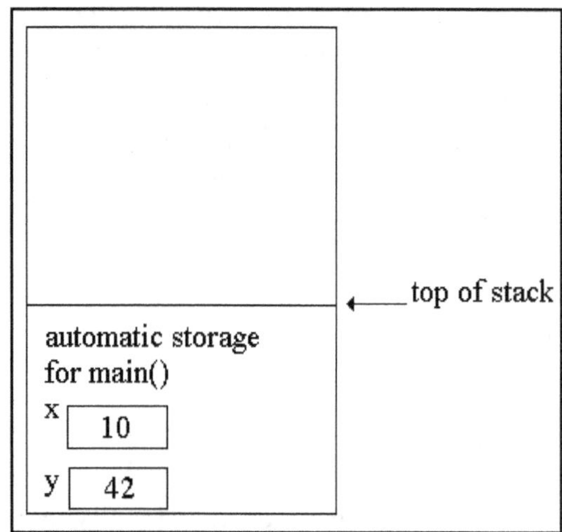

Figure 6.10 The Stack Before the Call to Higher

In this example, a register cannot be used to return a **double** since the **double** is larger than 4 bytes. Hence, immediately at the top of the stack, the compiler reserves some space for the return value that **higher()** will eventually be returning back to **main()**. Next, it places the parameters for

higher() onto the stack and copies **main()**'s **x** and **y** values into **higher()**'s **x** and **y** parameters. So that the computer knows where within the calling function to return back to when **higher()** issues its **return** instruction, the return address to go back to within **main()** is stored on the stack next.

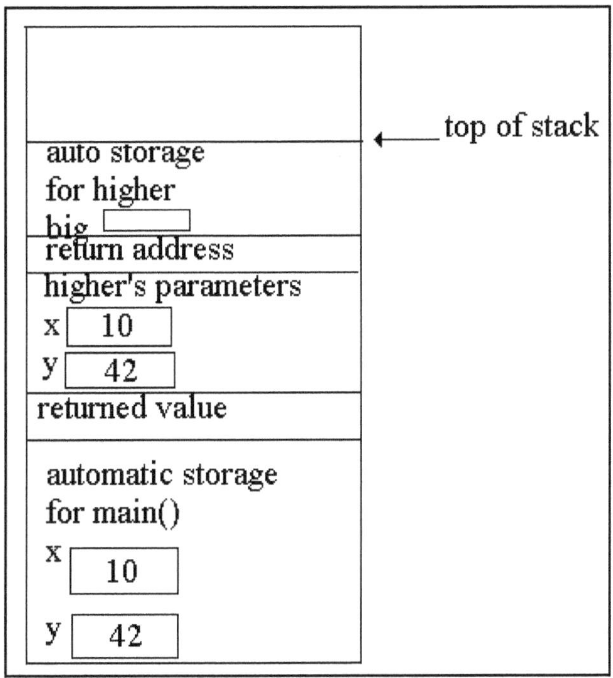

Figure 6.11 The Stack Upon Entry to Higher

Finally, it allocates space for the automatic storage variables of **higher()**, here variable **big**. Figure 6.11 represents what the stack looks like when the program has entered **higher()** and is about to test **higher()**'s **x** and **y** values to place the larger into variable **big**. The new top of the stack is now as shown in the figure.

When the **higher()** function executes, the return **big** instruction, a copy of the contents of **higher()**'s **big** is placed into that special save area just above automatic storage for **main()**. Now, one by one in reverse order, the various items are removed from the stack and the top of the stack is lowered back to where it was before **higher()** was called. Thus, this is how all automatic and parameter class variables are destroyed when the end brace } is executed. They are removed from the stack. Well, they are actually not removed. Rather the top of the stack pointer is adjusted downward, effectively making that space available for another function to use. Figure 6.12 shows what the stack looks like upon the return back to the **main()** function.

The return value of 42 is sitting right at the top of the stack ready for the assignment into **bigger**. It also shows what happens if no use is made of the return value from a function. The memory it occupies is overlaid by the next function call.

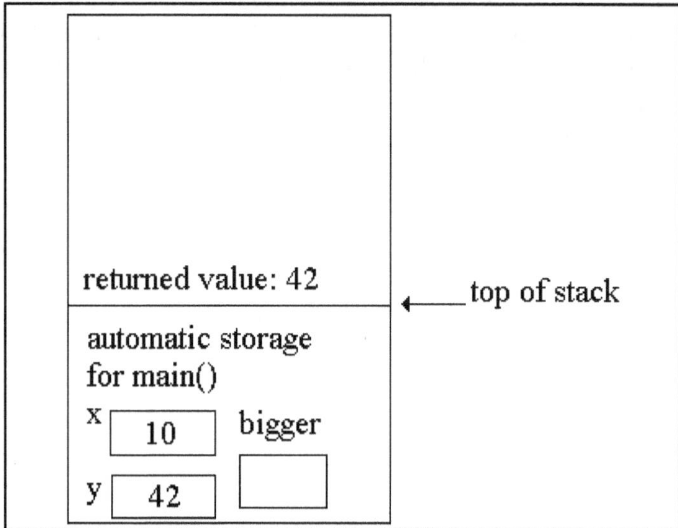

Figure 6.12 The Stack Upon the Return to main

Thus, storage on the stack is a very dynamic affair. When functions get called, the stack grows in size as parameters, return address and automatic variables for that function are placed on the stack. When the end brace } of the function is executed, it is all removed from the stack.

Automatic storage and parameter class variables are always stored on the stack. Can you see now why the lifetime of automatic and parameter class variables is just for the duration of the defining block of code? It makes sense when you know what is going on with the stack.

More on the bool Data Type and Functions that Return a bool

Sometimes a variable is meant to hold a simple yes/no true/false type answer. We saw in Chapter 4 that there is boolean data type, **bool**. A variable of the **bool** type can contain only the values **true** and **false**. Here are some variables that may easily be declared as **bool**.

```
bool isWindowVisible;
bool isLeapYear;
bool isAvailable;
bool isVoter;
bool passingGrade;
bool ok;
bool error;
```

Sometimes a function needs to return a simple yes/no or true/false result. A function may also be passed a **bool** parameter and can return a **bool** as well. Sometimes this makes good sense.

Consider a function that is to determine if a person is a potential voter. It might be called **isVoter()**. It is passed the person's age and citizenship status. While the age might be an integer, the citizenship ought to be a **bool** as well. The prototype is then

```
bool isVoter (int age, bool citizenship);
```

The **main()** function and the **isVoter()** function can be coded this way. Of course, the test condition in the function could be shortened into one line if desired.

```
int main () {
  bool citizenship;
  int age;
  bool potentialVoter;
  potentialVoter = isVoter (age, citizenship);
  if (potentialVoter) { // here: a possible voter
 ...
}

bool isVoter (int age, bool citizenship) {
  if (age < 18)
    return false;
  if (!citizenship)
    return false;
  return true;
}
```

Also **main()** does not need to actually store the **bool** return value from **isVoter()** if it is not going to be needed beyond the single test. In such a case **main()** could be done this way.

```
int main () {
  bool citizenship;
  int age;
  if (isVoter (age, citizenship)) {
 ...
}
bool isVoter (int age, bool citizenship) {
  return (age < 18 ||!citizenship) ? false : true;
}
```

The Shipping Cost Function

Look back at program **Cs04a** Customer Order on pages 120-121. We could create a function to calculate the shipping cost. The function **CalcShippingCost** would need only the total before tax amount in order for it to find the correct shipping charges. It can return the calculated shipping cost. Its prototype is coded this way.

```
double CalcShippingCost (double total);
```

It is implemented as follows.

```
double CalcShippingCost (double total) {
 double shippingCost = 0;
 if (total < 100) {    // need to figure shipping costs
  shippingCost = total * .005;
  if (shippingCost < 4.00) // if it is less than minimum amt
   shippingCost = 4.00;    // reset shipping to minimum amt
 }
 return shippingCost;
}
```

Then, back in **main()** we would replace lines 58 through 62 with a simple function call.

```
shippingCost = CalcShippingCost (totalBeforeTax);
```

Functions that Return No Value

Sometimes a function does its work and has no value to return at all. Suppose that a program needed a function to print headings. Reports typically have one or more heading lines that identify the company and the report type. Also, homework assignments typically require an initial top line with the assignment number and student name on it. A headings function might not be passed any variables nor does it have anything to return; it just prints headings.

When a function has no parameters, nothing is coded in the prototype or header—just the pair of parentheses (). When a function returns nothing, the keyword **void** must be used for the return data type.

The prototype for a headings function that took no parameters and returned no value is as follows.

```
void headings ();
```

The prototype of an **outputLine()** function that took several variables and displayed them might be

```
void outputLine (double cost, int quantity,
                 long itemNumber);
```

A **void** function can return back to the caller by coding

```
return;
```

or by reaching the end brace } of the function. Either of the following is acceptable.

```
void headings () {
  cout << "Assignment 6   by J.J. Student\n\n";
  cout << "       Acme Sales Report\n\n";
}
```

or

```
void headings () {
  cout << "Assignment 6   by J.J. Student\n\n";
  cout << "       Acme Sales Report\n\n";
  return;
}
```

Where Should Error Messages Be Displayed?

When a program detects an error situation while it is running, it usually must display an appropriate error message for the user. Often those errors are fatal, meaning the program cannot continue to run and must terminate.

Up to this point, the error messages have been displayed on the **cout** output stream. However, C++ and DOS provide another output stream specifically designed for displaying error messages. This is the output stream **cerr**.

Any message displayed to the stream **cerr** always goes to the screen. In contrast, the normal output stream, **cout**, can be redirected to the printer or a disk file using DOS output redirection

```
C:\pgm1\debug>pgm1 >> results.txt
```

(In Visual C++ 6.0, set the program arguments edit control found under Project—Settings—Debug tab to **>> results.txt**. In Visual C++7.0, choose properties on the project in Project View and go to the Debug section.)

Error messages must be seen by the user. Thus, it is always a wise practice to display error messages to **cerr** instead of **cout** because **cout** is often redirected to an output file.

```
cerr << "Error: invalid data in the input file on line 42\n";
```

Frequently the program's output is directly written to an output file. In such a case, it is prudent to display the error message to both **cerr** and the output file streams. The user of the program then sees the error message on the screen. If the user opens the output result file, the error message is there as well, indicating the set of results being viewed are not correct. For example,

```
if (!infile.eof() && infile.fail ()) {
  cerr << "Error: bad data in the input file; results are not correct\n";
  cout << "Error: bad data in the input file; results are not correct\n";
  ...
}
```

Note that there is another error stream instance, **clog**, which also displays only on the DOS error device, the screen. However, **clog** messages are held in an internal buffer area and only displayed when the buffer is full, the program ends, or a flush the buffer instruction is executed.

Thus, error messages might not appear as soon as they happen. You should normally use the **cerr** stream for error messages.

Controlling Leading 0's on Output—the setfill() Function

Sometimes the output format requires fields to have leading zeros instead of blanks. This is quite common when dealing with dates. For example, month numbers are commonly displayed as 01, 02, 09, 10, and 12. The following does not work.

```
int month = 2;
cout << setw (2) << month;
```

The output would be a blank followed by the '2' digit. The fill character for leading zeros is a blank. That is, all leading zeros in a number are replaced by blanks on output. The fill character can be changed using the **setfill()** function, which takes one parameter, the character to be used as the fill. The following produces the correct output of 02 for the month.

```
int month = 2;
cout << setw (2) << setfill ('0') << month << setfill (' ');
```

Once the fill character is set, it remains in force for all numerical fields until it is changed back to a blank. Thus, when you are done using a '0' as a fill character, change it back to the default of ' ', a blank as shown above. A fill character of '*' is often used when printing numerical values on checks: $*****1.42 for example.

Inputting Integers that have Leading Zeros—The dec Manipulator Function

Sometimes the input data contains leading zeros. Dates are commonly entered with leading zeros; for example, 01 09 2000, representing January 9, 2000. One might expect that the sequence to input just such a date would be given as follows.

```
int month;
int day;
int year;
cin >> month >> day >> year;
```

or

```
infile >> month >> day >> year;
```

While the **month** is input successfully, garbage results in the **day** variable. Why?

C++ supports the input of numbers in three number schemes, **decimal**, **octal,** and **hexadecimal. Decimal** numbers are base 10 and valid digits range from 0 through 9. **Octal** numbers are base 8; that is, valid digits range from 0 through 7. **Hexadecimal** numbers are base 16. The input stream uses a clever method to detect the difference between the input of a decimal-based number and an octal number. The rule that the input streams use is: if the number begins with a 0 digit and is not just the number 0, then that number is considered to be an octal number. In the above example, when the extraction operator encounters the 01 for January, it assumes that it is an octal number. However, 1 in octal is equivalent to 1 in decimal and all is well. But when it extracts the day, it encounters 09 and therefore assumes an octal number. Since a 9 digit is an invalid octal digit, trouble arises.

To input or specify a number in hexadecimal, prefix it with 0x.

There is a function available that tells the input stream to change its assumptions about the inputting of numbers with leading zeros. It is the **dec** manipulator function. Within the input stream there is a flag that controls this assumption regarding leading zeros. In order for us to input decimal numbers that contain leading zeros, we only need to change this flag to accept decimal numbers. Thus, one time only usually at the start of the program, we change the flag by coding

```
cin >> dec;
```

or

```
infile >> dec;
```

Notice that you must set the flag on the input stream you are actually using to input those decimal numbers and that you only need to do it one time.

Section B: Computer Science Example

Cs06-1—Employee Payroll Program

Acme Company wants a program to compute the monthly payroll for its employees. The input file, **employee.txt**, contains the employee's social security number, the hours worked, the pay rate, the pay type and the shift worked. The hours worked is in the format of hh:mm. The pay type contains a one if this employee is salaried, which means their pay is just the flat pay rate independent of hours worked; a zero means this is an hourly worker. The shift worked is a number between one and three. For all employees, there is a 5% bonus for working 2nd shift and a 12% bonus for working 3rd shift. Overtime is paid at time and a half. For each employee, display their social security number, hours worked, pay rate, pay type, shift and pay.

Begin by examining the output of the program, the report itself.

Output from Cs06a Employee Payroll Program

```
             Acme Employee Payroll Report

  Social     Hours       Pay   Salaried  Shift      Gross
  Security   Worked      Rate      ?     Worked     Pay
  Number

 333333333  40.00   $  10.00     No         1    $  400.00
 333445555  40.00   $  10.00     No         2    $  420.00
```

```
 231444556  40.00   $  10.00    No         3    $  448.00
 334534456  35.50   $  10.00    No         1    $  355.00
 234560934  35.17   $ 450.00    Yes        1    $  450.00
 959649449  60.50   $ 554.00    Yes        2    $  581.70
 683433344  40.00   $ 350.00    Yes        3    $  392.00
 434433242  60.00   $  10.00    No         1    $  700.00
 423425699  60.00   $  10.00    No         2    $  735.00
 534432832  60.00   $  10.00    No         3    $  784.00
                                                ----------
                                               $   5265.70
```

Notice that the Salaried column is Yes or No. It makes sense to convert this input value of zero or one into a **bool** data type for our convenience. Note that a **bool** data type cannot be input or output directly. Now look at what one line of input contains.

```
333333333 40:00  10.00 0 1
```

The hours can be input directly and the colon ends the extraction of the hours. By extracting a single character, we can input the colon itself. Then, the minutes can be extracted.

Next, design a solution. Since this problem has some involved calculations, let's have a **calcPay()** function. Also, let's have a print **headings()** function to handle setting up the floating point formats and printing the heading and column headings; these are all done one time at the start of the program. The Top-Down Design is shown in Figure 6.13.

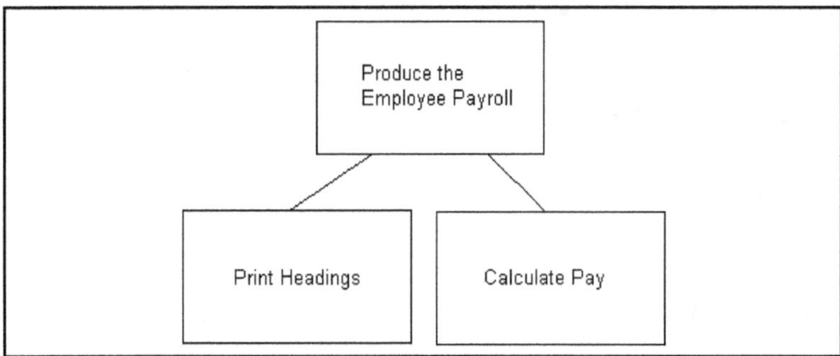

Figure 6.13 Top-Down Design for Payroll Program

Now design the **main()** function that represents the top box in the design. For input, we need these variables: **ssno**, **hoursWorked** (which will be created from variables hh and mm), **payRate**, **paytype** to hold the 0 or 1, **salaried** (the **bool** conversion from pay type), and **shiftWorked**. We also need a single character, **c**, to hold the colon separator between the hours and minutes integers. The calculation result field is **pay**. Finally, add a box for the grand total pay, **grandTotal**. Figure 6.14 shows the main storage diagram for the program.

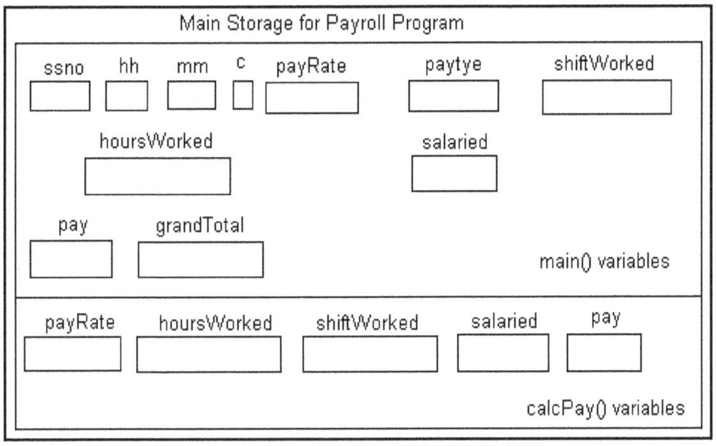

Figure 6.14 Main Storage for Payroll Program

The sketch of the sequence of instructions for **main()** is as follows.
print headings
open input file, displaying an error message if it cannot be opened and abort program
while the input of **ssno, hh**, **c**, **mm**, **payRate**, **paytype** and **shiftWorked** is ok do these
    convert **paytype** to a bool and store in **salaried**
    convert **hh:mm** to **hoursWorked** (**hh** + **mm** / 60.)
    let **pay** = **calcPay (payRate, hoursWorked, shiftWorked, salaried);**
    accumulate **grandTotal** (add in this **pay**)
    display this employee's pay line: **ssno**, **hoursWorked**, **payRate**,
        salaried ? " Yes" : " No ", **shiftWorked** and **pay**
end **while**
check for bad input data and abort with an error message if so
display **grandTotal** payroll amount
infile.close ();

The **headings()** function is next. It is passed nothing and consists of a simple sequence.
Function: **headings()**
    setup floating point output for two digits of accuracy
    print headings and column headings

Finally, let's write the sequences needed for the **calcPay** function. It needs one variable besides those passed to it, the **pay** answer variable. Assume the names that we intend to call the parameters are: **payRate**, **hoursWorked**, **shiftWorked** and **salaried**. The sequence of steps is as follows.

Function: **calcPay** is given: **payRate**, **hoursWorked**, **shiftWorked** and **salaried**
    if (**salaried**) then **pay** = **payRate**;
    else do the following:
        if (**hoursWorked** > 40.)
            pay = **payRate** * (40 + 1.5 * (**hoursWorked** - 40.));
        else **pay** = **payRate** * **hoursWorked**;

end else do
// apply the shift bonus to all employees
if (**shiftWorked** == 2) then **pay** *= 1.05;
else if (**shiftWorked** == 3) then **pay** *= 1.12;
return **pay** to caller

After thoroughly desk checking the program, code it into C++. When making up your own test data to test the program thoroughly, be sure to test all If-Then-Else paths. The test data set I provided does just that. Here is the completed program, **Cs06a**.

Cs06a Employee Payroll Program

```
/***************************************************************/
/*                                                             */
/* Cs06a Employee Payroll Program                              */
/*                                                             */
/***************************************************************/

#include <iostream>
#include <iomanip>
#include <fstream>
using namespace std;

void   headings ();
double calcPay (double payRate, double hoursWorked,
                int shiftWorked, bool salaried);

int main () {

 // input data
 long   ssno;         // social security number
 double hoursWorked;  // hours worked converted from hh:mm
 int    hh, mm;       // work fields to input time hh:mm
 char   c;            // to hold the : separator
 double payRate;      // hourly pay rate or flat rate
 int    paytype;      // 0 or 1, converted into salaried bool
 bool   salaried;     // true if salaried
 int    shiftWorked;  // the shift worked 1, 2 or 3
 double pay;          // employee's pay

 double grandTotal = 0; // grand total sales

 headings ();  // print the headings of the report

 // open input file
 ifstream infile ("EmployeeData.txt");
 if (!infile) {
  cerr << "Error: cannot open EmployeeData.txt file\n";
  return 1;
 }

```

```
 // process all employee data
 while (infile >> ssno >> hh >> c >> mm >> payRate
               >> paytype >> shiftWorked) {
  // convert paytype to a bool
  salaried = paytype ? true : false;
  // convert hh:mm to double total hours worked
  hoursWorked = hh + mm / 60.;

  // calculate employee pay
  pay = calcPay (payRate, hoursWorked, shiftWorked, salaried);

  // accumulate grand total payroll
  grandTotal += pay;

  // display this employee's pay line
  cout << setw (10) << ssno << setw (7) << hoursWorked << "   $"
       << setw (7) << payRate
       << (salaried ? "    Yes" : "    No ")
       << setw (8) << shiftWorked << "    $"
       << setw (8) << pay << endl;
 }

 // check for bad input data - abort with an error message if so
 if (!infile.eof()) {
  cerr << "Error: bad data on input\n";
  infile.close ();
  return 2;
 }

 // display grand total payroll
 cout <<
   "                                                ----------\n";
 cout << "                                             $"
      << setw (10) << grandTotal << endl;

 infile.close ();
 return 0;
}

/***************************************************************/
/*                                                             */
/* headings: print headings for the report                     */
/*                                                             */
/***************************************************************/

void  headings () {
 // setup floating point output for 2 digits of accuracy
 cout << fixed << setprecision (2);

 // print headings and column headings
 cout << "         Acme Employee Payroll Report\n\n"
   << "  Social    Hours      Pay   Salaried  Shift      Gross\n"
   << "  Security  Worked     Rate     ?      Worked     Pay\n"
```

```
 94     << "  Number\n\n";
 95 }
 96
 97 /***************************************************************/
 98 /*                                                             */
 99 /* calcPay: calculate the actual pay for this employee         */
100 /*                                                             */
101 /***************************************************************/
102
103 double calcPay (double payRate, double hoursWorked,
104                 int shiftWorked, bool salaried) {
105  double pay;      // will hold the person's pay
106
107  if (salaried) { // salaried are paid flat rate
108   pay = payRate;
109  }
110  else {           // hourly are paid overtime
111   if (hoursWorked > 40.) {
112    pay = payRate * (40 + 1.5 * (hoursWorked - 40.));
113   }
114   else {          // hourly but no overtime
115    pay = payRate * hoursWorked;
116   }
117  }
118
119  // apply the shift bonus to all employees
120  if (shiftWorked == 2)
121   pay *= 1.05;
122  else if (shiftWorked == 3)
123   pay *= 1.12;
124
125  return pay;
126 }
```

Notice how on line 44 the **bool** salaried is given its more convenient value. See how it is passed to the **calcPay()** function and subsequently used on line 107. Also, notice how the corresponding Yes and No are displayed on line 57.

Section C: An Engineering Example

Introduction to Numerical Analysis

Numerical analysis is the study of procedures, which give an approximate answer to problems that cannot be expressed in simple algebraic expressions. Frequently, real world problems do not have a simple algebraic answer.

A study of mathematics leads one to believe that there is always a neat precise mathematical answer to the problem at hand, such as summing a series from one to infinity. While this is mathematically sound and precise, real world applications cannot sum to infinity or the bridge would never be built. Thus, we must settle for an approximate answer that is as accurate as we need for the job at hand.

The approximation often has three aspects.

a. Done over a limited range
b. Done to the desired degree of accuracy
c. With some estimate of the error from the precise answer

Let's look at these points one by one.

Computer programs cannot sum to infinity, but they can sum a finite number of terms. When looking for the roots of an equation, such as sin x, while there are an infinite number of values of x where sin x becomes zero, a program can be written to find one of these roots within a certain range of x values. Thus, the first step in numerical analysis often involves some kind of range reduction.

Critical to any numerical analysis is obtaining an answer that is sufficiently accurate enough for our needs at hand. This is frequently expressed as obtaining an answer to a desired number of decimal places. Recall in the last chapter when evaluating a polynomial, if the next term in the series did not appreciably add any further accuracy, we could terminate the summing process with a sufficiently accurate answer. Again, if one has no idea of the needed accuracy, use .000001 as a beginning point for the analysis.

If our task was to calculate the volume of cubic yards of concrete to place into one of our cement mixer trucks to deliver to a construction site, an accuracy of .1 cubic yard is sufficient. If you have even assisted in pouring a concrete driveway, recall how it comes out of the truck. It is nearly impossible for the truck delivery system to unload mixed cement in any more accurate volume. Always keep in mind how accurate the results need to be.

Finally, when given the approximate numerical analysis answer, sometimes it is wise to know some estimate of just how accurate that answer really is. Often it is possible to apply mathematical procedures to calculate an estimate of the error. However, since this is just a beginning examination of numerical analysis, no estimates of roundoff errors are presented in this text. They are completely covered in a text devoted to the study of numerical analysis.

When attempting to create numerical analysis tools on the computer, one other factor may be important to the solution.

d. The rapidity of convergence to the approximate answer over the desired range. In other words, does the method or algorithm being implemented yield the result sufficiently rapidly? Usually, this is measured by the number of iterations of the main processing loop needed to obtain the result. This also translates into the actual amount of time required to obtain that answer.

For this class, rapidity of convergence is negligible. In the real world, such is not always the case. Back when I began my computer career in astronomy, a major problem to be solved on the computer was the calculation of the intensities of hydrogen spectral lines. When a hydrogen atom's electron is hit by a photon of light, the electron can be energized into a higher orbit about the proton, in the Bohr model. Over time, that unstable orbit decays and as the electron drops back toward its original normal orbit, it releases light energy of a precise frequency. The series of frequencies emitted is called the hydrogen spectral lines. In astronomy back then, it was vital that we know the theoretical intensities. Knowing the laboratory values, astronomers could then determine many properties of stars and gaseous clouds throughout the universe. In 1964, the first numerical methods were applied to the exceedingly complex equations needed to predict the intensities of the first seven lines or frequencies of hydrogen. The solution produced the results but the program ran on the computer for 48 hours nonstop! The problem was that the lines or frequencies that were most needed were not the first seven but those around 50! Here is an extreme case where faster convergence was needed.

Another example is NASA's real-time flight simulator for the space shuttles. When a shuttle is in orbit, one major concern is collision with space debris. On earth, if you are driving a car down the road and debris is in the way, you just swerve out of the way. In orbit about the earth, one cannot just swerve out of the way because that swerve might put the shuttle into orbit about the sun instead without sufficient fuel to ever return to earth! Thus, ground control has a flight simulator that can be used to determine just how to best swerve out of the way. That program, then, must have rapid convergence or by the time that the solution is relayed to the shuttle, the collision has already occurred. Hence, in the real world, sometimes the rapidity of convergence is extremely important.

Our first numerical analysis procedure will be to find the root(s) of a function. In this chapter, the simplest method is employed. However, in the next chapter, alternative methods will be seen to converge far more rapidly to the answer.

Numerical Analysis: Root Solving, the Bisection Method

Engineering, science, and math problems frequently need a method to find the roots of an equation. That is, find one or more values of x such that f(x) = 0. The restriction we must place on this problem is that the user knows or suspects that there is a root of f(x) that lies somewhere between points A and B along the x-axis. In other words, given the left and right endpoints along the x-axis (A and B) and given the function f(x) and desired degree of accuracy, we can determine if there is a root within that interval and find it, if it exists. Figure 6.15 shows the general situation.

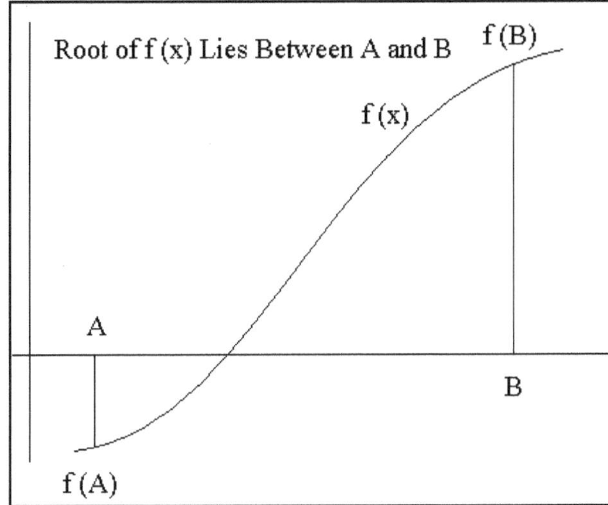

Figure 6.15 The Root of f(x)

The root lies about 1/3 the way from point A to B. The key concept that allows us to find that root is that the function evaluated at A and the function evaluated at B changes sign. That is, f (A) has a negative value, while f (B) has a positive value. If point A was moved to about 1/2 of the current distance from point B, then f (at that A) would be positive. If the user asked for a root between that new A and B, then there is no root in that interval. Likewise, if the user specified a point B that was about 1/4 of the distance to the right of the current point A, then f (at that B) would be negative, and again no root is in that interval. The fact that the sign of the f (x) changes between points A and B is the basis of our ability to find the desired root.

The Bisection Method of root solving requires only f (x), points A and B, and the desired degree of accuracy of that root. Thus, it requires minimal knowledge of the situation. The procedure is as follows. Let's call the left x endpoint, x1 and the right endpoint x3; the value of f (x1) is called f1 while the value of f (x3) is called f3. Now how can we determine if there is any root within that interval to be found? If we multiply f1 by f3 and that product is negative, then there is a root to be found—the sign changed. If both f1 and f3 were positive or both negative, the product would be positive indicating no root in the interval.

Now divide the interval x1 to x3 in half and call that new point x2. It is found by taking (x3 + x1) / 2. The function evaluated at x2 is called f2. Figure 6.16 shows the solution thus far.

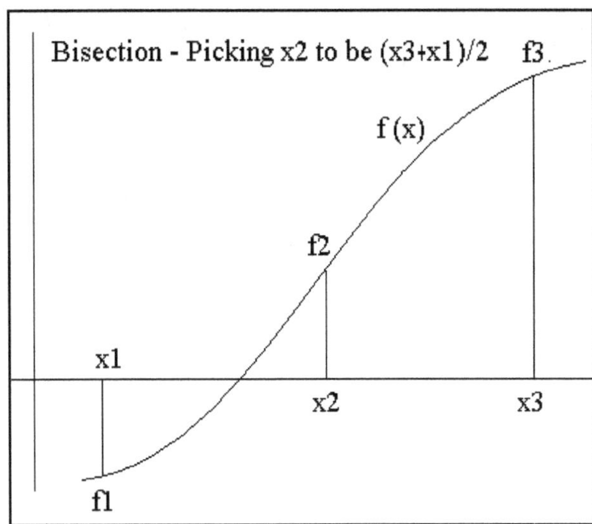

Figure 6.16 Bisection — Picking x2

Next, examine the two intervals, x1–x2 and x2–x3. In which half does the root lie? From the figure, the root lies in the left half, between x1–x2. How can a computer program tell which half the root is in? If we check the products f1f2 and f2f3, one of these will be negative, the other positive; the root is in the interval whose product is negative.

Now we need to formulate this into an iterative procedure or a series of steps that we can repetitively execute. Since the root is in the left interval this time, reassign the right endpoint x3 to be x2 and f3 to be f2. And repeat the process by computing a new x2 that is halfway between the x1 and new x3. This is shown in Figure 6.17.

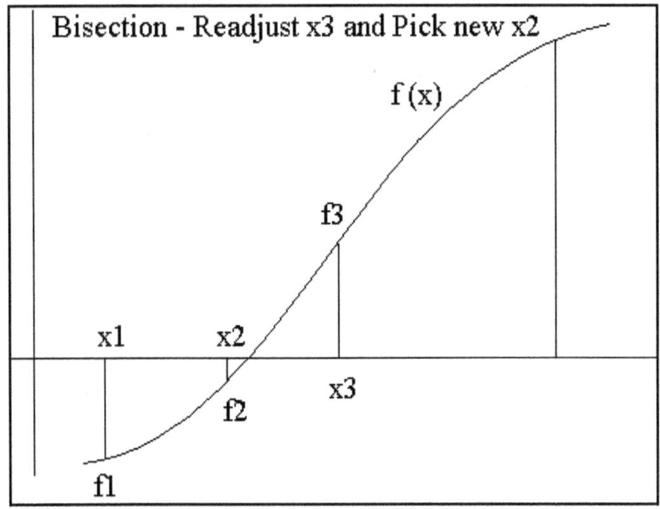

Figure 6.17 Readjusting x3 with New x2

Repeat the process. This time the root is in the x2x3 interval or the right half because f2*f3 is negative. We move the left x1 point; x1 becomes x2 and f1 becomes f2. Again, calculate a new x2 halfway between the new x1–x3 interval. This is shown in Figure 6.18.

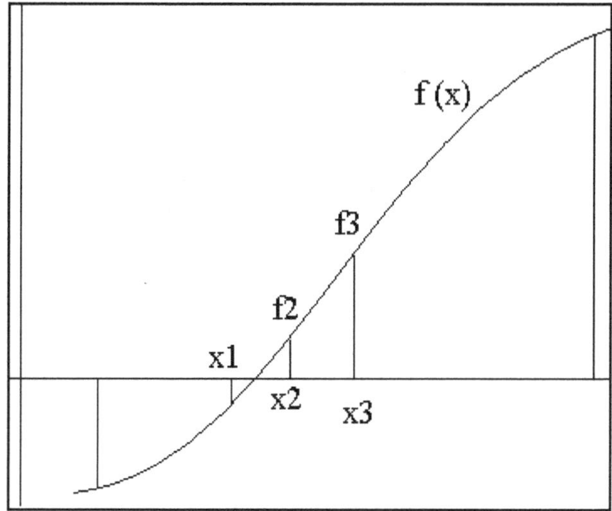

Figure 6.18 The Third Iteration Results

How do we know when to quit? When the new width of the interval is less than or equal to the desired accuracy, it is time to quit and the root is that value of x2.

Engr06a—Root Solving, the Bisection Method

The f(x) equation whose root we wish to find is

$$f(x) = e^{-x} - \sin\left(\frac{PI}{2}x\right)$$

The program should prompt the user to enter the left and right endpoints (A and B), the desired degree of accuracy and the maximum number of iterations to attempt before aborting the attempt should something go wrong.

The Top-Down Design shown in Figure 6.19 includes two functions besides **main()**: the function **f(x)** and **bisect()**.

The **main()** function needs variables **a**, **b**, **eps** for the desired degree of accuracy and it needs **imax**, which is the maximum number of iterations **bisect()** should attempt to do. Variable **root** holds the answer. The design is simple for **main()**.

prompt and input user choices for **a**, **b**, **eps** and **imax**
let **root** = **bisect** passing it **a**, **b**, **eps** and **imax**.

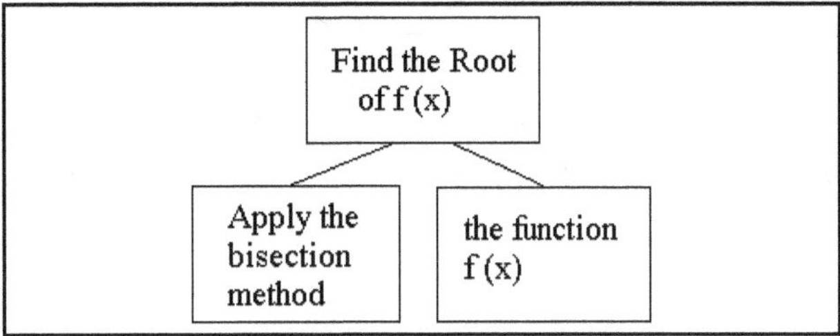

Figure 6.19 Top-Down Design for Bisect

The **f(x)** function is also simple. While one could use a one-line return expression, I store the result in a variable **ansr** and return **ansr**. This way, if something went wrong, you could either insert some **cout** instructions within the function to display values useful in finding the bug. If it was written as a one line return expression, then only the parameters could be displayed.

Function **f** is given **x**
  let **ansr** = exp (–**x**) – sin (.5 PI **x**)
  return **ansr**

The **bisect()** function raises some new details. Initially, we have this line.

Function **bisect** is given **a**, **b**, **eps** and **imax** parameters

Now determine what additional variables are going to be needed. From the algorithm discussed above, we need to define variables for **x1**, **x2**, **x3**, **f1**, **f2**, **f3** and the distance or width of the current interval, **d**. The function counts the number of iterations, **I**, that it takes to find the root. This is done for two reasons. First, users always like to know how many iterations it took to find the answer. Second, in case something goes wrong, we can test the current number of iterations against **imax** and avoid an infinite loop by shutting down. Figure 6.20 shows the main storage diagram.

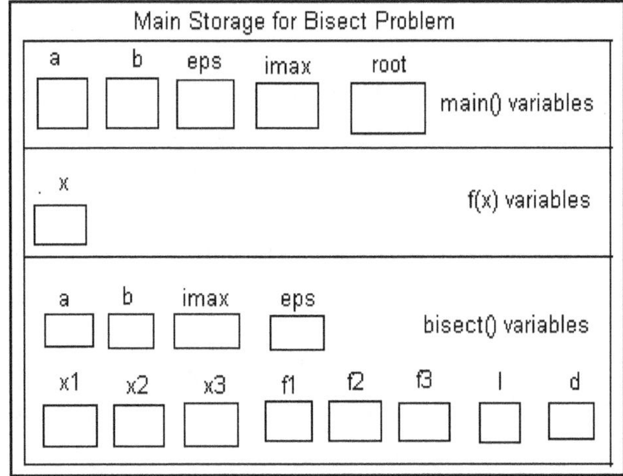

Figure 6.20 Main Storage for Root Solver

Next, using the variable names in the main storage diagram, write out the **bisect()** sequence. The initial steps of **bisect()** are

let **x1** = **a**;
let **x3** = **b**;

let **x2** = (**b** + **a**) * .5;
let **f1** = **f** (**x1**);
let **f2** = **f** (**x2**);
let **f3** = **f** (**x3**);
let **d** = (**x3** – **x1**) * .5, which is the width of the interval
let **I** = 0; which is the current number of iterations

The first action must be to verify that there is a root within this interval.
is **f1*f3** >= 0 ? If so do
    display using **cerr** "Error: no root in the interval:", **a** to **b**
    display also some reasons why such as the function may be miscoded or the values of the end points are incorrect
    return back to the caller a 0

Here we have a slight problem. We really need to be able to abort the program since no solution is possible. A way to do that is covered in the next chapter, so for now, return zero to the caller. The error messages should suffice to alert them.

The main loop must check both for a sufficiently accurate result and for too many iterations.
do the following **while I** < **imax** and **d** > **eps**
    check to see if root is in left half (**f1** * **f2** < 0) if so
        Let **x3** = **x2**;
        Let **f3** = **f2**;
    end then clause
    otherwise it is in right half so do the following
        Let **x1** = **x2**;
        Let **f1** = **f2**;
    end otherwise
    calculate new midpoint and width of interval by
    let **x2** = (**x3** + **x1**) * .5;
    let **f2** = **f** (**x2**);
    let **d** = (**x3** – **x1**) * .5;
    I++; increment number of iterations
end main do while loop
is **I** == **imax** meaning it has not converged? If so then do
    display Warning: after **imax** iterations, bisection has not converged
    display the results so far, which is **x2**
end then
otherwise **x2** is the answer so do
    display Root is: **x2** and was found after **I** iterations
end otherwise
return **x2** back to caller

Next, desk check the solution thoroughly and then convert it into the program. Here are the complete program and a couple test executions.

Engr06a - Bisect Root Solver

```
/***************************************************************/
/*                                                             */
/* Engr06a - Bisection to find root of f(x)=exp(-x)-sin(.5PIx) */
/*                                                             */
/***************************************************************/

#include <iostream>
#include <iomanip>
#include <cmath>
using namespace std;
double f (double x);
double bisect (double a, double b, double eps, int imax);

const double PI = acos (-1.);

int main () {

 double a;    // left x endpoint - root is between a and b
 double b;    // right x endpoint
 double eps;  // the desired degree of accuracy
 int    imax; // maximum number of iterations to try
 double root; // the answer, the root of the equation

 // setup floating point output for 5 digits of accuracy
 // on cout and cerr since bisect is sending error msgs to cerr
 cout << fixed << setprecision (5);
 cerr << fixed << setprecision (5);

 cout << "Finding roots of exp (-x) - sin (.5 PI x)\n\n";
 cout << "Enter the interval in which to search for a root\n"
      << "Enter the left endpoint:  ";
 cin >> a;
 cout << "Enter the right endpoint: ";
 cin >> b;
 cout<<"Enter the desired degree of accuracy, such as .000001\n";
 cin >> eps;
 cout << "Enter the maximum number of iterations to attempt: ";
 cin >> imax;
 cout << endl;

 root = bisect (a, b, eps, imax);

 return 0;
}

/***************************************************************/
/*                                                             */
/* bisect: function to find the root of function f(x)          */
```

```
/*                                                             */
/***************************************************************/

double bisect (double a, double b, double eps, int imax) {
 double x1 = a;
 double x3 = b;
 double x2 = (b + a) * .5;
 double f1 = f (x1);
 double f2 = f (x2);
 double f3 = f (x3);

 double d = (x3 - x1) * .5; // the width of the interval
 int    i = 0;              // the current number of iterations

 // verify there is a solution
 if (f1*f3 >= 0) {
  cerr << "Error: no root in the interval: "
       << a << " to " << b << endl
       << "The function may be miscoded or\n"
       << "the values of the end points are incorrect\n";
  return 0;
 }

 // find the root, stop when the root is sufficiently accurate
 // or imax iterations have been done
 while (i < imax && d > eps) {

  if (f1 * f2 < 0) { // is root in left half?
   x3 = x2;          // yes, so move right end point leftwards
   f3 = f2;
  }
  else {             // root in right half
   x1 = x2;          // so move left end point rightwards
   f1 = f2;
  }

  // calculate new midpoint and width of interval
  x2 = (x3 + x1) * .5;
  f2 = f (x2);
  d = (x3 - x1) * .5;
  i++;
 }

 // check if it converged or not - either way, display results
 if (i == imax) {
  cerr << "Warning: after " << imax
       << " iterations, bisection has not converged\n"
       << "Root thus far is: " << x2 << endl;
 }
 else {
  cout << "Root is: " << x2
       << " found after " << i << " iterations\n";
 }
```

```

 return x2; // return root of function
}

/***************************************************************/
/*                                                             */
/* f(x): exp(-1) - sin (.5 PI x)                               */
/*                                                             */
/***************************************************************/

double f (double x) {
 double ansr;
 ansr = exp (-x) - sin (.5 * PI * x);
 return ansr;
 // return exp (-x) - sin (.5 * PI * x);
}
```

```
Two Sample Test Runs - Engr06a - Bisect Root Solver
```

```
Finding roots of exp (-x) - sin (.5 PI x)

Enter the interval in which to search for a root
Enter the left endpoint:  .4
Enter the right endpoint: .5
Enter the desired degree of accuracy, such as .000001
.000001
Enter the maximum number of iterations to attempt: 100

Root is: 0.44357 found after 16 iterations

==== second test run ==================================

Finding roots of exp (-x) - sin (.5 PI x)

Enter the interval in which to search for a root
Enter the left endpoint:  .1
Enter the right endpoint: .2
Enter the desired degree of accuracy, such as .000001
.000001
Enter the maximum number of iterations to attempt: 100

Error: no root in the interval: 0.10000 to 0.20000
The function may be miscoded or
the values of the the end points are incorrect
```

Some of the awkwardness of the solution will be alleviated with the new C++ features covered in the next chapter. The largest limitation to this solution is that the function **f(x)** must be self-contained. In other words, **main()** cannot input values for some other variables that are needed in the function **f(x)**. If it did, then with just what we know now, we would have to pass those variables to **bisect()**, which would in turn pass them onto **f(x)**. And if we did that, we would not have a generalized **bisect()** function that can find the root of any function, we would have to write lots of specialized **bisect()** functions that took all sorts of other parameters just to pass on to the more specialized **f(x)** function. The new features covered in the next chapter will handle this situation.

Design Exercises

1. Acme Company is planning to create a Shapes Helper Package that consists of a number of helpful graphical drawing functions. Write the pseudocode for each of these functions. The rectangle functions are passed a length and width. The circle functions are passed the radius.

getRectangleArea() returns the area of the rectangle.
getRectanglePerimeter() returns the perimeter of the rectangle.
getCircleArea() returns the area of the circle (PI * radius * radius)
getCircleCircum() returns the circumference (2 * PI * radius)

2. A billing application needs frequently to determine the number of days between a pair of dates. A single date is stored as three integers for month, day, and year. The billing program needs to know the number of days between pairs of dates for every set of data in the master file. Thus, it would be desirable for the main program to do something like

if (numDays (.....) > 30) { // print a bill

In order to calculate the number of days between two dates, it is usually more convenient to convert the date into a Julian day number, which is the number of days since noon on January 1, 4713 B.C. The following sequence converts a date (month, day, year) into the corresponding Julian day.

if the month is 1 or 2, add 12 to month and subtract 1 from the year
Julian day = 1720994.5 + day + (int) ((month + 1) * 30.6001) +
(int) (365.25 * year)
if the original date is greater than October 15, 1582, then add one more term to the above Julian day equation: (int) (2 – year / 100 + year / 400).

Since the **numDays()** function needs to convert two dates into the Julian day equivalent, it makes sense to also have a **toJulian()** function. Write out the pseudocode for each of the two functions: **numDays()** and **toJulian()**. Be sure to indicate what variables are being passed to your functions and what is being returned.

Stop! Do These Exercises Before Programming

Correct the syntax and logical goofs in the following problems one through seven.

1. The compiler issues an error on this one. Why? How can it be fixed?

```
#include <iostream>
#include <iomanip>
using namespace std;

int main () {
 double x = 99;
 double y;
 y = fun (x);
 cout << y;
 return 0;
}
double fun (double x) {
 return x * x * x;
}
```

2. The linker issues an error on this one. Why? How can it be fixed?

```
#include <iostream>
#include <iomanip>
using namespace std;

fun1 (double x);

int main () {
 double x = 99;
 double y;
 y = fun1(x);
 cout << y << endl;
 return 0;
}
double fun1 (double x) {
 return x * x * x;
}
```

3. This one does not work right. Why? How can it be fixed?

```
#include <iostream>
#include <iomanip>
using namespace std;

int fun2 (double x);
int main () {
 double x = 99;
 double y;
 fun2 (x);
 cout << y << endl;
 return 0;
}

int fun2 (double x) {
 return x * x * x;
}
```

4. This one creates a compiler error. Why? How can it be fixed?

```
#include <iostream>
#include <iomanip>
using namespace std;

double fun3 (double x);

int main () {
 double x = 99;
 double y;
 y = fun3 (x);
 cout << y << endl;
 return 0;
}
double fun3 (double x) {
 double sum = x * x * x;
}
```

5. This one does not produce the correct output. Why? How can it be fixed?

```
#include <iostream>
#include <iomanip>
using namespace std;

double fun4 (double x);

int main () {
 double x = 99;
 double y;
 y = double fun4 (double x);
 cout << y << endl;
 return 0;
}

double fun4 (double x) {
 return x * x * x;
}
```

6. This one produces the wrong results. Why? How can it be fixed?

```
#include <iostream>
#include <iomanip>
using namespace std;

double fun5 (double x, int power);

int main () {
 double x = 99;
 double y;
 y = fun5 (x);
 cout << y << endl;
 return 0;
}

double fun5 (double x, int power) {
 double ansr = pow (x, power);
 return power;
}
```

7. This one creates a compiler error about local functions not supported. Why? How can it be fixed?

```
#include <iostream>
#include <iomanip>
using namespace std;

double fun6 (double x);

int main () {
 double x = 99;
 double y;
 y = fun6 (x);
     double fun6 (double x) {
      return = x * x * x;
     }
 cout << y << endl;
 return 0;
}
```

8. What will the **cout** display for the variables **a**, **b** and **c**?

```
#include <iostream>
#include <iomanip>
using namespace std;

int  fun (int a, int b);
int main () {
 int a = 1;
 int b = 2;
 int c = 3;
 c = fun (a, b);
 cout << c << " " << b << " " << a << endl;
 return 0;
}
int  fun (int a, int b) {
 a = 42;
 b = 42;
 return 42;
}
```

9. What will the **cout** display for the variables **a**, **b** and **c**?

```
#include <iostream>
#include <iomanip>
using namespace std;

int  fun (int a, int b);

int main () {
 int a = 1;
 int b = 2;
 int c = 3;
 if (a == 1) {
  int d = 42;
  int c;
  c = fun (d, a);
 }
 cout << c << " " << b << " " << a << endl;
 return 0;
}

int  fun (int a, int b) {
 return a + b;
}
```

Programming Problems

Problem Cs06-1—Leap Year Determination Program

Write a function called **isLeap()** that takes one integer parameter, the year, and returns a **bool** value of **true** if the parameter **year** is indeed a leap year and **false** if it is not a leap year. No data is either input or output from within this function.

A year IS a leap year if it satisfies EITHER of these rules:
(1) the year is evenly divisible by 4 but not by 100
(2) the year is evenly divisible by 400

These years are leap years: 1600, 1988, 1992, 2000, 2400.
These years are not leap years: 1900, 1991, 1994, 2200.

Write a **main()** function to input a year, call the **isLeap()** function and output that year plus the text either "Leap Year" or "Not a Leap Year." It should loop and repeat until the end of file is signaled by the user pressing the ^Z key (CTRL-Z). Test with the above nine values.

Problem Cs06-2—Determining the Number of Days in a Month

Write a function, **daysInMonth()**, that is passed a pair of integers, the **year** and the **month**, and returns an integer representing the number of days in that month. The function does not read any input nor write any output. Note that February has 28 days except in a leap year when it has 29 days.

The **daysInMonth()** function must call **isLeap()** function when it is necessary to determine if this is a leap year or not. **Use the exact same isLeap() function coded in Problem Cs06-1; no changes to it are needed or wanted.**

Write a **main()** function to input the month and year, call **daysInMonth()** to get the number of days in that month and output the number of days in that month. It should repeat the process until the end of file is signaled.

Test with the following runs:

```
02 1600
02 1991
12 1990
01 1976
06 1776
```

Problem Cs06-3—The Valid Date Program

Write a function, named **isDate()**, that takes three integer arguments representing a calendar date as month, day, and year. The function returns a **bool**—**true** if the date is valid and returns **false** if the date is invalid. The function does not read any input or write any output.

The date is valid if the year is between 1600 and 2400, inclusive, the month is between 1 and 12, inclusive, and the day is within the appropriate range for the month. The **isDate()** function must call the **daysInMonth()** function from Problem Cs06-2 to determine the number of days in a month. The function, **isDate()**, does not have any input or output statements in it. **Note, you should use the exact same daysInMonth() and isLeap() functions copied exactly as they are in the previous two problems with NO changes.**

Write a **main()** function to input a date (as three integers, month, day, and year), call the **isDate()** function and write the output. Do not use any prompts; all input comes from the file **dates.txt**.

Write the output in this format:

```
02-09-1995
06-31-1993    INVALID DATE
10-01-2000
13-15-1999    INVALID DATE
```

Always print two digits for the month and day, and separate the month, day, and year with hyphens. To produce the leading 0's, you may use the **setfill ('0')** function. If the date is invalid, write "INVALID DATE" on the same line after the date, but if the date is valid, leave the rest of the line blank.

Problem Cs06-4—Checking Account Monthly Report

Write a Top-Down Design and a C++ program with functions to create a checking account monthly balance report. The first line of input contains the account number and the beginning balance. On the subsequent lines are a variable number of checking account transactions. There are two types, a deposit entry, and a check entry. The first character is 1 for a check or 2 for a deposit. Next on the line is the monetary amount of that transaction.

A simple test run might consist of the following

```
11234152  879.46
1 400.00
2 100.00
```

For each transaction, service charges must be calculated and applied to the running account balance. For a deposit, there is a 10-cent charge. For a check, there is a 15-cent charge. Also, should the balance ever drop below $500, then there is a one-time monthly $5.00 service charge. If the current balance should ever fall below $50, display a warning message. If the current balance should ever become negative (overdrawn), then apply a $10 service charge per each check written until the balance becomes positive again.

Finally, when the end of file occurs, display the ending monthly balance, the total monthly deposits, total monthly checks, and the total service charges applied that month. Test the program with file **account.txt**.

The above simple set of transactions would be displayed as follows.

```
Beginning balance:            $ 879.46

Check amount:                 $ 400.00
Service charge:               $   0.15
Service charge below $500:    $   5.00
Total service charges:        $   5.15
Current Balance:              $ 474.31

Deposit amount:               $ 100.00
Service charge:               $   0.10
Total service charges:        $   0.10
Current Balance:              $ 574.21

Beginning balance:            $ 879.46
Total checks:                 $ 400.00
Total deposits:               $ 100.00
Total service charges:        $   5.25

Ending balance:               $ 574.21
```

Problem Cs06-5—The Factorial Function

Write a function called **factorial()** that is passed a long integer number and returns that number's factorial. That is, if **factorial()** is passed 5, it should return 5! or 5 * 4 * 3 * 2 * 1.

Next, write a **main()** function that prompts the user for a number and then displays its factorial. Repeat the process until the user enters a –1 to quit. The output should be formatted similar to this.

5! = 120

Problem Engr06-1—Function Evaluation, Min/Max and Files

Part A. Given the function:

$$f(x) = 4e^{-\frac{x}{2}} \sin(2x - .3)$$

Write a program to evaluate the function beginning at x = –2.0 through +4.0 in steps of .2. On each iteration, call an **f(x)** function to calculate the function at the current x value. Then, display **x** and **f(x)** both to the screen and to a file called **result.txt**. The screen output only should contain column headings, nicely centered above the columns of data. The **result.txt** file should just contain the two numerical values separated by blanks on each line. Use a precision of five decimal places for both the screen and file output.

Part B. Given the file **result.txt**, write another program that reads in the file of results; each line of that file should contain a pair of values **x** and **f(x)**. For each pair of values, display them in a columnar format as was done in Part A.

The main program should determine both the maximum and minimum values of **f(x)**. Do not hard code the number of lines to input; we might change the evaluation range in Part A. When the end of file is reached, display the results similar to the following:

```
The function was evaluated from x = aaaaa to x = bbbbb
The function has a minimum value of nnnnn at x = mmmmm
The function has a maximum value of rrrrr at x = qqqqq
```

Note that you will need to save both the first and last values of **x** to create the first line of output.

Problem Engr06-2—Probability Theory

In probability theory, one problem that often arises is how many combinations of **n** objects taken **p** at a time are there? The combinatorial function is C (n,p) and is given by

$$C(n,p) = \frac{n!}{(n-p)!p!}$$

Write a function **C()** that is passed the two integers, **n** and **p**, and returns the number of combinations based on the formula. Do not just calculate the equation as is. Instead, first work out the ratio of successive C's for a given **n**—that is on paper work out the ratio of C(n,p+1)/C(n,p). Your implementation of the function **C()** should make use of this ratio. Note that C(n,0) is defined to be 1.

Write a **main()** function that prompts the user for values of **n** and **p** and then displays the number of combinations. Repeat the process until the user enters ^Z for end of file.

Test your program with these entries and any others that you deem appropriate to demonstrate that the C(n,p) function works properly in all cases.

N	P	C(n,p)
0	0	1
1	0	1
1	1	1
4	2	6

Problem Engr06-3—Prime Number Function

Write a function **isPrime()** that is passed a long integer number and returns a **bool** whose value is **true** if that number is a prime number and whose value is **false** if it is not a prime number. A number **x** is a prime number if it is not evenly divisible by any other number between 2 and **sqrt (x)**. Note that 1 is a prime number as is 2 and 3 but 4 is not a prime number.

Write a **main()** function that prompts the user to input a number and then display that number along with a message indicating whether or not it is a prime number. Your output should look something like this.

```
1 is prime
4 not prime
5 is prime
6 not prime
```

Test your program with these values:

1, 4, 5, 6 100, 101, 94274, 93743, 2147000, 2147001

Problem Engr06-4—Root Solving

Modify the sample program **Engr06a** to use bisection to find the roots of these functions. In both cases, five digits of accuracy are required. Limit the maximum number of iterations to 100.

A. f (x) = x2 + 2x – 15, where a = 2.8 and b = 3.1
B. f (x) = sin (x), where a = 170 degrees and b = 190 degrees

Problem Engr06-5—Re-forming of Cyclohexane into Benzene (Chemical Engineering)

Chemical engineers often encounter difficult equations to solve when calculating the mass balances of chemical reactions. For example, the conversion of hydrocarbons to other hydrocarbons with higher octane numbers is called re-forming. For a simple example, Cyclohexane re-forms into benzene. The reaction equation based on lb-moles is given by

$$\frac{(4+3n)^3 n}{\frac{(1-n)}{13}(5+3n)^3} = 14.7$$

where n is the volume of benzene produced in lb-mole.

Solving for n is difficult. However, we can use our bisect root solving method to find n. Rearrange the equation into the format of f(n) = 0, by moving the 14.7 to the other side.

Create a function **f(n)** that computes the above formula. Then, modify the **Engr06a** sample program. Look for a root between .5 and 1.0 using an accuracy of .000001 and a maximum number of iterations of 100. You should get the result of .64345 for the resulting value of **n**.

Chapter 7—More on Functions

Section A: Basic Theory

Introduction

When one starts using functions, more often than not, one encounters circumstances in which a function needs to return more than one result. Yet, a function can only return a single value. A **reference variable**, which is the memory address of the passed argument, is used to allow a function to directly modify the contents of a calling function's variable. Reference variables are a powerful feature of the language.

The remaining storage classes of data are discussed along with more applications for functions.

Reference Variables

A **reference variable** is the memory address of the argument being passed to a function. The compiler is responsible for the implementation details. Instead of passing a copy of the contents of the variable, C++ passes a copy of its memory location so that the function may change it directly. Before we dive into the details, let's see why they are needed.

The Need for Reference Variables

Suppose that the program needed to input a starting time. Often, people encode a time in the format of hh:mm:ss, such as 10:42:15 meaning 10 hours, 42 minutes and 15 seconds. How can these integers be input when there is a colon separating them instead of a blank? We must define a character to hold that single colon character and input that character. The input stream's **get()** function can input one single character. Assume that we have defined three integers to hold this starting time.

```
int shrs;
int smin;
int ssec;
```

Consider where the input stream current position is when the extraction of the hours is completed:

```
cin >> shrs;
```

Remember that the extraction operator skips over white space (there is none initially), then inputs successive characters that can be part of an integer, including a sign and the digits 0 through 9. It terminates the extraction when it reaches the end of file, white space or a character that cannot be in an integer. In this case, the colon cannot be part of an integer and thus the 10 hours is inputted into **shrs** and the current position in the input stream is pointing to the colon.

Thus, if we defined a character **c** as

```
char c;
```

then we can input that colon as follows.

```
cin.get (c);
```

The **get()** function inputs the next character no matter what it is, blank, a letter, a colon, a <CR>. If you input the <CR>, it is stored as the new line code, **'\n'**.

Alternatively, we can input that character using the extraction operator

```
cin >> c;
```

because the current character is not white space. Thus, the complete sequence to input the time could be either of these.

```
cin >> shrs;
cin.get (c);
cin >> smin;
cin.get (c);
cin >> ssec;
```

or

```
cin >> shrs >> c >> smin >> c >> ssec;
```

One caution. When requesting that the user use something other than a blank to separate values on input, please include very specific details in your prompt to the user. Otherwise, users get very frustrated trying every imaginable possibility except the right one. Suppose for a moment that the user accidentally entered instead

```
10 42 15
```

What would the lengthy sequence of input instructions using the **get()** function produce for input? Precisely the same results because the **get()** inputs the blank. However, if we used the single chained series of extraction operators, what would result? Disaster, because the extraction of the first character **c** skips over white space and inputs the 4 digit into **c**. The 2 digit then is input for the minutes and so on.

Now if there is a starting time, there is also likely to be a finish time. So we can add

```
int fhrs;
int fmin;
int fsec;
```

and input those

```
cin >> shrs >> c >> smin >> c >> ssec;
```

Let's say the user entered 11:15:08 for the finish time.

And if you have a finish time and a start time, what do you suppose that the user would like to know next? The elapsed time. Okay, so how do you do the subtraction?

```
 11:15:08
-10:42:15
---------
```

This would not be a fun thing to do! While we could write a block of coding to do so, there is a far easier way. The technique often used is to convert the times into the total number of seconds since midnight. Since we need to do this conversion at least twice, a function is desired. Always use a function when facing coding the same thing twice.

What would be the data type of the total number of seconds? If we have 10 hours, this would be 10 * 60 * 60 or 36000 seconds. This exceeds an **int** type under old DOS. Thus, the platform independent method would be to make these total seconds variables be **longs**. Hence, define three longs as follows.

```
long stotsec; // start total seconds
long ftotsec; // finish total seconds
long etotsec; // elapsed total seconds
```

At this point, we need to write a function call to convert the times.

```
stotsec = function . . .
```

Let's follow the procedure developed in the last chapter. First, we define the prototype by inventing a good name for the function, by creating the parameter list and then by adding the return data type. The function's name can be **hms_to_totsec()** and it is passed three integers representing the hours, minutes and seconds; it must return the **long** total seconds since midnight.

```
long hms_to_totsec (int hrs, int min, int sec);
```

Next, define the function header and then code its body. As a first approximation, we can write

```
long hms_to_totsec (int hrs, int min, int sec) {
 return hrs * 3600L + min * 60 + sec;
}
```

Why is the constant written as 3600L? Remember that if the suffix type cast to a **long** is not used, then the constant would be an **int** type. The multiplication would then be **int** * **int**, which yields overflow errors if this program were compiled under old DOS, since on that platform an **int** can only hold 32,767.

Next, we can tentatively write the function invocation as

```
stotsec = hms_to_totsec (shrs, smin, ssec);
```

However, since we are going to be asking a user to enter a time, this is absolutely not the way to do this. What would our function do if the user enters

```
100:-88:99
10:99:61
24:00:10
00:00:00
-10:42:22
```

Naturally, all of these are not valid times on a twenty-four hour basis. If the user enters such, we need instead to reject those. Certainly we can do the following within **hms_to_totsec().**

```
 if (hrs > 24 || hrs < 0 ||
```

```
        min > 59 || min < 0 ||
        sec > 59 || sec < 0) {
```

but then what do we do if it is true, the time is in error? We can return an error code. No valid total number of seconds since midnight could ever be negative. So to indicate an error, let's return a negative number. Which one? It is up to you; it is an arbitrary; any negative value works. Usually, a programmer would pick –1 for the first error type. But we should not just write

```
return -1;
```

Instead, we should return a constant integer that is defined once and used throughout the program as needed. Let's call it **TIME_ERROR**. Its definition is

```
const int TIME_ERROR = -1;
```

and our return instruction is now

```
 if (hrs > 24 || hrs < 0 ||
     min > 59 || min < 0 ||
     sec > 59 || sec < 0)
  return TIME_ERROR;
```

Is this sufficient testing to be done? Reexamine the above four incorrect user entries. It handles all of them except two, 24:00:10 and 00:00:00. Additional testing is needed. We can add a test for all zeros as follows.

```
if (hrs == 0 && min == 0 && sec == 0) // disallow 0:0:0
 return TIME_ERROR;
```

However, the 24:00:10 is more difficult to test. Taking it bit by bit, we can write straightforwardly

```
if (hrs == 24)
 if (min == 0 && sec == 0)
  ; // all is ok
 else
  return TIME_ERROR;
else
 ; // all is ok
```

The final **else ;** can be eliminated—I used it solely for clarity. The other test for **min** and **sec** being 0 is also verbose with a needed null statement for the then-clause. We can eliminate the null then-clause by reversing the test condition result; this is done using the ! operator.

```
if (hrs == 24)
 if (!(min == 0 && sec == 0))
  return TIME_ERROR;
```

Finally, the two test conditions can be merged into one, yielding the following streamlined version

```
if (hrs == 24 && !(min == 0 && sec == 0))
  return TIME_ERROR;
```

Our completed function is

```
long  hms_to_totsec (int hrs, int min, int sec) {
 if (hrs > 24 || hrs < 0 || min > 60 || min < 0 ||
     sec > 60 || sec < 0)
  return TIME_ERROR;
 if (hrs == 0 && min == 0 && sec == 0)
  return TIME_ERROR;
 if (hrs == 24 && !(min == 0 && sec == 0))
```

```
  return TIME_ERROR;
 return 3600L * hrs + 60 * min + sec;
}
```

Now back to the calling function, **main()**. Once we make the assignment to **stotsec**, we must check for the error value.

```
stotsec = hms_to_totsec (shrs, smin, ssec);
if (stotsec == TIME_ERROR) {
 cout << "Error: start time is invalid.\n";
 return 1;
}
```

Once again, C++ programmers are likely to take a shortcut on this sequence by coding the assignment and test into one instruction.

```
if ((stotsec =hms_to_totsec (shrs, smin,ssec))==TIME_ERROR){
 cout << "Error: start time is invalid.\n";
 return 1;
}
```

Notice the boldfaced ( ) parentheses. These are mandatory if this code is to function properly. Consider what it would look like without the extra parenthesis.

```
if (stotsec = hms_to_totsec (shrs, smin, ssec)== TIME_ERROR)
```

Recall the precedence of operators. What is done first?

Always function calls must be evaluated first so that it has the value it represents to use in the rest of the statement. **hms_to_totsec()** is going to be called first. What is always done dead last? Assignments. Thus, the return value from the **hms_to_totsec()** is compared against the **TIME_ERROR** and then the result of that test, either true (1) or false (0) is copied into **stotsec**! The parenthesis forces the assignment to be done first and the test of the value copied into **stotsec** to be done last.

Applying the same technique to the finish time, we have

```
if ((ftotsec =hms_to_totsec (fhrs, fmin,fsec))==TIME_ERROR){
 cout << "Error: finish time is invalid.\n";
 return 1;
}
```

And now we can easily calculate the elapsed time as

```
etotsec = ftotsec - stotsec;
```

I think you can see that we could also do any number of other actions to times in this format, such as adding 30 minutes to one time, subtracting an hour from another time, comparing two times to see if they were the same and so on. All can be very easily implemented.

Let's say that the result was 3601 total seconds. Notice one detail. You cannot just display the result as 3601 total seconds difference! The user would like the result to be 01:00:01 for example. No problem. We'll just apply our standard function creation steps. Invent a good name,

totsec_to_hms() and pass it only the **long** total seconds to convert.

```
... totsec_to_hms (long totsec);
```

Then figure out what it is to return. Here it must return the hours, minutes, and seconds that the **long** total seconds represents. Oops! A function can return nothing or one single value, not three values! Here we run into the brick wall.

Two solutions exist to enable us to get around the barrier that a function can only return a single value. The most optimum method is discussed first, the use of reference variables.

The Reference Variable Solution

When a reference variable is used as a parameter, the compiler passes the memory location of the calling function's variable to the called function. Within the called function all accesses of that parameter reference variable are actually accessing directly the calling function's variable's contents. Thus, if the called function assigns a value to the reference parameter variable, that new value is really being stored in the calling function's variable. Figure 7.1 illustrates this.

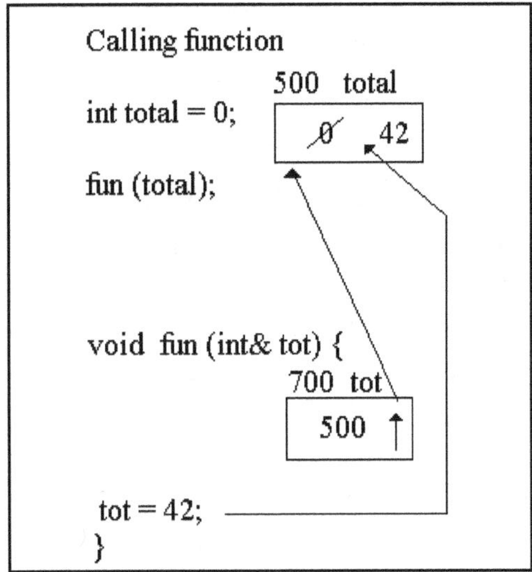

Figure 7.1 Reference Variable

The calling function's **total** is located at memory location 500 and contains 0 when it calls function **fun()**. Function fun's parameter **tot** is a reference to **total** and contains that memory location of 500. Note that **tot** itself is located at some other memory location, 700. When the assignment of 42 to **tot** occurs, the value 42 is actually placed into the calling function's **total** as shown. The compiler handles all of the details for us.

To make a reference variable, simply add the & symbol after the data type and before the name. Both of the following are correct.

```
void fun (int& tot);
void fun (int &tot);
```

When invoking a function and passing a reference to a variable, the calling program is giving the called function total access to its variable. The called function can alter its contents if it desires. Normally, when designing functions, only pass references to variables that the function must alter. In the last chapter's **higher()** function, duplicate copies of the **main()** function's **x** and **y** variables were passed. It is a design error to pass references to **main()**'s **x** and **y** variables to **higher()**; **higher()** has no business altering **main()**'s **x** and **y** contents! Only pass by reference when the called function must logically alter the original values of the calling function.

Reference variables handle the problem of how to return three integers from our **totsec_to_hms()** function. In addition to passing the **long** total seconds, we must pass three references to the three integer answer variables of **main()**. The prototype is

```
void totsec_to_hms (long totsec,
                    int& hrs, int& min, int& sec);
```

And **main()** calls the function like this.

```
totsec_to_hms (etotsec, ehrs, emin, esec);
```

The actual conversion back into hours, minutes and seconds is very easy.

```
void  totsec_to_hms (long totsec,
                     int &hrs, int &min, int &sec) {
 hrs = totsec / 3600;
 min = totsec % 3600 / 60;
 sec = totsec % 60;
}
```

Let's say that the **totsec** contained 3601 or one hour and one second. The result of the division of **totsec** by 3600 seconds per hour is 1. The 1 is stored in **hrs**, which is a reference to **main()**'s **ehrs**; thus the 1 is stored in **main()**'s **ehrs** variable. The 0 minutes is then stored in **min**, which is a reference to **main()**'s **emin**; the 0 is stored in **main()**'s **emin**. Finally, the 1 second is stored in **sec**, which is a reference to **main()**'s **esec** and is stored there.

Basic07a - Using Reference Variables to Find the Elapsed Time

```
#include <iostream>
#include <iomanip>
using namespace std;
/***************************************************************/
/*                                                             */
/* Reference Variables Example: finding the elapsed time       */
/*                                                             */
/***************************************************************/

// global error value
const int TIME_ERROR = -1;

// function prototypes
long  hms_to_totsec (int hrs, int min, int sec);
```

```
void  totsec_to_hms (long totsec, int &hrs, int &min, int &sec);


int main () {

 int shr, smin, ssec, // starting hours, minutes, seconds
     fhr, fmin, fsec, // finish hours, minutes, seconds
     ehr, emin, esec; // elapsed hours, minutes, seconds

 long stotsec, ftotsec, etotsec; // total seconds
 char c;

 // input the starting time
 cin >> dec; // allow for 08:09:09 leading 0's
 cout << "Enter starting time (hh:mm:ss): ";
 cin >> shr;
 cin.get (c);
 cin >> smin;
 cin.get (c);
 cin >> ssec;

 // input the ending time

 cout << "Enter finish time (hh:mm:ss):   ";
 cin >> fhr >> c >> fmin >> c >> fsec;

 // validate both times and convert valid times to total seconds

 if ((stotsec = hms_to_totsec (shr, smin, ssec)) == TIME_ERROR) {
  cout << "Error: start time is invalid.\n";
  return 1;
 }

 if ((ftotsec = hms_to_totsec (fhr, fmin, fsec)) == TIME_ERROR) {
  cout << "Error: finish time is invalid.\n";
  return 1;
 }

 // calculate the elapsed total seconds

 etotsec = ftotsec - stotsec;

 // convert elapsed total seconds back to hms

 totsec_to_hms (etotsec, ehr, emin, esec);

 // display the elapsed hms-each part is 2 characters zero filled

 cout << "Elapsed time is:             "
      << setfill('0') << setw(2) << ehr << ':'
      << setw(2) << emin << ':'
      << setw(2) << esec << endl << setfill(' ');
 return 0;
```

```
}

/***************************************************************/
/*                                                             */
/* hms_to_totsec: converts hh:mm:ss to total seconds           */
/*                                                             */
/***************************************************************/

long  hms_to_totsec (int hrs, int min, int sec) {
 // verify time is valid
 if (hrs>24 || hrs<0 || min>60 || min<0 || sec>60 || sec<0)
  return TIME_ERROR;
 if (hrs == 0 && min == 0 && sec == 0) // disallow 0:0:0
  return TIME_ERROR;
 if (hrs == 24 && !(min == 0 && sec == 0)) // disallow > 24:0:0
  return TIME_ERROR;

 // return total seconds
 return 3600L * hrs + 60 * min + sec;
}

/***************************************************************/
/*                                                             */
/* totsec_to_hms: converts total seconds back to               */
/*                hh:mm:ss in reference flds                   */
/*                                                             */
/***************************************************************/

void totsec_to_hms (long totsec, int &hrs, int &min, int &sec) {
 hrs = totsec / 3600;
 min = totsec % 3600 / 60;
 sec = totsec % 60;
}
```

The Static Storage Class

Sometimes we would like to have a function's variable remember the last value it had from the previous call of that function. To see why we might like this kind of behavior, let's examine a typical program application that needs just such a behavior.

When producing reports that fill more than one page, just displaying a title and column headings on the first page is insufficient. Every page of a multiple page report must contain the report title, column headings, and a page number. Obviously, page numbers must begin with page 1 and increase sequentially page by page. We know how to display headings and column headings on the first page of a report. These principles have to be extended to multiple paged reports. Commonly, a **headings()** function is used to encapsulate all of the details of printing the headings, column headings and page numbers.

For the main program to know when it is time to call the **headings()** function, it must know when a page is full and can contain no further lines. This is done by counting the total number of lines written on a page. The variable is often called **lineCount**. Before writing any line to the report, the program must check **lineCount** to see if there are sufficient lines remaining. The number of lines that can be written on a page depends upon several factors including the font size used and the height of the paper. Typical reports have around 55 lines per page; the remaining space is used for margins. Every time the program displays a line on the report, it must add the number of lines just written to **lineCount**. Also, headings must be written on the first page as the program begins. Thus, **lineCount** is often initialized to 99, indicating a full page so that headings are printed at once on the first page. Here is the **main()** function's logic to handle multiple paged reports.

```
int main () {
  int lineCount = 99;
  ...
  // input a set of data
  while (there is more data) {
    if (lineCount > 55) {
     headings (.....);
    }
    // process this record
    // output one line of this set of data and results
    lineCount++;
    // input next set of data
  }
```

Now desk check this coding through the main loop. Initially, **lineCount** contains 99 so that the first pass through the loop, it is larger than 55 lines and **headings()** is called to generate the various heading lines. Then the first set of data and results are displayed and **lineCount** is incremented by one. What is its value now? 100! Oops. Clearly, either **main()** must reset **lineCount** back to the number of heading and column heading and blank lines written or else **headings()** must do so. It is lousy design to have **main()** reset **lineCount** because **main()** has no idea how many lines that **headings()** actually has written. It is much better to let **headings()** reset **lineCount**. Thus, again, a reference parameter variable must be used. The prototype for **headings()** is

```
void headings (int& lineCount);
```

How is **headings()** implemented? The first action must be to eject to a new page. Frequently, the reports are printed and thus with a full page, the printer must be told to eject to a new page. This is done using the escape sequence **\f** for **formfeed** as it is known. Wherever there is a **\f** code, the printer does a page eject and the characters after the **\f** code are then printed at the top of the next page. To see how this is done, let's assume that the report is to appear as follows.

```
 Acme Daily Sales Report     Page: 1

 Item   Quantity   Unit    Total
Number    Sold     Cost    Cost

 1234       10    42.00   420.00
 ...
```

To produce the first line at the top of a new page, **headings()** could do the following.

```
cout << "\f Acme Daily Sales Report       Page: "
```

Next, comes the page number. Let's have **headings()** define and initialize an integer to represent the page number. Each time **headings()** is entered, the page number is incremented.

```
void headings (int& lineCount) {
 int pageNum = 0;
 pageNum++;
 cout << "\f Acme Daily Sales Report       Page: "
      << setw (3) << pageNum << endl << endl;
 cout << " Item   Quantity   Unit    Total\n"
      << "Number    Sold     Cost    Cost\n\n";
 lineCount = 5;
}
```

After displaying the five lines, **lineCount** is set to five total lines used so far. The first page now looks great.

However, after the **main()** function fills up the page with 50 more lines of sales data, **main()** calls **headings()** to eject to the second page and print headings once more. Now what prints for the page number? What is the storage class of **headings()**'s **pageNum** variable? What happens to its storage when the end block } is executed? What happens when **headings()** is reentered the second time?

The **pageNum** variable is automatic storage. As soon as the end brace } is executed, the storage for **pageNum** is destroyed. When **headings()** is entered the second time, storage is reallocated and the new **pageNum** is reinitialized to 0 and then incremented to 1. This version displays page number 1 for every page in the report.

What is needed is a kind of variable, which remembers its previous value so that when **headings()** is reentered, the previous value is available to be incremented to 2 and so on. This is the behavior of data of the **static** storage class. The scope of a static variable is the same as automatic, from the point of definition to the end of the defining block of code. That is, it is **headings()**'s **pageNum**. No other function can directly access it by using its name. (Note that a function can pass it as a reference parameter to a function and then the function can alter it, but that called function is doing so using its own separate parameter reference variable.)

The lifetime of a static variable is totally different from the automatic and parameter classes. The lifetime of a static variable is the duration of the whole program! The storage for a static variable is not destroyed until the entire program is finished and returns to DOS.

Initialization is done one time by the compiler at compile time. It is never initialized at run time when the function is invoked. Contrast this behavior with that of automatic storage, which gets initialized at run time every time the block that contains the variable is entered.

Static variables then can be thought of as remembering the previous values that they had from the last call to the function that defines them. To create a static variable, just add the keyword **static** before the data type. In this example,

```
static int pageNum = 0;
pageNum++;
```

Now the **headings()** function operates properly. Page number 1 prints on the first page. When the function is called to produce headings on the second page, **pageNum** now contains the last value it held, which was the 1. The increment instruction sets **pageNum** to 2, and so on for additional calls to **headings()**. Here is the correct version of the function.

```
void headings (int& lineCount) {
 static int pageNum = 0;
 pageNum++;
 cout << "\f Acme Daily Sales Report      Page: "
      << setw (3) << pageNum << endl << endl;
 cout << " Item   Quantity   Unit    Total\n"
      << "Number    Sold     Cost    Cost\n\n";
 lineCount = 5;
}
```

There are very few variables that must be made **static** in programs. The page number is one such case. They are handy in the right circumstances.

The Global/External Storage Class

The fourth storage class is called **global/external storage**. To make a variable global, simply define that variable outside of any block of coding. The scope of a global variable is from the point of its definition to the end of that cpp file and even beyond into additional cpp files (external). Generally, global variables are defined near the beginning of the cpp file containing the **main()** function so that **main()** and all other functions can get access to that variable. Here is the only type of variable that can be referenced directly using its name anywhere in the program from its point of definition onwards.

The lifetime of a global/external variable is the duration of the entire program. The storage for global variables, like static variables, is not destroyed until the program terminates and returns to DOS. Also like static variables, initialization is done one time at compile time and never at execution or run time.

We have been using global constant items since the beginning. However, non-constant global variables can also be used. Using global variables represents the second way that the elapsed time problem could have been solved. Recall that the **totsec_to_hms()** function could not return three integers for the hours, minutes and seconds. Another way to handle the problem is to create three global variables defined above the **main()** function. Then have the **totsec_to_hms()** store the results in them and have the **main()** function retrieve the results from them.

Here is how they could be defined and positioned within the cpp file. Note that global variables ought to be readily identifiable; I have uppercased their names.

```
#include <iostream>
#include <iomanip>
using namespace std;

// global error value
const int TIME_ERROR = -1;
// function prototypes
long  hms_to_totsec (int hrs, int min, int sec);
void  totsec_to_hms (long totsec);

// global variables
int GHR, GMIN, GSEC; // global hours, minutes and seconds
int main () {
```

From this point onward, all functions can directly access these three global variables. Specifically, **totsec_to_hms()** can directly place new results in them.

```
void  totsec_to_hms (long totsec) {
  GHR = totsec / 3600;
  GMIN = totsec % 3600 / 60;
  GSEC = totsec % 60;
}
```

Back in **main()**, the contents can be copied to other automatic storage variables.

```
ehr  = GHR;
emin = GMIN;
esec = GSEC;
```

Or they may be displayed directly.

```
cout << GHR << ':' << GMIN << ':' << GSEC << endl;
```

It is usually a wise idea to copy the results from the global results variables into some local automatic variables. In this case, the program might need to more elapsed times. The next call to **totsec_to_hms()** erases the current values in these global variables and places the new results in them. Here is the complete program **Basic07b**.

Basic07b - Using Global Variables to Find the Elapsed Time

```
/***************************************************************/
/*                                                             */
/* Basic07b: using global variables to find the elapsed time   */
/*                                                             */
/***************************************************************/

#include <iostream>
#include <iomanip>
using namespace std;
// global error value
const int TIME_ERROR = -1;

// function prototypes
```

```
long  hms_to_totsec (int hrs, int min, int sec);
void  totsec_to_hms (long totsec);

// global variables
int GHR, GMIN, GSEC; // global hours, minutes and seconds


int main () {

 int shr, smin, ssec, // starting hours, minutes, seconds
     fhr, fmin, fsec, // finish hours, minutes, seconds
     ehr, emin, esec; // elapsed hours, minutes, seconds

 long stotsec, ftotsec, etotsec; // total seconds
 char c;

 // input the starting time

 cout << "Enter starting time (hh:mm:ss): ";
 cin >> shr;
 cin.get (c);
 cin >> smin;
 cin.get (c);
 cin >> ssec;

 // input the ending time

 cout << "Enter finish time (hh:mm:ss):   ";
 cin >> fhr >> c >> fmin >> c >> fsec;

 // validate both times and convert valid times to total seconds

 if ((stotsec = hms_to_totsec (shr, smin, ssec)) == TIME_ERROR) {
  cout << "Error: start time is invalid.\n";
  return 1;
 }

 if ((ftotsec = hms_to_totsec (fhr, fmin, fsec)) == TIME_ERROR) {
  cout << "Error: finish time is invalid.\n";
  return 1;
 }

 // calculate the elapsed total seconds

 etotsec = ftotsec - stotsec;

 // convert elapsed total seconds back to hms

 totsec_to_hms (etotsec);

 // save a local copy of global values in case we wish to recall
 // totsec_to_hms for another set of elapsed times

```

```
 ehr  = GHR;
 emin = GMIN;
 esec = GSEC;

 // display the elapsed hms-each part is 2 characters zero filled

 cout << "Elapsed time is:                 "
      << setw(2) << setfill('0') << ehr << ':'
      << setw(2) << setfill('0') << emin << ':'
      << setw(2) << setfill('0') << esec << endl;
 return 0;
}

/***************************************************************/
/*                                                             */
/* hms_to_totsec: converts hh:mm:ss to total seconds           */
/*                                                             */
/***************************************************************/

long  hms_to_totsec (int hr, int min, int sec) {
 // verify time is valid
 if (hr>24 || hr<0 || min>60 || min<0 || sec>60 || sec<0)
  return TIME_ERROR;
 if (hr == 0 && min == 0 && sec == 0) // disallow 0:0:0
  return TIME_ERROR;
 if (hr == 24 && !(min == 0 && sec == 0)) // disallow > 24:0:0
  return TIME_ERROR;

 // return total seconds
 return 3600L * hr + 60 * min + sec;
}

/***************************************************************/
/*                                                             */
/* totsec_to_hms: converts total seconds back to hh:mm:ss      */
/*                in Global fields                             */
/*                                                             */
/***************************************************************/

void  totsec_to_hms (long totsec) {
 GHR = totsec / 3600;
 GMIN = totsec % 3600 / 60;
 GSEC = totsec % 60;
}
```

Using Global Variables in Other Cpp Files—the extern Keyword

In larger programs, all of the coding is not placed into one cpp file. Rather than create a scrolling nightmare, each function or series of related functions is placed into a separate cpp file, and the project is adjusted to include not only the **main()** cpp file, but also all of the other cpp files. This poses a problem for global variables. Suppose that **Basic07b.cpp** was broken into two separate cpp files. That is, let's remove the **totsec_to_hms()** function that **main()** calls and place it into a separate cpp file called **totsec_to_hms.cpp**.

When the **main()** function compiles, the compiler encounters the definitions for the three global variables and creates space for them. However, when **totsec_to_hms.cpp** compiles, errors occur because **GHR**, **GMIN,** and **GSEC** are not defined anywhere in this cpp file. So one could remove the compile time errors by copying their definitions from the main cpp file as shown.

```
// global variables
int GHR, GMIN, GSEC; // global hours, minutes and seconds

void  totsec_to_hms (long totsec) {
  GHR = totsec / 3600;
  GMIN = totsec % 3600 / 60;
  GSEC = totsec % 60;
}
```

Now it compiles without errors. The compiler also creates the three global variables. However, when the linker executes combining all the parts into the final executable file, errors occur. The linker is responsible for actually placing the global variables into their final locations within the data segment. However, after it creates space for the three globals, **GHR**, **GMIN,** and **GSEC**, along comes the second cpp file asking the linker to make space for three more global variables with the exact same names! There can only be one global variable with a specific name.

The answer is to tell the compiler and linker what we are really wanting to do inside of the **totsec_to_hms.cpp** file. We really want this cpp file to be using the three global variables that are defined in the **main.cpp** file. Hence, append the **extern** keyword before their definitions. The **extern** stands for external reference. We are saying that these three are external references to the global variables of the same name located in another cpp file.

```
extern int GHR, GMIN, GSEC;

void  totsec_to_hms (long totsec) {
  GHR = totsec / 3600;
  GMIN = totsec % 3600 / 60;
  GSEC = totsec % 60;
}
```

Where are Global and Static Variables Actually Stored?

Again, knowing a bit about how the computer is really operating helps immensely one's understanding of how the storage classes operate. We have seen that automatic and parameter variables are stored in the program's stack save area. Global and static variables are stored in the program's **data segment**. The following Figure 7.2 represents what a program's exe file looks like as well as what the program looks like when it is actually loaded into memory to execute.

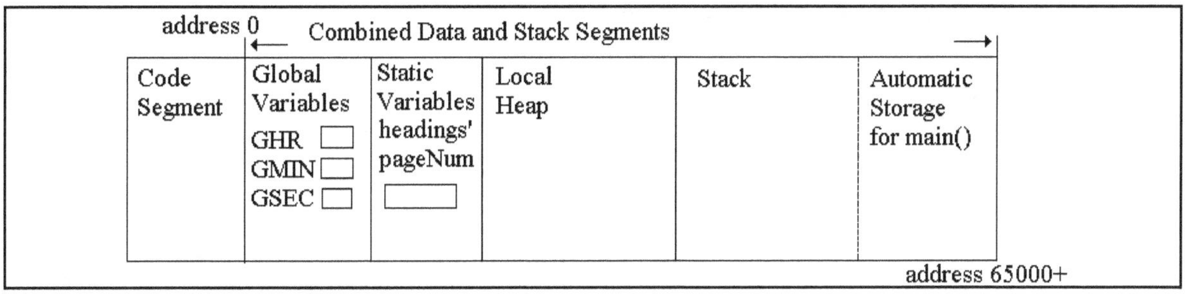

address 0 ← Combined Data and Stack Segments →

Code Segment	Global Variables GHR ☐ GMIN ☐ GSEC ☐	Static Variables headings' pageNum ☐	Local Heap	Stack	Automatic Storage for main()

address 65000+

Figure 7.2 Memory Layout of a Program

The Data and Stack segments are combined into one large segment. The stack is located at the higher memory address while the data segment begins at an offset address 0 within the segment. All global variables are stored in the global variable section of the data segment beginning at address 0. They are followed by the static variables section. The remainder of the segment that is not part of the global, static or stack is called the **local heap**, meaning large pile of unused memory available for our use. Note that all of the actual program instructions are located in the code segment along with the code for our functions and those that are built into the language, such as **sqrt()**.

Now you can see why the lifetime of static and global variables is for the duration of the entire program. The compiler reserves space in the data segment for these variables, and they remain there until DOS removes the program from memory when the program terminates. Storage on the stack is very dynamic in contrast to global and static types. Table 7.1 shows a summary of the main storage classes.

Storage Class	Where Located	Scope	Lifetime	Initialization
Automatic	on the stack	from the point of definition to the end of the defining block of code	to the end of the defining block of code	run time at block entry
Parameter	on the stack	from the point of definition in the function header to the end of the function	to the end of the function	run time when function is invoked
Static	in the data segment	from the point of definition to the end of the defining block of code	duration of whole program	one time at compile time
Global	in the data segment	from the point of definition to the end of the entire program	duration of whole program	one time at compile time

Table 7.1 The Main Storage Classes

Philosophy on the Use of Global Variables

Using global **constants** is highly recommended, such as

```
const double PI = 3.14159;
```

Using global **variables** is highly NOT recommended. Using global variables is generally very bad program design and should be avoided at all costs if possible. Let's see why it is such a bad design idea. When global data are used, there are no longer any controls over who can access and change the data or when and so on.

At a company that remains forever nameless, the accountants wanted every report to be stored on a reel of magnetic tape and kept in the destruction-proof bunkers for ten years just in case the government wished to audit their policies and practices. On the printed version of the report, in the title had to be the volume serial number of that reel of tape that the report was also being written along with the date. IBM tape open programmers supplied a revised tape open function that returned the date and the serial number of the tape volume so that the information could be printed in the heading. All went well until one February 29. On that date, the report said the date was March 1. IBM had an error in their date/time routines and did not calculate leap years correctly.

Within that operating system program, the date/time was stored as global data so that every function of the operating system could get at it. Thus, the tape open programmers quickly fixed the date and sent out a fix to this nameless company and the world. Several months later, a new version of the operating system was installed, and the accountants complained once again that the date was wrong, it was now ahead an entire day. What had happened is that IBM's date programmers discovered their error and applied a fix to the date so that it was now correct. They did not know about the previous fix applied to the same global date done by the tape open programmers. Thus, the date ended up being doubly fixed! Hence, in the next version of the operating system the tape open programmers then removed their fix.

When using global data, all control over who can use it and when and why and where are lost entirely. The result can be chaos. Had the date been passed by reference, then the caller can tightly control who has the rights actually to alter that data. There are many, many more horror stories that have occurred because of global data. Try to avoid using global variables as much as possible. Until the object oriented classes are covered, there can be some circumstances in which global variables are the lesser of several evils and are therefore used. The Engineering application's section illustrates this situation.

How to Pass iostreams to Functions

Commonly, instances of the **iostreams** or file versions of them must be passed to functions and perhaps even returned from functions. How must they always be passed? Let's explore this a bit.

Suppose that we pass **cin** to a function called **fun()** as follows.

```
int main () {
 int x, y;
 fun (cin);
 cin >> x >> y;
}
void fun (istream input) { // a disaster...
  int a, b;
  input >> a >> b;
}
```

Notice that a copy of the input stream is passed. Also, assume that the other variables are defined to be integers. What occurs? When **main()** calls **fun()** and executes the extraction of the integers **a** and **b** from the input stream, all is well. The first two integers are input from the keyboard. However, remember what happens with an input stream. There is a current position in the input stream that is updated as characters are extracted from the stream. There are many other variables that are also updated such as the end of file state and bad data and so on. But what happens to the copy of **cin** that is passed and used within **fun()** when **fun()** returns? It is pitched! Now what is the state of **cin** back in **main()** just as it is about to extract the values for **x** and **y**? It believes **cin** has not even been used yet to obtain any data! Oops! It was a copy of the **cin** object that was used within function **fun()**.

This is a recipe for disaster when passing **iostreams** to functions. And yet, very frequently **ifstreams** and **ofstreams** need to be passed to input and output type functions. The answer is to pass them by reference. If they are passed by reference, no copy is made. Rather, any changes made to their contents are made to the real, original stream. The correct way to code function **fun()** above is as follows.

```
void fun (istream& input) {
  int a, b;
  input >> a >> b;
}
```

Rule: **Always** pass **iostreams** and file streams by reference to functions; if a function is to return one, make it return a reference to the passed **iostream**.

Input type functions are often written to unclutter the **main()** function. Similarly, output type functions are written to also streamline the **main()** function. If you review many of the previous programs in this text, the largest percentage of instructions in the **main()** function have dealt with input and output.

Suppose that the program needed conversationally to prompt the user to enter four values from the keyboard, such as

```
cout << "Enter item number: ";
cin >> itemNum;
cout << "Enter quantity:    ";
cin >> qty;
cout << "Enter unit cost:   ";
cin >> cost;
cout << "Enter state code:  ";
cin >> stateCode;
```

This sequence tends to clutter up the **main()** function making it harder to read. It is even more cluttered if a primed loop approach is taken in which the above sequence is done once before the loop and then again at the very bottom of the loop.

Consider the simplification that the following function call to **inputData()** has on the **main()** function's processing loop.

```
inputData (cin, itemNum, qty, cost, stateCode);
while (cin) {
  ... process and output this set of data
  inputData (cin, itemNum, qty, cost, stateCode);
}
```

Now **main()** is much more readable and streamlined.

How would the **inputData()** function be written? First, develop its prototype. In this case, since it is inputting the actual values to be stored in **main()**'s variables, all of the parameters must be passed by reference.

```
void inputData (istream& in, long& itemNum, int& qty,
                double& cost, int& stateCode);
```

The body of the function is just the original sequence, assuming the prompts go to the screen.

```
void inputData (istream& in, long& itemNum, int& qty,
                double& cost, int& stateCode){
 cout << "Enter item number: ";
 in >> itemNum;
 cout << "Enter quantity:    ";
 in >> qty;
 cout << "Enter unit cost:   ";
 in >> cost;
 cout << "Enter state code:  ";
 in >> stateCode;
}
```

However, using an input file is far more useful and practical. Since a file stream, **ifstream**, is derived from an **istream**, it may be passed either as a reference to an **ifstream** or as a reference to an **istream**. Often it is passed using an **istream&** so that more flexibility can be gained. In other words, either an opened input file stream can be passed to the function or **cin** can be passed. Also, from a design of the function point of view, if the function returns a reference to the input stream it was given, then the calling functions gain more flexibility. If our prototype is

```
istream& inputData (istream& in, long& itemNum, int& qty,
                    double& cost, int& stateCode){
```

then the user can do any of the following to invoke our input function.

```
inputData (infile, itemNum, qty, cost, stateCode);
```

or

```
if (inputData (infile, itemNum, qty, cost, stateCode)) {
```

or

```
while (inputData (infile, itemNum, qty, cost, stateCode)) {
```

The **while** clause is most often coded by programmers.

If one is using a file for input, then there is no need for the prompts and the function can be coded as follows.

```
istream& inputData (istream& in, long& itemNum, int& qty,
                    double& cost, int& stateCode){
 in >> itemNum >> qty >> cost >> stateCode;
 return in;
}
```

Yet when the function is reduced to just this, it does not seem worthwhile to even do all this, since it is replacing only one input instruction that could have been coded more easily in the **main()** function! True at this point. However, in a later chapter the input operation of one set of data will become much more complex and expand to fill several instructions. At that point, this type of an input function is very valuable in reducing complexity.

The same principles apply to output functions. Suppose that a program's report was supposed to be written to a file and not to the screen. The **headings()** function above must now be passed the output file upon which to write the headings. Here is a revised version that displays headings but displays them on the passed output stream.

```
ostream& headings (ostream& out, int& lineCount) {
 static int pageNum = 0;
 pageNum++;
 out << "\f Acme Daily Sales Report      Page: "
     << setw (3) << pageNum << endl << endl;
 out << " Item   Quantity   Unit    Total\n"
     << "Number    Sold     Cost    Cost\n\n";
 lineCount = 5;
 return out;
}
```

Once again, by making the parameter **out** be a reference to an **ostream**, then the caller can pass either **cout** or an instance of an **ofstream** class, such as **outfile**. By returning that same **ostream** reference, we give the user the option of chaining a function call to **headings()** with some other output actions.

Section B: Computer Science Examples

Cs07c—Acme Ticket Sales Report—a Multi-page Report

Let's return to **Cs05a**, the Ticket Sales program. This time because of the rather large volume of tickets sold, we need to print a multi-page detail report of the sales. Recall that each input line consists of the number of adult tickets sold, the number of child tickets, the number of senior tickets sold and the basic cost of a ticket.

Assuming that each page of the report can hold 41 lines, here is the output of the program.

```
Output from Cs07c Acme Ticket Sales Multi-page Report
```

```
          Acme Ticket Sales Summary Report      Page:    1

          Number of Tickets Sold     Total Cost
          Adult   Child   Senior     Of Tickets

              2       2        2     $  42.00
              2       0        0     $  20.00
...
              2       0        0     $  20.00
         Acme Ticket Sales Summary Report      Page:    2

          Number of Tickets Sold     Total Cost
          Adult   Child   Senior     Of Tickets

              2       2        2     $  42.00
...
              2       0        0     $  20.00
        Acme Ticket Sales Summary Report      Page:    3

          Number of Tickets Sold     Total Cost
          Adult   Child   Senior     Of Tickets

              2       2        2     $  42.00
...
              2       0        0     $  20.00
             ---     ---      ---     --------
 Totals:   204     264       48     $3024.00
 Percents: 40%      51%       9%

 Average cost of ticket:             $   5.86
```

The Top-down design that I have chosen is shown below.

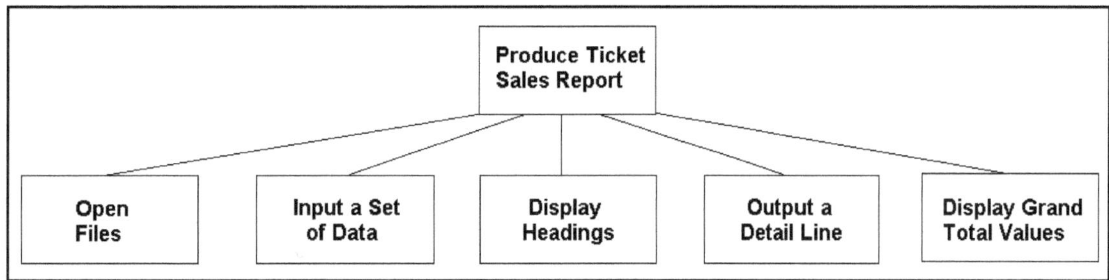

Top-down Design for Program Cs07c

My objective is to migrate as much of the processing details out of the main function as possible. In order to implement the **OpenFiles** function, we must pass a reference to the two file streams, **infile** and **outfile**. This function then attempts to open both files. If a file cannot be opened, an error message is shown. **OpenFiles** returns a **bool**. If both files are successfully opened, it returns **true**. If one could not be opened, it returns **false**.

As you study this example, notice how the actual workload is spread out among the various functions. Each function is short and simple. By designing programs this way, the entire problem is greatly simplified and far more easily written and debugged.

Cs07c Acme Ticket Sales Multi-page Report

```
#include <iostream>
#include <iomanip>
#include <fstream>
using namespace std;

//        prototypes
bool      OpenFiles (ifstream& infile, ofstream& outfile);

istream& InputData (istream& is, int& numAdult, int& numChild,
                     int& numSenior, double& cost);
void      Headings (ostream& os, int& lineCount);
ostream& OutputLine (ostream& os, int numAdult, int numChild,
                      int numSenior, double cost, int& lineCount);
ostream& DisplayTotals (ostream& os, int totAdult, int totChild,
                         int totSenior, double totalCost);

/***************************************************************/
/*                                                             */
/* Cs07c: Acme Ticket Sales Multiple Page Report               */
/*                                                             */
/***************************************************************/
int main () {

 // input fields
 int    numAdult;  // number adult tickets sold to this customer
 int    numChild;  // number child tickets sold to this customer
```

```
int    numSenior; // number senior tickets sold to this customer
double cost;      // total cost of this customer's tickets

// calculation fields
int    totNumAdult = 0;  // total adult tickets sold
int    totNumChild = 0;  // total child tickets sold
int    totNumSenior = 0; // total senior tickets sold
double totalCost = 0;    // total cost of all tickets sold

int lineCount = 99;      // number of lines written on the page
int lines = 1;           // line count of total lines for errors

ifstream infile;         // the input file
ofstream outfile;        // the output file

// attempt to open the files
if (!OpenFiles (infile, outfile))
 return 1;

// process all the input sets of data
while (InputData (infile, numAdult, numChild, numSenior, cost)){
 lines++; // increment count of total lines in case of errors
 // accumulate totals
 totNumAdult += numAdult;
 totNumChild += numChild;
 totNumSenior += numSenior;
 totalCost += cost;

 // eject to new page if needed
 if (lineCount > 40) {
  Headings (outfile, lineCount);
 }

 // output this line
 OutputLine (outfile, numAdult, numChild, numSenior, cost,
             lineCount);
}

// check for bad data on input
if (!infile.eof()) {
 cerr << "Error: bad data in the input file on line "
      << lines << endl;
 outfile << "Error: bad data in the input file on line "
      << lines << endl;
 infile.close ();
 outfile.close ();
 return 4;
}

// display the grand totals and results
DisplayTotals (outfile, totNumAdult, totNumChild, totNumSenior,
               totalCost);

```

```
 infile.close ();
 outfile.close ();
 return 0;
}

/***************************************************************/
/*                                                             */
/* OpenFiles: attempt to open input and output files           */
/*            returns false if one could not be opened         */
/*                                                             */
/***************************************************************/
bool     OpenFiles (ifstream& infile, ofstream& outfile) {
 // attempt to open the input file
 infile.open ("ticket-sales.txt");
 if (!infile) { // failed, so display an error message and quit
  cerr << "Error: cannot open file ticket-sales.txt\n";
  return false;
 }

 // attempt to open the output file
 outfile.open ("results.txt");
 if (!outfile) { // failed, so display error, close and quit
  cerr << "Error: cannot open the output file results.txt\n";
  infile.close ();
  return false;
 }

 // setup floating point format for output of dollars
 outfile << fixed << setprecision (2);
 return true;
}


/***************************************************************/
/*                                                             */
/* InputData: input a set of data                              */
/*                                                             */
/***************************************************************/
istream& InputData (istream& is, int& numAdult, int& numChild,
                    int& numSenior, double& cost) {
 is >> numAdult >> numChild >> numSenior >> cost;
 return is;
}

/***************************************************************/
/*                                                             */
/* OutputLine: output a detail line                            */
/*                                                             */
/***************************************************************/
ostream& OutputLine (ostream& os, int numAdult, int numChild,
                     int numSenior, double cost, int& lineCount){
 os << setw (12) << numAdult <<  setw (8) << numChild
    << setw (9)  << numSenior << "    $" << setw (7)
```

```
    << cost << endl;
 lineCount++;
 return os;
}

/***************************************************************/
/*                                                             */
/* Headings: eject to new page and display headings and pagenum*/
/*                                                             */
/***************************************************************/
void Headings (ostream& os, int& lineCount) {
 static int pageNumber = 0;
 pageNumber++;

 os << "\f      Acme Ticket Sales Summary Report     Page: "
    << setw (3) << pageNumber << "\n\n"
    << "       Number of Tickets Sold    Total Cost\n"
    << "       Adult   Child   Senior    Of Tickets\n\n";
 lineCount = 5; // reset number of lines written on this page
 return;
}

/***************************************************************/
/*                                                             */
/* DisplayTotals: calcs and displays the grand total values    */
/*                                                             */
/***************************************************************/
ostream& DisplayTotals (ostream& os, int totAdult, int totChild,
                        int totSenior, double totalCost) {
 int    grandTotalTicketsSold;// total number of all tickets sold
 double percentAdult;         // percent adult of total tickets
 double percentChild;         // percent child of total tickets
 double percentSenior;        // percent senior of total tickets
 double avgCost;              // average cost of one ticket

 // display first totals line
 os << "          ---     ---      ---    --------\n";
 os << "Totals:" << setw (5) << totAdult << setw (8)
    << totChild << setw (9) << totSenior
    << "    $" << setw (7) << totalCost << endl;

 // calculate and display the percentages line
 grandTotalTicketsSold = totAdult + totChild +totSenior;
 percentAdult = totAdult * 100. / grandTotalTicketsSold;
 percentChild = totChild * 100. / grandTotalTicketsSold;
 percentSenior = totSenior * 100. / grandTotalTicketsSold;
 os << setprecision (0);
 os << "Percents:" << setw (3) << percentAdult << "%"
    << setw (7) << percentChild << "%" << setw (8)
    << percentSenior << "%" << endl << endl;
 os << setprecision (2);

 // calculate and display the average cost of a ticket
```

```
 avgCost = totalCost / grandTotalTicketsSold;
 os << "Average cost of ticket:          $" << setw (7)
    << avgCost << endl;
 return os;
}
```

Cs07a—Multiple Level Control Break Processing The Policies Sold by State and by Agent Report

Commonly, reports need to be broken down into smaller groupings. Consider a national insurance company, which has many agents in many states selling insurance policies. The company needs the very lengthy report broken down into smaller portions. The input data has already been sorted into increasing state code order and then into agent number order within each state. Here is what the report looks like.

```
Output from Cs07a - Policy Report by State and by Agent Number
```

```
Acme Insurance Policies Sold   Page   1

State Code:  1          Agent:   1

 Policy Number      Premium

   1234567        $ 250.00
   1234346        $ 345.44
   1233455        $ 454.45

Total Policies for this agent:     3
Total Premiums for this agent:  1049.89
----------------------------------------
Acme Insurance Policies Sold   Page   2

State Code:  1          Agent:   2

 Policy Number      Premium

   2343233        $ 433.44
   3453453        $ 345.22
   3453455        $ 356.99

Total Policies for this agent:     3
Total Premiums for this agent:  1135.65

Total Policies for this state:     6
Total Premiums for this state:  2185.54
----------------------------------------
Acme Insurance Policies Sold   Page   3
```

```

State Code:  2          Agent:   1

 Policy Number      Premium

   3245674        $ 564.33
   4375645        $ 334.55

Total Policies for this agent:     2
Total Premiums for this agent:   898.88
-------------------------------------------
Acme Insurance Policies Sold  Page   4

State Code:  2          Agent:   2

 Policy Number      Premium

   3476557        $ 235.55
   2453534        $ 456.88

Total Policies for this agent:     2
Total Premiums for this agent:   692.43

Total Policies for this state:     4
Total Premiums for this state:  1591.31

Company Total Policies:            10
Company Total Premiums:         3776.85
```

When printing the data for a specific agent within a state, if the number of lines exceeds 55, the program must eject the printer to a new page. Whenever the agent within a state changes, the program must print that agent's total number of policies and the total premium. Begin the new agent on the next page. Whenever the state changes, also print the state total policies and total premiums. At the end of the file, print the company total policies and total premiums.

The state code and the agent number are called **control fields** because their contents are going to control the way the report is created.

A state code change is referred to as the **major level break** and an agent number change is called the **minor level break**. The detection of a full page is sometimes called a **page break**. In this problem, there are three events that must be detected and handled as we input each line of input data: a state break, an agent break, and a page break. We can use a variable called **lineCount** to check for a full page. But to check for a change in the other two input variables, we must keep track of the previous state and previous agent number. Whenever the previous value does not equal the current one just input, a break occurs in which alternative processing is done, such as printing the totals for the now finished agent or state.

When checking for the occurrence of the breaks, the rule is always check for breaks from major to minor. That is, after inputting a new set of data, first check if the state code has changed. If not, then check to see if the agent number has changed. If not, then check to see if we need a new page because this one is full.

When processing breaks, such as the current state is not equal to the previous state, the rule is always process the breaks from minor to major. That is, if the state changed, then first display the totals for the last agent we were working on when the state code changed. Then the state totals can be done.

The processing steps usually found when a break in a control field has occurred include the following.

1. Rolling any totals into the next higher set of totals, such as adding this agent's totals into the state totals.
2. Displaying this set of totals
3. Resetting this set of totals back to 0
4. Resetting the previous value of this control field
5. Ejecting to a new page to begin this new group on a new page.

Rolling totals makes good sense. Suppose that there are 1,000,000 policies (lines in this case) in the file. If after inputting each set of data, we added that premium to the agent's total premium, the state's total premium and the company total premium, then 3,000,000 additions need to be done. On the other hand, if there are only 50 states and 1,000 agents involved, then by rolling totals, only 1,001,050 additions need to be done. That is, after inputting a set of data, add the premium to the agent's total premium. When the agent number changes, add that agent's total premium into the state total premium. Later on when the state changes, add that state's total premium into the company total premium. This becomes a significant factor when there are a large number of sets of data involved.

The Top-Down Design shows a function for handling the state break, agent break, and headings. These functions are going to be called from several points in the program.

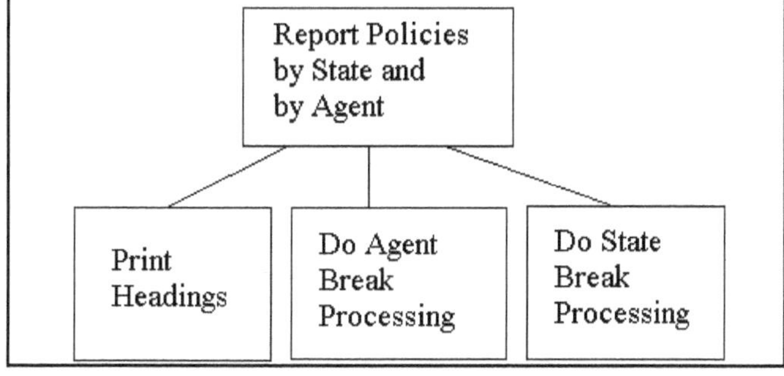

Figure 7.3 Top-Down Design for Policy Program

Next, design the solution. The key variables needed to hold the input set of data include: **policyNumber**, **stateCode**, **agentNumber** and **premium**. A pair of variables is needed to store the previous values of the state code and agent number: **previousStateCode** and

previousAgentNumber. Three sets of totals are needed, one for the agent, one for the state and one for the company. So that these can easily be kept straight in the program, very descriptive names are chosen: **totalPoliciesAgent**, **totalPremiumsAgent**, **totalPoliciesState**, **totalPremiumsState**, **totalPoliciesCompany** and **totalPremiumsCompany**. Finally, **lineCount** is used to track the number of lines written. Figure 7.4 shows main storage for function **main()**.

Now sketch the sequences of instructions needed in the **main()** function.
open the input and output files, displaying an error message and quitting if they cannot
    be opened
initialize all totals
    totalPoliciesAgent = 0
    totalPremiumsAgent = 0
    totalPoliciesState = 0
    totalPremiumsState = 0

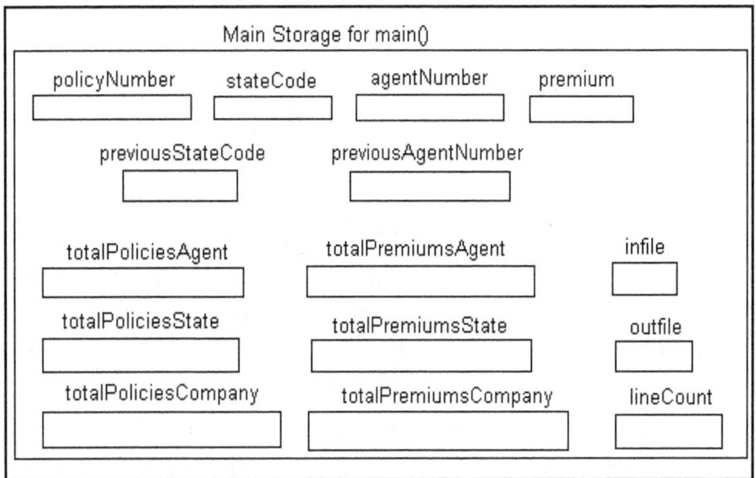

Figure 7.4 Main Storage for Function **main()**

    totalPoliciesCompany = 0
    totalPremiumsCompany = 0
input the first set of data from **infile**, aborting if the file is empty
set **previousAgentNumber** to **agentNumber**
set **previousStateCode** to **stateCode**
call **headings()** to get headings on the first page
while infile is still ok, do the following
    if **previousStateCode** is not the same as **stateCode**, then do
        do an agent break to display agent totals
        do a state break to display state totals
        reset **previousStateCode** to the new **stateCode**
        reset **previousAgentNumber** to the new **agentNumber**
        do **headings()** again
    end do
    else if the **previousAgentNumber** is not the same as **agentNumber**, do these

do an agent break to display agent totals
reset **previousAgentNumber** to the new **agentNumber**
do **headings()** again
end do
else if **lineCount** is > 55, then do these
do **headings()** again
end do
increment **totalPoliciesAgent**
add **premium** to **totalPremiumsAgent**
display this set of data, **policyNumber** and **premium**
increment **lineCount** by one
input next set of data from **infile**
end **while** loop
do an agent break to display agent totals
do a state break to display state totals
display company totals
close the files and return to dos

Continue to sketch the sequences needed for the other three functions. Here are the steps needed for **doAgentBreak()**. For brevity, I have not shown the main storage diagrams for these.

Function **doAgentBreak()** is given the output stream out, **totalPoliciesAgent**, **totalPremiumsAgent**, **totalPoliciesState** and **totalPremiumsState**.
totalPoliciesState += **totalPoliciesAgent**;
totalPremiumsState += **totalPremiumsAgent**;
output **totalPoliciesAgent** and **totalPremiumsAgent**
set **totalPoliciesAgent** = 0;
set **totalPremiumsAgent** = 0;

Function **doStateBreak()** is given the output stream **out**, and **totalPoliciesState**, **totalPremiumsState**, **totalPoliciesCompany** and **totalPremiumsCompany**
totalPoliciesCompany += **totalPoliciesState**;
totalPremiumsCompany += **totalPremiumsState**;
using file **out**, display **totalPoliciesState** and **totalPremiumsState**
set **totalPoliciesState** = 0;
set **totalPremiumsState** = 0;

Here is the completed program. Notice how closely it follows our design.

Cs07a - Policy Report by State and by Agent Number

```
/***************************************************************/
/*                                                             */
/* Cs07a: Policy Report By State Code and By Agent Number      */
```

```
/*                                                                   */
/*********************************************************************/

#include <iostream>
#include <iomanip>
#include <fstream>
using namespace std;

const int LinesPerPage = 55; // the maximum lines on a page

void doStateBreak (ostream& out, long& totalPoliciesState,
          double& totalPremiumsState, long& totalPoliciesCompany,
          double& totalPremiumsCompany);
void doAgentBreak (ostream& out, long& totalPoliciesAgent,
          double& totalPremiumsAgent, long& totalPoliciesState,
          double& totalPremiumsState);
void headings (ostream& out, short& lineCount, char stateCode,
               short agentNumber);

int main () {
 // input data
 long   policyNumber;
 char   stateCode;
 short  agentNumber;
 double premium;

 // previous control field values
 char   previousStateCode;
 short  previousAgentNumber;

 // totals
 long   totalPoliciesAgent = 0;
 double totalPremiumsAgent = 0;
 long   totalPoliciesState = 0;
 double totalPremiumsState = 0;
 long   totalPoliciesCompany = 0;
 double totalPremiumsCompany = 0;

 short  lineCount;

 // attempt to open input master file
 ifstream infile ("PolicyFile.txt");
 if (!infile) {
  cerr << "Error: cannot open PolicyFile.txt file\n";
  return 1;
 }

 // get first set of data - be alert for an empty file
 infile >> policyNumber >> stateCode >> agentNumber >> premium;
 if (!infile) {
  cerr << "Error: no data or bad data\n";
  infile.close ();
  return 2;
```

```
}

// open output report file
ofstream report ("PolicyReport.txt");
if (!report) {
 cerr << "Error: cannot open PolicyReport.txt file\n";
 infile.close ();
 return 3;
}
// setup floating point output format for dollars
report << fixed << setprecision (2);

// set previous values to the initial data
previousStateCode = stateCode;
previousAgentNumber = agentNumber;

// print headings for first page
headings (report, lineCount, stateCode, agentNumber);

while (infile) {
 // has the state code changed?
 if (stateCode != previousStateCode) {
  doAgentBreak (report, totalPoliciesAgent, totalPremiumsAgent,
                totalPoliciesState, totalPremiumsState);
  doStateBreak (report, totalPoliciesState, totalPremiumsState,
                totalPoliciesCompany, totalPremiumsCompany);
  previousStateCode = stateCode;
  previousAgentNumber = agentNumber;
  headings (report, lineCount, stateCode, agentNumber);
 }
 // has the agent number changed?
 else if (agentNumber != previousAgentNumber) {
  doAgentBreak (report, totalPoliciesAgent, totalPremiumsAgent,
                totalPoliciesState, totalPremiumsState);
  previousAgentNumber = agentNumber;
  headings (report, lineCount, stateCode, agentNumber);
 }
 // is the current page full?
 else if (lineCount > LinesPerPage) {
  headings (report, lineCount, stateCode, agentNumber);
 }

 // accumulate agent totals
 totalPoliciesAgent++;
 totalPremiumsAgent += premium;

 // display this set of data
 report << setw (10) << policyNumber << "        $"
        << setw (7) << premium << endl;
 lineCount++;

 // get next set of data
 infile >> policyNumber >> stateCode >> agentNumber >> premium;
```

```
 }

 // process totals for the last agent
 doAgentBreak (report, totalPoliciesAgent, totalPremiumsAgent,
               totalPoliciesState, totalPremiumsState);
 // process totals for the last state code
 doStateBreak (report, totalPoliciesState, totalPremiumsState,
               totalPoliciesCompany, totalPremiumsCompany);
 // display final company totals
 report << "\nCompany Total Policies:        " << setw (5)
        << totalPoliciesCompany << endl
        << "Company Total Premiums:        " << setw (8)
        << totalPremiumsCompany << endl;

 infile.close ();
 report.close ();
 return 0;
}

/***************************************************************/
/*                                                             */
/* headings: display all heading lines                         */
/*                                                             */
/***************************************************************/

void headings (ostream& out, short& lineCount, char stateCode,
               short agentNumber) {
 static int pageNum = 0;
 pageNum++;
 out << "\fAcme Insurance Policies Sold  Page " << setw (3)
     << pageNum << endl << endl;
 out << "State Code: " << setw (2) << stateCode
     << "          Agent: " <<setw(3) << agentNumber<<endl<<endl;
 out << " Policy Number     Premium\n\n";
 lineCount = 6;
}

/***************************************************************/
/*                                                             */
/* doAgentBreak: process and display agent totals              */
/*                                                             */
/***************************************************************/

void doAgentBreak (ostream& out, long& totalPoliciesAgent,
                   double& totalPremiumsAgent,
                   long& totalPoliciesState,
                   double& totalPremiumsState) {
 totalPoliciesState += totalPoliciesAgent;
 totalPremiumsState += totalPremiumsAgent;
 out << "\nTotal Policies for this agent: " << setw (5)
     << totalPoliciesAgent << endl
     << "Total Premiums for this agent: " << setw (8)
     << totalPremiumsAgent << endl;
```

```
 totalPoliciesAgent = 0;
 totalPremiumsAgent = 0;
}

/***************************************************************/
/*                                                             */
/* doStateBreak: process and display state totals              */
/*                                                             */
/***************************************************************/

void doStateBreak (ostream& out, long& totalPoliciesState,
                   double& totalPremiumsState,
                   long& totalPoliciesCompany,
                   double& totalPremiumsCompany) {
 totalPoliciesCompany += totalPoliciesState;
 totalPremiumsCompany += totalPremiumsState;
 out << "\nTotal Policies for this state: " << setw (5)
     << totalPoliciesState << endl
     << "Total Premiums for this state: " << setw (8)
     << totalPremiumsState << endl;
 totalPoliciesState = 0;
 totalPremiumsState = 0;
}
```

There remains one small detail that can turn this program into a "mostly working" program. Can you spot that detail? Here is a hint. Suppose that we have just displayed the last set of data for some state and that **lineCount** now is 55. At the bottom of the loop, the next set of data is input, and it is for the next state. What happens next? Both break functions are called to display the additional total lines, as they should. But have you spotted the problem? The page is full, so where are those totals going to be displayed? On a new page—one that has no headings, page numbers or column headings! Oops. One really ought to check on **lineCount** each time to see if there are going to be enough lines to print totals and if not, call **headings()** again.

Cs07b—Summary Reports Based upon Control Break Processing The Summary Report by State Program

Summary reports are often closely related to control break programs. The difference is that a summary report program only prints the totals when the control field(s) change. Consider the following output from program **Cs07b**.

```
Output from Cs07b - Summary Report by State
```

```
Acme Insurance Summary Report   Page   1

State    Total     Total
Code     Policies  Premium

```

```
 6   1         6      2185.54
 7   2         4      1591.31
 8           -----   --------
 9            10      3776.85
```

This time, the program is not printing anything from each set of input data. Rather, it simply accumulates the totals. When the state code changes, then, in the state break function, a total line is written, lines 6 and 7 in the above report.

The agent break function is removed along with the agent totals. The main processing loop now accumulates the state totals instead. Nothing is printed within the main loop. The **headings()** function becomes simpler since the state code and agent number no longer need to be passed. However, the state break function now needs the state code in order to display the total line. When a change in state occurs, we must pass the **previousStateCode** because the current **stateCode** is that of the new state. Also at the end of the file when the main loop terminates, the state break function is called one more time to produce totals for that last state. Notice that **previousStateCode** is also passed since nothing was input into **stateCode** when the end of file is reached.

Here is the variation program **Cs07b Summary Report by State**. To save some pages, I have removed some of the lines that are duplicates of program **Cs07a**.

```
Cs07b - Summary Report by State
```

```
...
/* Cs07b: Summary Report By State Code and By Agent Number     */
...
void doStateBreak (ostream& out, long& totalPoliciesState,
                   double& totalPremiumsState, long& totalPoliciesCompany,
                   double& totalPremiumsCompany, char stateCode);
void headings (ostream& out, short& lineCount);

int main () {
 // input data
 long   policyNumber;
 char   stateCode;
 short  agentNumber;
 double premium;

 // previous control field value
 char   previousStateCode;

 // totals
 long   totalPoliciesState = 0;
 double totalPremiumsState = 0;
 long   totalPoliciesCompany = 0;
 double totalPremiumsCompany = 0;

 short  lineCount;
```

```

// attempt to open input master file
...
// get first set of data - be alert for an empty file
infile >> policyNumber >> stateCode >> agentNumber >> premium;
...
// set previous values to the initial data
previousStateCode = stateCode;

// print headings for first page
headings (report, lineCount);

while (infile) {
 // has the state code changed?
 if (stateCode != previousStateCode) {
  doStateBreak (report, totalPoliciesState, totalPremiumsState,
                totalPoliciesCompany, totalPremiumsCompany,
                previousStateCode);
  previousStateCode = stateCode;
  lineCount++;
 }
 // is the current page full?
 else if (lineCount > LinesPerPage) {
  headings (report, lineCount);
 }

 // accumulate agent totals
 totalPoliciesState++;
 totalPremiumsState += premium;

 // get next set of data
 infile >> policyNumber >> stateCode >> agentNumber >> premium;
}

// process totals for the last state code
doStateBreak (report, totalPoliciesState, totalPremiumsState,
              totalPoliciesCompany, totalPremiumsCompany,
              previousStateCode);
// display final company totals
report << "   "
       << "     -----    --------\n"
       << "   "
       << setw (10) << totalPoliciesCompany
       << setw (12) << totalPremiumsCompany << endl;
...
void headings (ostream& out, short& lineCount) {
 static int pageNum = 0;
 pageNum++;
 out << "\fAcme Insurance Summary Report  Page " << setw (3)
     << pageNum << endl << endl;
 out << "State   Total     Total\n"
     << "Code    Policies  Premium\n\n";
 lineCount = 5;
```

```
}
...
void doStateBreak (ostream& out, long& totalPoliciesState,
          double& totalPremiumsState, long& totalPoliciesCompany,
          double& totalPremiumsCompany, char stateCode) {
 totalPoliciesCompany += totalPoliciesState;
 totalPremiumsCompany += totalPremiumsState;
 out << setw (3)  << stateCode
     << setw (10) << totalPoliciesState
     << setw (12) << totalPremiumsState << endl;
 totalPoliciesState = 0;
 totalPremiumsState = 0;
}
```

Section C: Engineering Examples

Bisection Revisited—Writing a Generic Bisection Function

In the last chapter, we examined the bisection method for root solving. The **bisect()** function we wrote then was severely limited. Now that references and global variables are understood, a much better bisection function can be written. The ideal scene is to have a generic **bisect()** function that can be given any function what so ever and have it find the root. In other words, once we have coded the **bisect()** function, we should be able to just copy and paste **bisect()** as is with no alterations into any other program that needs a root of some equation found.

The first deficiency of **bisect()** from Chapter 6 is that it needs really to return the root and the number of iterations needed by way of reference variables. That then frees up the function's return data type. An improved **bisect()** function ought to return **true** when a root is found or **false** when a **root** is not found.

The second deficiency is that the parameters to the function whose root is to be found may have only one parameter, the **double x**. In reality, functions are much more complex, often requiring a number of other parameters as well. These additional parameters, while constant in terms of the root solving process, are variables because the user might wish to enter their specific values. For example, a function might also be a function of time as well as **x**, that is, **f (x, t)**. The user enters the specific value desired for **t** and then **bisect()** finds the **x** value. How does the **main()** function get that value of **t** to the function?

One poor method would be to pass the value of **t** to **bisect()**. That requires changing the prototype and function header of **bisect()** as well as finding every function call to function **f()** and also relaying parameter **t** to that function. This defeats the idea of a generic function in which we write it once and use it over without changes.

A far better approach is to make use of global variables. The benefits of using global variables to allow **bisect()** to remain a generic function (code it once—then use over and over) outweigh their disadvantages, in my opinion. Thus, the time variable would be defined as a global variable, assigned its current value from user input, and used directly in the **f (x, t)** function.

The third deficiency of the old **bisect()** function is that the name of the function must be **f()** and nothing else. If we wanted to bisect the **sin()** function or any other function that is not called **f()**, then all calls to that function **f()** within **bisect()** must be altered to use the new name of the function to be used this time. Clearly, this is not a generic way to do things. The solution is actually a simple one—just pass to **bisect()** the name of the function to be used. Let's say that the name of the function to be used was passed as the last parameter to **bisect()**. Here are several possible calls to **bisect()**. (The . . . indicates the omission of the other usual parameters to **bisect()**.)

```
bisect (. . . , f);
bisect (. . . , sin);
bisect (. . . , tan);
bisect (. . . , meltingPoint);
bisect (. . . , heatFlow);
```

While the function might be called **f (x)**, it could also be one of the built-in functions such as **sin()** or **tan()**. It could also be any other function we might write, such as **heatFlow()**. This gives **bisect()** maximum flexibility.

But it brings up a new fundamental rather advanced C++ issue. What is the data type of the name of a function? The **name of a function** is the memory address of where that code or instructions are located in memory. Further, the data type of a function used as a parameter is its prototype. And at this point the syntax is awful as well as advanced. In the next chapter, we will see how a programmer can invent a new name for some more cumbersome data types. So for now, just accept the magical line of coding that generates a reasonable data type that we can use for our function headers and prototypes in which a function is to be passed.

Here are the magical line and the new complete prototype for a generic **bisect()** function.

```
// creates a data type for a parameter function value for bisect
typedef double (*function) (double);

bool bisect (double a, double b, double eps, int imax,
             double& root, int& I, function f);
```

The **typedef** is short for type define. The **typedef** line is defining a more convenient data type called **function** that we can use as a data type for a function being passed as a parameter. We know that the **f (x)** function has the prototype of

```
double f (double);
```

The * in the definition means pointer to or memory address of. Given that **typedef** line, then the last parameter to **bisect()**, which is the function to be used, has a data type of **function**.

Notice that **bisect()** now returns a **bool**, **true** if a root is found, **false** if not. The two answers are **root** and **i**, which contain the root and the number of iterations needed to find that root.

With these changes understood, examine **Engr07a**, which is a rewrite of our previous program from Chapter 6, **Engr06a**.

Engr07a—Using a Generic bisect() Function

The function now called **fun()** is

$$fun(x) = e^{-x} - \sin(.5\ PI\ x)$$

The **main()** function still prompts the user for the interval **a** to **b** along with the desired accuracy and the maximum number of iterations to try. If **bisect()** returns **true**, the root is displayed.

Here is the competed new version of **bisect()**. I have highlighted in bold face the significant changes of our improved program. Notice that in **main()** the function to be bisected is called **fun()** and is defined beginning on line 124. However, on line 47 where **bisect()** is invoked, **fun** is passed as the last parameter. Within **bisect()**, that parameter is known as **f (x)** as before.

Engr07a - Generic bisect Function

```
 1 /***************************************************************/
 2 /*                                                             */
 3 /* Engr07a - Finding roots using a generic function bisect    */
 4 /*                                                             */
 5 /***************************************************************/
 6
 7 #include <iostream>
 8 #include <iomanip>
 9 #include <cmath>
10 using namespace std;
11 // creates a data type for a parameter function value for bisect
12 typedef double (*function) (double);
13
14 bool bisect (double a, double b, double eps, int imax,
15              double& root, int& i, function f);
16
17 double fun (double x);
18
19 const double PI = acos (-1.);
20
21 int main () {
22
23  double a;     // left x endpoint - root is between a and b
24  double b;     // right x endpoint
25  double eps;   // the desired degree of accuracy
26  int    imax;  // maximum number of iterations to try
27  int    i;     // number of iterations actually done
28  double root;  // the answer, the root of the equation
29
30  // setup floating point output for 5 digits of accuracy
31  cout << fixed << setprecision (5);
34
```

```
 cout << "Finding roots of exp (-x) - sin (.5 PI x)\n\n";
 cout << "Enter the interval in which to search for a root\n"
      << "Enter the left endpoint:  ";
 cin >> a;
 cout << "Enter the right endpoint: ";
 cin >> b;
 cout<<"Enter the desired degree of accuracy, such as .000001\n";
 cin >> eps;
 cout << "Enter the maximum number of iterations to attempt: ";
 cin >> imax;
 cout << endl;

 if (bisect (a, b, eps, imax, root, i, fun)) {
  cout << "Root is: " << root
       << " found after " << i << " iterations\n";
 }

 return 0;
}

/***************************************************************/
/*                                                             */
/* bisect: function to find the root of function f(x)          */
/*         parameter function f must be of the form            */
/*         double funct (double);                              */
/*                                                             */
/***************************************************************/

bool bisect (double a, double b, double eps, int imax,
             double& root, int& i, function f) {
 double x1 = a;
 double x3 = b;
 double x2 = (b + a) * .5;
 double f1 = f (x1);
 double f2 = f (x2);
 double f3 = f (x3);

 double d = (x3 - x1) * .5; // the width of the interval
 i = 0;                     // the current number of iterations

 // verify that there is a solution
 if (f1*f3 >= 0) {
  cerr << "Error: no root in the interval: "
       << a << " to " << b << endl
       << "The function may be miscoded or\n"
       << "the values of the end points are incorrect\n";
  return false;
 }

 // find the root, stop when the root is sufficiently accurate
 // or imax iterations have been done
 while (i < imax && d > eps) {

```

```
  if (f1 * f2 < 0) { // is root in left half?
   x3 = x2;          // yes, so move right end point leftwards
   f3 = f2;
  }
  else {             // root in right half
   x1 = x2;          // so move left end point rightwards
   f1 = f2;
  }

  // calculate new midpoint and width of interval
  x2 = (x3 + x1) * .5;
  f2 = f (x2);
  d = (x3 - x1) * .5;
  i++;
 }

 // check if it converged or not - either way, display results
 if (i == imax) {
  cerr << "Warning: after " << imax
       << " iterations, bisection has not converged\n"
       << "Root thus far is: " << x2 << endl;
  root = x2;
  return false;
 }

 // here we have found a root, i is set to number of iterations
 root = x2;    // store x2 in the caller's answer variable
 return true;
}

/***************************************************************/
/*                                                             */
/* fun(x): exp(-1) - sin (.5 PI x)                             */
/*                                                             */
/***************************************************************/

double fun (double x) {
 double ansr;
 ansr = exp (-x) - sin (.5 * PI * x);
 return ansr;
 // return exp (-x) - sin (.5 * PI * x);
}
```

Engr07b—Molar Volume of Non-Ideal Gases (Chemical Engineering)

The chemical and physical interactions between gases and liquids are commonly encountered in chemical engineering. For a specific substance, the mathematical description of the transition from gas to liquid is vital. The basic ideal gas equation for one mole of gas is

$$p = \frac{nRT}{V}$$

where p is the pressure, V is the volume of one mole, n is the number of moles, T is the temperature in degrees K (kelvin) and R is the ideal gas constant of .082054 L-atm/(mol-K).

This ideal gas equation assumes low pressures and high temperatures such that the liquid state is not present at all. However, this assumption often is not a valid one; many situations exist where there is a combination of a substance in both its gaseous and liquid state present. This situation is called an imperfect gas. Empirical formulas have been discovered that model this behavior. One of these is Van der Waal's equation of state for an imperfect gas. If the formula is simplified, it is

$$\left(p + \frac{a}{v^2}\right)(v - b) = RT$$

where v is the molar volume or V/n and the values of a and b are empirical values or constants that are dependent upon the gas at hand. These critical measurements correspond to that point where equal masses of the gas and liquid phase have the same density. The critical values are tabulated for many substances. See, for example, the Critical Constants for Gases section in the *Handbook of Chemistry and Physics.*

Sending space probes to other planets with higher gravities than the earth poses problems in gas containment of the onboard fuels. In this problem, the user wishes to enter the temperature in Kelvin and the pressure in atmospheres. The program must display the volume as given by the ideal gas equation and then by Van der Waal's equation. While the ideal gas formula is a simple calculation, root solving must be used to determine v. By moving the RT term to the left side, we get the usual f (x) format needed for bisection.

$$van(v) = \left(p + \frac{a}{v^2}\right)(v - b) - RT = 0$$

For oxygen, the **a** value is 1.360 and the **b** value is 0.03183.

The **bisect()** function is copied exactly as-is from program **Engr07a**. A pair of global variables, **p** and **t**, hold the pressure and temperature respectively. The **main()** function prompts the user to enter the two end points, **a** and **b**, and then the pressure in atmospheres and the temperature in kelvin.

If the bisection function returns **true**, the results are displayed along with the volume result given from the ideal gas equation.

Here are the complete program **Engr07b** and a set of sample results.

Engr07b - Volume of Oxygen (van der Waal) using bisect

```
/***************************************************************/
/*                                                             */
/* Engr07b - Finding roots of van der Waal's gas equation      */
/*                                                             */
/***************************************************************/

#include <iostream>
#include <iomanip>
#include <cmath>
using namespace std;
// creates a data type for a parameter function value for bisect
typedef double (*function) (double);

bool bisect (double a, double b, double eps, int imax,
             double& root, int& i, function f);

double van (double x);

const double R = 0.082054; // ideal gas constant

double p; // pressure in atmospheres
double t; // temperature in K

int main () {

 double a;             // left x endpoint - root is between a and b
 double b;             // right x endpoint
 double eps = .000001;  // the desired degree of accuracy
 int    imax = 1000;    // maximum number of iterations to try

 int    i;    // number of iterations actually done
 double v;    // the answer, the volume of gas

 // setup floating point output for 5 digits of accuracy
 cout << fixed << setprecision (5);

 cout <<
   "Finding roots of van der Waal's gas equation for Oxygen\n\n";
 cout <<
   "Enter the left endpoint, right endpoint, pressure in atm\n"
      << "and temperature in Kelvin - separated by blanks\n"
      << "Press ^Z to quit\n";
 while (cin >> a >> b >> p >> t) {
  cout << endl;
  if (bisect (a, b, eps, imax, v, i, van)) {
```

```
   cout << "At pressure of:      " << p << endl
        << "At temperature of:   " << t << endl
        << "The volume is:       " << v
        <<  " (" << i << " iterations)\n"
        << "Ideal Gas volume is: " << R * t / p << endl;
  }
  cout << endl;
  cout << "Enter another set or ^Z to quit\n";
 }

 return 0;
}

/***************************************************************/
/*                                                             */
/* bisect: function to find the root of function f(x)          */
/*         parameter function f must be of the form            */
/*         double funct (double);                              */
/*                                                             */
/***************************************************************/

bool bisect (double a, double b, double eps, int imax,
             double& root, int& i, function f) {
 double x1 = a;
 double x3 = b;
 double x2 = (b + a) * .5;
 double f1 = f (x1);
 double f2 = f (x2);
 double f3 = f (x3);

 double d = (x3 - x1) * .5; // the width of the interval
 i = 0;                     // the current number of iterations

 // verify that there is a solution
 if (f1*f3 >= 0) {
  cerr << "Error: no root in the interval: "
       << a << " to " << b << endl
       << "The function may be miscoded or\n"
       << "the values of the end points are incorrect\n"
       << "F(a) = " << f1 << endl
       << "F(b) = " << f3 << endl;
  return false;
 }

 // find the root, but when the root is sufficiently accurate
 // or imax iterations have been done
 while (i < imax && d > eps) {

  if (f1 * f2 < 0) { // is root in left half?
   x3 = x2;          // yes, so move right end point leftwards
   f3 = f2;
  }
  else {             // root in right half
```

```
     x1 = x2;           // so move left end point rightwards
     f1 = f2;
    }

    // calculate new midpoint and width of interval
    x2 = (x3 + x1) * .5;
    f2 = f (x2);
    d = (x3 - x1) * .5;
    i++;
   }

   // check if it converged or not - either way, display results
   if (i == imax) {
    cerr << "Warning: after " << imax
         << " iterations, bisection has not converged\n"
         << "Root thus far is: " << x2 << endl;
    root = x2;
    return false;
   }

   // here we have found a root, i is set to number of iterations
   root = x2;    // store x2 in the caller's answer variable
   return true;
  }

  /***************************************************************/
  /*                                                             */
  /* van(x): van der waals gas equation                          */
  /*                                                             */
  /***************************************************************/

  double van (double v) {
   double a = 1.360;
   double b = 0.03183;
   double ansr;
   ansr = (p + a / (v * v)) * (v - b) - R * t;
   return ansr;
  }
```

Sample run - Engr07b - Volume of Oxygen (van der Waal) using bisect

```
Finding roots of van der Waal's gas equation for Oxygen

Enter the left endpoint, right endpoint, pressure in atm
and temperature in Kelvin - separated by blanks
Press ^Z to quit
24 26 1 300

At pressure of:       1.00000
At temperature of:    300.00000
The volume is:        24.59280 (20 iterations)
Ideal Gas volume is: 24.61620
```

```

Enter another set or ^Z to quit
2.3 2.6 10 300

At pressure of:       10.00000
At temperature of:    300.00000
The volume is:        2.43840 (18 iterations)
Ideal Gas volume is: 2.46162

Enter another set or ^Z to quit
.2 .3 100 300

At pressure of:       100.00000
At temperature of:    300.00000
The volume is:        0.22636 (16 iterations)
Ideal Gas volume is: 0.24616

Enter another set or ^Z to quit
^
```

Faster Alternative Root Solving Methods

The major problem with the bisection technique is that it can take a relatively large number of iterations to get the answer. If the **f (x)** was a complex one and if performance was a design factor, then alternative methods can be used to obtain the root in far fewer iterations. Performance can be a crucial design issue in real-time applications. For example, in a space flight simulator program, roots may need to be found repetitively as the path of the space ship is plotted. The alternative methods generally require knowing more about the behavior of the function around the interval in question. Let's look at three alternative methods.

The Regula Falsi Root Solving Method

The Regula Falsi method is a refinement of the bisection approach. Instead of arbitrarily dividing the interval **x3–x1** in half, let's interpolate where the line between **f (x1)** and **f (x3)** crosses the x-axis.

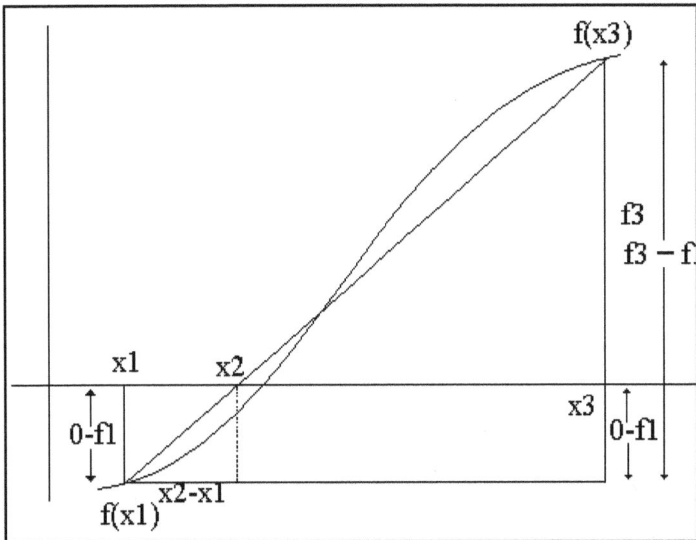

Figure 7.5 The Regula Falsi Method

From Figure 7.5, we have the following relationship

$$\frac{0-f1}{f3-f1}=\frac{x2-x1}{x3-x1}$$

And solving for x2,

$$x2 = x1-(x3-x1)\frac{f1}{(f3-f1)}$$

Thus, all that must be done to change bisect into Regula Falsi is to alter how **x2** is chosen.

Engr07c—Molar Volume of Non-Ideal Gases—Using Regula Falsi Method

In this version of Regula Falsi, I added a slight change to better assist in detection of the ending conditions. If by chance **f1** or **f3** ever becomes 0, then **x1** or **x3** is the precise answer. At the start of each iteration, I check for this possibility and quit if true. All coding in the **main()** function and the **van()** function remain the same, except for the new name of the function, **falsi()**.

```
Engr07c - Volume of Oxygen (van der Waal) using Regula Falsi Method
```

```
/***************************************************************/
/*                                                             */
/* Engr07c - Regula Falsi Method of root solving               */
/*                                                             */
/***************************************************************/

#include <iostream>
#include <iomanip>
#include <cmath>
using namespace std;
// creates a data type for a parameter function value for bisect
typedef double (*function) (double);

bool falsi (double a, double b, double eps, int imax,
            double& root, int& i, function f);

double van (double x);

const double R = 0.082054; // ideal gas constant

double p; // pressure in atmospheres
double t; // temperature in K

int main () {

 double a;           // left x endpoint - root is between a and b
 double b;           // right x endpoint
 double eps = .000001;  // the desired degree of accuracy
 int    imax = 1000;    // maximum number of iterations to try

 int    i;    // number of iterations actually done
 double v;    // the answer, the volume of gas

 // setup floating point output for 5 digits of accuracy
 cout << fixed << setprecision (5);

 cout <<
   "Finding roots of van der Waal's gas equation for Oxygen\n\n";
 cout <<
   "Enter the left endpoint, right endpoint, pressure in atm\n"
      << "and temperature in Kelvin - separated by blanks\n"
      << "Press ^Z to quit\n";
 while (cin >> a >> b >> p >> t) {
  cout << endl;
  if (falsi (a, b, eps, imax, v, i, van)) {
   cout << "At pressure of:       " << p << endl
        << "At temperature of:    " << t << endl
        << "The volume is:        " << v
        <<  " (" << i << " iterations)\n"
        << "Ideal Gas volume is: " << R * t / p << endl;
  }
  cout << endl;
  cout << "Enter another set or ^Z to quit\n";
```

```
 }

 return 0;
}

/***************************************************************/
/*                                                             */
/* falsi:   function to find the root of function f(x)         */
/*          parameter function f must be of the form           */
/*          double funct (double);                             */
/*                                                             */
/***************************************************************/

bool falsi (double a, double b, double eps, int imax,
             double& root, int& i, function f) {
 double x1 = a;
 double x3 = b;
 double x2;
 double f1 = f (x1);
 double f2;
 double f3 = f (x3);

 double d = x3 - x1;        // width of the current interval
 i = 0;                     // the current number of iterations

 // verify that there is a solution
 if (f1*f3 >= 0) {
  cerr << "Error: no root in the interval: "
       << a << " to " << b << endl
       << "The function may be miscoded or\n"
       << "the values of the end points are incorrect\n"
       << "F(a) = " << f1 << endl
       << "F(b) = " << f3 << endl;
  return false;
 }

 // find the root, but when the root is sufficiently accurate
 // or imax iterations have been done
 while (i < imax && d > eps) {
  // alternate done checks
  if (fabs (f1) < eps) {
   root = x1;
   return true;
  }
  if (fabs (f3) < eps) {
   root = x3;
   return true;
  }

  x2 = x1 - (x3 - x1) * f1 / (f3 - f1);
  f2 = f (x2);

  if (f1 * f2 < 0) { // is root in left half?
```

```
     x3 = x2;            // yes, so move right end point leftwards
     f3 = f2;
    }
    else {               // root in right half
     x1 = x2;            // so move left end point rightwards
     f1 = f2;
    }

    // calculate new width
    d = (x3 - x1);
    i++;
   }

   // check if it converged or not - either way, display results
   if (i == imax) {
    cerr << "Warning: after " << imax
         << " iterations, Regula Falsi has not converged\n"
         << "Root thus far is: " << x2 << endl;
    root = x2;
    return false;
   }

   // here we have found a root, i is set to number of iterations
   root = x2;    // store x2 in the caller's answer variable
   return true;
  }

  /***************************************************************/
  /*                                                             */
  /* van(x): van der waals gas equation                          */
  /*                                                             */
  /***************************************************************/

  double van (double v) {
   double a = 1.360;
   double b = 0.03183;
   double ansr;
   ansr = (p + a / (v * v)) * (v - b) - R * t;
   return ansr;
  }
```

The Regula Falsi method finds the roots much more quickly than bisection. Here are the results from a similar test run as was done for the bisection version above.

```
Sample Run - Engr07c - Volume using Regula Falsi Method
```

```
Finding roots of van der Waal's gas equation for Oxygen

Enter the left endpoint, right endpoint, pressure in atm
and temperature in Kelvin - separated by blanks
Press ^Z to quit
```

```
24 26 1 300
At pressure of:       1.00000
At temperature of:    300.00000
The volume is:        24.59280 (2 iterations)
Ideal Gas volume is: 24.61620
Enter another set or ^Z to quit
2.3 2.6 10 300
At pressure of:       10.00000
At temperature of:    300.00000
The volume is:        2.43840 (3 iterations)
Ideal Gas volume is: 2.46162
Enter another set or ^Z to quit
.2 .3 100 300
At pressure of:       100.00000
At temperature of:    300.00000
The volume is:        0.22636 (5 iterations)
Ideal Gas volume is: 0.24616
Enter another set or ^Z to qui
```

Newton's Method of Root Solving

Newton's method is another approach to finding the roots of an equation that yields an accurate and fast solution. However, to enable it to obtain the more accurate root more quickly, more must be known about the function and its behavior.

Newton's method begins with an initial guess for the root, $\mathbf{x_0}$. A tangent line is passed through the function at point $f(x_0)$. Where that tangent line crosses the x-axis becomes the new guess of the root. This is shown in Figure 7.6.

The slope of the tangent line at point $f(x_0)$ is f', the first derivative of $f(x)$ with respect to x. Using the equation of a straight line, we have $f(x_0) + f'(x_0)(x - x_0) = 0$. Solving for the new guess, x, we get

$$x = x_0 - f(x_0) / f'(x_0)$$

The actual mathematical derivation begins with rewriting the function as a Taylor series. Assuming $|x - x_0|$ is small, only the first two terms of the series are used.

$$f(x) = 0 = f(x_0) + f'(x_0)(x - x_0)$$

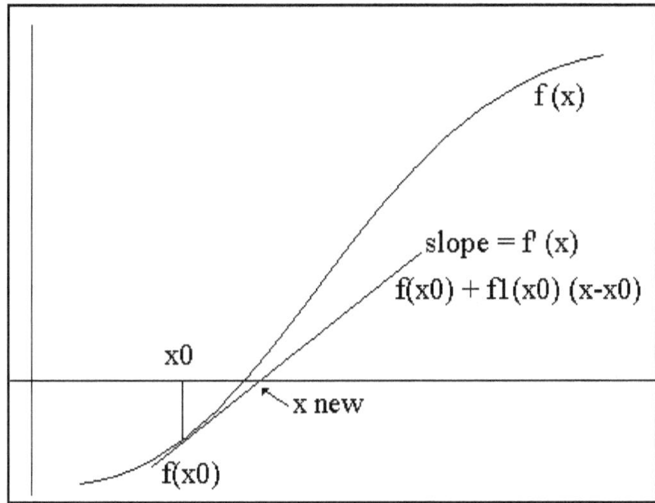

Figure 7.6 Newton's Method of Root Solving

The complete derivation is found in most numerical analysis texts. For our use, it is sufficient to say that we are approximating the function by a straight line passing through f (x_0), which has the same slope as a tangent line through the point (x_0, f_0). Thus, Newton's method requires an initial guess and the first derivative function instead of the interval **a** to **b**. However, care must be exercised when using Newton's method. A poor initial guess can lead to finding the wrong root or worse. The next series of three figures illustrates some of the results of making a poor initial guess.

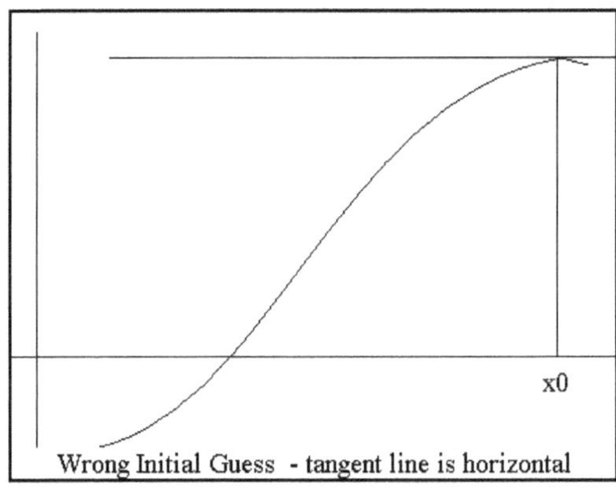

Figure 7.7 Newton — Bad Initial Guess

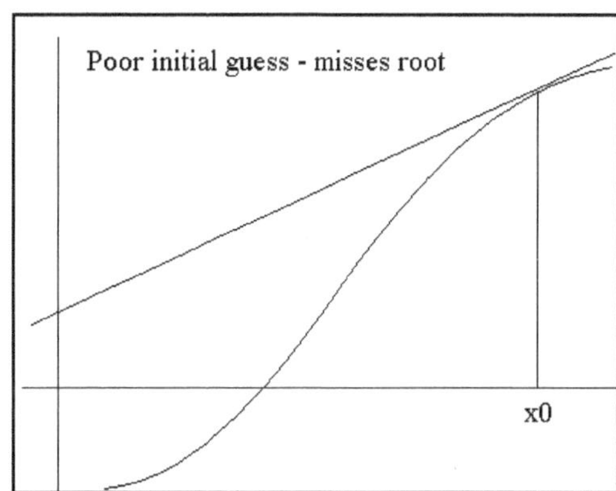

Figure 7.8 Newton — Poor Initial Guess

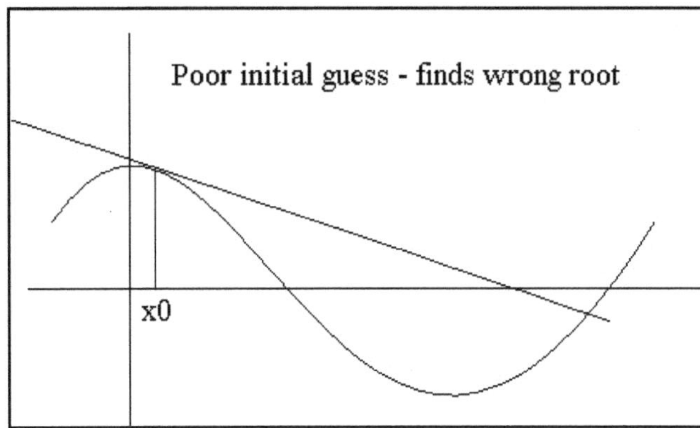

Figure 7.9 Newton — Poor Initial Guess

Another factor is needed for effective use of Newton's method, the multiplicity factor. Suppose that the function f(x) was this one.

$$f(x) = x^3 - 5x^2 + 7x - 3 = (x - 3)(x - 1)(x - 1)$$

Here there are two identical roots at x = 1. A plot of this function around x=1 is shown in Figure 7.10.

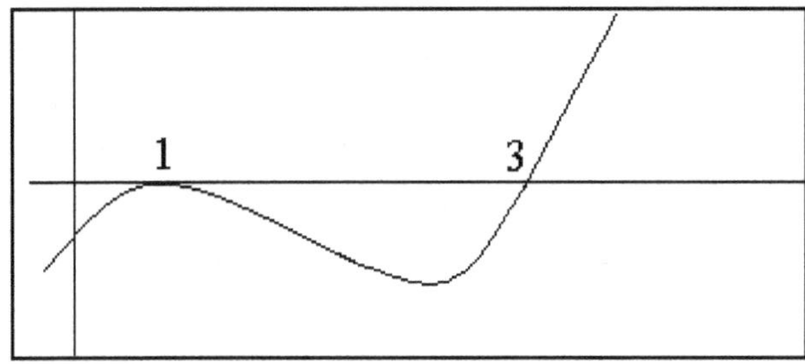

Figure 7.10 Newton — Multiple Roots

Engr07d—Molar Volume of Non-Ideal Gases—Using Newton's Method

To use Newton's method, the first derivative function must be found. It is

$$f'(x) = p - \frac{a}{v^2} + \frac{2ab}{v^3}$$

Another consideration, when coding an implementation of Newton's method is divergence. If the next increment to be added to **x** to get the next guess for the root is greater than some value, say called **divergeAmt**, then the process is diverging. Quite often, that value **divergeAmt** is twice the width of the interval in which a root might lie. In other words, commonly, the left endpoint, **a**, is passed as the initial guess and **2*(b – a)** is passed as the divergence value. If |delta x|, the next amount to be added to the current guess to obtain the next guess at the root, is larger than this divergence amount, then we should display a warning message. It is also quite likely that within an iteration or two, Newton's method will fail anyway.

This implementation uses the Do Until loop because always one iteration must be done before checking upon ending conditions. The steps within the loop consist of

```
do {
    calculate the value of dfdx (x)
    if that value is sufficiently close to zero then
        display an error message to avoid division by zero
    calculate the next amount to add to x to get the next guess
    if that next amount > diverge amount then
        display a diverging warning message
    root += that next amount
    I++
} while (I<imax && the next amount > eps);
```

Here are the complete program and the sample test runs using the same three test cases of oxygen.

Engr07d - Newton's Method to Find Roots of van der Wall's Equation

```
/***************************************************************/
/*                                                             */
/* Engr07d - Newton's Method of root solving                   */
/*                                                             */
/***************************************************************/

#include <iostream>
#include <iomanip>
#include <cmath>
using namespace std;
// creates a data type for a parameter function value for bisect
typedef double (*function) (double);

bool Newton (double x, int mult, double eps, int imax,
             double divergeAmt, double& root, int& i,
             function fx, function dfdx);

double van (double x);
double vandfdx (double x);

const double R = 0.082054; // ideal gas constant

double p; // pressure in atmospheres
double t; // temperature in K

int main () {

 double x;                   // initial guess for root, often a
```

```
 double divergeAmt;      // maximum amount to add to get to next
                         // guess, usually 2 * (b-a)
 int    mult;            // number of multiple roots at this root
 double eps = .000001;   // the desired degree of accuracy
 int    imax = 1000;     // maximum number of iterations to try

 int    i;    // number of iterations actually done
 double v;    // the answer, the volume of gas

 // setup floating point output for 5 digits of accuracy
 cout << fixed << setprecision (5);

 cout <<
   "Finding roots of van der Waal's gas equation for Oxygen\n\n";
 cout << "Enter the initial guess, the multiplicity factor\n"
      << "the divergence check amount, the pressure in atm\n"
      << "and the temperature in Kelvin - separated by blanks\n"
      << "Press ^Z to quit\n";
 while (cin >> x >> mult >> divergeAmt >> p >> t) {
  cout << endl;
  if (Newton (x, mult, eps, imax, divergeAmt, v,i,van,vandfdx)) {
   cout << "At pressure of:        " << p << endl
        << "At temperature of:     " << t << endl
        << "The volume is:         " << v
        <<  " (" << i << " iterations)\n"
        << "Ideal Gas volume is: " << R * t / p << endl;
  }
  cout << endl;
  cout << "Enter another set or ^Z to quit\n";
 }

 return 0;
}

/***************************************************************/
/*                                                             */
/* Newton: function to find the root of function f(x)          */
/*         parameter function f must be of the form            */
/*         double funct (double);                              */
/*                                                             */
/***************************************************************/

bool Newton (double x, int mult, double eps, int imax,
             double divergeAmt, double& root, int& i,
             function fx, function dfdx) {
 double df; // the value of dfdx (x)
 double dx; // the next increment

 root = x;
 i = 0;
 do {
  df = dfdx (root);
  // avoid division by zero
```

```
  if (fabs (df) < .0000001) {
   cerr << "Error: fatal error in Newton.\n"
        << "The dfdx function returned a value nearly 0\n"
        << "dfdx was: " << df << " at x: " << root << endl
        << "On iteration number " << i << endl;
   return false;
  }
  // calculate the next increment to the root
  dx = - mult * fx (root) / df;
  // display warning if starting to diverge
  if (fabs (dx) > divergeAmt)
   cerr << "Warning: function is diverging.\n"
     << "The current delta x to be added to get the next guess\n"
     << "is greater than the specified diverge amount\n"
     << "|delta x|: " << fabs (dx) << " and diverge amount: "
     << divergeAmt << endl
     << "On iteration number " << i << endl;
  // obtain new guess for the root
  root += dx;
  i++;
 } while (i < imax && fabs (dx) > eps);

 // check and display a message if it did not converge in time
 if (i == imax) {
  cerr << "Warning: after " << imax
       << " iterations, Newton has not converged\n"
       << "Root thus far is: " << root << endl;
  return false;
 }

 // here we have found a root, i is set to number of iterations
 return true;
}

/***************************************************************/
/*                                                             */
/* van(x): van der waals gas equation                          */
/*                                                             */
/***************************************************************/

double van (double v) {
 double a = 1.360;
 double b = 0.03183;
 double ansr;
 ansr = (p + a / (v * v)) * (v - b) - R * t;
 return ansr;
}

/***************************************************************/
/*                                                             */
/* vandfdx(x): van der waals gas equation -first deriv.function*/
/*                                                             */
/***************************************************************/
```

```

double vandfdx (double v) {
 double a = 1.360;
 double b = 0.03183;
 double v2 = v * v;
 double v3 = v2 * v;
 double ansr;
 ansr = p - a / v2 + 2 * a * b / v3;
 return ansr;
}
```

Sample Run - Engr07d - Using Newton's Method to Find Roots

```
Finding roots of van der Waal's gas equation for Oxygen

Enter the initial guess, the multiplicity factor
the divergence check amount, the pressure in atm
and the temperature in Kelvin - separated by blanks
Press ^Z to quit
24 1 4 1 300

At pressure of:       1.00000
At temperature of:    300.00000
The volume is:        24.59280 (3 iterations)
Ideal Gas volume is: 24.61620

Enter another set or ^Z to quit
2.3 1 .6 10 300

At pressure of:       10.00000
At temperature of:    300.00000
The volume is:        2.43840 (3 iterations)
Ideal Gas volume is: 2.46162

Enter another set or ^Z to quit
.2 1 .2 100 300

At pressure of:       100.00000
At temperature of:    300.00000
The volume is:        0.22636 (3 iterations)
Ideal Gas volume is: 0.24616
```

The Secant Method of Root Solving

The major problem with Newton's method is the first derivative function. Sometimes the derivative of f (x) is very hard to create. The Secant method is an alternative that does not require that derivative function.

The secant method is passed an initial guess and a delta x to add to the initial guess to get to the next guess. Often this translates into the left end point, **a**, and the width of the interval, **b** – **a**, that has been used with bisection and Regula Falsi methods. Let's call that delta x value the correction to add to the guess to obtain the next guess at the root.

The process starts with the basic idea behind Newton's method.

$$x_{i+1} = x_i - \frac{f(x_i)}{f'(x_i)}$$

If delta x_i is sufficiently small then an approximation for $f'(x_i)$ is given by

$f'(x_i) = (f(x_{i-1}) - f(x_i)) / (x_{i-1} - x_i)$

yielding

$$x_{i+1} = x_i - f(x_i)\frac{(x_{i-1} - x_i)}{(f(x_{i-1}) - f(x_i))}$$

or simpler

$$x_{i+1} = x_i + \frac{(x_i - x_{i-1})}{\frac{f(x_{i-1})}{f(x_i)} - 1}$$

Secant is given the initial guess for the root **x** and the correction to add to it to get to the next **x**. Given those two values and the function **f(x)**, we can calculate the next guess for the root. Pictorially, secant method gets its name from the fact that what we are in effect doing is replacing the **f(x)** with a line through the points (x_0, f_0) and (x_1, f_1), which is a secant line. This is shown in Figure 7.11.

The secant method suffers from poor choices of the initial guess just as does Newton's method. If the secant line should ever become nearly horizontal, for example, the next delta x to add to the guess is gargantuan, clearly diverging. Also, any implementation must guard against division by zero should $f(x_1)$ become 0, which indicates that x_1 is the precise root.

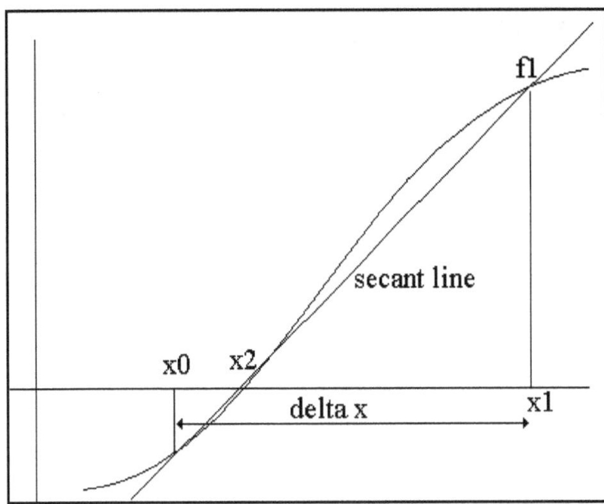

Figure 7.11 The Secant Method

Engr07e—Molar Volume of Non-Ideal Gases—Using the Secant Method

This version uses the secant method to find the roots. The function requires the initial guess **x** and the delta x value to be added to the initial guess to get to the next guess. Usually, the left end point, **a**, is passed as the guess and the width of the search interval, **b** – **a**, is passed for the delta x value. Additionally, the function is passed a maximum amount for the delta x values that are calculated. During any iteration, should the next delta x value ever exceed this maximum amount, then secant displays a diverging message and terminates. Usually, that maximum amount is set to two times the initial search interval.

Since there are four criteria to check during an iteration, I left the four checks within the loop body. Before a new delta x value can be calculated, **f1** must be checked for zero to avoid division by zero errors. Also, if **f1** is zero, we have landed exactly upon the root. If the next delta x value is less than the error precision, we have found the root. If that delta x value is greater than the maximum the user has passed, the diverging error message is displayed. Finally, if that new delta x is twice the previous delta x, then a warning message is displayed about possible divergence. It is very likely that such a warning message will be shortly followed by the failure message when it diverges even more and goes beyond the maximum allowed. Here are the secant program and test run.

Engr07e - Using the Secant Method to Find Roots

```
/***************************************************************/
/*                                                             */
/* Engr07e - Secant Method of root solving                     */
/*                                                             */
/***************************************************************/
```

```

#include <iostream>
#include <iomanip>
#include <cmath>
using namespace std;
// creates a data type for a parameter function value for secant
typedef double (*function) (double);

bool Secant (double x, double deltaX, double eps, int imax,
           double divergeAmt, double& root, int& i, function fx);

double van (double x);

const double R = 0.082054; // ideal gas constant

double p; // pressure in atmospheres
double t; // temperature in K

int main () {

 double x;               // initial guess for root, often a
 double divergeAmt;      // maximum amount to add to get to next
                         // guess, usually 2 * (b-a)
 double dx;              // amount to add to x to get to next guess
 double eps = .000001; // the desired degree of accuracy
 int    imax = 1000;     // maximum number of iterations to try

 int    i;     // number of iterations actually done
 double v;     // the answer, the volume of gas

 // setup floating point output for 5 digits of accuracy
 cout << fixed << setprecision (5);

 cout <<
   "Finding roots of van der Waal's gas equation for Oxygen\n\n";
 cout <<
   "Enter the initial guess, the amount to add to get to the\n"
      << "next guess, the divergence amount, pressure in atm\n"
      << "and the temperature in Kelvin - separated by blanks\n"
      << "Press ^Z to quit\n";
 while (cin >> x >> dx >> divergeAmt >> p >> t) {
  cout << endl;
  if (Secant (x, dx, eps, imax, divergeAmt, v, i, van)) {
   cout << "At pressure of:       " << p << endl
        << "At temperature of:    " << t << endl
        << "The volume is:        " << v
        <<  " (" << i << " iterations)\n"
        << "Ideal Gas volume is: " << R * t / p << endl;
  }
  cout << endl;
  cout << "Enter another set or ^Z to quit\n";
 }

```

```
 return 0;
}

/***************************************************************/
/*                                                             */
/* Secant: function to find the root of function f(x)          */
/*         parameter function f must be of the form            */
/*         double funct (double);                              */
/*                                                             */
/***************************************************************/

bool Secant (double x, double deltaX, double eps, int imax,
           double divergeAmt, double& root, int& i, function f) {
 double x0 = x;  //
 double dx0 = deltaX; // the next increment
 double f0 = f (x0);
 double x1;
 double f1;
 double dx1;

 i = 0;
 while (i < imax) {
  x1 = x0 + dx0;
  f1 = f (x1);
  if (f1 == 0) {
   root = x1;
   return true;
  }
  // calculate the next increment to the root
  dx1 = dx0 / (f0/f1 -1);
  if (fabs (dx1) < eps) {
   root = x1 + dx1;
   return true;
  }
  // display an error message and abort if diverging
  else if (fabs (dx1) > divergeAmt) {
   cerr << "Error: function is diverging.\n"
     << "The current delta x to be added to get the next guess\n"
     << "is greater than the specified diverge amount\n"
     << "|delta x|: " << fabs (dx1) << " and diverge amount: "
     << divergeAmt << endl
     << "On iteration number " << i << endl;
   return false;
  }
  else if (fabs (dx1) > 2 * fabs (dx0)) {
   cerr << "Warning: function is diverging.\n"
     << "The current delta x to be added to get the next guess\n"
     << "is greater than twice the previous amount\n"
     << "|delta x|: " << fabs(dx1) <<" and the previous amount: "
     << dx0 << endl
     << "On iteration number " << i << endl;
  }
  x0 = x1;
```

```
   dx0 = dx1;
   f0 = f1;
   i++;
  }
  // display a message that it did not converge in time
  root = x0 + dx0;
  cerr << "Warning: after " << imax
       << " iterations, Secant has not converged\n"
       << "Root thus far is: " << root << endl;
  return false;
 }

 /***************************************************************/
 /*                                                             */
 /* van(x): van der waals gas equation                          */
 /*                                                             */
 /***************************************************************/

 double van (double v) {
  double a = 1.360;
  double b = 0.03183;
  double ansr;
  ansr = (p + a / (v * v)) * (v - b) - R * t;
  return ansr;
 }
```

```
Test Run - Engr07e - Using the Secant Method to Find Roots
```

```
Finding roots of van der Waal's gas equation for Oxygen

Enter the initial guess, the amount to add to get to the
next guess, the divergence amount, pressure in atm
and the temperature in Kelvin - separated by blanks
Press ^Z to quit
24 4 8 1 300

At pressure of:       1.00000
At temperature of:    300.00000
The volume is:        24.59280 (2 iterations)
Ideal Gas volume is: 24.61620

Enter another set or ^Z to quit
2.3 .6 1.2 10 300

At pressure of:       10.00000
At temperature of:    300.00000
The volume is:        2.43840 (3 iterations)
Ideal Gas volume is: 2.46162

Enter another set or ^Z to quit
.2 .2 .4 100 300

```

```
At pressure of:         100.00000
At temperature of:      300.00000
The volume is:          0.22636 (3 iterations)
Ideal Gas volume is:    0.24616
```

Summary of Root Solving Techniques

Table 7.2 shows a summary of the results of the different root solving methods. Notice that each method yields the correct results. They differ in how many iterations it took to arrive at the result.

	1 atm @ 300	10 atm @ 300	100 atm @ 300
Ideal Gas	24.61620	2.46162	0.24616
Bisection	24.59280 20 iterations	2.43840 18 iterations	0.22636 16 iterations
Falsi	24.59280 2 iterations	2.43840 3 iterations	0.22636 5 iterations
Newton	24.59280 3 iterations	2.43840 3 iterations	0.22636 3 iterations
Secant	24.59280 2 iterations	2.43840 3 iterations	0.22636 3 iterations

Table 7.2 Results of the Root Solving Methods

All methods require the **f(x)** function, the degree of accuracy and the number of iterations to attempt. The more advanced methods require greater knowledge of the behavior of the function. The Bisection and Regula Falsi Methods require only the left and right end points enclosing a root. The Secant Method requires an initial guess for the root and an interval to add to get the next guess at the root. Newton's Method requires an initial guess, an interval, the number of roots at this location and the first derivative function. Secant and Newton's Methods are both very sensitive to the initial guess; a poor choice can yield a total miss of the root.

Looking over the results and the function requirements, it is easy to see why the Secant Method is one of the most popular methods for root solving applications.

Design Exercises

1. Design an function called **inputData()**. From the passed input file stream, it is to extract a set of data. The data include the employee Id number (9 digits long), the employee's age in years, and the date that the employee was hired. The hired date is input in the form of mm:dd:yyyy. However, if the year is less than 100, it is not "year 2000 compliant." In that case, add 1900 to the year. The user expects to use the function as follows.

```
    while (inputData (infile, id, age, month, day, year)) {
```

2. Design a function called **circleProperties()**. It is passed the circle's radius. It must calculate the area of the circle and the circumference of the circle. However, if the radius is within .001 from being 0, then return **false** along with zeros for the two properties. If the radius is not 0, then return **true**. The calling function expects to use it similar to this.

```
    if (circleProperties (radius, circum, area)) {
```

Stop! Do These Exercises Before Programming

1. Consider the following program to input a date in the format of mm-dd-yyyy, such as `10-22-2001`. What happens if the user inputs by accident `10 22-2001`? What happens if the user enters `10-22 2001`? What happens if the user enters `10a22a2001`?

```
    int month, day, year, c;
    cin >> month >> c >> day >> c >> year;
```

What would be the results of these three user entries if the input operation had been coded this way?

```
    cin >> month;
    cin.get (c);
    cin >> day;
    cin.get (c);
    cin >> year;
```

2. Why does this program create a linker error when building the program? How should it be fixed?

```
#include <iostream>
using namespace std;

int sumFunction (int& counter);
int main () {
 int x = 42;
 int sum = sumFunction (x);
 return 0;
}

int sumFunction (int counter) {
 int j;
 int sum = 0;
 for (j=0; j<counter; j++)
  sum += j;
 return sum;
}
```

3. What is wrong with the first **if** statement? How can it be made to work correctly so that **result** contains the correct value, ignoring leap year troubles?

```
#include <iostream>
using namespace std;
const int ERROR = -1;
int validateDate (int month, int day, int year);
int main () {
 int mon = 10;
 int day = 32;
 int yr = 2000;
 int result;
 if (result = validateDate (mon, day, yr) == ERROR)
  cout << "Bad Date\n"
 ...
int validateDate (int m, int d, int y) {
 if (m < 1 || m > 12 || d < 1 || d > 31 || y < 1900)
   return ERROR;
 else
  return 1;
}
```

4. When this program is executed, why do very unpredictable actions occur? How can it be fixed so that it works properly?

```
#include <iostream>
using namespace std;

void inputDate (iostream in, int& month, int& day,
                int& year);
int main () {
 int month, day, year, quantity;
 double cost;
 inputDate (cin, month, day, year);
 cin >> quantity >> cost;
 ...
void inputDate (iostream in, int& month, int& day,
                int& year) {
 char c;
 in >> month;
 in.get (c);
 in >> day;
 in.get (c);
 in >> year;
}
```

5. When this program is executed, why do very unpredictable actions occur? How can it be fixed so that it works properly?

```
#include <iostream>
using namespace std;
iostream inputDate (iostream& in, int& month, int& day,
                    int& year);
int main () {
 int month, day, year, quantity;
 double cost;
 while (inputDate (cin, month, day, year)) {
  cin >> quantity >> cost;
 ...
iostream inputDate (iostream& in, int& month, int& day,
                    int& year) {
 char c;
 in >> month;
 in.get (c);
 in >> day;
 in.get (c);
 in >> year;
 return in;
}
```

6. When this program runs, why does **main()**'s **cout** produce erroneous results? How can it be fixed?

```
#include <iostream>
using namespace std;
```

```
void inputDate ();
int month, day, year;
int main () {
 int month, day, year;
 inputDate ();
 cout << month << '-' << day << '-' << year;
 ...
void inputDate () {
 char c;
 in >> month >> c >> day >> c >> year;
}
```

7. When this program runs, why does **main()**'s **cout** produce erroneous results? How can it be fixed?

```
#include <iostream>
using namespace std;

void inputDate ();
int month, day, year;
int main () {
 int month, day, year;
 inputDate ();
 cout << month << '-' << day << '-' << year;
 ...
void inputDate () {
 int month, day, year;
 char c;
 in >> month >> c >> day >> c >> year;
}
```

8. This **outputDate()** function is badly designed. Why? How can it be repaired?

```
#include <iostream>
#include <iomanip>
using namespace std;

ostream& outputDate (ostream& out, int& m, int& d, int& y);

int main () {
 int month, day, year;
 ...
 outputDate (cout, month, day, year);
 ...
}

ostream& outputDate (ostream& out, int& m, int& d, int& y){
 out << setw (2) << setfill ('0') << m << '-'
     << setw (2) << d << '-' << setw (4) << y
     << setfill (' ');
 return out;
}
```

9. When this program is run, a strange, often large, number appears after the correct date on the screen. Why? How can it be removed?

```
#include <iostream>
#include <iomanip>
using namespace std;

ostream& outputDate (ostream& out, int& m, int& d, int& y);

int main () {
 int month, day, year, quantity;
 ...
 cout << outputDate (cout, month, day, year) << " "
      << setw (10) << quantity;
 ...
}

ostream& outputDate (ostream& out, int& m, int& d, int& y){
 out << setw (2) << setfill ('0') << m << '-'
     << setw (2) << d << '-' << setw (4) << y
     << setfill (' ');
 return out;
}
```

10. What will **cout** display for the variable **c**? for **b**? for **a**?

```
#include <iostream>
```

```
#include <iomanip>
using namespace std;

int  fun (int a, int &b);

int main () {
 int a = 1;
 int b = 2;
 int c = 3;
 c = fun (a, b);
 cout << c << " " << b << " " << a << endl;
 return 0;
}

int  fun (int a, int &b) {
 a = 42;
 b = 42;
 return 42;
}
```

11. What are the contents of **main()**'s variables **a** and **b** after the first call to **fun()**? What are the contents of **a** and **b** after the second call to **fun()**?

```
#include <iostream>
using namespace std;

void fun (double &x, double y);

int main() {
 double a = 1, b = 2;
 fun (a, b);
 fun (b, a);
}

void fun (double &x, double y) {
 x += y;
 return;
}
```

12. What values are printed for **x**, **y** and **z** in **some_fun()** the first time that function is called? What values are printed the second time it is called?

```
#include <iostream>
#include <iomanip>
using namespace std;

void some_fun ();

int x = 1;

int main(){
 int y = 2;
 static int z = 3;
 some_fun();
 x +=10;
 y +=10;
 z +=10;
 some_fun();
 return 0;
}

void some_fun () {
 int y = 2;
 static int z = 3;
 cout << x << "  " << y << "  " << z << endl;
 x++;
 y++;
 z++;
}
```

Programming Problems

Problem Cs07-1—The Grande Pumpkin Shoot (Game Design)

In fall, amid our pumpkin festivals, pumpkin tossing contests are held. Each contestant spends the year designing the best contraption to lob pumpkins the farthest. This year, the target is set up at a specific distance from the shooters. Each contestant gets up to five attempts to hit the target with a pumpkin toss. There are two variables that the contestants can change in order to hit the target: the initial velocity of the launch and the angle of the launch.

The distance, **dist**, to the landing point of a fired pumpkin is given by

$$dist = \frac{velocity^2 \sin(2angle)}{32.2}$$

Note that we are ignoring air friction effects and other aerodynamics of flying pumpkins. The angle is in radians, which is given by

radians = degrees * PI / 180

Write a program that first, one time only, inputs the distance to the target. Then, notify the user that he or she has five attempts to hit the target and to enter a pair of values for the velocity and the angle in degrees. All distances are in feet.

For each set of input data, the **main()** function calls a function, **toRadians()**, that returns the angle converted into radians. Then, the **main()** function calls another function, **computeDistance()**, that calculates both the distance this shot travels and the difference between this distance and the target's distance. Next, the **main()** function displays the distance this shot traveled and by how much it missed the target. If the absolute value of the distance traveled minus the target distance is less than .1% of the target distance, display a message that this shot hit the target and that they win the game; then quit the program. If it misses the target, prompt for another set of initial velocity and angle values. Repeat the process five times. If they have not hit the target after five tries, display a message that they have lost and quit.

Problem Cs07-2—Marketing Sales Summary (Control Break Processing)

Acme Telemarketing Sales has produced a summary sales information file. Each line in the file contains the telemarketer's id number and the total sales they made on that transaction. The file, **summary.txt**, contains all of the summarized data for one week and has been sorted into id number order.

Write a program that produces the marketing sales summary report. The report should be laid out as follows.

```
 Acme Marketing Sales Summary Report    Page 1

     Id        Number       Weekly
     Number    of Sales      Sales

     12334       10      $ 1234.00
...
               ----      ---------
                999     $ 99999.99
```

The program should accumulate a count of the number of sales and the total weekly sales for a specific id. When the id changes, display the summary line as shown above. At the end of the file, display a dashed line and the total number of sales for the company and the grand weekly sales.

The program should count the number of lines displayed and allow for a maximum of 10 lines per page (very small paper). You should have at least a **headings()** function and a **doSalesBreak()** function. Test the program with the provided data file, **summary.txt**.

Problem Cs07-3—A swap() Function

Write a function called **swap()** that swaps the contents of two **doubles**. The function prototype is

```
     void swap (double& x, double& y);
```

Then, write a **main()** function that prompts the user to enter two numbers, storing them in **x** and **y**. It then displays these original contents of **x** and **y**. The **main()** function then calls **swap()** and displays the new contents of **x** and **y** when it returns. Do not define any global variables. The display should appear similar to the following. (Note numbers are shown with two decimal digits.)

```
     Before swap. x = 999.99
                  y = 111.11
     After swap.  x = 111.11
                  y = 999.99
```

Problem Cs07-4—A sortTwo() Function

Write a function called **sortTwo()** that is passed two **doubles**, **x** and **y**. The function places the smaller of the two into **x** and the larger into **y**. Use the **swap()** function written in Problem **Cs07-3** within **sortTwo()** if the contents of **x** and **y** need to be switched. The prototype of the **sortTwo()** function is

```
void sortTwo (double& x, double& y);
```

Then write a **main()** function to input a pair of values for **x** and **y**. Display the original contents of **x** and **y**. Then, call the **sortTwo()** function and redisplay the values of **x** and **y** when the function returns. Repeat for additional pairs of numbers until the user presses ^Z. The display results should appear as follows.

```
Before sorting: x = 999.99  y = 111.11
After sorting:  x = 111.11  y = 999.99
```

Problem Cs07-5—A sortThree() Function

Write a function called **sortThree()** that is passed three **doubles**, **x**, **y** and **z**. The function places the smallest of the three values into **x**, the next smallest into **y** and the largest value into **z**. Use three calls to the **sortTwo()** function written in Problem **Cs07-4** within **sortThree()**. Do not define any global variables. The prototype of the **sortThree()** function is

```
void sortThree (double& x, double& y, double& z);
```

Then write a **main()** function to input a trio of values for **x**, **y** and **z**. Display the original contents of **x**, **y** and **z**. Then, call the **sortThree()** function and redisplay the values of **x**, **y** and **z** when the function returns. Repeat for additional trios of numbers until the user presses ^Z. The display results should appear as follows.

```
Before sorting: x = 999.99  y = 111.11  z =  88.99
After sorting:  x =  88.99  y = 111.11  z = 999.99
```

Problem Cs07-6—A quadratic() Function

Write a function called **quadratic()** that finds both roots of the quadratic equation. The **main()** function prompts and inputs the values for **a**, **b** and **c**.

$$\frac{-b \pm \sqrt{b^2 - 4ac}}{2a}$$

If **a** is zero, display an error message to **cerr** and return **false**. If the discriminant is negative, display an error message to **cerr** and return **false**. Otherwise, calculate the two roots and return **true**. The function prototype is

```
bool quadratic (double a, double b, double c,
                double& root1, double& root2);
```

Next write a **main()** function that inputs a trio of values for **a**, **b** and **c**. Then, **main()** calls **quadratic()**. If there are roots, **main()** displays the two roots. Finally, **main()** inputs another trio of values until the user signals the end of file by pressing ^Z. Note that the only displaying that is done within the **quadratic()** function is to **cerr** for error messages.

Problem Engr07-1—Vibration Studies (Mechanical Engineering)

In the Midwest, after the spring thaw, potholes form in many roads. When a car hits a pothole, the springs and shock absorbers get a workout dampening out the sudden jolt. Of course, if the shock absorbers need replacing, the oscillations continue for a much longer time. The basic idea is that the spring-shock absorber combination should rapidly dampen out that sudden jolt.

Given a car of mass **m** in grams, we can find the equation that defines the vertical motion as a function of time, **x (t)**. At any point in time, the forces operating on the mass of the car are the resistance of the spring and the dampening force of the shock absorber. The spring force is **-kx**, where **k** is the spring constant and it is negative indicating it is returning the car toward equilibrium. The dampening force is given by **-c x'** where **x'** is the first derivative of **x** with respect to time or the vertical velocity. Using Newton's second law (f=ma), and using **x''** for the second derivative, the equation becomes

m x'' = -cx' + (-kx)

Rewriting it into a form that can be used for root solving,

x'' + c x' / m + k x / m = 0

This is a second order differential equation. If the car hits a hole in the road at time 0 and is displaced $\mathbf{x_0}$ then the equation we need to solve is given below.

$$x(t) = e^{-nt}(x_0 \cos(pt) + x_0 \frac{n}{p} \sin(pt))$$

$$n = \frac{c}{2m}$$

$$p = \sqrt{\frac{k}{m} - \frac{c^2}{4m^2}}$$

Assume that the spring constant **k** = 1.25E9 g/s/s and that the dampening constant **c** = 1.4E7 g/s. The mass and the initial depth of the pothole, **m** and $\mathbf{x_0}$, are input values from the user.

The program should ask the user to enter the weight of the car in pounds and the depth of the pothole in inches. The program must convert those into grams and meters.

The program is to display the first three roots that represent the amount of time that the car takes to get back to the equilibrium point. Figure 7.12 shows a graph of the equation using a 3000-pound car hitting a 10-inch pothole.

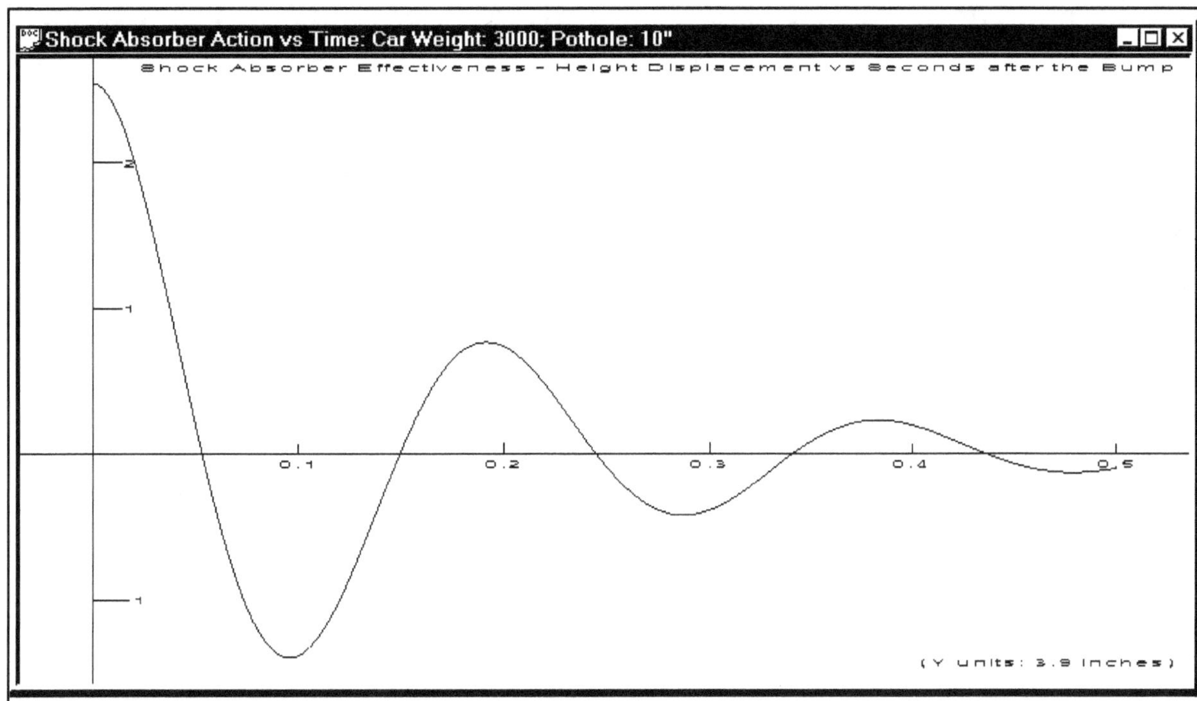

Figure 7.12 Shock Absorber Displacement as a Function of Time

The program should call **bisect()** three times to find the first three roots. Then, call **falsi()** to find the same three roots and finally call **secant()** to find the same roots. The program should display the three roots found by each of the three methods. Design the output to look something like this. Test your program with a 3000-pound car hitting a 10-inch pothole.

```
         Root 1         Root 2         Root 3
Bisect   0.05xxxx 11    0.15xxxx 10    .25xxxx 9
Falsi    0.05xxxx 11    0.15xxxx 10    .25xxxx 9
Secant   0.05xxxx 11    0.15xxxx 10    .25xxxx 9
```

Show six digits of accuracy and show the number of iterations the method required to find the root.

Problem Engr07-2—Electrical Circuit Design (Electrical Engineering)

Consider a capacitor, resistor, and an inductor in a circuit. If the capacitor alone is given some initial charge from a power supply, and then that supply is cut off and the circuit is activated by some switching mechanism, the circuit undergoes a series of oscillations until a new steady state is reached. The length of the oscillations is related to the charge-storing properties of the capacitor and the energy storage by the inductor; the resistance in the circuit dissipates the magnitude of the oscillations. The problem to solve is to find that resistance required to dissipate the energy in a given circuit at a specified rate.

The equations involved begin with the basics. The flow of current through a resistor creates a voltage drop given by V = iR, where V is in volts, i is in amperes and R is in ohms. The inductor voltage drop is given by V = Li' where L is the inductance in henrys and i' is the first derivative of the current flow with respect to time. The voltage drop over the capacitor is V = q/C where C is the capacitance in farads and q is the charge in coulombs. Kirchoff's second law says that the sum of the voltage drops in a closed circuit is zero. So we have

$$L\,i' + R\,i + q/C = 0$$

The current is related to the charge by i = q' where q' is the first derivative of q with respect to time. The equation is really a second order differential equation. The calculus solution then yields

$$q(t) = q_0 e^{\frac{-Rt}{2L}} \cos\left(t\sqrt{\frac{1}{LC} - \left(\frac{R}{2L}\right)^2}\right)$$

In order to find a root, we need an equation f(R) = 0. Moving q(t) to the right side and dividing by q_0, we get our function.

$$f(R) = e^{\frac{-Rt}{2L}} \cos\left(t\sqrt{\frac{1}{LC} - \left(\frac{R}{2L}\right)^2}\right) - \frac{q}{q_0}$$

Write a program that repeatedly prompts the user to input the four values: time **t**, **L**, **C** and the dissipation ratio **q/q_0**. Then use one of the root solving techniques to find the resistance needed to make the circuit work. Repeat the process until the end of the file occurs, that is, the user presses ^Z. Test your program with these test cases.

	t (sec)	L	C	q/q0	A	B
Case 1:	.05	5 H	1E-4	.01	0	400
Case 2:	.05	5.1 H	1E-4	.01	0	400
Case 3:	.05	8 H	.5E-4	.05	0	400
Case 4:	.1	10 H	1E-5	.1	0	400

If Case 3 or Case 4 should fail to find a root, explain what has occurred. Can you devise a better method for determining the end point B. Hint, examine the contents of the square root term in the equation.

Problem Engr07-3—Doppler Effects—Using Radar to Find a Vehicle's Speed

The radar guns used by the state police to monitor a vehicle's speed uses the principles of Doppler shift in frequency. The gun emits a beam at a given frequency f_0. The beam bounces off the moving vehicle, which then adds or subtracts its speed from the frequency, yielding either an increased or decreased frequency when measured by the radar gun. This same effect can be heard with approaching sirens. The frequency increases in pitch as the vehicle approaches and then decreases as it moves away from the observer. The Doppler shift formula is

$$v = \frac{c}{n} \frac{f - f_0}{f + f_0}$$

where c is the speed of light, n is the index of refraction of radar microwaves in the air and f is the final received frequency. The radar gun emits microwaves at a frequency f_0 of 2E10 cycles per second. The speed of light c is 2.99792458E8 meters per second. The index of refraction n is 1.00031. Finally, the radar gun's manufacturer claims that the gun can measure an absolute value of $|f - f_0|$ to one part in 10^4 or 0.01% accuracy.

The speed limit widely adopted is now just 55 miles an hour. An overzealous officer, from your point of view, has been ticketing motorists whose speed is greater than or equal to 55.01 miles per hour. Your claim is that the gun is not sufficiently accurate to measure such a small change in speed as 0.01 miles per hour.

To prove or disprove your claim, find the two frequencies, $f_{55.00}$ and $f_{55.01}$. Use one of the root solving methods to find these frequencies. Use .0001 as the desired accuracy and let A be .99 f_0 and B be 1.01 f_0. Note in order to create the **velocity (f)** function to solve, you must move the velocity term to the other side of the equation.

Calculate the frequency differences $df1 = |f_{55.00} - f_0|$ and $df2 = |f_{55.01} - f_0|$. Finally if $|df1 - df1| < .0001$, then the radar gun is not sufficiently accurate. Display the two roots found and the final $|df1 - df2|$ result along with a message "pay the ticket" or "Judge dismisses the case."

Chapter 8—Character Processing and Do Case

Section A: Basic Theory

Introduction

This chapter begins with an in depth look at the processing of character data. Exactly how a character is stored in memory is shown. Some of the more frequently used character processing functions are discussed. Next, the Do Case decision making structure is presented as an alternative to lengthy If-Then-Else constructs. Finally, enumerated data types are presented as a way to better handle numerical quantities that are used in some kind of control situation.

The Processing of Character Data

This chapter examines the processing of single characters of data. Already we have used character constants or literals such as 'A'. Note that coding "A" is not the same; the double quote marks indicate this is a string of characters. "A" is not the same thing as 'A'. Character strings are covered after the chapter on array processing because a string is stored as a series of characters and includes a special byte to denote the end of the string.

Defining Variables to Hold a Character of Data

A character variable is often defined using the **char** data type. Here coding

```
char c;
```

defines **c** to be a variable capable of holding a single character of data. Similarly, one can define other commonly used variables such as

```
char sex;             // a person's sex: M or F
char payType;         // a person's pay type: S or H
                      //   salaried or hourly
char maritalStatus;   // S single, M married, D divorced,
                      // W widowed
char grade;           // a person's grade in a course
```

A character variable can be initialized when it is defined. Suppose that we wished to define a variable to hold an employee's pay type and initialize it to the letter H for hourly worker. The following accomplishes this.

```
char payType = 'H';
```
Or one might wish to define a variable to hold a person's grade and initialize it to the letter A.
```
char grade = 'A';
```

Inputting Character Data

There are two methods for inputting a character of data: the extraction operator >> and the **get()** function. The effects of these two methods differ. Let's begin with the extraction operator.

Using the Extraction Operator to Input a Character

A character of data can be input using the extraction operator; the rules parallel those for the numerical data types. Assume that one has coded the following.
```
char grade;
cin >> grade;
```
The extraction operator first skips over white space to the first nonwhite space character. Then that next nonwhite space character is input and stored in the **grade** variable. The input stream is positioned to the next character in the input stream after the grade letter. If the end of file is reached instead of a nonwhite space character, then the input action fails and the end of file flag is turned on. Thus, the extraction of a character of data is no different from the extraction of a numerical value.

Assume that one needs to input the item number, quantity, tax type, and the cost values from an input file. The tax type contains an F for food item and N for non-food item; it is used to calculate the tax on the item purchased. The following could be the main loop coding.
```
long   itemNumber;
int    quantity;
char   taxType;
double cost;
...
while (infile >>itemNumber >> quantity >> taxType >> cost) {
 ...
}
```
And an input line might look like this.
```
1234567 10 F 14.99<CR>
```
In other words, there are no surprises with the extraction operator.

However, please note that the input line could also have been written as follows.
```
1234567 10F14.99<CR>
```
Notice that there are no blanks or white space on either side of the tax type value F in this case. The data would still be inputted correctly. Remember that the extraction of an integer, **quantity**, is ended by the detection of the F in the input stream; the 10 is input for the **quantity**. Since the next item to be extracted is a character, the F is inputted into the **taxType** variable. However, running the data together is not a good idea because a person would have difficulty reading that line of input when

doing a visual check of their data entry typing.

Running the data together does occur with both dates and times. For example as we have already seen a time expressed as hours, minutes and seconds frequently contains a colon (:) to separate the three values, 10:14:42. Dates expressed as three integers, month, day and year, might appear as 10-01-2000. When dates are in this format, both the month and day integers have leading zeros present if needed.

Inputting values in this format brings up an additional consideration. In chapter 6, we saw that the default for input streams is to assume numbers beginning with a 0 digit are in the octal number system. One time only we must call the **dec** manipulator function to notify the input stream that numbers with leading 0's are in fact decimal numbers.

```
char c;
int month, day, year;
ifstream infile ("aFileOfDates.txt");
if (!infile) {
 ... output an error message and abort the program
}
infile >> dec;
```

If one is inputting dates that have leading 0’s before some month and day values, then the input stream must have the decimal flag turned on for them to be properly inputted. Failure to do so results in 08 and 09 are not being properly input.

Hexadecimal Numbers

As long as we are on the topic of number systems, the third number system in C++ is the hexadecimal number system or base 16. In hex, valid digits range from 0 through F. There is the system

```
hex  decimal
 0      0
 1      1
 2      2
 3      3
 4      4
 5      5
 6      6
 7      7
 8      8
 9      9
 A     10
 B     11
 C     12
 D     13
 E     14
 F     15
```

C++ uses a 0x identifier to signal that the following number is actually a hexadecimal number: 0x20 defines a hexadecimal value of 32 in decimal. 0x10 defines a hex value of 16 decimal. 0x1F defines a decimal 31. Just as in the decimal system when you add 9 + 1 you get 10, in the hexadecimal system adding 0xF + 0x1 gives 0x10. Fortunately, hexadecimal values are seldom needed in programming. They are found heavily in system programs, such as code that is a part of the operating system programs.

Using the get() Function

The **get()** function represents an alternative method to input a character. Its operation differs significantly from the extraction operator. The **get()** function inputs the next character no matter what it might be. It only fails if the end of file is reached. The syntax is simple

```
cin.get (c);
```

or

```
infile.get (c);
```

Notice that it is a function call and is therefore not chainable as the extraction operator is. The following is illegal.

```
infile >> month >> infile.get (c) >> day;
```

If one wanted to input the date using the **get()** function to input the dashes, the sequence would be

```
infile >> month;
infile.get (c);
infile >> day;
infile.get (c);
infile >> year;
```

Clearly, the extraction operator is superior in this case, unless you are being paid for the number of lines of coding you produce.

There are, however, some circumstances in which the use of the **get()** function is mandatory. Suppose that you needed to input the answers to a multiple choice test. There are say five questions whose answers are A through E. The following coding is a potential disaster for the grading program.

```
char answer;
for (int j=0; j<5; j++) {
 infile >> answer;
 ... use answer
}
```

Suppose one student's answer line was as follows.

```
ABCDE<CR>
```

Then the above coding would correctly input each question's letter choice. However, what can occur on a test? Sometimes a student omits a question for one reason or another. What would the above coding input if the following two lines were entered?

```
 B D <CR>
ABCDE<CR>
```

The first line shows that the student failed to answer the first and third and fifth question. But what does the extraction code actually input for the five answers? B, D, A, B, and C! Remember that the extraction operator skips over white space and a blank is white space. Here is a classic opportunity in which the **get()** function must be used to properly input the data. The following sequence is a proper way to input the five answers.

```
char answer;
char endOfLine;
for (int j=0; j<5; j++) {
 infile.get (answer);
 ... use answer
}
infile.get (endOfLine);
```

Within the loop, five characters are input. Thus, the first character would contain the blank, then the B, then the blank, then the D and then the blank. However, at this point, the input stream is now pointing to the newline code, the <CR> carriage return, and line feed bytes. If we assume that the program soon will input the next student's answers as represented by the next line of input, that <CR> must be input. Failure to do so would mean that it would be input as the first answer for the next student!

Hence, the following guideline might help you decide whether or not a **get()** function is needed to input a character.

Rule: If a valid character to be input could contain white space, then the **get()** function must be used. Otherwise, the extraction operator can be used.

Output of Character Data—the put() Function

The insertion operator can be used to output character data. The **setw()** function operates as usual with the character being right aligned by default within the specified width. Assume a person's **grade** variable contains an 'A'; the following code

```
cout << setw (5) << grade << endl;
```

produces

```
bbbbA
```

where the b represents a blank.

The **put()** function can also be used to output a character. It is given a character to output and it outputs that character to the indicated stream. For example, the following code displays the letter A. For more on the **put()** function, see the **Plot()** function below.

```
cout.put (grade);
outfile.put (grade); // where outfile = an ofstream instance
```

How Are Character Data Stored?

Character data are stored using their ASCII values. ASCII stands for the American Standard Codes for Information Interchange. The basic idea behind the storing of character data is “agreement.” For example, suppose that you are designing a computer system and wish to find a way to store a character of data, such as the letter A. A byte contains 8 bits that are on or off, 1 or 0. The possible bit patterns of 1's and 0's range from

0000 0000
0000 0001
0000 0010
0000 0011
0000 0100
...
1111 1111

For fun, you might write out all the unique possibilities that there are in one byte. There are, in fact, 256 possible unique bit patterns in a byte.

So to store the letter A, pick one, say for example
0100 0001

And then get everyone else to agree with you so that, when they encounter that bit pattern, they display, print and so on a letter A. That is all that the ASCII scheme really is—an agreed upon scheme of bit patterns to represent the letters. Here are the first few ASCII bit patterns for some letters.

A 0100 0001
B 0100 0010
C 0100 0011
D 0100 0100

and so on.

Of course, with any agreed upon pattern, there are always those that do not agree. On some computers, such as IBM mainframes, there is a completely different agreed upon scheme called EBCDIC, Extended Binary Coded Decimal Interchange Codes. On an IBM mainframe, the letter A is encoded as

A 1100 0001

Thus, when a PC is communicating with a mainframe computer, some form of translation must occur as they are speaking different languages, so to speak. This ASCII to EBCDIC translation can be done using a hardware circuit board placed between the two computers or it can be done using software.

Another interesting point is that the bit pattern holding the letter A is 0100 0001. That bit pattern is also the decimal number 65 ($1x2^0 + 1x2^6 = 1 + 64 = 65$). Here is the complete ASCII table for my PC running Windows NT, Table 8.1.

0 ^@ nul	1 ^A	2 ^B	3 ^C	4 ^D	65 ^E	6 ^F	7 ^G
8 ^H bs	9 ^I	10 ^J lf	11 ^K	12 ^L ff	13 ^M cr	14 ^N	15 ^O
16 ^P	17 ^Q	18 ^R	19 ^S	20 ^T	21 ^U	22 ^V	23 ^W
24 ^X	25 ^Y	26 ^Z eof	27 ^[esc	28 ^\	29 ^|	30 ^^	31 ^
32	33 !	34 "	35 #	36 $	37 %	38 &	39 '
40 (	41)	42 *	43 +	44 ,	45 -	46 .	47 /
48 0	49 1	50 2	51 3	52 4	53 5	54 6	55 7
56 8	57 9	58 :	59 ;	60 <	61 =	62 >	63 ?
64 @	65 A	66 B	67 C	68 D	69 E	70 F	71 G
72 H	73 I	74 J	75 K	76 L	77 M	78 N	79 O
80 P	81 Q	82 R	83 S	84 T	85 U	86 V	87 W
88 X	89 Y	90 Z	91 [	92 \	93]	94 ^	95 _
96 `	97 a	98 b	99 c	100 d	101 e	102 f	103 g
104 h	105 I	106 j	107 k	108 l	109 m	110 n	111 o
112 p	113 q	114 r	115 s	116 t	117 u	118 v	119 w
120 x	121 y	122 z	123 {	124 |	125 }	126 ~	127 ⌂ ^bs

upper ASCII (Graphics)

128 Ç	129 ü	130 é	131 â	132 ä	133 à	134 å	135 ç
136 ê	137 ë	138 è	139 ï	140 î	141 ì	142 Ä	143 Å
144 É	145 æ	146 Æ	147 ô	148 ö	149 ò	150 û	151 ù
152 ÿ	153 Ö	154 Ü	155 ¢	156 £	157 ¥	158 ₧	159 ƒ
160 á	161 í	162 ó	163 ú	164 ñ	165 Ñ	166 ª	167 º
168 ¿	169 ⌐	170 ¬	171 ½	172 ¼	173 ¡	174 «	175 »
176 ░	177 ▒	178 ▓	179 │	180 ┤	181 ╡	182 ╢	183 ╖
184 ╕	185 ╣	186 ║	187 ╗	188 ╝	189 ╜	190 ╛	191 ┐
192 └	193 ┴	194 ┬	195 ├	196 ─	197 ┼	198 ╞	199 ╟
200 ╚	201 ╔	202 ╩	203 ╦	204 ╠	205 ═	206 ╬	207 ╧
208 ╨	209 ╤	210 ╥	211 ╙	212 ╘	213 ╒	214 ╓	215 ╫
216 ╪	217 ┘	218 ┌	219 █	220 ▄	221 ▌	222 ▐	223 ▀
224 α	225 ß	226 Γ	227 π	228 Σ	229 σ	230 µ	231 τ
232 Φ	233 Θ	234 Ω	235 δ	236 ∞	237 φ	238 ε	239 ∩
240 ≡	241 ±	242 ≥	243 ≤	244 ⌠	245 ⌡	246 ÷	247 ≈
248 °	249 ·	250 ·	251 √	252 ^{n}	253 ^{2}	254 ■	255

Table 8.1 The ASCII Codes

When IBM invented the very first PC, they completely filled up all possible ASCII table values. The values corresponding to decimal numbers below 32 are known as the **control codes**. For example, if you press ^C (Ctrl + C key), the actual decimal value input and stored is 3. The Carriage Return code is 13 and the Line Feed code is a 10. Remember that C++ inputs both bytes, 13 and 10, but it stores only the line feed code, the 10. On output of a new line code, C++ also outputs the CR or 13 first and then outputs the LF code of 10. The formfeed code, a 12, causes a printer to eject to a new page.

A blank or space is stored as a decimal 32. Above the blank are the numbers 0 through 9 stored as a 48 through 57. Beginning at a decimal 65 are the uppercase letters and the lowercase letters begin at 97. Interspersed are the special characters, such as + – , $ % and the period.

All characters whose decimal values are above 127 are known as the upper ASCII codes or the graphics codes. Some of these can be used to draw text boxes on the screen in either a single line or double line version. Additionally, there are many foreign language characters stored in the remaining values. In short, when the first PC appeared, all 256 possible values were filled and used. Of course, this then led to a major problem when the 101 special keys were developed, such as the arrow keys, function keys, insert, delete, page up and down for example. IBM had used all the slots so some other scheme had to be devised to input these keys.

The Escape Sequences

The escape sequences allow us to enter some of these unusual codes by directly entering their ASCII code numbers. Table 8.2 shows the complete escape sequences.

Table 8.2 The Escape Sequences

Escape Sequence	ASCII Code	Meaning
\a	7	alert—sounds the bell making a beep sound
\b	8	backspace-rub out
\f	12	form feed—printer eject to new page
\n	10	newline code (a line feed)
\r	13	carriage return code
\t	9	tab—horizontal
\v	11	vertical tab
\\	92	backslash
\’	39	single quote mark
\”	34	double quote mark
\?	63	question mark
\nnn	nnn	the character whose code number is specified by this octal number
\xnnn	0xnnn	the character whose code number is specified by this hexadecimal number

Sometimes these codes are needed. When creating the full path of a filename, the \\ is used, C:\\Cmpsc125\\test.dat. When a double quote mark is needed within a string, the \" is used, “He said, \"Hello.\".” When a character literal is to contain a single quote mark, the \' is used, ‘\'‘ creates a byte containing a single quote mark.

When the program needs to display an important error message, including anywhere in the message string the \a code causes the PC also to beep to catch the user’s attention. For example

```
cerr << "The data contains invalid codes!\a\n";
```

Numbers and Letters

The **char** data types, including **char**, **signed char** and **unsigned char**, cause much confusion for everyone including the computer itself. Suppose that one had defined the following fields (recall that **char** is short for **signed char**)

```
char letter;
char num1; // which is the same as a signed char num1;
unsigned char num2;
letter = 'A';
num1 = +65;
num2 = 65;
```

How are these three values, the letter A, the +65 and the unsigned 65, actually stored in memory? All three variables occupy just one byte. Here are their bit patterns

```
letter 0100 0001
num1   0100 0001
num2   0100 0001
```

For signed numbers, the sign is the very first bit of the field; a 0 bit means + and a 1 bit means –. For unsigned numbers the first bit is part of the number. Had the leftmost bit of **num2**, the unsigned number, been a 1 bit, it would represent $1x2^7$ or 128 added into the value represented by the bits.

What is startling is that all three completely different values appear absolutely identical in memory! In other words, if a byte contains 0100 0001, no PC can tell whether that value is the letter A, a +65 or an unsigned 65! Therefore, the computer depends upon the **context** of the instructions to give it a clue as to the meaning of the value.

When you use the extraction or insertion operators or the **get()** and **put()** functions, the computer assumes that the value is to be the ASCII code or letter. Thus, if you write

```
cin >> letter;
```

and the user enters

```
A
```

then the value stored is considered to be the ASCII value of the letter A, or the 65. This makes sense if we are to input character data.

However, it can sometimes get a programmer into trouble. Consider this user entry.

```
1
```

Now what is stored in the variable letter? It stores the ASCII value for the character '1', which is a decimal 49. It does not store the numerical binary equivalent of 0000 0001! In other words, the following two inputs give very different results.

```
char x;
int y;
cin >> x >> y;
```

where the user enters

```
1 1
```

The contents of **x** contain 0011 0001 while **y** contains 0000 0000 0000 0001 (Assuming an **int** occupies 2-bytes.) The variable **x** holds the ASCII value of '1' while the variable **y** holds the numerical binary value of 1.

On output, if you want the computer to consider the contents of the **char** to be a numerical value, use a typecast. I produced the ASCII table by

```
cout << (int) letter << " " << letter;
```

where **letter** is defined as a **char**. If you want the ASCII letter displayed from an integer type, use a typecast.

```
cout << num1 << " " << (char) num1;
```

The computer takes its clue from your coding. If you perform any math operations on the **char** variable, the computer assumes that the value is a numerical one. Thus, if we wrote

```
letter += 1;
```

when done, **letter** contains 0100 0010 or the letter 'B';

Occasionally in older coding, you may run across math operations on obviously character data.

```
letter += 32;
letter -= 32;
```

If **letter** contained 'A', then adding 32 to the ASCII value of 65 yields 97, which is the ASCII code for the letter 'a'. Similarly, if the contents of **letter** was an ASCII 97, the second line above produces a 65 or the letter 'A'. These two lines are changing the case of a letter. However, these two lines to change case are NOT platform independent. Rather, they only work correctly on a computer that is using the ASCII encoding scheme. There are some built-in character processing functions that properly change the case of a letter independent of the encoding scheme.

Suppose that the program needed to verify that a letter only was input. It could be checked using some ranges.

```
if ( (letter >= 'A' && letter <= 'Z') ||
     (letter >= 'a' && letter <= 'z')) {
 // here it is a letter
}
```

But there are also some character processing functions to do this for us that are not dependent upon the data being encoded in ASCII.

The Character Processing Functions

All character processing function prototypes are in the header file **<ctype.h>** or in **<cctype>** when using the **namespace std**. Some functions convert case independent of the platform. Some report whether or not the character is a letter, number, and so on. Table 8.3 shows many of the more frequently used functions.

Table 8.3 Some Commonly Used Character Processing Functions

function	returns
toupper (c)	returns the uppercase letter equivalent of the lowercase letter in c, otherwise returns the character it was given
tolower (c)	returns the lowercase letter equivalent of the uppercase letter in c, otherwise returns the character it was given
isupper (c)	returns non-zero value if c contains an uppercase letter; otherwise, returns 0
islower (c)	returns non-zero value if c contains a lowercase letter; otherwise, returns 0
isalpha (c)	returns non-zero value if c is a letter; otherwise, returns 0
isdigit (c)	returns non-zero value if c contains a digit (0-9); otherwise, returns 0

Basic08a—A Word Counter Program

To illustrate these character processing functions as well as character I/O, let's write a program that inputs a text file, finds, and displays each word. At the end of file, display a total of all words found. By definition, a word consists of a series of letters. Any non-letter separates the words.

In terms of design, let's have two functions: **skipToStartOfWord()** and **getRestOfWord()**. The **skipToStartOfWord()** is to input characters until it finds a letter; then it returns the first letter of a new word. The **getRestOfWord()** inputs and displays each successive letter until the end of the word is found. Figure 8.1 shows the main storage drawing for the three functions.

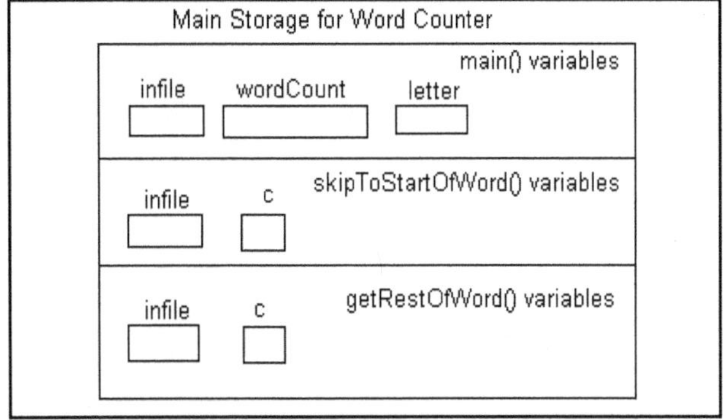

Figure 8.1 Main Storage for Word Counter

Here is the design sketch for the **main()** function.
define **infile** and open the file
if it fails, display error message and quit
set **wordCount** to 0

let **letter** = **skipToStartOfWord (infile)**;
while (**infile**) do the following
    display **letter** on a new line
    wordCount++
    getRestOfWord (infile);
    let **letter** = **skipToStartOfWord** (**infile**);
end **while**
display **wordCount**
close **infile**

The sequence for **skipToStartOfWord()** that is passed **infile** is
infile.get (**c**)
while infile and **c** is not a letter do the following
    infile.get (**c**)
end do **while**
if **infile** is good, **return c**
otherwise **return** 0

The sequence for **getRestOfWord()** that is passed **infile** is
infile.get (**c**)
while infile and **c** is a letter do the following
    output **c**
    infile.get (**c**)
end do **while**
output a newline code

Here are the completed program and a sample test run.

```
Basic08a - displays words in a file and counts them
```

```
/***************************************************************/
/*                                                             */
/* Basic08a: displays words in a file and counts them          */
/*                                                             */
/***************************************************************/

#include <iostream>
#include <fstream>
#include <cctype>
using namespace std;
char skipToStartOfWord (istream& infile);
void getRestOfWord (istream& infile);

int main () {
 ifstream infile ("sample.txt");
 if (!infile) {
  cerr << "Error: cannot open the input file sample.txt\n";
```

```
   return 1;
  }

  char letter;
  long wordCount = 0;
  letter = skipToStartOfWord (infile);
  while (infile) {
   cout << letter;
   wordCount++;
   getRestOfWord(infile);
   letter = skipToStartOfWord (infile);
  }
  cout << endl << "Total Words: " << wordCount << endl;
  infile.close();
  return 0;
 }

 /***************************************************************/
 /*                                                             */
 /* skipToStartOfWord: skips over non-letters until it          */
 /*                    finds 1st letter                         */
 /*                                                             */
 /***************************************************************/

 char skipToStartOfWord (istream& infile) {
  char c;
  infile.get (c);
  while (infile && !isalpha (c)) {
   infile.get (c);
  }
  return infile ? c : 0;
 }

 /***************************************************************/
 /*                                                             */
 /* getRestOfWord: get and display rest of a word               */
 /*                                                             */
 /***************************************************************/

 void getRestOfWord (istream& infile) {
  char c;
  infile.get (c);
  while (infile && isalpha (c)) {
   cout << c;
   infile.get (c);
  }
  cout << endl;
 }
```

Output from Basic08a - displays words in a file and counts them

```
Define
```

```
infile
and
open
the
file
if
it
fails
display
error
message
...
end
do
while
output
a
newline
code

Total Words: 116
Press any key to continue
```

The Do Case Structure

Sometimes a variable must be tested for a number of possible values and alternative processing done for each possibility. For example, assume that a company has five departments numbered 1 through 5. The cost of supplies must be charged back to the specific department. Thus, such a program would have five department total variables and the charge back coding might be as follows.

```
if (deptno == 1) {
 total1 += cost;
}
else if (deptno == 2) {
 total2 += cost;
}
else if (deptno == 3) {
 total3 += cost;
}
else if (deptno == 4) {
 total4 += cost;
}
else if (deptno == 5) {
 total5 += cost;
}
else {
 cerr << "Error: incorrect department number. It was: "
      << deptno << endl;
}
```

Such decision-making logic works fine, but is cumbersome when the number of possibilities is large. The Do Case structure represents a convenience method to shorten this.

The circumstances that allow a Do Case structure to be used are twofold: one variable, **deptno**, is being checked for values and that variable is an integer. Figure 8.2 shows the industry standard Do Case structure. However, the C++ default implementation does not follow that standard but introduces more flexibility. Figure 8.3 shows the C++ Do Case structure.

Notice that by default, when the special processing for a specific case is completed, the C++Do Case falls into the next case! When the special processing for a specific case is completed, the normal industry Do Case leaves and goes to the next instruction after the Do Case. C++ introduces a **break** statement to enable a program to break out of a loop or a Do Case structure so that we can implement the industry normal Do Case if desired. Normally, that is precisely what is desired. When we are finished with the special processing for a given case, we do not wish to fall through and do all the other cases' special processing.

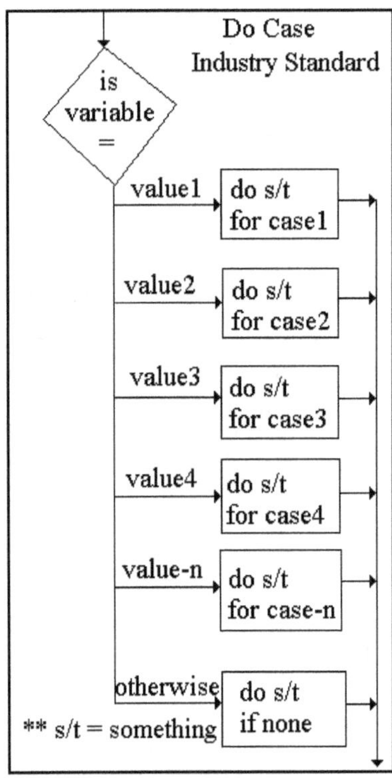

Figure 8.2 Industry Do Case

Do Case
C++ Default
is
variable
=
value1
do s/t
for case1
value2
do s/t
for case2
value3
do s/t
for case3
value4
do s/t
for case4
value-n
do s/t
for case-n
otherwise
do s/t
if none
** s/t = something

Figure 8.3 C++ Do Case

The Do Case syntax is

```
switch (integer variable or expression) {
  case value1:
    special processing when the variable contains value1
    break;
  case value2:
    special processing when the variable contains value2
```

```
      break;
    ...
    case valuen:
      special processing when the variable contains valuen
      break;
    default:
      special processing when the variable is none of these
      break;
  }
```

Returning to the opening situation of five departments and their charge back totals, assuming that **deptno** was defined to be an integer type, then the following represents the Do Case solution. Notice it simplifies all the If-Then-Else statements.

```
switch (deptno) {
  case 1:
    total1 += cost;
    break;
  case 2:
    total2 += cost;
    break;
  case 3:
    total3 += cost;
    break;
  case 4:
    total4 += cost;
    break;
  case 5:
    total5 += cost;
    break;
  default:
    cerr << "Error: incorrect department number. It was: "
         << deptno << endl;
}
```

When the **switch** statement is encountered, the compiler evaluates the contents of **deptno**. Depending upon the current contents of **deptno**, it then goes to the corresponding **case**. So if **deptno** contains a 4, then **case 4** is executed adding the **cost** to **total4** and then the **break** causes it to leave the entire Do Case statement.

Here is another example. Suppose that the program needed to display the day of the week. Assume that variable **day** is an integer type. The following shows how this can easily be done using a Do Case.

```
cin >> day;
switch (day) {
  case 1:
    cout << "Sunday" << endl;
    break;
```

```
  case 2:
    cout << "Monday" << endl;
    break;
  case 3:
    cout << "Tuesday" << endl;
    break;
  case 4:
    cout << "Wednesday" << endl;
    break;
  case 5:
    cout << "Thursday" << endl;
    break;
  case 6:
    cout << "Friday" << endl;
    break;
  case 7:
    cout << "Saturday" << endl;
    break;
  default:
    cerr << "Error: incorrect day: must be 1-7. It was: "
         << day << endl;
}
```

Now consider this version of the program. What is the output when the user enters a 4 for the day?

```
cin >> day;
switch (day) {
  case 1:
    cout << "Sunday" << endl;
  case 2:
    cout << "Monday" << endl;
  case 3:
    cout << "Tuesday" << endl;
  case 4:
    cout << "Wednesday" << endl;
  case 5:
    cout << "Thursday" << endl;
  case 6:
    cout << "Friday" << endl;
  case 7:
    cout << "Saturday" << endl;
  default:
    cerr << "Error: incorrect day: must be 1-7. It was: "
         << day << endl;
}
```

It produces

```
Wednesday
Thursday
```

```
Friday
Saturday
Error: incorrect day: must be 1-7. It was 4
```

This is because the **break;** statements were left out. When it finishes one case, it falls on down into the next case's set of things to do.

The **switch** can be on any integer type of variable (**char**, **short**, **int** or **long**) and even an expression that results in an integer value. It can also be used on ASCII characters since they are stored in a **char** type. The values used in the **case** statements do not need to be in increasing or even sequential order, but often are for readability. The values can also be ASCII characters.

Suppose that the tax on an item is based upon whether or not the item is classified as a food item or a non-food item. Assume that the following variables have been defined and values inputted for a specific purchase.

```
char   taxtype; // F or N
short  quantity;
double cost;
double taxrate;
double tax;
```

The following **switch** statement obtains the correct tax.

```
switch (taxtype) {
  case 'F':
    taxrate = .01;
    break;
  case 'N':
    taxrate = .07;
    break;
  default:
    taxrate = 0;
}
tax = quantity * cost * taxrate;
```

When would the C++ fall through and do the next **case**'s statements ever be useful? That is, are there any circumstances when **break** statements are not desired? Yes, there can be some situations where the basic behavior is desirable. Suppose that we needed to write a **daysInMonth()** function that returned the number of days in a month. Notice how streamlined the coding can be by making use of **switch** statement and the default C++ behavior.

```
int daysInMonth (int month) {
 int days;
 switch (month) {
   case 1:
   case 3:
   case 5:
   case 7:
   case 8:
   case 10:
   case 12:
```

```
        days = 31;
        break;
      case 2:
        days = 28;
        break;
      default:
        days = 30;
    }
    return days;
  }
```

One can nest additional **switch** statements within a **case** clause as long as that inner Do Case structure is entirely contained in the outer **case** clause. However, no new variables can be defined within a Do Case statement.

The Do Case structure is entirely a matter of convenience. A series of If-Then-Elses can accomplish the same task.

More on the break Statement and the continue Statement

The **break** statement has additional uses. It causes control to leave the current block of coding. Suppose that we wish to write a "Guess the Letter" game in which the user tries to guess which letter you have chosen. The main loop centers on the input of the next guess, repeating while the guess is not correct. The user gets 10 tries. One way to write such a loop is as follows.

```
char theLetter; // the original letter to be guessed
char guess;
int tries = 0;
cout << "Guess my letter. Enter a letter: ";
cin >> guess;
while (cin && tries < 10) {
  if (guess == theLetter)
    break;
  tries++;
  cout << "Try again. Enter a letter: ";
  cin >> guess;
}
if (cin) { // if not eof or user giving up
 if (tries == 10)
   cout << "You lose\n";
 else
   cout << "You win in " << tries << " attempts\n";
}
```

Here, if the user's guess ever equals the letter, the **break** statement terminates the loop. One could have just as easily written the **while** clause as

```
while (cin && tries < 10 && guess != theLetter) {
```

And this would have been a much clearer way to have written it. The **break** statement does have valid uses in later chapters in which the alternate loop termination condition does not fit particularly well in a **while** clause.

The **continue** statement causes control to go to the bottom of the loop. If it is a **for** loop, then the bump expression(s) is(are) activated. The **continue** statement provides a means of skipping the body of a loop on a specific iteration, yet not terminate the loop. Suppose that a **sumNumber()** function is passed a number between one and one hundred. The function is to return the sum of all integers between one and one hundred but not including the passed number. Here is a good use of the **continue** statement.

```
long sumNumber (long number) {
 long sum = 0;
 long j;
 for (j=1; j<101; j++) {
  if (j == number)
    continue; // bypass adding this j to sum; go do next j
  sum += j;
 }
 return sum;
}
```

Enumerated Data Types

Many integer variables hold key values that a program checks within **while**, If-Then-Else and Do Case statements. Take the department number example in which the company has five that are identified by values ranging from one to five. Throughout a program, one might see these numbers appearing for various processing needs. However, these abstract numbers bear little relation to what they represent. For example, it is not obvious to anyone that department number 1 represents the Appliance department; 2, the Automotive department and so on. To make the program clearer, one can add comments such as these.

```
case 1: // appliance department
if (deptno == 2) { // the automotive department
```

A better approach would be to make a set of **#define** symbols or constant **int**s such as these two versions.

```
#define Appliances 1
#define Automotive 2
...
case Appliances:
if (deptno == Automotive) {
```

or

```
const int Appliances = 1;
const int Automotive = 2;
...
case Appliances:
if (deptno == Automotive) {
```

The **#define** creates a symbolic name that represents the value that comes after the name. It is a preprocessor directive. The preprocessor handles all the lines that begin with a # sign. It includes the various header files. In the case of **#defines**, it does a text substitution. That is, the preprocessor looks for all occurrences of **Appliances** within the program and replaces that symbol with its corresponding value, 1. Because the **#define** is just a simple text substitution, the **const int** approach is preferred because the **Appliances** is actually an instance of the integer data type.

Please note that although **Appliances** is a "variable" it really is a constant integer. The values on the **case** statements cannot be variables. That is, the following is invalid because in this case **appliances** is a variable, not a constant.

```
int appliances = 1;
...
case appliances: // error not a constant value
```

For many uses, using either a **const int** or a **#define** to create a more meaningful name is extremely important for readability. However, when there are more than just a few possibilities, errors can occur with this approach. What would result if the user coded the following and then used these as the values in a Do Case statement?

```
const int Appliances = 1;
const int Automotive = 2;
const int Housewares = 3;
const int Toys = 3;
const int Accounting = 5;
```

Because **Toys** was accidentally given the wrong value, incorrect results will occur that are difficult to find. There is a better way.

An **enumerated data type** allows us to create a "new" data type and specify precisely what possible values that variables of this new type can contain. The syntax is

```
enum new_data_type {enumerator-1, enumerator-2,
                    ..., enumerator-n };
```

where the form of the enumerators is

```
identifier = integer value
```

Usually the new data type is capitalized as are the enumerator identifiers. If the integer values are not coded, the first one is given the value 0, the next one is given a value of 1, and so on. Specifically, to handle these department numbers, an **enum** is a terrific way to proceed. Consider this version.

```
enum DeptNum {Invalid, Appliances, Automotive,
              Housewares, Toys, Accounting};
```

This creates a new data type known as **DeptNum**. Variables of this type can only have the six indicated values represented by **Invalid**, **Appliances** and so on.

Actually, an **enum** is implemented as an **int**, so you can look upon an **enum** as a "disguised **int**." By default, the first value the **enum** can hold is given the value 0. Thus, in the above definition, **Invalid** represents a 0; **Appliances**, a 1; **Automotive**, a 2; and so on. That is, the compiler from the point of definition of this **enum** now knows to replace all occurrences of **Appliances** with its value 1.

Where are most all **enum** definitions placed within a program? They, like **#define**s and **const int**s, must be defined before their first use. They are usually placed after the **#include**s and before the prototypes of our functions.

How do we create an instance of a **DeptNum**? One is created precisely the same way we create an instance of a **double** or a **long**. The following creates several instances of the **enum DeptNum**.

```
DeptNum deptnum;
DeptNum previousDeptNum;
DeptNum x;
```

Given these new variables, then the following are valid.

```
if (deptnum == Appliances)
if (x == Automotive)
case Toys:
```

But these are invalid because specific integer values are being used.

```
if (deptnum == 1)
if (x == 2)
case 3:
```

An **enum** can be passed to a function and one can be returned by a function. The prototypes require a data type and that is simple to code.

```
DeptNum someFunction (DeptNum z);
```

In other words, we use our new **enum** just as if it were any other intrinsic or built-in data type.

Here is the total view of how the **enum** fits into the program. The function **getAlternativeDept()** returns an alternative department number; perhaps the item desired is located in that department, and so on.

```
#include <iostream>
using namespace std;

enum DeptNum {Invalid, Appliances, Automotive,
              Housewares, Toys, Accounting};

DeptNum getAlternativeDept (DeptNum thisDept);

int main () {
 DeptNum thisDept;
 ...
 switch (thisDept) {
  case Appliances:
    ...
    break;
  case Automotive:
```

```
      ...
      break;
  }
  DeptNum altDept = getAlternativeDept (thisDept);
  ...
}

DeptNum getAlternativeDept (DeptNum thisDept) {
 switch (thisDept) {
  case Appliances:
    return Housewares;
  case Automotive:
    return Appliances;
 ...
 }
 ...
}
```

As you look this rather contrived example over, notice one major feature. Nowhere in it are the actual numerical values that would have had to be there if **enum**s were not used! Also note that since the first **enum** symbol has the value 0 by default and since no department number can have the value 0, I chose to place another identifier to represent the value 0, **Invalid**. Thus, **Appliances** has the value 1 as required.

Here is another example of an **enum**. This time, I use convenient names for the month.

```
enum Month {Invalid, Jan, Feb, Mar, Apl, May, Jun,
            Jul, Aug, Sep, Oct, Nov, Dec};
```

Then within **main()** an instance can be created and used.

```
Month month;
...
if (month == Jun || month == Jul || month == Aug)
  cout << "Vacation Time!\n";
```

An **enum** can be very useful in the right circumstance. A store might use an **enum** to represent its products:

```
enum ProductId {Coffee, Tea, Milk, Soda};
```

Or a pet shop program could define an **enum** to help identify all the animals it has for sale:

```
enum Pets {Cat, Dog, Hamster, Snake, Goldfish, Bird};
```

The bottom line is simple: an English identifier that is easily read replaces abstract numerical values. The result is far fewer errors in such programs!

There must be a catch you say. Well, yes, there is a catch. **enum**s are implemented as an integer data type internally. No I/O operations use **enum**s directly; instead, all I/O operations read and write the integer value. Using the **Pet enum** above, if one coded

```
Pets myNewPet;
```

```
cin >> myNewPet; // error - cannot I/O an enum value
```

The user would have to key in the integer 1 if the new pet was a dog, for instance. Ugh.

Likewise, if you outputted

```
cout << myNewPet; // error - cannot I/O an enum value
```

and if the pet was a dog, then a 1 appears on the output, not "Dog." Ugh. (Note that the newer **ostream** implementation now gives a compiler error message on the above line.)

For clear output, there is an easy way around the **enum** problem. Use a Do Case statement and display the appropriate string.

```
switch (myNewPet) {
 case Cat:
   cout << "Cat"; break;
 case Dog:
   cout << "Dog"; break;
 ...
}
```

This is very commonly done for output. It makes the output very readable.

How can the input operation be accomplished and still be readable? There is nothing to prevent the user from inputting 42 when asked to enter the new pet number! Instead of inputting the enumerated value directly, input something more meaningful and use a Do Case to assign the correct **enum** value. One way would be to use a single letter for the pet type, 'D' for Dog, 'C' for Cat and so on. Here is a way it can be written.

```
#include <iostream>
#include <cctype>
using namespace std;

enum Pets {Cat, Dog, Hamster, Snake, Goldfish, Bird};

istream& getPet (istream& infile, Pets& newPet);

int main () {
 Pets thePet;
 while (getPet (cin, thePet)) {
  ... here we have a valid thePet
 }
 ...
 return 0;
}

istream& getPet (istream& infile, Pets& newPet) {
 char c;
 bool validEntry = false;
 while (infile && !validEntry) {
  cout << "Enter Pet type - C (for cat), D (for dog),\n"
     << "H (for hamster), S (for snake), G (for goldfish)\n"
```

```
     << "B (for bird)\n";
  infile >> c;
  if (!infile)
   return infile;
  c = toupper (c);
  switch (c) {
    case 'C':
      newPet = Cat;
      validEntry = true;
      break;
    case 'D':
      newPet = Dog;
      validEntry = true;
      break;
    case 'H':
      newPet = Hamster;
      validEntry = true;
      break;
    case 'S':
      newPet = Snake;
      validEntry = true;
      break;
    case 'G':
      newPet = GoldFish;
      validEntry = true;
      break;
    case 'B':
      newPet = Bird;
      validEntry = true;
      break;
    default:
      cout << "Invalid entry - try again\n";
  }
 }
 return infile;
}
```

In the **getPet()** function, the boolean variable **validEntry** is initialized to **false**. If the user ever enters a valid pet character, then the **validEntry** is set to **true**. The **while** loop repeats the sequence as long as **infile** is still in the good state and a valid entry has not yet been made. After prompting the user and getting their input, if the end of file has been reached, the function returns at once. Otherwise, the character is converted to uppercase and a Do Case sorts out the possibilities. If the user entry matches one of the valid characters, the reference parameter **enum newPet** is assigned the corresponding value and **validEntry** is set to **true**. If no match occurs, then after an error message is displayed, the loop repeats until the user enters a proper pet code.

Thus we have ways of inputting and outputting these enumerated values in a much more readable, user-friendly manner than just a set of abstract numbers.

Suppose that a program must deal with coins at a financial institution. Here is another way the **enum** can be setup in which each identifier is given its value instead of taking the default.

```
enum CoinAmt {Penny = 1, Nickel = 5, Dime = 10,
              Quarter = 25, HalfDollar = 50,
              SilverDollar = 100};
```

Given these values, one can now use them anywhere an integer data type could be used. For example

```
long totalAmount = 124; // total pennies

// the number of quarters in the change
int numQuarters = totalAmount / Quarter;

// remaining change
totalAmount %= Quarter;
```

Once one stops providing unique values, the next enumerator's values go up by one from the previous ones. With the department number **enum**, if one did not wish to have **Invalid** be a part of the enumerated values, then it could have been coded this way.

```
enum DeptNum {Appliances = 1, Automotive, Housewares, Toys,
              Accounting};
```

The month **enum** could have been done this way.

```
enum Month {Jan = 1, Feb, Mar, Apl, May, Jun,
            Jul, Aug, Sep, Oct, Nov, Dec};
```

In these two cases, **Automotive** and **Feb** are given the value of 2; **Housewares** and **Mar**, 3; and so on.

Finally, if no instances of the enumerated data type are ever going to be created, the name can be omitted. This is called an **anonymous enum**. Of course, the enumerated values can be used wherever an integer type can be used. In the coin amount example above, I did not create any instances of **CoinAmt**. I did, however, make use of the enumerated values. It could have been defined this way.

```
enum {Penny = 1, Nickel = 5, Dime = 10, Quarter = 25,
      HalfDollar = 50, SilverDollar = 100};
```

Anonymous **enums** are often used to create good symbolic names for numerical values.

When an application has need of a series of numerical values that are used for some form of identification purposes, consider making those values as part of an enumerated data type to increase readability of the program and lessen the chance for errors.

Aborting the Program

Sometimes a function detects that an error has arisen that it cannot handle. One action the function could to is to return a special error value, such as TIME_ERROR back in chapter 7. However, if a function that is to open a file discovers it cannot be opened, the function may wish to abort the program, to terminate it, instead of returning back to its caller. This is done using the **exit()** function whose sole parameter is the integer return code to give back to DOS.

```
exit (1); // aborts the program with a return code of 1
```

Section B: Computer Science Examples

Cs08a—Inventory on Hand Program

To illustrate many of the principles found in this chapter, let's examine the inventory on hand problem at Acme Chocolates Company. They make chocolate candies that are coated with a thin shell of these colors: yellow, red, blue, green, and brown. The **master.file** contains the current quantity on hand of each of the different colors. Each line in the master file contains first a letter that corresponds to a color (Y, R, U, G, B where U is blue) followed by the number of that color on hand.

At the end of the workday, two additional files have been produced from other programs: **orders.txt** and **made.txt**, representing the orders that have been taken throughout the day for chocolates and the number of new ones made that day. Both of these files have the same form as the master file; that is, first is a letter identifying the color and then the number of that color.

The program should begin by inputting the current **master.txt** file. Next, the program inputs the **made.txt** file and adds the number of the specific colors made today to the corresponding number on hand. Then the program inputs the **orders.txt** file and subtracts the number sold of each color from the number on hand. Finally, the program then writes a new master file of the quantity on hand, called **newmaster.txt**. Note, should the final quantity on hand even become negative, a special line is written to the file **makeAtOnce.txt**, indicating the deficit information so that the manufacturing group can make those kinds immediately the next shift to catch up with the demand.

In this case, an **enum** for the colors simplifies things. Let's make an **enum** like this.

```
enum Color {Yellow, Red, Blue, Green, Brown};
```

Each line in the three files has a character color abbreviation followed by an integer number. Notice the commonality here. Rather than write independent coding for each of the three files, since they all have a common line characteristic, let's write one function, **getLine()**, that can be used to input a line of data from any of the three files. Since for each file the character color must be converted into a **Color enum** type, let's have a function **convertToColor()** to do that coding one time only. Let's also make four other functions that parallel the work to be done: **loadMaster()**, **addMades()**, **subOrders()** and **makeNewMaster()**. The Top-Down Design is thus shown in Figure 8.4.

The **main()** function is really simple in this program. It must define the five totals variables and then call each of the four functions in turn. The variables are: **totalYellow**, **totalRed**, **totalBlue**, **totalGreen** and **totalBrown**. The instruction sequence is just:

loadMaster (**totalYellow**, **totalRed**, **totalBlue**, **totalGreen**, **totalBrown**);
addMades (**totalYellow**, **totalRed**, **totalBlue**, **totalGreen**, **totalBrown**);
subOrders (**totalYellow**, **totalRed**, **totalBlue**, **totalGreen**, **totalBrown**);
makeNewMaster (**totalYellow**, **totalRed**, **totalBlue**, **totalGreen**, **totalBrown**);

The variables must be passed by reference to the first three functions since those functions are altering their contents. However, **makeNewMaster()** can just be passed a copy.

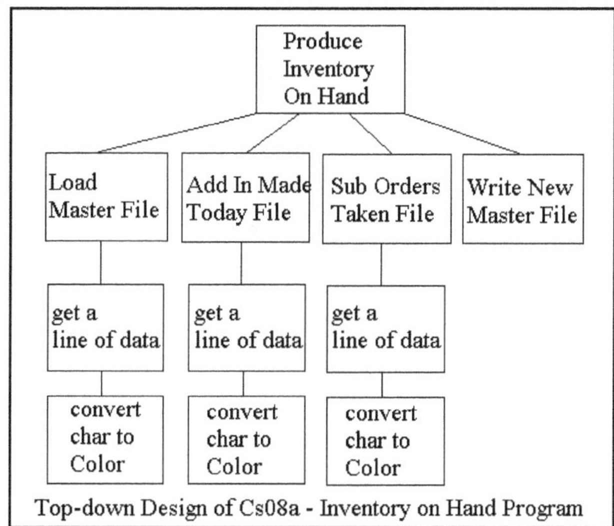

Figure 8.4 Top-Down Design of Cs08a

The sequence for **loadMaster()**, which is passed the five variables by reference is as follows.
define a **Color** variable called **color**
define a **long** variable to hold the incoming quantity, **thisCount**.
open the master file, displaying an error message and aborting if it cannot be opened.
get a line of data filling **color** and **thisCount**.
while the input stream is still good do the following
 switch (**color**) {
  for case **Yellow**, do this
   totalYellow = **thisCount**;
  end do this
  repeat for other 4 color cases
 end **switch**
 get another line of data
end **while**
close the file

The sequence for **addMades()** is exactly the same as **loadMaster()**, except that within the **switch** statement, a calculation must be done like this.

totalYellow += **thisCount**.

The sequence for **subOrders()** is also the same except the calculation is **totalYellow -= thisCount**.

The sequence for **makeNewMasterFile()** is also simple. It simply writes a line for each type consisting of the color letter and the amount on hand. Then, it checks to see if the amount for a given color is less than zero and, if so, displays a message to the make now file.

The sequence for the **getLine()** function, which is passed a reference to the **Color** and **amount**, is as follows.

define a variable to hold the character color called **col**
input **col** and the **amount**
if the file is not in the good state, return the file
assign to the passed **color** reference parameter the returned value from
  convertToColor giving it the **col** character to convert.
return the file reference

The sequence for the **convertToColor()** function first converts the color character to uppercase and then does a **switch** on the character color variable. For each color case, it returns the correct enumerated value.

Figure 8.5 shows the main storage diagram for the program. An easy way to handle the reference variables in the functions is to place "ref" within the reference variable boxes. Then when you are desk checking a call to a function, which has one or more reference variables, draw a line from the reference variable box with the ref in it to the calling function's variable to which it is a reference.

Main Storage for Inventory Program

main(): totalYellow, totalRed, totalGreen, totalBlue, totalBrown

getline(): infile (ref), color (ref), amount (ref), col

convertToColor(): color

loadMaster(): totalYellow (ref), totalRed (ref), totalGreen (ref), totalBlue (ref), totalBrown (ref), color, thisCount, masterFile

addMades(): totalYellow (ref), totalRed (ref), totalGreen (ref), totalBlue (ref), totalBrown (ref), color, thisCount, madeFile

subOrders(): totalYellow (ref), totalRed (ref), totalGreen (ref), totalBlue (ref), totalBrown (ref), color, thisCount, ordersFile

makeNewMaster(): totalYellow (ref), totalRed (ref), totalGreen (ref), totalBlue (ref), totalBrown (ref), makeNowFile, newMasterFile

Figure 8.5 Main Storage for Inventory Program

Here is the completed program. Notice how easy the **enums** make reading the coding.

Cs08a - Inventory on Hand

```
/***************************************************************/
/*                                                             */
/* Cs08a: Inventory On Hand Program                            */
/*                                                             */
/***************************************************************/

#include <iostream>
#include <iomanip>
#include <fstream>
#include <cctype>
using namespace std;

enum Color {Yellow, Red, Blue, Green, Brown};

istream& getLine (istream& infile, Color& color, long& amount);
Color    convertToColor (char color);

void loadMaster (long& totalYellow, long& totalRed,
            long& totalBlue, long& totalGreen, long& totalBrown);
void addMades (long& totalYellow, long& totalRed,
            long& totalBlue, long& totalGreen, long& totalBrown);
void subOrders (long& totalYellow, long& totalRed,
            long& totalBlue, long& totalGreen, long& totalBrown);
void makeNewMaster (long totalYellow, long totalRed,
            long totalBlue, long totalGreen, long totalBrown);

int main () {

 // total quantity on hand of each color
 long totalYellow = 0;
 long totalRed = 0;
 long totalBlue = 0;
 long totalGreen = 0;
 long totalBrown = 0;

 // main processing steps
 loadMaster (totalYellow, totalRed, totalBlue, totalGreen,
             totalBrown);
 addMades (totalYellow, totalRed, totalBlue, totalGreen,
           totalBrown);
 subOrders (totalYellow, totalRed, totalBlue, totalGreen,
            totalBrown);
 makeNewMaster (totalYellow, totalRed, totalBlue, totalGreen,
                totalBrown);

 return 0;
}

```

```
/***************************************************************/
/*                                                             */
/* getLine: input a line: Color and amount from a file         */
/*                                                             */
/***************************************************************/

istream& getLine (istream& infile, Color& color, long& amount) {
 char col; // color letter
 infile >> col >> amount; // input one line
 if (!infile)
  return infile;
 color = convertToColor (col);
 return infile;
}

/***************************************************************/
/*                                                             */
/* convertToColor: given a char color letter, return           */
/*                 corresponding Color enumeration value       */
/*                                                             */
/***************************************************************/

Color convertToColor (char color) {
 color = toupper (color);
 switch (color) {
  case 'Y':
   return Yellow;
  case 'R':
   return Red;
  case 'G':
   return Green;
  case 'U':
   return Blue;
  case 'B':
   return Brown;
  default:
   cerr << "Invalid color letter. It was: " << color << endl;
   exit (1);
 }
}

/***************************************************************/
/*                                                             */
/* loadMaster: load master file of qty on hand for each color  */
/*                                                             */
/***************************************************************/

void loadMaster (long& totalYellow, long& totalRed,
           long& totalBlue, long& totalGreen, long& totalBrown) {
 Color color;     // color of current one
 long thisCount; // quantity of current one

 //open the master file
```

```
 ifstream masterFile ("master.txt");
 if (!masterFile) {
  cerr << "Error: unable to open master.txt file.\n";
  exit (2);
 }

 // input the amount on hand for each color
 while (getLine (masterFile, color, thisCount)) {
  switch (color) {
  case Yellow:
   totalYellow = thisCount; break;
  case Red:
   totalRed = thisCount; break;
  case Green:
   totalGreen = thisCount; break;
  case Blue:
   totalBlue = thisCount; break;
  case Brown:
   totalBrown = thisCount; break;
  }
 }
 masterFile.close ();
}

/***************************************************************/
/*                                                             */
/* addMades: add in the totals that were made today            */
/*                                                             */
/***************************************************************/

void addMades (long& totalYellow, long& totalRed,
           long& totalBlue, long& totalGreen, long& totalBrown) {
 Color color;    // color of current one
 long thisCount; // quantity of current one

 //open the made today file
 ifstream madeFile ("made.txt");
 if (!madeFile) {
  cerr << "Error: unable to open made.txt file.\n";
  exit (3);
 }

 //for each one made today, add amount made to total for color
 while (getLine (madeFile, color, thisCount)) {
  switch (color) {
  case Yellow:
   totalYellow += thisCount; break;
  case Red:
   totalRed += thisCount; break;
  case Green:
   totalGreen += thisCount; break;
  case Blue:
   totalBlue += thisCount; break;
```

```
  case Brown:
   totalBrown += thisCount; break;
  }
 }
 madeFile.close ();
}

/***************************************************************/
/*                                                             */
/* subOrders: subtract out the current orders to be filled     */
/*                                                             */
/***************************************************************/

void subOrders (long& totalYellow, long& totalRed,
           long& totalBlue, long& totalGreen, long& totalBrown) {
 Color color;    // color of current one
 long thisCount; // quantity of current one

 // open the orders file
 ifstream ordersFile ("orders.txt");
 if (!ordersFile) {
  cerr << "Error: unable to open orders.txt file.\n";
  exit (4);
 }

 // process each line
 while (getLine (ordersFile, color, thisCount)) {
  // subtract total that corresponds to each color
  switch (color) {
  case Yellow:
   totalYellow -= thisCount; break;
  case Red:
   totalRed -= thisCount; break;
  case Green:
   totalGreen -= thisCount; break;
  case Blue:
   totalBlue -= thisCount; break;
  case Brown:
   totalBrown -= thisCount; break;
  }
 }
 ordersFile.close ();
}

/***************************************************************/
/*                                                             */
/* makeNewMaster: makes new master file with errors reported   */
/*                                                             */
/***************************************************************/

void makeNewMaster (long totalYellow, long totalRed,
              long totalBlue, long totalGreen, long totalBrown) {
 // open both files
```

```
  ofstream makeNowFile ("makeAtOnce.txt");
  ofstream newMasterFile ("newmaster.txt");

  // make a new master file
  newMasterFile << 'Y' << " " << totalYellow << endl;
  newMasterFile << 'R' << " " << totalRed    << endl;
  newMasterFile << 'G' << " " << totalGreen  << endl;
  newMasterFile << 'U' << " " << totalBlue   << endl;
  newMasterFile << 'B' << " " << totalBrown  << endl;
  newMasterFile.close ();

  // report on deficits that must be made at once
  if (totalYellow < 0) {
   makeNowFile << "Yellow is short: " << setw(6) << totalYellow
               << endl;
  }
  if (totalRed < 0) {
   makeNowFile << "Red is short:    " << setw(6) << totalRed
               << endl;
  }
  if (totalGreen < 0) {
   makeNowFile << "Green is short:  " << setw(6) << totalGreen
               << endl;
  }
  if (totalBlue < 0) {
   makeNowFile << "Blue is short:   " << setw(6) << totalBlue
               << endl;
  }
  if (totalBrown < 0) {
   makeNowFile << "Brown is short:  " << setw(6) << totalBrown
               << endl;
  }
  makeNowFile.close ();
}
```

Cs08b—Inventory on Hand Program—Using a Generic processFile() Function

Note that there is still some redundant coding in **Cs08a**. Namely, **loadMaster()** and **addMades()** are nearly identical. They could be reduced to a single function by some slight changes. If **main()** initialized the five totals to zero and passed a controlling parameter in addition to the five references to the long amounts, then one function could be used to handle both situations. Taking it one step further, if that common function was also passed a way to determine if it was a subtraction that was needed, then it could also be used for the **subOrders()** as well.

Suppose we made another **enum** that identifies which file we want to process. Let's call it **FileType** and it is defined as

```
enum FileType {Master, Mades, Orders};
```

Now the prototype for the generic single function to read and process a file of these data could then be

```
void processFile (FileType which, long& totalYellow,
                  long& totalRed, long& totalBlue,
                  long& totalGreen, long& totalBrown);
```

Then the correct file can be opened this way.

```
ifstream infile;
switch (which) {
 case Master:
  infile.open ("master.txt");
  break;
 case Mades:
  infile.open ("made.txt");
  break;
 case Orders:
  infile.open ("orders.txt");
  break;
 default:
  cerr << "Error: incorrect parameter to processFile\n";
  exit (3);
}
if (!infile) {
 cerr << "Error cannot open the input files\n";
 exit (2);
}
```

Within the **switch** on the **Color enum**, a slight change handles all three cases:

```
case Yellow:
 if (which == Orders)
    totalYellow -= thisCount;
 else
   totalYellow += thisCount;
 break;
```

And so on with the other four cases. In other words, we can write only one input a file and process its data function, streamlining the program significantly. Here is the revised program **Cs08b**.

Cs08b - Inventory on Hand - Generic Process Function

```
/***************************************************************/
/*                                                             */
/* Cs08b: Inventory On Hand Program                            */
/*                                                             */
/***************************************************************/

#include <iostream>
#include <iomanip>
#include <fstream>
#include <cctype>
using namespace std;
```

```

enum Color {Yellow, Red, Blue, Green, Brown};
enum FileType {Master, Mades, Orders};

istream& getLine (istream& infile, Color& color, long& amount);
Color    convertToColor (char color);

void processFile (FileType which, long& totalYellow,
               long& totalRed, long& totalBlue, long& totalGreen,
               long& totalBrown);
void makeNewMaster (long totalYellow, long totalRed,
               long totalBlue, long totalGreen, long totalBrown);

int main () {
 // total quantity on hand of each color
 long totalYellow = 0;
 long totalRed = 0;
 long totalBlue = 0;
 long totalGreen = 0;
 long totalBrown = 0;

 // main processing steps
 processFile (Master, totalYellow, totalRed, totalBlue,
              totalGreen, totalBrown);
 processFile (Mades, totalYellow, totalRed, totalBlue,
              totalGreen, totalBrown);
 processFile (Orders, totalYellow, totalRed, totalBlue,
              totalGreen, totalBrown);
 makeNewMaster (totalYellow, totalRed, totalBlue,
                totalGreen, totalBrown);

 return 0;
}

/***************************************************************/
/*                                                             */
/* getLine: input a line: Color and amount from a file         */
/*                                                             */
/***************************************************************/

istream& getLine (istream& infile, Color& color, long& amount) {
 char col; // color letter
 infile >> col >> amount; // input one line
 if (!infile)
  return infile;
 color = convertToColor (col);
 return infile;
}

/***************************************************************/
/*                                                             */
/* convertToColor: given a char color, return corresponding    */
/*                 Color enumeration value                     */
```

```
/*                                                              */
/****************************************************************/

Color convertToColor (char color) {
 color = toupper (color);
 switch (color) {
  case 'Y':
   return Yellow;
  case 'R':
   return Red;
  case 'G':
   return Green;
  case 'U':
   return Blue;
  case 'B':
   return Brown;
  default:
   cerr << "Invalid color letter. It was: " << color << endl;
   exit (1);
 }
}

/****************************************************************/
/*                                                              */
/* processFile: process a file of colors and amounts            */
/*                                                              */
/****************************************************************/

void processFile (FileType which, long& totalYellow,
                  long& totalRed, long& totalBlue, long& totalGreen,
                  long& totalBrown) {
 Color color;    // color of current one
 long thisCount; // quantity of current one

 //open the master file
 ifstream infile;
 switch (which) {
  case Master:
   infile.open ("master.txt");
   if (!infile) {
    cerr << "Error: unable to open master.txt file.\n";
    exit (2);
   }
   break;
  case Mades:
   infile.open ("made.txt");
   if (!infile) {
    cerr << "Error: unable to open made.txt file.\n";
    exit (3);
   }
   break;
  case Orders:
   infile.open ("orders.txt");
```

```
    if (!infile) {
     cerr << "Error: unable to open orders.txt file.\n";
     exit (4);
    }
    break;
   default:
    cerr << "Error: incorrect parameter to processFile\n";
    exit (5);
  }

  // input the amount on hand for each color
  while (getLine (infile, color, thisCount)) {
   switch (color) {
   case Yellow:
    if (which == Orders)
     totalYellow -= thisCount;
    else
     totalYellow += thisCount;
    break;
   case Red:
    if (which == Orders)
     totalRed -= thisCount;
    else
     totalRed += thisCount;
    break;
   case Green:
    if (which == Orders)
     totalGreen -= thisCount;
    else
     totalGreen += thisCount;
    break;
   case Blue:
    if (which == Orders)
     totalBlue -= thisCount;
    else
     totalBlue += thisCount;
    break;
   case Brown:
    if (which == Orders)
     totalBrown -= thisCount;
    else
     totalBrown += thisCount;
   }
  }
  infile.close ();
 }

/***************************************************************/
/*                                                             */
/* makeNewMaster: makes new master file with errors reported   */
/*                                                             */
/***************************************************************/

```

```
void makeNewMaster (long totalYellow, long totalRed,
                    long totalBlue, long totalGreen, long totalBrown) {
 // open both files
 ofstream makeNowFile ("makeAtOnce.txt");
 ofstream newMasterFile ("newmaster.txt");
if (!makeNowFile || !newMasterFile) {
 cerr << "Cannot open either newMasterFile or newmaster.txt\n";
  exit (6);
  }
 // make a new master file
 newMasterFile << 'Y' << " " << totalYellow << endl;
 newMasterFile << 'R' << " " << totalRed    << endl;
 newMasterFile << 'G' << " " << totalGreen  << endl;
 newMasterFile << 'U' << " " << totalBlue   << endl;
 newMasterFile << 'B' << " " << totalBrown  << endl;
 newMasterFile.close ();

 // report on deficits that must be made at once
 if (totalYellow < 0) {
  makeNowFile << "Yellow is short: " << setw(6) << totalYellow
              << endl;
 }
 if (totalRed < 0) {
  makeNowFile << "Red is short:    " << setw(6) << totalRed
              << endl;
 }
 if (totalGreen < 0) {
  makeNowFile << "Green is short:  " << setw(6) << totalGreen
              << endl;
 }
 if (totalBlue < 0) {
  makeNowFile << "Blue is short:   " << setw(6) << totalBlue
              << endl;
 }
 if (totalBrown < 0) {
  makeNowFile << "Brown is short:  " << setw(6) << totalBrown
              << endl;
 }
 makeNowFile.close ();
}
```

The **rule** of thumb to follow in programming is this. **If you find that you are coding nearly the same exact coding in more than one function, see if there is a way that coding can easily be factored out and done just once.**

Section C: Engineering Examples—Numerical Integration

The Trapezoid Method of Numerical Integration

Often a programmer is called upon to integrate a function f(x). While the computer cannot integrate from zero to infinity or from minus infinity to plus infinity, if there are some limits, say integrating from point A to point B, then the computer can easily perform the integration. The first method of handling the integration is called the trapezoid method.

A way of looking at the integration of

$$I = \int_A^B f(x)$$

is that the result is actually the area under the curve as shown in Figure 8.6.

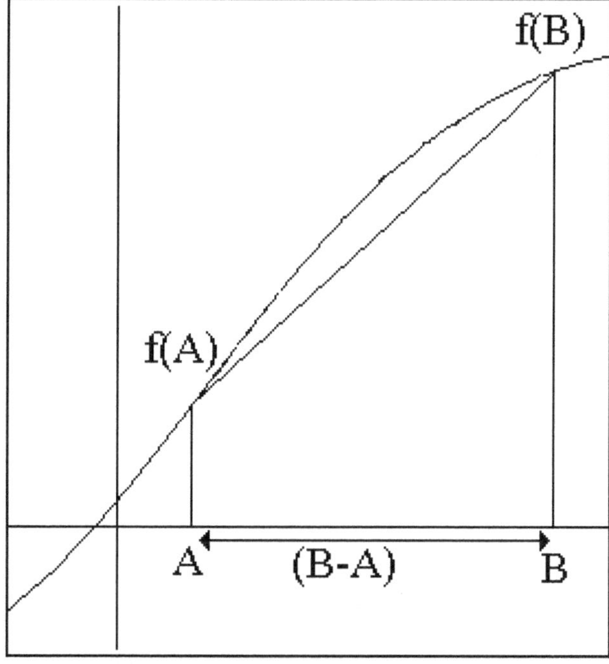

Figure 8.6 Integration Using One Trapezoid

The trapezoid method divides the interval A to B into a number of trapezoids and calculates the area of the trapezoids, which becomes the area under the curve or the result of the integration. In Figure 8.6, there is one trapezoid. The area of that trapezoid is given by

$$A = \frac{1}{2}(F(A) + F(B))(B - A)$$

One trapezoid does not provide a very accurate value for the area under the curve. In Figure 8.7, the interval A to B is divided into four equal portions. The sum of the areas of these trapezoids is a closer approximation to the area under the curve.

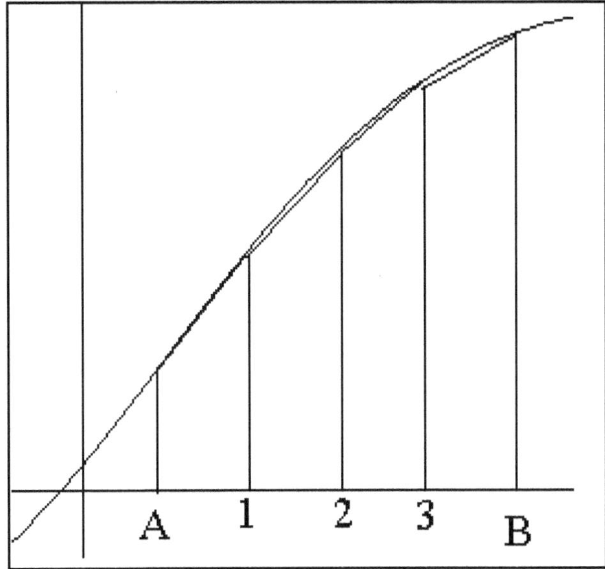

Figure 8.7 Integration Using Four Trapezoids

When there are four evenly spaced trapezoids, let **w** be the uniform width of each trapezoid. The area becomes

.5 * w * (f(a) + f(1))   + .5 * w * (f(1) + f(2))
+ .5 * w * (f(2) + f(3))   + .5 * w * (f(3) + f(b))

If we group these, we have
I = .5 * w * (f(a) + f(b) + 2 (f(1) + f(2) + f(3)))
From this, we can generalize the solution using n total trapezoids as

$$I = .5w\left(f(a) + f(b) + 2\sum_{i=1}^{n-1} f(x_i) \right)$$

This equation can be used to perform the integration. However, one major difficulty remains. How do we know how many trapezoids are sufficient to yield an accurate solution? Certainly, one could solve the equation using one trapezoid, and then do it again for two, and then three and so on. Eventually, adding one more trapezoid should make no appreciable impact upon the resulting answer, to the desired degree of accuracy. While this would work, it is going to be a very slow method doing many redundant calculations. There is a better way to proceed. In other words, if we have already calculated the area using one number of trapezoids, is there a way we can use that result in the next iteration so as to avoid recalculating the entire summation each time? If so, then when the next iteration's result is less than the desired degree of accuracy from the previous result, we have found the answer.

One thing that can be done to more quickly zero in on the result is to increase the number of trapezoids by a power of 2. Let's let n, the number of trapezoids, be given by

$$n = 2^k$$

where k begins at 0 and goes up by one each time. Thus, the number of trapezoids goes rapidly up: 1, 2, 4, 8, 16, 32, 64, 128, 256, 1024,...

Also by doubling the number of trapezoids each time, we introduce some interesting aspects. The width of the trapezoids, **w**, is given by

$$x = \frac{B - A}{2^k}$$

The implication is that the width of the kth trapezoids is ½ of the $(k-1)^{th}$ trapezoids. But there is also an even more important aspect that this doubling of the number of trapezoids has on the calculation. If we go from two to four trapezoids, then two of the points have already had their f(x)'s calculated and added into the result. Compare Figure 8.7 with four trapezoids to Figure 8.8, which uses two trapezoids. Notice that point 2 in Figure 8.7 is the same as point 1 in Figure 8.8.

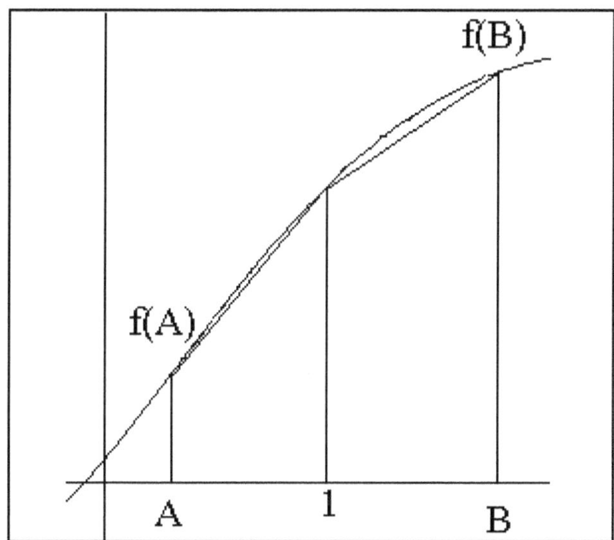

Figure 8.8 Integration Using Two Trapezoids

We have then the two areas given by

$T_2 = \frac{1}{2} w_2 (f(a) + f(b) + 2 (f1))$

$T_4 = \frac{1}{2} w_4 (f(a) + f(b) + 2 (f1 + f2 + f3))$

but w_4 is ½ w_2 and f2 of T_4 is the same point as f1 of T_2. So substituting we get

$T_4 = \frac{1}{2} T_2 + w_4 (f1 + f3)$

From this, we can generalize based on k, the power of 2:

$$T_k = \frac{T_{k-1}}{2} + w_k \sum_{i=1,odd-only}^{n-1} f(a + iw_k)$$

This is the version that we can efficiently use to integrate a function on the computer.

Engr08a—Numerical Integration with the Trapezoid Rule

Let's integrate a simple function that has a known answer so that we can compare the results. The function is

$$I = \int_1^2 \frac{1}{x} dx$$

This yields ln(x); ln(1) is 0, and ln(2) is .69314718. Here is the output from running the program.

Output from Engr08a - Integration using Trapezoid Method

```
Integration of 1/x
Enter the range a and b, the desired degree of accuracy
such as 1E-6, and the maximum number of iterations
separated by blanks
1 2 .000001 50
The result is:  0.6931464 found after 25 iterations
```

The **main()** function does nothing more than prompt the user to enter the four needed values, calls the **Trap()** function and displays the results. Function **F()** is trivial. All of the work is done in the **Trap()** function. The logic within **Trap()** follows very similarly to that used in root solving. The main loop is executed as long as **k** is less than the maximum number of iterations and the difference between this result and the previous result is greater than the desired accuracy. Here is the complete program.

Engr08a - Integration using Trapezoid Method

```
/***************************************************************/
/*                                                             */
/* Engr08a Integrate f(x) using the Trapezoid Method           */
/*                                                             */
/***************************************************************/

#include <iostream>
#include <iomanip>
#include <cmath>
using namespace std;
double Trap (double a, double b, int imax, double eps, int& i);
double F (double x);
```

```
int main () {

 double a, b;
 int imax;
 double eps;
 cout << "Integration of 1/x\n"
   << "Enter the range a and b, the desired degree of accuracy\n"
   << "such as 1E-6, and the maximum number of iterations\n"
   << "separated by blanks\n";
 cin >> a >> b >> eps >> imax;
 if (!cin)
  return 1;

 double answer;
 int    numberIterations;
 answer = Trap (a, b, imax, eps, numberIterations);
 cout << "The result is: " << setw(10) << setprecision (7)
      << answer << " found after " << numberIterations
      << " iterations\n";

 return 0;
}

/***************************************************************/
/*                                                             */
/* Trap: integrates F(x) using the trapezoid method            */
/*                                                             */
/***************************************************************/

double Trap (double a, double b, int imax, double eps, int& k) {

 const double wba = b-a; // original width of integration
 double prevT = 0;       // the previous integration result
 double newT = .5 * wba * (F(a) + F(b)); // current result
 double sum;
 double w;
 int n;
 int i;

 k = 1;                  // number of iterations

 while (k < imax && fabs (newT - prevT) > eps) {
  prevT = newT;           // save prev result for this iteration
  n = (int) (pow (2., (double) k)); // new number of trapezoids
  w = wba / n;            // get new uniform width of trapezoids
  sum = 0;                // find sum of all odd terms
  for (i=1; i<n-1; i+=2) {
   sum = sum + F(a + i * w);
  }
  newT = .5 * prevT + w * sum; // calc new area
  // for debugging, display these intermediate results
  //cout << k << " " << setprecision (8) << newT << endl;
```

```
   k++;
  }
  // check for non-convergence
  if (k == imax) {
   cerr << "After " << imax
        << " iterations, Trap has not converged.\n"
        << "The result so far is " << setprecision (8) << newT
        << endl << "The accuracy is " << fabs (newT - prevT)
        << endl;
  }
  return newT;
 }

/*************************************************************/
/*                                                           */
/* F - the function to integrate - here 1/x                  */
/*                                                           */
/*************************************************************/

double F (double x) {
 return 1/x;
}
```

Integration Using Simpson's Rule

Simpson's Rule fits a parabola to three equally spaced points instead of the simple trapezoid. The general form of the parabola is

$$y(x) = a\,(x - x_0)^2 + b\,(x - x_0) + c$$

Again if we use the number of panels as given by

$$n = 2^k$$

and the uniform width, w, as (b-a) / n, then Simpson's Rule becomes

$$S = \frac{1}{3} w \left[f(a) + f(b) + 4 \sum_{i=1,odd-only}^{n-1} f(a+iw) + 2 \sum_{i=2,even-only}^{n-2} f(a+iw) \right]$$

Since the derivation is commonly found in Calculus books, it is not shown here.

To use Simpson's Rule to perform the integration, we must enter the **k** term, which is the power of 2 that determines the number of panels in which to divide the interval **a** to **b**. The programming solution of this equation is straightforward. Two summations must be done; both are extremely straightforward.

Engr08b—Numerical Integration with Simpson's Rule

The function **Simp()** performs the calculation or integration. It is passed the two limits **a** and **b** along with the **k** term, which is the power of two specifying the number of panels to use. The only refinement from the original equation above is the calculation of the next **x** term to be used in the call to **F(x)** within the summations. As the equation is written, for each term, the new **x** value is given by **a + i * w**. Performing a multiplication each time is a slow operation. It is far faster to obtain the next **x** value by adding **deltaX** to the previous **x** where **deltaX** is 2***w**.

Here is the result of a program execution. So that we can compare the results, I have entered a **k** value of 25, identical to what the **Trap()** function found for the integration result.

```
Output from Engr08b - Integration using Simpson's Rule
```

```
Integration of 1/x using Simpson's Rule
Enter the range a and b and enter the number of iterations
separated by blanks
1 2 25
The result is:  0.6931472 found using k of 25
```

Compare this result to that from the trapezoid method and to the precise mathematical calculated result:

```
precise value: 0.69314718
Trapezoid:     0.6931464
Simpson's:     0.6931472
```

Simpson's rule provides a more accurate value than does the trapezoid method, which is one reason that this method is a popular one for integration work.

Here is the complete program.

```
Engr08b - Integration using Simpson's Rule
```

```
/***************************************************************/
/*                                                             */
/* Engr08b Integrate f(x) using Simpson's Rule                 */
/*                                                             */
/***************************************************************/

#include <iostream>
#include <iomanip>
#include <cmath>
using namespace std;
double Simp (double a, double b, int k);
double F (double x);

int main () {

 double a, b;
 int k;
```

```
 cout << "Integration of 1/x using Simpson's Rule\n"
 <<"Enter the range a and b and enter the number of iterations\n"
      << "separated by blanks\n";
 cin >> a >> b >> k;
 if (!cin)
  return 1;

 double answer;
 answer = Simp (a, b, k);
 cout << "The result is: " << setw(10) << setprecision (7)
      << answer << " found using k of " << k << endl;
 return 0;
}

/***************************************************************/
/*                                                             */
/* Simp: integrates F(x) using Simpson's Rule                  */
/*                                                             */
/***************************************************************/

double Simp (double a, double b, int k) {

 int n = (int) (pow (2., (double) k)); // new number of panels
 double w = (b-a) / n;        // get the uniform width

 // calculate first sums of odd terms
 int i;
 double sum2 = 0;
 double deltaX = 2 * w;    // amount to add to x to get next odd x
 double x = a + w;         // initial x to use
 for (i=1; i<n-1; i+=2) {  // do all odd terms
  sum2 += F(x);            // add in this term
  x += deltaX;             // find next odd x
 }
 sum2 *= 4;                // multiply sum by 4

 // calculate second sum of even terms
 double sum4 = 0;
 x = a + deltaX;           // initial x to use
 for (i=2; i<n-2; i+=2) {  // do all even terms
  sum4 += F(x);            // add in this term
  x += deltaX;             // find next even term
 }
 sum4 *= 2;                // multiply sum by 2

 // create final sum of all terms
 double sum = F(a) + F(b) + sum2 + sum4;
 return w * sum / 3;       // return Simpson's Rule for the area
}

/***************************************************************/
/*                                                             */
/* F - the function to integrate - here 1/x                    */
```

```
/*                                                                    */
/**********************************************************************/

double F (double x) {
 return 1/x;
}
```

Engr08c—Using Menus to Control Program Operation

A major use of character data in scientific type programming involves menus and menu choices. The following represents the main menu presented to the user.

```
Integration of F(x)

A. Perform the integration using the Trapezoid method
B. Perform the integration using Simpson's method
C. Quit the program

Enter the letter of your choice: _
```

The user then enters their choice and the program performs the requisite action and then redisplays the main menu. A character is input as the user's choice.

To be compatible, the original Trapezoid method is used so that it can be directly compared to the results from Simpson's Rule.

The coding to display a menu is a straightforward series of text lines to be displayed. They are encapsulated in a function called **ShowMenu()**. The function **GetMenuChoice()** must obtain a valid choice, A, B or C. I initialized the character **choice** with a 0 so that within the loop, if **choice** is ever anything else, an invalid entry error message can be displayed and a prompt to reenter the letter can be done. If the user presses Ctrl-Z for end of file, **GetMenuChoice()** simply sets **choice** to C; the main loop handles the termination request as if a 'C' had been pressed.

Here is a sample run of what the program produces.

Output from - Engr08c - Using a Menu to Control Program Actions

```



       Integration of F(x)

       A. Perform the integration using the Trapezoid method
       B. Perform the integration using Simpson's method
       C. Quit the program

       Enter the letter of your choice: a
       Enter k factor 10
```

```

Integration of 1/x using Trapezoid method with k of 10 = 0.69265872


          Integration of F(x)

          A. Perform the integration using the Trapezoid method
          B. Perform the integration using Simpson's method
          C. Quit the program

          Enter the letter of your choice: b
          Enter k factor 10

Integration of 1/x using Simpson's method with k of 10 = 0.69216998


          Integration of F(x)

          A. Perform the integration using the Trapezoid method
          B. Perform the integration using Simpson's method
          C. Quit the program

          Enter the letter of your choice: q
Choice must be A, B or C. Try again
```

Here is the completed menu driven program.

Engr08c - Using a Menu to Control Program Actions

```
/***************************************************************/
/*                                                             */
/* Engr08c Menu Choices for Integration                        */
/*                                                             */
/***************************************************************/

#include <iostream>
#include <iomanip>
#include <cmath>
#include <cctype>
using namespace std;
double Simp (double a, double b, int k);
double Trap (double a, double b, int k);
double F (double x);

void ShowMenu ();
void GetMenuChoice (char& choice);

int main () {

 const double a = 1;  // fixed limits on a and b
 const double b = 2;
 int k;
```

```
 cout << setprecision (8);
 char choice;

 ShowMenu ();             // display menu
 GetMenuChoice (choice); // get initial choice
 while (choice != 'C') {
  cout << "\tEnter k factor "; // get k factor
  cin >> k;
  if (!cin) break;
  // perform the integration; display results
  switch (choice) {
   case 'A':
    cout <<
         "\nIntegration of 1/x using Trapezoid method with k of "
         << k << " = " << Trap (a, b, k);
    break;
   case 'B':
    cout <<
         "\nIntegration of 1/x using Simpson's method with k of "
         << k << " = " << Simp (a, b, k);
    break;
  }
  ShowMenu ();             // redisplay menu
  GetMenuChoice (choice); // get next choice
 }
 return 0;
}

/***************************************************************/
/*                                                             */
/* ShowMenu: displays the menu of choices                      */
/*                                                             */
/***************************************************************/

void ShowMenu () {
 cout << endl << endl << endl;
 cout << "\tIntegration of F(x)\n\n"
   << "\tA. Perform the integration using the Trapezoid method\n"
   << "\tB. Perform the integration using Simpson's method\n"
   << "\tC. Quit the program\n\n"
   << "\tEnter the letter of your choice: ";
}

/***************************************************************/
/*                                                             */
/* GetMenuChoice: get the user's menu choice                   */
/*                                                             */
/***************************************************************/

void GetMenuChoice (char &choice) {
 choice = 0;
 while (choice < 'A' || choice > 'C') {
  if (choice)
```

```
   cout << "Choice must be A, B or C. Try again ";
  cin >> choice;
  if (!cin)
   choice = 'C';
  else
   choice = toupper (choice);
 }
}

/***************************************************************/
/*                                                             */
/* Simp: integrates F(x) using Simpson's Rule                  */
/*                                                             */
/***************************************************************/

double Simp (double a, double b, int k) {

 int n = (int) (pow (2., (double) k)); // new number of panels
 double w = (b-a) / n;       // get the uniform width

 // calculate first sums of odd terms
 int i;
 double sum2 = 0;
 double deltaX = 2 * w;    // amount to add to x to get next odd x
 double x = a + w;         // initial x to use
 for (i=1; i<n-1; i+=2) { // do all odd terms
  sum2 += F(x);            // add in this term
  x += deltaX;             // find next odd x
 }
 sum2 *= 4;                // multiply sum by 4

 // calculate second sum of even terms
 double sum4 = 0;
 x = a + deltaX;           // initial x to use
 for (i=2; i<n-2; i+=2) { // do all even terms
  sum4 += F(x);            // add in this term
  x += deltaX;             // find next even term
 }
 sum4 *= 2;                // multiply sum by 2

 // create final sum of all terms
 double sum = F(a) + F(b) + sum2 + sum4;
 return w * sum / 3;       // return Simpson's Rule for the area
}

/***************************************************************/
/*                                                             */
/* Trap: integrates F(x) using the trapezoid method            */
/*                                                             */
/***************************************************************/

double Trap (double a, double b, int k) {

```

```
 int n = (int) (pow (2., (double) k)); // number of trapezoids
 double w = (b-a) / n;           // get the uniform width of traps
 double x = a + w;               // get the initial x to use
 double sum = 0;
 int i;
 for (i=1; i<n-1; i++) {         // sum all terms
  sum += F(x);
  x += w;
 }
 sum *= 2;                       // create 2 times the sum
 sum = sum + F(a) + F(b);        // add up all the other terms
 return .5 * w * sum;            // return the integration result
}

/***************************************************************/
/*                                                             */
/* F - the function to integrate - here 1/x                    */
/*                                                             */
/***************************************************************/

double F (double x) {
 return 1/x;
}
```

Design Exercises

1. Design a Weekly Sales Summary Program

Acme Music Company handles violins, cellos, drums, guitars, and pianos. When the weekly sales summary report program is run, the sales file is input and summarized.

Each line in the sales file represents sales in which the customer purchased an item that was in the store. A line contains the quantity sold, its cost, its id number, a letter code indicating which kind of instrument it is, and finally a nine-digit customer id number. This letter code consists of one of these letters: V, C, D, G, and P—taken from the first letter of each musical instrument type

The summary report should accumulate the total sales of each instrument type. When the end of the file is reached, display a summary of the sales for each instrument type. The report looks like this.

```
     Acme Music Company
     Weekly Sales Summary

Instrument Quantity    Total
             Sold      Sales
  Violin      999    $9,999.99
  Cello       999    $9,999.99
```

```
Drum            999     $9,999.99
Guitar          999     $9,999.99
Piano           999     $9,999.99
                        ---------
                       $99,999.99
```

Design the program. First, do a Top-Down Design of the problem to isolate what functions are needed. Next, decide upon whether or not to use an **enum**—that is, how you wish to handle the instrument codes. Then, layout main storage for your functions. Finally, pseudocode the functions needed.

2. Design a **petTypeConversion()** function

Acme Pet Shop handles many kinds of pets. Each is identified in many of their data files by a single letter, either upper or lowercase. Having heard about **enums**, management has decided to convert all of their programs over to using a **Pet enum**. A single function is to be written that all the programs can use to handle this process. The **Pet enum** handles the following: dog, cat, bird, rat, hamster, snake, and gerbil. The letter codes consist of the first letter of the animal types.

The **petTypeConversion()** function is passed four parameters. The first parameter is a **bool** called **which** that indicates which way the conversion is to go. If **which** is **true**, convert the second parameter, a **char** pet code letter, into the appropriate **enum** value and store it in the third parameter which is a reference to a **Pet enum** called **pet**. If **which** is **false**, then display the English word, such as dog, for the passed **Pet enum**, **pet**. The display is done using the fourth parameter, a reference to an **ostream**, **outfile**.

Stop! Do These Exercises Before Programming

1. The following program segment does not produce the correct results. Why? How can it be fixed?

```
char quantity;
double cost;
cin >> quantity >> cost;
cout << "Total is " << quantity * cost << endl;
```

2. Acme Department Store has new product information stored in a file whose lines consist of product id, product type, and cost. The product id is a **long** integer while the cost is a **double**. The product type is a letter code indicating the category of merchandise, such as A (automotive), C (clothing), S (sports) and so on. A typical line looks like this with one blank on either side of the product type letter.

```
23455 A 4.99
```

However, since these are new items, sometimes the type of product has not yet been determined and that field is blank in that line. The programmer wrote the following input function. It does not work. Why? What can be done to fix it up so that it properly inputs the data whether or not the product type is temporarily blank?

```
istream& getData (istream& infile, long& id, char& type,
                  double& cost) {
 infile >> id >> type >> cost;
 return infile;
}
```

3. Another Acme programmer attempted to fix the program in Problem 2 above by coding the following function. It does not work properly either. Why? How could it be fixed to work correctly?

```
istream& getData (istream& infile, long& id, char& type,
                  double& cost) {
 infile >> id;
 infile.get (type);
 infile >> cost;
 return infile;
}
```

4. What is wrong with the following Do Case coding? How can it be fixed up so that it would work?

```
double month;
switch (month) {
 case 1:
 case 2:
 case 12:
   // winter costs are 25% higher
   double sum;
   sum = qty * cost * 1.25;
   break;
 default:
   double sum;
   sum = qty * cost;
   break;
}
cout << sum;
```

5. The programmer goofed while coding this Do Case to calculate the shift bonus for the employee payroll. What is wrong and how can it be fixed?

```
char shift;
switch (shift) {
 case '1':
  pay = hours * rate;
```

```
  case '2':
   pay = hours * rate * 1.05;
  case '3':
   pay = hours * rate * 1.12;
}
cout << pay;
```

6. The programmer wanted to setup an enumerated data type to handle the employee's shift. However, the following coding fails. Why? How can it be repaired?

```
Enum ShiftType = First, Second, and Third;
```

7. A programmer setup the following **enum** to handle the product types.

```
enum ProductTypes {Games, Auto, Clothing, Appliances};
```

In the input a set of data function, the user is instructed to enter a letter for the product type: G, A, C or A. What is the design flaw and why does not the following input coding work? How can it be repaired?

```
ProductTypes prodType;
infile >> prodType;
```

8. In Problem 7, the programmer got frustrated and then did the following, which does not compile. Why? Can this coding be repaired?

```
ProductTypes prodType;
char c;
infile >> c;
if (c == 'A')
 prodType = 1;
if (c == 'G')
 prodType = 0;
```

Programming Problems

Problem Cs08-1—Triangle Processing

A triangle has three sides. If all three sides are equal, it is called an equilateral triangle. If any two sides are equal, it is an isosceles triangle. If none of the three sides is equal, it is called a scalene triangle. For a triangle even to exist, the sum of any two sides must be longer than the remaining side.

Write a program inputs a set of three potential sides of a triangle; use **double**s for their data type. After processing a set of sides, input another set of sides until end-of-file occurs. For each set of data, echo print the original values, and then call two functions and display the results accordingly. The first function is called **IsTriangle()** that is passed the three sides and returns a **bool**: either **true** if they make a triangle or **false** if they do not make a triangle. If the three sides do not make a triangle, display "Not a triangle" and get the next set of data.

If they form a triangle, then call a function **GetTriangleType()** that is passed the three sides and returns an enumerated value. You need to setup an enumerated type whose values are Scalene, Isosceles, Equilateral. Store the return value in an instance of this **enum**. Next, the main program switches on the stored return value (a Do Case) and displays an appropriate message based on the kind of triangle. For example, "This is an isosceles triangle."

Thoroughly test your program.

Problem Cs08-2—Tax Rate Processing

Acme Sales operates stores in a number of states. Each state has its own tax rate. When a set of sales data is input, the state abbreviation is stored in two character variables, **stateLetter1** and **stateLetter2.** Each line of input contains the order id number (a **long**), the two letters of the state code, and the total cost of the order before taxes are applied (a **double**). For example, an input line might be

123456 IL 42.00

The following table shows the states in which Acme is currently selling and the corresponding tax rates.

State	Two Letter Input Code	Tax Rate
Illinois	IL	7.5%
Iowa	IA	7%
Idaho	ID	6.5%
Indiana	IN	8%
Hawaii	HI	8%
Georgia	GA	6.5%

The program should input the file, **Sales.txt**, that is provided in the test data accompanying the book, and produce a sales report that looks like this.

```
   Acme Sales Report

Order    State  Total
Number   Code   Sales
12345     IL    42.33
```

The program must use a Do Case to sort out the state code abbreviations. Use a **switch** on the first letter. If the letter is an I, then **switch** on the second letter to sort out those that begin with the letter I. Realistically, Acme may end up selling in all fifty states and the switching logic would then be expanded to include all fifty states. Make sure your solution would be easily expandable to include additional states.

Note that the input may contain lowercase letters and may contain invalid state codes. If the code is not valid (perhaps a new state not yet in the program tables), display an error message to **cerr** including the order number and the offending state code letters and go on to get the next input line.

Problem Cs08-3—Fun with Phone Numbers

A telephone number can utilize letters. The conversion is
ABC = 2, DEF = 3, GHI = 4, JKL = 5, MNO = 6, PRS = 7, TUV = 8, WXY = 9

Write a function called **digitToLetter()** that is passed an ASCII digit, '0' through '9' and returns the character letter that corresponds to the number. If there is no corresponding letter, return the ASCII digit instead. Use a Do Case to sort out the possibilities.

Write a function called **letterToDigit()** that is passed a letter and returns the ASCII digit that corresponds to that letter. If there is no corresponding digit for a letter, such as Q, then return a '*' character. Use a Do Case to sort out the possibilities.

Now write a **main()** function that inputs a phone number in ASCII format. The number might be entered as 228-7387 or as CAT-PETS. On a new line, echo print the original number and then display " = " and then display the reverse of each digit or character of the number. For example, if the CAT-PETS was entered, you program should display
CAT-PETS = 228-7387
Or if 555-4242 were entered
555-4242 = JJJ-GAGA
Repeat until the end of the file is reached. Thoroughly test the program.

Problem Cs08-4—Areas of Shapes

The areas of some shapes are given below.
Triangle: A = ½ base * height
Rectangle: A = height * width
Circle: A = PI * radius^2
Square: A = side^2

Define an **enum** called **Shapes** that has the following values: **Triangle**, **Rectangle**, **Square**, **Circle**. Then define five **doubles**: **base**, **height**, **width**, **radius**, and **side**. Next, input a shape, calculate and display its area. The first item on each line is a letter indicating, which shape the line represents. The character is T, R, C or S. The rest of the line contains the relevant information for that shape. If it is a triangle, then after the T character comes the **base** and **height**. If it is a rectangle, after the R character comes the **height** and **width**. If it is a circle, after the C character comes the **radius**. If it is a square, after the S comes the **side**.

The program should input the character and then based upon its value, input the remaining items and calculate the area accordingly. A **switch** statement can be used. Assume that all data lines contain correct data. To test the program, use the provided file, **shapes.txt**.

Problem Engr08-1—Integrate F(x) = sin (x) / x

Modify the **Trap()** and **Simp()** functions to perform integrations of

$$F(x) = \frac{\sin(x)}{x}$$

Specifically, use first 10 panels or trapezoids and then use 20 for both **Trap()** and **Simp()**. Display the results so that they can be easily compared. Format the output similar to this

```
Integration Results of F(x)  = sin (x) / x

From xxxx to yyyy

method         10 panels       20 panels
Trap           nnnnnnnnn       nnnnnnnnn
Simp           nnnnnnnnn       nnnnnnnnn
```

Test the program with a = 1 and b = 6.5.

Then, test the program with a = –3 and b = 3. Caution: you must modify the **F(x)** function; the second test will crash at **x = 0**. However, the function **F (x = 0)** does have a value in this particular case. Use that special value at point x = 0.

Problem Engr08-2—Find the Integrals of Functions

Write a program(s) to integrate the following equations:

$$\int_0^1 xe^{-x}\,dx \qquad \int_0^{\frac{PI}{2}} x\sin(x)dx \qquad \int_0^{PI} (4 + 2\sin(x))dx$$

Use the **Trap()** function with a desired accuracy of .00001.

Problem Engr08-3—Determine the RMS Current (Electrical Engineering)

Alternating currents or oscillating currents produce a positive current flow and then a negative flow. Over the course of one period, which may appear as a sine wave if monitored on an oscilloscope, the average current flow may be zero since the positive values cancel the negative ones out. Despite the fact that the average flow is zero does not mean that no work can be done by that current. It does create heat and can do work. However, when working with such circuits, one utilizes not the average current but the root mean square current flow.

The RMS current flow is given by the following equation.

$$I_{RMS} = \sqrt{\frac{\int_0^T i^2(t)dt}{T}}$$

where T is the period.

By using the square of the current **i**, the problem of positive and negative values canceling each other out is eliminated. However, an integration is always involved when calculating I_{RMS}. For this problem, the i(t) function is given as

$$i(t) = 10e^{\frac{-t}{T}}\left(\sin\left(\frac{2\pi t}{T}\right)\right)$$

for 0 <= t <= T/2 and I(t) = 0 for T/2 <= t <=T.

Thus, we need to integrate from a=0 through b=T/2. Assume that the period is to be one second, so the T = 1 sec for this analysis. Write a program to calculate the I_{RMS} in this case. To assist you in debugging, the resultant integral of

$$I = \int_0^{.5} (10e^{-t}\sin(2\pi t))^2\,dt$$

equals 15.41261. Use a desired accuracy of .00001.

Problem Engr08-4—Find the Cross-sectional Area of a River (Water Resource Engineering)

To predict flooding effects of a river, a water resource engineer measures the cross-sectional area of a riverbed. Using a boat, they have measured the depth of the river at uniform intervals across its width. These depths have been tabulated below. All measurements are in meters. Write a program to compute the cross-sectional area of the river from these data. Use the **Trap()** function with the required number of trapezoids to match the data.

```
distance        depth
from            of
left bank       river
 0               0
 2               2
 4               3
 6               6
 8              10
10              12
12              10
14               8
16               6
18               4
20               0
```

Problem Engr08-5—Menu for Volume of Shapes

Write a program that displays the following menu, gets the user's choice, and performs the indicated calculation. Note additional prompts are needed to input the dimensions shown in parentheses.

```
Volume of Shapes Calculator

A. Find the volume of a cube (side)
B. Find the volume of a rectangular block (height, width, length)
C. Find the volume of a sphere (radius)
D. Quit the program

Enter a letter choice:
```

Chapter 9—Arrays

Section A: Basic Theory

Definitions and Need for Arrays

An **array** is a consecutive series of data objects of the same data type. It represents a collection of similar objects. For example, your local post office has an array of postal boxes, each identical in size and shape (usually). Each object in the array is known as an array **element**. An element is accessed by providing its **subscript** or **index**, which is a numerical value beginning with the value zero. Similarly, at the post office, to access the contents of a specific postal box, one must know its box number. All box numbers must be unique; there cannot be two boxes with the same number at a given post office. Subscripts follow a similar pattern; they must be unique, and they always begin with value zero. This is sometimes called zero-based offsets.

Why are arrays needed? Consider this problem. The Weather Service monitors the temperatures at a particular location at six-minute intervals, yielding ten temperature measurements every hour. They have collected a 24-hour period worth of observations, or a total of 240 values. Now suppose they wish the report to display the average, the highest and the lowest temperatures on the first line of the report followed by all of the actual temperatures measured. The program needs to input and store all 240 observations so that the results can be calculated and displayed first before it displays all of the data. If the result's line could be displayed last instead of first, then we could have just one input field, and write a simple loop to input a temperature, perform the needed calculations and comparisons and then display that value on the report. Clearly, one would not want to define 240 separate variables, write 240 separate input operations. Imagine what the calculations coding would be like! Instead, here is an ideal application for an array. We simply define one array of **doubles** to hold the temperatures; input all of the temperatures into the array; then do our calculations and make the report, using and reusing the values stored in the array.

Defining Arrays

To define an array, follow the variable name with [maximum number of elements].

```
double temps[240];
```

This defines **temps** to be an array of 240 **doubles**. Similarly, consider these array definitions

```
long  total[10];
char  tally[50];
short count[100];
```

Here, **total** is an array of 10 **longs**; **tally** is an array of 50 characters; **count** is an array of 100 **shorts**.

However, good programming practice dictates that the numerical values should be replaced by a more maintainable method. The array bounds should be either a **#define** symbol or a **const int** variable. For example,

```
#include <iostream>
using namespace std;

const int MAXTEMPS = 240; // maximum number of temperatures

int main () {
     double temps[MAXTEMPS];
```

Why use the constant integer **MAXTEMPS** instead of hard coding 240? From a program maintenance point of view, array bounds often change. Suppose that the weather service went to 5-minute intervals instead of the 6-minute ones. Now there are 12 observations per hour or a total of 288. With the constant integer approach shown above, all that would need to be done is change the initial value from 240 to 288 and rebuild the program. If one had hard coded the 240, then a thorough search of the entire program for all numerical values of 240 would have to be made; such action is tedious and error prone.

Accessing Array Elements

An array is accessed by an integer type subscript that can be a constant, variable or an expression. The subscript is also enclosed inside of [] brackets. The following are valid array references

```
temps[0]   temps[i]   temps[j + 1]
```

where **i** and **j** are both integer types. Subscripts are like post office box numbers, specifying which element to access.

The following are valid.

```
temps[i] = 42;     // stores 42 in the ith element
temps[i]++;        // adds 1 to the ith element of temps
cin >> temps[i];   // input the ith element of temps
cout << temps[i];  // output the ith element of temps
```

The following are invalid.

```
cin >> temps;
cout << temps;
```

An array cannot be input as a group in a single input statement. All assignment and math operations must be done on an individual element basis. So these are invalid as well.

```
temps += count;
temps++;
```

One array cannot be assigned to another array; instead, a loop must be written to copy each element.

```
double save_temps[MAXTEMPS];
save_temps = temps; // illegal - use a loop instead
```

Rather, if a copy of the array is needed, then the following loop accomplishes it.

```
for (i=0; i<MAXTEMPS; i++) {
     save_temps[i] = temps[i];
}
```

When using subscripts, it is vital that the subscript be within the range defined by the array. In the case of the 240 temperatures, valid subscripts are in the range from 0 to 239. Note a common cause of errors is to attempt to access **temps[240]**, which does not exist as it would be the 241st element. This attempt to access an element that is beyond the bounds of the array is called **subscript out of bounds**.

What exactly happens when one uses a subscript that is out of bounds? To see the effect, let's examine how memory is laid out for an array. Suppose our company had five departments and we wished to store the total income for each department. We might have the following.

```
const int MAX_DEPTS = 5;
int main () {
     long totals[MAX_DEPTS];
```

The array **totals** consists of 5 **long** integers in a row. Assume that each long occupies 4 bytes of memory and that the array begins at memory address 100.

```
Memory
Address
100       104       108      112       116      120
---------------------------------------------------------------
|         |         |         |         |         |         |     |
|         |         |         |         |         |         |     |
---------------------------------------------------------------
   [0]       [1]        [2]       [3]       [4]     x
```

The array ends at "x" marks the spot. Memory beginning at address 120 is beyond the end of the array. What is there? It could be the memory of some other variable in the program; it may not even be a part of your program.

Now if the subscript out of bounds is in retrieval mode, such as

```
grandtotal += totals[5];
```

Then the computer attempts to access what it thinks is element 6 at memory address 120 and retrieves the four bytes there, assumes that it is a **long**, and adds it into **grandtotal**. Even though it is effectively a garbage value, any combination of bits turned on within the byte corresponds to an integer value of some kind. So if the memory exists, something, usually quite bizarre, is added into **grandtotal**. However, if **totals** were an array of **doubles**, then not every possible combination of bits within an 8-byte memory area corresponds to a valid floating point number. In such cases, a runtime error can result with a message of floating point overflow or underflow.

On the other hand, if the subscript out of bounds is in a storage mode, such as

```
total[5] = 42;
```

then things become more unpredictable. If the memory is occupied by another program variable, then that variable is overlaid. On Windows 95/98 systems, if that memory is actually part of some Windows system code (part of a runtime dll, for example), then the code is overlaid. Further, if that

Windows code is ever actually subsequently executed, wildly unpredictable things can occur, from a simple page fault exception, to a system lock up and reboot, to a resetting of the computer's CMOS settings, to a reformatting of hard drives, and so on. Under Windows NT, any attempt to overlay system code is automatically handled by terminating the offending program with a system exception.

Thus, when using arrays, the programmer must always be certain that subscripts are within the bounds of the array.

Methods of Inputting Data into an Array

Okay, so with that in mind, how can these 240 temperatures be input into the array **temps**? Consider the following methods.

Method A: Inputting a Known Number of Elements

```
ifstream infile;
infile.open ("myfile.txt");
if (!infile) {
     cerr << "Cannot open myfile.txt\n";
     return 1;
}
int i;
for (i=0; i<MAXTEMPS && infile; i++) {
     infile >> temps[i];
}
if (!infile) {
     cerr << " Error: Could not input " << MAXTEMPS
          << " temperatures\n";
     infile.close ();
     return 1;
}
infile.close ();
```

This method can be used only when there are precisely **MAXTEMPS**, 240, long values in the file. Memory cannot be overwritten because of the **for** loop's test condition. To guard against bad data, the loop's test condition also checks on **infile**'s goodness.

Unfortunately, there are not many circumstances in which the precise number of data values to be input is known at compile time or when the program is written. An alternative that is often used is to make the first line of the input file contain the number of items in the array that follows in the file.

Method B: Inputting the Number of Array Elements To Be Input

Here, the number of temperatures in the file is inputted first. If that number exceeds the maximum size of the array, then an error message is printed. One could abort the program or test it using the maximum number of temperatures the array can hold. What is very important in this example is the use of the variable **numTemps** that is to hold the actual number of temperatures in the array on THIS run of the program.

```
ifstream infile;
infile.open ("myfile.txt");
if (!infile) {
     cerr << "Cannot open myfile.txt\n";
     return 1;
}
int i;
int numTemps;
infile >> numTemps;
if (numTemps > MAXTEMPS) {
     cerr << "Error: too many temperatures\n"
          << "  using the first " << MAXTEMPS << endl;
     numTemps = MAXTEMPS;
}
for (i=0; i<numTemps && infile; i++) {
     infile >> temps[i];
}
if (!infile) {
     cerr << " Error: Could not input " << numTemps
          << " temperatures\n";
     infile.close ();
     return 1;
}
infile.close ();
```

The drawback of this approach is that it can place a terrible burden on the user to count accurately the number of temperatures to be input. While this is fine when the numbers are small, I would not want to count to 240! Instead, the most common approach is to have the program input all values until it reaches the end of the file.

Method C: Inputting an Unknown Number of Elements Until EOF Is Reached

```
ifstream infile;
infile.open ("myfile.txt");
if (!infile) {
     cerr << "Cannot open myfile.txt\n";
     return 1;
```

```
}
int i = 0;
int numTemps;
while (i<MAXTEMPS && infile >> temps[i]) {
      i++;
}
// guard against too many temperatures in the file
if (i == MAXTEMPS && infile >> ws && infile.good()) {
      cerr << "Error: too many temperatures\n";
      infile.close ();
      return 2;
}
// guard against bad data in the input file
else if (!infile.eof() && infile.fail()) {
      cerr << "Error: bad data in the file\n";
      infile.close ();
      return 3;
}
// set the number of temps in the array on this run
numTemps = i;
infile.close ();
```

In the **while** loop, notice that the first test condition guarantees that the subscript must be within the bounds of the array. Recall the effect of the **&&** operator—the second half of the test condition is never executed when **i** becomes equal or exceeds **MAXTEMPS**. The second half of the test condition inputs a single temperature and returns a good state if successful. The loop ends when the end of file is reached or bad data occurs or the array bound is exceeded.

Note the **infile >> ws && infile.good()** action. The **ws** is another manipulator function that skips over white space. It provides us a convenient way to find out if there are more data still in the input stream. If it can successfully skip over white space, then there are more data to be input and the stream is in the good state. If it is not successful, then it is most likely the end of file. Remember that the current position in an input stream is located right after the last character that was input. Often the current position in the input stream is pointing to the <cr> at the end of the line that was just input or is pointing to the EOF code (the hidden ^Z byte). Consider the following two circumstances.

Assume that the program inputs pairs of **quantity** and **cost** values and has just finished this instruction.

```
infile >> quantity >> cost;
```

Assume the following is in the file being read. After inputting the first line, the current position in the input stream is pointing to the boldfaced <cr>.

```
123 42.50<cr>
345 99.99<cr>
^Z
```

Coding
```
infile >> ws;
```
successfully skips over white space and positions the current position to the 3 digit of the 345 quantity value on the next line. After inputting the second line, the current position is now pointing to the second line's <cr>. Now executing
```
infile >> ws;
```
is unsuccessful as the end of file is reached and **infile** goes into the EOF state.

Next, the two error circumstances are sorted out, bad data and too much data. If the count equals **MAXTEMPS** then two possibilities exist. The program may have just inputted the last value in the file and the current position in the input stream is on the <CRLF> before the EOF marker. Or there actually are some more data in the file. To sort out which is the case, attempt to skip over whitespace. If there are no more data, the stream goes into the non-good state and all is well. On the other hand, if there are more values in the input file, then the skip over whitespace succeeds and the stream is in the good state, triggering the error message. The bad data circumstance is easily checked by calling the **fail()** function.

An alternative method to detecting too much data in the file is to define a character, say **c**, and attempt to extract it. If it is successful, then there are more data in the file.
```
// guard against too many temperatures in the file
char c;
if (i == MAXTEMPS && infile >> c) {
     cerr << "Error: too many temperatures\n";
     infile.close ();
     return 2;
}
```

Again, it is vital to save the number of values actually inputted on this run. In this example, it is saved in the variable **numTemps**;

Working with Arrays—The Calculations

With the array loaded with either **MAXTEMPS** or **numTemps** worth of temperatures, a program often does one or more calculations using the array element values. Quite often,every element in the array must be used. In this example, the average temperature must be found. If the program adds each temperature to a **sum** and then divides that **sum** by the number of temperatures, the average can be found. In the following coding, it is assumed that **numTemps** holds the actual number of temperatures inputted in this execution of the program.

```
double sum = 0;
for (i=0; i< numTemps; i++) {
     sum += temps[i];
}
double average = sum / numTemps;
```

How are the highest and lowest temperatures found? Assuming that high and low variables are to contain the results, each element in the array, that is, each temperature, must be compared to these two values. If the next temperature is greater than or less than the corresponding high or low temperature, then that value replaces the current high or low value. This can be done as follows.

```
double high = temps[0];
double low = temps[0];
for (i=1; i<numTemps; i++) {
     if (temps[i] > high)
          high = temps[i];
     if (temps[i] < low)
          low = temps[i];
}
// here high and low have the largest and smallest
// temperatures in the array
```

Here is a common coding error that yields a mostly-working program. Can you spot the error?

```
double high = 0;
double low = 0;
for (i=0; i<numTemps; i++) {
     if (temps[i] > high)
          high = temps[i];
     if (temps[i] < low)
          low = temps[i];
}
```

If not, suppose the location is Florida in the summer. What will this code produce as the low temperature for the day? A temperature of 0 degrees would mark a catastrophe for the citrus crops! Now suppose that this location is Fairbanks, Alaska in the dead of winter. What will this code produce for highest temperature? Hint: 0 degrees would be considered a heat wave.

Working with arrays: the Output Process

Frequently all the elements of the array must be displayed. Writing another loop, outputting each element in turn does this.

```
cout << setprecision (1);
for (i=0; i<numTemps; i++) {
     cout << setw(12) << temps[i] << endl;
}
```

Initializing an Array

When an array is defined or declared, it may also be initialized if desired. Suppose that one needed to define an array of **totals** to hold the total sales from each of ten departments within a store. One could code

```
double totals[10];
```

However, in practice, the first usage of any element in the array is likely to be of the form

```
total[j] = total[j] + sales;
```

This requires that each element in the array be initialized to zero. The initialization syntax in general is

```
data type variable-name[limit] = {value0, value1,
                                  value2, … valuen};
```

Initialization of arrays begins with a begin brace { and ends with an end brace }. The syntax provides for giving each element its unique initial value. In the example of store **totals**, one could code

```
double totals[10] = {0, 0, 0, 0, 0, 0, 0, 0, 0, 0};
```

However, C++ provides a default value of 0 for all elements not specifically initialized. In reality, one would define totals this way

```
double totals[10] = {0};
```

This tells the compiler to place a 0 in the first element and then to place a default value (that happens to also be 0) in all remaining elements. Once you stop providing initial values, all remaining elements are defaulted to a 0 starting value. Values neither can be omitted nor can there be more values than array elements. The following coding is illegal, since once you stop providing values (after element zero in this case) you cannot later on resume providing explicit values.

```
double totals[10] = {0, , , 0};// error - cannot omit values
```

Passing Arrays to Functions

Very commonly, arrays are passed to functions so that the workload can be broken down into more manageable units. Often a program has a **loadArray()** function whose purpose is to encapsulate the entire array's input operation. The **main()** function is then left with just a single function call to **loadArray()**, thereby streamlining **main()**. What would **main()** need to give **loadArray()** and what should the function return? The **loadArray()** function must be given the array to fill up and the maximum number of elements in the array; it must return the actual number of elements inputted on this run. Thus, if we were to write a **loadArray()** function to load the array of temperatures, the only coding in **main()** would now be

```
int numTemps = loadArray (temps, MAXTEMPS);
```

This immediately raises the question how are arrays passed to functions. The answer lies in asking what is the data type of the name of an array? The data type of the name of an array is always a constant pointer or memory address to the first element. Thus, in the above temperature's example, the name **temps** is a **const double***. This reads backwards "is a pointer to a **double** that is constant." A pointer is just the memory address of something. In this context, when used without the **[i]** notation, **temps** is just a memory address where the 240 **doubles** begin. So when **main()** calls **loadArray()**, it is not passing a copy of the entire array of 240 **doubles**, but rather just the memory location at which the array begins. This is highly desirable; consider the overhead of actually trying to pass a copy of the entire array—that is, 240 **doubles** or 1920 bytes, assuming a **double** occupies 8 bytes. When coding the prototype for **loadArray()**, two different notations can be used.

```
int loadArray (double temps[], int limit);
int loadArray (double* temps, int limit);
```

In the first version, the **[]** tells the compiler that the preceding symbol **temps** is not just a **double** but is also an array of **doubles**, which therefore means that this parameter is really just the memory address where the array begins.

Notice one significant detail when setting up the prototype of a function that has an array as a parameter. The actual array bound is not used as it was when defining the array. Compare the two statements in **main()**:

```
// defines storage for the array
double temps[MAXTEMPS];
// prototype for the loadArray function
int loadArray (double temps[], int limit);
```

The first defines the array and allocates space for 240 doubles. The second line says that within **loadArray()**, the **temps** parameter is an array of **doubles**. The compiler never cares how many elements are in this passed array, only that it is an array of **doubles**. One could also have coded the prototype as

```
int loadArray (double temps[MAXTEMPS], int limit);
```

However, the compiler simply ignores the array bounds; only the **[]** is important, for the **[]** tells the compiler that the symbol is an array. As usual, the programmer must be vigilant in making sure that the array bound is not exceeded by passing in that maximum number of elements as the second parameter and using it to avoid inputting too many values.

Next, let's see how the **loadArray()** function could be implemented. The changes from the previous version are in boldface.

```
int loadArray (double temps[], int limit) {
     ifstream infile;
     infile.open ("myfile.txt");
     if (!infile) {
          cerr << "Cannot open myfile.txt\n";
          exit (1);
     }
     int i = 0;
     while (i<limit && infile >> temps[i]) {
          i++;
     }
     // guard against too many temperatures in the file
     if (i == limit && infile >> ws && infile.good()) {
          cerr << "Error: too many temperatures\n";
          infile.close ();
          exit (2);
     }
     // guard against bad data in the input file
     else if (!infile.eof() && infile.fail ()) {
          cerr << "Error: bad data in the file\n";
          infile.close ();
          exit (3);
     }
     // set the number of temps in the array on this run
     infile.close ();
     return i;
}
```

The first change to notice is the reference to the constant integer **MAXTEMPS** is replaced with the parameter **limit**, which should contain the value **MAXTEMPS** has in it. However, one could have just used the global constant integer **MAXTEMPS** and not even bothered passing it as the second parameter, **limit**. But doing so is not the optimum method. Very often in larger applications, many of the functions are actually stored in their own separate cpp files. If **loadArray()** were in its own file, **LoadArray.cpp**, then the compiler would not have access to the constant integer **MAXTEMPS**. By passing its value of 240 as the parameter **limit**, all dependencies upon the symbol **MAXTEMPS** defined in the **main.cpp** file have been removed. This makes a better design and a more flexible program.

The other change arises from the detection of error situations, such as, being unable to open the file, or having too much data. When the coding to load the array is found in the **main()** program, after displaying the error message, the instruction

```
return 1;
```

causes the program to return back to DOS and terminate. However, in **loadArray()**, any return statement causes the computer to return back into **main()** at the point where **main()** calls or invokes the **loadArray()** function and then copies the returned integer into the variable **numTemps**! Oops! This is not what is desired at all. A function can directly invoke program termination by calling the **exit()** function, which takes one parameter, the integer return code to give to DOS. The coding

```
exit (1);
```

immediately terminates the program without ever returning to the calling function and gives a return code of 1 to DOS.

The **main()** function could be streamlined even further by creating three more functions, **findAverage()**, **findRanges()** and **printResults()**. The prototypes for **findAverage()** and **printResults()** are straightforward.

```
double findAverage (double temps[], int num_temps);
void   printResults(double temps[], int num_temps,
                    double avg, double high, double low);
```

The **findRanges()** function cannot return two values, that is, the highest and lowest temperatures, so these two variables must be passed by reference.

```
void FindRanges (double temps[], int num_temps,
                  double& high, double& low);
```

With these changes, **main()** now becomes very streamlined.

```
int main () {
     double temps[MAXTEMPS];
     int numTemps;
     double average;
     double high;
     double low;

     numTemps = LoadArray (temps, MAXTEMPS);
     average = FindAverage (temps, numTemps);
     FindRanges (temps, numTemps, high, low);
     PrintResults (temps, numTemps, average, high, low);

     return 0;
}
```

Here is the complete program listing for **Basic09a**. Pay particular attention to how the array of temperatures is passed to the functions and how it is then used within the functions.

Basic09a - Produce Temperature Statistics

```
/***************************************************************/
/*                                                             */
/* Basic09a Produce temperature statistics from a set of temps */
/*                                                             */
/*  Inputs up to 240 temperatures and calculates the average,  */
/*  highest and lowest temperatures and then displays the      */
/*  temperatures as inputted                                   */
/*                                                             */
/***************************************************************/
```

```

#include <iostream>
#include <iomanip>
#include <fstream>
using namespace std;

const int MAXTEMPS = 240; // the maximum number of temperatures

int    LoadArray    (double temps[], int limit);
double FindAverage  (double temps[], int numTemps);
void   FindRanges   (double temps[], int numTemps,
                     double& high, double& low);
void   PrintResults (double temps[], int numTemps,
                     double avg, double high, double low);

int main () {
 double temps[MAXTEMPS]; // the array of temperatures
 int numTemps;           // the actual number inputted
 double average;         // the average of all temperatures
 double high;            // the highest temperature input
 double low;             // the lowest temperature input

 cout << fixed;          // setup floating point output format

 numTemps = LoadArray (temps, MAXTEMPS);  // load the array
 if (!numTemps) { // guard against no data
  cout << "No temperatures in the file\n";
  return 1;
 }
 average = FindAverage (temps, numTemps); // calc the average
 FindRanges (temps, numTemps, high, low); // find high and low
 PrintResults (temps, numTemps, average, high, low);

 return 0;
}

/***************************************************************/
/*                                                             */
/* LoadArray: load an array of temperatures                    */
/*                                                             */
/***************************************************************/

int LoadArray (double temps[], int limit) {
 // open the data file - abort the program if not found
 ifstream infile;
 infile.open ("temperatures.txt");
 if (!infile) {
  cerr << "Cannot open temperatures.txt\n";
  exit (1);
 }

 // input all the temperatures upto limit total
 int i = 0;
```

```
 while (i<limit && infile >> temps[i]) {
  i++;
 }

 // guard against too many temperatures in the file
 if (i == limit && infile >> ws && infile.good()) {
  cerr << "Error: too many temperatures\n";
  infile.close ();
  exit (2);
 }

 // guard against bad data in the input file
 else if (!infile.eof() && infile.fail()) {
  cerr << "Error: bad data in the file\n";
  infile.close ();
  exit (3);
 }
 infile.close ();

 // return the number of temperatures in the array on this run
 return i;
}

/****************************************************************/
/*                                                              */
/* FindAverage: determines the average temperature              */
/*                                                              */
/****************************************************************/

double FindAverage (double temps[], int numTemps) {
 double sum = 0;
 for (int i=0; i< numTemps; i++) {
  sum += temps[i];      // accumulate all temperatures
 }
 return sum / numTemps; // return the average temperature
}

/****************************************************************/
/*                                                              */
/* FindRanges: determines the highest and lowest temperatures   */
/*                                                              */
/****************************************************************/

void FindRanges (double temps[], int numTemps,
                 double& high, double& low) {
 high = temps[0]; // initialize high to the first temperature
 low  = temps[0]; // initialize low to the first temperature

 // now check all other temperatures against these
 for (int i=1; i<numTemps; i++) {
  if (temps[i] > high)
   high = temps[i];   // replace high with the larger temperature
  if (temps[i] < low)
```

```
    low = temps[i];    // replace low with the lower temperature
  }
  // high & low now have the largest & smallest temps in the array
}

/***************************************************************/
/*                                                             */
/* PrintResults: prints the complete report                    */
/*                                                             */
/***************************************************************/

void PrintResults (double temps[], int numTemps,
                    double avg, double high, double low) {
 cout << setprecision (1);

 // display heading of report
 cout << "Temperature Analysis\n\n";

 // display the statistical results lines
 cout << "Average: " << setw (6) << avg  << endl
      << "Highest: " << setw (6) << high << endl
      << "Lowest:  " << setw (6) << low  << endl << endl;

 // display column heading
 cout << "Observations\n";

 // display all temperatures as entered
 for (int i=0; i<numTemps; i++) {
  cout << setw(7) << temps[i] << endl;
 }
}
```

Here is a sample test run showing the output of the program.

Basic09a - Sample Test Run

```
Temperature Analysis

Average:   95.0
Highest:  100.0
Lowest:    90.0

Observations
   91.0
   92.0
   93.0
   94.0
   95.0
   96.0
   97.0
   98.0
```

```
   99.0
  100.0
   99.0
   98.0
   97.0
   96.0
   95.0
   94.0
   93.0
   92.0
   91.0
   90.0
```

Section B: Computer Science Examples

Cs09a—Sales Data Analysis

Acme Sales wishes a statistical analysis of their monthly sales data. The input file contains the sales person's id number and their sales for that transaction. The sales person ids range from 1 to 10 inclusively. Each person is paid a commission based on the total of those sales as follows:

if the sales are less than 100.00, commission is 5%
if the sales are 100.00 or above but less than 500.00, commission is 6%
if the sales are 500.00 or above, the commission is 7%

Accumulate the sales for each sales person and their commission. When all sales data have been input, produce the sales analysis report, which lists the results for each person on one line. Print that sales person's id number, their total sales, their average sales, their total commission, their average commission, and their percentage their average commission from the company average commission. At the end of the report, show the grand totals for each of the four dollar amounts. Note that any given sales person might not have sold anything in this particular month.

Since this report is rather complex, here is the output from the sample run.

Cs09a Sales Data Analysis - Sample Report

```
                  Acme Monthly Sales Analysis Report

 ID  Number    Total     Average     Total     Average    Percentage
      Sales    Sales      Sales   Commission Commission of Avg Comm


  1     4    1300.00    325.00      88.00      22.00      -46.43
  2     6    2600.00    433.33     173.00      28.83      -29.79
  3     6    3200.00    533.33     217.00      36.17      -11.93
  4     5    3200.00    640.00     220.00      44.00        7.15
  5     6    4400.00    733.33     308.00      51.33       25.00
```

```

   6     5     3800.00     760.00     266.00      53.20     29.55
   7     6     3300.00     550.00     228.00      38.00     -7.46
   8     0        0.00       0.00       0.00       0.00      0.00
   9     4     2100.00     525.00     143.00      35.75    -12.94
  10     4     3600.00     900.00     246.00      61.50     49.76
       -----   -------    -------    -------    -------
          46  27500.00     597.83    1889.00      41.07
```

Let's examine some of the needed processing details before making the Top-Down Design. It's clear that the input operation must bring in each set of sales data, add the sales to the corresponding salesperson's total, and increment that sales person's number of sales. At that time, we can easily calculate the commission on that sale and add it into that sales person's total commission. Effectively, we are just accumulating the basic data, hence an **Accumulate()** function.

The calculations pose a more interesting situation. Once all the data have been accumulated, we can traverse each sales person in the array and determine their two averages, average sales and average commission. However, to obtain the percentage of average commission, the grand totals must first be determined so that the company average commission, here $41.07 can be found. Once that is known, we can go back through each sales person and calculate their percentage. So a **DoCalcs()** function is definitely in order. With the values known, it is a simple matter to print the contents of all the arrays and grand total fields in a **PrintReport()** function. This yields our Top-Down Design shown in Figure 9.1.

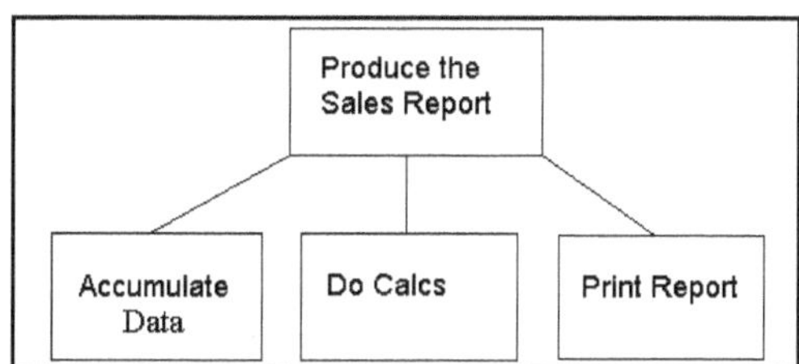

Figure 9.1 Top-Down Design

Examine first the coding for the **main()** function given below in the **Cs10a** listing. The **main()** function defines all of the arrays and totals, initializing all to 0. Notice that the array bounds is set to 11. The element at subscript 0 is being ignored in this example. A variation might be to instead use the subscript 0 elements in the arrays to contain the grand totals, thereby reducing the number of variables that need to be passed to the functions. **main()** then simply calls in turn **Accumulate()**, **DoCalcs()** and **PrintReport()**, very streamlined indeed.

What will main storage look like for function **main()**? How do we draw effective graphical representations for an array? Remember, one of the purposes of drawing the memory layouts is to have a convenient way to desk check the solution. If an array were defined to contain 100 elements, then theoretically, one would have to draw 100 adjacent and connected boxes to represent that array. However, such is not really needed. I usually just include several representing the first few and the last one. The **main()** function needs a const int for the array bounds, say **MAXID**. It needs six arrays for the accumulated results for each salesperson. Let's call these: **totalSales**, **totalComm**, **numSales**, **avgSales**, **avgComm** and **percent**. Additionally, there are five grand total fields called **grandNum**, **grandSales**, **grandComm**, **grandAvgSales** and **grandAvgComm**—all of which must be initialized to 0. Main storage for the **main()** function appears in Figure 9.2.

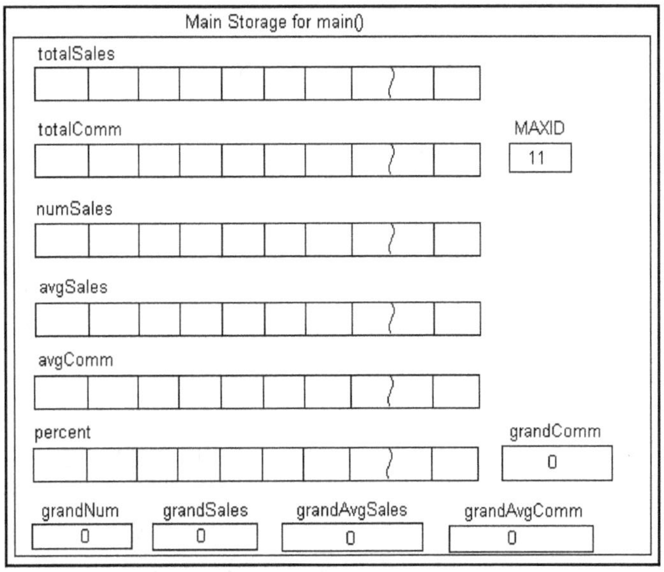

Main Storage for main()

totalSales

totalComm

MAXID 11

numSales

avgSales

avgComm

percent

grandComm 0

grandNum 0

grandSales 0

grandAvgSales 0

grandAvgComm 0

Figure 9.2 Main Storage for Function **main()**

In **Accumulate()**, the input fields, **id** and **sales**, will hold the data actually input from the input file. Then, if the id number is invalid, an error message is written to the **cerr** stream and is visible onscreen, not in the report. Realistically, the error message should also appear in the report. Once validated, the sales person's id is used as the subscript into the arrays. Note that no checking is done for the possibility of bad data being entered. In reality, one should check **infile.fail()** and report on that circumstance when the loop has finished. If the id number is within range, then accumulate the totals and calculate the commission and accumulate it as well.

The **Accumulate()** function's parameters are the three arrays—**totalsales**, **totalcomm**, and **numsales**—and a copy of the **const int MAXID** here called **limit** is as follows. Notice how I have laid out main storage for the array parameters in Figure 9.3. Notice how I set up the arrays in **main()** and in **Accumulate()**.

Remember when an array is passed, only the memory location of that array is actually passed, so **Accumulate()**'s **numsales** is really pointing to **main()**'s **numSales** as shown. Here is the coding sequence for **Accumulate()**.

open **infile**
if it fails to open, display an error message on **cerr** and exit the program
while (**infile** >> **id** >> **sales**) do the following
  if (**id** < 0 || **id** > **limit**) then display an error message to **cerr** and skip this set
  otherwise do these steps

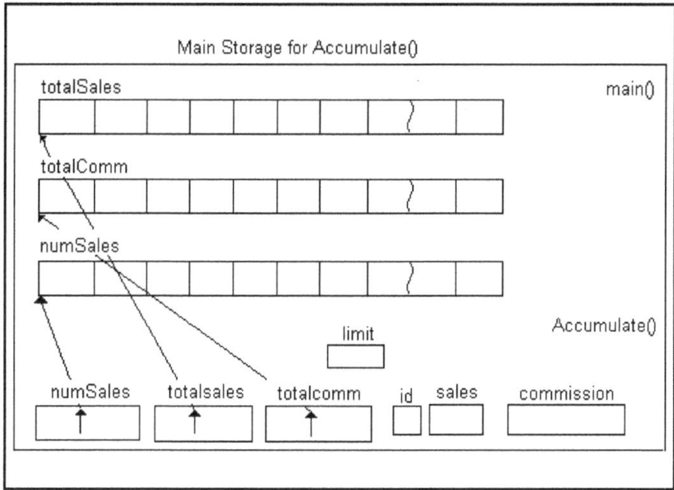

Figure 9.3 Main Storage for **Accumulate()**

numsales[id] = **numsales[id]** + 1
totalsales[id] = **totalsales[id]** + **sales**
if (**sales** < 100.00) then **commission** = .05 * **sales**
else if (**sales** < 500.00) then **commission** = .06 * **sales**
else commission = .07 * **sales**
totalcomm[id] = **totalcomm[id]** + **commission**;
end otherwise clause
end **while**
close **infile**

The other functions can similarly be sketched out. The function **DoCalcs()** is passed arrays: **totalSales**, **totalComm**, **numSales**, **avgSales**, **avgComm**, and **percent**. It is passed the **limit**, and a reference to the grand totals: **grandNum**, **grandSales**, **grandComm**, **grandAvgSales**, and **grandAvgComm**. The sequence of steps are as follows.

for i=1 and continuing until **i<limit** each time through the loop increment **i**
if (**numSales**[i] != 0) then
avgSales[i] = **totalSales**[i] / **numSales**[i];
avgComm[i] = **totalComm**[i] / **numSales**[i];
end the if
add **numSales**[i] to **grandNum**
add **totalSales**[i] to **grandSales**
add **totalComm**[i] to **grandComm**
end the for loop
// find the grand averages
grandAvgSales = **grandSales** / **grandNum**;
grandAvgComm = **grandComm** / **grandNum**;
// use the grand averages to calculate each sales person's percentage

for (i=1; i<limit; i++) do the following
  if (**numSales**[i] != 0)
      percent[i] = (**avgComm**[i] – **grandAvgComm**) * 100 / **grandAvgComm**;
end the for loop

The function **PrintReport()** is straightforward with one exception. We are to leave a blank line every 5 detail lines. This is easily done by
    if ((i-1) % 5 == 0) // insert blank line every five lines

This implementation of **Cs09a** shown below is an example of a "mostly working" program. Specifically, one possible situation was NOT checked. If that condition should occur, then the program would crash with a divide by zero fatal error at run time. Can you spot what that situation is? Clue: the run time error would occur at line 114. Okay. If the input file contains no valid data (is empty or otherwise goofed up with all wrong data), the **Accumulate()** function does not check for this possibility. Neither does the **main()** function, which then calls **DoCalcs()**. Since all arrays and variables are initialized to zero, the disaster does not occur until line 114. Here, **grandNum** still contains 0 and is used as the divisor. How can the program be bulletproofed against such occurrences? There are several ways. See if you can find one or more ways to fix **Cs09a**.

Cs09a Produce the monthly sales analysis report

```
  1 /***************************************************************/
  2 /*                                                             */
  3 /* Cs09a Produce the monthly sales analysis report             */
  4 /*                                                             */
  5 /***************************************************************/
  6
  7 #include <iostream>
  8 #include <iomanip>
  9 #include <fstream>
 10 using namespace std;
 11
 12 const int MAXID = 11; // the maximum number sales persons
 13                       // their id's range from 1 to 10
 14                       // ignore element [0]
 15
 16 void Accumulate   (double totalSales[], double totalComm[],
 17                    int    numSales[],   int limit);
 18 void DoCalcs (double totalSales[], double totalComm[],
 19              int numSales[], double avgSales[], double avgComm[],
 20              int limit, double percent[], int& grandNum,
 21              double& grandSales, double& grandComm,
 22              double& grandAvgSales,
 23              double& grandAvgComm);
 24 void PrintReport (double totalSales[], double totalComm[],
 25               int numSales[], double avgSales[],double avgComm[],
 26               int limit, double percent[], int grandNum,
 27               double grandSales, double grandComm,
```

```
               double grandAvgSales, double grandAvgComm);

int main () {
 double totalSales[MAXID] = {0}; // total sales of each person
 double totalComm[MAXID] = {0};  // total commission each person
 int    numSales[MAXID] = {0};   // number of sales each person
 double avgSales[MAXID] = {0};   // average sales of each person
 double avgComm[MAXID] = {0};    // average commission per sale
 double percent[MAXID] = {0};    // percent of avg commission
 int    grandNum = 0;            // grand number of sales
 double grandSales = 0;          // grand total sales of everyone
 double grandComm = 0;           // grand commission paid
 double grandAvgSales = 0;       // average amount of each sale
 double grandAvgComm = 0;        // average comm paid per sale

 Accumulate (totalSales, totalComm, numSales, MAXID);
 DoCalcs (totalSales, totalComm, numSales, avgSales, avgComm,
          MAXID, percent, grandNum, grandSales, grandComm,
          grandAvgSales, grandAvgComm);
 PrintReport (totalSales, totalComm, numSales, avgSales, avgComm,
              MAXID, percent, grandNum, grandSales, grandComm,
              grandAvgSales, grandAvgComm);
 return 0;
}

/***************************************************************/
/*                                                             */
/* Accumulate: input the data, accumulating all data           */
/*                                                             */
/***************************************************************/

void Accumulate  (double totalsales[], double totalcomm[],
                  int    numsales[],   int limit) {
 // open the data file - abort the program if not found
 ifstream infile;
 infile.open ("SalesData.txt");
 if (!infile) {
  cerr << "Cannot open salesdata.txt\n";
  exit (1);
 }

 int id;
 double sales;
 int lineNumber = 1;
 while (infile >> id >> sales) {
  if (id < 1 || id >= limit) {
   cerr << "Error: invalid sales person number. It was " << id
        << " on line " << lineNumber
        << "\nAction taken - skipping this person\n";
  }
  else {
   numsales[id]++;          // increment their number of sales
   totalsales[id] += sales; // accumulate their sales
```

```
    double commission;        // calculate the comm on this sales
    if (sales < 100.00)
     commission = .05 * sales;
    else if (sales < 500.00)
     commission = .06 * sales;
    else
     commission = .07 * sales;
    totalcomm[id] += commission; // accumulate commission
   }
   lineNumber++;
  }
  if (!infile.eof()) {
   cerr << "Error - bad data in the input file on line "
        << lineNumber << endl;
   infile.close ();
   exit (1);
  }
  infile.close ();
 }

/***************************************************************/
/*                                                             */
/* DoCalcs: find the averages, grand totals and percentage     */
/*                                                             */
/***************************************************************/

void DoCalcs (double totalSales[], double totalComm[],
              int numSales[], double avgSales[], double avgComm[],
              int limit, double percent[], int& grandNum,
              double& grandSales, double& grandComm,
              double& grandAvgSales, double& grandAvgComm) {
 int i;
 // calculate all sales person's average sales and commission
 for (i=1; i<limit; i++) {
  if (numSales[i] != 0) {
   avgSales[i] = totalSales[i]/numSales[i];
   avgComm[i] = totalComm[i]/numSales[i];
  }
  grandNum += numSales[i];      // accumulate the grand totals
  grandSales += totalSales[i];
  grandComm += totalComm[i];
 }
 // find the grand averages
 grandAvgSales = grandSales / grandNum;
 grandAvgComm = grandComm / grandNum;
 // use the grand averages to calculate sales person's percentage
 for (i=1; i<limit; i++) {
  if (numSales[i] != 0) {
   percent[i] = (avgComm[i] - grandAvgComm) * 100 / grandAvgComm;
  }
 }
}
```

```
/***************************************************************/
/*                                                             */
/* PrintReport: prints the complete report                     */
/*                                                             */
/***************************************************************/

void PrintReport (double totalSales[], double totalComm[],
                  int numSales[], double avgSales[], double avgComm[],
                  int limit, double percent[], int grandNum,
                  double grandSales, double grandComm,
                  double grandAvgSales, double grandAvgComm) {
 ofstream outfile ("SalesReport.txt");
 // setup floating point output format
 outfile << fixed << setprecision (2);

 // display heading of report and column headings
 outfile <<
        "                   Acme Monthly Sales Analysis Report\n\n";
 outfile << " ID  Number   Total    Average    Total    Average"
           "   Percentage\n"
        << "      Sales    Sales     Sales  Commission Commission"
           " of Avg Comm\n\n";
 // print each sales person's results
 for (int i=1; i<limit; i++) {
  if ((i-1) % 5 == 0) // insert blank line every five lines
   outfile << endl;
  outfile << setw(3) << i << setw(5) << numSales[i]
          << setw(11) << totalSales[i] << setw(10) << avgSales[i]
          << setw(10) << totalComm[i]  << setw(10) << avgComm[i]
          << setw(10) << percent[i]    << endl;
 }
 outfile <<"     -----  -------   -------   -------   -------\n";
 outfile << "   " << setw (5) << grandNum
          << setw (11) << grandSales
          << setw (10) << grandAvgSales
          << setw (10) << grandComm
          << setw (10) << grandAvgComm << endl;
 outfile.close();
}
```

Section C: Engineering Examples

Engr09a —Vector Coordinate Conversions

A vector has both a magnitude and a direction. Unlike a scalar, a quantity that can be represented by a single number, a vector requires two numbers. Vectors can be defined by either their magnitude and direction (in polar coordinates) or the projection of the vector along the axis of a rectangular coordinate system. The two representations are equivalent. Frequently, one needs to convert a vector from one coordinate system to another. These quantities are conveniently stored in an array. For a two-dimensional vector, the conversions are represented by the following equations derived from Figure 9.4.

$\mathbf{V} = V_x \mathbf{i} + V_y \mathbf{j}$ where **i** and **j** are the unit vectors in the x and y directions
$V_x = V \cos theta$
$V_y = V \sin theta$

$$V = \sqrt{V_x^2 + V_y^2}$$

theta $= \text{atan}(V_y / V_x)$

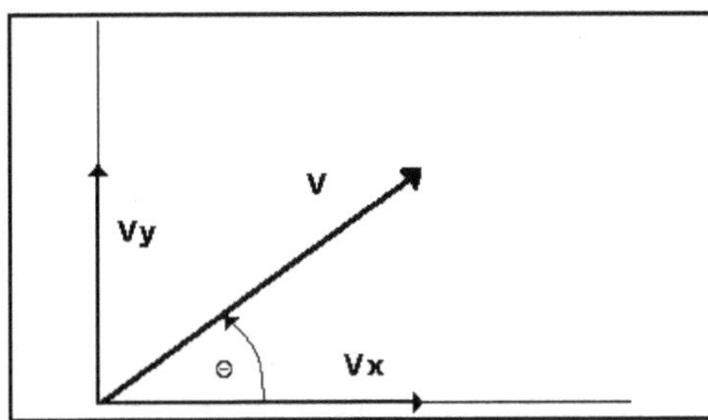

Figure 9.4 Vector

The two conversion functions are passed the rectangular coordinate's array and the polar coordinate's array. Element 0 represents V_x in rectangular coordinates or V in polar. Similarly, element 1 represents the V_y or the angle.

Another use of arrays is to lower the total number of parameters, by collecting similar, related items into one array. Here, we can consider the **rect** array to be a vector containing the x and y axis components. Likewise, the array **polar** can be though of containing the vector in polar coordinates.

Examine the **PolarConvert()** function first, which is passed the arrays **rect** and **polar**. The magnitude is calculated; the angle is found and then converted into degrees.

```
polar[0] = sqrt (rect[0] * rect[0] + rect[1] * rect[1]);
radians = atan (rect[1] / rect[0]);
polar[1] = ToDegrees (radians);
```

The function **RectConvert()** passed **polar** and **rect** arrays first converts the **angle** into

radians and then calculates the V_x and V_y quantities as follows.

radians = **ToRadians** (**polar**[1]);
rect[0] = **polar**[0] * cos (**radians**);
rect[1] = **polar**[0] * sin (**radians**);

Notice that constant subscripts, 0 and 1, are used to access the specific elements.

Again in the radian conversion helper functions, the value of PI is found by **acos(-1.)**, which gives the most nearly accurate value of PI as a **double**.

Listing **Engr09a** shows the complete program including a small test main program. A test run is also shown below.

Listing for Program Engr09a - Vector Conversions

```
/***************************************************************/
/*                                                             */
/*  Engr09a  Vector Conversions                                */
/*                                                             */
/*  Convert a vector from rectangular coords to polar coords   */
/*  Convert a vector from polar coords to rectangular coords   */
/*                                                             */
/***************************************************************/

#include <iostream>
#include <iomanip>
#include <cmath>
using namespace std;
void PolarConvert (double rect[], double polar[]);
void RectConvert (double polar[], double rect[]);

double ToRadians (double angle);
double ToDegrees (double radians);

int main () {

 double rect[2];
 double polar[2];
 double rect2[2];

 // setup floating point output format
 cout << fixed << setprecision (3);

 // input a vector in rectangular coordinates
 cout << "Enter the Vector in rectangular coordinates\n"
   << "X axis value first, then Y axis - separated by a blank\n";
 cin >> rect[0] >> rect[1];

 // convert vector to polar and then use polar to convert back
 PolarConvert (rect, polar);
 RectConvert (polar, rect2);
```

```

 // display results
 cout << "Original rect   " << setw (8) << rect[0]  << " "
      << setw (8) << rect[1] << endl;
 cout << "Polar           " << setw (8) << polar[0] << " "
      << setw (8) << polar[1] << endl;
 cout << "Rect from polar " << setw (8) << rect2[0] << " "
      << setw (8) << rect2[1] << endl;
 return 0;
}

/***************************************************************/
/*                                                             */
/* PolarConvert: convert vector in rectangular coords to polar */
/*                                                             */
/*  polar[0] = V    polar[1] = angle                           */
/*  rect[0]  = Vx   rect[1]  = Vy                              */
/*                                                             */
/***************************************************************/

void PolarConvert (double rect[], double polar[]) {
 polar[0] = sqrt (rect[0] * rect[0] + rect[1] * rect[1]);
 double radians = atan (rect[1] / rect[0]);
 polar[1] = ToDegrees (radians);
}

/***************************************************************/
/*                                                             */
/* ToRadians: convert an angle in degrees into radians         */
/*                                                             */
/***************************************************************/

double ToRadians (double angle) {
 double pi = acos (-1.);
 return angle / 180. * pi;
}

/***************************************************************/
/*                                                             */
/* ToDegrees: convert an angle in radians to degrees           */
/*                                                             */
/***************************************************************/

double ToDegrees (double radians) {
 double pi = acos (-1.);
 return radians * 180. / pi;
}

/***************************************************************/
/*                                                             */
/* RectConvert: convert a vector in polar coords to rect coords*/
/*                                                             */
/*  polar[0] = V    polar[1] = angle                           */
```

```
/*   rect[0]   = Vx   rect[1]   = Vy                              */
/*                                                                */
/******************************************************************/

void RectConvert (double polar[], double rect[]) {
 double radians = ToRadians (polar[1]);
 rect[0] = polar[0] * cos (radians);
 rect[1] = polar[0] * sin (radians);
}
```

Sample Execution of Program Engr09a - Vector Conversions

```
Enter the Vector in rectangular coordinates
X axis value first, then Y axis - separated by a blank
5 5
Original rect       5.000    5.000
Polar               7.071   45.000
Rect from polar     5.000    5.00
```

Engr09b—Plotting Graphs

Plotting graphs uses arrays in other ways. Typically, the function to be plotted is evaluated at a number of uniformly spaced points. The x and y values are stored in a pair of arrays and passed to a plotting function along with the number of points in the arrays.

The plotting function must scale the range of x and y values so that the graph can be displayed within the dimensions of the screen or printer. If you have access to a plotter device, high quality plots can be made and there often is a library of graphics or plotting functions available for your program to invoke. If not, one can make a crude plot using the * character to represent a point. This sample does just that to illustrate the basic mechanics of plotting a graph using arrays of x and y values. Here is the sample output from this program.

```
Plot of the function

        Ymin                                              Ymax
        0.00                                              1.00
   X    +                        +                           +
       |--------------------------------------------------|
 0.00  |*                                                  |
 0.06  |  *                                                |
 0.12  |     *                                             |
 0.17  |        *                                          |
 0.23  |           *                                       |
 0.29  |              *                                    |
 0.35  |                 *                                 |
 0.41  |                   *                               |
```

```
0.47  |                      *                           |
0.52  |                        *                         |
0.58  |                           *                      |
0.64  |                             *                    |
0.70  |                                *                 |
0.76  |                                  *               |
0.81  |                                    *             |
0.87  |                                      *           |
0.93  |                                        *         |
0.99  |                                         *        |
1.05  |                                           *      |
1.11  |                                            *     |
1.16  |                                             *    |
1.22  |                                              *   |
1.28  |                                               *  |
1.34  |                                                * |
1.40  |                                                 *|
1.45  |                                                 *|
1.51  |                                                 *|
1.57  |                                                 *|
1.63  |                                                 *|
1.69  |                                                 *|
1.75  |                                                 *|
1.80  |                                                * |
1.86  |                                               *  |
1.92  |                                              *   |
1.98  |                                             *    |
2.04  |                                            *     |
2.09  |                                           *      |
2.15  |                                         *        |
2.21  |                                        *         |
2.27  |                                      *           |
2.33  |                                    *             |
2.39  |                                  *               |
2.44  |                                *                 |
2.50  |                             *                    |
2.56  |                           *                      |
2.62  |                         *                        |
2.68  |                      *                           |
2.73  |                   *                              |
2.79  |                 *                                |
2.85  |              *                                   |
2.91  |           *                                      |
2.97  |        *                                         |
3.03  |     *                                            |
3.08  |  *                                               |
3.14  |*                                                 |
      |--------------------------------------------------|
```

Let's begin with what a user of a plotting function would need to do to be able to plot a graph of some function. Assume that the prototype for the **Plot()** function is

```
    void Plot (double x[], double y[], int numpts, ostream& out);
```

The **Plot()** function is given an array of x and y points along with the number of points in these arrays. **Plot()** displays the graph on the passed output stream, which can be either a file on disk or **cout** for screen displays. Clearly, all that the user of the **Plot()** function must do is define and fill an array of points that represent the function's behavior over the desired interval. Assume that we wish to plot the **sin** function from 0 to PI. Since the points along the x axis must be uniformly spaced, first calculate a delta x value, that is the incremental x amount to add to the previous point's x value to get to the next x point to plot. The magnitude of delta x is determined by the total range of x values to be plotted and the number of points desired. Since in this simple plot, one line represents one point's x value, the number of points should be fairly small.

```
const int MaxPts = 55;
int main () {
 double x[MaxPts];   // contains the  points to plot
 double y[MaxPts];
 double pi = acos (-1.);
 double deltax = pi / (MaxPts - 1);
```

The basic algorithm to calculate the ith x,y pair is to add delta x to the previous point's x value to give the new x value. Thus, the initial x value must be set by hand.

```
 x[0] = 0;
 y[0] = sin (x[0]);
```

Now a loop can be done to automatically determine the next point's x value from the previous point’s x value and then the new y value.

```
 int i = 1;
 while (i<MaxPts) {
  x[i] = x[i-1] + deltax;
  y[i] = sin (x[i]);
  i++;
 }
```

When the loop is complete, the x and y arrays are ready to be graphed.

```
 Plot (x, y, MaxPts, out);
```

Thus, the user of a plotting function only needs to create the array of points.

Writing the **Plot()** function is more difficult, especially if it is to handle all possible graphical situations. The fundamental principle is that the range of y values must be scaled to fit within the available physical space. In this case, all y values must lie within 50 columns so that the graph may be displayed on the screen or on a printed page. In this simple plotting function, each line represents the next x value. In a more robust plotting function, the x values would also be scaled to fit the available space.

The minimum y value would be in the first column and the maximum y value would be in the 50th column. The **Plot()** function begins by finding the maximum and minimum values of the array of y values using the two helper functions, **FindMax()** and **FindMin()**.

```
double ymax = FindMax (y, numpts);
double ymin = FindMin (y, numpts);
double scale_denom = ymax - ymin;
```

The **columns** array is defined as follows

```
char columns[50];
```

It must hold 49 blanks plus one *, where the * represents the actual point being plotted. To initialize all 50 characters to blanks, use a short loop assigning a blank to each element.

Let's examine the main processing loop of the **Plot()** function as it plots a single point, the ith one. First, the **y[i]** value must be scaled and converted into a subscript that lies between 0 and 49.

```
ratio = (y[i] - ymin) / scale_denom;
int j = (int) (50. * ratio);
```

However, it is always wise practice when calculating a subscript to guarantee that the final result lies within the range of the array, columns in this case.

```
if (j < 0)
 j = 0;
else if (j > 49)
 j = 49;
```

Now it is a simple matter of inserting the * character in the jth element.

```
columns[j] = '*';
```

The next issue is how to display that array of characters. One cannot just do

```
out << columns;
```

because the **ostream** considers that this is a character string, which ends with a byte of 0. Strings are discussed in a later chapter. Thus, the **columns** array must be outputted one character at a time in a short loop, which is followed by outputting the newline code.

```
for (int k=0; k<50; k++)
 out.put (columns[k]);
out << "|\n";
```

Finally, the * character must be replaced by a blank so that the **columns** array is ready for the next point.

```
columns[j] = ' ';
```

Listing **Engr09b** contains the complete Plot program.

Listing for Program Engr09b - Plot Function

```
/***************************************************************/
/*                                                             */
/* Engr09b Plot Function - display a simple text graph of a fun*/
/*                                                             */
/***************************************************************/

#include <iostream>
#include <iomanip>
```

```
#include <fstream>
#include <cmath>
using namespace std;
void Plot (double x[], double y[], int numpts, ostream& out);
double FindMax (double x[], int numpts);
double FindMin (double x[], int numpts);

const int MaxPts = 55;

int main () {

 ofstream out ("Engr09b.txt"); // send the plot to this file

 double x[MaxPts];  // contains the  points to plot
 double y[MaxPts];

 double pi = acos (-1.);
 double deltax = pi / (MaxPts - 1); // uniform x interval

 // plot sin(x) from 0 to pi - assign the starting point values
 x[0] = 0;
 y[0] = sin (x[0]);
 int i = 1;
 // calculate all other points in the range
 while (i<MaxPts) {
  x[i] = x[i-1] + deltax;
  y[i] = sin (x[i]);
  i++;
 }

 // plot the graph
 Plot (x, y, MaxPts, out);

 return 0;
}

/***************************************************************/
/*                                                             */
/* Plot: display a text style graph of a set of x,y points     */
/*       on the passed output stream                           */
/*                                                             */
/*                                                             */
/***************************************************************/

void Plot (double x[], double y[], int numpts, ostream& out) {
 // setup floating point output format
 out << fixed <<setprecision (2);

 // get max range so that we can scale each point to fit ourrange
 double ymax = FindMax (y, numpts);
 double ymin = FindMin (y, numpts);
 double scale_denom = ymax - ymin;
 double ratio;
```

```

 char columns[50]; // will hold 49 blanks and one * per point
 int i;
 for (i=0; i<50; i++) {
  columns[i] = ' ';
 }

 // display title and headings
 out << "Plot of the function\n\n";
 out <<
  "       Ymin                                          Ymax\n";
 out << setw (12) << ymin << setw (46) << ymax << endl;
 out <<
  "   X    +                       +                        +\n";
 out <<
 "       |--------------------------------------------------|\n";
 // plot each point
 for (i=0; i<numpts; i++) {
  out << setw (5) << x[i] << "  |";
  // scale this point
  ratio = (y[i] - ymin) / scale_denom;
  int j = (int) (50. * ratio);
  // force j to not exceed the boundaries of the columns array
  if (j < 0)
   j = 0;
  else if (j > 49)
   j = 49;
  // insert * character for this point
  columns[j] = '*';
  // display all 50 characters one at a time
  for (int k=0; k<50; k++)
   out.put (columns[k]);
  out << "|\n";
  // remove * character for this point
  columns[j] = ' ';
 }
 out <<
 "       |--------------------------------------------------|\n";
}

/***************************************************************/
/*                                                             */
/* FindMin: finds the minimum value of an array of numpts vals */
/*                                                             */
/***************************************************************/

double FindMin (double x[], int numpts) {
 double min = x[0];
 for (int i=1; i<numpts; i++) {
  if (x[i] < min)
   min = x[i];
 }
 return min;
```

```
}

/***************************************************************/
/*                                                             */
/* FindMax: finds the maximum value of an array of numpts vals */
/*                                                             */
/***************************************************************/

double FindMax (double x[], int numpts) {
 double max = x[0];
 for (int i=1; i<numpts; i++) {
  if (x[i] > max)
   max = x[i];
 }
 return max;
}
```

Design Exercises

1. Mail Sorting Statistics

Design a program that displays mail sorting statistics for the Post Office. At the end of each worker's shift at the mail sorting room, that mail sorter's id and the number of pieces of mail they have sorted are appended to the **DailyStats.txt** file. At the end of the day, this program is run to produce the Mail Sorting Stats Report.

```
The Average Number Sorted Today: 999999

Sorter   Number   Percentage
  Id     Sorted   of Average
 9999     99999    999.99%
 9999     99999    999.99%
 9999     99999    999.99%
```

Allow for a maximum of 100 workers. The percentage of the average sorted is given by that workers number sorted * 100 / average number sorted.

2. The Optimum Hours

A fast food restaurant has installed a traffic counter to count the number of cars driving by its store. It logs a count of the number of cars in each ten-minute period from 8am to 10pm. Each line contains a time of the form of hh:mm followed by the count of the cars passing during that interval. The program should first load the file **counts.txt** into three arrays, hour, minute, count. Find the average number of cars per ten-minute interval throughout the day. Now display that average count and the three highest counts that were observed along with their time. The report appears similar to this.

```
Summary of Passing Cars
 Average count: 9999
 hh:mm   count
 99:99     9999
 99:99     9999
 99:99     9999
```

Based upon these results, management will ensure that more employees are working during the potential higher traffic times.

Stop! Do These Exercises Before Programming

1. This attempt to input the five tax rates for the states in which ACME sells products won't compile. Why? How can it be repaired so that it works?

```
int main () {
 double taxrates[5];
 cin >> taxrates;
 ...
```

2. This attempt also does not work properly, though it compiles. Why? How can it be fixed?

```
int main () {
 double taxrates[5];
 for (int j=1; j<6; j++)
  cin >> taxrates[0];
 ...
```

3. This attempt compiles fine, but at run time it crashes. Why? How can it be fixed so that it works properly?

```
int main () {
 double taxrates[5];
 for (int j=1; j<6; j++)
  cin >> taxrates[j];
 ...
```

4. Now that the tax rates have been correctly input, a major design flaw surfaced. If the main program inputs a state code, such as 13 (for Illinois), how can the corresponding tax rate from the array of five tax rates be found? A file was created in which each input line of the **taxrates.txt** file contains the integer state code and the corresponding tax rate. This attempt at making a function to load the arrays fails to work properly. Why? How can it be fixed?

```
int main () {
 double taxrates[5];
 int    states[5];
 loadArray (states[], taxrates[5]);
 ...
void loadArray (int states[], double taxrates) {
 ifstream infile ("taxrates.txt");
 int j=0;
 while (infile >> states[j] >> taxrates) {
  j++);
 }
 infile.close();
}
```

5. Since the previous attempt to make the load function failed, the programmer threw the whole thing away and started over. This is the next attempt, also doomed, though the programmer finally got it to compile nearly. Why? How can it be fixed up?

```
const int MAX = 5
int main () {
 double taxrates[MAX];
 int    states[MAX];
 loadArray (states[MAX], taxrates[MAX], MAX);
 ...
void loadArray (int states, double taxrates, int MAX) {
 ifstream infile ("taxrates.txt");
 int j=0;
 while (infile >> states >> taxrates && j < MAX) {
  j++);
 }
 infile.close();
}
```

6. Undaunted by his previous difficulties, the programmer decided that a **matchState()** function was needed. Here is the first attempt. It compiles but does not work. Why? How can you fix it so that it does work properly?

```
int matchState (int states[], int state) {
 int j = 0;
 while (state != states[0])
  j++;
 }
 return j;
}
```

7. With a working way to find the matching state, work began on the main function's calculation's loop. This is what the programmer produced. It fails to work properly. Why? How can it be repaired?

```
int    statecodes[5];
double taxrates[5];
double cost;
int    quantity;
int    statecd;
double tax;
double total;
double grandTotal;
int    matchingStateCodeSubscript;
while (infile2 >> quantity >> cost >> statecd) {
 total = quantity * cost;
 matchState (statecodes, statecd);
 tax = total * taxrates[matchingStateCodeSubscript];
 grandTotal = total + tax;
 cout << grandTotal << endl;
}
```

8. A programmer was asked to make a program to convert students' final raw grades into a letter grade. The specifications called for the use of arrays. One array holds the lowest possible score for a particular letter grade and the other array holds the corresponding letter grade. The programmer produced the following coding. While it works, his boss immediately ordered a revision, telling him to initialize the arrays, and not assign them values at run time. How can this be done?

```
int main () {
 int  rawScores[5];
 char grades[5];
 rawScores[0] = 90;
 grades[0] = 'A';
 rawScores[1] = 80;
 grades[1] = 'B';
 rawScores[2] = 70;
 grades[3] = 'C';
 rawScores[3] = 60;
 grades[3] = 'D';
 rawScores[4] = 0;
 grades[4] = 'F';
```

9. Next, having gotten the two arrays loaded properly, the programmer proceeded to write the code to convert students' raw scores into letter grades. The students complained bitterly about the results. Desk check with a grade of 94.78. What is wrong with this and how can it be fixed to work properly?

```
int main () {
 int rawScores[5]....
 char grade[5]....
 double rawscore;
 long idNum;
 char grade;
 while (cin >> idNum >> rawscore) {
  for (int j=4; j>=0; j++)
   if (rawscore > rawScores[j]) break;
  }
  grade = grades[j];
  cout << idNum << ' ' << grade << endl;
 }
```

10. Hastily, the programmer spotted his errors and recoded the program as follows. This is now a "mostly working" program. Far fewer students were complaining about their grades. Can you spot the remaining error? One of the students complaining bitterly about their grade received a raw score of 89.997. How can the program now be fixed?

```
int main () {
 int rawScores[5]....
 char grade[5]....
 double rawscore;
 long idNum;
 char grade;
 while (cin >> idNum >> rawscore) {
  for (int j=0; j<5; j++)
   if (rawscore >= rawScores[j]) break;
  }
  grade = grades[j];
  cout << idNum << ' ' << grade << endl;
 }
```

Programming Problems

Problem CS09-1—Write a Program to Grade a Multiple Choice Test

All input lines except the first line contain a 9-digit student ID number followed by one blank followed by their letter answers to the questions. The first line of input contains a dummy student ID, a blank space and then the answer key. For example,

```
000000000 ABCDABCDABCD
123123123 ABDCABACDDAD
143434193 BACDACDABACD
323737347 B A D D AAAA
```

In this example, there were 12 test questions. Please allow for up to 100 test questions. All answers will be in uppercase letters. Please note that students sometimes fail to answer a question. Their corresponding letter is a blank. This means you must use the **get()** function to retrieve each letter (or blank).

After inputting the dummy ID number and using **get()** to retrieve the blank, make a loop to input each letter answer key and store it in an array called **answer_key**. You need only this ONE array in this problem. The bounds of the **answer_key** array should be 100. However, you must know how many answers there really are on this particular test. Thus, continue inputting answer characters and storing them into the array until you input a \n, the new line code. At this point, you know the number of questions and their answers.

Now write a loop that goes until the end of the file is reached. Input the student ID number (nine digits long) and then write a loop to input their answers. Since you now know how many questions there are, you can use a **for** loop. As an answer comes in, compare it to the correct answer letter and accumulate totals of correct answers for that student. After inputting all the student answers, print on line that contains the student ID number followed by the percent correct answers. (Remember when converting into a percentage, to multiply by 100 before you divide.)

Finally, when the end of the file is reached, print the average percentage correct found by totaling the individual percent correct scores and dividing by the number of students. Your output should look something like:

```
 STUDENT     PERCENT
   ID        CORRECT
xxxxxxxxx    xxx.xx
xxxxxxxxx    xxx.xx
xxxxxxxxx    xxx.xx

AVERAGE      xxx.xx
```

Test your program with the 2 provided test files, **TestGrading1.txt** and **TestGrading2.txt**.

Problem CS09-2—The ComputeAverage() Function

Write a function to find and return the average of the numbers in an array of **double** type elements. Name the function **ComputeAverage()**. The function is passed two arguments: the array, and the count of the number of elements in the array. Test your function using the **main()** function provided on disk contained in file **CS09-2.cpp**. Here are the results you should get.

```
Average of numbers in array x = 51.11
Average of numbers in array y = 5.50
Average of numbers in array z = 429.50
```

Problem CS09-3—FindHighest() and FindLowest() Functions

Write a function to find and return the largest number in an array of **double** type elements. Name the function **FindHighest()**. The function will be passed two arguments: the array, and the count of numbers in the array. Also write a function to find and return the smallest number in an array of **double** type elements. Name the function **FindLowest()**. The function is passed the same arguments as **FindHighest()**. Test your function using the **main()** function provided on disk contained in the file **CS09-3.cpp**. Here are the results you should get.

```
Array x:  high = 88.88   low = 11.11
Array y:  high = 9.00   low = 2.00
Array z:  high = 789.00 low = 102.00
```

Problem CS09-4—FindIndexHighest() Function

Write a function to find and return the index of the largest number in an array of **double** type elements. That is, if the largest number in the array is in the element with the subscript 7, then the function should return 7. Name the function **FindIndexHighest()**. Decide what the return data type ought to be. The function is passed two arguments: the array, and the count of numbers in the array. Test your function using the **main()** function provided on disk called **CS09-4.cpp**. Here are the results you should get.

```
Array x:  element index = 2  element contents = 88.88
Array y:  element index = 0  element contents = 9.00
Array z:  element index = 7  element contents = 789.00
```

Problem CS09-5—Occurrences() Function

Write a function that may be called like this:

```
int n = Occurrences (array, count, target);
```

The first argument is an array of **double** type elements. The second argument is the count of number of elements used in the array. The function counts how many times the third argument appears in the array and then returns that number of occurrences. Test your function using the **main()** function provided on disk in file **CS09-5.cpp**. Here are the results you should get.

```
11.11 occurs 1 time(s) in array x.
11.11 occurs 2 time(s) in array y.
11.11 occurs 0 time(s) in array z.

33.33 occurs 2 time(s) in array x.
33.33 occurs 0 time(s) in array y.
33.33 occurs 3 time(s) in array z.

88.88 occurs 5 time(s) in array x.
88.88 occurs 2 time(s) in array y.
88.88 occurs 1 time(s) in array z.
```

Problem Engr09-1—Vector Cross Product

Given two vectors in three-dimensional space, the cross product is often needed. Assuming the two vectors are V1 and V2 and are defined in rectangular coordinates as

V1 = Vx1**i** + Vy1**j** + Vz1**k**
V2 = Vx2**i** + Vy2**j** + Vz2**k**

The cross product is given by

V1 x**V2** = (Vy1 Vz2 – Vy2 Vz1) **i** +
(Vz1 Vx2 – Vz2 Vx1) **j** +
(Vx1 Vy2 – Vx2 Vy1) **k**

Write a function, **CrossProduct()**, that is passed three arrays, each with three elements. The first array is V1, the second is V2 and the third is the answer vector. Write a main program to prompt the user to input the two vectors V1 and V2 and then output the results. The general format to output a vector to follow is

V1 [–2.5, 4.3, 6.7]

Test your program with the two vectors: V1 [–2.5, 4.3, 6.7], V2 [.05, 3.1, 2.2]

Problem Engr09-2—Cross Product Application —Velocity of an Orbiting Satellite

A satellite is in orbit around the earth at a radius **r** from the center of the earth and has a known angular velocity. Determine the velocity of the satellite. The angular velocity omega of an object moving with a velocity **v** at distance **r** from the origin of the coordinate system is

v = **r** x omega

Write a program that inputs the distance vector and the angular velocity vector into two arrays of three elements each. Then calculate the velocity vector using the previous problem's cross product function.

Test your program with a satellite that is at r = 350000i + 450000**j** + 55000**k** meters with an angular velocity of –6.1E–3i + 2.3E–3**j** + –9.2E–4**k** radians per second. The resulting velocity is in meters per second.

Problem Engr09-3—Vector Dot Products

Given two vectors in three-dimensional space, the dot product is often needed. Assuming the two vectors are V1 and V2 and are defined in rectangular coordinates as

V1 = Vx1**i** + Vy1**j** + Vz1**k**
V2 = Vx2**i** + Vy2**j** + Vz2**k**

The dot product scalar is given by

V1 · **V2** = Vx1 Vx2 + Vy1 Vy2 + Vz1 Vz2

Write a function, **DotProduct()**, that is passed the arrays, each with three elements. The first array is V1, and the second is V2. The function returns the dot product as a double.
Write a main program to prompt the user to input the two vectors V1 and V2 and then output the results. The general format to output a vector to follow is

V1 [–2.5, 4.3, 6.7]

Test your program with the two vectors: V1 [–2.5, 4.3, 6.7], V2 [.05, 3.1, 2.2]

Problem Engr09-4—Dot Product Application – Power Supplied to an Object

From physics, if an object is being pushed by a force of F at a velocity of v, then the power being supplied to the object by that force is

$p = F \cdot v$

Write a program that inputs the force vector and the velocity vector into two arrays of three elements each. Then calculate the power being supplied by using the previous problem's dot product function, **Engr09-3**.

Test your program with an object that has a velocity of v = 7.5i + 4.56**j** + 5.5**k** meters per second with a force of 6.1i + 2.3**j** + 9.2**k** newton. The resulting power is in watts.

Problem Engr09-5—Plotting the Cosine Function

Modify the **Plot()** graph function to plot the cosine function across the range 0-2pi. Since the plot function used an array of 50 columns and since this function is uniformly spaced across the positive and negative y axis over this range, make the columns array contain 51 elements. Let 0 be the array element in the middle.

Problem Engr09-6—Gaussian (Normal) Distribution Function

The Gaussian distribution is a random distribution with the classic bell-shape curve. If the distribution has an average of zero and a standard deviation of 1.0, it is called the standardized normal distribution. The probability of any given value occurring in this standardized distribution is given by the formula

$$p(x) = \frac{1}{\sqrt{2PI}} e^{-\frac{x^2}{2}}$$

Use the **Plot()** function to graph this equation over the range from –4 to +4 in 51 intervals.

Chapter 10—Using Arrays

Section A: Basic Theory

Introduction

Arrays are widely used in programming. Sometimes a single-dimensioned array is called a **list** or a **table**. Thinking in general about an abstract list of things, there are a number of actions that might commonly be done to and with and a list. Lists may be unsorted (unordered) or they may be sorted into some order, numerically low to high or perhaps alphabetically. An unordered list may need to be sorted into some order. A new item may be added to either an ordered or unordered list. A list may be searched for a matching item; this is sometimes called a **table lookup**. Two lists may be related; these are called **parallel arrays**. For example, one array might hold the student id number while the parallel array holds the student grades for a course. In such a case, a specific element of one array corresponds to that same element in another array. That is, element 0 of the id array contains the id of the student whose grade is in the corresponding element 0 of the grades array. In this chapter, we explore these different uses of arrays.

Using an Array for Direct Lookup Operations

When working with dates, one often needs to know how many days there are in a given month. Using an array can streamline such operations. Given the month number (1 through 12), the program should be able to access directly the array element that contains the number of days in that month. If the month number is 1 for January, then **days_in_month[1]** should contain 31 days. When setting up the **days_in_month** array, since all arrays begin with element 0 and since 0 is not normally a month number, it is permissible to make the array one element larger, placing a dummy value in the never-to-be-used element 0. The array could be defined as follows

```
const int days_in_month[13] = {0, 31, 28, 31, 30, 31, 30,
                               31, 31, 30, 31, 30, 31}
```

Notice also the usage of the **const** keyword. Once the array elements are given their initial values, they should never be changed. Making the array constant ensures that no accidental changes to these values can be made.

In this example, the month number is used as the subscript to directly access the correct number of days in that month. The following illustrates this.

```
int month;
cout << "Enter a month number: ";
cin >> month;
while (month < 1 || month > 12) {
 cout << "Invalid month number - please re-enter: ";
```

```
 cin >> month;
}
cout << "Month " << month << " contains "
     << days_in_month[month] << " days\n"
```

Parallel Arrays and Sequential Searches—Inquiry Programs

Consider two single-dimensioned arrays; one contains the student id number, and the other contains their course grade. Clearly, the two arrays must be kept synchronized at all times. The grade stored in element 1 of the **grade** array corresponds to the student whose id is stored in element 1 of the **id** array. Once the information is loaded into the two arrays, then the inquiry operations can begin. An **inquiry program** is one in which the user is prompted to enter a specific id of some kind and the program then finds the corresponding data and displays it. Inquiry programs are widespread in the modern world. Checking on your bank account balance, credit card limit, and even the grade that you received in a course—all are inquiry type programs.

Let's first examine how the inquiry array is loaded and then how it is used or searched. Assume that each line of input contains a long student id number followed by the letter grade they received. The following loads both arrays

```
long id[MaxStudents];
char grade[MaxStudents];
int numberStudents;
int j = 0;
while (j < MaxStudents && cin >> id[j] >> grade[j]) {
 j++;
}
numberStudents = j;
```

Notice the **while** test condition checks first to see if there is still another available element and if so, attempts the input operation and if successful, increments the subscript for the next iteration. Assume that the following Illustration 10.1 represents the arrays after all the data have been input. The variable **numberStudents** contains the number actually input into the arrays and is 5.

Illustration 10.1 The Id and Grades Arrays

subscript	id array	grade array
0	111111111	A
1	444444444	B
2	222222222	A
3	555555555	C
4	333333333	B

Next, the inquiry program prompts the user to enter the id of the student whose grade is to be found.

```
long studentId;
char studentGrade;
```

```
cout << "Enter student id number: ";
cin >> studentId;
```

Now the objective is to search the id array looking for a match on **studentId**, obtain the subscript of the matching id and use that subscript to get at that student's grade. Let's encapsulate the matching process in a function, **MatchId()**, whose header begins

```
int  MatchId (const long id[], int num, long findId) {
```

MatchId() must be passed the array of id numbers whose data are constant in this function and the current number in the array along with the id number to find, **findId**. It should return the subscript of that element of the id array that matched **findId**.

Look over Illustration 10.1 above; suppose that the user enters an id number of 555555555. Counting down the array elements, the **MatchId()** function should return 3.

But what would happen if the user asks **MatchId()** to find a student id of 666666666? That id number is not in the list. Thus, when **MatchId()** ends, if there is no match on the **findId**, **MatchId()** must have a way to notify the caller of that fact. Because no subscript can ever be a negative integer, we can adopt some negative number to return to indicate no match found. Commonly –1 is used for this purpose.

Following good programming practice, define a constant integer for to represent it and place it in the global namespace above the main function.

```
const int NoMatch = -1;
```

The logic of the **MatchId()** function is

```
int  MatchId (const long id[], int num, long findId) {
 for (int j=0; j<num; j++) {
  if (findId == id[j])
   return j;
 }
 return NoMatch;
}
```

The **main()** program then invokes **MatchId()** as follows.

```
int match = MatchId (id, numberStudents, studentId);
if (match != NoMatch) {
 studentGrade = grade[match];
 cout << studentID << "received a grade of "
      << studentGrade << endl;
}
else {
 cout << "Error: invalid student id\n";
}
```

Inserting Another Element into an Unsorted Array

Suppose that a student with an id number of 666666666 takes a make-up exam and scores a grade of B. One could alter the input file to add this sixth line and rerun the program. However, in some applications, it is neither possible nor desirable to terminate the program and restart it just to reload the arrays. Instead, the new information is additionally inserted into the array. In an unsorted array, the new information added into the first empty element. Make sure that the total number of elements in the array is incremented. The following **InsertStudent()** function illustrates how this may be done. Notice this time, the arrays are not constant.

```
bool  InsertStudent (long id[], char grade[],
                     int& num, int maxlimit,
                     long newid, char newgrade) {
 if (num >= maxlimit) return false;
 id[num] = newid;
 grade[num] = newgrade;
 num++;
 return true;
}
```

Notice that the function returns **false** if there is no more room left in the array. Observe that the number in the array, **num**, must be passed by reference so that the number in **main()** can be incremented. The two arrays now appear as follows as shown in Illustration 10.2.

Illustration 10.2 Updated Id and Grade Arrays
numberStudents is 6 - **main()**'s variable

subscript	id array	grade array
0	111111111	A
1	444444444	B
2	222222222	A
3	555555555	C
4	333333333	B
5	666666666	B

Ordered (Sorted) Lists

One problem of unsorted lists is the time that it takes to search through the array sequentially looking for a matching value in the array. If there are only a few elements, the amount of time is negligible. However, suppose that these arrays contained a store's inventory numbers, quantity on hand and unit cost. Further, suppose that the store handles 100,000 separate items. If the item number desired was the last one in the list, a significant amount of time is needed to find that match. The answer is not "Get a faster computer" but rather devise a better algorithm. If the list is sorted into numerical or alphabetical order depending upon the type of data the array contains, then far faster searches can be devised. Returning to the student id and grades arrays, let's assume that the arrays have been sorted into increasing numerical order on the ids. The arrays appear as shown in Illustration 10.3.

Illustration 10.3 Sorted Id and Grade Arrays
numberStudents is 6 - **main()**'s variable

```
subscript  id array  grade array
     0     111111111     A
     1     222222222     A
     2     333333333     B
     3     444444444     B
     4     555555555     C
     5     666666666     B
```

The array of ids can still be matched sequentially. However, we can take advantage of the ordered nature to detect no matching id number more quickly. Suppose that the **findId** this time was 345678999. Notice that when we are at subscript 3, which contains id 444444444, we know for certain that this id is not in the array and can return **false** at once without having to check any further subscripts. The slight modification is in boldface

```
int  MatchSortedId (const long id[], int num, long findId) {
 for (int j=0; j<num && findId >= id[j]; j++) {
  if (findId == id[j])
   return j;
 }
 return NoMatch;
}
```

On the average, some increase in speed results. However, for items near the end of the array are still going to take a large number of iterations through the loop to find them.

The **binary search** method uses a different searching algorithm, one that drastically reduces the number of comparisons that need to be done to find the match. Before looking at the coding for the search, let's examine in detail how the binary search works. Let N represent the number of ids in the array. The first subscript to use in the search is N/2—the midpoint. We compare the **findId** to the element in the middle. If we are lucky, we have an exact match and are done. More likely, it does not match, but if the **findId** is smaller than the one in the middle, we can eliminate the entire higher half of the array from further consideration. Likewise, if the **findId** is greater than that in the middle, we can eliminate all those values in the lower half. Thus, on one test, we have eliminated one-half of the array from further consideration! Now that same process is repeated, halving the new interval and testing the one in the middle again, and so on until we find the match or run out of array, indicating no match.

Let's do a concrete example using the student data above in Illustration 10.3. Say the **findId** is 22222222. The first subscript to try is (0 + 5) / 2 or index 2, which stores id 333333333. The **findId** is smaller so if this one is in the array it must lie in the lower half, between indexes 0 and 1.

The new index to try is halfway between. At subscript 1, we have our match.

The binary search function should be designed so that it returns **true** if it finds a match; the index of the match is stored in a reference parameter for use by the caller. However, if it does not find a match, the index stored in the passed reference parameter should be the index of where that value ought to have been if it was in the list. Why? Code reuse. True, for a simple query, match this id, just a return value of **false** for not present is sufficient. But the next feature one might need to implement is to add this id into the sorted list where it belongs. Thinking ahead, when an id is not in the list, it is a simple matter also to provide the index of where this element should be if it were in the list. Then only one **BinarySearch()** function need be written.

```
bool  BinarySearch (const long id[], int num,
                    long findId, int& foundIndex) {
 int firstidx = 0;
 int lastidx = num - 1;
 int middleidx = 0; // in case array is empty
 bool foundMatch = false;
 while (lastidx >= firstidx && !foundMatch) {
  middleidx = (firstidx + lastidx) / 2;
  if (findId < id[middleidx])
    lastidx = middleidx - 1;
  else if (findId > id[middleidx])
    firstidx = middleidx + 1;
  else foundMatch = true;
 }
 foundIndex = middleidx;
 return foundMatch;
 // note that if there is no match, then this new value
 // goes either before or after the returned foundIndex
 // and an insertion should check which - done in the caller
}
```

The main function would then do the following to obtain the corresponding subscript in **match**.

```
if (BinarySearch (id, numberStudents, studentId, match))
 cout << studentID << "received a grade of "
      << grade[match]<< endl;
```

Inserting New Data into a Sorted List

Inserting new elements into a sorted array is more difficult. Consider the above **id** and **grade** arrays with the six elements currently in it, Illustration 10.3. Suppose that a student id of 255555555 with a grade of B needs to be inserted. What would have to be done to actually insert this new student?

First, we would have to find the subscript where that id would be the proper sequence. In this case, 255555555 belongs in the element with a subscript of 2, between the values 222222222 and 333333333. Since element 2 is already occupied, that element and all others must be moved down one element. That is, the data at index 2 must be moved into subscript 3; 3 must be moved into index

4; 4 into 5 and 5 into the unoccupied 6.

Caution. The movement of elements must be done in reverse order. If we move 33333333 into the **id** array at subscript 3, it replaces the data that is there, id 444444444. Thus, the movement must be 5 into 6, 4 into 5, 3 into 4 and finally 2 into 3. Once the data in the element of index 2 has been copied into element 3, we can then copy in the new id of 255555555 into the element at index 2.

Of course, nothing can be inserted if all the elements are used. To be robust, the insert function should also make sure the requested id is not already in the list. Remember too when parallel arrays are involved, what is done to one array must be echoed in the other parallel arrays.

For this example, assume the following const int definitions are available in the global namespace.

```
const int InsertErrorBoundsExceeded = -1;
const int InsertErrorDuplicateId = -2;
const int InsertSuccess = 0;
```

Further assume that the new data to be inserted into the list are contained in the following **main()** program's variables

```
long newId;
char newGrade;
```

The **main()** function invokes the **InsertStudent()** function as follows

```
int retcd = InsertStudent (id, grade, numberStudents,
                           MaxStudents, newId, newGrade);
if (retcd == InsertErrorBoundsExceeded) {
  cout << "Error: Cannot add more students\n"
       << "The list is full\n";
}
else if (retcd == InsertErrorDuplicateId) {
  cout << "Error: student id " << newId
       << " is already present in the list\n";
}
```

The coding for the robust **InsertStudent()** function is as follows.

```
int InsertStudent (long id[], char grade[],
                   int& num, int maxlimit,
                   long newId, char newGrade) {
 if (num >= maxlimit) // out of elements
  return InsertErrorBoundsExceeded;
 int index; // subscript where id belongs
 if (BinarySearch (id, num, newId, index))
  return InsertErrorDuplicateId; // found this id
 if (num && newId > id[index]) // is insert after this one?
  index++;// yes, so move index down one for move operations
```

```
 if (index != num) { // do we need to move elements down?
  // yes, so move all items down one index to make room
  for (int j=num-1; j >= index; j--) {
   id[j+1] = id[j];
   grade[j+1] = grade[j];
  }
 }
 // copy new data into lists
 id[index] = newid;
 grade[index] = newgrade;
 num++;
 return InsertSuccess;
}
```

Sorting an Array

The next question is how is an array sorted into numerical or alphabetical order? There are numerous sorting algorithms; each offers benefits under proper circumstances. One method of sorting may work well on a list that is in more or less random order, yet be dismal when perhaps only one element in the list is actually out of order. Another method may work very well when only one element in the list is out of sequence, but performs badly if the list is in random order.

The Straight Selection Sort, is the easiest to remember how to code. Begin with the first element in the list. Compare the initial element with all the other elements in the list below it. Any time one below it is smaller than that initial element, switch them, placing the smallest valued element in that initial position in the list. When the end of the list is reached on that pass, the smallest valued element is in the first element. Proceed to the second element, look through all the remaining elements, and place the next smallest remaining element in it. Once the next-to-the-last row has been done, all the elements are now in low to high order, either numerically or alphabetically.

When performing an exchange because the next element is smaller than the one at hand, the swap action must use a temporary variable. For example, supposing one wanted to swap the contents of **int** variables **x** and **y**. You must also have a temporary **int** variable as shown.

```
int temp = x;
x = y;
y = temp;
```

If sorting parallel arrays such as the **id** and **grade** lists, if you swap a pair of elements in the **id** array, you must also swap the same elements in the **grade** array to maintain the corresponding values.

Here is a simple **SortArrays()** function that sorts the **id** and **grade** arrays into increasing id number order.

```
void  SortArrays (long id[], char grade[], int num) {
```

```
 long tempid;
 char tempgrade;
 int i, j;
 for (i=0; i<num-1; i++) {
  // look through all elements below this one
  // place smallest one in this the ith one
  for (j=i+1; j<num; j++) {
   if (id[j] < id[i]) {
    // jth one is smaller, so swap them
    tempid = id[i];
    id[i] = id[j];
    id[j] = tempid;
    // also swap parallel grade array
    tempgrade = grade[i];
    grade[i] = grade[j];
    grade[j] = tempgrade;
   }
  }
 }
}
```

There are many other sorting algorithms. Each has specific benefits in certain circumstances.

Arrays are very useful aggregates of data. Unsorted lists are often used to look up information, to find matching items and can easily have new items added to them by appending them onto the end of the list. Lists can be sorted into numerical order. Matching with sorted lists can be highly optimized for speed of lookup but inserting a new item into the list requires more work. Parallel arrays of data provide a convenient means of keeping related information organized.

Section B: A Computer Science Example

Cs10B—Account Processing using a Menu and Sorted Arrays

In this example, all of the techniques of array processing are combined into a working example along with a menu. The objective is to store an array of account numbers and their account balances for our credit card company. When the company first opens for business, there are no accounts in the main file. However, soon, the accounts file will exist. Thus, when the program first begins, it attempts to load the parallel arrays from the master file, if it exists.

A menu of choices is shown. If another customer is added, the two arrays must be kept in increasing account number order. Hence, a binary search is used to find the correct insertion point for the new account number. Provisions are made to display all accounts on the screen and to look up the balance of a specific account. At the end of the run, a new master file can be written.

Here is a sample run of the program.

Cs10b Sample Test Run

```
  Acme Loan Services
        1 Add a New Account
        2 Find an Account Balance
        3 Display All Accounts
        4 Save the Accounts Data
        5 Quit the Program
Enter the number of your choice: 1
Enter the new account number and balance: 10
1000
Data has been added successfully
  Acme Loan Services
        1 Add a New Account
        2 Find an Account Balance
        3 Display All Accounts
        4 Save the Accounts Data
        5 Quit the Program
Enter the number of your choice: 1
Enter the new account number and balance: 20
2000
Data has been added successfully
  Acme Loan Services
        1 Add a New Account
        2 Find an Account Balance
        3 Display All Accounts
        4 Save the Accounts Data
        5 Quit the Program
Enter the number of your choice: 1
Enter the new account number and balance: 30 3000
Data has been added successfully
  Acme Loan Services
```

```
        1 Add a New Account
        2 Find an Account Balance
        3 Display All Accounts
        4 Save the Accounts Data
        5 Quit the Program
Enter the number of your choice: 1
Enter the new account number and balance: 5 500
Data has been added successfully
  Acme Loan Services
        1 Add a New Account
        2 Find an Account Balance
        3 Display All Accounts
        4 Save the Accounts Data
        5 Quit the Program
Enter the number of your choice: 1
Enter the new account number and balance: 25 2500
Data has been added successfully
  Acme Loan Services
        1 Add a New Account
        2 Find an Account Balance
        3 Display All Accounts
        4 Save the Accounts Data
        5 Quit the Program
Enter the number of your choice: 3
Account Number   Balance
         5   $    500.00
        10   $   1000.00
        20   $   2000.00
        25   $   2500.00
        30   $   3000.00
  Acme Loan Services
        1 Add a New Account
        2 Find an Account Balance
        3 Display All Accounts
```

```
        4 Save the Accounts Data
        5 Quit the Program
Enter the number of your choice: 2
Enter the account number to look up: 5
Account Number 5 has a balance of $500.00
  Acme Loan Services
        1 Add a New Account
        2 Find an Account Balance
        3 Display All Accounts
        4 Save the Accounts Data
        5 Quit the Program
Enter the number of your choice: 2
Enter the account number to look up: 30
Account Number 30 has a balance of $3000.00
  Acme Loan Services
        1 Add a New Account
        2 Find an Account Balance
        3 Display All Accounts
        4 Save the Accounts Data
        5 Quit the Program
Enter the number of your choice: 2
Enter the account number to look up: 42
Error: account 42 is not in the database
  Acme Loan Services
        1 Add a New Account
        2 Find an Account Balance
        3 Display All Accounts
        4 Save the Accounts Data
        5 Quit the Program
Enter the number of your choice: 4
Data saved in file newAccounts.txt
  Acme Loan Services
        1 Add a New Account
```

```
          2 Find an Account Balance
          3 Display All Accounts
          4 Save the Accounts Data
          5 Quit the Program

Enter the number of your choice: 5
```

Here is the Top-down design for Cs10b.

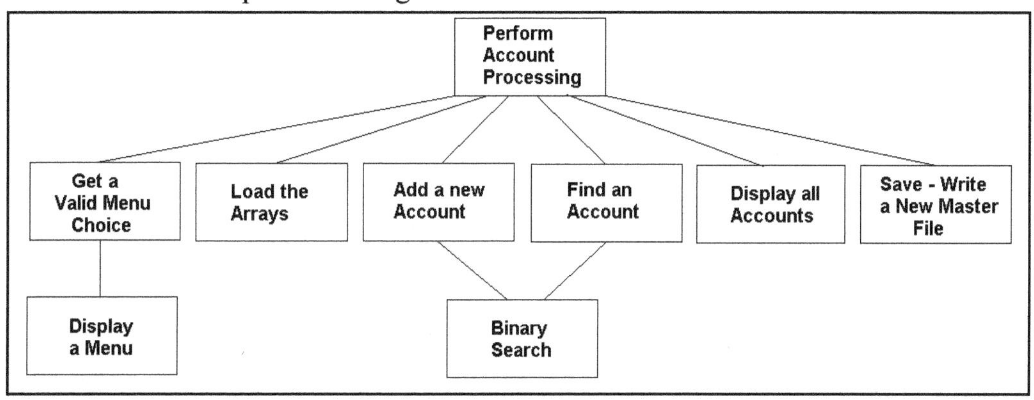

Cs10b Top-down Design

To better handle responding to menu choices, an enum is used:

```
enum Choice {AddNewAccount = 1, FindAccount, DisplayAccounts,
             Save, Quit};
```

The main function becomes very streamlined and is just this.

```
long   accountNum[MAX];
double balance[MAX];

// load the initial accounts array
int    numAccounts = LoadAccounts (accountNum, balance, MAX);

// process menu choices until Quit is chosen
Choice c = GetValidMenuChoice ();
while (cin && c != Quit) {
 switch (c) {
  case AddNewAccount:
   AddAccount (accountNum, balance, numAccounts);
   break;
  case FindAccount:
   FindTheAccount (accountNum, balance, numAccounts);
   break;
  case DisplayAccounts:
   DisplayAllAccounts (accountNum, balance, numAccounts);
   break;
  case Save:
   SaveAccounts (accountNum, balance, numAccounts);
   break;
 }
 c = GetValidMenuChoice ();
}
```

Each of the functions is very simple and straightforward. Here is the complete Cs10b program. Notice that by using many functions, the problem has become relatively easy to code.

Cs10b Account Processing with Menu

```
#include <iostream>
#include <iomanip>
#include <fstream>
using namespace std;

/***************************************************************/
/*                                                             */
/* Cs10b: Account Processing                                   */
/*                                                             */
/***************************************************************/

const int MAX = 100;

enum Choice {AddNewAccount = 1, FindAccount, DisplayAccounts,
             Save, Quit};

int    LoadAccounts (long accountNum[], double balance[],
                     int limit);
void   DisplayMenu ();
Choice GetValidMenuChoice ();
bool   AddAccount (long accountNum[], double balance[],
                   int& limit);
void   FindTheAccount (long accountNum[], double balance[],
                       int limit);
void   DisplayAllAccounts (long accountNum[], double balance[],
                           int limit);
bool   SaveAccounts (long accountNum[], double balance[],
                     int limit);
bool   BinarySearch (long id[], int num, long findId,
                     int& foundIndex);

int main () {
 cout << fixed << setprecision (2);

 long   accountNum[MAX];
 double balance[MAX];

 // load the initial accounts array
 int    numAccounts = LoadAccounts (accountNum, balance, MAX);

 // process menu choices until Quit is chosen
 Choice c = GetValidMenuChoice ();
 while (cin && c != Quit) {
  switch (c) {
   case AddNewAccount:
    AddAccount (accountNum, balance, numAccounts);
    break;
```

```
   case FindAccount:
    FindTheAccount (accountNum, balance, numAccounts);
    break;
   case DisplayAccounts:
    DisplayAllAccounts (accountNum, balance, numAccounts);
    break;
   case Save:
    SaveAccounts (accountNum, balance, numAccounts);
    break;
  }
  c = GetValidMenuChoice ();
 }

 return 0;
}

/***************************************************************/
/*                                                             */
/* LoadAccounts: loads arrays from the file of accounts        */
/*               returns the number in the array               */
/*                                                             */
/***************************************************************/
int LoadAccounts (long accountNum[], double balance[],
                  int limit) {
 ifstream infile ("Accounts.txt");
 if (!infile)
  return 0; // no accounts sold as yet
 int i = 0;
 while (i<limit && infile >> accountNum[i] >> balance[i])
  i++;
 if (i == limit && infile >> ws) {
  cerr << "Error: too many accounts for the program to handle\n";
  infile.close ();
  exit (1);
 }
 if (!infile.eof() && infile.fail()) {
  cerr << "Error: bad data in the accounts file\n";
  infile.close ();
  exit (2);
 }
 infile.close ();
 return i;
}

/***************************************************************/
/*                                                             */
/* DisplayMenu: shows the menu on the screen                   */
/*                                                             */
/***************************************************************/
void DisplayMenu () {
 cout << "\n\n\n  Acme Loan Services\n\n"
      << "\t1 Add a New Account\n"
      << "\t2 Find an Account Balance\n"
```

```
       << "\t3 Display All Accounts\n"
       << "\t4 Save the Accounts Data\n"
       << "\t5 Quit the Program\n\n"
       << "Enter the number of your choice: ";
}

/***************************************************************/
/*                                                             */
/* GetValidMenuChoice: returns a valid menu choice             */
/*                                                             */
/***************************************************************/
Choice GetValidMenuChoice () {
 int num;
 do {
  DisplayMenu ();
  cin >> num;
 } while ((num < AddNewAccount || num > Quit) && cin);
 if (!cin) num = Quit;
 return (Choice) num;
}

/***************************************************************/
/*                                                             */
/* AddAccount: adds another account to the array - ret false   */
/*             if it could not add another                     */
/*                                                             */
/***************************************************************/
bool AddAccount (long accountNum[], double balance[],
                 int& limit) {
 if (limit == MAX) {
  cerr << "Error: accounts array size at maximum capacity\n";
  return false;
 }
 long newAcctNum;
 double newBalance;
 cout << "Enter the new account number and balance: ";
 cin >> newAcctNum >> newBalance;
 if (!cin) {
  cout << "Error: bad data inputted\n";
  return false;
 }
 int index;
 if (BinarySearch (accountNum, limit, newAcctNum, index)) {
  cerr << "Error: account " << newAcctNum
       << " is already in the database\n";
  return false;
 }
 if (limit && newAcctNum > accountNum[index])
  index++;
 if (index != limit) { // do we need to move elements down?
  // yes, so move all items down one index to make room
  for (int j=limit-1; j >= index; j--) {
   accountNum[j+1] = accountNum[j];
```

```
    balance[j+1] = balance[j];
   }
  }
  accountNum[index] = newAcctNum;
  balance[index] = newBalance;
  limit++;
  cout << "Data has been added successfully\n";
  return true;
}

/***************************************************************/
/*                                                             */
/* FindTheAccount: displays account info for this account      */
/*                                                             */
/***************************************************************/
void FindTheAccount (long accountNum[], double balance[],
                     int limit) {
 long findAcctNum;
 cout << "Enter the account number to look up: ";
 cin >> findAcctNum;
 if (!cin) {
  cout << "Error: bad data inputted\n";
  return;
 }
 int index;
 if (BinarySearch (accountNum, limit, findAcctNum, index))
  cout << "Account Number " << findAcctNum
       << " has a balance of $" << balance[index] << endl;
 else
  cerr << "Error: account " << findAcctNum
       << " is not in the database\n";
}

/***************************************************************/
/*                                                             */
/* DisplayAllAccounts: on-screen display of all accounts       */
/*                                                             */
/***************************************************************/
void DisplayAllAccounts (long accountNum[], double balance[],
                         int limit) {
 cout << "Account Number   Balance\n\n";
 for (int i=0; i<limit; i++)
  cout << setw(10) << accountNum[i] << "   $" << setw (10)
       << balance[i] << endl;
 cout << endl << endl;
}

/***************************************************************/
/*                                                             */
/* SaveAccounts: returns true if data is saved to a file       */
/*                                                             */
/***************************************************************/
bool SaveAccounts (long accountNum[], double balance[],
```

```
                   int limit) {
 ofstream outfile ("newAccounts.txt");
 if (!outfile) {
  cerr << "Error: cannot open the newAccounts.txt file\n";
  return false;
 }
 for (int i=0; i<limit; i++)
  outfile << setw(10) << accountNum[i] << setw (10)
          << balance[i] << endl;
 outfile.close();
 cout << "Data saved in file newAccounts.txt\n";
 return true;
}

/***************************************************************/
/*                                                             */
/* BinarySearch: returns true if found; foundIndex has the idx */
/*      of the matching one or the insertion point if not fnd  */
/*                                                             */
/***************************************************************/
bool BinarySearch (const long id[], int num, long findId,
                   int& foundIndex) {
 int firstidx = 0;
 int lastidx = num - 1;
 int middleidx = 0;
 bool foundMatch = false;
 while (lastidx >= firstidx && !foundMatch) {
  middleidx = (firstidx + lastidx) / 2;
  if (findId < id[middleidx])
   lastidx = middleidx - 1;
  else if (findId > id[middleidx])
    firstidx = middleidx + 1;
  else foundMatch = true;
 }
 foundIndex = middleidx;
 return foundMatch;
 // note that if there is no match, then this new value
 // goes either before or after the returned foundIndex
 // and an insertion should check which
}
```

Cs10A—Merging Arrays

In this example, some methods of merging two arrays into one final array are examined. While this problem could be solved a number of different ways, here, let's use arrays to illustrate how arrays can be merged.

Acme Salvage Company has just bought out one of their competitor's companies, Jones Salvage. Both are supplying parts and management wishes to merge their master file of parts into one new file. Each line in each company's master file of parts consists of a part id, quantity on hand, manufacturer id, and cost. Originally, both companies' master files are sorted into increasing part id order. Write a program to merge the two separate master files into one new master file, again in increasing part id order.

Two complexities arise. In a few cases, both companies carry a specific manufacturer's part. If a part in the Jones master file has a manufacturer id that matches one that is already in the Acme master file, simply add the Jones quantity on hand to that of the Acme quantity. The other potential problem is duplicate id numbers. When adding a Jones set of data to the merged arrays, if the Jones id number is the same as an Acme id number, then go ahead and add the Jones data using that duplicate id number. However, write out an error message to a log file so that management can review the magnitude of the problem and recommend appropriate steps.

In this problem, while we could write a **LoadAcmeArrays()** and a **LoadJonesArrays()** pair of functions, this is not good programming design. Since both master files contain the same fields in the same order, one should write one **LoadArrays()** function that can input either master file. The **main()** function first calls **LoadArrays()** twice, once for each company's master file. Then **main()** calls **MergeArrays()** and finally **OutputArrays()**.

In **main()**, notice that both files should be opened and tested before calling the **LoadArrays()** function. It would be a waste of computer resources to open one file and input its data before attempting to open the second file only to find that the file is not present.

How is the merge operation handled? If there were no duplicate manufacturer id numbers, it would be simple. We would define three subscripts, each initialized to zero; one for the Acme arrays, one for the Jones arrays and one for the merged arrays. Next, compare the current id numbers and copy the set of data with the lower id numbers into the merged arrays. If the id numbers were the same, copy both sets of data and write an error log message.

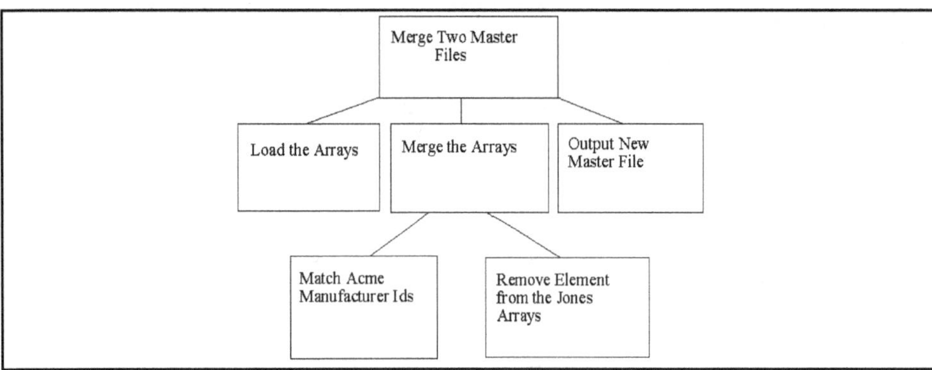

Figure 10.1 Top-Down Design for Merge Program

However, the possibility of duplicate manufacturer id numbers requires an additional step. The simplest method is to traverse all of the Jones manufacturer ids looking for a corresponding match in the Acme array. If a duplicate is found, add the Jones quantity to the corresponding Acme quantity. Thus, **MergeArrays()** needs a **MatchAcmeManuId()** function to check for matches and a **RemoveJonesElement()** function to remove one set of data from the Jones arrays. Figure 10.1 shows the Top-Down Design.

Here are the Acme input file and the Jones input file that we can use for desk checking.

```
The Input file: Cs10a-AcmeMaster.txt
```

```
111111  10   11223344  42.00
111112 100   11323355 445.55
111113 200   13223366  88.99
111222 300   14223377 123.45
111224 110   51223388 234.22
222221  33   51223399  19.99
222222  42   21224411  24.99
222223  55   14424444 255.55
333331  84   31225544  35.99
444444  55   61226644  55.49
555555 444   21227744  56.31
777777  13   41228833  88.88
999995  15   61229944  84.84
```

```
The Input file: Cs10a-JonesMaster.txt
```

```
111112 100   11323355 445.55
111113 200   22323366  88.99
131111  10   11233444  42.00
141222 300   14453377 123.45
151224 110   51224444 234.22
252221  33   51223399  19.99
262222  42   25624411  24.99
272223  55   14656444 255.55
383331  84   31225666  35.99
```

```
10 484444   55   61226688   55.49
11 595555 444   21456454   56.31
12 787777   13   41223633   88.88
13 988995   15   61244944   84.84
```

The **main()** function defines the arrays as shown in Figure 10.2. Its coding steps are as follows.

In order to display the final summary of the results, **main()** must have the three counters as shown in Figure 10.2, initialized to 0. Here is the sketch of the **main()** function.

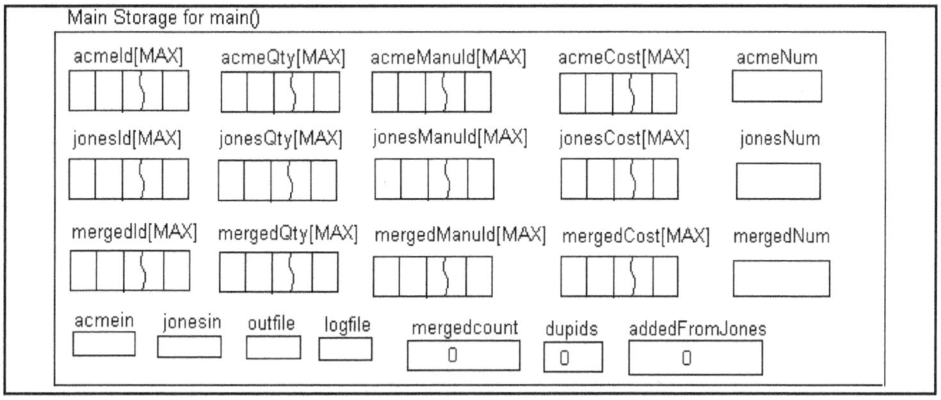

Main Storage for main()

acmeId[MAX] acmeQty[MAX] acmeManuId[MAX] acmeCost[MAX] acmeNum

jonesId[MAX] jonesQty[MAX] jonesManuId[MAX] jonesCost[MAX] jonesNum

mergedId[MAX] mergedQty[MAX] mergedManuId[MAX] mergedCost[MAX] mergedNum

acmein jonesin outfile logfile mergedcount 0 dupids 0 addedFromJones 0

Figure 10.2 Main Storage for **main()**

attempt to open **acmein** and **jonesin**
if either fail to open, display an error message and quit
let **acmeNum** = **LoadArrays (acmeId, acmeQty, acmeManuId, acmeCost, MAX, acmein)**
close **acmein**
let **jonesNum** = **LoadArrays (jonesId, jonesQty, jonesManuId, jonesCost, MAX, jonesin)**
close **jonesin**
open the **logfile**
let **mergedNum** = **MergeArrays** (
acmeId, acmeQty, acmeManuId, acmeCost, acmeNum,
jonesId, jonesQty, jonesManuId, jonesCost, jonesNum,
mergedId, mergedQty, mergedManuId, mergedCost, MAX,
mergedcount, dupids, addedFromJones, logfile)
open **outfile**
OutputArrays (mergedId, mergedQty, mergedManuId, mergedCost, mergedNum, outfile)
close **outfile**
display on the **logfile** the **mergedcount**, the **dupids** and **addedFromJones**
close **logfile**

The **LoadArrays()** function is very simple. It is given: **id**[], **qty**[], **manufid**[], **cost**[],

limit and **infile**.

let **i** = 0;
while (i < limit && infile >> **id[i]** >> **qty[i]** >> **manufid[i]** >> **cost[i]**)
i++;
if (i == **limit && infile** >> **ws**) then display an error and exit
return i;

The merge operation has four loops. Initially, we must look through all of the Jones array for duplicate manufacturer id numbers. If any are found, the Jones quantity must be added to the Acme quantity and that entry must be removed from the Jones arrays. The actual merging can then take place. The second loop continues while there still exists at least one set of data in both Acme and Jones arrays. When the first loop ends, there could still be additional items in the Acme array or there could still be items left in the Jones arrays that have not yet been added. Thus, two additional loops are needed to add these to the new arrays. Here is the sequence of **MergeArrays()**, which is passed:

aid[], aqty[], **amanuid**[], **acost**[], **numAcme**,
jid[], jqty[], **jmanuid**[], **jcost**[], **numJones**,
mid[], mqty[], **mmanuid**[], **mcost**[], **limit**,
mergedcount, **dupids**, **addedFromJones** and **logfile**

let **ida** and **idj** and **idm** = 0 - our subscripts for the three arrays
// look through all of the Jones arrays to find and remove all those with duplicate
// manufacturer id numbers
while (**idj** < **numJones**) do the following to look for duplicate manufacturer ids
let **match** = **MatchAcmeManuId** (**amanuid**, **numAcme**, **jmanuid**[**idj**])
if match >= 0, then we have found a duplicate
aqty[match] += **jqty[idj]**; // add Jones's qty to Acme's qty
And remove this entry from the Jones arrays
RemoveJonesElement (**idj, jid, jqty, jmanuid, jcost, numJones**);
increment **mergedcount**
end if
else increment the Jones subscript **idj**
end while
reset the Jones array subscript **idj** back to 0

The second loop continues while there still exists at least one set of data in both Acme and Jones arrays. We want to add the smaller of the two current id numbers (between Acme and Jones) into the resultant merged arrays. Thus, we check to see which is smaller and move the data accordingly.

while (**ida** < **numAcme** && **idj** < **numJones**) {
if the Acme product id smaller than Jones—**aid[ida] < jid[idj]**? If so then do
// copy this Acme item into the merged arrays
mid[idm] = **aid[ida]**;
mqty[idm] = **aqty[ida]**;
mmanuid[idm] = **amanuid[ida]**;
mcost[idm] = **acost[ida]**;

increment both the Acme and the merged array subscripts, **ida** and **idm**
end the then clause
otherwise see if the Jones id is smaller **aid[ida] > jid[idj]**? If so then do
// copy this Jones item into the merged arrays
mid[idm] = **jid[idj]**;
mqty[idm] = **jqty**[idj];
mmanuid[idm] = **jmanuid[idj]**;
mcost[idm] = **jcost[idj]**;
increment both the subscripts, **idj** and **idm**
increment the count of those added from Jones, **addedFromJones**
end the otherwise clause
else here they are duplicate product id numbers

If they are duplicate numbers, then we must add both to the merged arrays and write an informatory message to the log file.

mid[idm] = **aid[ida]**; // add in Acme's first
mqty[idm] = **aqty**[ida];
mmanuid[idm] = **amanuid[ida]**;
mcost[idm] = **acost[ida]**;
increment the merged array subscript for the next entry, **idm**
mid[idm] = **jid[idj]**; // add in Jones
mqty[idm] = **jqty[idj]**;
mmanuid[idm] = **jmanuid[idj]**;
mcost[**idm**] = **jcost[idj]**;
increment the merged array subscript for the next entry, **idm**
log an error message about these duplicate product ids to **logfile**
increment the duplicates count, **dupids**
increment the Jones and Acme subscripts, **ida** and **idj**
end the else
end the **while** loop

When the first loop ends, there could still be additional items in the Acme array or there could still be items left in the Jones arrays that have not yet been added. Thus, two additional loops are needed to add any remaining in these to the new arrays.

while (ida < numAcme) do the following
mid[idm] = **aid[ida]**;
mqty[idm] = **aqty[ida]**;
mmanuid[idm] = **amanuid[ida]**;
mcost[idm] = **acost[ida]**;
increment both **ida** and **idm**
end the while loop for extra Acme products

Now add in any left over Jones products

while (idj < numJones) do the following
mid[idm] = **jid[idj]**;

mqty[idm] = **jqty[idj]**;
mmanuid[idm] = **jmanuid[idj]**;
mcost[idm] = **jcost[idj]**;
increment both **idj** and **idm**
increment **addedFromJones**
end the while loop for extra Jones products
return the total number in the new arrays, **idm**

The **MatchAcmeManuId()** function is very straightforward. It is given **manuid**[], **num**, **matchmanuid**. Its sequence is as follows.

for (**int j**=0; **j<num**; **j**++) do the following
if (**manuid[j]** == **matchmanuid**) then
simply **return j**, which is the subscript of the matching manufacturer id
end the for loop
return NoMatch;

The **RemoveJonesElement()** function must remove the data at the passed **thisone** subscript from the Jones arrays. It is passed **thisone**, **jid**[], **jqty**[], **jmanuid**[], **jcost**[] and **numJones**. The method of removal is to move all the elements above this one down one row in the arrays. Thus, it is a simple loop. The subscript of the last row in the arrays is **numJones – 1**.

for (**int j**=**thisone**; **j<numJones**–1; **j**++) {
jid[j] = **jid[j**+1];
jqty[j] = **jqty[j**+1];
jmanuid[j] = **jmanuid[j**+1];
jcost[j] = **jcost[j**+1];
end the for loop
lower the **numJones** count by one element

The **OutputArrays()** function must write the new master file. It is given **id**[], **qty**[], **manuid**[], **cost**[], **limit** and **outfile**. The sequence of steps is short.

setup floating point output format on outfile
for (int **i**=0; **i<limit**; **i**++) {
display to **outfile id[i]**, **qty[i]**, **manuid[i]** and **cost[i]**

Here are the log report and the merge error report produced when the program runs.

```
Cs10a - Merge Master Files - Output Log Report

Error: duplicate product ids: 111113
       Acme manufacturer id:  13223366
       Jones manufacturer id: 22323366

   2 Duplicate Jones manufacturer ids
   1 Duplicate product ids to be examined
  10 New products added from Jones
```

The Output file: MergeErrorLog.txt

```
Error: duplicate product ids: 111113
 Acme manufacturer id: 13223366
 Jones manufacturer id: 22323366
```

Here is the completed program, **Cs10a**. Notice how easy it is to convert the sketch into the actual program coding.

Cs10a - Merge Master Files

```
/***************************************************************/
/*                                                             */
/* Cs10a Merge Master Files                                    */
/*                                                             */
/***************************************************************/

#include <iostream>
#include <iomanip>
#include <fstream>
using namespace std;

const int MAX = 100;     // the maximum number of parts
const int NoMatch = -1;  // code for no match found

int LoadArrays  (long id[], int qty[], long manufid[],
                 double cost[], int limit, istream& infile);
int MergeArrays (long aid[], int aqty[], long amanuid[],
                 double acost[], int numAcme,
                 long jid[], int jqty[], long jmanuid[],
                 double jcost[], int& numJones,
                 long mid[], int mqty[], long mmanuid[],
                 double mcost[], int limit,
                 int& mergedcount, int& dupids,
                 int& addedFromJones, ostream& logfile);
int  MatchAcmeManuId (long manuid[], int num, long matchmanuid);
void RemoveJonesElement (int thisone, long jid[], int jqty[],
                         long jmanuid[], double jcost[],
                         int& numJones);
void OutputArrays (long id[], int qty[], long manuid[],
                   double cost[], int limit, ostream& outfile);

int main () {
 long   acmeId[MAX];     // the Acme master file data
 int    acmeQty[MAX];
 long   acmeManuId[MAX];
 double acmeCost[MAX];
 int    acmeNum;

```

```
long   jonesId[MAX];     // the Jones master file data
int    jonesQty[MAX];
long   jonesManuId[MAX];
double jonesCost[MAX];
int    jonesNum;

long   mergedId[MAX];    // the merged file data
int    mergedQty[MAX];
long   mergedManuId[MAX];
double mergedCost[MAX];
int    mergedNum;

// attempt to open both master files
ifstream acmein ("Cs10a-AcmeMaster.txt");
if (!acmein) {
 cerr << "Error: cannot open Cs10a-AcmeMaster.txt file\n";
 return 1;
}
ifstream jonesin("Cs10a-JonesMaster.txt");
if (!jonesin) {
 cerr << "Error: cannot open Cs10a-JonesMaster.txt file\n";
 acmein.close ();
 return 1;
}

// load both files of data
acmeNum = LoadArrays (acmeId, acmeQty, acmeManuId, acmeCost,MAX,
                      acmein);
acmein.close ();
jonesNum = LoadArrays (jonesId, jonesQty, jonesManuId,jonesCost,
                       MAX, jonesin);
jonesin.close ();

int mergedcount = 0;    // count of duplicate Jones products
int dupids = 0;         // count of duplicate product ids
int addedFromJones = 0;// count of new products added from Jones
ofstream logfile ("results-log.txt");

// merge both sets together, updating results counts
mergedNum = MergeArrays (
            acmeId, acmeQty, acmeManuId, acmeCost, acmeNum,
            jonesId, jonesQty, jonesManuId, jonesCost, jonesNum,
            mergedId, mergedQty, mergedManuId, mergedCost, MAX,
            mergedcount, dupids, addedFromJones, logfile);
ofstream outfile ("master-new.txt");

// write out new master file
OutputArrays (mergedId, mergedQty, mergedManuId, mergedCost,
              mergedNum, outfile);
outfile.close ();

// print final results to log file
logfile << endl << setw (4) << mergedcount
```

```
         << " Duplicate Jones manufacturer ids\n"
         << setw (4) << dupids
         << " Duplicate product ids to be examined\n"
         << setw (4) << addedFromJones
         << " New products added from Jones\n";
 logfile.close ();
 return 0;
}

/****************************************************************/
/*                                                              */
/* LoadArrays: input the data                                   */
/*                                                              */
/****************************************************************/

int LoadArrays  (long id[], int qty[], long manufid[],
                 double cost[], int limit, istream& infile) {
 int i = 0;
 while (i < limit &&
        infile >> id[i] >> qty[i] >> manufid[i] >> cost[i]) {
  i++;
 }
 if (i == limit && infile >> ws) {
  cerr << "Error: array bounds exceeded\n";
  exit (1);
 }
 // not checking for bad input data - these are production files
 return i;
}

/****************************************************************/
/*                                                              */
/* MergeArrays: merge the two arrays together but check for     */
/*         duplicate manufacturer id values - if found,         */
/*         add jones to acme                                    */
/*                                                              */
/****************************************************************/

int MergeArrays (
  long aid[], int aqty[], long amanuid[], double acost[],
  int numAcme,
  long jid[], int jqty[], long jmanuid[], double jcost[],
  int& numJones,
  long mid[], int mqty[], long mmanuid[], double mcost[],
  int limit,
  int& mergedcount, int& dupids, int& addedFromJones,
  ostream& logfile) {
 int ida = 0, idj = 0, idm = 0;
 // find all duplicate manufacturer id numbers and add Jones
 // into corresponding Acme qty and remove the dupe from Jones
 while (idj < numJones) {
  int match = MatchAcmeManuId (amanuid, numAcme, jmanuid[idj]);
  if (match >= 0) {          // found a duplicate
```

```
  aqty[match] += jqty[idj]; // add to Acme's qty
  RemoveJonesElement (idj, jid, jqty, jmanuid, jcost, numJones);
  mergedcount++;            // increment merged into Acme count
 }
 else idj++;
}
idj = 0;
// perform main merge of Jones and Acme into new arrays
// preserving sort order on product id array
while (ida < numAcme && idj < numJones) {
 if (aid[ida] < jid[idj]) {  // Acme prod id is smaller
  mid[idm] = aid[ida];       // copy over this Acme item
  mqty[idm] = aqty[ida];
  mmanuid[idm] = amanuid[ida];
  mcost[idm] = acost[ida];
  ida++;
  idm++;
 }
 else if (aid[ida] > jid[idj]) { // Jones prod id is smaller
  mid[idm] = jid[idj];           // copy over this Jones item
  mqty[idm] = jqty[idj];
  mmanuid[idm] = jmanuid[idj];
  mcost[idm] = jcost[idj];
  idj++;
  idm++;
  addedFromJones++;              // increment count of added ones
 }
 else {                          // error - duplicate prod ids
  mid[idm] = aid[ida];           // add in Acme's first
  mqty[idm] = aqty[ida];
  mmanuid[idm] = amanuid[ida];
  mcost[idm] = acost[ida];
  idm++;
  mid[idm] = jid[idj];           // add in Jones
  mqty[idm] = jqty[idj];
  mmanuid[idm] = jmanuid[idj];
  mcost[idm] = jcost[idj];
  idm++;
  // log an error message about these duplicate product ids
  logfile << "Error: duplicate product ids: " << aid[ida]
          << endl;
  logfile << "       Acme manufacturer id:  " << amanuid[ida]
          << endl;
  logfile << "       Jones manufacturer id: " << jmanuid[idj]
          << endl;
  dupids++;              // increment the duplicates count
  ida++;
  idj++;
 }
}
while (ida < numAcme) { // add in any left over Acme products
 mid[idm] = aid[ida];
 mqty[idm] = aqty[ida];
```

```
  mmanuid[idm] = amanuid[ida];
  mcost[idm] = acost[ida];
  ida++;
  idm++;
 }
 while (idj < numJones) { // add in any left over Jones products
  mid[idm] = jid[idj];
  mqty[idm] = jqty[idj];
  mmanuid[idm] = jmanuid[idj];
  mcost[idm] = jcost[idj];
  idj++;
  idm++;
  addedFromJones++;
 }
 // return the total number in the new arrays
 return idm;
}

/***************************************************************/
/*                                                             */
/* MatchAcmeManuId: match this jones manufacturer id to acme's */
/*                                                             */
/***************************************************************/

int  MatchAcmeManuId (long manuid[], int num, long matchmanuid) {
 for (int j=0; j<num; j++) {
  if (manuid[j] == matchmanuid) {
   return j; // return subscript of the matching manufacturer id
  }
 }
 return NoMatch;
}

/***************************************************************/
/*                                                             */
/* RemoveJonesElement: remove this one from jones arrays       */
/*                                                             */
/***************************************************************/

void RemoveJonesElement (int thisone, long jid[], int jqty[],
                         long jmanuid[], double jcost[],
                         int& numJones) {
 // move all elements down one
 for (int j=thisone; j<numJones-1; j++) {
  jid[j] = jid[j+1];
  jqty[j] = jqty[j+1];
  jmanuid[j] = jmanuid[j+1];
  jcost[j] = jcost[j+1];
 }
 numJones--; // reset the number of elements in the arrays
}

/***************************************************************/
```

```
/*                                                                  */
/* OutputArrays: rewrite the new master file                        */
/*                                                                  */
/********************************************************************/

void OutputArrays (long id[], int qty[], long manuid[],
                   double cost[], int limit, ostream& outfile) {
 // setup floating point output format
 outfile << fixed << setprecision (2);

 // write a new master file
 for (int i=0; i<limit; i++) {
  outfile << setw (10) << id[i]     << setw (10) << qty[i]
          << setw (10) << manuid[i] << setw (10) << cost[i]
          << endl;
 }
}
```

Section C: An Engineering Example

Engr10a—Statistical Computations

Single dimensioned arrays are often used in statistical applications. We have seen that determining the average, the highest and lowest values of an array are simple to calculate. If the array is subsequently sorted, the **mean value**, that is, the value in the middle, can be found. Given the average of a distribution, one can then calculate the **standard deviation** from the average, which represents the spread of the data about the average. If the data are tightly grouped about the mean, the deviation is small. The **variance** is defined to be the square of the deviation. The final statistic is the **coefficient of variance**, which is a ratio of the standard deviation to the mean often in the form of a percentage.

To find the median or middle value of a distribution, the values must be sorted into numerical order. If a distribution of values has N elements or values in it, then the median value is located at element N/2 if N is an odd number. Assume N is 3, then 3/2 yields subscript 1 for the median value. However, if N is an even number, say 4 for example, then N/2 yields a subscript of 2. But there are effectively two elements in the middle. Thus, if N is even, the median value must be the average of the two elements in the middle. For example, suppose that N is 4. The median would be the average of the values of the elements located at index 1 and 2. Thus, we have

median value is array[N/2] when N is odd
median value is (array[N/2] + array[(N–1)/2]) / 2. when N is even

The standard deviation from the mean or average is given by the formula

$$std\_dev = \sqrt{\frac{\sum_{i=1}^{N}(x_i - xmean)^2}{(N-1)}}$$

Here x_i is the ith observation and xmean is the mean or average value. Notice that the divisor is N–1. There is no such thing as a spread of values about a single point.

Our example this time comes from Electrical Engineering. The electrical resistance for a circuit element has been measured in the laboratory. The file **resist.txt** contains an unknown number of these measurements. The company wishes to publish its findings. The published value of the resistance is the mean of these values, but the standard deviation and coefficient of variance must be published as well, providing an estimate of the accuracy of this resistance value.

Engr10a provides a solution to this problem. The **main()** function calls **LoadArray()** first to input the values. Next, **SortArray()** is called to get them into order as required by the formula. Now the mean value can be found and the **FindStdDev()** function can be called to find the standard deviation from the mean. Then the results are printed. Since the problem is so similar to the coding samples presented in the Basic Section above, I have only reproduced the final program and results.

Engr10a - Statistics on a set of resistance observations

```
/***************************************************************/
/*                                                             */
/* Engr10a: Statistics on a set of resistance observations     */
/*      Finds the mean, std deviation, and                     */
/*      coefficient of variance                                */
/*                                                             */
/*                                                             */
/***************************************************************/

#include <iostream>
#include <iomanip>
#include <fstream>
#include <cmath>
using namespace std;

int    LoadArray (double resist[], int limit);
double FindAverage (const double resist[], int numpts);
void   SortResist (double resist[], int numpts);
double FindStdDev (const double resist[], int numpts,double avg);

const int MaxPts = 1000;

int main () {

 // setup floating point output format
 cout << fixed << setprecision (2);

 double resist[MaxPts]; // array of resistance values
 double mean;           // final resistance, the mean value
 double stdDev;         // standard deviation of the mean
 double cv;             // percentage coefficient of variance
 int    numpts;         // number of resistance values in array

 numpts = LoadArray (resist, MaxPts); // load resistance values
 double average = FindAverage (resist, numpts); // find average
 SortResist (resist, numpts);   // sort resistances low to high
 // find the median resistance
 if (numpts % 2) { // odd number of points
  mean = resist[numpts/2];
 }
 else { // even number of points
  mean = (resist[numpts/2] + resist[(numpts-1)/2]) / 2.;
 }
 stdDev = FindStdDev (resist, numpts, average);
 cv = (stdDev*stdDev) / mean * 100;  // find cv in percentage

 //display results
 cout << "Mean Resistance: " << setw (10) << mean   << " ohms\n";
 cout << "Std Deviation:   " << setw (10) << stdDev << endl;
 cout << "CV:              " << setw (10) << cv << '%' << endl;
```

```

 return 0;
}

/***************************************************************/
/*                                                             */
/* LoadArray: load an array of resistance values               */
/*    aborts program is file not found, too much data, bad data*/
/*                                                             */
/***************************************************************/

int LoadArray (double resist[], int limit) {
 ifstream infile;
 infile.open ("resist.txt", ios::in);
 if (!infile) {
  cerr << "Error: cannot open file resist.txt\n";
  exit (1);
 }
 int i = 0;
 while (i<limit && infile >> resist[i]) {
  i++;
 }
 if (i == limit && infile >> ws) {
  cerr << "Error: too many resistance values - maximum is "
       << limit << endl;
  infile.close ();
  exit (2);
 }
 infile.close ();
 if (!infile.eof() && infile.fail()) {
  cerr << "Error: bad data on line " << i+1 << endl;
  infile.close ();
  exit (2);
 }
 infile.close ();
 return i;
}

/***************************************************************/
/*                                                             */
/* SortResist: sorts the array into low to high order          */
/*                                                             */
/***************************************************************/

void SortResist (double resist[], int numpts) {
 int i, j;
 double temp;
 for (i=0; i<numpts-1; i++) {
  for (j=i+1; j<numpts; j++) {
   if (resist[j] < resist[i]) {
    temp = resist[i];
    resist[i] = resist[j];
    resist[j] = temp;
```

```
    }
   }
  }
 }

/***************************************************************/
/*                                                             */
/* FindAverage: finds the average resistance        r          */
/*                                                             */
/***************************************************************/

double FindAverage (const double resist[], int numpts) {
 double sum = 0;
 for (int i=0; i<numpts; i++) {
  sum += resist[i];
 }
 return sum / numpts;
}

/***************************************************************/
/*                                                             */
/* FindStdDev: finds the standard deviation from the average   */
/*             aborts the program if the number of points is 1 */
/*                                                             */
/***************************************************************/

double FindStdDev (const double resist[], int numpts,
                   double avg) {
 // guard against a no solution
 if (numpts == 1) {
  cerr <<
    "Error: data has only one point, cannot calculate std dev\n";
  exit (3);
 }
 double dev;
 double factor;
 double sum = 0;
 // compute the sum of the square of the differences
 for (int i=0; i<numpts; i++) {
  factor = resist[i] - avg;
  sum += factor * factor;
 }
 // calculate the std dev
 dev = sqrt (sum / (numpts - 1));
 return dev;
}
```

The **resist.txt** file contains these data:

128.35
130.44
129.33
128.75
129.22

130.21
128.56
129.45
129.88
129.12

The program produces these results:

```
Mean Resistance:      129.28 ohms
Std Deviation:          0.69
CV:                     0.37%
```

Least Squares Curve Fitting

Perhaps one of the most important numerical analysis tools is least squares curve fitting, a process that determines the best fitting straight line to a set of observational data. Plotting a "best fit" curve to data is an important facet of research. It is done by regression analysis; one postulates a mathematical model that will model the data and by regression find the set of coefficients that will minimize some measurement of the deviation from that model—the best fit for that model. Often the model is a linear one; straight lines are the easiest to utilize:

$$y = f(x) = ax + b$$

Linear regression is used to find the best set of a and b values such that the square of the distances between the line and the observed data is minimized. The raw data consists of points (x_1,y_1), (x_2,y_2), ... (x_n,y_n)—for a total of n sets. We wish to minimize the distances (d) of the observed points from the theoretical line.

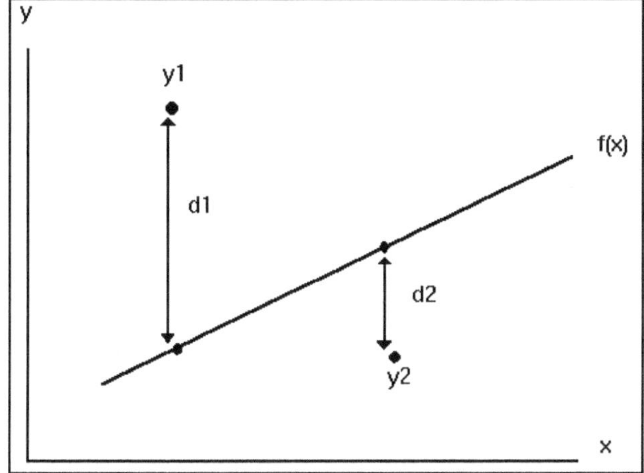

Figure 10.3 Least Squares Derivation

The formula for the distance d is:

$$d = y - f(x) = y - (ax + b)$$

d = y – ax – b

We wish to minimize these distances. But if we just sum the distances, some are likely positive and some negative. They would tend to cancel each other out leaving us with an incorrect measurement. Instead, we minimize the squares of the distances. This is shown in Figure 10.3.

The total error E is then the sum of all distances squared is given by

$$E = \sum_{k=1}^{N} d_k^2$$

Substituting for d, we get

$$E = \sum_{k=1}^{N} (y_k - ax_k - b)^2$$

How do we minimize E? Use differential calculus to get the partial derivatives of E with respect to the two unknown coefficients a and b. A minimum of a function occurs when the derivative is 0.

$$\frac{dE}{da} = -2\sum_{k=1}^{N} x_k(y_k - ax_k - b)$$

$$\frac{dE}{db} = -2\sum_{k=1}^{N} (y_k - ax_k - b)$$

Set these two equations to 0 and reduce and rearrange to get

$$a\sum_{k=1}^{N} x_k^2 + b\sum_{k=1}^{N} x_k = \sum_{k=1}^{N} x_k y_k$$

$$a\sum_{k=1}^{N} x_k + bN = \sum_{k=1}^{N} y_k$$

Thus, we have two equations in two unknowns. Using Cramer's Rule to solve for a and b, we get the following values.

$$a = \frac{N\sum_{k=1}^{N} x_k y_k - \sum_{k=1}^{N} x_k \sum_{k=1}^{N} y_k}{N\sum_{k=1}^{N} x_k^2 - \left(\sum_{k=1}^{N} x_k\right)^2}$$

$$b = \frac{\sum_{k=1}^{N} y_k \sum_{k=1}^{N} x_k^{\,2} - \sum_{k=1}^{N} x_k \sum_{k=1}^{N} x_k y_k}{N \sum_{k=1}^{N} x_k^{\,2} - \left(\sum_{k=1}^{N} x_k \right)^2}$$

Thus, given a set of observations, we can find the best fitting curve rather easily. This theory is used in several problems below.

Design Exercises

1. Reverse Order

Acme Corporation has a **master.txt** file of item numbers and their corresponding costs. The file has been sorted into ascending order on the item numbers. However, in order to compare their items with a competitor, the printout must be in high to low order based on the item numbers. Management does not want to spend the computer time actually to resort the file because it is a very large one. Write a program that inputs the **long** item numbers and **float** costs into two arrays that can handle a maximum of 10,000 items. Then print the report listing the item number and associated cost.

2. Statistical Study of a Car's Mpg (miles per gallon)

For 36 months, a record has been kept of gas station fill-ups. Specifically, the driver logged the date (mm-dd-yyyy), the odometer reading in miles and the number of gallons of gas it took to fill the car. It is postulated that one can use the average monthly mile per gallons (mpg) figures to determine when the car needs maintenance. That is, when the mpg decreases substantially, it is indicative of at least a tuneup being required. Write a program to prove or disprove the theory.

Input the **log.txt** file whose lines consist of the date, the mileage, and the number of gallons. For each line, calculate the mpg. Accumulate the mpg figures until the month changes and then find that month's average mpg. Store that month's average mpg into an array, which can hold up to 36 values. The very first line of the file is special. It represents the very first full tank of gas, so no average can be calculated for this entry.

Now print a report listing each month's average mpg and print a ** beside that mpg, which is more than 20% different from the previous month. The report might appear like this.

```
Avg Monthly Mpg
    35.6
    36.5
    25.5 **
    34.5 **
    33.9
```

Stop! Do These Exercises Before Programming

1. Acme National Sales expanded and their parallel arrays of state codes and corresponding tax rates have grown larger. The programmer has coded the following to load the tables. Why does it not work? What must be done to fix the coding so that the tables are correctly loaded?

```
const int MaxLimit = 50;
int LoadArrays (int stateCode[], taxRate[], int limit);
int main () {
 double taxRate[50];
 int stateCode[50];
 int numValues;
 LoadArrays (stateCode, taxRate, 50);
 ...
int LoadArrays (int stateCode[], taxRate[], int limit) {
 ...// gets infile opened
 int j=0;
 while (infile >> stateCode[limit] >> taxRate[limit])
  j++;
 infile.close();
 return limit;
}
```

2. With the arrays loaded, the programmer embarked on the writing of a sort function to get the state codes in numerical order for faster table look ups within the main program. The following function is to sort the state codes into increasing numerical order. It does not work properly. Why? How can it be fixed up?

```
void SortStateCodes (int state[], int limit) {
 int j, k, temp;
 for (j=0; j<limit; j++) {
  for (k=j; k<limit; k++) {
   state[j] = temp;
   temp = state[k];
   state[k] = state[j];
  }
 }
}
```

3. Now that the states are sorted successfully, the programmer realized that the tax rates needed to be sorted as well. Tired at the end of a long day, he produced the following patch to his program. Assume that the **SortTaxRates()** function now works perfectly.

```
const int MaxLimit = 50;
int LoadArrays (int stateCode[], taxRate[], int limit);
void SortStateCodes (int states[], int limit);
void SortTaxRates (double rates[], int limit);
int main () {
 double taxRate[MaxLimit];
 int stateCode[MaxLimit];
 ...
 SortStateCodes (stateCode, numValues);
 SortTaxRates (taxrate, numValues);
 ...
```

When he tested the program, all of the taxes were completely wrong. What is wrong with the design of the entire sorting method? How can it be fixed? Write the sorting code that would enable the program, given a state code, find the correct tax rate. (However, do not write any table look up coding.)

4. Grateful for your assistance in bailing him out of his coding mess yesterday, the programmer today has embarked upon construction of a fast matching function that is given the two arrays and the number of elements in it and returns the tax rate. This is what has been produced thus far.

```
double FindTaxRate (int states[], double rates[], int num,
                    int findState) {
 int j = 0;
 double taxRate;
 while (j<num) {
  if (findState == states[num]) {
   taxRate = rates[j];
  }
  j++;
 }
 return taxRate;
}
```

The function has serious design flaws and of course does not work properly. Why? What must be done to correct this coding so that it produces the correct taxes in all circumstances?

5. Looking over Problem 4 just above, the **FindTaxRate()** function does not in any way make use of the fact that the state codes are sorted into numerical order. Using a binary search function would provide the speed up desired. Assume that the **BinarySearch()** function presented earlier in this chapter has been rewritten using an array of **int**s instead of **long**s. Rewrite the **FindTaxRate()** function above to use the **BinarySearch()** in finding the tax rate to return.

Programming Problems

Problem Cs10-1—Array Manipulations

The included file **Cs10-1.cpp** provides the **main()** function and some helper functions that enable it to thoroughly test your coding. In this problem, you are going to practice various array manipulations. You are to write each of the six functions described below. Do NOT define any additional arrays inside your functions; work only with the array(s) passed as the argument(s).

1. Write the **LoadData()** function whose prototype is

```
int LoadData (istream &infile, int array[], int arraySize,
              int &count);
```

The **LoadData()** function reads integers from the passed stream and loads them into the successive elements of the array passed as the second argument. The third argument specifies the size of the array (number of elements). The function loads data into the array until the array is full or the end of the file is reached, whichever occurs first. The function assigns the count of integers stored into the array to the fourth argument. The function must not overflow the boundary of the array or read any more data after the array is full. The function returns a status code: 0 if the whole input file is successfully loaded into the array, 1 if the input file is too large to fully load into the array (the array is full but there are more data in the file), or –1 if there is invalid (non-integer) data in the input file. In all cases, the **count** parameter must be assigned the correct count of numbers stored in the array.

2. Write the **List()** function whose prototype is

```
void List (const int array[], int count);
```

The **List()** function prints the numbers in the array passed as the first argument; the second argument is the count of numbers in the array. Print each number in a three-column field and print a newline character after each set of twenty numbers. After all the numbers are printed, print one blank line.

3. Write the **CopyArray()** function whose prototype is

```
void CopyArray (int destArray[], const int srcArray[], int count);
```

The **Copy()** function copies the contents of one array to another. The first argument is the destination array and the second argument is the source array. The third argument specifies the number of elements to copy.

4. Write the **RotateLeft()** function whose prototype is

```
void RotateLeft (int array[], int count);
```

The **RotateLeft()** function shifts each number in the array, except the first, one element to the "left" (the element with the next lower subscript). The first number in the array is shifted to the last element in the array.

5. Write the **RotateRight()** function whose prototype is

```
void RotateRight (int array[], int count);
```

The **RotateRight()** function shifts each number in the array, except the last, one element to the "right" (the element with the next higher subscript). The last number in the array is shifted to the first element. (Note: you can **RotateRight()** by repeating **RotateLeft()** for count – 1 times. However, this is extremely inefficient. Use an efficient method for rotating to the right; do not repeatedly rotate the array to left.)

6. Write the **Reverse()** function whose prototype is

```
void Reverse (int array[], int count);
```

The **Reverse()** function reverses the sequence of the numbers in the array. (Note: you can reverse an array by repeating **RotateLeft()** or **RotateRight()** for **count** – 1 times, while at the same time decreasing the count after each repetition. However, this is extremely inefficient. Use an efficient method for reversing; do not repeatedly rotate the array.)

Test your program on the provided test files **Cs10-1a.txt**, **Cs10-1b.txt**, **Cs10-1c.txt**, **Cs10-1d.txt** and **Cs10-1e.txt**. Here are the outputs you should get (I have single-spaced the output to reduce lines here in the book.)

```
Enter input file name: CS10-1a.txt

status = 0  count = 9

load:      99 88 77 66 55 44 33 22 11
copy:      99 88 77 66 55 44 33 22 11
left:      88 77 66 55 44 33 22 11 99
right:     11 99 88 77 66 55 44 33 22
reverse:   11 22 33 44 55 66 77 88 99

Enter input file name: CS10-1b.txt

status = 0  count = 20

load:       1  2  3  4  5  6  7  8  9 10 11 12 13 14 15 16 17 18 19 20
copy:       1  2  3  4  5  6  7  8  9 10 11 12 13 14 15 16 17 18 19 20
left:       2  3  4  5  6  7  8  9 10 11 12 13 14 15 16 17 18 19 20  1
right:     20  1  2  3  4  5  6  7  8  9 10 11 12 13 14 15 16 17 18 19
reverse:   20 19 18 17 16 15 14 13 12 11 10  9  8  7  6  5  4  3  2  1

Enter input file name: CS10-1c.txt

status = 1  count = 20

load:       2  4  6  8 10 12 14 16 18 20 22 24 26 28 30 32 34 36 38 40
copy:       2  4  6  8 10 12 14 16 18 20 22 24 26 28 30 32 34 36 38 40
left:       4  6  8 10 12 14 16 18 20 22 24 26 28 30 32 34 36 38 40  2
right:     40  2  4  6  8 10 12 14 16 18 20 22 24 26 28 30 32 34 36 38
reverse:   40 38 36 34 32 30 28 26 24 22 20 18 16 14 12 10  8  6  4  2

Enter input file name:CS10-1d.txt

status = -1  count = 5

load:      90 80 70 60 50
copy:      90 80 70 60 50
```

```
left:       80 70 60 50 90
right:      50 90 80 70 60
reverse:    50 60 70 80 90
```

Problem Cs10-2—Acme Sales Summary

The Acme has a master file, **Cs10-2-master.txt**, that contains the information on all the products that they sell. Each line represents a specific product and includes an item number and the cost. Item numbers can be up to six digits long. The file is in increasing item number order. Allow for a maximum of 500 products.

Each day, Acme stores all of their daily sales in the **Cs10-2-transactions.txt** file. It includes the invoice number (up to nine digits), the product id (the item number) and the quantity ordered.

After loading the master file of data, input each transaction line, and calculate the total cost of that order and print it nicely formatted. When you reach the end of the transaction file, display the grand total sales figure beneath the total cost column. The report should look something like this.

```
                 Acme Sales Summary

Invoice     Product Id     Quantity     Unit         Total
                                        Cost         Cost
999999999    999999          999     $999999.99  $999999.99
999999999    999999          999     $999999.99  $999999.99
                                                 ----------
                                                $9999999.99
```

Note that you need parallel arrays for the item number and cost arrays. In addition, the match function should take advantage of the fact that the file is sorted into item number order.

If a given product id cannot be found in the master file, print that invoice, id, and quantity as usual in the report, but instead of printing the cost, display “error” in the cost column.

Problem Cs10-3—Acme Sales Inventory Update

Continuing work with the Acme master file described in Problem **Cs10-2**, each week Acme adds new products to their line. Occasionally, they drop a line of products. The file **Cs10-3-update.txt** contains the week's purchasing transactions.

The first character on each update transaction line contains an uppercase letter that describes this transaction. If the character is 'A', then this is an 'add new product' transaction and the next two numbers represent the product id and its cost. If the character is a 'D', then this is a deletion request and the next number is the product id.

Write a program to perform this master file update process. When processing an add request, insert that product id and its cost into the correct position in the sorted arrays. When processing a deletion request, remove that product id and its cost from the arrays.

Your program should produce a **log.txt** file of the requested transaction and its results, similar to the following.

```
Acme Weekly Update Master File Log

Action   Product Id      Cost    Result
  A        123434      444.44    Success
  A        123434      444.44    Error: duplicate product id
  D        234444                Removed
```

Finally, when the update transactions have all been processed, output the new modified master file (call it **master-new.txt**). For debugging purposes, also print the contents of the two arrays in columnar format.

Problem Cs10-4—Grade Statistics

Write a program that calculates the results of a test. Sample output is shown below. Each line of input contains a student identification number and a test score. The identification number is a one to nine digit whole number; the test score may contain a decimal point. The input file may contain from zero to fifty students. Write separate functions as follows:

1. The **ReadInput()** function reads the input file, counts the number of students and stores all the identification numbers and test scores in two arrays.

2. The **OutputReport()** function prints the report. Notice that the program prints one asterisk for students who made a B on the test, and prints two asterisks for students who made an A on the test.

3. The **AverageScore()** function finds and returns the average test score in the array of test scores; the function does not read any input or write any output.

4. The **HighScore()** function finds and returns the highest test score in the array of test scores; the function does not read any input or write any output.

5. The **LetterGrade()** function is passed two arguments: an individual test score (not an array) and the group average. The function returns the student's letter grade according to this scale:
A = 20 points or more above average
B = 10 or more but less than 20 points above average
C = less than 10 points above or below the average
D = 10 or more but less than 20 points below average
F = 20 points or more below average

6. The **main()** function simply calls the other functions; **main()** does not perform any input, calculations, or output. Test your program using each of the provided data files: **Cs10-4a.txt**, **Cs10-4b.txt** and **Cs10-4c.txt**. Write the grade report to a disk output file. Input the file names from the keyboard at run-time. Print both the screen output and the file output.

```
Average score = 75.00
Highest score = 100.00

      ID           SCORE    GRADE

   100000000       54.00      F
   100000001       70.00      C
   111111111       65.00      D
  *200000000       89.00      B
   200000001       55.00      F
   222222222       72.00      C
   300000000       66.00      C
 **300000003       96.00      A
   333333333       50.00      F
 **400000000       95.00      A
   400000001       76.00      C
  *400000004       85.00      B
  *444444444       94.00      B
   500000000       84.00      C
   500000001       80.00      C
   500000005       59.00      D
   555555555       74.00      C
   600000000       61.00      D
   600000001       56.00      D
 **600000006      100.00      A
  *666666666       94.00      B
```

Problem Engr10-1—Other Statistical Means

There are three other statistical means that are sometimes used. These include the geometric mean, the harmonic mean and the root-mean-square (RMS) average. They are given by the following formulas.

$$GeometricMean = \sqrt[N]{x_1 * x_2 * x_3 * \ldots x_N}$$

$$HarmonicMean = \frac{N}{\frac{1}{x_1} + \frac{1}{x_2} + \frac{1}{x_3} + \ldots + \frac{1}{x_N}}$$

$$RMS\_Average = \sqrt{\frac{1}{N} \sum_{i=1}^{N} x_i^2}$$

Write a program to calculate the average, mean, standard deviation from the mean, geometric mean, harmonic mean, and RMS average. Use the **resist.txt** data file from program **Engr10a**. Format the results similar to **Engr10a**.

Problem Engr10-2—Random Distributions

C++ has a function that generates random numbers. However, the random number generator required an initial seed value. For any given seed value, the sequence of numbers generated are always the same. If a program desires truly random integer numbers each time the program executes, the seed value must be different for each run of the program. Programmers often use the computer's time of day clock to create the initial seed value because it would be very unlikely to launch the program at precisely the same second on two successive runs. The random function is called **rand()** and the seed function is **srand()**. Both functions' prototypes are in **<iostream>**. Calling the **time()** function with a parameter of 0 results in the current time of day being returned; its prototype is in **<ctime>**. The seed value is normally given only once per run of the program. The following sets the seed to the current time and then generates 10 random numbers.

```
#include <iostream>
#include <ctime>
using namespace std;
int main () {
 srand ((unsigned) time (0)); // current time as seed
 for (int j=0; j<10; j++)
 cout << rand () << endl;
 return 0;
}
```

Game designers often require a random die roll. Engineering applications sometimes need a set of random values within a specified range. To create a random die roll on a 6-sided die, use **(rand() % 6) + 1** to generate numbers between 1 and 6, for example.

Write a program that inputs a specific unsigned seed value, generates the first 1,000 random numbers between 0 and 10 based on that seed. The question to explore is "for a specific seed, are these numbers truly random?" Create a frequency count array of 11 elements initialized to 0. For each of the 1,000 random numbers, increment the corresponding frequency count as the random number is found. For example, if the random number is 3, then add one to the frequency count of subscript 3.

If the distribution were truly random, one might expect to see all frequency counts approximately the same value, if the sample size is sufficiently large. Calculate the average and standard deviation of the frequency counts. The theoretical average for random numbers in the range (0, 10) is 5. The theoretical standard deviation is .289.

The program should output the seed used, the average, the standard deviation and then the frequency counts for all 11 values. Caution, the standard deviation requires that the array be sorted. Thus, before calling the sort function, copy the frequency array into a new temporary array and use the temporary array to sort and to find the standard deviation. Keep the original frequency array so that the original values may be printed.

Run the program using 5 different seed values. Does the seed value affect the results?

Problem Engr10-3—Least Squares Curve Fitting

The resistance characteristics of a given thermistor can be found by placing it on an oven, setting the oven at various known temperatures, and measuring the resistance of the thermistor at each of the known temperatures. This was done for a series of temperatures. The data, pairs of temperature and resistance, are

```
100 25580
120 14430
140  8576
160  5328
180  3446
200  2308
220  1578
240  1132
260   826
280   616
300   469
```

Assuming that temperature is the independent variable, write a program to find the best linear fit. Print the results, slope and intercept, nicely formatted. Then, modify the **Plot()** function from Chapter 10 to plot two sets of data. Use '*' characters to represent the observed data and use the 'x' character to represent the least squares best-fit curve. Using your best fit solution, calculate the resistance at the same temperatures as the original data and pass these as the second array pair to **Plot()**.

Problem Engr10-4—Exponential Curves and Least Squares Best Fitting Lines

In the previous problem **Engr10-3**, the best fitting straight line is not a good fit because the thermistor resistance versus temperature is not linear. Rather, it is exponential in nature. Thus, fitting an exponential curve to the observed data yields a better result. The general exponential curve to use is given by

$$R = be^{mT}$$

However, an examination of the data shows that the simple slope intercept method will fail because the curve never reaches the x axis; it is asymptotic at around 100 ohms. In such cases, one can employ the trick of converting to x versus log y space—that is, plot the graph using x and log y. If the data were asymptotic to both axises, one could try a plot in log x versus log y space. In other words, we plot x as before, but use log y for each y value.

Rewrite the least squares best-fit program to find the best fitting straight line in x versus log y space. As you input the Y data points, take the log of them. When plotting the two graphs, plot log (y) instead of y values for the vertical axis.

Chapter 11—Strings

Section A: Basic Theory

Defining Character Strings

A character string in C++, such as "Hello World," is stored in an array of characters with an extra byte on the end marking the end of the string. This extra end of string marker is called the null terminator and consists of a byte whose value is zero, that is, all the bits are zero. In C++, nearly all strings ever used are null-terminated. However, the language provides for non-null terminated strings as well. But, in C++, unlike C, these are seldom used.

Suppose for example that you used the string literal value "Sam." We know that if we had written

```
cout << "Sam";
```

then the output stream displays

```
Sam
```

But how does the computer know how long the literal string is and where it ends? The answer is that the literal "Sam" is a null-terminated string consisting of four bytes containing 'S', 'a', 'm', and 0. This null-terminator can be represented by a numerical 0 or by the escape sequence \0. Most all of the C++ functions that take a character string as an argument expect that string to be null-terminated.

The null-terminator marks the end of the characters in the variable. For example, suppose that a variable is defined to hold a person's name as follows

```
char name[21];
```

This definition is saying that the maximum number of characters that can be stored is twenty plus one for the null-terminator. This maximum length is different from the number of characters actually stored when a person's name is entered. For example, assume that the program has inputted the name as follows

```
cin >> name;
```

Assume that the user has entered "Sam" from the keyboard. In this instance, only four of the possible twenty-one are in use with the null terminator in the 4th character. Make sure you understand the distinction between the maximum size of a string and the actual size in a specific instance.

When defining a string variable, it makes good programming sense not to hard-code the array bounds but to use a **const int**, just as is done with other kinds of arrays. Thus, the **name** variable ought to have been coded like this

```
const int NAMELENGTH = 21;
int main () {
 char name[NAMELENGTH];
```

If later you decide that twenty character names are too short, it is a simple matter of changing the constant value and recompiling.

When character string variables are defined, they can also be initialized. However, two forms are possible. Assume that when the name variable is defined, it should be given the value of "Sam." Following the initialization syntax for any other kind of array, one could code

```
char name[NAMELENGTH] = {'S', 'a', 'm', '\0'};
```

Here each specific character is assigned its starting value; do not fail to include the null terminator. However, the compiler allows a string to be initialized with another literal string as follows

```
char name[NAMELENGTH] = "Sam";
```

Clearly this second form is much more convenient.

With all forms of arrays, when defining and initializing an array, it is permissible to omit the array bounds and let the compiler determine how many elements the array must have based on the number of initial values you provide. Thus, the following is valid.

```
char name[] = "Sam";
```

However, in general, this approach is lousy programming style and error prone. Why? In the above case, the compiler allocates an array just large enough to hold the literal "Sam." That is, the **name** array is only four characters long. What would happen if later on one attempted to input another name that needed more characters? Disaster. Always provide the array bounds whenever possible.

Inputting Character Strings

Using the Extraction Operator

The extraction operator can be used to input character strings. The specific rules of string extraction follow those for the other data types we have covered. It skips over whitespace to the first non-whitespace character, inputs successive characters storing them into successive bytes in the array until the extraction operator encounters whitespace or the end of file. Lastly, it stores the null terminator. Two aspects of this input operation frequently make the use of the extraction operator useless.

Notice that the extraction operator does not permit a blank to be in the string. Suppose that you prompted the user to input their name and age and then used **cin** to input them as follows

```
cin >> name >> age;
```

What results if the user enters the following data?

```
Sam Spade  25
```

The input stream goes into the bad or fail state. It inputs the characters "Sam" and stores them along with the trailing null-terminator into the **name** field. It skips over the blank, attempts to input the character S of Spade into the **age** integer, and goes immediately into the bad state. If you reflect upon all the different kinds of strings that you might encounter in the real world of programming (names, product descriptions, addresses, cities), the vast majority may have embedded blanks in them. This rules out the extraction operation as a method of inputting them.

The other part of the extraction operator rules is quite destructive, especially if you are running on the Windows 95/98 platform. It inputs all characters until it finds whitespace or EOF. Now suppose that the field **name** is defined to be an array of 21 characters. What happens if in response to the prompt to enter a name, the user enters the following name.

```
Rumplestillskinchevskikov
```

The computer attempts to store 26 characters into an array that is only 21 characters long. Four bytes of memory are now overlaid. What happens next is unpredictable. If another variable in your program occupies that overlaid memory, its contents are trashed. If that memory is not even part of your program, but is part of some other program, such as a Windows system dll, it is overlaid; even wilder things can happen! Under Windows NT/2000, if you attempt to overlay memory that is not part of your data segment, the program is aborted instead. This is one reason for so many system crashes under Windows 95/98.

One way to get around the extraction operator's disadvantages is to use either the **get()** or **getline()** function. The **get()** function can be used in one of two ways. Note: while I am using **cin** in these examples, any **ifstream** instance can be used as well.

```
cin.get (string variable, sizeof (string variable));
cin.get (string variable, sizeof (string variable),
         delimiter character);
```

These input all characters from the current position in the stream until either the maximum number of characters including the null terminator has been read or EOF or the delimiter is found. By default the delimiter is a new line code. The delimiter is **not** extracted but remains in the input stream.

```
cin.getline (string variable, sizeof (string variable));
cin.getline (string variable, sizeof (string variable),
             delimiter character);
```

This function works the same way except the delimiter **is** removed from the input stream but never stored in the string variable. It also defaults to the new line code.

Method A—All Strings Have the Same Length

This is a common situation. In the input set of data or file, all character strings are the same length, the maximum. Shorter strings have blanks added onto the end of the character series to fill out the maximum length. Assume that a cost record input set of data contains the item number, quantity, description and cost fields. The program defines the input fields as follows.

```
const int DescrLimit = 21;
long   itemnumber;
long   quantity;
char   description[DescrLimit];
double cost;
```

The **description** field can hold up to twenty characters plus one for the null terminator. The input set of data would appear as

```
12345   10 Pots and Pans        14.99
34567  101 Cups                  5.99
```

```
45667    3 Silverware, Finished 10.42
```

Notice how the shorter strings are padded with blanks so that in all circumstances the **description** field is 20 characters long.

The data is then input this way.

```
infile >> itemnumber >> quantity >> ws;
infile.get (description, sizeof (description));
infile >> cost;
```

Observe that the first line ends by skipping over whitespace to position the input stream to the first character of the description field. **sizeof()** always returns the number of bytes the variable occupies. In the case of the **description** field, it yields twenty-one. If one used **sizeof(quantity)**, it would return four bytes, since longs occupy four bytes. One could also use the constant integer **DescrLimit** instead of the **sizeof()**; this subtle difference will be important shortly.

Many company input data files are set up in this manner. What is input and stored in the **description** field when the second line of data above is input? The **description** contains: "Cups   "—that is, the characters C-u-p-s followed by sixteen blanks and then the null terminator.

There is one drawback to this method. The blanks are stored. Shortly we will see how character strings can be compared to see if two contain the same values. Clearly, if we compared this description to the literal "Cups," the two would not be equal. Can you spot why? The inputted description contains sixteen blanks that the literal does not contain! Thus, if the trailing blanks are going to present a problem to the processing logic of the program, they need to be removed. On the other hand, if the description field is only going to be displayed, the presence of the blanks is harmless.

With a few lines of coding, the blanks can be removed. The idea is to begin at the end of the string and if that byte contains a blank, back up another byte until a byte that is non-blank is found. Then place a null terminator in the last blank position. Since the length of all strings must be twenty characters (after the **get()** function is done, the null terminator is in the twenty-first position), the location of the last byte that contains real data must be subscript 19. The null terminator must be at subscript 20. The following coding can be used to remove the blanks at the end, if any.

```
int index = DescrLimit - 2; // or 19
while (index >= 0 && description[index] == ' ')
 index--;
// here index = subscript of the first non-blank char
index++;
description[index] = 0; // insert a null-terminator
                        // over last blank a '\0' or 0
```

If the **description** contains all blanks or if the string contains a non-blank character in the 20th position, this coding still works well.

The main problem to consider when inputting strings with the **get()** function is handling the detection of the end of file properly. We are used to seeing coding such as

```
while (cin >> itemnumber >> quantity) {
```

But in this case, the input operation cannot be done with one chained series of extraction operators. Rather, it is broken into three separate statements. Consider replacing the three lines of coding with a new user helper function.

```
while (GetData (infile, itemnumber, quantity,
                description, cost, DescrLimit)) {
```

The function would be

```
istream& GetData (istream& infile, long& itemnumber,
                  long& quantity, char description[],
                  double& cost, int descrLimit) {
 infile >> itemnumber >> quantity >> ws;
 if (!infile) return infile;
 infile.get (description, descrLimit);
 if (!infile) return infile;
 infile >> cost;
 if (!infile) return infile;
 int index = descrLimit - 2;
 while (index >= 0 && description[index] == ' ')
  index--;
 index++;
 description[index] = 0;
 return infile;
}
```

Vitally important is that the number of bytes to use in the **get()** function this time is not **sizeof(description)**. Why? Within the function, the **description** is the memory address of where the first element of the array of characters is located. Memory addresses are always four bytes in size on a 32-bit platform. Thus, had we used **sizeof(description)**, then 4 bytes would have been the limit!

Method A, where all strings are the same length, also applies to data files that have more than one string in a line of data. Consider a customer data line, which contains the customer number, name, address, city, state, and zip code. Here three strings potentially contain blanks, assuming the state is a two-digit abbreviation. Thus, Method A is commonly used.

Method B – String Contains Only the Needed Characters, But Is the Last Field on a Line

In certain circumstances, the string data field is the last item on the input data line. If so, it can contain just the number of characters it needs. Assume that the cost record data were reorganized as shown (<CRLF> indicates the enter key).

```
12345   10 14.99 Pots and Pans<CRLF>
34567  101  5.99 Cups<CRLF>
45667    3 10.42 Silverware, Finished<CRLF>
```

This data can be input more easily as follows.

```
infile >> itemnumber >> quantity >> cost >> ws;
infile.get (description, sizeof (description));
```

Alternately, the **getline()** function could also be used. There are no excess blanks on the end of the descriptions to be removed. It is simpler. However, its use is limited because many data entry lines contain more than one string and it is often impossible to reorganize a company's data files just to put the string at the end of the data entry lines.

Method B works well when prompting the user to enter a single string. Consider the action of asking the user to enter a filename for the program to use for input. Note on the **open** function call for input, we can use the **ios::in** flag, and for output, we use the **ios::out** flag.

```
char filename[_MAX_PATH];
cin.getline (filename, sizeof(filename));
ifstream infile;
infile.open (filename, ios::in);
```

When dealing with filenames, one common problem to face is just how many characters long should the **filename** array actually be? The compiler provides a **#define** of **_MAX_PATH** (in the header file **<iostream>**) that contains the platform specific maximum length a complete path could be. For Windows 95, that number is 256 bytes.

Method C—All strings Are Delimited

The problem that we are facing is knowing where a string actually ends because a blank is not usually a good delimiter. Sometimes quote marks are used to surround the string data. Here a " mark begins and ends a string. Suppose that the input data appeared as follows.

```
12345   10 "Pots and Pans" 14.99
34567  101 "Cups" 5.99
45667    3 "Silverware, Finished" 10.42
```

When a string is delimited, the data can be input rather easily if we use the alternate form of the **get()** function, supplying the delimiter '\"'.

```
char junk;
infile >> itemnumber >> quantity >> junk;
infile.get (description, sizeof (description), '\"');
infile >> junk >> cost;
```

Notice that we must input the beginning quote mark. The **get()** function leaves the delimiter in the input stream, so we must extract it before continuing on with the next field, **cost**.

On the other hand, the **getline()** function removes the delimiter. Coding becomes simpler.

```
char junk;
infile >> itemnumber >> quantity >> junk;
infile.getline (description, DescrLimit, '\"');
infile >> cost;
```

Outputting Character Strings

Outputting strings presents a different set of problems, ones of spacing and alignment. In most all cases, the insertion operator handles the output of strings quite well. In the most basic form one might output a line of the cost record as follows

```
     cout << setw (10) << itemnumber
          << setw (10) << quantity
          << description
          << setw (10) << cost << endl;
```

If the entire program output consisted of one line, the above is fine. Usually, the output consists of many lines, columnarly aligned. If so, the above fails utterly.

With a string, the insertion operator outputs all of the characters up to the null terminator. It does not output the null terminator. With strings of varying length, there is going to be an unacceptable jagged right edge in the description column. On the other hand, if Method A was used to input the strings and all strings are of the same length, all is well until the **setw()** function is used to define the total field width. Suppose that the **description** field should be displayed within a width of thirty columns. One might be tempted to code

```
     cout << setw (10) << itemnumber
          << setw (10) << quantity
          << setw (30) << description
          << setw (10) << cost << endl;
```

The default field alignment of an **ostream** is right alignment. All of our numeric fields display perfectly this way. But when right alignment is used on character strings, the results are usually not acceptable as shown below

```
     12345    10                 Pots and Pans 14.99
     34567   101                          Cups  5.99
     45667     3         Silverware, Finished 10.42
```

Left alignment must be used when displaying strings. Right alignment must be used when displaying numerical data. The alignment is easily changed by using the **setf()** function.

```
     cout << setw (10) << itemnumber
          << setw (10) << quantity;
     cout.setf (ios::left, ios::adjustfield);
     cout << setw (30) << description;
     cout.setf (ios::right, ios::adjustfield);
     cout << setw (10) << cost << endl;
```

In the call to **setf()**, the second parameter **ios::adjustfield** clears all the justification flags—that is, turns them off. Then left justification is turned on. Once the string is output, the second call to **setf()** turns right justification back on for the other numerical data. It is vital to use the **ios::adjustfield** second parameter. The Microsoft implementation of the **ostream** contains two flags, one for left and one for right justification. If the left justification flag is on, then left justification occurs. Since there are two separate flags, when setting justification, failure to clear all the flags can lead to the weird circumstance in which both left and right justification flags are on. Now you have left-right justification (a joke)—from now on, the output is hopelessly messed up justification-wise.

Alternatively, one can use the much more convenient manipulator functions: **`left`** and **`right`**.

```
cout << setw (10) << itemnumber << setw (10) << quantity
     << left << setw (30) << description << right
     << setw (10) << cost << endl;
```

Finally, the insertion operator displays all characters in a string until it encounters the null terminator. What happens if by accident a string is missing its null terminator? Simple, the insertion operator displays all bytes until it finds a null terminator. I often refer to this action as a "light show." Yes, one sees the contents of the string appear, but "garbage" characters follow that. If a line gets full, DOS line wraps and continues on the next line. If the screen fills, DOS scrolls. All of this occurs at a blazing speed. Sit back and relax; don't panic if this happens to you. It is harmless. Enjoy the show. It will stop eventually when it finds a byte with a zero in it.

Passing a String to a Function

When passing a string to a function, the prototype of the string is just like that of any other array. Suppose that we have a **PrintRecord()** function whose purpose was to display one cost record. The **description** string must be passed. The prototype of the **PrintRecord()** function is

```
void PrintRecord (const char description[],...
```

and the **main()** function could invoke it as

```
PrintRecord (description,...
```

Recall that the name of an array is always the memory address of the first element, or a pointer. Sometimes you may see the prototype for a string using pointer notation instead of array notation.

```
void PrintRecord (const char* description, ...
```

These are entirely equivalent notations when passing a string to a function.

Remember, if a function is not going to alter the caller's character string, it should have the const qualifier.

Working with Strings

Working with character string fields presents some new problems that we have not encountered before. Suppose that we have the following fields defined and have inputted some data into them.

```
const int NameLen = 21;
char previousName[NameLen];
char currentName[NameLen];
```

Suppose that we needed to compare the two names to see if they were equal or not—that is, they contain the same series of characters. Further, suppose that if they are not the same, we needed to copy the current name into the previous name field. One might be tempted to code the following.

```
if (previousName != currentName) {
 previousName = currentName;
```

Coding the above cannot possibly work. Why? Remember that the name of an array is the memory address where that array begins in memory. For the sake of illustration, assume that the **previousName** array begins at memory address 5000 and that the **currentName** array begins at memory location 8000. If you substitute these values for the variable array names in the above coding as the compiler does, you end up with this

```
if (5000 != 8000) {
 5000 = 8000;
```

In all cases, the test condition is always true, for 5000 is not 8000, ever. But look at the assignment, it is ludicrous. Although the test condition compiles with no errors, the assignment line generates an error message.

To our rescue comes the library of string functions. The prototypes of all of these string functions are in the header file **<string>**.

Comparing Strings

Here is where the new changes Microsoft has made in .NET 2005 come to the forefront. Older code now recompiled using .NET 2005 will produce a large number of warning message about function calls now being depricated, that is, obsolete. First, let's examine the older versions and then see why Microsoft has made unilateral, not yet in the C++ Standard, changes.

The Old Way: To compare two strings, use either **strcmp()** or **stricmp()**. **strcmp()** is a case sensitive string compare function. **stricmp()** is a case insensitive string compare function. Both functions return an integer indicating the result of the comparison operation. The prototype of the string comparison function is this.

```
int strcmp (const char* string1, const char* string2);
```

It is showing that we pass it the two strings to be compared. However, the notation, **const char*** also indicates that the string's contents are constant. That is, the comparison function cannot alter the contents of either string. If the parameters were just **char* string1**, then potentially the contents of the string we passed could be altered in some way. The **const char*** notation is our guarantee that the function cannot alter the contents of the string we pass. It is rather like making the string "read-only."

The integer return code indicates the result:

0 => the two strings are the same
positive => the first string is larger
negative => the first string is smaller

The New Way: To compare two strings, use either **strcmp()** or **_stricmp()**. **strcmp()** is a case sensitive string compare function. **_stricmp()** is a case insensitive string compare function. Both functions return an integer indicating the result of the comparison operation. The prototype of the string comparison function is this.

```
int strcmp (const char* string1, const char* string2);
int _stricmp (const char* string1, const char* string2);
```

It is showing that we pass it the two strings to be compared. Both functions abort the program if either of the two passed memory addresses is zero or NULL.

While the meaning of the result's phrase, "the two strings are the same," is obvious, the other two results might not be so clear. Character data is stored in an encoding scheme, often ASCII, American Standard Code for Information Interchange. In this scheme, the decimal number 65 represents the letter 'A'. The letter 'B' is a 66; 'C', a 67, and so on. If the first string begins with the letter 'A' and the second string begins with the letter 'B', then the first string is said to be smaller than the second string because the 65 is smaller than the 66. The comparison function returns the value given by 'A' – 'B' or (65 – 66) or a negative number indicating that the first string is smaller than the second string.

When comparing strings, one is more often testing for the equal or not equal situation. Applications that involve sorting or merging two sets of strings would make use of the smaller/larger possibilities. To fix up the previous example in which we wanted to find out if the **previousName** was not equal to the **currentName**, we should code the following assuming that case was important.

```
if (strcmp (previousName, currentName) != 0) {
```

If we wanted to ignore case sensitivity issues, then code this.

```
if (_stricmp (previousName, currentName) != 0) {
```

Copying Strings

The **older** function to copy a string is **strcpy()**. Its prototype is

```
char* strcpy (char* destination, const char* source);
```

It copies all characters including the null terminator of the source string, placing them in the destination string. In the previous example where we wanted to copy the **currentName** into the **previousName** field, we code

```
strcpy (previousName, currentName);
```

Of course, the destination string should have sufficient characters in its array to store all the characters contained in the source string. If not, a memory overlay occurs. For example, if one has defined the following two strings

```
char source[20] = "Hello World";
char dest[5];
```

If one copies the source string to the destination string, memory is overlain.

```
strcpy (dest, source);
```

Seven bytes of memory are clobbered in this case and contain a blank, the characters "World" and the null terminator.

This clobbering of memory, the core overlay, or more politically correct, buffer overrun, has taken its toll on not only Microsoft coding but many other applications. Hackers and virus writers often take advantage of this inherently insecure function to overwrite memory with malicious machine instructions. Hence, Microsoft has unilaterally decided to rewrite the standard C Libraries to prevent such from occurring. As of this publication, Microsoft's changes are not in the ANSII C++ standard.

The new string copy function looks like this.

```
char* strcpy_s (char* destination, size_t destSize,
                const char* source);
```

It copies all characters including the null terminator of the source string, placing them in the destination string, subject to not exceeding the maximum number of bytes of the destination string. In all cases, the destination string will be null terminated. However, if the source or destination memory address is 0 or if the destination string is too small to hold the result, the program is basically terminated at run time. In a later course, a program can prevent this abnormal termination and do something about the problem.

In the previous example where we wanted to copy the **currentName** into the **previousName** field, we now code

```
strcpy_s (previousName, sizeof (previousName), currentName);
```

This text will consistently use these new Microsoft changes. If you are using another compiler, either use the samples provided in the 2002-3 samples folder or remove the sizeof parameter along with the _s in the function names.

Getting the Actual Number of Characters Currently in a String

The next most frequently used string function is **strlen()**, which returns the number of bytes that the string currently contains. Suppose that we had defined

```
char name[21] = "Sam";
```

If we code the following

```
int len  = strlen (name); // returns 3 bytes
int size = sizeof (name); // returns 21 bytes
```

then the **strlen(name)** function would return 3. Notice that **strlen()** does NOT count the null terminator.

The **sizeof(name)** gives the defined number of bytes that the variable contains or 21 in this case. Notice the significant difference between these two operations!

Concatenating or Joining Two Strings into One Larger String

Again, there is a new version of this function in .NET 2005. The older function is the **strcat()** function, which appends one string onto the end of another string forming a concatenation of the two strings. Suppose that we had defined

```
char drive[3] = "C:";
```

```
char path[_MAX_PATH] = "\\Programming\\Samples";
char name[_MAX_PATH] = "test.txt";
char fullfilename[_MAX_PATH];
```

In reality, when users install an application, they can place it on nearly any drive and nearly any path. However, the application does know the filename and then has to join the pieces together. The objective here is to join the filename components into a complete file specification so that the **fullfilename** field can then be passed to the **ifstream open()** function. The sequence would be

```
strcpy (fullfilename, drive); // copy the drive string
strcat (fullfilename, path);  // append the path
strcat (fullfilename, "\\");  // append the \
strcat (fullfilename, name);  // append filename
infile.open (fullfilename, ios::in); // open the file
```

The new version is **strcat_s()**, which now takes the destination maximum number of bytes as the second parameter before the source string. The above sequence using the newer functions is this.

```
strcpy_s (fullfilename, _MAX_PATH, drive); // copy the drive
strcat_s (fullfilename, _MAX_PATH, path);  // append the path
strcat_s (fullfilename, _MAX_PATH, "\\");  // append the \
strcat_s (fullfilename, _MAX_PATH, name);  // append filename
infile.open (fullfilename, ios::in); // open the file
```

The String Functions

There are a number of other string functions that are available. The next table lists some of these and their use. The prototypes of all of these are in **<string>**. The data type size_t is really an unsigned integer.

```
Name: strlen
Meaning: string length function
Prototype: size_t strlen (const char* string);
Action done: returns the current length of the string. size_t is
             another name for an unsigned int.
Example: char s1[10] = "Sam";
              char s2[10] = "";
              strlen (s1) yields 3
              strlen (s2) yields 0
```

```
Name-old: strcmp and stricmp
Meaning: string compare, case sensitive and case insensitive
Prototype: int strcmp (const char* string1, const char* string2);
           int stricmp (const char* string1, const char* string2);
Action done: strcmp does a case sensitive comparison of the two
             strings, beginning with the first character of each
```

```
            string. It returns 0 if all characters in both
            strings are the same. It returns a negative value if
            the different character in string1 is less than that
            in string2. It returns a positive value if it is
            larger.
Example: char s1[10] = "Bcd";
         char s2[10] = "Bcd";
         char s3[10] = "Abc";
         char s4[10] = "Cde";
         char s5[10] = "bcd";
         strcmp (s1, s2) yields 0 - stings are equal
         stricmp (s1, s5) yields 0 - strings are equal
         strcmp (s1, s3) yields a + value—s1 > s3
         strcmp (s1, s4) yields a - value—s1 < s4
```

Name-new: **strcmp** and **_stricmp**

```
Meaning: string compare, case sensitive and case insensitive
Prototype: int strcmp (const char* string1, const char* string2);
         int _stricmp (const char* string1, const char* string2);
Action done: strcmp does a case sensitive comparison of the two
            strings, beginning with the first character of each
            string. It returns 0 if all characters in both
            strings are the same. It returns a negative value if
            the different character in string1 is less than that
            in string2. It returns a positive value if it is
            larger. Both functions abort the program if the
            memory address is null or 0.
Example: char s1[10] = "Bcd";
         char s2[10] = "Bcd";
         char s3[10] = "Abc";
         char s4[10] = "Cde";
         char s5[10] = "bcd";
         strcmp (s1, s2) yields 0 - stings are equal
         _stricmp (s1, s5) yields 0 - strings are equal
         strcmp (s1, s3) yields a + value—s1 > s3
         strcmp (s1, s4) yields a - value—s1 < s4
```

Name-old: **strcat**

```
Meaning: string concatenation
Prototype: char* strcat (char* desString, const char* srcString);
Action done: The srcString is appended onto the end of the
            desString. Returns the desString address
Example: char s1[20] = "Hello";
         char s2[10] = " World";
         strcat (s1, s2); yields "Hello World" in s1.
```

```
Name-new: strcat_s
Meaning: string concatenation
Prototype: strcat (char* desString, size_t maxDestSize,
                   const char* srcString);
Action done: The srcString is appended onto the end of the
             desString. Aborts the program if dest is too small.
Example: char s1[20] = "Hello";
         char s2[10] = " World";
       strcat_s (s1, sizeof(s1), s2); yields "Hello World" in s1.
Name-old: strcpy
Meaning: string copy
Prototype: char* strcpy (char* desString, const char* srcString);
Action done: All bytes of the srcString are copied into the
             destination string, including the null terminator.
             The function returns the desString memory address.
Example: char s1[10];
         char s2[10] = "Sam";
         strcpy (s1, s2); When done, s1 now contains "Sam".
```

```
Name-new: strcpy_s
Meaning: string copy
Prototype: char* strcpy (char* desString, size_t maxDestSize,
                         const char* srcString);
Action done: All bytes of the srcString are copied into the
             destination string, including the null terminator.
             The function returns the desString memory address.
             It aborts the program if destination is too small.
Example: char s1[10];
         char s2[10] = "Sam";
         strcpy_s (s1, sizeof (s1), s2);
When done, s1 now contains "Sam".
```

```
Name: strchr
Meaning: search string for first occurrence of the character
Prototype: char* strchr (const char* srcString, int findChar);
Action done: returns the memory address or char* of the first
             occurrence of the findChar in the srcString. If
             findChar is not in the srcString, it returns NULL
             or 0.
Example: char s1[10] = "Burr";
         char* found = strchr (s1, 'r');
         returns the memory address of the first letter r
         character, so that found[0] would give you that 'r'.
```

```
Name: strstr
Meaning: search string1 for the first occurrence of find string
Prototype: char* strstr (const char* string1,
                         const char* findThisString);
Action done: returns the memory address (char*) of the first
             occurrence of findThisString in string1 or NULL (0)
             if it is not present.
Example: char s1[10] = "abcabc";
         char s2[10] = "abcdef";
   char* firstOccurrence = strstr (s1, "abc");
         It finds the first abc in s1 and firstOccurrence has the
         same memory address as s1, so that s1[0] and
         firstOccurrence[0] both contain the first letter 'a' of
         the string
   char* where = strstr (s2, "def");
         Here where contains the memory address of the 'd' in the
         s2
```

```
Name-old: strlwr
Meaning: string to lowercase
Prototype: char* strlwr (char* string);
Action done: All uppercase letters in the string are converted
             to lowercase letters. All others are left untouched.
Example: char s1[10] = "Hello 123";
         strlwr (s1);
         Yields "hello 123" in s1 when done.
```

```
Name-new: strlwr_s
Meaning: string to lowercase
Prototype: char* strlwr (char* string, size_t maxSizeOfString);
Action done: All uppercase letters in the string are converted
             to lowercase letters. All others are left untouched.
Example: char s1[10] = "Hello 123";
         strlwr_s (s1, sizeof (s1));
         Yields "hello 123" in s1 when done.
```

```
Name-old: strupr
Meaning: convert a string to uppercase
Prototype: char* strupr (char* string);
Action done: Any lowercase letters in the string are converted
             to uppercase; all others are untouched.
Example: char s1[10] = "Hello 123";
         strupr (s1);
         When done, s1 contains "HELLO 123"
```

```
Name-new: strupr_s
Meaning: convert a string to uppercase
Prototype: char* strupr_s (char* string, size_t maxSizeOfString);
Action done: Any lowercase letters in the string are converted
             to uppercase; all others are untouched.
Example: char s1[10] = "Hello 123";
         strupr_s (s1, sizeof(s1));
         When done, s1 contains "HELLO 123"
```

```
Name-old: strrev
Meaning: string reverse
Prototype: char* strrev (char* string);
Action done: Reverses the characters in a string.
Example: char s1[10] = "Hello";
         strrev (s1);
         When done, string contains "olleH"
```

```
Name-new: _strrev
Meaning: string reverse
Prototype: char* _strrev (char* string);
Action done: Reverses the characters in a string. It aborts the
program if the memory address passed is null or 0;
Example: char s1[10] = "Hello";
         _strrev (s1);
         When done, string contains "olleH"
```

How Could String Functions Be Implemented?

Next, let's examine how the **strcpy()** and **strcmp()** functions could be implemented using array notation. The **strcpy()** function must copy all bytes from the **srcString** into the **desString**, including the null-terminator. It could be done as follows.

```
char* strcpy (char* desString, const char* srcString) {
 int i = 0;
 while (desString[i] = srcString[i])
  i++;
 return desString;
}
```

The **while** clause first copies a character from the source into the destination string. Then it compares the character it just copied. If that character was not equal to zero, the body of the loop is executed; **i** is incremented for the next character. If the character just copied was the null terminator, the test condition is false and the loop ends.

Here is how the **strcmp()** function might be implemented using array notation.

```
int strcmp (const char* string1, const char* string2) {
 int i=0;
 while (string1[i] && string1[i] == string2[i])
  i++;
 return string1[i] - string2[i];
}
```

The first test in the **while** clause is checking to see if we are at the null terminator of **string1.** If so, the loop ends. If not, then the corresponding characters of **string1** and **string2** are compared. If those two characters are equal, the loop body is executed and **i** is incremented. If the two characters are different, the loop also ends. To create the return integer, the current characters are subtracted. If the two strings are indeed equal, then both bytes must be the null terminators of the respective strings; the return value is then 0. Otherwise, the return value depends on the ASCII numerical values of the corresponding characters.

Section B: A Computer Science Example

Cs11a—Character String Manipulation—Customer Names

One task frequently encountered when applications work with people's names is that of conversion from "firstname lastname" into "lastname, firstname." This problem explores some techniques to handle the conversion. There are many ways to accomplish splitting a name apart. Since the use of pointer variables (variables that contain the memory addresses of things), have not yet been discussed, the approach here is to use subscripting to accomplish it. Indeed, a programmer does need to be able to manipulate the contents of a string as well as utilize the higher lever string functions. This example illustrates low-level character manipulation within strings as well as utilizing some commonly used string functions.

The problem is to take a customer name, such as "John Jones" and extract the first and last names ("John" and "Jones") and then to turn it into the alternate comma delimited form, "Jones, John." Alternatively, take the comma form and extract the first and last names. At first glance, the approach to take seems simple enough. When extracting the first and last names from the full name, look for a blank delimiter and take what's to the left of it as the first name and what's to the right as the last name.

But what about names like "Mr. and Mrs. John J. Jones?" To find the last name portion, begin on the right or at the end of the string and move through the string in reverse direction looking for the first blank. That works fine until one encounters "John J. Jones, Jr.". So we must make a further qualification on that first blank, and that is, there must not be a comma immediately in front of it. If there is, ignore that blank and keep moving toward the beginning of the string.

When extracting the first and last names from the comma version (such as "Jones, John J."), we can look for the comma followed by a blank pair. However, what about this one, "Jones, Jr., John

J.?" Clearly, we need to start at the end of the string and work toward the beginning of the string in the search for the comma-blank pair.

Once we know the subscript of the blank or the comma-blank pair, how can the pieces be copied into the first and last name strings? This is done by copying byte by byte from some starting subscript through some ending subscript, appending a null terminator when finished. In this problem, I have made a helper function, **CopyPartialString()** to do just that.

The function **NameToParts()** takes a full name and breaks it into first and last name strings. The original passed full name string is not altered and is declared constant.

The function **NameToCommaForm()** takes the first and last names and converts them into the comma-formatted name, last, first. Since the first and last names are not altered, those parameters are also declared constant.

The function **CommaFormToNames()** converts a comma-formatted name into first and last names. Since the comma-formatted name is not altered, it is also declared constant.

Let's begin by examining the output of the program to see what is needed. Here is the test run of **Cs11a**.

```
Cs11a Character String Manipulation - Sample Execution
```

```
Original Name: |John J. Jones|
   First Name: |John J.|
   Last  Name: |Jones|
   Comma Form: |Jones, John J.|
   First and Last from comma form test ok

Original Name: |Betsy Smith|
   First Name: |Betsy|
   Last  Name: |Smith|
   Comma Form: |Smith, Betsy|
   First and Last from comma form test ok

Original Name: |Mr. and Mrs. R. J. Smith|
   First Name: |Mr. and Mrs. R. J.|
   Last  Name: |Smith|
   Comma Form: |Smith, Mr. and Mrs. R. J.|
   First and Last from comma form test ok

Original Name: |Prof. William Q. Jones|
   First Name: |Prof. William Q.|
   Last  Name: |Jones|
   Comma Form: |Jones, Prof. William Q.|
   First and Last from comma form test ok

Original Name: |J. J. Jones|
   First Name: |J. J.|
```

```
   Last  Name: |Jones|
   Comma Form: |Jones, J. J.|
   First and Last from comma form test ok

Original Name: |Jones|
   First Name: ||
   Last  Name: |Jones|
   Comma Form: |Jones|
   First and Last from comma form test ok

Original Name: |Mr. John J. Jones, Jr.|
   First Name: |Mr. John J.|
   Last  Name: |Jones, Jr.|
   Comma Form: |Jones, Jr., Mr. John J.|
   First and Last from comma form test ok

Original Name: |Mr. John J. Jones, II|
   First Name: |Mr. John J.|
   Last  Name: |Jones, II|
   Comma Form: |Jones, II, Mr. John J.|
   First and Last from comma form test ok

Original Name: |Mr. John J. Jones, MD.|
   First Name: |Mr. John J.|
   Last  Name: |Jones, MD.|
   Comma Form: |Jones, MD., Mr. John J.|
   First and Last from comma form test ok

Original Name: |The Honorable Betsy Smith|
   First Name: |The Honorable Betsy|
   Last  Name: |Smith|
   Comma Form: |Smith, The Honorable Betsy|
   First and Last from comma form test ok

Original Name: |Betsy O'Neill|
   First Name: |Betsy|
   Last  Name: |O'Neill|
   Comma Form: |O'Neill, Betsy|
   First and Last from comma form test ok

```

Program **Cs11a** is going to input a file of customer names. For each name, it first converts that full name into first and last names. Then, it forms the comma-blank version of the full name. And finally, it extracts the first and last names from the comma-blank string. If the first and last names from the two approaches do not agree, an error is written. If they agree, an "Okay" message is displayed. Since blanks are important to this problem and since a blank is hard to spot, the | character is printed before and after each string, making errant blanks quite visible. The Top-Down Design is shown in Figure 11.1.

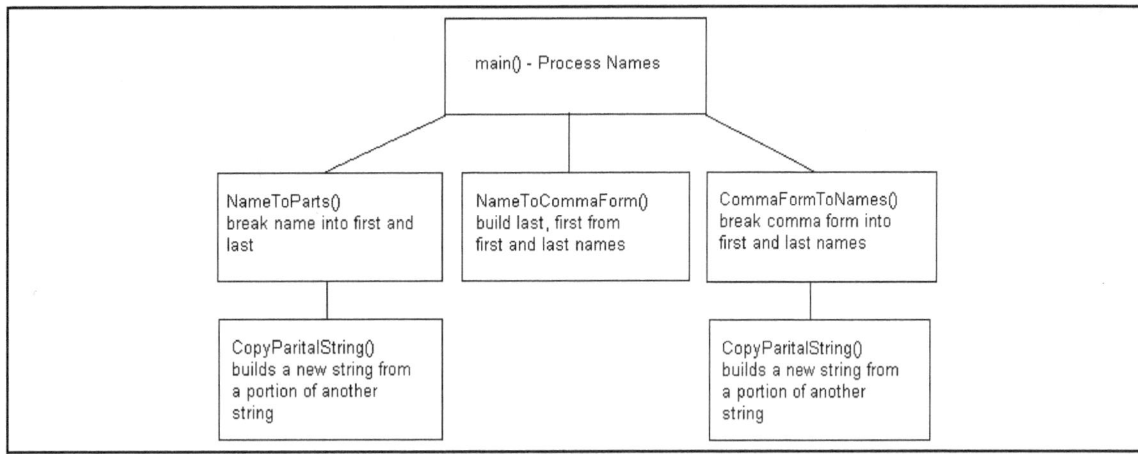

Figure 11.1 Top-Down Design of Name Program

The **main()** function defines the arrays as shown in Figure 11.2. The sequence of processing steps for **main()** is as follows.

open the input file, if it fails, display an error message and quit
while we have successfully inputted a line into **fullName** do the following
  call **NameToParts (fullName, firstName, lastName, MaxNameLen)**;
  call **NameToCommaForm (commaName, firstName, lastName)**;
  call **CommaFormToNames (commaName, firstFromCommaForm,**
          lastFromCommaForm);
  output the results, which include **fullName**, **firstName**, **lastName** and **commaName**
  if **firstName** and **firstFromCommaForm** are the same as well as
    lastName and **lastFromCommaForm** then output an Ok message
  else display an error message and the **firstFromCommaForm** and
    lastFromCommaForm
end the **while** clause
close the input file

Main Storage for main ()
fullName[MaxNameLen]
firstName[MaxNameLen]
lastName[MaxNameLen]
commaName[MaxNameLen]
MaxNameLen
51
firstFromCommaForm[MaxNameLen]
lastFromCommaForm[MaxNameLen]

Figure 11.2 Main Storage for **main()**

NameToParts() must break a full name into first and last names and is passed four parameters: **fullName**, **firstName**, **lastName**, and **limit**. As we work out the sequence of coding, let's work with a specific example. Suppose that **fullName** contains the following, where the $_0$ indicates the null terminator. I have written the subscripts below the corresponding characters.

```
Mr. John J. Jones, MD.0
0000000000111111111222
01234567890123456789012
```

The **strlen(fullName)** yields 22 characters as the current length and the subscript for the last character in the string is thus 21. So working from the end of the string, look for a blank that does not have a comma immediately in front of it.

```
i = strlen (fullName) – 1;
while (i >= 0) do the following
  does fullName[i] == ' '? If so do the following
    if there is a previous character—that is, is i>0 and
      if that previous character is not a comma, fullName[i – 1] != ',' then
        // we have found the spot—so we need to break out of the loop
        break;  with i on the blank
    end the if test
  end the does clause
  back up to the previous character, i--;
end the while clause
```

Now split out the two names. Notice we pass **i**+1, which is the first non-blank character in the last name.

```
CopyParitalString (lastName, fullName, i+1, strlen (fullName));
CopyParitalString (firstName, fullName, 0, i);
```

The **CopyParitalString()** function's purpose is to copy a series of characters in a source string from some beginning subscript through an ending subscript and then insert a null terminator. It is passed the **dest** string, the **src** string, **startAt** and **endAt**.

```
is startAt >= endAt meaning we are starting at the ending point, there is nothing
        to copy, so just make the dest string a properly null-terminated string.
  dest[0] = 0
  and return
end is
```

To copy the characters, we need a subscript variable for each string, **isrc** and **ides**.

```
let isrc = startAt
let ides = 0;
```

Now copy all characters from **startAt** to **endAt**

```
while  isrc < endAt do the following
  dest[ides] = src[isrc];
  increment both isrc and ides
end while
```

Finally, insert the null terminator

```
dest[ides] = 0;
```

The **NameToCommaForm()** function is comparatively simple. From two strings containing the first and last names, make one combined new string of the form last name, first name. However, in some cases, there might not be any first name. In that case, the result should just be a copy of the last name string. **NameToCommaForm()** is passed three strings: the answer string to fill up—**commaName**—and the two source strings—**firstName** and **lastName**. The sequence is as follows.

strcpy (**commaName**, **lastName**);
if a first name exists—that is, does **strlen** (**firstName**) != 0, if so do
  append a comma and a blank—**strcat** (**commaName**, ", ")
  append the first name—**strcat** (**commaName**, **firstName**)
end if

The **CommaFormToNames()** function must convert a single string with the form of "last name, first name" into first and last name strings. It is passed **commaName** to convert and the two strings to fill up - **firstName** and **lastName**. This time, we again begin at the end of the string looking for the first comma followed by a blank. Consider these two cases.

```
Jones, Jr., Mr. John J.0
Jones, Prof. William Q.0
```

Clearly, we want to stop at the first ", " occurrence to avoid problems with "Jr.".

let **len** = **strlen** (**commaName**)
let **commaAt** = **len** – 2
while commaAt > 0 do the following
  if the current character at **commaAt** is a ',' and
    the character at **commaAt** + 1 is a blank, then break out of the loop
  back up **commaAt**
end the **while** clause

However, this could be compacted a bit more by using ! (not) logic in the **while** test condition.

while commaAt > 0 and
    !(**commaName[commaAt]** == ',' && **commaName[commaAt**+1] == ' ')) {

When the loop ends, we must guard against no comma and blank found.
if (**commaAt** <= 0) then there is no comma so do the following
  strcpy (**lastName**, **commaName**)
  firstName[0] = 0
  and return
end the if

Finally, at this point, we have found the ", " portion; copy the two portions as follows.

CopyParitalString (**lastName**, **commaName**, 0, **commaAt**)
CopyParitalString (**firstName**, **commaName**, **commaAt**+2, **len**)

As you study the coding, draw some pictures of some test data and trace what is occurring if you have any doubts about what is going on. Here is the complete program.

```
Cs11a Character String Manipulation
```

```
/***************************************************************/
/*                                                             */
/* Cs11a Character String Manipulation - Customer Names        */
/*                                                             */
/***************************************************************/

#include <iostream>
#include <iomanip>
#include <fstream>
#include <string>
using namespace std;

const int MaxNameLen = 51;     // the maximum length of names

void NameToParts (const char fullName[],// converts a full name
                  char firstName[],     // to first & last names
                  char lastName[],
                  int limit);

void NameToCommaForm (char commaName[], // converts a first and
                 const char firstName[], // last name into a
                 const char lastName[]); // full name string

void CommaFormToNames (const char commaName[],// converts a comma
                 char firstFromCommaForm[], // form of name into
                 char lastFromCommaForm[]); // first & last names

void CopyParitalString (char dest[], // copies a part of the src
                  const char src[],  // string into the dest
                        int startAt, // beginning at startAt and
                        int endAt);  // ending at endAt

int main () {
 char fullName[MaxNameLen];         // original full name as input
 char firstName[MaxNameLen];        // first name from full name
 char lastName[MaxNameLen];         // last name from full name
 char commaName[MaxNameLen];        // full name in comma form
 char firstFromCommaForm[MaxNameLen];// first name from commaform
 char lastFromCommaForm[MaxNameLen]; // last name from comma form

 ifstream infile ("Cs11a-Names.txt");
 if (!infile) {
  cerr << "Error: cannot find the names file\n";
  return 1;
 }
 ofstream out ("results.txt");

 while (infile.getline (fullName, sizeof (fullName))) {
  // break full name inputted into first and last names
  NameToParts (fullName, firstName, lastName, MaxNameLen);

  // turn first and last names into a comma form of full name
```

```
  NameToCommaForm (commaName, firstName, lastName);

  // break comma form of full name into first and last names
  CommaFormToNames (commaName, firstFromCommaForm,
                    lastFromCommaForm);

  // output results
  out << "Original Name: |" << fullName  << '|' << endl;
  out << "   First Name: |" << firstName << '|' << endl;
  out << "   Last  Name: |" << lastName  << '|' << endl;
  out << "   Comma Form: |" << commaName << '|' << endl;

  // test that first and last names agree from both forms
  // of extraction
  if (strcmp (firstName, firstFromCommaForm) == 0 &&
      strcmp (lastName, lastFromCommaForm) == 0)
   out << "   First and Last from comma form test ok" << endl;
  else {
   out << "   Error from comma form - does not match\n";
   out << "   First Name: |" << firstFromCommaForm << '|' <<endl;
   out << "   Last  Name: |" << lastFromCommaForm  << '|' <<endl;
  }
  out << endl;
 }
 infile.close ();
 out.close ();
 return 0;
}

/***************************************************************/
/*                                                             */
/* CopyParitalString: copies src from startAt through endAt   */
/*                                                             */
/***************************************************************/

void CopyParitalString (char dest[], const char src[],
                        int startAt, int endAt) {
 if (startAt >= endAt) { // avoid starting after ending
  dest[0] = 0;           // just set dest string to a null string
  return;
 }

 int isrc = startAt;
 int ides = 0;
 // copy all needed chars from startAt to endAt
 for (; isrc<endAt; isrc++, ides++) {
  dest[ides] = src[isrc];
 }
 dest[ides] = 0; // insert null terminator
}

/***************************************************************/
/*                                                             */
```

```
/* NameToParts: break a full name into first and last name     */
/*                                                              */
/***************************************************************/

void NameToParts (const char fullName[], char firstName[],
                  char lastName[], int limit) {
 // working from the end of the string, look for blank separator
 // that does not have a , immediately in front of it
 int i = (int) strlen (fullName) - 1;
 while (i >= 0) {
  if (fullName[i] == ' ') {            // found a blank and
   if (i>0 && fullName[i-1] != ',') { // earlier char is not a,
    break;                             // end with i on the blank
   }
  }
  i--;
 }
 CopyParitalString (lastName,fullName i+1,(int)strlen(fullName));
 CopyParitalString (firstName, fullName, 0, i);
}

/***************************************************************/
/*                                                              */
/* NameToCommaForm: from first & last names, make last, first  */
/*                                                              */
/***************************************************************/

void NameToCommaForm (char commaName[], const char firstName[],
                      const char lastName[]) {
 strcpy_s (commaName, MaxNameLen, lastName);
 if (strlen (firstName)) {       // if a first name exists,
  strcat_s (commaName, MaxNameLen, ", "); // add a , and blank
  strcat_s (commaName, MaxNameLen, firstName); // add first name
 }
}

/***************************************************************/
/*                                                              */
/* CommaFormToNames: convert a last, first name to first & last*/
/*                                                              */
/***************************************************************/

void CommaFormToNames (const char commaName[], char firstName[],
                       char lastName[]) {
 // begin at the end and look for a ,blank
 int len = (int) strlen (commaName);
 int commaAt = len - 2;
 while (commaAt > 0 &&
   !(commaName[commaAt] == ',' && commaName[commaAt+1] == ' ')) {
  commaAt--;
 }
 if (commaAt <= 0) {             // here there is no comma so
  strcpy_s (lastName, MaxNameLen, commaName);
```

```
  firstName[0] = 0;          // set first name to null string
  return;
 }
 CopyParitalString (lastName, commaName, 0, commaAt);
 CopyParitalString (firstName, commaName, commaAt+2, len);
}
```

Section C: An Engineering Example

Engineering problems primarily make use of strings as labels or identifiers associated with a set of numerical values.

Engr11a—Weather Statistics Revisited

On a daily basis, weather statistics for cities scattered around the state are collected, summarized, and forwarded to our center for processing. Our company maintains an Internet web page that lists the unusual weather occurrences within the last 24-hour period. Write a program that inputs the daily weather file and displays those cities with unusual weather in a nicely formatted report.

An input line consists of the city surrounded by double quote marks, such as "Peoria." Next, come the high and low temperatures, the rainfall amount, the snowfall amount, and wind speed. Unusual weather is defined to be a high temperature above 95, a low temperature below 0, a rainfall amount in excess of two inches, snowfall accumulations in excess of six inches or a wind speed greater than 45 mph.

Since each day's data is stored in a different file, the program first should prompt the user to enter the filename to be used for the input. Also, prompt the user for the output file to which the report is to be written.

An output line might appear as

```
City                Hi   Low   Rain  Snow   Winds

Peoria              85   55     0     0      55*
Washington          99*  75     0     0     10
```

A * character is placed after the weather statistic that is unusual.

Since this problem is quite basic, I have not included the coding sketch. By now, the logic should be obvious. Here are the program listing and the sample output. Make sure you examine the instructions that process the new string variables.

```
Listing for Program Engr11a - Unusual Weather Statistics
```

```
/***************************************************************/
/*                                                             */
/* Engr11a: Unusual Weather Statistics report                  */
/*                                                             */
/***************************************************************/

#include <iostream>
#include <iomanip>
#include <fstream>
#include <string>
using namespace std;

const int MaxCityLen = 21; // city name length is 20 chars

int main () {

 char infilename[_MAX_PATH];
 char reportname[_MAX_PATH];
 cout << "Enter the filename with today's weather data\n";
 cin.getline (infilename, sizeof (infilename));
 cout << "\nEnter the report filename\n";
 cin.getline (reportname, sizeof(reportname));

 ifstream infile;
 infile.open (infilename);
 if (!infile) {
  cerr << "Error: cannot open file: " << infilename << endl;
  return 1;
 }

 ofstream outfile;
 outfile.open (reportname, ios::out);
 if (!outfile) {
  cerr << "Error: cannot open file: " << reportname << endl;
  return 1;
 }
 // setup floating point output format
 outfile << fixed << setprecision (1);

 outfile << "Unusual Weather Report\n\n";
 outfile<<"City                    High     Low    Rain    Snow"
          "    Wind\n";
 outfile<<"                                         Fall    Fall"
          "   Speed\n\n";

 char city [MaxCityLen]; // string to hold city name
 float high;             // high temperature of the day - F
 float low;              // low temperature of the day - F
 float rainfall;         // rainfall in inches
 float snowfall;         // snowfall in inches
 float windspeed;        // wind speed in mph

```

```
char  junk;                // to hold the " around city names
int   line = 0;            // line count for error processing

while (infile >> junk) { // input the leading " of city
 infile.get (city, sizeof (city), '\"');
 infile.get (junk);
 infile >> high >> low >> rainfall >> snowfall >> windspeed;
 // abort if there is incomplete or bad data
 if (!infile) {
  cerr << "Error: incomplete city data on line " << line <<endl;
  infile.close ();
  outfile.close ();
  return 2;
 }
 if (high > 95 || low < 0 || rainfall > 2 || snowfall > 6 ||
  windspeed > 45) {
  // unusual weather - display this city data
  outfile << left << setw (22) << city << right
          << setw (7) << high;
  if (high > 95)
   outfile << '*';
  else
   outfile << ' ';
  outfile << setw (7) << low;
  if (low < 0)
   outfile << '*';
  else
   outfile << ' ';
  outfile << setw (7) << rainfall;
  if (rainfall > 2)
   outfile << '*';
  else
   outfile << ' ';
  outfile << setw (7) << snowfall;
  if (snowfall > 6)
   outfile << '*';
  else
   outfile << ' ';
  outfile << setw (7) << windspeed;
  if (windspeed > 45)
   outfile << '*';
  else
   outfile << ' ';
  outfile << endl;
 }
}
infile.close ();
outfile.close ();
return 0;
}
```

```
Engr11a - Unusual Weather Report Output
```

```
Unusual Weather Report

City                     High      Low      Rain     Snow     Wind
                                            Fall     Fall     Speed

Washington               99.0*    70.0      0.0      0.0      20.0
Morton                   85.0     65.0      5.0*     0.0      40.0
Chicago                  32.0     -5.0*     0.0      8.0*     25.0
Joliet                   88.0     70.0      2.0      0.0      60.0*
Springfield              99.0*    75.0      3.0*     0.0      55.0*
New Salem                 0.0     -3.0*     0.0      9.0*     55.0*
```

Design Exercises

1. Design a Grade Book Program

The Grade Book Program inputs a set of students grades for a semester. First, design the layout of the data file to be used for input and then design the program to produce the Grade Report shown below.

The data consists of a student id number, which is their social security number, their name, which can be up to 20 characters long, the course name, which can be up to 10 characters in length, the course number and finally the letter grade earned. Design how the input lines must be entered. Include in what order they are entered; pay particular attention to specifically how the student names are going to be entered on your lines.

The Grade Report produced by the program that is to input your data file appears as follows.

```
     Student Grade Report

Student     Student                    ----Course-----
   Id       Name                       Name      Number Grade
111111111   Sam J. Jones               Cmpsc       125    A
...
```

2. Design the Merge Conference Roster Program

Two sections of a conference course have been merged into one larger section. Each original section has a file of the attendee names. You are to write a program that merges the two into one new file. Each original file contains, in alphabetical order, the attendee names, which can be up to 30 characters long, one name per line. The new file this program creates must also be in alphabetical order.

Stop! Do These Exercises Before Programming

1. A programmer needs to input the day of the week as a character string. The following coding failed to run properly. Why? What must be done to fix it up?

```
char dayName[9];
cin >> dayName;
```

2. A program needs to input the chemical compound names of two substances and then compare to see if the names are the same. The following was coded and compiles without errors but when run always produces the wrong results. Why? How can it be fixed?

```
char compound1[40];
char compound2[40];
infile1.get (compound1, sizeof (compound1));
infile2.get (compound2, sizeof (compound2));
if (compound1 == compound2) {
  cout << "These compounds match\n";
else
  cout << "These compounds do not match\n";
```

3. The programmer inputted a compound name and its cost and then wanted to check to see if it was equal to "Sodium Chloride." The following coding compiles with no errors but when it runs, it fails to find Sodium Chloride when that is input. The input line is

```
Sodium Chloride      4.99
```

What is wrong and how can it be fixed?

```
char compound[20];
double cost;
cin.get (compound, sizeof (compound));
cin >> cost;
if (stricmp (compound, "Sodium Chloride") == 0) {
 cout << "Found\n";
}
```

4. The input file consists of a **long** student id number followed by a blank and then the student's name. The following coding does not input the data properly. Why? What specifically is input when the user enters a line like this?

```
1234567 Sam Spade<cr>
```

How can it be fixed so that it correctly inputs the data?

```
long id;
char name[20];
while (cin >> id) {
  cin.get (name, sizeof (name));
 ...
}
```

5. A file of student names and their grades is to be input. The programmer wrote a **GetNextStudent()** function. It does not work. How can it be fixed so that it does work properly?

```
char name[20];
char grade;
while (GetNextStudent (infile, name, grade, 20)) {
...
istream GetNextStudent (istream infile, char name[],
                        char grade, int maxLen) {
 infile.get (name, sizeof (name));
 infile.get (grade);
 return infile;
}
```

6. The proposed Acme Data Records consist of the following.

```
12345 Pots and Pans 42 10.99
23455 Coffee #10 can 18 5.99
32453 Peanuts 20 1.25
```

The first entry is the item number, the second is the product description, the third is the quantity on hand, and the fourth is the unit cost. Assume that no description can exceed 20 characters. The programmer wrote the following code to input the data.

```
int main () {
 long   id;
 char   description[21];
 int    quantity;
 double cost;
 ifstream infile ("master.txt", ios::in | ios::nocreate);
 while (infile >> id >> description >> quantity >> cost) {
...
```

However, it did not run at all right. What is wrong with it? Is it possible to fix the program so that it would read in that data file? What would you recommend?

Programming Problems

Problem Cs11-1—Life Insurance Problem

Acme Life Insurance has asked you to write a program to produce their Customer's Premium Paid Report. The report lists the person's name, age, and yearly premium paid. Yearly premiums are based upon the age when the person first became a customer.

The table of rates is stored in the file **Cs11-1-rates.txt** on disk. The file contains the age and the corresponding premium on a line. Since these rates are subject to change, your program should read these values from the file. In other words, do not hard code them in the program. Currently, the data appears as follows (column headings have been added by for clarity).

```
  Age     Premium
 Limit    Dollars
  25      277.00
  35      287.50
  45      307.75
  55      327.25
  65      357.00
  70      455.00
```

The ages listed are the upper limits for the corresponding premium. In other words, if a person took out a policy at any age up to and including 25, the premium would be $277.00. If they were 26 through 35, then their premium would be $287.50. If they were above 70, use the age 70 rate of $455.00.

Your program should begin by inputting the two parallel arrays, **age** and **premium**. Allow for a maximum of 20 in each array. Load these arrays from a function called **LoadArrays()** that is passed the two arrays and the limit of 20. It returns the number of elements in the parallel arrays.

After calling the **LoadArrays()**, the **main()** function, inputs the customers' data from the **Cs11-1-policy.txt** file. Each line in this file contains the policy number, name, and age fields. The policy number should be a **long** and the name can be up to 20 characters long. The customer names contain the last name only with no imbedded blanks. For each customer, print out their name, their age and their premium. The report should have an appropriate title and column headings.

Problem Cs11-2—Acme Personnel Report

Write a program to produce the Acme Personnel Report from the **Cs11-2-personnel.txt** file. In the file are the following fields in this order: employee name (20 characters maximum), integer years employed, the department (15 characters maximum), and the year-to-date pay. The report should look like this.

```
                Acme Personnel Report

Employee                Years  Department          Year to
Name                     Emp.                      Date Pay

xxxxxxxxxxxxxxxxxxxx     99    xxxxxxxxxxxxxxx    $99999.99
xxxxxxxxxxxxxxxxxxxx     99    xxxxxxxxxxxxxxx    $99999.99
```

The employee name and the department should be left aligned while the numeric fields should be right aligned.

Problem Cs11-3—Palindrome Analysis

A palindrome is a string that is the same whether read forward or backwards. For example, "level" and "Nod Don" and "123454321" are all palindromes. For this problem, case is not important. Write a function **IsPalindrome()** that takes a constant string as its only argument and returns a **bool**, **true** if the word is a palindrome or **false** if it is not.

Then write a **main()** function that inputs file **Cs11-3-words.txt**. A line in this file cannot exceed 80 characters. For each line input, print out a single line as follows

```
Yes--Nod Don
No---Nod Jim
```

Problem Cs11-4—Merging Customer Files

Write a Merge Files program to merge two separate customer data into one file. Each file contains the following fields: the customer's number (up to 7 digits), the customer's last name (20 characters maximum), the customer's first name (15 characters maximum), the address (20 characters maximum), the city (15 characters maximum), the state code (2 characters), and the zip code (5 digits).

The resulting file should be in order by customer last names (a through z). If there are two identical last names, then check the first names to decide which to insert into the new master file first. Names should be case insensitive.

Normally, the only output of the merge program is the new master file called **newMaster.txt**. However, for debugging purposes, also echo print to the screen the customer last and first names as they are written to the new master file.

The two input files are called **Cs11-4-mast1.txt** and **Cs11-4-mast2.txt**.

Problem Engr11-1—Liquids and Gases in Coexistence (Chemical Engineering)

The chemical and physical interactions between gases and liquids are commonly encountered in chemical engineering. For a specific substance, the mathematical description of the transition from gas to liquid is vital. The basic ideal gas equation for one mole of gas is

P = RT / V

where P = pressure in N/m^2

V = volume of one mole in m^3

T = temperature in degrees K

R = ideal gas constant of 8.314 J/mol-K

This ideal gas equation assumes low pressures and high temperatures such that the liquid state is not present at all. However, this assumption often is not a valid one; many situations exist where there is a combination of a substance in both its gaseous and liquid state present. This situation is called an imperfect gas. Empirical formulas have been discovered that model this behavior. One of these is Van der Waal's equation of state for an imperfect gas. If the formula is simplified, it is

$$p = \frac{\frac{8}{3}t}{\left(v - \frac{1}{3}\right)} - \frac{3}{v^2}$$

where p, v and t are scaled versions of the pressure, volume and temperature. The scaling is done by dividing the measurement by a known, published critical value of that measurement. These scaled equations are

p = P/Pc   v = V/Vc   t = T/Tc

These critical measurements correspond to that point where equal masses of the gas and liquid phase have the same density. The critical values are tabulated for many substances. See for example the *Handbook of Chemistry and Physics*—"Critical Constants for Gases" section.

Since there are actually three variables, v, p and t, the objective for this problem is to see how this equation behaves at that boundary where gas is turning into a liquid. To do so, plot p versus v versus t. An easy way that this can be accomplished is to choose a specific t value and calculate a set of p versus v values. Then change t and make another set of p versus v values. All told, there are to be three sets of p versus v values.

The three t values to use are 1.1, 1.0, and 0.9. For all three cases, the v values range from 0.4 through 3.0; divide this range into 100 uniformly spaced intervals. Then for each of the 100 v values, calculate the corresponding p value. This means that you should define a v array that holds 100 elements. Define three p arrays, one for each of the three t values, each p array to hold 100 elements. One of the p arrays represents the t = 1.1 results; another, the t = 1.0 results; the third, the t = 0.9 results. Create one for loop that calculates all of these values. It is most convenient to define also a function p (v, t) to handle the actual calculation of one specific pressure at a specific volume and temperature.

Since these results are scaled values, they can then be applied to any specific substance. Prepare an input data file for the substances listed below. Enter the four fields in this order, substance, Tc, Pc, Vc. Your program should input each of these lines. For each line, in other words each substance, the four arrays are printed in a columnar format, with the scaled t, v, p values converted into T, V and P. In the table below, Tc is in degrees Kelvin; Pc is in atmospheres; Vc is in cubic meters per mole.

```
Substance            Tc        Pc        Vc
Water              647.56   217.72 0.00000721
Nitrogen           126.06    33.5  0.00000436
Carbon dioxide 304.26    73.0  0.0000202
```

The report for a specific substance should appear similar to the following

```
Substance: Carbon dioxide

Critical Volume          Critical Pressures for 3 temps
cubic meters/mole        T = 334.69  T = 304.26  T = 273.83

    0.00000808              1551.24     1843.23     1259.24
    ...
```

If you have access to a plotter, for each substance, plot all three sets of **p** versus **v** curves on the same graph.

Problem Engr11-2—Chemical Formula

Each line of the **E11-2-formula.txt** file contains the chemical formula for a compound. A blank separates the formula from the compound name. For example, one line could be
NaClO3 Sodium Chlorate. In the formula, there can be no blanks; allow for a maximum of 40 characters in the formula and another 40 in the compound name. Further, in the formula, case is significant. The atom identification is one or two characters long, the first of which must be uppercase and the second, if any, must be lowercase. That is, the atom is identified by an uppercase letter. Any trailing numbers represent the number of those atoms at that point in the formula. In the above example, there is one Na (Sodium), one Cl (Chlorine) and three O (Oxygen) atoms in the compound.

For each compound, print a line detailing its component atoms such as this.

```
Sodium Chlorate
    1 Na
    1 Cl
    3 O
```

Sum all like atoms into a single total. For example, if we had Methanol—CH3OH, the totals would be

```
     1 C
     4 H
     1 O
```

Chapter 12—Multidimensional Arrays

Section A: Basic Theory

Introduction

Multidimensional arrays, that is, arrays with two or more dimensions, are extremely valuable in many applications. A two-dimensional array can be thought of as having a number of rows each with the same number of columns.

One common application of two-dimensional arrays is a spreadsheet. In a monthly budget spreadsheet, for example, the rows represent the income and expenses while the columns represent the monthly expenses. Consider the following budget.

```
item              June     July    August
income         1500.00  1550.00   1500.00
rent            500.00   500.00    500.00
utilities       200.00   200.00    200.00
phone            40.00    40.00     40.00
movies           20.00    30.00     25.00
```

All of the above numerical values are **doubles**. While one could create five single-dimensioned arrays, each containing three elements to hold the sets of monthly values, a single two-dimensional array of five rows each with three columns greatly simplifies the programming logic.

Defining Multidimensional Arrays

The above budget two-dimensional array is defined as

```
double budget[5][3];
```

In general, the syntax is

```
datatype name[limit1][limit2][limit3]…[limitn];
```

The number of dimensions is unlimited; however, for practical purposes, the amount of memory available for a program to use on a specific platform becomes the limiting factor. How much memory does the above budget array occupy? Assuming that a **double** occupies 8 bytes, then budget takes 5 x 3 x 8 bytes, or 120 bytes.

When defining multidimensional arrays, each array bound or limit should be either a **#define** value or a **const int**. These limit values are likely to be used throughout the program. If a symbolic limit is used, it is easier later to modify the limits to allow for more or less data. The above budget array can be defined as follows.

```
const int NumberItems = 5;
const int NumberMonths = 3;
...
double budget[NumberItems][NumberMonths];
```

Consider another example. Suppose that we needed to accumulate the total sales from various cash registers located in three different stores and that each store had four departments each. We could define three separate total arrays, one for each store; each array would have four elements, one for each department. However, defining one two-dimensional array of three stores each with four departments greatly simplifies programming. The **totals** array could be defined as follows.

```
#define STORES 3
#define DEPTS 4
...
double totals[STORES][DEPTS];
```

Suppose further that, within each department, there are always two cash registers. Now the array would contain a third dimension.

```
#define REGS 2
...
double regtotals[STORES][DEPTS][REGS];
```

How are the individual elements within a multidimensional array accessed? By providing all the needed subscripts. Remember that all subscripts begin with element 0. The following are valid.

```
totals[0][1] = 5.;  // store 0, dept 1
totals[1][3] = 10.; // store 1, dept 3
totals[0][0] = 0;   // the first element in the array
x = totals[2][3];   // the last element in the array
regtotals[1][2][0] = 42; // store 1, dept 2, reg 0
```

The following are invalid.

```
totals[0,1] = 5; // each subscript must be within []
totals[1] = 1;   // this only specifies row 1 -
                 // which has 4 columns
totals = 0;      // unfortunately not allowed either
```

Normally, the subscripts are variables and not constants. The subscripts may also be integer expressions. The following are valid.

```
totals[i][j]++;  // increments this specific total
totals[k][0] = 5;
totals[k+j][j/2] = 5;
```

The following are invalid.

```
totals[k++][0]; // incs k not the element in total
totals++[k][0]; // ++ op comes after the subscripts
totals[.5][.3] = 5; // subscripts must be integers
```

Physical Memory Layout versus Logical Layout

The physical memory layout always follows the same sequence. In a two-dimensional array, all of the columns of row 0 come first followed by all the columns for row 1 and so on. This is called **row-major order**. Figure 12.1 shows how memory is laid out for the **totals** array.

Figure 12.2 shows how the **regtotals** array is stored in memory.

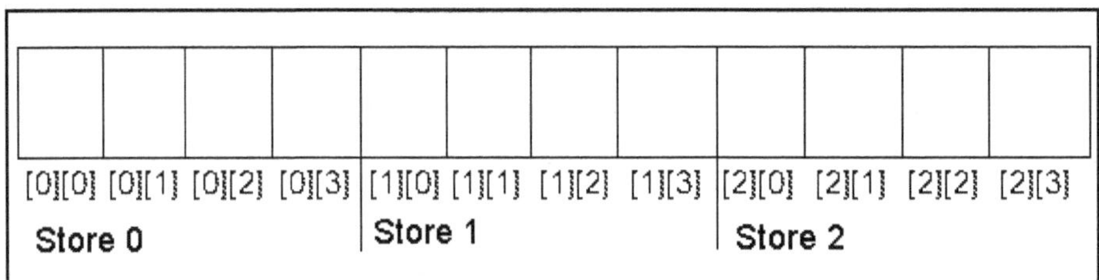

Figure 12.1 Memory Layout for **totals**

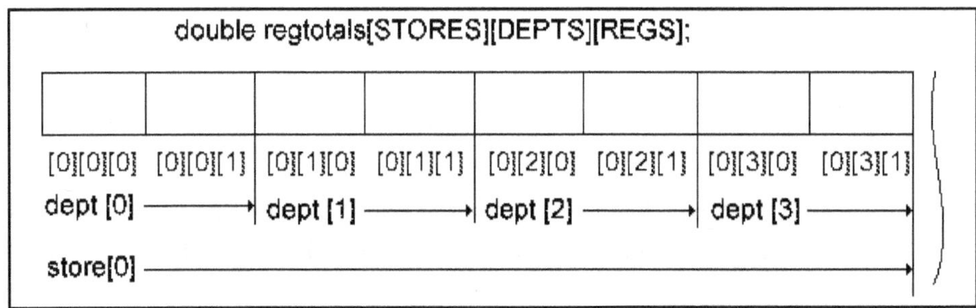

Figure 12.2 Memory Layout for **regtotals**

Programmatically, two-dimensional arrays are often thought of as having rows and columns, rather like a table. It is more useful to take the following logical viewpoint of the **totals** array, where the x-axis represents the columns and the y-axis represent the rows. This is shown in Figure 12.3.

In a similar manner, a three-dimensional array has the first or leftmost dimension on the z-axis (coming into or out of the page), its second dimension is along the y-axis, and the rightmost dimension is along the x-axis.

rows \ columns-->	0	1	2	3
0	totals[0][0]	totals[0][1]	totals[0][2]	totals[0][3]
1	totals[1][0]	totals[1][1]	totals[1][2]	totals[1][3]
2	totals[2][0]	totals[2][1]	totals[2][2]	totals[2][3]

Figure 12.3 The Logical Rows and Columns View

Initialization of Multidimensional Arrays

The basic concept of single-dimensioned array initialization is extended in a similar fashion to multidimensional arrays. Consider the totals array of 3 rows by 4 columns. First, all of row 0 is initialized. However, since row 0 is an array of 4 columns, the array notation is used.

```
double totals[3][4] = { {1, 2, 3, 4}, {11. 12. 13. 14},
                         row 0          row 1

                        {21, 22, 23, 24} };
                         row 2
```

If all of the elements of a single-dimensioned array are not initialized, the default value of 0 is used for the remaining unspecified elements. Thus, if **totals** were to be initialized to 0, it could be done as follows.

```
double totals[3][4] = { {0}, {0}, {0} };
```

To initialize all the elements of **regtotals** to 0, one could do the following.

```
double regtotals[3][4][2] = { { {0}, {0}, {0}, {0} },
//                          dept 0    1    2    3
//                           -- store 0 ---------
 { {0}, {0}, {0}, {0} }, { {0}, {0}, {0}, {0} } };
// ----- store 1 -----     ----- store 2 -----
```

As the number of dimensions increases, the initialization syntax becomes awful! Frequently, it is much simpler just to write some loops to initialize the arrays at run time. The **regtotals** array can be initialized as follows.

```
for (int i=0; i< STORES; i++) {
 for (int j=0; j<DEPTS; j++) {
  for (int k=0; k<REGS; k++) {
   regtotals[i][j][k] = 0;
  }
 }
}
```

Passing Multidimensional Arrays to Functions

With single-dimensioned arrays, the name of the array is a constant pointer or memory address of the first element of the array. The same is true of a multidimensional array; its name is a constant pointer or memory address of the first element. If the **totals** array were to be passed to a function, say **calcs()**, the prototype is

```
void calcs (double totals[][DEPTS]);
```

It would not be wrong to provide all dimensions though, as in

```
void calcs (double totals[STORES][DEPTS]);
```

However, the compiler always ignores the leftmost dimension's value. However, all other dimensions must be specified. The **main()** function would then invoke the **calcs()** function by

```
calcs (totals);
```

The following is in error—why?

```
void calcs (double totals[][]);
```

To see why, suppose that within **calcs()** one coded the following.

```
totals[1][0] = qty * sales;
```

How does the compiler locate the specific element to assign the calculation result? The compiler finds the start of the 2nd row (subscript 1) by multiplying the number of elements in any row times the size of the data type of the array. This is called the **row offset** from the start of the array. It then finds the **column offset** by multiplying the column number by the size of the data type of the array. Finally, the compiler adds the starting address of the array with the row offset and then the column offset to yield the memory address of the requested element. Thus, to find the row offset, the compiler must know how many elements are in a row, that is, the second dimension.

Suppose that the array **regtotals** is to be passed to the **calcs2()** function. The prototype is

```
void calcs2 (double regtotals[][DEPTS][REGS]);
```

In all cases, it is permissible to omit only the leftmost dimension. However, it is always permissible to provide all the dimension limits; this is also less error prone.

```
void calcs2 (double regtotals[STORES][DEPTS][REGS]);
```

The **main()** function would then invoke **calcs2()** by the following.

```
calcs2 (regtotals);
```

Loading a Multidimensional Array from an Input File

Consider again the **budget** array with which the chapter began. It was defined as

```
double budget[NumberItems][ NumberMonths];
```

Suppose that the data were stored in a file called **budget.txt** and that a **LoadArray()** function is to read this data filling up the **budget** array. Recall with a single-dimensioned array, typically, not all potential elements were used in a given execution of a program. We commonly track the number of elements actually input with an integer, **numElements**, for example. The input of a multidimensional array presents some additional complications.

Suppose in true generality that not every column of every row was present. That is, for row 0, we might only have the first two columns; for row 1, all three columns are present; for row 2, only the first column's data is present; and so on. How could this be represented in the input data and worse still, how would the program know when accessing a specific row how many columns of data were actually in that row? True, we could input on a line-by-line basis and say all columns for a given row were on one line so that line breaks ended that row's input, but there is no easy way to "remember" how many elements each row has. If this needed to be done, a parallel second array of integer column counts would have to be constructed in which the number of elements actually in row 0 of the budget array was stored in element 0 of the counts array. Notice how fast the complexity is rising!

In reality, very often the input of multidimensional arrays is simplified to one of two approaches:

All elements of every row and all rows are entered
All elements of every row are entered, but not all rows are input

In other words, only the leftmost dimension can have a variable number input. For instance, with the **budget** array, we could store the number of rows of budget items actually input in the integer **numItems**. However, every row entered must have all three monthly values present.

The **main()** function calls **LoadBudget()** as follows.

```
int numItems = LoadBudget (budget, NumberItems,
                           NumberMonths);
```

Here is the **LoadBudget()** function that returns the number of items or rows actually input.

```
int LoadBudget (double budget[NumberItems][NumberMonths],
                int itemLimit, int monthLimit) {
 ifstream infile ("budget.txt");
 if (!infile) {
  cerr << "Error: cannot open budget.txt\n";
  exit (1);
 }
 int j = 0;
 int k;
 while (j<itemLimit && infile >> ws && infile.good()) {
  for (k=0; k<monthLimit && infile; k++) {
   infile >> budget[j][k];
  }
  if (!infile) {
   cerr << "Error: unexpected end of a budget row "
        << j+1 << endl;
   exit (2);
  }
  j++;
 }
 infile.close ();
 return j;
}
```

Working with Multidimensional Arrays

When working with two-dimensional arrays, a programmer is frequently called upon to sum the contents of an entire row (summing all the columns of that row) or to sum the contents of a specific column (summing that column in all the rows). Let's examine the straightforward approach to these two problems and then see what can be done to improve execution speed of the operations. The **main()** function defines the array to use and calls the simple **sumrow1()** function to sum all of the values in a row and display that sum.

```
#include <iostream>
#include <iomanip>
using namespace std;
```

```
const int NUMROWS = 3;
const int NUMCOLS = 4;

int sumrow1 (int x[][NUMCOLS], int whichrow);
int sumrow2 (int x[NUMCOLS]);

int sumcol1 (int x[][NUMCOLS], int whichcol);
int sumcol2 (int x[NUMCOLS], int whichcol);

int main() {
 int n;
 int array[NUMROWS][NUMCOLS] = { {1,2,3,4}, {11,12,13,14},
                                 {21,22,23,24} };
 // Method 1: normal sumrow function
 for (n=0; n<NUMROWS; n++) {
   cout << "sumrow1 = " << sumrow1(array,n) << endl;
 }
```

The function **sumrow1()** is straightforward. For the given row, simply add up each column.

```
int sumrow1 (int x[][NUMCOLS], int whichrow) {
 int i, sum = 0;
 for (i=0; i<NUMCOLS; i++) {
  sum += x[whichrow][i];
 }
 return sum;
}
```

How can this coding be speeded up at execution time? First, if the bounds are small and the sum is invoked only one time, there is no need to try to improve its efficiency. However, if the bounds are large and this function is to be invoked many times, then a speed up is in order. What is slowing down the **sumrow1()** function is the need for two subscripts. Remember that to find the current element to add to the sum, the compiler must first calculate the row offset and then the column offset and add those to values to the beginning memory address of the array in order to find the requested element. Both offset calculations involve multiplying by the size of the data type, the **sizeof** a **double** or 8 in this case. The multiplication machine instruction is fairly slow, though on the Pentium class chips, it has been drastically speeded up. If we can reduce the number of multiplies, the function executes more quickly.

When summing a row, all the columns of that row are in consecutive memory locations, that is, it can be thought of as a single-dimensioned array of four columns in this case. Thus, we pass only the current row **n** of four columns. The notation is

```
array[n]
```

Here I have provided only the first subscript of the two-dimensional array. The compiler assumes that I am specifying only the nth row, which is a single-dimensioned array of four **double**s.

The **main()** function now does the following.

```
 // results in 25% less code, 4% faster execution
 for (n=0; n<NUMROWS; n++) {
  cout << "sumrow2 = " << sumrow2(array[n]) << endl;
 }
```

The **sumrow2()** function is now very simple indeed.

```
int sumrow2 (int x[NUMCOLS]) {
 int i, sum = 0;
 for (i=0; i<NUMCOLS; i++) {
  sum += x[i];
 }
 return sum;
}
```

The other common operation is summing columns. For a specific column, find the sum of that column by accumulating the sum of that column in every row. The **main()** function calls **sumcol1()** illustrating the straightforward approach. Note that no matter which vertical column whose sum is desired, the entire array is passed.

```
 for (n=0; n<NUMCOLS; n++) {
  cout << "sumcol1 = " << sumcol1(array,n) << endl;
 }
```

The basic **sumcol1()** function is as follows. Here we simply go through each row adding up the desired column.

```
int sumcol1 (int x[][NUMCOLS], int whichcol) {
 int i, sum = 0;
 for (i=0; i<NUMROWS; i++) {
  sum += x[i][whichcol];
 }
 return sum;
}
```

If performance requires the **sumcol()** function to be more efficient, how can it be improved? The objective is once more to reduce the number of multiplication machine instructions it takes to find the desired element. In this case, we cannot just pass the needed row as an array of four column values; we need to go vertical through the rows summing the specific column in each row. However, there is a trick that we can use. Recall that the compiler never checks for the "subscript out of range" condition. Assume that we have passed only the very first row of the two-dimensional array, so that the **sumcol2()** function sees only a single-dimension array of four elements, those of row 0. Set the initial subscript to the desired column that we are to sum—for example column 2. Then, to get to the next row's corresponding column, to our subscript add the number of columns in a row. In this case, there are four columns per row. The next subscript is 2 + 4 or 6, which is, in fact, really in column 2 of the next row.

```
// The results: it has 2% faster execution
for (n=0;n<NUMCOLS;n++) {
 cout << "sumcol2 = " << sumcol2(array[0],n) << endl;
}
```

The improved **sumcol2()** function is shown below.

```
int i, j = whichcol, sum = 0;
for (i=0; i<NUMROWS; i++) {
 sum += x[j];
 j = j + NUMCOLS;
}
```

Here are the complete program listing and sample output for **Basic12a** that implements all these functions. Multidimensional arrays have many uses. Some of these are explored in the next sections.

Listing for Basic12a - Working with two-dimensional arrays

```
/***************************************************************/
/*                                                             */
/* Basic12a Working with 2-dimensional arrays                  */
/*                                                             */
/***************************************************************/
#include <iostream>
#include <iomanip>
using namespace std;
const int NUMROWS = 3;
const int NUMCOLS = 4;

int sumrow1 (int x[][NUMCOLS], int whichrow);
int sumrow2 (int x[NUMCOLS]);

int sumcol1 (int x[][NUMCOLS], int whichcol);
int sumcol2 (int x[NUMCOLS], int whichcol);

int main() {
 int n;
 int array[NUMROWS][NUMCOLS] = { {1,2,3,4}, {11,12,13,14},
                                 {21,22,23,24} };

 // Method 1: normal sum the rows function
 for (n=0; n<NUMROWS; n++) {
  cout << "sumrow1 = " << sumrow1(array,n) << endl;
 }
 cout << endl;

 // To get it faster, pass a single dimensioned array of 4 cols
 // that is the row to sum up. Access is now by  a single
 // subscript array[n] is an array of 4 ints
 // The results: takes 25% less code and has 4% faster execution
 for (n=0; n<NUMROWS; n++) {
  cout << "sumrow2 = " << sumrow2(array[n]) << endl;
 }
 cout << endl;

 // Normal sum the columns approach
 for (n=0; n<NUMCOLS; n++) {
```

```
   cout << "sumcol1 = " << sumcol1(array,n) << endl;
  }
  cout << endl;

  // To get it faster, pass only the address of start of the first
  // row as a single dimension array of 4 columns
  // The results: it has 2% faster execution
  for (n=0;n<NUMCOLS;n++) {
   cout << "sumcol2 = " << sumcol2(array[0],n) << endl;
  }
  cout << endl;

  return 0;
 }

/***************************************************************/
/*                                                             */
/* sumrow1: basic method to sum the contents of a specific row */
/*                                                             */
/***************************************************************/

int sumrow1 (int x[][NUMCOLS], int whichrow) {
 int i, sum = 0;
 for (i=0; i<NUMCOLS; i++) {
  sum += x[whichrow][i];
 }
 return sum;
}

/***************************************************************/
/*                                                             */
/* sumrow2: faster method to sum the contents of a specific row*/
/*                                                             */
/***************************************************************/

int sumrow2 (int x[NUMCOLS]) {
 int i, sum = 0;
 for (i=0; i<NUMCOLS; i++) {
  sum += x[i];
 }
 return sum;
}

/***************************************************************/
/*                                                             */
/* sumcol1: basic method to sum the contents of a specific col */
/*                                                             */
/***************************************************************/

int sumcol1 (int x[][NUMCOLS], int whichcol) {
 int i, sum = 0;
 for (i=0; i<NUMROWS; i++) {
  sum += x[i][whichcol];
```

```
  }
 return sum;
}

/**************************************************************/
/*                                                            */
/* sumcol2: fater method to sum the contents of a specific col */
/*                                                            */
/**************************************************************/

int sumcol2 (int x[], int whichcol) {
 int i, j = whichcol, sum = 0;
 for (i=0; i<NUMROWS; i++) {
  sum += x[j];
  j = j + NUMCOLS;
 }
 return sum;
}
```

Output from Basic12a - Working with two-dimensional arrays

```
sumrow1 = 10
sumrow1 = 50
sumrow1 = 90

sumrow2 = 10
sumrow2 = 50
sumrow2 = 90

sumcol1 = 33
sumcol1 = 36
sumcol1 = 39
sumcol1 = 42

sumcol2 = 33
sumcol2 = 36
sumcol2 = 39
sumcol2 = 42
```

Some More Examples of Array Processing

Let's assume that we have defined a two-dimensional array this way.

```
const int MAX = 20;
int array[MAX][MAX];
```

Also, assume that there is a value in all twenty rows and all twenty columns of each row. And let's perform some actions on the array. First, set all elements of the 3rd row to 0.

```
for (col=0; col<MAX; col++) {
 array[2][col] = 0;
}
```

Next, let's set all the 2nd column values to 1.

```
for (row=0; row<MAX; row++) {
 array[row][1] = 1;
}
```

Let's set each element of the main diagonal from (0,0) to (19,19) to 42.

```
for (row=0; row<MAX; row++) {
 array[row][row] = 42;
}
```

Let's set each element of the back diagonal from (0,19) to (19,0) to 5.

```
for (row=0; row<MAX; row++) {
 array[row][MAX-row-1] = 5;
}
```

Section B: A Computer Science Example

Cs12a—Arrays of Strings

Suppose that we wished to store an array of character strings, such as the month names. Notice that since a string is a single-dimensioned array of **char**, then the array of strings must therefore be really a two-dimensioned array of characters. Here is how the array of month names could be defined and initialized.

```
const char monthNames[13][10] = { "",
     "January", "February", "March", "April", "May",
     "June", "July", "August", "September", "October",
     "November", "December" };
```

When initializing an array of strings, it is permissible to use "strings" as element values. Since month numbers normally range from one through twelve, I have "wasted" element 0, storing a null string in it. Also, notice that I made the array constant. Thus, these values cannot be accidentally altered by the program.

For this example, let's write a word counter program. Our input can be a sample chapter of someone's writing. We must construct a table of the words that we find (ignoring case) and a parallel array of frequencies of those words.

Initially, **numWords**, which holds the number of words in the table, is zero. The two-dimensional array **words** holds all of the found words. The array **freq** holds the corresponding frequency counts. The array **word** holds the current word that has been input.

What constitutes a "word?" My definition is overly simplified. It is any consecutive series of letters only. Hyphenated words become two separate words. The **main()** program then defines these as follows.

```
const int MaxWords = 1000;
const int WordLen = 20;
char words[MaxWords][WordLen]; // the table of found words
int freq[MaxWords] = {0};
char word[WordLen];            // place to input the next word
int numWords = 0;              // number of words in the table
```

Figure 12.4 shows main storage for the **main()** function. The basic operation of the program is to input a word and find out if it is in the table. If it is in the table already, then increment that word's corresponding frequency. If it is not yet in the table of words, add it to the table and set its frequency count to one. This process is repeated until the end of the text file occurs. The results are sorted into frequency of use order and printed. This then suggests the following Top-Down Design shown in Figure 12.5.

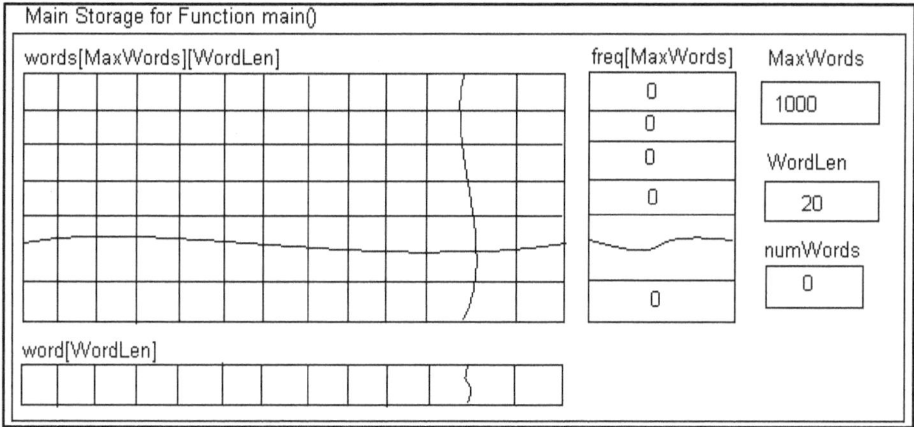

Figure 12.4 Main Storage for Word Program

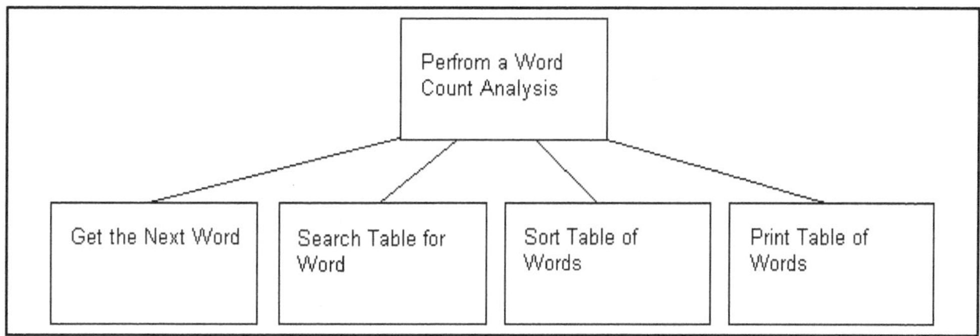

Figure 12.5 Top-Down Design of Word Counter Program

From a design point of view, the **GetNextWord()** function should return the **istream** reference from which it is inputting the new word. That way, we can test for the end of file condition in the **main()** function's **while** clause. **SearchTableForWord()** should return the subscript of the matching word or the current number of words in the table if the new word is not in the table. This allows the **main()** function to become very simple indeed. Here is the sequence.

open **infile**; if it fails to open, display an error message and quit
while (**GetNextWord** (**infile**, **word**, **WordLen**)) do the following
  i = **SearchTableForWord** (**words**, **numWords**, **word**);
  if i == **numWords**, then the word is not in the table, so do these steps
    add this word by doing **strcpy** (**words[i**], **word**);
    let **freq[i**] = 1;
    increment the **numWords** in the table
  end then clause
  otherwise it is in the table, so increment its count: **freq[i**]++
end the **while** clause
sort the **words** array into order by calling into frequency by calling **SortArray** passing it **words**, **freq** and **numWords**
call **PrintArray** passing it **words**, **freq**, **numWords**, and a string containing the filename to use for the display.

The **GetNextWord()** function retrieves the next word. It must skip over non-letters to next letter; then get and store each letter until it either encounters a non-letter or reaches the maximum word length – 1. Finally, it must insert the null terminator.

GetNextWord() is passed **infile**, **word**[] and the **wordlen**. Its sequence is as follows.
To skip over everything but a letter:
while (**infile.get** (**c**)) do the following
if c < 'A' || (**c** > 'Z' && **c** < 'a') || **c** > 'z' then it is not a letter, so continue
else break out of the loop with **c** containing the letter
end **while**
if !**infile** then it is EOF and no word was found, so do these steps
word[0] = 0 to null terminate the string
return **infile**
end the if
Now insert successive letters into the **word** array until a non-letter or **wordlen** – 1 is reached or EOF occurs:
word[count++] = **c**;
while count < **wordlen** -1 && **infile.get** (**c**) do the following
is **c** < 'A' || (**c** > 'Z' && **c** < 'a') || **c** > 'z' then it is not a letter so **break**
word[count++] = **c** to insert the letter into the array
end **while** loop
word[count] = 0 to null terminate the string
return infile;

The **SearchTableForWord()** function is passed **table**[][**WordLen**], **count** and the new **word**. It must return the subscript of the matching word in the table or **count** if **word** is not in the table yet. It is case insensitive.
for (**int i**=0; **i<count**; **i**++) do the following
if (**stricmp** (**word**, **table[i]**) == 0) then it is a match, so **return i**;
end **for** loop
no match, so **return count**

The **SortArray()** function sorts the table of words and frequencies into frequency order from highest to lowest. It is passed the **table**[][**WordLen**], **freq**[] and **count**. Because **table** and **freq** are parallel arrays, swapping must be done together. Assuming that **temp** and **tfreq** are the temporary variables to hold a string and a frequency, the following represents the sorting sequence.
for (**int i**=0; **i<count**-1; **i**++) do the following
for (**int j**=**i**+1; **j<count**; **j**++) do the following
is **freq[j]** > **freq[i]**? If so, then we have found a larger frequency, so swap
tfreq = **freq[i]**; // exchange frequencies
freq[i] = **freq[j]**;
freq[j] = **tfreq**;
strcpy (**temp**, **table[i]**); // exchange words in the table
strcpy (**table[i]**, **table[j]**);

strcpy (**table[j]**, **temp**);
end if
end inner loop
end outer loop

The **PrintArray()** function prints out a nicely formatted set of results and is passed the **table**[][**WordLen**], **freq**[], **count** and the **filename** string to use for output.

attempt to open **out**; if it fails, display an error message and quit
display a title
for (**int i**=0; **i<count**; **i**++)
output the **table[i]** word and its frequency **freq[i]**
close **out**

Here are the completed program **Cs12a** and the abbreviated output for the first few page of this chapter used as input.

Cs12a - Word Usage Frequency Analysis

```
/***************************************************************/
/*                                                             */
/* Cs12a Word frequency of use in the first part of Chapter 12 */
/*                                                             */
/***************************************************************/

#include <iostream>
#include <iomanip>
#include <fstream>
#include <string>
#include <cctype>
using namespace std;

const int MaxWords = 1000;
const int WordLen = 20;

istream& GetNextWord (istream& infile, char word[], int wordlen);
int      SearchTableForWord (char table[][WordLen], int count,
                             char word[]);
void     SortArray(char table[][WordLen], int freq[], int count);
void     PrintArray(char table[][WordLen], int freq[], int count,
                    const char filename[]);

int main () {
 char words[MaxWords][WordLen]; // the table of found words
 int freq[MaxWords] = {0};      // corresponding frequencies
 int numWords = 0;              // number of words in the table

 char word[WordLen];            // an inputted word

 const char filename[] = "Cs12a-text.txt";
 ifstream infile (filename);
```

```
 if (!infile) {
  cerr << "Error: cannot open input file " << filename << endl;
  return 1;
 }

 // input words and accumulate frequency of occurrence
 while (GetNextWord (infile, word, WordLen)) {
  int i = SearchTableForWord (words, numWords, word);
  if (i == numWords) {      // word not in the table yet
   strcpy_s (words[i], sizeof(words[i]), word); // add this word
   freq[i] = 1;              // set count to 1 time
   numWords++;               // increment total word count
  }
  else freq[i]++;            // is in the table, so inc frequency
 }
 infile.close ();

 // sort into frequency of use order
 SortArray (words, freq, numWords);

 // print the results
 PrintArray (words, freq, numWords, filename);

 return 0;
}

/***************************************************************/
/*                                                             */
/* GetNextWord: retrieves the next word                        */
/*    skip over non-letters to next letter                     */
/*    get and store each letter until either it encounters a   */
/*    non-letter or reaches max word length -1                 */
/*    null terminates the string                               */
/*                                                             */
/***************************************************************/

istream& GetNextWord (istream& infile, char word[],
                      int wordlen) {
 char c;
 int count = 0;
 while (infile.get (c)) { // skip over everything but a letter
  if (c < 'A' || (c > 'Z' && c < 'a') || c > 'z')
   continue;
  else
   break;
 }

 if (!infile) { // if eof & no word, at least return null string
  word[0] = 0;
  return infile;
 }

 // insert successive letters until a non-letter is found or
```

```
// it reaches wordlen - 1 or hits eof
word[count++] = c;
while (count < wordlen -1 && infile.get (c)) {
 if (c < 'A' || (c > 'Z' && c < 'a') || c > 'z')
  break;
 word[count++] = c;
}

word[count] = 0; // null terminate string
return infile;
}

/***************************************************************/
/*                                                             */
/* SearchTableForWord: returns subscript of matching word      */
/*            in table or count if it is not in the table yet  */
/*                      case insensitive comparison            */
/*                                                             */
/***************************************************************/

int SearchTableForWord (char table[][WordLen], int count,
                        char word[]) {
 for (int i=0; i<count; i++) {
  if (_stricmp (word, table[i]) == 0)
   return i;
 }
 return count;
}

/***************************************************************/
/*                                                             */
/* SortArray: sorts the table of words & frequencies into freq */
/*            order from highest to lowest                     */
/*                                                             */
/***************************************************************/

void SortArray (char table[][WordLen], int freq[], int count) {
 char temp[WordLen];
 int  tfreq;
 for (int i=0; i<count-1; i++) {
  for (int j=i+1; j<count; j++) {
   if (freq[j] > freq[i]) {  // found a larger freq, so swap
    tfreq = freq[i];          // exchange frequencies
    freq[i] = freq[j];
    freq[j] = tfreq;
    strcpy (temp, WordLen, table[i]); // exchange words in table
    strcpy (table[i], WordLen, table[j]);
    strcpy (table[j], WordLen, temp);
   }
  }
 }
}

```

```
/***************************************************************/
/*                                                             */
/* PrintArray: print out a nicely formatted set of results     */
/*                                                             */
/***************************************************************/

void PrintArray (char table[][WordLen], int freq[], int count,
                 const char filename[]) {
 ofstream out ("Cs12a-results.txt");
 if (!out) {
  cerr<<"Error: cannot open the output file Cs12a-results.txt\n";
  exit (1);
 }
 out << "Word frequencies found in " << filename << endl << endl;
 for (int i=0; i<count; i++) {
  out << setw (4) << i+1 << ". " << left << setw (WordLen+5)
      << table[i] << right << setw (6) << freq[i] << endl;
 }
 out.close ();
}
```

Abbreviated output of Cs12a - Word Usage Frequency Analysis

```
Word frequencies found in Cs12a-text.txt

   1. the                            40
   2. array                          15
   3. A                              15
   4. totals                         15
   5. of                             12
   6. each                           12
   7. are                            10
   8. is                              9
   9. be                              8
  10. Arrays                          8
  11. budget                          8
  12. for                             8
  13. two                             8
  14. to                              7
  15. In                              7
  16. dimensional                     6
  17. following                       6
  18. dimensioned                     6
  19. limit                           6
  20. columns                         6
  21. subscripts                      6
  22. three                           5
  23. One                             5
  24. double                          5
  25. with                            5
  26. memory                          5
  27. that                            5
```

```
  28. define                  5
  29. total                   5
  30. stores                  5
  31. store                   5
  32. Multi                   5
  33. All                     5
  34. k                       5
...
 227. out                     1
```

Section C: Engineering Examples

Matrix Algebra

Multiple dimensioned arrays open new vistas in the types of problems that can be solved. Specifically, matrices can be stored in two-dimensional arrays. Matrices can be used to solve linear simultaneous equations, such as **n** equations in **n** unknowns. The starting point is a brief review of the rules of Matrix Algebra.

Suppose that we had the following simultaneous equations.

$$5x + 4y + 3z = 40$$
$$9y + 3z + 8x = 10$$
$$4z + 3x + 6y = 20$$

They must be rearranged into the proper format.

$$5x + 4y + 3z = 40$$
$$8x + 9y + 3z = 10$$
$$3x + 6y + 4z = 20$$

In matrix notation, this becomes the following.

$$\begin{pmatrix} 5 & 4 & 3 \\ 9 & 3 & 8 \\ 4 & 3 & 6 \end{pmatrix} x \begin{pmatrix} x \\ y \\ z \end{pmatrix} = \begin{pmatrix} 40 \\ 10 \\ 20 \end{pmatrix}$$

Or **A X** = **B**; so the solution is **X** = **B/A**

The normal matrix notation for this case of 3 equations in 3 unknowns is show below.

$$\begin{pmatrix} a11 & a12 & a13 \\ a21 & a22 & a23 \\ a31 & a32 & a33 \end{pmatrix} . \begin{pmatrix} x1 \\ x2 \\ x3 \end{pmatrix} = \begin{pmatrix} b1 \\ b2 \\ b3 \end{pmatrix}$$

Notice that the math matrix notation parallels C++ subscripts, but begins with subscript 1 not 0. Always remember to subtract 1 from the matrix math indices to get a C++ array subscript.

In this example, the **a** matrix is composed of 3 rows or row vectors, and 3 columns or column vectors. In general, a matrix is said to be an **m** by **n** matrix, **m** rows and **n** columns. When **m** = **n**, it is called a **square** matrix. A matrix with only one row is a **row** matrix; one with only one column is a **column** matrix. The **x** and **b** matrices are both column matrices.

Matrix Math Operations Summary

1. Two matrices are said to be equal if and only if they have the same dimensions and all corresponding elements are equal.

aij = **bij** for all **i**=1,**m** and **j**=1,**n**

2. Addition and Subtraction operations require that the matrices involved have the same number of rows and columns. To compute **C** = **A** + **B** or **C** = **A** – **B**, simply add or subtract all corresponding elements. This can be implemented in C++ as follows.

```
for (int I=0; I<M; I++) {
 for (int J=0; J<N; J++) {
  C(I,J) = A(I,J) + B(I,J);
 }
}
```

3. Multiplication of a matrix by a number is commutative. That is, **rA** is the same as **Ar.** The result is given by **r** times each element.

```
for (int I=0; I<M; I++) {
 for (int J=0; J<N; J++) {
  A(I,J) = A(I,J) * r;
 }
}
```

For example, assume **A** is defined to be the following.

$$A = \begin{pmatrix} 2.7 & -1.8 \\ 0.9 & 3.6 \end{pmatrix}$$

Then 2**A** would be

$$A = \begin{pmatrix} 5.4 & -3.6 \\ 1.8 & 7.2 \end{pmatrix}$$

and 10/9**A** would be

$$A = \begin{pmatrix} 3 & -2 \\ 1 & 4 \end{pmatrix}$$

4. A **diagonal** matrix is one whose elements above and below the principal diagonal are 0: namely **aij**=0 for all **i**!=**j**

$$diagonal \begin{pmatrix} 3 & 0 & 0 \\ 0 & 4 & 0 \\ 0 & 0 & 5 \end{pmatrix}$$

5. An **identity** matrix is a diagonal matrix whose principal diagonal elements are all 1.

$$identity \begin{pmatrix} 1 & 0 & 0 \\ 0 & 1 & 0 \\ 0 & 0 & 1 \end{pmatrix}$$

6. Matrix multiplication says that the product of a square matrix times a column matrix is another column matrix. It is computed as follows: for each row in the square matrix, sum the products of each element in the square matrix's row by the corresponding element in the column matrix's column.

$$\begin{pmatrix} a11 & a12 & a13 \\ a21 & a22 & a23 \\ a31 & a32 & a33 \end{pmatrix} . \begin{pmatrix} b1 \\ b2 \\ b3 \end{pmatrix} = \begin{pmatrix} \mathrm{a11*b1+a12*b2+a13*b3} \\ \mathrm{a21*b1+a22*b2+a23*b3} \\ \mathrm{a31*b1+a32*b2+a33*b3} \end{pmatrix}$$

For a square matrix times a square matrix, the result is a square matrix of the same dimensions, each element of the result is the sum of the products of each element of the corresponding row of one matrix times each element of the corresponding column of the other matrix

C = A * B

where **Cij** = i^{th} row of **A** * j^{th} column of **B** or in coding

```
for (int I=0; I<3; I++) {
 for (int J=0; J<3; J++) {
  C(I,J) = 0;
  for (int K=0; K<3; K++) {
   C(I,J) = C(I,J) + A(I,K)*B(K,J);
  }
 }
}
```

7. Determinants form a crucial aspect in solving systems of equations. What we are after is the ability to solve: **A*X = B** so that we can solve it as **X = B/A**. However, matrix division is a real problem and really is not needed because there is a simpler method. A determinant can be pictorially thought of as rather like a "greatest common denominator."

If we had this simple two equations in two unknowns problem

```
a11x1 + a12x2 = b1
a21x1 + a22x2 = b2
```

then the long hand solution would be

```
x1 = (b1a22 - b2a12)          x2 = (b2a11 - b1a12)
     ----------------              ----------------
     (a11a22 - a21a12)             (a11a22 - a21a12)
```

assuming the denominator, called the **determinant**, is not zero; Note that the determinant is a single number. Notice that the determinant can be considered as the sum of the right slanted diagonals—sum of the left slanted diagonals.

It is notated as |**a**|, the determinant of **a**. For a 3x3 matrix, the determinant is given by the following number.

```
  a11a22a33 + a12a23a31 + a13a32a21
- a11a23a32 - a21a12a33 - a31a22a13
```

For a larger matrix, that is, the general case, the Cofactor Matrix concept is used. Consult a matrix math text for details. Normally another approach is used when the number of dimensions becomes four or more.

Mathematical Theorems of Determinants

The following summarize the rules that apply to working with determinants. We will apply these to the problem of solving simultaneous equations shortly.

1. The value of a determinant is not altered if its rows are written as columns in the same order.

$$\begin{pmatrix} 1 & 3 & 0 \\ 2 & 6 & 4 \\ -1 & 0 & 2 \end{pmatrix} = \begin{pmatrix} 1 & 2 & -1 \\ 3 & 6 & 0 \\ 0 & 4 & 2 \end{pmatrix} = -12$$

2. If all the elements of one row (or one column) of a determinant are multiplied by the same factor **k**, the value of the determinant is **k** times the value of the determinant. Notice the difference between **k|D|** and **kA**, where |**D**| is a determinant and **A** is a matrix. The operation **k|D|** multiplies just one row or column by **k** but **kA** multiplies all elements by **k**.

3. If all elements of a row or column of a determinant are zero, the value of the determinant is zero.

4. If any one row is proportional to another row (or one column is proportional to another column), then the determinant is zero.

5. If the elements of any one row are identical (in the same order) to another row, the determinant is zero. Likewise for columns.

6. Any two rows or columns may be interchanged, and the determinant just changes sign.

7. The value of a determinant is unchanged if the elements of a row (or column) are altered by adding to them any constant multiple of the corresponding elements in any other row (or column).

Given these basic principles, we can examine the two common methods used to solve linear equations. The Gauss Method is perhaps the simplest procedure used to solve linear equations. The Gauss-Jordan Method, which is a refinement of the Gauss Method, makes the process even easier.

The Gauss Method for Solving a System of Linear Equations

Suppose we had to solve:

```
    2x + 3y -  z =  1
    3x + 5y + 2z =  8
     x - 2y - 3z = -1
```

Gauss elimination begins by using the first equation to eliminate the first variable x in the second and other equations. By the theorems above, we can add, subtract, and multiply without altering the results. So we choose to subtract some multiple of the first equation to the remaining equations to bring about 0x in the remaining equations:

```
  3x +5.0y + 2.0z = 8.0    second equation
-(3x +4.5y - 1.5z = 1.5)   subtract the first equation * 1.5
-----------------------
  0x +0.5y +3.5z  = 6.5    the replacement second equation
```

So we now have the following.

```
2x +  3y -    z =  1
0x + .5y + 3.5z =  6.5
 x -  2y -   3z = -1
```

Next we do the same for the third equation.

```
  x - 2.0y - 3.0z = -1   third equation
-(x + 1.5y - 0.5z = .5)  subtract first equation * .5
-----------------------
 0x -3.5y  - 2.5z = -1.5
```

So now we have these results.

```
2x +   3y -    z =  1
0x +  .5y + 3.5z =  6.5
0x - 3.5y - 2.5z = -1.5
```

Now we move down to row 2 and repeat the process for all those equations that lie below row 2 - here, only row 3. Notice that column 1, the x column, is 0x for all rows from 2 on down. Hence, we only need to consider column 2 downward.

```
  - 3.5y - 2.5z = -1.5  third equation
-(- 3.5y -24.5z =-45.5) subtract second equation *-7
-----------------------
    0y   +22.0z = 44
```

So now we have the following.

```
2x +    3y -      z =   1
0x +   .5y + 3.5z =   6.5
0x +    0y +   22z =   44
```

We can back solve for the answers at this point. Beginning at the bottom, that is, row 3, we get the following.

```
z = 44/22 = 2
y = (6.5 - 3.5*2)/.5 = -1
x = (1 + 2 - 3*(-1))/2 = 3
```

Before we implement this procedure, let's study the effects. In the Gauss method, the "pivot row" is defined to be that row at which we are currently using to eliminate elements in the equations below. The pivot row begins at row 1 and runs to the n–1 row. The last row is complete—here 22z = 44. The "pivot coefficient" is the multiplicative factor we need to force zero in the "pivot column" of the lower rows. How did we determine what the pivot coefficient should be? Look again at the first step above. We took the second equation's pivot column's number (3x) and divided it by the first equation's pivot column's number (2x) to get 1.5.

Now you can see the problem. What happens if the current pivot row's pivot column contains zero? A divide by zero problem! The second problem is round off. If we divide by a tiny number, we will get a large result that is then used to multiply all other elements. Clearly the errors introduced will mushroom.

A better approach is known as "pivoting." We know that we can reorder the equations without altering the solution. So the idea is that, when reaching a specific pivot row and corresponding pivot column, we scan on down to the nth row and replace the current pivot row with that lower row that has the largest absolute magnitude pivot column number. Not only will this reduce round off errors, it will help avoid dividing by zero as well.

Gauss-Jordan Method of Solving Simultaneous Linear Equations

The Gauss-Jordan method is very similar to Gauss except that the elimination is carried further. The objective is to turn matrix **A** into an identity matrix, in which case, the coefficient matrix **B** actually holds the results.

For each pivot row **r** from 1 to **n** do the following two steps.

1. The pivot element is **a(r,r)**; normalized by dividing all elements of pivot row **r** and the **b(r)** by the pivot element **a(r,r)**. This gets the pivot element set to 1.

2. Next add multiples of the pivot row **r** to every other row in such a manner so that the pivot column **r** (the same number as the pivot row) has all zeros in it.

When the process is done, the matrix **A** will have become the identity matrix with the answers in the **B** column matrix. Usually, the **B** matrix is copied into the **X** answer matrix for consistency.

Listing Engr12a shows both the **Gauss()** and **GaussJordan()** functions. The **main()** function is discussed next.

Engr12a Gauss and GaussJordan Solutions of Equations

```
/***************************************************************/
/*                                                             */
/* Engr12a Gauss and GaussJordan Solutions of Equations        */
/*                                                             */
/***************************************************************/

#include <iostream>
#include <fstream>
#include <iomanip>
#include <cmath>
using namespace std;

const int MaxDim = 25;
bool Gauss (double A[][MaxDim], double B[], double X[], int N);
bool Reorder (double A[][MaxDim], double B[], int N, int pivot);
void Elim (double A[][MaxDim], double B[], int N, int pivot);
void Backsub (double A[][MaxDim], double B[], int N, double X[]);
bool GaussJordan (double A[][MaxDim], double B[], double X[],
                  int N);
void ElimJordan (double A[][MaxDim], double B[], int N,
                 int pivot);

int main () {
 // the arrays - one for Gauss and one for GaussJordan
 double A[MaxDim][MaxDim], B[MaxDim], X[MaxDim];
 double AJ[MaxDim][MaxDim], BJ[MaxDim], XJ[MaxDim];
 int i, j, N;

 // setup floating point output format
 ofstream out ("GaussResults.txt");
 out << fixed << setprecision (5);

 // open input file
 ifstream infile ("mirror.dat");
 if (!infile) {
  cerr << "Error: cannot open file mirror.dat\n";
  out.close ();
  return 1;
 }
 // input the number of equations in n unknowns
 infile >> N;
 if (N > MaxDim) {
```

```
   cerr << "Error: array dimensions exceeded - can handle 25\n";
   out.close ();
   infile.close ();
   return 2;
  }
  // input the arrays and copy into arrays for GaussJordan
  for (i=0; i<N; i++) {
   for (j=0; j<N; j++) {
    infile >> A[i][j];
    AJ[i][j] = A[i][j];
   }
   infile >> B[i];
   BJ[i] = B[i];
  }
  infile.close ();

  // do both the Gauss and Gauss Jordan solutions
  if (Gauss (A, B, X, N)) {
   if (GaussJordan (AJ, BJ, XJ, N)) {
    // print the results
    out << "The solutions are\n\n  I        Gauss   Gauss Jordan"
        << endl << endl;
    for (i=0; i<N; i++) {
     out << setw (3) << i+1 << setw (13) << X[i] << setw (15)
         << XJ[i] << endl;
    }
   }
  }
  out.close ();
  return 0;
 }

/***************************************************************/
/*                                                             */
/*  Gauss function                                             */
/*                                                             */
/*  Problem Definition: Perform a Gauss Elimination to find    */
/*  the solution of a set of n linear equations.               */
/*                                                             */
/*  Pass array of coefficients A, column array of answers B    */
/*  and a column array X to hold the solution                  */
/*  Pass N number dims in use this run                         */
/*                                                             */
/*  The answer is placed in the array X, with original arrays  */
/*  A and B being destroyed in the process                     */
/*                                                             */
/*  The solution utilizes pivoting and reordering to bring the */
/*  largest coefficient to the current pivot row on each       */
/*  iteration reducing round off errors and                    */
/*  avoiding division by 0                                     */
/*                                                             */
/*  However, should the pivot divisor become too small 1.E-5 or*/
/*  actually be 0, then no solution is possible and Gauss      */
```

```
/*  returns false.                                               */
/*  If all is well, Gauss returns true, solution found           */
/*                                                               */
/***************************************************************/

bool Gauss (double A[][MaxDim], double B[], double X[], int N) {
 int pivot = 0;       // begin on the first row and go til N-1 row
 while (pivot < (N-1)) {
  if (!Reorder (A, B, N, pivot)) {; // bring largest to pivot row
   cerr << "Error - no solution is possible\n";
   return false;
  }
  Elim (A, B, N, pivot); // perform the elimination
  pivot++; // and go on to the next row
 }
 Backsub (A, B, N, X); // now calculate the solution
 return true;
}

/***************************************************************/
/*                                                               */
/* Reorder: find the largest pivot element in this pivot row    */
/*          if it is not in the current pivot row,               */
/*          replace the pivot rowand this larger one's row      */
/*                                                               */
/***************************************************************/

bool Reorder (double A[][MaxDim], double B[], int N, int pivot) {
 int maxrow = pivot; // assume this one is the largest
 int row, col;
 double temp;
 // find if any other row has a larger one
 for (row=pivot+1; row<N; row++) {
  if (fabs (A[row][pivot]) > fabs (A[maxrow][pivot]))
   maxrow = row;
 }
 // error check - is the largest one 0 or too small to continue?
 if (fabs (A[maxrow][pivot]) < 1.E-5) return false;
 // no, so check to see if rows will need to be swapped
 if (maxrow != pivot) { // yes, swap rows in A and also in B
  for (col=0; col<N; col++) {
   temp           = A[maxrow][col];
   A[maxrow][col] = A[pivot][col];
   A[pivot][col]  = temp;
  }
  temp      = B[maxrow];
  B[maxrow] = B[pivot];
  B[pivot]  = temp;
 }
 return true; // all is ok
}

/***************************************************************/
```

```
/*                                                              */
/* Elim: replace all rows below pivot row,                      */
/*       forcing 0 into the pivot col                           */
/*                                                              */
/****************************************************************/

void Elim (double A[][MaxDim], double B[], int N, int pivot) {
 int row, col;
 double factor;
 for (row=pivot+1; row<N; row++) {
  factor = A[row][pivot] / A[pivot][pivot];
  A[row][pivot] = 0;
  for (col=pivot+1; col<N; col++) {
   A[row][col] -= A[pivot][col] * factor;
  }
  B[row] -= B[pivot] * factor;
 }
}

/****************************************************************/
/*                                                              */
/* Backsub: perform back substitution to create answer array    */
/*                                                              */
/****************************************************************/

void Backsub (double A[][MaxDim], double B[], int N, double X[]){
 int row, col;
 // calculate directly the last one
 X[N-1] = B[N-1] / A[N-1][N-1];
 // now repetatively substitute found X's to create next one
 for (row=N-2; row>=0; row--) {
  for (col=N-1; col>row; col--) {
   B[row] -= X[col] * A[row][col];
  }
  X[row] = B[row] / A[row][row];
 }
}

/****************************************************************/
/*                                                              */
/*  GaussJordan function                                        */
/*                                                              */
/*  Problem Definition: Perform a Gauss Jordan Elimination      */
/*  to determine the solution of a set of n linear equations.   */
/*                                                              */
/*  Pass array of coefficients A, column array of answers B     */
/*  and a column array X to hold the solution                   */
/*  Pass N number dims in use this run                          */
/*                                                              */
/*  The answer is placed in the array X, with the original      */
/*  A and B being destroyed in the process                      */
/*                                                              */
/*  The solution utilizes pivoting and reordering to bring the */
```

```
/*  largest coefficient to current pivot row on each iteration */
/*  thereby reducing round off errors and avoiding dividing by0*/
/*                                                             */
/*  However, should the pivot divisor become too small 1.E-5 or*/
/*  actually be 0, then no solution is possible and it returns */
/*  false. If all is well, returns true, solution found        */
/*                                                             */
/***************************************************************/

bool GaussJordan (double A[][MaxDim], double B[], double X[],
                  int N) {
 int pivot = 0;       // begin on the first row and go til N-1 row
 while (pivot < N) {
  if (!Reorder (A, B, N, pivot)) { // bring largest to pivot row
   cerr << "Error - no solution is possible\n";
   return false;
  }
  ElimJordan (A, B, N, pivot);  // perform the elimination
  pivot++;                      // and go on to the next row
 }
 for (int i=0; i<N; i++) {      // copy results back into X array
  X[i] = B[i];
 }
 return true;
}

/***************************************************************/
/*                                                             */
/* ElimJordan: replace all rows above and below pivot row      */
/*             forcing 1 into main diagonal and 0 in all others*/
/*                                                             */
/***************************************************************/

void ElimJordan (double A[][MaxDim], double B[], int N,
                 int pivot) {
 int row, col;
 // normalize pivot row, so A(pivot,pivot) = 1
 for (col=pivot+1; col<N; col++) {
  A[pivot][col] = A[pivot][col] / A[pivot][pivot];
 }
 B[pivot] = B[pivot] / A[pivot][pivot];
 A[pivot][pivot] = 1.;
 // eliminate pivot column in all other rows, except pivot row
 for (row=0; row<N; row++) {
  if (row == pivot || A[row][pivot] == 0) continue;
  for (col=pivot+1; col<N; col++) {
   A[row][col] -= A[row][pivot] * A[pivot][col];
  }
  B[row] -= B[pivot] * A[row][pivot];
  A[row][pivot] = 0;
 }
}
```

Engr12a—Aligning the Mirrors of a Telescope (Astronomy)

Finally, we need a set of equations to solve. In astronomy, the larger the diameter of the mirror, the better the performance. However, using glass mirrors beyond about 200 inches in diameter is not feasible due to overall weight, cost, and other factors. One way around this is to make an array of inexpensive 12-inch mirrors and align them to focus at a single point, as if they were sections of one large diameter mirror. Small servomotors can be used to keep all of the smaller mirrors in precise alignment. Periodically, a set of optical sensors detect the current alignment. In this example, there are 25 mirrors hooked together. Thus, one sample time period yields 25 coefficients of current alignment. When inserted into the corresponding 25 equations, and solved, the resulting values are sent to the servomotors to bring each mirror into correct alignment. This process is repeated periodically to keep the scope properly aligned.

The only difficulty in writing a **main()** function to do Gauss elimination is knowing in advance how many equations and unknowns there are going to be. When we define the A, B, and x matrices, we must provide the maximum number. In this example, I used an arbitrarily high number, **const int MaxDim** = 25. Then, the program expects the very first number to be input to contain the real number of unknowns on this particular test run. The real number of unknowns must be less than or equal to 25. This **MaxDim** could have been set far higher on a Win32 platform because up to 2G of memory are potentially available. If **MaxDim** had been set to 100 unknowns, then the amount of memory used by the arrays would be 160k all told.

In this case, the first line in the test file **mirror.dat** contains the number of equations, 25. Next comes the data for row 0's 25 column coefficients followed by the corresponding **B** value. Next come row 1's 25 coefficients and its **B** value and so on. The **main()** function inputs the **A** and **B** matrices and does both a Gauss and Gauss-Jordan elimination, printing the solutions side by side. Examine the above **Engr12a.cpp** file above for the coding in the **main()** function. Here is the output of the program.

```
The output from Engr12a - Gauss and Gauss-Jordan Methods
```

```
The solutions are

  I        Gauss    Gauss Jordan

  1     -0.91555        -0.91555
  2     -0.40311        -0.40311
  3      0.00197         0.00197
  4      0.39354         0.39354
  5      0.92317         0.92317
  6     -0.81407        -0.81407
  7     -0.16746        -0.16746
  8     -0.00308        -0.00308
  9      0.17736         0.17736
 10      0.75808         0.75808
 11     -0.85436        -0.85436
 12     -0.26967        -0.26967
```

```
13      -0.00471       -0.00471
14       0.28572        0.28572
15       0.86823        0.86823
16      -0.81815       -0.81815
17      -0.17053       -0.17053
18      -0.00129       -0.00129
19       0.15691        0.15691
20       0.80501        0.80501
21      -0.91745       -0.91745
22      -0.39403       -0.39403
23       0.00120        0.00120
24       0.39109        0.39109
25       0.91720        0.91720
```

Design Exercises

1. Spreadsheet Design

You want to track your budget for a year's time on a monthly basis. You have categorized your expenses into ten categories and have only one job producing income. The input file consists of 11 lines. The first is the income line. It contains a character string description, "Monthly Income," which is then followed by 12 monthly income figures. The next 10 lines contain the expense description, such as "House Rent" followed by the 12 monthly figures for that expense. Sketch out the Top-Down Design and pseudo coding to produce your budget report shown below.

```
                 My Budget Report

Item                  Jan     Feb     Mar    ... Dec
Monthly Income     999.99  999.99  999.99     999.99
House Rent         999.99  999.99  999.99     999.99
...
                   ------  ------  ------     ------
Total Expenses    9999.99 9999.99 9999.99    9999.99
Net Profit        9999.99 9999.99 9999.99    9999.99
```

You should make effective use of functions to eliminate as many repetitive actions as possible.

Stop! Do These Exercises Before Programming

1. The programmer wanted to define a two-dimensional array of grades. There are five sections of twenty-four students each. What must be done to the following to get it defined correctly?

```
const int Sections = 5;
const int Students = 24;
int main () {
 char grades[Students, Sections];
```

Which array bounds should come first, assuming that the normal processing handles all of the students within a given section at one time? Why?

2. Since not every section has 24 students in it, the programmer decided to have another array called **numberStudentsInThisSection**, which is an array of five integers, one for each section. Thus, **numberStudentsInThisSection[0]** contains the number of students in that section. With this defined, a **LoadStudentArrays()** function was written but does not compile or work. Why? What must be done to make this work properly?

```
const int Sections = 5;
const int Students = 24;
int LoadStudentArrays (char grades[][Students],
                       numberStudentsInThisSection[],
                       int maxSections, int maxStudents);
int main () {
 char grades[Sections, Students];
 int numberStudentsInThisSection[Sections];
 int numSections = LoadStudentArrays (grades[][Students],
        numberStudentsInThisSection[], Sections, Students);
...
int LoadStudentArrays (char grades[][Students],
                       numberStudentsInThisSection[],
                       int maxSections, int maxStudents){
 int j = 0;  // section subscript
 while (cin >> ws) {
  int k = 0; // student subscript
  while (cin >> grades[k][j]) {
   k++;
  }
  numberStudentsInThisSection[j] = j;
  j++;
 }
 return j;
}
```

3. Next the **main()** function attempted to printout all of the grades to see if they had been input properly. The following coding does not work properly. Why? What must be done to get it to properly print out the grades as entered?

```
const int Sections = 5;
const int Students = 24;
int LoadStudentArrays (char grades[][Students],
                       numberStudentsInThisSection[],
                       int maxSections, int maxStudents);
int main () {
 char grades[Sections, Students];
 int numberStudentsInThisSection[Sections];
 int numSections = LoadStudentArrays (grades[][Students],
        numberStudentsInThisSection[], Sections, Students);
 for (int j=0; j<numSections; j++) {
  cout << "\n\nSection: " << j << endl;
  for (int k=0; k<numberStudentsInThisSection[k]; k++) {
   cout << grades[k][j] << endl;
  }
 }
```

4. With the data properly input and printed, the next step is to calculate the average grade for each section. Since the grades are letter grades, assume that a 4.0 system is in use. That is, an A is worth 4 points, B is 3 and so on. The **FindAvgGrades()** function does not compile. Why? How can it be made to work properly?

```
const int Sections = 5;
const int Students = 24;
void FindAvgGrades (char grades[][Students],
                    numberStudentsInThisSection[],
                    int numSections, double avgs[]);
int main () {
 char grades[Sections, Students];
 int numberStudentsInThisSection[Sections];
 int numSections;
 double averages;
 ...
 FindAvgGrades (grades, numberStudentsInThisSection[],
                int numSections, averages);
 ...
void FindAvgGrades (char grades[][Students],
                    int numberStudentsInThisSection[],
                    int numSections, double avgs[]){
 double sum;
 for (j=0; j<numberStudentsInThisSection[j]; j++) {
  sum = 0;
  for (k=0; k<numberStudentsInThisSection[j]; k++) {
   switch (grades[j[k]) {
    case 'A':
```

```
        sum += 4;
      case 'B':
        sum += 3;
      case 'C':
        sum += 2;
      case 'D':
        sum += 1;
      case 'F':
        sum += 0;
     }
   }
   avgs[k] = sum / numberStudentsInThisSection[j];
  }
 }
```

5. Sorting of a two-dimensional array usually means sorting each row's worth of column values into order. Assume that there are 10 rows of raw scores and each row has 20 columns and that all elements are present. That is, there are 200 values in the array. The following coding to sort the array fails. Why? How can it be fixed so that the data are sorted properly?

```
const int Rows = 10;
const int Cols = 20;
double rawScores[Rows][Cols];
for (int j=0; j<Rows; j++) {
 double temp;
 for (int k=0; k<Cols; k++) {
  for (int m=k; m<Cols; m++) {
   if (rawScores[j][k] < rawScores[j][m]) {
    temp = rawScores[k][j];
    rawScores[j][k] = rawScores[j][m];
    rawScores[j][m] = temp;
  }
 }
}
```

Programming Problems

Problem Cs12-1—Two-Dimensioned Array—Star Graph

The Jet Propulsion Laboratory wishes you to write a Star Graph program quickly to verify that their digital images coming back from a spacecraft are operational. The spacecraft's digital images are focused onto a two-dimensional array of photo sensors, 30 rows of 30 columns of sensors. Each sensor records the intensity of light hitting its surface during the exposure. The intensity ranges from 0 to 20. Due to imperfections in the device, some stray light will scatter about. Thus, a star is likely to be found at a given location only when the average of that sensor and the surrounding 4 sensors intensity is greater than 6.0.

Create an array of integers that is 30 x 30 in size. The 4 surrounding neighbors would be the same row but in the previous and in the next column as well as in the row above and below in the same column as the reference intensity. In other words, no diagonals are used. Do not try to find the intensity of the 4 surrounding neighbors on the outer rows and outer columns. There are not 4 neighbors!

Call a function known as **LoadArray()** to actually input the basic intensities into the array. Assume that there are 30 rows of 30 columns of data. However, guard against too many rows and columns in the input data. The test data file is called **Cs12-1-starplot.txt**. The **LoadArray()** prototype should be something like this.

```
bool LoadArray (int intensity[30][30]);
```

However, you should use a constant integer for the bounds of 30. If the function fails (cannot find the file, for example), return **false**. If the array is loaded successfully, return **true**.

Next, the **main()** program should call a **Plot()** function whose prototype should be something like this.

```
void   Plot (int intensity[30][30]);
```

For each intensity in the array, print a '*' character if there is a star at that location. Print a blank if there is no star in that location. Thus, each row of intensities uses 30 columns and there is 30 rows. Additionally, draw a frame around the image using the '-' character for the horizontal lines and a '|' character for the vertical lines. Print your usual student id information first before the graph is printed. The output, for example, might begin something like this:

Caution: you must consider the special cases of the top and bottom rows and the left and right columns in the intensity averaging process. In these cases, there are not four nearest neighbors. Also note that the 4 corners are different still.

Problem Cs12-2—Store Statistical Comparison

Acme Incorporated owns five chain stores located in five different states. Each of their stores has five departments. To avoid checkout lines, each department has two cash registers. Acme Incorporated has collected together all of the monthly sales figures from all stores, all departments, and all registers within each department. The data is stored in master file **Cs12-2-sales.txt**. The individual data items are total sales figures.

Define an array of **doubles** to hold the data. Each line of the file contains all the data for one store and consists of ten sales amounts. The first pair represents the total sales from the two cash registers within the first department within that store. The second pair represents the register totals for the second department, and so on.

The desired report concerns a comparison of department sales from store to store. The report appears as follows.

```
Acme Sales Analysis - Sales Figures
Department        Store                                                Grand
                  Alabama   Illinois  New York  Virginia     Texas    Total
Automotive        99999.99  99999.99  99999.99  99999.99  99999.99  999999.99
Appliances        99999.99  99999.99  99999.99  99999.99  99999.99  999999.99
Clothing          99999.99  99999.99  99999.99  99999.99  99999.99  999999.99
Sporting Goods    99999.99  99999.99  99999.99  99999.99  99999.99  999999.99
Toys              99999.99  99999.99  99999.99  99999.99  99999.99  999999.99
Grand Totals      99999.99  99999.99  99999.99  99999.99  99999.99  999999.99

Acme Sales Analysis - Sales Percentages
Department        Store
                  Alabama   Illinois  New York  Virginia     Texas
Automotive          99.9      99.9      99.9      99.9        99.9
Appliances          99.9      99.9      99.9      99.9        99.9
Clothing            99.9      99.9      99.9      99.9        99.9
Sporting Goods      99.9      99.9      99.9      99.9        99.9
Toys                99.9      99.9      99.9      99.9        99.9
```

The store that corresponds to subscript 0 is Alabama; subscript 4, Texas. The automotive department is subscript 0; Toys is subscript 4, and so on. On the detail lines, the "Grand Total" column represents the sum of all of the store's automotive departments, for example. The last line of totals represents each store's total sales in all departments. The appearance of the first report is similar to a spreadsheet. Once the grand totals are known, then the relative percentages of each department can be calculated, store by store. For Alabama's Automotive department, multiply its total sales by 100 and divide by the grand total sales for the Automotive department. The others are done similarly.

Problem Cs12-3—Tic-Tac-Toe Game

Write a program to play a tic-tac-toe game. The playing board consists of boxes laid out in three rows of three columns. One player places X's and the other player places O's in the boxes. The first player to have three in a row—horizontally, diagonally or vertically—wins the game. If neither player wins, it is a draw. Store the "boxes" as a 3x3 array of char values. Initialize all elements to a blank. When the X player places an X in a box, store the character 'X' in that box. Use an 'O' character for the other player. Begin the game with the X player and take turns until someone wins or it becomes a draw.

The interactive dialog should be something like this:

X player—enter row and column numbers (1 1 through 3 3): 2 2

Now place an X in **array[1][1]**. Notice that the array is zero-based, while the coordinates that the players enter are one-based. A box is empty and available for a player to choose if it contains a blank. After getting a valid choice from player X and placing the X in the correct box, determine if that player has won. If so, the game ends with a winning message of your design. If not, then repeat the sequence using the O player. Also, print out the final box representation showing the placement of the X's and O's.

After a player has won or the game is a draw and the appropriate messages have been shown, then ask the users if they want to play another game. If so, clear the array and repeat the game.

Design your solution first. Notice that there are many common operations going on. Try to design your game to minimize duplicate coding, that is, doing a complete set of operations for player X and then coding that same set for player O. Instead, write generalized functions that can take a player's mark, the X or O as a parameter and code the sequence one time as a function.

Problem Engr12-1—Weather Statistics using Arrays

Do some research on the weather. Pick a city in the northern hemisphere and obtain a series of daily temperatures covering a 30-day period. Create a file containing these temperatures. Enter one day's set of temperature observations per line. Use a uniform number of temperatures for each day. For example, you might have 10 daily temperature recordings each day for 30 days.

1. Read the temperatures into a two-dimensioned array, defined for example as:
`double temps[NumDays][NumObservations];`
where **NumDays** might be 30 and **NumObservations** might be 10. Use values that are appropriate to your data.

2. Print a nicely formatted report with column heading headings listing the temperatures for each day. Begin each day's series on a new page. Remember printing a '\f' code causes the printer to eject to a new page.

3. Create single-dimensioned arrays to hold the daily high temperature, low temperature, average temperature, the median temperature (the one in the middle), and the standard deviation. These arrays should have **NumDays** elements, one for each day. Now, calculate these values.

4. Print a nicely formatted report; each line on the report represents the above five values for that day. Begin this section of the report on a new page.

5. Also turn in a printout of the original data file used; for example:
C>COPY TEMPS.DAT PRN

6. Cite your source for the temperatures that you find. The following is an example of some data you might find.

```
50 54 56 60 67 69 74 78 73 74 60 55
52 55 58 62 66 69 73 75 74 73 65 60
55 59 60 66 71 75 75 72 70 65 61 50
45 44 43 49 53 52 51 49 45 42 42 41
35 36 40 45 55 57 55 53 45 47 40 37
33 35 39 42 44 48 50 53 49 45 42 38
29 28 29 33 37 38 37 36 39 39 37 33
32 30 32 35 39 40 40 39 39 38 38 37
33 30 29 30 30 33 35 34 33 32 31 30
30 29 28 28 27 27 26 25 23 22 21 20
19 20 22 24 28 28 29 27 24 22 20 19
18 17 19 20 21 22 24 25 23 22 20 15
15 17 20 21 23 23 23 24 22 20 19 10
5  10 11 13 15 15 15 14 13 13 12 11
4   9 10 11 13 13 13 12 11 10  9  7
-1  0  2  1  0  1  2  4  3  2  1 -2
-4 -3 -2  1  1  3  4  2 -1 -1 -3 -5
-8 -5 -4 -5 -3 -2 -1 -2 -3 -3 -4 -9
```

```
-11-3 -1  1  2  3  4  5  5  6  7  7
9  10 15 20 16 11 10  7  2 -1  0  1
```

Here are some URLs for the Internet to try out. There is no guarantee that they still exist. Internet sites come and go.

For New Mexico, try entering this in the Location box:
http://weather.nmsu.edu/stations.html
This is the New Mexico State University database. There is a "click here" to get the layout of the hourly data. Pick a location; there's many data.

For Utah, try entering this in the Location box:
http://climate.usu.edu/
Then pick "hourly data." It is not as fancy an interface as New Mexico's.

For Fairbanks, Alaska, try
http://newnet.jdola.lanl.gov/sel1705.html
Then choose Listing.

Problem Engr12-2—Analysis of Static Truss (Civil Engineering)

In structural engineering, the calculations of the forces and reactions on a static truss are important. In the following figure of a section of a bridge, Point 3 is constrained only to transmit forces vertically to the pier, while Point 2 also can transmit in the horizontal direction. If an external load of 1000 pounds downward is applied at Point 1, the load is distributed among the various beams of the truss.

One can construct free-body-force diagrams for each of the three points. Since the system is at rest, the sum of all the forces at each of the three node points must be 0. This leads then to six equations that describe the situation.

```
-F1 cos 30 + F3 cos 60 + F1h = 0
-F1 sin 30 - F3 sin 60 + F1v = 0
F2 + F1 cos 30 + F2h + H2 = 0
F1 sin 30 + F2v + V2 = 0
-F2 -F3 cos 60 + F3h = 0
F3 sin 60 + F3v + V3 = 0
```

In this problem, F1v is –1000 pounds. F1h, F2h, F2v, F3h, F3v are 0. If we insert these numerical values into the six equations and represent them in matrix format, we have the following system of equations to solve.

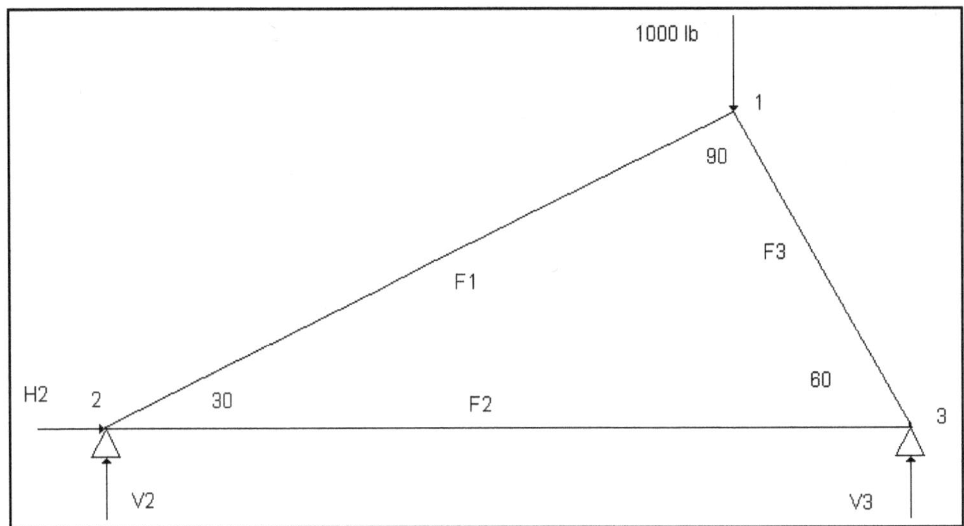

Figure 12.6 The Force Diagram

$$\begin{pmatrix} 0.866 & 0 & -0,5 & 0 & 0 & 0 \\ 0.5 & 0 & 0.866 & 0 & 0 & 0 \\ -0.866 & -1 & 0 & -1 & 0 & 0 \\ -0.5 & 0 & 0 & 0 & -1 & 0 \\ 0 & 1 & 0.5 & 0 & 0 & 0 \\ 0 & 0 & -0.866 & 0 & 0 & -1 \end{pmatrix} \begin{pmatrix} F1 \\ F2 \\ F3 \\ H2 \\ V2 \\ V3 \end{pmatrix} = \begin{pmatrix} 0 \\ -1000 \\ 0 \\ 0 \\ 0 \\ 0 \end{pmatrix}$$

Figure 12.7 The System of Equations

Use the data in the above matrix notation to make a data file to be used as input to the main program. Write a program to input these data into arrays and perform both a Gauss and a Gauss-Jordan elimination to solve for the six unknowns. For each variable, such as F1, print side by side the formatted results from the Gauss and Gauss Jordan methods.

Problem Engr12-3—A Matrix Math Package

When dealing with problems that involve matrices, it is convenient to have a set of canned functions to handle the common matrix math operations. For simplicity, assume that all two-dimensional matrices are square and that any corresponding column or row vectors have the same dimension as their corresponding square matrix. Thus, one constant integer can provide dimensions for the arrays, **MaxDim** in this case.

1. Write an **IsEqual()** function that returns **true** if the two square matrices are equal. Its prototype should be

```
bool IsEqual (double A[MaxDim][MaxDim],
              double B[MaxDim][MaxDim], int limit);
```

2. Write an **Add()** function to add two square matrices **A** and **B**, placing the result in matrix **C**. Its prototype is

```
void Add (double A[MaxDim][MaxDim],
          double B[MaxDim][MaxDim],
          double C[MaxDim][MaxDim], int limit);
```

3. Write a **Subtract()** function to subtract two square matrices (**C** = **A** – **B**) placing the result in matrix **C**. Its prototype is

```
void Subtract (double A[MaxDim][MaxDim],
               double B[MaxDim][MaxDim],
               double C[MaxDim][MaxDim], int limit);
```

4. Write a **MultiplyByConstant()** function to multiply the matrix **A** by the value **b** and place the result in matrix **C**. The prototype is

```
void MultiplyByConstant (double A[MaxDim][MaxDim],
                         double b,
                         double C[MaxDim][MaxDim],
                         int limit);
```

5. Write a function **IsDiagonal()** that returns **true** if the matrix is a diagonal matrix. Its prototype is

```
bool IsDiagonal (double A[MaxDim][MaxDim], int limit);
```

6. Write a function **IsIdentity()** that returns **true** if the matrix is an identity matrix. Its prototype is

```
bool IsIdentity (double A[MaxDim][MaxDim], int limit);
```

7. Write a function **MatrixBySquare()** that multiplies the square matrix **A** by the column matrix **B** yielding the column matrix **C**. Its prototype is

```
void MatrixBySquare (double A[MaxDim][MaxDim],
                     double B[MaxDim],
                     double C[MaxDim], int limit);
```

8. Finally, write a function **MatrixByMatrix()** that multiplies the square matrix **A** by square matrix **B**, yielding square matrix **C**. Its prototype is

```
void MatrixByMatrix (double A[MaxDim][MaxDim],
                     double B[MaxDim][MaxDim],
                     double C[MaxDim][MaxDim], int limit);
```

Now write a main function to test all of these. Thoroughly test all functions.

Chapter 13—Structures

Section A: Basic Theory

Introduction

Suppose that a program needed to process car insurance premiums. Each line of input represented one policyholder's information about their insurance. Take a minute and reflect on what fields of information might be needed. Certainly the line would contain the policy number, the policy holder's first and last name, their address, city, state, zip code, phone number, car make, car model, VIN number, color, year, and so on. There could easily be more than two dozen individual fields. Following the principles of good programming design, the problem would undoubtedly be functionally decomposed into several functions, for example input a set of data. Can you imagine the function prototypes and headers required to pass two dozen fields? It would be a nightmare.

Structures

What is needed is a way to group all these related fields into one large aggregate and then to be able to use that aggregate to simplify the programming. This is exactly what a **structure** is and does for us. A **structure** is a grouping of related fields of information that is often called a record of data. Many convenient operations can be performed using this structure aggregate. If we had a car insurance structure, we can pass this one instance of the large group to the functions instead of the dozens of individual fields. The structure provides means for us to access the individual member fields as needed.

Defining Structures

The starting point is to define the model or blueprint that the compiler uses when it needs to create an actual instance of the structure in memory. This model is called the **structure template** or definition. The template includes the keyword **struct** followed by the **structure tag**, which is the name that is used to identify this structure from all others. This is followed by all of the member field definitions surrounded by braces {…} and ends with a semicolon.

Suppose that the program is to process cost records. Each cost record includes the item number, quantity on hand, product description and its cost. Here is what the structure template looks like.

```
const int DescrLen = 21; // max length of description

struct COSTREC {
  long   itemNum;          // item number
  short  qty;              // quantity on hand
  char   descr[DescrLen]; // item description
  double cost;             // item cost
};
```

The structure tag, **COSTREC** in this case, is used to identify this particular structure. By convention, all structure tags either are wholly uppercase names (usually) or are capitalized.

The four data items contained between the braces { } are called the **structure members**. Each structure member is a normal variable data definition. Notice that constant integers or **#defines** can be used for array bounds as usual, but those definitions must precede the structure template, following the "defined before first use" rule.

When any instance of **COSTREC** is created or used, the member fields are always created and stored in the order shown in the template. The order of the structure members can sometimes be important. If this program is part of a collection of programs, all sharing the same files, such as a payroll system of programs, or if the data file to be input is in binary format, then the structure members must be in the same order that the data is in the binary file. A **binary** file is one in which all data is stored in internal format; binary files cannot be viewed with text editors such as Notepad. They are discussed in detail near the end of this chapter. For most problems, the fields can be in any order you choose.

Suppose that when recording weather statistics, data is measured and recorded every hour. A daily weather record might be defined as follows.

```
const int NumObs = 24;
const int StationLen = 21;

struct WEATHER {
 char  stationName[StationLen]; // reporting location
 float temps[NumObs];           // degrees Centigrade
 float humidity[NumObs];        // such as 50%
 float rainfall[NumObs];        // in millimeters
 float windspeed[NumObs];       // in m/s
};
```

Notice that a structure can contain arrays.

Where are the structure templates located in a program? As with all data definitions, a structure template must be defined before its first use. Where is its first usage? In a modular program, structures or references to structures are commonly passed to other functions. Thus, the structure templates must come before function prototypes that use them. The sequence is often

```
#includes
const ints or #defines
```

```
structure templates
int main () {
```

Creating Instances of a Structure

With the structure template defined, how are instances of it created? It is done in a manner similar to any other intrinsic data type. For example, how would one define an instance of a **double** called **cost**?

```
double cost;
```

The data type precedes the desired name of the variable. Structure instances follow the same pattern. The data type is the structure tag in C++. The following creates a **structure variable** called **costRec** and a structure variable called **weaRec**. A structure variable is just an instance of a structure in memory.

```
COSTREC costRec;
WEATHER weaRec;
```

What does the structure variable **costRec** look like in memory when it is created by the compiler? Figure 13.1 shows the memory layout of **costRec** and its member fields. Notice that the fields are in the same order as in the **COSTREC** template.

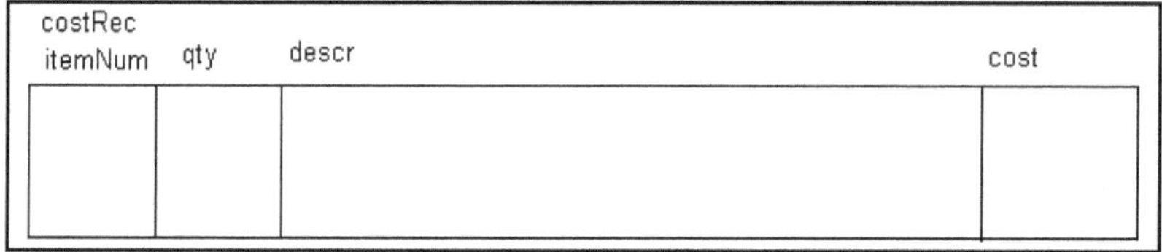

Figure 13.1 The **costRec** Memory Layout

One can have arrays of structures as well. Suppose that the program needed to store a maximum of 1000 cost records and a maximum of 500 weather records. The following defines these two arrays and shows the location of all the parts of the structure definitions.

```
#define MAXRECS 1000
const int DescrLen = 21;  // max length of description

struct COSTREC {
  long   itemNum;           // item number
  short  qty;               // quantity on hand
  char   descr[DescrLen]; // item description
  double cost;              // item cost
};

int main () {
 COSTREC arec[MAXRECS];  // array of 1000 cost records
 ...
```

or

```
#define LIMIT 500
const int NumObs = 24; // number observations per day
```

```
const int StationLen = 21; // max len of station

struct WEATHER {
 char  stationName[StationLen]; // reporting location
 float temps[NumObs];           // degrees Centigrade
 float humidity[NumObs];        // such as 50%
 float rainfall[NumObs];        // in millimeters
 float windspeed[NumObs];       // in m/s
};

int main () {
 WEATHER weaArray[LIMIT];
```

A structure can also contain instances of other structures and arrays of other structures. For example, consider a **DATE** structure, which represents a calendar date. Using instances of a **DATE** structure would make passing dates very convenient. Further, consider an employee record that contained the employee's id number, their salary, and the date that they were hired. The **EMPLOYEE** structure contains an instance of the **DATE** structure as shown below.

```
struct DATE {
  char month;
  char day;
  short year;
};

struct EMPLOYEE {
  long id;
  double salary;
  DATE hireDate;
};
```

Suppose that a **CARMAINT** structure must be defined to represent the periodic maintenance requirements for a new car. Here the **CARMAINT** structure contains an array of **DATE** structures.

```
const int numMaint = 10;
struct CARMAINT {
 bool maintenanceDone[numMaint];    // true if the work was done
 int  maintenanceCode[numMaint];    // manufacturer's maint. codes
 DATE maintenanceDueDate[numMaint];// date maintenance is due
};
```

How are Structures Initialized?

An instance of a structure can be initialized when it is defined, just as any other variable. However, since a structure typically has a number of data members, the values are surrounded by braces {} as are single dimensioned arrays. The following structure represents a quarter coin initialized as it is defined within **main()**.

```
const int MaxLen = 10;
struct COIN {
 int denomination;
 char singular[MaxLen];
 char multiple[MaxLen];
};
int main () {
 COIN quarter = {25, "Quarter", "Quarters"};
```

How are Structure Members Accessed?

Having defined the structure template and created instance(s) of it, the next action is to utilize the members within the structure. This is done by using the **dot (.)** operator. To the left of the **dot** operator must be a **structure variable** and to the right must be a **member variable** of that structure.

To access the **qty** member of the **costRec** instance, one codes

```
costRec.qty
```

To calculate the **totalCost** using the **cost** and **qty** members of the **costRec** instance, do the following.

```
double totalCost = costRec.qty * costRec.cost;
```

To display the description, use

```
cout << costRec.descr;
```

To increment the **costRec**'s quantity member or add another variable to it, one can code

```
costRec.qty++;
costRec.qty += orderedQty;
```

To input a set of data into the **costRec** variable, there are a number of ways. Here is one.

```
cin >> costRec.itemNum >> costRec.qty >> ws;
cin.get (costRec.descr, DescrLen);
cin >> costRec.cost;
```

The above assumes that no description field in the input data contains all blanks. It also assumes that all descriptions contain **DescrLen – 1** number of characters.

As you look these over, notice that there are no differences at all on input or output of structure members, other than the requisite **dot** operator qualification with the structure variable.

Rules of Use for Structure Variables

Structure variables can be used for only five actions. These are the following.

A structure variable can be used to access structure members.

A structure variable or reference to one can be passed to a function.

A function can return a structure variable.

The address operator & returns the memory address of a structure variable

A structure variable can be assigned to another structure variable as long as they both have the same structure tag.

We have already examined the first one, using the structure variable to access the individual members, as in **costRec.qty**. The **address** operator & returns the address of the structure variable. If one codes

```
&costRec
```

then the compiler provides the memory location where the instance begins. Normally, the compiler does this automatically for us when we use reference variables.

Assume that the program also had defined another instance of the **COSTREC**.

```
COSTREC previousRec;
```

The fifth rule says that a complete copy of a structure variable can be done as follows.

```
previousRec = costRec;
```

This is very powerful indeed. Consider the alternative if this were not allowed. One would have to write an assignment for each of the three numeric fields and then use **strcpy()** to copy the string as shown below.

```
previousRec.itemNum = costRec.itemNum;
previousRec.qty = costRec.qty;
previousRec.cost = costRec.cost;
strcpy (previousRec.descr, costRec.descr);
```

Clearly, the ability to assign one structure variable to another instance can be a terrific operation when it is needed.

A structure variable can be passed to a function or a reference to one can be passed. Passing by reference is the best approach to take. Likewise, a function can return a copy of a structure. However, in reality, returning a structure and passing a structure and not using reference to a structure instance is generally avoided. Let's examine these two issues in detail.

Suppose that the **main()** program defined the cost record structure as we have been using it thus far. Suppose further that the **main()** function then wanted to call a **PrintRec()** function whose task is to print the data nicely formatted. The **main()** function does the following.

```
int main () {
COSTREC crec;
...
PrintRec (outfile, crec);
```

The **PrintRec()** function begins as follows.

```
void PrintRec (ostream& outfile, COSTREC crec) {
  outfile << crec.itemNum...
```

When the compiler generates the instructions to make the call to **PrintRec()**, it must make a new parameter instance of the **COSTREC** structure and then spend execution time to copy all the data from the **main()**'s **costRec** instance into **PrintRec()**'s **crec** parameter instance. For structures that contain a large number of members, this is wasteful of both memory (the parameter copy) and execution speed (making the copy every time the function is called).

A far better approach is to pass the structure variable by reference. A simple change to **PrintRec()** vastly improves both memory utilization and execution speed.

```
void PrintRec (ostream& outfile, COSTREC& crec) {
  outfile << crec.itemNum...
```

Here the compiler actually passes only the memory address of **main()**'s **costRec**. **PrintRec()**'s **crec** parameter is now a reference variable (usually occupying 4 bytes of memory). No copy of the data is made.

Okay. But what about good programming design? **PrintRec()** should not be allowed to modify the contents of **main()**'s **costRec** in any way. It should have read-only access, for example. This can be enforced by using the **const** keyword as follows.

```
void PrintRec (ostream& outfile, const COSTREC& crec) {
  outfile << crec.itemNum...
```

Here, the data being referenced is constant and cannot be changed within **PrintRec()**. If **PrintRec()** were to attempt to assign 42 to the **qty** field as in

```
crec.qty = 42;
```

the compiler generates a compile time error. Thus, you should always use constant references in functions that should not be allowed to alter the data. A **ReadRec()** function would certainly not be passed a constant **COSTREC** reference. It should be filling up the structure instance with input data.

This brings up the **ReadRec()** function whose job it is to input the data and somehow fill up the **main()**'s **costRec** with that data. One way that the **ReadRec()** function can be defined is to have it return a **COSTREC** structure. This is not a good way to do it, but let's see how a function can return a structure instance. Then, we will see how to better design the **ReadRec()** function. If **ReadRec()** returns a structure, then **main()** would have to assign it to **main()**'s **costRec** variable. From a design point of view, since **main()** is passing **ReadRec()** a reference to the input stream, **ReadRec()** lets the **main()** function decide on what to for I/O errors, bad data and EOF detection. The coding for **main()** is as follows.

```
int main () {
 COSTREC costRec;
 costRec = ReadRec (infile);
 // now check on infile's state
```

Now in **ReadRec()**, the coding can be done this way.

```
COSTREC ReadRec (istream& infile) {
```

```
 COSTREC temp = {0};
 if (infile >> ws && !infile.good()) {
  return temp;
 }
 infile >> temp.itemNum >> and so on
 return temp;
}
```

Here the structure variable **temp** is filled with the input file's next set of data and then a complete copy of **temp** is returned to **main()**. However, since EOF can occur as well as bad data and since we have to return an instance of the **COSTREC** structure, **temp** is initialized to zeros. Back in **main()**, when the function call to **ReadRec()** is completed, the compiler then must copy that returned copy of **temp** into **main()**'s **costRec** variable. If the structure contained a large number of member fields, memory is being wasted. In all cases, execution speed is going to suffer because of all the copying operations needed to move the data from **temp** into **costRec**.

While there can be times when this overhead cannot be avoided, usually the answer is to pass a reference to the **ReadRec()** function and have the function fill up **main()**'s **costRec** directly. This then frees up the return value for other uses. And by now returning a reference to the input stream being used for input, the caller of the **ReadRec()** function can make more effective use of the language.

Suppose that **ReadRec()** was rewritten to be passed a reference to the caller's **COSTREC** structure variable to be filled with the input data. The improved function is shown below.

```
istream& ReadRec (istream& infile, COSTREC& crec) {
 if (infile >> ws && !infile.good()) {
  return infile;
 }
 infile >> crec.itemNum >> and so on
 return infile;
}
```

Now the **main()** function has more ways that it can utilize the **ReadRec()** function. Here is the improved **main()** function.

```
int main () {
 COSTREC costRec;
 ...
 while (ReadRec (infile, costRec)) {
```

Certainly **main()** benefits from the change. The **while** clause is basically testing the goodness of the input stream after the input operations are complete. Also, **ReadRec()** now avoids both the extra memory overhead of returning a structure instance and the execution time needed to make the copies.

User-Written Header Files

A programming application may involve a series of programs. A payroll application typically consists of several individual programs to accomplish the total task of managing a company's payroll needs. One program might input the weekly time sheets and store the data into a master file on disk. The next program in the series might calculate the wages of all the employees from that master file on disk. Another program might input that master file and produce IRS reports, and so on. All of these programs must use an **EMPLOYEE** structure to group the fields into a manageable aggregate.

If each program defined its own version of the **EMPLOYEE** structure, chaos arises. Suppose a simple change was requested—increase the size of the employee's name field from 20 characters to 30. The programmers would have to go into every program in the system and make that same change in every version of the **EMPLOYEE** structure. This is simply not practical or feasible. Instead, the **EMPLOYEE** structure definition or template and related items such as the **const int**s or **#define**s are stored in a separate file, a header file with the extension **.h**. Each program that wishes to use the **EMPLOYEE** structure only has to code a **#include** for it.

The syntax for user header files differs slightly from system header files. The <> on the **#include** compiler directives notify the compiler that the filename within the angle brackets is in the system include folder(s). To include user header files, use double quote marks instead of the angle brackets—"filename" for example.

```
#include "Employee.h"
```

This instructs the compiler to copy the contents of the file **Employee.h** into the program at this point. The compiler assumes that the **Employee.h** file is located in the same folder as the project cpp file(s).

If the header file is not in the project folder, a partial path, a relative path or a full path can be included. The following are all valid, assuming the file is located in the indicated place.

```
#include "Employee.h"
#include "Include\\Employee.h"
#include "..\\IncludeFiles\\Employee.h"
#include "D:\\Programming\\Include\\Employee.h"
```

The first one implies the header is in the project folder. The second one implies that the header file is in a subfolder of the project called **Include**. The third one implies that the header is in the **IncludeFiles** folder located in the parent folder of the project folder. The fourth one provides an absolute path.

In general, do not use absolute paths because the project is not portable. One cannot move the project to other drives, other computers or other folders and still compile properly. User headers are often found in the project folder.

The header file is built just like a cpp file. If you are working with the Microsoft Visual C++ compiler, choose File-New and pick header file and enter the name desired.

If we wanted to place the **COSTREC** structure template into a header file, the contents of the header file **CostRec.h** would be as follows.

```
const int DescrLen = 21;   // max length of description

struct COSTREC {
  long   itemNum;             // item number
  short  qty;                 // quantity on hand
  char   descr[DescrLen]; // item description
  double cost;                // item cost
};
```

In the **main()** function, you should include first all of the needed C++ standard library header files that the program requires and then include all of the user header files.

```
#include <iostream>
#include <iomanip>
#include <cmath>
using namespace std;
#include "Costrec.h"
```

Why? Accidentally, you might have used a name that is already in use by the system functions and system coding contained in the system header files. If you include the system headers first, the compiler points to your accidental redefinition in your header file. However, if you include the user headers first and the system headers second, then the compiler's error messages point to a redefinition error within the system headers!

Binary Files and Structures

Up to this point, every file of data that has been used is a text file. That is, the encoding scheme is that of pure ASCII text. Such files are easily viewed and created with Notepad or any other text editor. For example, suppose that the file contained the **quantity** of 1234. If you viewed this file and the line with this number on it, four characters are shown: '1', '2', '3' and '4'. The digits are stored using their ASCII decimal values of 49, 50, 51 and 52. If the **quantity** were defined to be a **short** and then inputted as usual with

cin >> quantity;

we know that **quantity** is stored in a binary format. In this case, since a **short** has 16 bits and since the sign occupies the first or leftmost position (0 meaning it is a positive number), then 15 bits remain to store the value.

In memory, the **quantity** variable appears this way.

```
0 0 0 0  0 1 0 0  1 1 0 1  0 0 1 0
```

This means the number stored is given by:

$$0x2^0 + 1x2^1 + 0x2^2 + 0x2^3 + 1x2^4 + 1x2^6 + 1x2^7 + 1x2^{10}$$

or

$$2 + 16 + 64 + 128 + 1024 = 1234$$

This is what is meant by internal numeric format. Floating point types have a different format.

When the input stream inputs the **quantity**, it brings in the ASCII text digits and must then convert those digits into the binary internal representation. This is a process known as **data conversion**. In general, data conversion is a slow, tedious process. It is very slow indeed for the floating point types.

A **binary** file is one in which all data are stored in internal format. If the **short quantity** were stored in a binary file, the two bytes would contain precisely the bit pattern that they would have if it were in memory, namely

```
0 0 0 0  0 1 0 0  1 1 0 1  0 0 1 0
```

It is indistinguishable from the **short quantity** in memory. If the **ifstream** was to input a **quantity** field from a binary file, no conversion is needed ever. It only has to input the two bytes that comprise a **short** and place then into the two bytes of the **quantity** field.

Binary file I/O is significantly faster than text file I/O. The larger the file, the more significant the speed difference. Consider some other examples: a **double** occupies eight bytes in a binary file; a **long**, four bytes. How about a character string? Suppose that the string was defined to contain a maximum of 20 bytes but that this particular instance currently is holding the string "Sam". Binary output of this string outputs all 20 bytes, not just the characters that are in use at the moment. Similarly, binary input of the string must input all 20 bytes. Contrast this with what would be output using a **cout** operation.

If a company is storing its data in a database or file, then it makes sense to store that data in a binary file. Consider for a moment the database or master file of a national car insurance company. One expects that the company to have a significant number of programs accessing that data for some purpose, such as billing and reporting. By making the master file be a binary file instead of a text file, their entire system of programs runs significantly faster.

Mechanics of Binary Files

The **iostreams** are capable of reading and writing binary files. When opening a file for binary operations, another flag must be set, **ios::binary**. If this flag is not set, the **iostream** assumes that it is a text type of file.

Two new functions actually handle the binary input and output operations, **read()** and **write()**. Let's begin by writing a short program that inputs a text file of temperatures and writes out a binary file of those same temperatures. When opening a binary file, normally we have used the flags **ios::in** or **ios::out**. Now we must OR in the **ios::binary** flag.

```
ofstream outfile;
outfile.open ("temps.dat", ios::out | ios::binary);
float temp;
while (cin >> temp) {
```

```
 outfile.write ((char*)&temp, sizeof (temp));
}
outfile.close ();
```

The new coding is in bold. First notice how **ios::binary** is ORed into the open flags.

The **write()** function looks complicated at first, but it really is simple. Its prototype is

```
ostream& write (char* buffer, unsigned int length);
```

The first parameter is the memory address from which the data is to be written and the second parameter is how many bytes are to be written starting at that location. The memory address it assumes is an array of characters or bytes. We use the address operator & to obtain the memory location of **temp**. The (**char***) typecast is used to convince the compiler that this memory address of a **float** is what is desired. The **sizeof()** macro is used to obtain the implementation defined number of bytes of the float variable **temp**.

Next, let's input the temperatures from the binary file we have just written. The short sequence is as follows.

```
ifstream infile;
infile.open ("temps.dat", ios::in | ios::binary);
float temp;
while (infile.read ((char*)&temp, sizeof (temp))) {
  do something with temp
}
infile.close();
```

Again, the new coding is in bold face. The **ios::binary** flag is ORed with **ios::in**.

The syntax of the **read()** function is

```
istream& read (char* buffer, unsigned int numBytes);
```

The **read()** function inputs the number of bytes indicated by the second parameter into consecutive bytes beginning with the memory address provided by the first parameter. It returns a reference to the original input stream.

When arrays are involved, binary I/O is even more powerful. Suppose that we had an array of up to 1000 temperatures with **numTemps** containing the number actually present on this execution. We can output the entire array with a single write function call!

```
float temps[1000];
int numTemps;
outfile.write ((char*) temps, numTemps * sizeof (float));
```

Or if all 1000 entries were filled, just

```
outfile.write ((char*) temps, sizeof (temps));
```

It gets even better when structures are involved. Suppose that we wanted to write our cost record instance, **costRec**, to a binary output file.

```
COSTREC costRec;
outfile.write ((char*) &costRec, sizeof (costRec));
```

One line and the entire structure with all of its member fields are written to disk. To input a single **COSTREC** structure instance into **costRec** from a binary file of data, it is as simple as

```
infile.read ((char*) &costRec, sizeof (costRec));
```

Binary data files using structures opens up new processing avenues and leads directly to inquiry and file update type applications. In an **inquiry** program, the user enters a key identifier, such as social security number, and the program finds that specific record in the binary master file, reads it into memory and typically displays the relevant information. In an **update** program, after inputting the data for the specific item, various fields are altered and the new modified data is rewritten to the master file, overlaying the previous contents. These types of applications are covered in my sequel book, Beginning Data Structures in C++. Structures represent the key to most all advanced processing circumstances. Structures led historically to the development of classes in object oriented programming.

Section B: Computer Science Examples

Cs13-1—Credit Card Application with Sorting

Acme Credit Company has a master file of its cardholders. Each record in the file **CreditMaster.txt** represents the data for one customer. The data consists of the account number (social security number), the customer name of up to 30 characters, a two-character state code abbreviation, the credit limit to be extended, and finally the current balance. The customer name is enclosed in quote marks, for example, "John Doe." The state codes are all uppercase letters. Design a credit structure and create an array that can hold a maximum of 500 cardholders. Note that the file is in no particular order.

The program is to input the master file and create the Credit Extended by State report. The report looks like this.

```
Output Report of Cs13a Credit Extended by State Program
```

```
Acme Credit Company - Credit Extended by State Report

State    Number of     Credit Totals Extended
Code     Accounts         Limit         Balance
  AL         4       $ 22100.00     $ 20500.00
  IA         5       $ 28300.00     $ 22642.42
  IL         7       $ 36500.00     $ 33500.00
  MO         4       $ 20200.00     $ 18500.00
  --       ---        ---------      ---------
   4        20       $107100.00     $ 95142.42
```

The program should have a **LoadArray()** function and a **SortArray()** function to subsequently sort the array of credit records into state code order. Once this has been done, the data can easily be accumulated and the report printed from a **PrintReport()** function.

The **main()** program should prompt the user for the master file name to be used and for the name of the report file to write. The screen display of the program should appear as follows; note that the user enters the file names to use.

```
Enter the name of the credit master file: CreditMaster.txt
Enter the name of the output report file: CreditReport.txt

Array loaded: nnn records input
Sorting the array
Printing the report
Finished
```

In this program, the report is sent to an output file. However, there is lots of processing going on during the execution of the program. Hence, to make the program more user-friendly, it must periodically display the last four lines, indicating the action that is occurring at that point. Otherwise, if the input file was large and the processing time therefore lengthy, the user would be staring at a blinking cursor wondering what was going on and perhaps panicking a bit.

Figure 13.2 shows the Top-Down Design for the program.

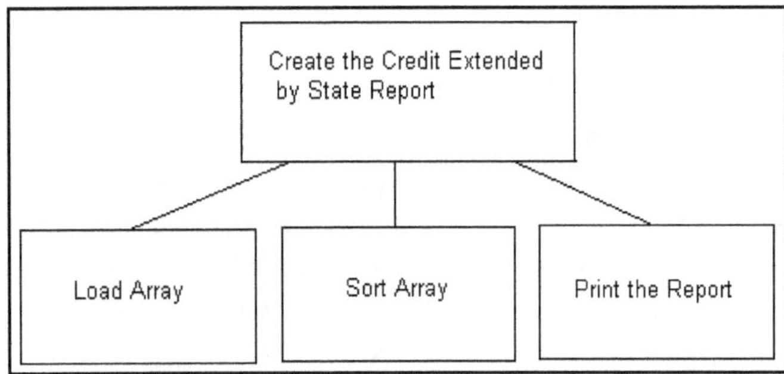

Figure 13.2 Top-Down Design for the Program

The data for a single card holder is stored in a **CREDITREC** structure. It is defined as follows.

```
struct CREDITREC {
 long   acctno;                    // account number =social security num
 char   custName[MaxNameLen];      // customer name up to 30 characters
 char   stateCode[MaxStCodeLen];// upper case state code
 double creditLimit;               // credit limit of customer
 double balance;                   // customer's current balance due
};
```

The **main()** function defines an array of **CREDITREC** structures called **creditRec** and **numRecs** contains the current number of elements actually in the array. Since the user must input the two file names, let's call them **inputFilename** and **reportFilename**. Main storage for **main()** is shown in Figure 13.3. Notice how I have drawn the array of **CREDITREC** structures. At the bottom of the array, I have included the member names.

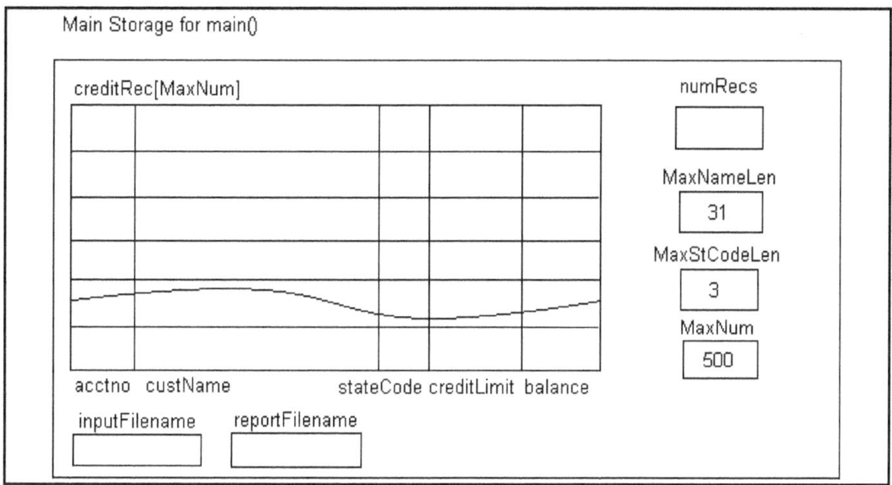

Figure 13.3 Main Storage for **main()**

The instruction sequence for **main()** is very simple, IPO as usual. First, it must obtain the input and report filenames from the user.

prompt for and input **inputFilename**
prompt for and input **reportFilename**
load the array of credit records by calling
  numRecs = **LoadArray** (**creditRec**, **MaxNum**, **inputFilename**)
display a message to the user that **numRecs** records were input
display a message that we are sorting the array into state code order
call **SortArray** (**creditRec**, **numRecs**)
display a message that we are printing the report
call **PrintReport** (**creditRec**, **numRecs**, **reportFilename**);
display a finished message

LoadArray() loads the passed array of credit records from the input file. It is given **crec**[], **limit** and **filename**. Its sequence is as follows. Notice how the **i**th element of the structure is referenced in the input operations. When the **custName** field is to be input, the leading double quotes mark is input into a character leaving the input stream pointing to the first character of the name. The **getline()** function is used to extract all characters of the name up to the trailing double quotes mark; **getline()** also removes this trailing character from the input stream.

define and open **infile (filename)**, if it fails to open, display an error message and abort
let **i** = 0;
while i<limit and an attempt to partially input the data by
  infile >> **crec[i].acctno** >> **c** is successful then do the following
 input the customer name by **infile.getline** (**crec[i]**.**custName**, **MaxNameLen**, '\"')
 input the next byte, which can be the " if the name is max length **infile.get** (c)
 then skip over whitespace to the start of the state code **infile >> ws**
 input the **stateCode** by calling **infile.get** (**crec[i].stateCode**, **MaxStCodeLen**)
 input the limit and balance by **infile** >> **crec[i].creditLimit** >> **crec[i].balance**

increment **i**
end **while** loop
guard against bad input data by checking **infile.fail()**—if bad, then do
display to **cerr** an error message stating what was the last good id
close the **infile**
abort the program
end the if bad block
guard against too many elements by checking **if i == limit** and
if infile >> ws is successful, then do the following
display an error message to **cerr** that the array size has been exceeded
close the **infile**
abort the program
end the **if**
close the **infile**
return **i**, which is the number of records input

The **SortArray()** sorts the credit records into state code order. It is passed **crec**[] and **numRecs**. In order to swap two elements of the array, a temporary **CREDITREC** called **temp** is needed. Since the field to be sorted is a character string, the **strcmp()** string function is used.

```
for (i=0; i<numRecs-1; i++) {
 for (j=i+1; j<numRecs; j++) {
  if (strcmp (crec[j].stateCode, crec[i].stateCode) < 0) {
   temp = crec[i];
   crec[i] = crec[j];
   crec[j] = temp;
  end if
 end inner for loop
end outer for loop
```

The **PrintReport()** function must summarize the data while printing the report. It is passed **crec**[], **numRecs** and the **filename** to use. This is essentially a control break problem. We must sum the number of accounts, their limits, and balances for each state. Since the array is now in state code order, the main loop just sums the values. When there is a change in state code, then we display the totals for the state we just summed and reset the totals and begin summing the next state.

Begin by identifying the key variables to hold our needed values. First, **prevState** should contain the previous state code; we check it against the current state code of the **i**th element in the array. The three state totals are **numAcctsInState**, **totalLimit** and **totalBalance**. The grand nationwide totals are **grandNumStates**, which is the total number of states serviced, **grandNumAccts**, **grandTotalLimit** and **grandTotalBalance**. All of these seven totals must be initialized to zero. Figure 13.4 shows the main storage layout for **PrintReport()**. Note for ease of debugging, I have recopied the actual array defined in the **main()** function here in the diagram for **crec**; in fact, **crec** is really just the memory address of **main()**'s **creditRec** array.

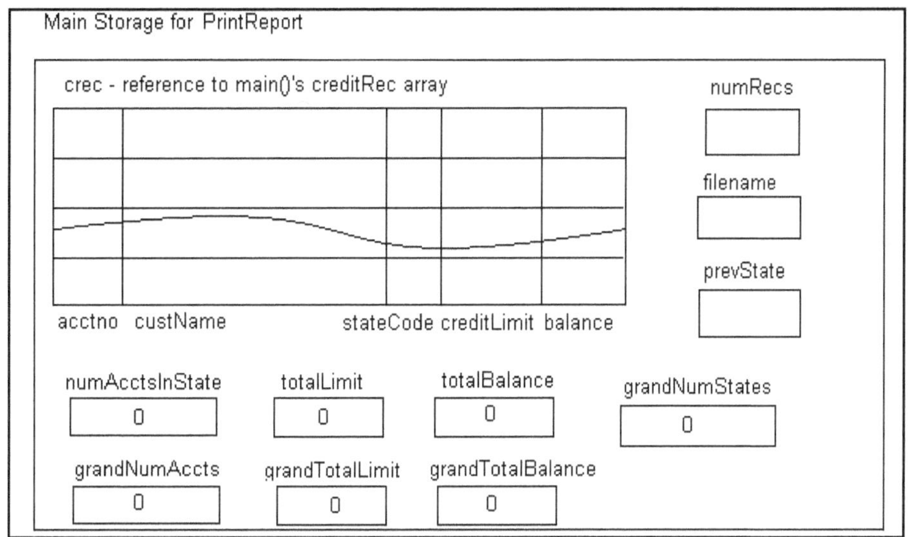

Figure 13.4 Main Storage for **PrintReport()**

The coding sequence for **PrintReport()** is as follows.
open **outfile**, but if it fails, display an error message to **cerr** and abort
output headings and column headings
if there are any elements in **crec**, then do the summation
  copy the first state code into **prevState—strcpy (prevState, crec[0].stateCode)**
  let **totalLimit** = **crec[0].creditLimit**
  let **totalBalance** = **crec[0].balance**
  and increment **numAcctsInState**
  loop through all the remaining credit records: **for i**=1; **i<numRecs**; **i**++ do
    has the state code changed—is **strcmp (prevState, crec[i].stateCode)** != 0—yes, do
      output the **prevState**, **numAcctsInState**, **totalLimit** and **totalBalance**
      // add this state set of totals to the grand totals
      grandNumAccts += **numAcctsInState**
      increment **grandNumStates**
      grandTotalLimit += **totalLimit**
      grandTotalBalance += **totalBalance**
      reset the previous state code—**strcpy (prevState, crec[i].stateCode)**
      // set totals back to zero
      numAcctsInState = 0;
      totalLimit = 0;
      totalBalance = 0;
    end **if** state changed
    increment **numAcctsInState**
    totalLimit += **crec[i].creditLimit**
    totalBalance += **crec[i].balance**
  end for loop
  // output last state's totals - **prevState**, **numAcctsInState**, **totalLimit** **totalBalance**

grandNumAccts += **numAcctsInState**
increment **grandNumStates**
grandTotalLimit += **totalLimit**
grandTotalBalance += **totalBalance**
end if there are any elements
output the dash line
output **grandNumStates**, **grandNumAccts**, **grandTotalLimit** and **grandTotalBalance**
close **outfile**

As usual, one should thoroughly desk check the solution before converting it into actual program coding. The complete program **Cs13a** is shown below.

Listing Cs13a - Credit Extended by State Program

```
/***************************************************************/
/*                                                             */
/*  CS13a - Credit Extended by State report program            */
/*                                                             */
/***************************************************************/

#include <iostream>
#include <fstream>
#include <iomanip>
#include <string>
using namespace std;

const int MaxNameLen = 31;     // maximum length of customer name
const int MaxStCodeLen = 3;    // maximum length of state code
const int MaxNum = 500;        // maximum number of credit records

struct CREDITREC {
 long   acctno;                    // account number = ss number
 char   custName[MaxNameLen];      // customer name up to 30 chars
 char   stateCode[MaxStCodeLen];// upper case state code
 double creditLimit;               // credit limit of customer
 double balance;                   // customer's current balance due
};

int  LoadArray  (CREDITREC crec[], int limit, char filename[]);
void SortArray  (CREDITREC crec[], int numRecs);
void PrintReport(CREDITREC crec[], int numRecs, char filename[]);

int main () {
 CREDITREC creditRec[MaxNum]; // array of customer credit records
 int       numRecs;           // current number of customers

 // obtain the input and report filenames from the user
 char inputFilename[_MAX_PATH];
 char reportFilename[_MAX_PATH];
 cout << "Enter the name of the credit master file: ";
```

```
 cin.getline (inputFilename, _MAX_PATH);
 cout << "Enter the name of the output report file: ";
 cin.getline (reportFilename, _MAX_PATH);

 // load the array of credit records
 numRecs = LoadArray (creditRec, MaxNum, inputFilename);
 cout << "\nArray loaded: " << numRecs << " records input\n";

 // sort the array into state code order
 cout << "Sorting the array\n";
 SortArray (creditRec, numRecs);

 // produce the report
 cout << "Printing the report\n";
 PrintReport (creditRec, numRecs, reportFilename);
 cout << "Finished\n";
 return 0;
}

/***************************************************************/
/*                                                             */
/* LoadArray: loads an array of credit records from the file  */
/*                                                             */
/***************************************************************/

int  LoadArray (CREDITREC crec[], int limit, char filename[]) {
 ifstream infile (filename);
 if (!infile) {
  cerr << "Error: cannot open " << filename << endl;
  exit (1);
 }
 int i = 0;
 char c;
 while (i<limit && infile >> crec[i].acctno >> c) {
  // input the customer name " delimited
  infile.getline (crec[i].custName, MaxNameLen, '\"');
  // input next byte which can be the " if the name is max length
  infile.get (c);
  // if it was the " then skip ws
  infile >> ws;
  infile.get (crec[i].stateCode, MaxStCodeLen);
  infile >> crec[i].creditLimit >> crec[i].balance;
  i++;
 }
 // guard against bad input data
 if (!infile.eof() && infile.fail()) {
  cerr << "Error: bad data in input file.\nLast good id was ";
  if ((i-1)==0)
   cerr << "the first line\n";
  else
   cerr << crec[i-1].acctno << endl;
  infile.close ();
  exit (2);
```

```
 }
 // guard against too much data for array size
 if (i == limit && infile >> ws && infile.good ()) {
  cerr << "Error: array size exceeded\n";
  infile.close ();
  exit (3);
 }
 infile.close ();
 return i; // return the number of records inputted
}

/***************************************************************/
/*                                                             */
/* SortArray: sorts the credit records into state code order   */
/*                                                             */
/***************************************************************/

void SortArray (CREDITREC crec[], int numRecs) {
 CREDITREC temp;
 int i, j;
 for (i=0; i<numRecs-1; i++) {
  for (j=i+1; j<numRecs; j++) {
   if (strcmp (crec[j].stateCode, crec[i].stateCode) < 0) {
    temp = crec[i];
    crec[i] = crec[j];
    crec[j] = temp;
   }
  }
 }
}

/***************************************************************/
/*                                                             */
/* PrintReport: summarize data while printing the report       */
/*                                                             */
/***************************************************************/

void PrintReport (CREDITREC crec[], int numRecs,
                  char filename[]) {
 char   prevState[MaxStCodeLen]; // previous state code for break
 int    numAcctsInState = 0;     // num of accounts in this state
 double totalLimit = 0;          // tot creditlimit in this state
 double totalBalance = 0;        // tot credit extended in  state
 int    grandNumStates = 0;      // tot number of states serviced
 int    grandNumAccts = 0;       // company total num of accounts
 double grandTotalLimit = 0;     // company total credit limit
 double grandTotalBalance = 0;   // company total credit extended

 // open report file and print headings and column headings
 ofstream outfile (filename);
 if (!outfile) {
  cerr << "Error: cannot open the output file: " << filename
       << endl;
```

```
 exit (2);
}
outfile <<
     "Acme Credit Company - Credit Extended by State Report\n\n"
        << "State   Number of     Credit Totals Extended\n"
        << "Code    Accounts        Limit        Balance\n";
outfile << fixed <<setprecision (2);

// guard against no records in the array
if (numRecs) {
 // initialize the previous state code to the first record
 // and initialize the initial state totals
 strcpy_s (prevState, sizeof(prevState), crec[0].stateCode);
 totalLimit = crec[0].creditLimit;
 totalBalance = crec[0].balance;
 numAcctsInState++;

 // loop through all the credit records
 for (int i=1; i<numRecs; i++) {
  // check for a change in state code
  if (strcmp (prevState, crec[i].stateCode) != 0) {
   // this state is the next state, print totals for prev state
   outfile << setw (4) << prevState
           << setw (9) << numAcctsInState
           << setw (7) << "$" << setw (9) << totalLimit
           << setw (6) << "$" << setw (9) << totalBalance
           << endl;
   // roll previous state totals into grand company totals
   grandNumAccts += numAcctsInState;
   grandNumStates++;
   grandTotalLimit += totalLimit;
   grandTotalBalance += totalBalance;
   // reset previous state code to the new one
   strcpy_s (prevState, sizeof(prevState), crec[i].stateCode);
   // reset this state totals to 0
   numAcctsInState = 0;
   totalLimit = 0;
   totalBalance = 0;
  }
  // accumulate this state values
  numAcctsInState++;
  totalLimit += crec[i].creditLimit;
  totalBalance += crec[i].balance;
 }
 // print last state in the set of data
 outfile << setw (4) << prevState
         << setw (9) << numAcctsInState
         << setw (7) << "$" << setw (9) << totalLimit
         << setw (6) << "$" << setw (9) << totalBalance << endl;
 grandNumAccts += numAcctsInState;
 grandNumStates++;
 grandTotalLimit += totalLimit;
 grandTotalBalance += totalBalance;
```

```
 }
 // print the grand company totals
 outfile << "   --       ---        ---------        ---------\n"
         << setw (4) << grandNumStates
         << setw (9) << grandNumAccts
         << setw (7) << "$" << setw (9) << grandTotalLimit
         << setw (6) << "$" << setw (9) << grandTotalBalance
         << endl;
 outfile.close ();
}
```

Cs13-2—Writing a Binary File

Let's examine how a binary file is created in the first place and then in the next example see how it can be read back into a program. For this program, we deal with Student Course Records. At the end of each semester, student grades are submitted. Each line of the input file contains the student's id number (social security number), the course (up to five characters), course number (three characters), section (one or two characters), and the letter grade earned. The binary master file that is output must contain these fields and a float for the grade points earned (based on the 4.0 scale). An A earns 4.0 points; a B earns 3.0, and so on. So first, let's create the structure to contain these fields. The structure **STUDREC** that meets these requirements is defined as follows.

```
const int CourseLen = 5;
const int CourseNumLen = 4;
const int SectionLen = 3;

struct STUDREC {
 long ssno;
 char course[CourseLen];
 char courseNum[CourseNumLen];
 char section[SectionLen];
 char grade;
 float gp;
};
```

The design is very simple. Whenever you need to input a set of data into a structure instance, it is usually very convenient to create a **GetData()** function that is passed a reference to the structure instance to fill up and a reference to the input stream to use, returning a reference to that stream back to the caller. Since this is the only function needed in this program, I have omitted the Top-Down Design drawing. The main storage diagram is also very tiny, containing just a single instance of the structure to be filled. I have omitted the main storage diagram as well.

The main processing loop is quite small. As long as the **GetData()** function is able to input another student record, the grade points earned for that course are figured and the binary record written to disk. Since the actual processing steps are so simple, I have omitted the pseudo coding also. Here are the key lines to look at. The items dealing with the binary file are shown in boldface.

```
STUDREC srec;
ofstream outfile ("Master.dat", ios::out | ios::binary);
while (GetData (infile, srec)) {
 count++;
 switch (srec.grade) { // figure grade points earned
  ...
 outfile.write ((char*) &srec, sizeof (srec));
}
```

Here is the complete listing of **Cs13b**.

Listing of Cs13b Student Records - build a binary master file

```
/***************************************************************/
/*                                                             */
/* Cs13b Student Records - build a binary master file          */
/*                                                             */
/***************************************************************/

#include <iostream>
#include <fstream>
using namespace std;
const int CourseLen = 6;
const int CourseNumLen = 4;
const int SectionLen = 3;

struct STUDREC {
 long ssno;                      // student id number
 char course[CourseLen];         // course taken: CSMPS
 char courseNum[CourseNumLen];   // course number: 125
 char section[SectionLen];       // course section: AA
 char grade;                     // letter grade received
 float gp;                       // grade point received-4.0 system
};

istream& GetData (istream& infile, STUDREC& srec);

int main () {
 STUDREC srec;

 ifstream infile ("Cs13b-student-records.txt");
 if (!infile) {
  cerr << "Error: cannot open file Cs13b-student-records.txt\n";
  return 1;
 }
 ofstream outfile ("Master.dat", ios::out | ios::binary);

 int count = 0;
 while (GetData (infile, srec)) {
  count++;
  switch (srec.grade) { // figure grade points earned
```

```
  case 'A':
   srec.gp = 4;
   break;
  case 'B':
   srec.gp = 3;
   break;
  case 'C':
   srec.gp = 2;
   break;
  case 'D':
   srec.gp = 1;
   break;
  default:
   srec.gp = 0;
  };
  outfile.write ((char*) &srec, sizeof (srec)); // binary write
 }
 infile.close ();
 outfile.close ();
 cout << count << " Student records written to the masterfile\n";

 return 0;
}

/***************************************************************/
/*                                                             */
/* GetData: input a student grade record                       */
/*                                                             */
/***************************************************************/

istream& GetData (istream& infile, STUDREC& srec) {
 infile >> srec.ssno >> ws;
 if (!infile) return infile;
 infile.get (srec.course, sizeof (srec.course));
 infile >> ws;
 infile.get (srec.courseNum, sizeof (srec.courseNum));
 infile >> ws;
 infile.get (srec.section, sizeof (srec.section));
 infile >> srec.grade;
 return infile;
}
```

Cs13-3—Reading a Binary File — Building a Consolidated Student GPA Binary File

Next, let's input the binary file of student course records just built with Program Cs13-2, accumulate the data for each student, and write a new binary file of **GPA** records. The student course records from the previous program are, in fact, in order by student id (social security number). For each student, accumulate their grade points and then calculate their **GPA**. The **GPA** record has just two members, the student id (social security number), and the overall GPA.

Actually, this problem is a control break problem. Input and accumulate a student's grade points until there is a change in social security number. The **ControlBreak()** function is called when there is a change in social security numbers. The break function fills in the **GPA** record, writes that record to disk, formats a brief log message, and resets the counter and sum fields to zero, ready for the next student. Don't forget to call the break function one more time when the main loop ends. Remember the program has been accumulating the grade points earned for the last student; that last student's **GPA** data must be written to disk as well.

The **GPA** structure is defined as

```
struct GPAREC {
 long ssno;   // student id number
 float gpa;   // grade point received - 4.0 system
};
```

As with all control break problems, the previous value of the control field, here the social security number, must be initialized with the value from the first student course record. Thus, we must use a primed loop approach, input the first record, and give the previous field its value.

Let's begin by examining the **main()** function's processing. The key variables are

```
STUDREC srec;          // student course record
int   count;           // count of courses of a student
float sum;             // sum of gp of a student
long  previousSsno; // the previous ssno
```

Next, **main()** reads in the first binary record and sets **previousSsno** variable and the accumulators.

```
infile.read ((char*) &srec, sizeof (srec));
previousSsno = srec.ssno;
sum = srec.gp;
count = 1;
```

After the **while** clause successfully reads in the next student record, the first action is to check and see if we are still working with the same student. If so, accumulate grade point information. If not, then the **ControlBreak()** function is called to generate and output the student **GPA** record. The **previousSsno** is reset to this new student.

```
while (infile.read ((char*) &srec, sizeof (srec))) {
 if (previousSsno != srec.ssno) {
  ControlBreak (outfile, previousSsno, sum, count, logfile);
  previousSsno = srec.ssno;
 }
 sum += srec.gp;
 count++;
}
ControlBreak (outfile, previousSsno, sum, count, logfile);
```

When the main loop ends, the **ControlBreak()** function is invoked one last time for that last student.

Control break logic always follows a quite standard sequence. First, roll (or add) any totals into any grand totals (there are none in this problem). Next, output this set of totals; here we calculate the GPA and fill in the **gpaRec** structure instance with this student's data and write it to the new binary master file. Next, the break function would zero the totals and counters. **ControlBreak()** is given **outfile**, **ssno**, **sum** and **count**. Its sequence is just this.

```
GPAREC gpaRec;
gpaRec.ssno = ssno;
gpaRec.gpa = sum / count;
outfile.write ((char*) &gpaRec, sizeof (gpaRec));
count = 0;
sum = 0;
```

Now we have a new binary file of student GPA values. The next step is to find out how an inquiry program can directly access a specific student's GPA record on disk. (Alas, you will have to get my sequel book to see this.) Here are the complete listing for **Cs13c** and a sample test run.

Listing of Cs13c Student GPA Builder Program - reads a binary file

```
/***************************************************************/
/*                                                             */
/* Cs13c Student GPA Builder Program- reads binary file of data*/
/*       writes another binary file of student gpa records     */
/*                                                             */
/***************************************************************/

#include <iostream>
#include <iomanip>
#include <fstream>
using namespace std;
const int CourseLen = 6;
const int CourseNumLen = 4;
const int SectionLen = 3;

struct STUDREC {
 long ssno;                     // student id number
 char course[CourseLen];        // course taken: CSMPS
 char courseNum[CourseNumLen];  // course number: 125
 char section[SectionLen];      // course section: AA
```

```
 char grade;                      // letter grade received
 float gp;                        // grade point received-4.0 system
};

struct GPAREC {
 long ssno;                       // student id number
 float gpa;                       // grade point received-4.0 system
};

void ControlBreak (ostream& outfile, long ssno, float& sum,
                   int& count, ostream& logfile);

int main () {
 ifstream infile ("Cs13c-StudentRecords.dat",
                  ios::in | ios::binary);
 if (!infile) {
  cerr << "Error: cannot open file Cs13c-StudentRecords.dat\n";
  return 1;
 }

 STUDREC srec;                    // student course record
 int   count;                     // count of courses of a student
 float sum;                       // sum of gp of a student
 long  previousSsno;              // the previous ssno
 int   totalStudents = 0;         // the total number of students

 // read first record and initialize counters and save areas
 infile.read ((char*) &srec, sizeof (srec));
 if (!infile) {
  cerr << "Masterfile is empty.\n";
  infile.close ();
  return 1;
 }
 previousSsno = srec.ssno;
 sum = srec.gp;
 count = 1;

 // open output files
 ofstream outfile ("GPA-Master.dat", ios::out | ios::binary);
 ofstream logfile ("LogResults.txt");
 // setup floating point output format
 logfile << fixed << setprecision (2);
 // display headings on the log file
 logfile << "      GPA Log File\n\n     Student ID   GPA\n\n";

 // process all student course records
 while (infile.read ((char*) &srec, sizeof (srec))) {
  // check for a change in student id (ssno)
  if (previousSsno != srec.ssno) {
   // finished with this student, so output their GPA record
   ControlBreak (outfile, previousSsno, sum, count, logfile);
   previousSsno = srec.ssno;
   totalStudents++;
```

```
   }
   // accumulate student grade points
   sum += srec.gp;
   count++;
  }
  // process last student being accumulated
  ControlBreak (outfile, previousSsno, sum, count, logfile);
  totalStudents++;

  infile.close ();
  outfile.close ();
  logfile << endl << totalStudents
          << " Student gpa records written\n";
  logfile.close ();
  return 0;
 }

/***************************************************************/
/*                                                             */
/* ControlBreak: fill in the GPA record and write it to master */
/*               and log files                                 */
/*                                                             */
/***************************************************************/

void ControlBreak (ostream& outfile, long ssno, float& sum,
                   int& count, ostream& logfile) {
 GPAREC gpaRec;

 // fillup gpaRec
 gpaRec.ssno = ssno;
 gpaRec.gpa = sum / count;

 // write the binary master file
 outfile.write ((char*) &gpaRec, sizeof (gpaRec));

 // write log information
 logfile << setw (15) << ssno << setw (6) << gpaRec.gpa << endl;

 // reset counters for next student
 count = 0;
 sum = 0;
}

```

Logfile for Cs13c Student GPA Builder Program

```
      GPA Log File

     Student ID   GPA

      111111111  4.00
      222222222  3.00
```

```
      333333333  2.00
      444444444  3.00
      555555555  2.50
      666666666  2.00

6 Student gpa records written
```

Section C: An Engineering Example

Engr13a—Weather Statistics Revisited

The major impact that structures have on engineering problems is primarily that of consolidating related fields. Weather statistics are far more involved than just merely recording hourly temperatures. A structure allows us to group all the related fields into one simple package and then to be able to pass a reference to the package to various statistical functions.

Assume that the weather stations are logging weather events on an hourly basis. For each feature measured, there are going to be twenty-four such observations per record. The following defines an advanced daily weather record for just one observing site within a state.

```
const int StationLen = 21;
const int NumObs = 24;
struct WEATHER_EVENTS {
 char station[StationLen];
 float temps[NumObs];
 float rainfall[NumObs];
 float pressure[NumObs];
 float relHumidity[NumObs];
 float windSpeed[NumObs];
 char windDir[NumObs][3];
};
```

Notice that the **WEATHER_EVENTS** record contains one string, five arrays of twenty-four elements each and one two-dimensional array of characters (in other words, a single-dimensioned array of strings). This **WEATHER_EVENTS** record represents 145 separate fields, occupying at least 573 bytes! Clearly, structures offer engineering programming a great value. In fact, if the data was stored in binary format, one read statement is all that is needed to input the entire set of fields!

This sample program is designed to show you how convenient arrays of structures can be. Let's modify Program Engr11a that produced a report of unusual weather conditions. If you look back at Program Engr11a, the **main()** function is a large wall of coding. The objective is to break this problem down into smaller units by using an array of weather structures. The **WEATHER** structure is defined as

```
const int MaxCityLen = 21; // city name length is 20 chars
const int MaxRecs = 100;   // max number of weather records
```

```
struct WEATHER {
 char city [MaxCityLen]; // string to hold city name
 float high;             // high temperature of the day - F
 float low;              // low temperature of the day - F
 float rainfall;         // rainfall in inches
 float snowfall;         // snowfall in inches
 float windspeed;        // wind speed in mph
};
```

The **main()** function defines an array of these weather records. After prompting the user to input the filenames to use both for input and for output, **main()** calls the **LoadArray()** function to input all the weather records into the array. Then, **main()** calls the **PrintReport()** function to print the actual report. Now **main()** is very streamlined and we have encapsulated the input and output operations in a pair of functions.

In the **LoadArray()** function, the key loop to input all the data is this.

```
 while (i < limit && infile >> junk) {
  // input of junk retrieved the leading " of city string
  infile.get (wrec[i].city, sizeof (wrec[i].city), '\"');
  infile.get (junk);
  infile >> wrec[i].high >> wrec[i].low >> wrec[i].rainfall
         >> wrec[i].snowfall >> wrec[i].windspeed;
  i++;
 }
```

Notice the syntax to access the individual members of the **i**th element of the **wrec** array is **wrec[i].city**, for example.

Here are the complete coding for **Engr13a** and the test run.

Engr13a: Unusual Weather Statistics report using a structure

```
/***************************************************************/
/*                                                             */
/* Engr13a: Unusual Weather Statistics report using a structure*/
/*                                                             */
/***************************************************************/

#include <iostream>
#include <iomanip>
#include <fstream>
#include <string>
using namespace std;

const int MaxCityLen = 21; // city name length is 20 chars
const int MaxRecs = 100;   // maximum number of weather records

struct WEATHER {
 char city [MaxCityLen]; // string to hold city name
```

```
 float high;              // high temperature of the day - F
 float low;               // low temperature of the day - F
 float rainfall;          // rainfall in inches
 float snowfall;          // snowfall in inches
 float windspeed;         // wind speed in mph
};

int  LoadArray (char filename[], WEATHER wrec[], int limit);
void PrintReport (char filename[], WEATHER wrec[], int limit);

int main () {

 // prompt user for filenames for input and output
 char infilename[_MAX_PATH];
 char reportname[_MAX_PATH];
 cout << "Enter the filename with today's weather data\n";
 cin.getline (infilename, sizeof (infilename));
 cout << "\nEnter the report filename\n";
 cin.getline (reportname, sizeof(reportname));

 WEATHER wrec[MaxRecs];
 int numRecs = LoadArray (infilename, wrec, MaxRecs);

 PrintReport (reportname, wrec, numRecs);
 return 0;
}

/***************************************************************/
/*                                                             */
/* LoadArray: loads an array of weather records                */
/*                                                             */
/***************************************************************/

int LoadArray (char filename[], WEATHER wrec[], int limit) {
 char junk; // to hold the " around city names
 int  i = 0;
 ifstream infile;
 infile.open (filename);
 if (!infile) {
  cerr << "Error: cannot open file: " << filename << endl;
  exit (1);
 }

 while (i < limit && infile >> junk) { // input leading " of city
  infile.get (wrec[i].city, sizeof (wrec[i].city), '\"');
  infile.get (junk);
  infile >> wrec[i].high >> wrec[i].low >> wrec[i].rainfall
         >> wrec[i].snowfall >> wrec[i].windspeed;

  // abort if there is incomplete or bad data
  if (!infile) {
   cerr << "Error: incomplete city data on line " << i+1 << endl;
   infile.close ();
```

```
   exit (2);
  }

  i++;
 }
 infile.close ();
 return i;
}
/***************************************************************/
/*                                                             */
/* PrintReport: prints a report of unusual weather             */
/*                                                             */
/***************************************************************/

void PrintReport (char filename[], WEATHER wrec[], int limit) {
 ofstream outfile;
 outfile.open (filename);
 if (!outfile) {
  cerr << "Error: cannot open file: " << filename << endl;
  exit (3);
 }
 // setup floating point output format
 outfile << fixed << setprecision (1);

 outfile << "Unusual Weather Report\n\n";
 outfile<<"City                     High     Low    Rain    Snow"
          "    Wind\n";
 outfile <<
          "                                         Fall    Fall"
          "   Speed\n\n";

 for (int i=0; i<limit; i++) {
  if (wrec[i].high > 95 || wrec[i].low < 0 ||
      wrec[i].rainfall > 2 || wrec[i].snowfall > 6 ||
      wrec[i].windspeed > 45) {
   // unusual weather - display this city data
   outfile << left << setw (22) << wrec[i].city << right
           << setw (7) << wrec[i].high;
   if (wrec[i].high > 95)
    outfile << '*';
   else
    outfile << ' ';
   outfile << setw (7) << wrec[i].low;
   if (wrec[i].low < 0)
    outfile << '*';
   else
    outfile << ' ';
   outfile << setw (7) << wrec[i].rainfall;
   if (wrec[i].rainfall > 2)
    outfile << '*';
   else
    outfile << ' ';
   outfile << setw (7) << wrec[i].snowfall;
```

```
    if (wrec[i].snowfall > 6)
     outfile << '*';
    else
     outfile << ' ';
    outfile << setw (7) << wrec[i].windspeed;
    if (wrec[i].windspeed > 45)
     outfile << '*';
    else
     outfile << ' ';
    outfile << endl;
  }
 }
 outfile.close ();

```

Output from Engr13a: Unusual Weather Statistics report using struct

```
Unusual Weather Report

City                       High     Low     Rain    Snow    Wind
                                            Fall    Fall   Speed

Washington                 99.0*   70.0     0.0     0.0    20.0
Morton                     85.0    65.0     5.0*    0.0    40.0
Chicago                    32.0    -5.0*    0.0     8.0*   25.0
Joliet                     88.0    70.0     2.0     0.0    60.0*
Springfield                99.0*   75.0     3.0*    0.0    55.0*
New Salem                   0.0    -3.0*    0.0     9.0*   55.0*
```

Design Exercises

1. Airline Scheduling Program

Acme Airline wants a new program to track their arrival and departure schedules. Create a **DATE** structure to contain a date that consists of three numbers: month, day and year. Create a **TIME** structure to contain a time that consists of two numbers: hours and minutes. All times are on a 24-hour basis; that is, 10:00 p.m. would be entered as 22:00. Next, create a **FLIGHT** structure that contains the departure date and time, the arrival date and time, the character string flight number, the maximum number of passengers and the current number of passengers. The arrival and departure dates and times should be instances of your **DATE** and **TIME** structures. The flight number is a string of 10 characters maximum including the null-terminator.

Now write the sketch for the program that inputs a set of data on flights, stores them in an array of **FLIGHT** structures. Then, print a report of the flights as entered. Each line of the input file consists of the flight number, departure date and time, arrival date and time, maximum passengers and current number of passengers.

2. Sports Event Reporting

For the time trails at a major sporting event, a series of programs needs to be designed and made to track the results of the contestants. The judges desire to store the contestant's three-digit id number, the contestant name of up to 30 characters, and the start and stop times. A time is input as hh:mm:ss.ssss. First, design a **TIME** structure to store the three portions of a time. Then, design an **EVENTREC** structure to store the basic information for one contestant. There is one additional field in the **EVENTREC**, the total elapsed time in seconds.

Now sketch the Data Entry program that inputs **EVENTREC** data and writes a binary master file of the contestant data. It must calculate the total elapsed time in seconds.

Now sketch an Event Summary Program that inputs the binary master file into an array of **EVENTREC** structures. The array should then be sorted into increasing total elapsed time order. The printed report displays the contestant id number, name, and total elapsed time.

Stop! Do These Exercises Before Programming

1. Acme wishes to make a database of all of its clients' TV preferences. A TV preference consists of the **short int** channel number, two **short ints** for the hour and minute the show is broadcast but are stored in 24-hour format (that is, 8pm is stored as 20 hours), a **short int** for the day of the week, and the name of the show, which can hold thirty characters. The programmer coded the following, which does not compile among other goofs. Correct this sequence so that it compiles and meets the specifications above.

```
Structure PREFERENCE {
     short channel
     short day
     short hr
     short min
     char name[MAXLEN]
}
const int MAXLEN = 30;
```

2. Just to test the structure coding, the programmer decided to see if he could input one set of preferences and then display it. However, his attempt met with complete failure and does not compile. Why? What would have to be done to make this work?

```
int main () {
  cin >> PREFERENCE.channel >>  PREFERENCE.day
      >> PREFERENCE.hr      >> PREFERENCE.min
      >> PREFERENCE.name;
  cout << PREFERENCE.channel << PREFERENCE.day
       << PREFERENCE.hr      << PREFERENCE.min
       << PREFERENCE.name << endl;
```

3. The problem specifications called for creating a **LoadPreferences()** function. Here the programmer ran into a great deal of difficulty. What is wrong with this function? How can it be fixed?

```
void LoadPreferences (PREFERENCE rec, int limit,
                      istream& infile) {
 for (int j=0; j<limit && infile >> ws; j++) {
  infile >> rec[j].channel >> rec[j].day >> rec[j].hr
         >> rec[j].min >>rec[j].name;
 }
}
```

Here are two typical data lines.

```
11 6 08:00pm Babylon 5
12 5 07:30pm Doctor Who
```

4. Having gotten the array loaded, the programmer decided to print what was in the array to be sure the data had been entered correctly. However, it does not compile. How can it be made to work properly?

```
int main () {
 PREFERENCE recs[1000];
 int numRecs;
 for (int j=0; j<numRecs; j++) {
  cout << recs.channel << setw (5) << recs.day << " "
       << setfill ('0') << setw (2) << recs.hr << ':'
       << recs.min << setfill (' ') << setw (40)
       << recs.name << endl;
 }
```

5. Next, management wanted the entire array sorted into order based on the TV show's name so that the program could then calculate frequencies of each TV show. The **sortArray()** function does not work properly, though it compiles. What is wrong and how can it be fixed?

```
void sortArray (PREFERENCE recs[], int numRecs) {
 PREFERENCES temp;
 for (int j=0; j<numRecs; j++) {
  for (int k=j; k<numRecs; k++) {
   if (recs[k].name < recs[j].name) {
    temp = recs[k];
    recs[k] = recs[j];
    recs[j] = temp;
   }
  }
 }
}
```

Programming Problems

Problem Cs13-1—Acme Payroll Program

The Acme Company has a master file of employee data that is already sorted by employee id number. Their employees work on various job sites around the city. At the end of the pay period, a transactions file is created that contains their hours worked. Our task is to calculate their pay.

Some employees are classified as time-card workers and are paid an hourly rate. Some are classified as salaried or management and are paid a fixed rate independent of hours worked. Define an enumerated data type, **PayType**, to reflect these two kinds, **Hourly** or **Salaried**.

Next, define an **EMPLOYEE** structure to hold the following fields in this order:
int id number
char name of maximum length of 20 chars +1 for the null-terminator
double pay rate
short int number of dependents
enum PayType, which can be **Salaried** or **Hourly**

In the **main()** function, create an array of these employee records and allow for a maximum of 500 employees. The **main()** function should first call the **LoadMaster()** function to load all of the employee master records into the array.

The **LoadMaster()** function is passed the **EMPLOYEE** array and the array bounds. It inputs the employee master file from a file called **Cs13-1-master.txt**. The function returns the number of employee records input. In the input file, the names are padded to twenty characters with blanks as needed. The **payType** input field contains an H for Hourly workers and S for Salaried workers.

Acme employees work on various job sites around the city. The second input file, **Cs13-1-jobsites.tx**t, contains the job site number and its corresponding name sorted into site number order. Create another structure called **JOBSITE** that contains these members.
int job site number
char sitename string of a maximum 20 chars plus 1 for the null-terminator

With the array loaded, the **main()** function should next define an array of 500 **JOBSITE** structures and an integer count of the number in the array. The **main()** function then calls the function **LoadSites()** to get that array filled. The **LoadSites()** function is passed the array of job sites and the maximum number. It returns the number of job sites actually input from the file.

With these initial setup actions done, **main()** is now ready to process the transactions file. The third file, **Cs13-1-transactions.txt,** contains the pay period information. Each line contains the following fields
int employee id number

int job site number
double hours worked
The transactions file is sorted into employee number order.

Your task in the **main()** function is to open this file and write a loop that inputs each employee and calculates their pay. The report is written to output file **pay.txt**. The report consists of one line per valid employee showing the id number, name, job site name, gross pay and net pay. Hence, two table look-ups must be done: one to obtain the employee's name and the other to get the job site name.

Create a pair of functions to do the table look ups: **MatchEmployee()** and **MatchSite()**. Each should return the index (integer) of the corresponding **EMPLOYEE** or **JOBSITE** structure for this employee's id or site number. Both functions must return a –1 for no matching record (invalid id or site number). If either the employee's id or the site number are invalid, then the **main()** function should print an error message to the error log file called **errors.txt**. It should print either

Error bad Id: then the employee's transaction record information

or

Error bad site Id: then the employee's transaction record information

An employee's pay is more complex. For Salaried workers, gross pay is the amount contained in the employee record's pay rate. For Hourly workers, the pay rate should be multiplied by the hours worked. However, they also get time and a half for all hours worked more than 40.

The net pay for any employee is gross pay minus tax. Here are the taxation rules:

if the number of dependents is 1, the tax rate is 15%
else the tax is the larger of these two amounts
gross pay x 2.5%
gross pay x 15% x (1 – number dependents/(number dependents – 6))

Finally, the last line of this report should list the number of employees paid and the total gross payroll.

Problem Cs13-2—Friends' Phone Number Database

The objective of this program is to aid you in maintaining a file of friends' phone numbers. The phone numbers contain three separate parts. For example, we are used to seeing phone numbers as (309) 699-9999. However, the program must store the phone number as three separate numbers: the area code (309), the prefix (699) and the main number (9999). Make a structure template called **FRIEND** that contains the following fields in this order.

Last name—up to 20 characters maximum + 1 for the null terminator
First name—up to 15 characters maximum + 1 for the null terminator
area code stored as a **short**
phone number prefix stored as a **short**
phone number main stored as a **short**

The **main()** function defines an array called **friends**; allow for a maximum of 200 entries.

The **main()** function begins by calling a **LoadFriends()** function that is passed the array and the maximum limit. **LoadFriends()** returns the number of friends actually input. In **LoadFriends()**, input all the data from the file **friends.txt**. Initially, the file does not exist, so no friend records are input and the function returns 0 elements are in the array.

With the array loaded, **main()** presents a short menu of options, similar to the following

```
Enter the number of your choice
     1. Add new friend
     2. Update a friend
     3. Save all the data
     4. Make a friends listing in Last Name order
     5. Make a friends listing in Area Code order
     6. Make a friends listing in Prefix order
     7. Quit the program
Enter your choice: _
```

Now get the user's choice.

The **friends** array is always saved on disk sorted into alphabetical order on last name and then first name, if there are two friends with the same last name. When the **friends** array is actually in memory, the array can be sorted into another order.

When the choice is "Add new friend," prompt the user for the needed information and input the data. Then, place that data into the array maintaining the correct alphabetical order.

When the choice is "Update a friend," prompt the user for the last and first names. Perform a match on last and first names to find that friend in the data base. If the entry is found, display the phone number three fields. Prompt and input the changes. Store the updated information in that friend's record.

When "Save" is selected, rewrite the **friends.txt** file from the **friends** array. Make sure that the array is sorted into order by last name and then first name, if two entries have the same last name.

For the three "Make a listing" actions, sort the array into the correct order. Sorting by area code means sort on area code first, but, when duplicate area codes occur, also sort on last name and then first name if the last names are the same. Sorting by prefix means to first sort on the prefix, but, when two prefixes are the same, use the main number portion next. If two main numbers are the same, do anything you desire. Note that the Sort on Name function must be done before a Save, Add or an Update operation can be done. To avoid needless sorting, have the **main()** program maintain a **bool**, **isInNameOrder**. It is **true** when the original input file is loaded. It is changed to **false** when any of the numerical sorts are done. It is reset back to **true** when the Sort on Name is subsequently done.

When the user chooses any of the Make a Friends Listing, prompt the user for the name of the output report file. Then sort the array as needed before producing the report.

Problem Cs13-3—Your Pet's Rabies Shot Is Due

Acme Animal Control maintains a database of all registered pets in the city. Each month, they send out a notice to all pet owners reminding them that the pet's rabies shot is due this month, but only of course if that pet is due for its rabies shot that month. Rabies shots are given yearly.

Define a structure template, **PETREC**, that contains the needed fields as follows. Be sure to add one to each of the character strings to get the needed array bounds. Each listed character string length represents the maximum number of characters it could hold.

Pet name—10 characters
Owner's name—40 characters
Address—30 characters
City—20 characters
State—2 characters
Zip—5 characters
Year of last vaccination
Month of last vaccination

The **main()** function defines an array of 100 pet records and calls the **LoadPets()** function. As usual, **LoadPets()** is passed the array of pet records and the array limit. It inputs the pet records in the file and returns the number actually input. Use the data file **Cs13-3-pets.txt**.

Next, the **main()** function prompts the user to enter the year and the month for the reminders. Given that reminder date, the **main()** function then checks each record in the array to see if that pet is due for its yearly rabies shot. If a pet is due, main calls **PrintReminder()** passing it a constant reference to the pet record and the output file stream on which to display the reminder.

PrintReminder() should display the reminder notice formatted as follows. (Assume that 10/2000 was the due date that was entered.)

```
Acme Animal Control
Spot is due for its annual rabies shot this month (10/2000).
```

```
John Smith
123 Somerville Ave
North Plains, TX 59685
```

Use the pet's name where I have used Spot. Insert the due date where I have 10/2000. Insert the owner's name, address, city, state, and zip. Print each reminder notice on a new page. (Remember that the escape sequence \f causes the printer to eject to a new page.)

Problem Cs13-4—Acme Grocery Store Sales Analysis

The Acme Grocery Store has inventory records that consist of these fields.

```
unsigned long  productId;
char           description[21];
unsigned short quantityOnHand;
double         cost;
```

Create an **INV_REC** structure to contain these four fields. In the **main()** function, create an array of a maximum of 100 **INV_REC** records. Then call a function, **loadArray()**, to input a file with up to 100 records in it. Use the provided file called **cs13-4-master.txt**.

Next, call a function, **findMin()**, that returns the subscript of the record that costs the least. Then, call a function, **findMax()**, that returns the subscript of the record that costs the most. Save these subscripts for later use in the final report.

Next, the **main()** function prompts the user to enter the markup percentage, such as 20.0, for 20%. For testing purposes, use 20.0 for the mark up percentage.

Now print a report similar to the one shown below. There are a title line and two column heading lines.

```
Acme Grocery Store Sales Analysis:   Mark up Percentage is  20%

Product Description       Quantity  Wholesale  Retail    Total
   ID                               Cost       Cost      Profit

9999999 Potatoes             10     $  6.00    $  7.20   $ 12.00
```

The retail cost is the inputted cost that has been marked up by the markup percentage. The profit is the difference between the retail and wholesale costs multiplied by the quantity.

Print a final summary set of lines. The first line shows the total expected profit if everything is sold. Follow that with two lines as follows:

```
The least expensive item is: nnnnnnnn $ nn.nn
The most expensive item is:  mmmmmmmm $ nn.nn
```

Finally, again prompt the user for another markup percentage and repeat the report using the new percentage. Continue until the user signals EOF by a ctrl-Z code. Begin each report on a new page.

Problem Engr13-1—Problem Engr07-2 Revisited (Electrical Circuit Design)

In Problem **Engr07-2**, an electronic circuit involving a resistor, capacitor and an inductor was designed according to the formula

$$f(R) = e^{\frac{-Rt}{2L}} \cos\left(t\sqrt{\frac{1}{LC} - \left(\frac{R}{2L}\right)^2} \right) - \frac{q}{q_0}$$

The resistance required was found using the bisection method. However, the problem with the **F(R)** function was the remaining variables, L, C, t and q/q_0. Those four values were input from the user in a function called **Input()**. However, they are actually used in *F(R)*. This was solved using four global variables.

A major use of structures is reducing the number of parameters needed to be passed or made available to functions. Create a structure to contain those four values. Then, create a global instance of that structure. Remove the other original four global variables. Rewrite the **Input()** function to fill up the global instance. Rewrite the **F(R)** function to use this global instance. Verify that all is working properly by running the same four test cases in the original problem.

Problem Engr13-2—Problem Engr07-1 Revisited—Vibration Studies

In Problem **Engr07-1**, various root solving methods were used to find the first three roots of the spring dampening function. The variables input by the user consisted of the car's mass and the depth of the pothole. Those were made global variables to facilitate communications to the **F(t)** function.

Remove those global variables. Create a structure whose two members are the mass of the car and the pothole depth. Then, create a global instance of the structure. Change the program to input the user's choices into the global instance. Modify the **F(t)** function to also access the two data members from the global instance. Then test the program in the same manner as given in **Engr07-1**

www.ingramcontent.com/pod-product-compliance
Lightning Source LLC
LaVergne TN
LVHW082125070326
832902LV00041B/3037
* 9 7 8 1 9 4 1 4 1 5 5 3 5 *